Why Do You Need This New Edition?

If you're wondering why you should buy this new edition of *Global Issues, Local Arguments*, here are nine great reasons!

❶ **Over 60 new readings** in this edition bring you up-to-date perspectives on a wide range of global issues.

❷ **A new chapter, Analyzing and Writing Arguments,** provides strategies to help you read and analyze the arguments in this book as well as to write summaries, rhetorical analyses, and arguments of your own (Ch. 2).

❸ **New assignments in each chapter (Analyzing Arguments Rhetorically)** help you identify strategies used by professional writers and improve your reading skills.

❹ **The addition of student essays** provides you with models for writing personal narratives, exploratory essays, rhetorical analysis essays, and arguments.

❺ **New researched student essays** model how to incorporate sources into your writing as well as to cite and document sources in the most current MLA style.

❻ **A new chapter on the current global economic crisis** shows how economic forces affect you personally through job losses, outsourcing, and credit tightening, deepening your financial literacy (Ch. 4).

❼ **Revised and updated Writing Assignments and For Class Discussion activities** throughout the text help you join conversations about the issues by presenting and supporting your own points of view.

❽ **New focus for the environment chapter** reflects changes in how Americans think about climate change, emphasizing proposals for sustainable energy technologies (Ch. 6).

❾ **A greater focus on music, television, and film in the global culture chapter** explores topics such as rap music, MTV, *Slumdog Millionaire,* and the globalization of culture (Ch. 8).

PEARSON
Longman

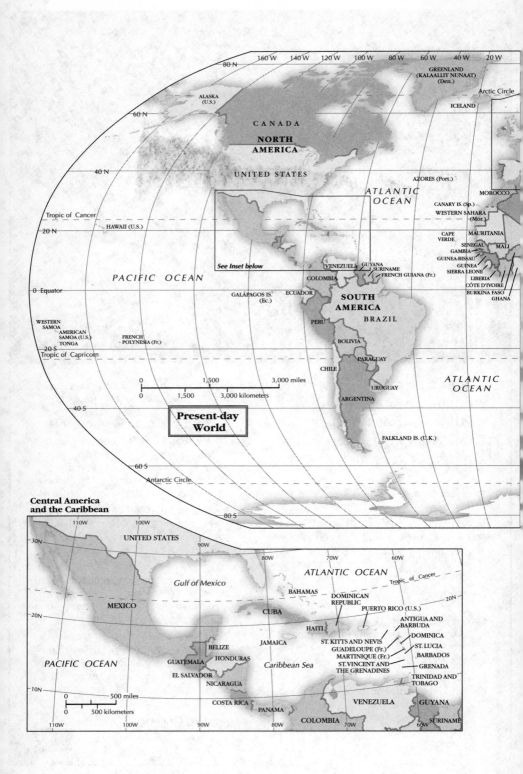

Present-day World

Central America and the Caribbean

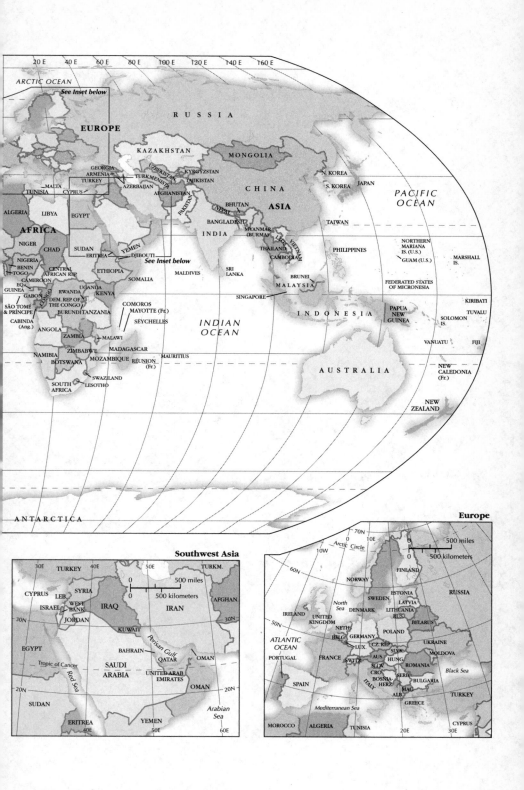

Global Issues, Local Arguments

Readings for Writing

Second Edition

June Johnson
Seattle University

Longman

Boston   Columbus   Indianapolis   New York   San Francisco   Upper Saddle River
Amsterdam   Cape Town   Dubai   London   Madrid   Milan   Munich
Paris   Montreal   Toronto   Delhi   Mexico City   Sao Paulo   Sydney
Hong Kong   Seoul   Singapore   Taipei   Tokyo

Acquisitions Editor: Lauren A. Finn
Senior Development Editor: Marion B. Castellucci
Senior Marketing Manager: Sandra McGuire
Senior Supplements Editor: Donna Campion
Senior Media Producer: Stefanie Liebman
Production Manager: Savoula Amanatidis
Project Coordination and Text Design: Elm Street Publishing Services
Electronic Page Makeup: Integra Software Services Pvt. Ltd.
Cover Design Manager: Nancy Danahy
Cover Images (clockwise from left): North Wales UK Three Wind turbine electricity generators
 on windfarm against blue sky © Alamy; Closing Down Posters in a Shop Window © Andrew
 Fox/Corbis; Starbucks Coffee Shop in the Forbidden City © Macduff Everton/Corbis
Photo Researcher: Rebecca Karamehdovis
Senior Manufacturing Buyer: Alfred C. Dorsey
Printer and Binder: R. R. Donnelley and Sons Company—Harrisonburg
Cover Printer: R. R. Donnelley and Sons Company—Harrisonburg

For permission to use copyrighted material, grateful acknowledgment is made to the copyright
holders on pp. 534–546, which are hereby made part of this copyright page.

Library of Congress Cataloging-in-Publication Data

Johnson, June, 1953–
 Global issues, local arguments: readings for writing/June Johnson.
  p. cm.
 Includes index.
 ISBN 0-205-73992-X
 1. History, Modern—21st century—Sources. 2. College readers. 3. Report writing.
 I. Title.
 D861.4.J65 2010
 320.6—dc22

                                                                        2009022316

Longman
is an imprint of

PEARSON

www.pearsonhighered.com

ISBN-13: 978-0-205-73992-9
ISBN-10:   0-205-73992-X

Brief Contents

Detailed Contents

3 Trading Goods
Consumerism, Free Trade, and Sweatshops   68

Readings   79

4 Trading Financial Risk and Jobs
The Global Economic Crisis   138

Readings   151

5 Crossing Borders
Immigration   217

6 Protecting the Environment
Water Issues and Emerging Energy Technologies   280

7 Feeding the World
Biotechnology, culture, and Local Food 341

Readings 352

8 Merging and Clashing Cultures
Media, Technology, Music, and Film   411

9 Defending Human Rights
Trafficking and Child Labor 471

Readings 481

Chapter Questions for Reflection and Discussion 514
Writing Assignments 515

Preface

A key question for writing instructors is no longer *whether* we should teach global issues in our writing classes but rather *how* to teach them. Many instructors have discovered that global issues spark students' interest and motivate learning. Still, the question is, How can we most productively enlist these issues in our writing classrooms?

Undoubtedly, students have both a need and a desire to understand the multiple ways that our states, regions, and country are part of the larger world. Daily, the media bombard us with stories and images that relate to controversies over global economic problems, free trade, outsourcing, immigration, energy, and food. In my writing classes, I have found that students welcome the opportunity to study, discuss, and write about these issues. Some of these controversies are new and intriguing to students: How does shopping at the local mall affect workers in clothing factories in China? How does the lack of safe water in Africa threaten global security? Some controversies are immediately relevant: How will sending businesses and jobs to Mexico and India affect the number of jobs available to young adults in the United States and Canada? Some have urgency: How can we stop the economic damage set off by the crash of the global financial system? In my classes, I have discovered that these issues, connecting "over there" with "home here," appeal to today's students, whose generation has been shaped by images from around the world.

Global Issues, Local Arguments is based on two main ideas. First, in today's world seeing how global issues touch us and how our local decisions as consumers and voters have far-reaching consequences is very important. Second, studying the public arguments on these issues in the writing classroom has great value. Unlike multicultural texts with readings about the world and perhaps by international writers, this text introduces students to global controversies and their local connections and focuses on readings *as* arguments. It helps students examine how arguments are constructed rhetorically. It encourages them to think their way through issues and contribute to the discussion of them in their writing.

WHAT'S NEW IN THE SECOND EDITION?

This second edition of *Global Issues, Local Arguments* preserves the approach and structure of the first edition, while it incorporates two new chapters and new features and substantially updates the readings on the issues to reflect current developments. Here are the major changes:

- **A new Chapter 2 on analyzing and writing arguments.** This new instructional chapter provides a condensed rhetoric that teaches the basics of argumentation and rhetorical analysis. It helps students understand how arguments are constructed and offers students guidance in writing their own. It teaches students to summarize arguments and to read and analyze them rhetorically by examining the way that rhetorical context and features of the writing itself shape the effect these arguments have on readers. In providing two professional arguments to analyze, two annotated student essays in MLA style, and numerous incremental exercises, this chapter prepares students to read and write summaries, rhetorical analyses, and arguments in response to the readings in this book.

- **New samples of student writing that show how students have engaged with and explored global issues.** In this edition, there are nine new "Student Voice" essays: three new personal narratives in chapter introductions; and an op-ed piece, a rhetorical analysis essay, a researched exploratory essay, and three researched arguments in MLA style in the readings sections of the chapters. Seven of these papers were written by students using the first edition of this book. They all exemplify students' idea-rich and often passionate responses to global issues and provide student readers with models of questions, topics, and strategies used effectively by their peers.

- **A new Chapter 4 on the current global financial crisis and the granting of work visas to international professionals.** This chapter on the global economic crash gives students background on the causes of this crisis and its global, national, and personal repercussions. Students encounter controversies over the global trade in financial risk; Americans' financial literacy; and the interrelationships among corporate responsibility, the outsourcing of white-collar jobs, the importation of professionals, and the national economy. Students explore how global economic forces can affect themselves and their families through job losses, mortgage foreclosures, credit card defaults, and poor employment prospects for graduates. A new "Student Voice" piece argues that the economic downturn is a wakeup call to return to basic financial responsibility and community values.

- **A new subissue about the development of sustainable energy technologies in Chapter 6 on the environment.** The global warming debate has changed from a discussion of causes to a debate over proposals for action, and the chapter emphasis has likewise shifted to arguments over the development of green energy technologies. A new essay by an international student arguing that the United States should adopt the wind turbine technology of her native Denmark and a humorous satirical argument arguing for "pedal power" enliven this topic with local perspectives.

- **A greater focus on music, television, and film in Chapter 8 on global culture.** While people continue to argue over the advantages and disadvantages of cross-cultural influence, the United States exports cultural forms that are taken up by people all over the world, especially young people, and imports cultural forms as well. New readings on the adaptation of rap music and MTV in Middle Eastern countries and the controversies over the film *Slumdog Millionaire* show students some of the issues raised by the globalization of culture.

- **Thoroughly updated readings.** This edition includes over 60 new professional visual and verbal arguments, representing multiple argument genres, diverse stakeholders, and current global and local developments on the issues. Readings chosen for high student appeal include controversies over crossover films from Bollywood, the disposal of electronic waste (cell phones, computer monitors, and televisions), possible energy technologies, and the advantages of local food.

- **New rhetorical analysis writing projects in every readings chapter.** Each readings chapter now includes one major "Analyzing Arguments Rhetorically" writing project and one or more shorter projects in the Brief Writing Projects that involve rhetorical analysis. These projects ask students to focus on how arguments achieve their rhetorical effects and help them expand their critical thinking skills.

- **A revised Chapter 1 explaining globalization and offering a new Global Pursuit quiz and a new exploratory exercise on "glocalization," based on two photos.** The chapter updates the presentation of globalization theory, offers a new, lively Global Pursuit quiz, and engages students in responding to photos of a Starbucks in Beijing, China, and of an advertisement for a restaurant in Dhaka, Bangladesh.

- **Revised headnotes, questions on readings, and writing projects throughout.** Revised headnotes provide current contextual information on the authors and the readings; new questions encourage students to analyze, reflect on, and personally apply the new readings to their lives; and new writing projects invite students to add their voices to the argumentative conversations of the readings.

WHAT *GLOBAL ISSUES, LOCAL ARGUMENTS* OFFERS WRITING INSTRUCTORS AND STUDENTS

Global Issues, Local Arguments has grown directly out of my experiences as a writing instructor grappling with the ongoing challenge of teaching my students to be successful writers. I have designed *Global Issues, Local Arguments* with the following goals in mind: reaching a wide range of students with current, high-interest material; encouraging students to be involved citizens; fostering critical thinking; and, most of all, helping students develop as writers and arguers.

Reaching a Wide Range of Students. Many instructors are looking for ways to teach college reading and writing to students heading for diverse fields and are seeking accessible, stimulating, current issues to explore in their courses. This text has grown out of my work in writing classrooms with students whose interests range widely, from social work to engineering, from environmental science to business, marketing, and law. The public controversies in this book provide significant, complex, and lively readings that span fields. The arguments in each chapter stimulate active reading and motivate students to respond with their own writing.

Encouraging Students to Be Involved Citizens. The local and global issues in this book exemplify argument as an active, productive instrument to build communities of supporters and bring about change. Understanding stakeholders' investments in issues—why they care—and how they try to change their readers' thinking and move them to action can help students find their own investment in arguments they write. In its chapter introductions, readings, discussion questions, and writing assignments, this text pushes students to ponder their local connection to global issues and in doing so forges fruitful links between academic writing and civic engagement.

Helping Students Develop as Critical. Thinkers Issues that bridge local and global communities are ideal for teaching critical thinking because these issues are complex, layered, and multifaceted. In preparation for writing about these issues, students are encouraged to examine and weigh multiple perspectives and to consider the emotional impact of arguments. Recognizing the controversial nature of these issues, in selecting readings I focused on representing multiple political perspectives and including international views. As students wrestle with multisided arguments and seek to identify, analyze, and synthesize viewpoints on these issues, they develop key critical thinking skills.

Helping Students Develop as Writers and Arguers. Most importantly, this book functions as a tool to teach writing in three main ways:

- *It helps students analyze the rhetorical power of arguments and think about how to infuse that power into their own arguments.* Chapter introductions, headnotes to readings, discussion questions, and writing assignments direct students' attention to the ways that the structure, content, and depth of arguments are shaped by the target audience and the genre and publication. The multisided arguments in each chapter demonstrate the importance of rhetorical context and are particularly good at showing how writers tailor their claims, reasons, evidence, and emotional and imaginative appeals to move their readers to think from new perspectives. In addition, each chapter's readings represent diverse argument genres for students to analyze and respond to, such as op-ed pieces, researched arguments, policy analyses from news commentary magazines, advocacy Web site policy statements, fliers, posters, and editorial cartoons.

- *This text works on the principle that students write best when they acquire a solid base of knowledge on issues.* More than in a traditional anthology of readings, each chapter gives students a running start on understanding the issues and prepares them to wrestle with the complexity of the arguments: Chapter introductions, headnotes, and questions provide context for the readings, help students understand the controversies and the stakeholders, and prepare students to find their own connections and delve deeply in their analyses. These local and global arguments and the suggestions for writing assignments growing out of them provide prime opportunities for using writing to learn and using rhetorical analysis of print and visual texts as preparation for students' writing of their own arguments.

- *Global Issues, Local Arguments helps students develop as arguers.* It moves them beyond the tendency to think of argument as pro-con debate or to reach closure quickly on issue questions. It pushes students to listen carefully to views and reflect on them in order to clarify their own values and deepen their own perspectives. Featuring global-local issues that do not have simple solutions, this book emphasizes the intellectual work involved in reading and writing arguments and shows how argument is connected to problem solving as well as persuasion. In studying multisided issues, students work their way toward more complex, informed views and toward writing richer arguments.

STRUCTURE OF *GLOBAL ISSUES, LOCAL ARGUMENTS*

This text is modularly structured for use in multiple writing courses. It offers instruction on argument, a rich variety of readings for analysis and discussion, and a range of writing assignments to foster intellectual engagement and quality writing. Both the readings and suggestions for writing assignments can be easily incorporated into various writing courses. The following overview of the features of this global argument reader shows how it can bring relevance, liveliness, and rigor to the writing classroom.

Chapter 1, "Exploring and Defining Globalization." This introductory chapter equips students with a big-picture understanding of globalization and eases them into the significant issues in the text's readings by showing how the term *globalization* itself is a subject of debate. It briefly sketches the major controversies that underlie global issues. It invites students to begin thinking about the relationship between their local space—city, region, country—and global issues through two challenging but fun exploration activities: "Exploration One: How Wide Is Your Global View?" is an informal Trivial Pursuit-type quiz that asks students to see how much they know about other countries and cultures; and "Exploration Two: Globalization at Work" is an activity that asks students to consider how two photos depict sites where globalization and local cultures meet.

Chapter 2, "Analyzing and Writing Arguments." This instructional chapter teaches students (1) the key rhetorical characteristics of argument, (2) how to summarize an argument, (3) how to write a rhetorical analysis, and (4) how to write an argument. "Discussing and Writing" exercises ask students to apply the writing concepts to the professional arguments and the two student pieces, a rhetorical analysis and a researched argument. Strategies charts highlight ideas and steps to help students with writing summaries, rhetorical analysis essays, and arguments.

Seven Chapters of Readings on Important Global Issues. The seven chapters of readings present a rich array of print and visual texts (political cartoons, posters, and photos) on global-local issues. All of these readings are nonfiction—arguments—representing many stakeholders and argument genres, from op-ed pieces to longer policy statements, testimonies before Congress, and scholarly arguments. These readings vary in length and complexity, with each chapter including several challenging pieces. Most importantly, the print and visual texts in each chapter exemplify multisided arguments. The chapters focus on seven main global topics, each a network of issues with local dimensions:

- Chapter 3, "Trading Goods: Consumerism, Free Trade, and Sweatshops"
- Chapter 4, "Trading Financial Risk and Jobs: The Global Economic Crisis"
- Chapter 5, "Crossing Borders: Immigration"
- Chapter 6, "Protecting the Environment: Water Issues and Emerging Energy Technologies"
- Chapter 7, "Feeding the World: Biotechnology, Culture, and Local Food"

- Chapter 8, "Merging and Clashing Cultures: Media, Technology, Music, and Film"
- Chapter 9: "Defending Human Rights: Trafficking and Child Labor"

Many of these chapters' issues intersect, creating even richer conversations and fuller pictures of these complex problems. For example, trading goods, trading financial risk, immigration, and cultural exchange involve global movements of goods, money, jobs, people, and cultural products across national borders, all of which are related to controversies over free trade. The questions and writing projects at the ends of chapters, as well as ideas in the *Instructor's Manual,* help students make connections among the chapters' issues.

PEDAGOGICAL FEATURES OF *GLOBAL ISSUES, LOCAL ARGUMENTS*

The pedagogical features of the text are designed to provide students with background information, help them relate personally to the issues, help them read the arguments analytically, and help them synthesize and evaluate what they have read through writing.

Chapter Introductions That Give Background Information and Context.
The introduction that opens each chapter has four main objectives: (1) to spark students' intellectual curiosity about each chapter's topic; (2) to make these global issues appealing and accessible to instructors and students; (3) to help students find their own personal engagement with these issues; and (4) to provide historical information, explanations, and definitions of terms to equip students with the knowledge base they will need to understand the readings and write about the issues. Each chapter introduction includes the following features:

- A **"Question to Ponder"** asks students to think about their connections to the chapter's global issues.
- **"Context for a Network of Issues"** sketches the current status of the issues, provides brief historical information, and explains key terms such as *free trade, nongovernmental organizations,* and *offshore outsourcing.*
- **"Stakes and Stakeholders"** illuminates some of the main controversies and issue questions that people are arguing about, starts students thinking about the global and local ties, and prepares students to analyze how people's investments in these issues shape their arguments.
- **"Student Voice"** presents a student's personal narrative response to, or reflection on, the issue to convey its experiential reality and to inspire students to look for their own connections with global issues.

- **"International Voices"** presents brief views from another part of the world in interviews and newspaper articles, bringing a concrete, human dimension to these issues.

- **"Global Hot Spot"** uses an excerpt from a foreign news service or Web site to zoom in on one of the main regions or countries grappling with this global issue to show its complexity and to engage students emotionally and intellectually.

Context and Discussion Questions for Each Reading. Brief introductory headnotes with preview questions and follow-up questions for discussion accompany each visual and verbal text to help students analyze the rhetorical context and the rhetorical features of these arguments. These "For Class Discussion" items focus students' attention on how each piece works as an argument, how each contributes to the global conversation on the issue, and often how readings talk to each other. Rhetorical terms are intentionally generic (for example, "author's reliability and credibility" instead of "appeals to *ethos*") to enable instructors to use this text in a range of writing courses.

Four Student Essays Using MLA Style. Chapters 2, 3, 4, and 6 offer student researched writing—three in the form of researched proposal arguments and one a researched exploratory essay driven by a significant, complex question. These papers offer examples of MLA documentation style.

Questions Concluding Each Chapter. Each chapter's "Chapter Questions for Reflection and Discussion" pose questions that encourage students to see relationships among readings, to explore points of agreement and disagreement among these arguments, and to frame their own questions for further research. These questions mention subissues and often Web sites for students to investigate and research on their own or in groups.

Chapter Suggestions for Multiple Writing Assignments. To give instructors maximum flexibility in using this text, the writing assignments at the end of each chapter offer options for instructors and students who are using the chapter's material early in the course as well as those using it later. "Brief Writing Assignments" include suggestions for short, informal writing; for reflective and narrative pieces; for writing-to-learn pieces; and for writing that can help students generate ideas for their longer, more formal writing assignments. These writing assignments also lead students to find their own local stakes in these global matters and to think out their own views.

The suggestions for "Writing Projects" also offer a range of writing assignments:

- **Analysis and synthesis prompts** ask students to rethink one reading in light of another and to draw their own conclusions based on both arguments.

- **Rhetorical analysis assignments** ask students to examine one or more arguments in terms of their rhetorical effect on particular audiences.

- **Argument assignments** ask students to construct their own arguments on one of the chapter's subissues for different audiences.
- **Civic argument assignments** foster civic engagement through letters to political representatives or op-ed pieces directed to university or regional newspapers.
- **Community-based assignments** lend themselves to service learning and call for fieldwork, interviews, surveys, and research into local conditions.
- **Research projects** broaden or deepen the chapter's issues, often through Web research on international and local organizations or advocacy groups.

Glossary and Films List. The Glossary of this text provides brief definitions of rhetorical analysis and argument terms and of key economic and political terms related to globalization. A list of films related to each chapter's issues provides ideas for further individual and class exploration. The *Instructor's Manual* discusses ways to incorporate these films.

STRATEGIES FOR USING THIS TEXT

Global Issues, Local Arguments can be used alone or in conjunction with any rhetoric text or writer's handbook. Instructors may choose to use the readings in the chapters in a number of ways: (1) as texts to analyze for their views on global issues; (2) as models of arguments that students can examine for their rhetorical features, argument genres, and argumentative strategies; and (3) as conversations about controversial issues that students can join with their own writing. The modular structure of *Global Issues, Local Arguments* as well as the multiple thematic threads running throughout the chapters enable this text to support many different course designs.

INSTRUCTOR'S MANUAL

The *Instructor's Manual* suggests ideas for course designs with sample syllabi, examines the many local-to-global connections in the readings, provides rhetorical approaches to the articles, and discusses how issues have potential for local community involvement. Additional suggestions for class discussion, in-class activities, and research activities out of class are provided to aid instructors in tailoring the text to different course designs.

MYCOMPLAB

PEARSON
mycomplab   MyCompLab empowers student writers and facilitates writing instruction by uniquely integrating a composing space and assessment tools with market-leading instruction, multimedia tutorials, and exercises for writing, grammar, and research.

Students can use MyCompLab on their own, benefiting from self-paced diagnostics and a personal study plan that recommends the instruction and practice each student needs to improve her writing skills. The composing space and its integrated resources, tools, and services (such as online tutoring) are also available to each student as he writes.

MyCompLab is an eminently flexible application that instructors can use in ways that best complement their course and teaching style. They can recommend it to students for self-study, set up courses to track student progress, or leverage the power of administrative features to be more effective and save time. The assignment builder and commenting tools, developed specifically for writing instruction, bring instructors closer to their student writers, make managing assignments and evaluating papers more efficient, and put powerful assessment within reach. Students receive feedback within the context of their own writing, which encourages critical thinking and revision and helps them to develop skills based on their individual needs.

Learn more at www.mycomplab.com.

Global Issues, Local Arguments invites students and instructors—all of us—to broaden and deepen our perspectives on the world and to use argument to think together about the opportunities before us and the problems that now pervade our own local spaces and others' local spaces around the globe.

ACKNOWLEDGMENTS

I have been very fortunate to have had a colleague at Seattle University, Hilary Hawley, working with me on this edition. Her experience teaching composition and argument, her strong rapport with her students, and her commitment to environmentalism contributed to this revision. The chapters on water and energy technologies and food especially reflect her writing courses on these themes. Other chapters and parts of the book also benefited from her expert research and pedagogical knowledge. Throughout this revision, her professional competence and equanimity provided welcomed encouragement.

This second edition has also been enriched by the insights and experience of other colleagues at Seattle University and around the country. I am especially grateful to Tara Roth, whose keen civic and cultural awareness inspired the parallel writing courses she and I taught for several years using this book. Tara's ability to design innovative assignments and to make students ponder issues deeply and creatively was instrumental in my revision plans for this book. I am also grateful to my colleague Geoffrey Grosshans for his timely help on this project, to Jenny Halpin for ideas for readings in the immigration chapter, and to John Bean for his photo from Dhaka, Bangladesh. Finally, John Holland teaching in California and Michael Ronan and his colleagues at the Houston Community College system offered enlightening feedback, sharing their lively pedagogical experiences using this book in their writing courses.

I am appreciative of my academic institution, Seattle University, particularly for its commitment to social justice, its support of first-year writing seminars, and its ever deeper investment in global education.

Recent and former students played a significant role in this revision through their responses to the book's material in class and in their writing. I am grateful to those students with origins outside the United States for constantly challenging my classes to see other and bigger pictures of the world than our local and national ones. I owe special thanks to the students who shared their narratives of the way global issues have touched their lives: Rahel Tesfahun, Michael Caster, and Victoria Herradura added their perspectives to this edition as "Student Voices" in chapter introductions; and Patrick Scholze and Nicole Cesmat shared their passionate questions and concerns in their exploratory essay and op-ed piece, respectively. Special thanks to Tyler Bernard, Lindsey Egan, Matthew Brady, and Tine Sommer for the intellectual curiosity and hard work they channeled into their researched writing; they were a pleasure to work with. I want to thank Michael Caster, who contributed the photo of Starbucks in Beijing, and Michael as well as Kelsey Peck and Sean McCreight, who provided visions of globalization from their traveling and living abroad.

I have great respect for the pedagogical experience of the people who reviewed this book. Whenever I could, I followed their insightful and very useful suggestions, and I am grateful to these scholars and teachers: Jia-Yi Cheng-Levine, College of the Canyons; Gail S. Corso, Neumann College; Jessica Matthews, George Mason University; Veronica Pantoja, Chandler-Gilbert Community College; Tim N. Taylor, Eastern Illinois University; and James Deaver Traywick, Jr., Black Hills State University.

My deep thanks go to my skillful Longman team: to Lauren Finn, my knowledgeable editor; to Marcy Lunetta, who worked on the literary permissions for this text; and to Martha Beyerlein, who shepherded the production stage. Marion Castellucci, my development editor, proved to be invaluable once again in the creation of the new parts of this text and the complex shaping of all the parts into a whole.

Finally, I want to thank my brother for encouraging this project and for enlarging my views as he commented on the global financial crisis from Australia and my parents for their support. My deepest gratitude goes to my husband, Kenneth Bube, who has been a wonderful intellectual and domestic partner, standing by me at every step of this project, and my daughter, Jane Ellen, who has also continuously supported and cheered me on.

JUNE JOHNSON
Seattle University

Exploring and Defining Globalization

Almost overnight, globalization has become the most pressing issue of our time, something debated from boardrooms to op-ed pages and in schools all over the world.*
—Joseph E. Stiglitz, Nobel Prize-winning economist

In this statement, Joseph E. Stiglitz succinctly articulates the immediacy, scope, and importance of globalization. **Globalization**—the increasing interconnectedness of all parts of the world in terms of communication, trade, business, politics, travel, and culture—affects us every day although its presence is sometimes masked. Globalization influences the food we eat, the clothing we wear, the jobs we have, the people we live near, and so on.

This text invites you to join worldwide conversations about globalization by reading, examining, and discussing many of the major global issues that people are arguing about, and by adding your own voice to the public dialogue through your writing about these issues. As you read and enter into these conversations, this text will continuously draw your attention to its overall thesis: that global issues affect us locally and that local matters have global consequences. For example, think about these hypothetical but realistic problems:

- The payroll department of a software company is moved overseas, causing your mother to lose her job, yet this outsourcing has brought new career opportunities and vital income to some workers in India.

- Your little brother's toys were made by a U.S. toy company's factory in China where use of lead in paint is unregulated and where workers toil seven days a week in rooms filled with poisonous fumes.

**Globalization and Its Discontents* (New York: W. W. Norton & Company, 2002), 4.

1

- Some of the fruits and vegetables you regularly eat were grown by chemical-using agribusinesses in Nicaragua that have displaced and impoverished small subsistence farmers. You wonder if you should investigate produce grown organically by local farmers.

- Your city has experienced an influx of immigrants from different parts of the world. You are interested in the new international restaurants, but you wonder what forces are driving these people to leave their countries and how the United States will integrate these people into life here—for instance, into the schools.

What do these experiences have in common? They are instances of the increasingly global connections that link the everyday lives of Americans with the lives of people around the world: In short, they are examples of globalization. They also suggest some of the problems of globalization that call on us to be informed, to seek solutions, and to make decisions.

Before you embark on your exploration of the global issues presented in later chapters of this text, you can begin thinking about the relationship between your local space and global concerns by doing two exploration activities. The first, a series of questions, resembles those informal, playful quizzes, often about global geography, which you might have seen in newspapers. The second activity asks you to examine two photos that visually represent some aspects of the process of globalization. Both exercises suggest significant questions about the mental, cultural, and geographical locations we inhabit. Both highlight our perceptions and introduce the idea of multiple perspectives. These activities are intended to stimulate your thinking about globalization and to be an enjoyable challenge.

Finally, this introduction asks you to consider what people mean by the term *globalization*. It briefly sketches the major controversies surrounding the concept of globalization itself and the big-picture questions that underlie global issues. Thinking about what scholars, analysts, and activists are saying about globalization will prepare you to explore the issues and arguments presented in the chapter readings.

EXPLORATION ONE: HOW WIDE IS YOUR GLOBAL VIEW?

As Americans, we sometimes forget that people living in other countries view the world differently than we do. Globalization draws all parts of the world closer together, and yet reduced transportation time and rapid communication should not fool us into believing that there is only one perspective on events, people, and problems. This first exploration activity resembles a newspaper quiz or Trivial Pursuit game with global subject matter. As you answer the questions that follow, explore how wide your global view is. Try to think beyond an American or Western-dominated perspective of the world. Working individually, with a partner, or with a group, you may want to search for answers to some of these questions by using the Web and by checking general reference books in a library.

Global Pursuit

1. Which of the following last names is the most common?
   a. Smith
   b. Suzuki
   c. Garcia
   d. Ng
   e. Johnson
   f. Wong
   g. Rodriguez
   h. Zhang
   i. Naidu

2. What is the Westminster System?
   a. An exercise program that its originator has claimed on the Oprah Winfrey show will ensure longer life
   b. An accounting practice blamed for the 2008 collapse of major American financial institutions such as Lehman Brothers
   c. A parliamentary form of government that developed in England and is now widespread in the former British colonies and around the globe
   d. A formula for calculating carbon emissions according to population

3. Match the name of the monetary currency with the country where it is used.

Baht	Sweden
Krona	China
Euro	Russia
Ruble	Thailand
Yuan	Slovenia

4. Which are the two principal denominations within the religious faith of Islam?
   a. Sunni
   b. Druze
   c. Kurd
   d. Shi'a

5. What is a "pide"?
   a. An endangered shellfish and the main export of Sri Lanka
   b. A military division of the Taliban in Afghanistan
   c. A type of Turkish food, similar to a small pizza
   d. A kind of scarf worn by Palestinian women

6. What do OECD and OPEC stand for?

7. On a per-capita basis, which nation consumes the highest percentage of global energy resources?

8. Which country has the strongest overall economy in South America?
   a. Peru
   b. Brazil
   c. Venezuela
   d. Argentina

9. NASDAQ ... HANG SENG ... FTSE 100 ... DEUTSCHE BÖRSE ... to what industry do these terms belong and which world cities are associated with each?

10. List the American states that border on Mexico.

11. Antarctica is the fifth largest continent on the planet. Which nation controls it?

12. True or false? If you have a French passport, you can live and work in Italy without additional visas or other documents.

13. With what country is the art form known as *manga* associated?
    a. China
    b. Japan
    c. Korea
    d. Spain

14. Hip-hop originated in New York City but its musical roots are mainly in which country?
    a. Congo
    b. West Africa
    c. Indonesia
    d. Cuba

15. In what major international sporting event is the "yellow jersey" prized?

16. If you were being addressed by a native speaker of Tagalog, in which country would you most likely be?
    a. Cambodia
    b. The Philippines
    c. Kazakhstan
    d. Kenya

17. What is a "blood diamond"?
    a. An especially valuable form of South African diamond with a distinct pinkish tint
    b. A synthetic diamond used in laser medical treatments to remove cancers
    c. A diamond mined in a war zone and used to fund an insurgency or an invasionary war effort
    d. A diamond that the family of a Masai bride gives to the family of the groom

18. The Dalai Lama is the spiritual leader of which nation?
    a. Nepal
    b. Laos
    c. Tibet
    d. Bangladesh

19. In which African country do you still have an opportunity to see a silverback gorilla in the wild?
    a. Rwanda
    b. Chad
    c. Mali
    d. Zimbabwe

20. During the last decade, which country had the lowest overall standard of living?
    a. Australia
    b. Denmark
    c. Japan
    d. United States

After you have located answers for the quiz, write informally for ten to fifteen minutes in response to these questions:

1. Which quiz questions and answers surprised you the most?
2. Why was (or was not) this information part of your regular cultural knowledge?
3. Have these questions made you think of other parts of the world as familiar or unknown, as close to home or far away?
4. How did searching for answers to these questions affect your thinking about the importance of being knowledgeable about the world?

After you have responded to these self-reflection questions, your class might discuss your quiz answers, where you found them, and what insights this activity has given you about other parts of the world.

EXPLORATION TWO: GLOBALIZATION AT WORK

One term that often comes up in discussions of globalization is **glocalization**. The Pulitzer Prize-winning journalist Thomas L. Friedman gives his explanation of glocalization in *The Lexus and the Olive Tree*:

> I define healthy glocalization as the ability of a culture, when it encounters other strong cultures, to absorb influences that naturally fit into and can enrich that culture, to resist those things that are truly alien and to compartmentalize those things that, while different, can nevertheless be enjoyed and celebrated as different. The whole purpose of glocalizing is to be able to assimilate aspects of globalization into your country and culture in a way that adds to your growth and diversity, without overwhelming it.*

Working individually or in groups, examine these two images of globalization: photos of a global franchise in Beijing, China, and an advertising banner for a global franchise that sells coffee, pizza, and books in Dhaka, Bangladesh. Then answer the following questions in preparation for a class discussion. (For the second photo, note that Ramadan is a month-long religious observance for Muslims that involves prayer and fasting from dawn till sunset. Iftar is the meal after sunset that breaks the fast.)

Starbuck's in Beijing, China

---

*Thomas L. Friedman, *The Lexus and the Olive Tree*. (New York: Random House, 1999), 295.

Sign in Dhaka, Bangladesh

1. Describe the visual details of each photo.
2. What influences of globalization do you see in these photos?
3. Now, consider whether these images do (or do not) represent successful examples of "healthy glocalization" according to Friedman's explanation. Create mini arguments for the following different audiences by formulating at least two reasons for each position you are taking: (a) a U.S. audience thinking about each business; (b) a group of Chinese citizens considering this Starbucks; and (c) a group of Bangladesh citizens considering the business advertising the "Ramadan Special."
4. What additional information about these photos would you find helpful in discussing them in terms of glocalization?

   The following sections offer several different definitions of globalization, introduce you to the disagreements over these definitions, and prepare you to think about arguments over global issues.

WHAT DOES *GLOBALIZATION* MEAN?

When people argue about globalization "from boardrooms to op-ed pages and in schools all over the world," what exactly are they arguing about? On the most general level, people are debating the meaning of globalization itself. Disagreements may focus on any or all of these major underlying questions about globalization:

Underlying Controversies About Globalization

- Is globalization a new phenomenon? Or is it simply an accelerated stage in a centuries-long process?
- What forces are driving globalization?
- Is globalization inevitable and uncontrollable? Or is it the product of human decisions and therefore controllable?
- Is globalization harmful or beneficial, a problem or the solution to problems?
- Are there clear winners and losers in globalization?
  - How can global and national interests be balanced?
  - How is globalization changing our perceptions and behavior, and most other aspects of our lives?
- Should we welcome, applaud, encourage, resist, protest, or seek to change globalization?

These questions are the foundation of all the global issues explored in this book. As you discuss the global-to-local connections in the chapters' readings, think about how specific issues and individual arguments tap into these foundational questions.

Controversies Over Definitions and Interpretations of Globalization

Most books about globalization begin with the author's definition of globalization as both a process and a phenomenon. Indeed, the term *globalization* has sparked intense discussion and argument. Let's consider three different definitions and a visual interpretation of globalization.

One common definition of globalization explains it as the new, defining phenomenon of our historical moment. Thomas L. Friedman, Pulitzer Prize-winning foreign affairs journalist and columnist for the *New York Times*, articulates this vision of globalization:

Thomas L. Friedman's Definition of Globalization

". . . it is the inexorable integration of markets, nation-states and technologies to a degree never witnessed before—in a way that is enabling individuals, corporations and nation-states to reach around the world farther, faster, deeper and cheaper than ever before and in a way that is enabling the world to reach into individuals, corporations and nation-states farther, faster, deeper, and cheaper than ever before."*

The Lexus and the Olive Tree (New York: Random House, 1999), 9.

Note that Friedman emphasizes "integration" and pervasive, expansive, and accelerated connections. In his view, all parts of the world are being drawn ever closer together by unstoppable historical processes.

Another common definition of globalization zeroes in on the *economic* features and forces of globalization. Jagdish Bhagwati, a professor of international economics and a former special advisor to the United Nations on globalization, distinguishes between cultural globalization, the revolution in communication of the recent past and present, and the profound, powerful economic changes referred to as **economic globalization**:

Jagdish Bhagwati's Definition of Economic Globalization

"Economic globalization constitutes integration of national economies into the international economy through trade, direct foreign investment (by corporations and multinationals), short-term capital flows, international flows of workers and humanity generally, and flows of technology. . . ."*

Still other prominent voices in the globalization debate emphasize the *problems of defining globalization.* Cynthia Moe-Lobeda, a professor of theology and ethics, argues that it is crucial that we distinguish between two main definitions of globalization: (1) the "intercontinental connections," the way that transportation, communication, and technology have facilitated the movement of materials, goods, and ideas around the world and among continents and countries (basically Friedman's definition), and (2) the dominant model and system of economic globalization (Bhagwati's definition). Moe-Lobeda asserts that the first kind of globalization describes a process of modernization and technological change that is inevitable and beneficial in many ways, whereas economic globalization is not inevitable and not universally beneficial. She contends that it matters *how* we define globalization because Friedman's definition of globalization masks the power dynamics driving global economic forces while Bhagwati's definition downplays who has control of economic forces and who is benefiting the most from the increased connections around the world. Moe-Lobeda and other opponents of economic globalization believe that it needs to be described in terms that reveal how it distributes economic and political power.† David Korten, a scholar, an activist, and one of the most vocal

---

In Defense of Globalization (New York: Oxford University Press, 2004), 3.
†"Defining Globalization: A Faculty Roundtable," in "Debating Globalization: An Interdisciplinary Dialogue" (conference, Seattle University, April 16–17, 2004).

and well-known critics of economic globalization, provides such a description:

David Korten's Definition of Economic Globalization

"[Economic globalization refers to] the forces of corporate globalization advanced by an alliance between the world's largest corporations and the most powerful governments. This alliance is backed by the power of money, and its defining project is to integrate the world's national economies into a single, borderless global economy in which the world's mega-corporations are free to move goods and money anywhere in the world that affords an opportunity for profit, without governmental interference."*

Economic globalization as an economic model and system is sometimes called "corporate globalization" or "neoliberalism." Among its main principles, **neoliberalism** as a political-economic philosophy maintains that governments should stay out of trade and give markets free rein; that resources and services such as railroads, electricity, and water should be controlled by private companies; and that capitalism and unregulated trade will lead to beneficial economic and social development.

In addition to verbal definitions, visual images define and interpret globalization. Scholar Wolfgang Sachs asserts that the "the image of the blue planet"† has become a rich symbol adopted by diverse stakeholders who assert different views of the globe and globalization. For example, for environmentalists, the image of the blue and green globe symbolizes the earth as a planet with limited water, air, livable land, and natural resources. Environmentalists want to convey that because the earth is all we have, we must work together to preserve it. However, for another group of stakeholders—the corporations who do business in countries all over the world—the image of the globe symbolizes the expansive potential of business territory and trade. Sachs explains that depicting the world in its entirety as a blue and green ball of continents and oceans with no country borders enables the business community to communicate the message that the entire world is open and available for economic growth.

In this text, the term *globalization* refers both to Friedman's definition of a technologically advanced, increasingly interconnected world, and to economic globalization. Several chapters specifically examine the interplay between globalization and the environment and globalization and culture. Although economic globalization influences globalization in all its forms,

---

When Corporations Rule the World (San Francisco: Berrett-Koehler Publishers, 2001), 4.
†"Globalization and Sustainability," in *The Globalization Reader*, ed. Frank J. Lechner and John Boli, 2nd ed. (Malden, MA: Blackwell, 2004), 398.

also keep in mind the other definitions as you read and discuss the arguments in this book.

Controversies Over Responses to Globalization

One reason that globalization is so controversial is that the lived experience of it differs depending on people's country, economic class and status, race, gender, age, and even religion. In the last three years, and especially since the global economic crisis of 2008 exploded, arguments about globalization have intensified as people world-wide ponder the positive and negative effects of globalization on their countries, cultures, and individual lives.

The responses to globalization and the suggestions for how to manage it range along a continuum.

Strong Supporters of Globalization. On one end of the continuum, supporters praise globalization's sharing of knowledge and technologies. They point to the growth of industries and new markets and the rate at which developing countries are being integrated into the international economy. Arguing that globalization has improved the standard of living and increased life-span for many, they promote expanded globalization. These most positive supporters of globalization argue that the problems come from people, institutions, and countries that try to interfere with globalization. Taking a strong stand in favor of economic globalization and open markets, they warn developing countries, as well as developed countries such as the United States, not to erect barriers to international trade that would interrupt the process of globalization but instead to welcome more open exchanges of goods, people, and culture.

Supporters of Globalization as a Process. Another group of globalization advocates emphasizes the process of globalization. They contend that most of the problems that countries are experiencing with globalization are temporary setbacks related to the current stage of globalization. They say that global trade must continue to grow and that developing nations must continue to push toward full economic and industrialized maturity. Advocates of globalization such as Jagdish Bhagwati argue that the problems people attribute to globalization, such as world poverty and hunger, will diminish and that more people will benefit from globalization as these developing countries participate more in the international economy.

Envisioning integration into the global economy as a "development ladder" that countries need to climb through the collaboration of governments and private business and the spreading of scientific and technological advances, economist Jeffrey Sachs offers a hopeful win-win vision of globalization that involves "shared prosperity" rather than simply a redistribution of wealth from rich countries to developing ones.*

Moderate Critics of Globalization. These people acknowledge the gains and benefits of globalization but voice objections, mainly about the unequal distribution of benefits and about problems with the global market. For example, George Soros, an entrepreneur, billionaire, activist, philanthropist, and author, sees globalization as an opportunity for greater freedom for everyone; however, he argues that the public good and social well-being of people in developing countries, especially, have been overrun by market forces. Similarly, Joseph E. Stiglitz, in his book *Making Globalization Work* (2006), argues that the way globalization has been conducted—rather than globalization itself—is at fault. He points out that economic globalization favors industrialized nations over developing nations, which lack the economic advantages to compete, and that globalization so far has resulted in "unbalanced outcomes, both between and within countries".[†] Soros, Stiglitz, and many other analysts of globalization call for a revision of the system, first by reforming the institutions of global governance such as the International Monetary Fund, the World Bank, and the World Trade Organization, which put decision-making power into the hand of an elite financial community unaccountable to the people whose lives are most directly affected. Pushing these organizations toward more democratic participation would provide checks and balances on market forces and protection for the public good of people in developing countries and poor people everywhere.

Strong Critics of Globalization. Toward the other end of the globalization continuum, some people vehemently challenge economic globalization. Environmentalists, advocates for social justice, spokespeople for preserving cultural identities and heritages, representatives of indigenous peoples and developing countries, political activists, and some economists see economic globalization as a warping of the market itself. Furthermore, Cynthia Moe-Lobeda, David Korten, Indian activist Vandana Shiva, and others believe that economic globalization, with its emphasis on immediate profits, is, in Korten's words, "enriching the few at the expense of the many, replacing democracy with rule by corporations and financial elites, destroying the real wealth of the planet and society to make money for the already wealthy. . . ."[‡] In short, they see economic globalization in its current form as inherently flawed, strongly antidemocratic, and harmful to

---

*Peter Sachs, *The End of Poverty: Economic Possibilities for Our Time* (New York: Penguin Press, 2005), 18. *Common Weath: Economics for a Crowded Planet* (New York: Penguin Press, 2008), 205.

[†]*Making Globalization Work* (NY: W. W. Norton, 2006), 8.

[‡]*When Corporations Rule the World*, 5.

people and the environment. They believe that people everywhere must reject the principle of economic growth, reduce consumption, and commit to preserving the environment and working for social justice in order to end world hunger and poverty.

Proponents of a Local Vision. On the far end of the globalization continuum, some critics are calling for a rethinking of globalization and new investment in local communities. Critics such as Gustavo Esteva and Madhu Suri Prakash focus on the ways that global forces have threatened "local spaces." They claim that it is arrogant and impossible to think "globally" because "[w]e can only think wisely about what we can know well." They say that global policies represent small groups foisting their local views and interests on other places and peoples. Esteva and Prakash envision an antiglobalization movement composed of "people thinking and acting locally, while forging solidarity with other local forces."* They urge all of us to resist global policies and forces at the local level as we make our decisions about what we eat, what we buy, and how we live.

Navigating the Controversies

As you read the arguments in this text about global issues and their local repercussions, you will see that these divergent definitions of and responses to globalization are embedded in these readings. Try to place the issues in the context of these big-picture questions about globalization: What assumptions have the writers made about the meaning of globalization? Are they assuming that globalization is inevitable? Do they believe that globalization is basically a good thing? Also examine the way their arguments pursue solutions to global problems and strive to win adherents to their views. After reading the multisided arguments in each chapter, consider how they have expanded and clarified your own thoughts and views about the way these issues influence your life.

---

*"From Global to Local: Beyond Neoliberalism to the International of Hope," in *The Globalization Reader*, 2nd ed. (Malden, MA: Blackwell, 2004), 412–16.

Analyzing and Writing Arguments

*Argument is an ethically powerful way of using conflict to conduct learning and inquiry, and to create change and newness.**

—James Crosswhite

Should U.S. cities follow Paris's example in becoming a bicycle zone with thousands of bikes to rent inexpensively? Should the United States grant more visas to highly educated immigrants? Who is responsible for the crisis in the global financial market that is affecting home mortgages, car loans, and retirement savings? Global issues like these, as you will discover as you read this book, are producing many public arguments.

Because arguments seek to shape readers' views of controversial issues, they can best be understood in rhetorical terms. The terms **rhetoric** and **rhetorical** refer to the persuasive use of language to accomplish certain ends in specific situations. Aristotle explained rhetoric as "the faculty of discovering in any particular case all the available means of persuasion." Scholar and rhetorician Lloyd Bitzer has expanded on Aristotle's definition and elaborated on the power and importance of rhetoric: "Rhetoric is a mode of altering reality, not by the direct application of energy to objects, but by the creation of discourse which changes reality through the mediation of thought and action."†

What these and many other definitions of rhetoric have in common is a focus on the use of language to persuade, to shape the way people see the world. Because rhetoric is enlisted all around us in arguments attempting to "change our reality," you as a citizen and a student will benefit from acquiring rhetorical skills to interpret and produce arguments.

To study arguments rhetorically means to realize that arguments are always produced in contexts. Reading rhetorically involves attending closely to the writer, the writer's purpose, the audience, and the genre or type of writing.

---

*James Crosswhite.*The Rhetoric of Reason: Writing and the Attractions of Argument.* (Madison: University of Wisconsin Press, 1996), 9.
†Quoted in Wayne Booth. *The Rhetoric of Rhetoric: The Quest for Effective Communication.* (Carlton, Victoria, Australia: Blackwell Publishing, 2004), 8.

When we think of an argument rhetorically, we think of it as written by someone who has a stake in the issue, to an audience, for a purpose, in a genre (from op-ed pieces to policy analyses to advocacy flyers to organizational and governmental white papers). Writers of arguments tailor their arguments to change readers' views and move them to action. However, these arguments can be skillfully, shoddily, responsibly, or deceptively constructed. Thinking rhetorically will enable you to examine arguments to determine how and why they are persuasive.

This chapter will introduce you to the main tools of civic and academic argument. First, it will explain the parts of an argument and the features to examine in analyzing an argument rhetorically. The second part of the chapter will provide some steps and strategies you can use to summarize arguments, write rhetorical analyses, and generate and structure your own arguments in response to the arguments you are reading. Knowing how to analyze arguments rhetorically will help you become a stronger, more sophisticated reader. Knowing how to speak back to texts and to construct your own reasoned and audience-based arguments will help you become a more confident, versatile writer.

A BRIEF INTRODUCTION TO ARGUMENT

The first step in understanding arguments rhetorically is to move beyond a casual understanding of argument. In everyday conversation, argument often refers to an opinion, a disagreement, or a fight. However, the discipline of writing and rhetoric has a more specialized and complete meaning for **argument:** a persuasive text that makes a claim and develops it with reasons and supporting evidence. In addition, argument is multisided, not merely two-sided. Usually, there are many positions that can be argued on any issue, not simply a pro and a con. Global issues tend to generate multiple views because these issues are complex and touch the lives of many people, groups, and institutions, all of whom have stakes in these issues.

Issue Questions, Claims, and Stakeholders

Arguments originate in issue questions. An **issue question** is a controversial question that could have many contestable answers. These controversial questions are behind every argument: no controversy, no argument. Writers form claims in answer to issue questions. You can think of a **claim** as a statement that asserts an arguable answer to an issue question.

Global issues are highly controversial and generate many issue questions. For example, urban farming is a controversial issue globally. Even though cities around the world—Vancouver, Canada; Beijing, China; Rosario, Argentina; Kyoto, Japan; and many others—are practicing urban farming, support for urban farming and systematic planning are lacking in many cities.

Some cities have outlawed agriculture and others consider it unimportant. Here are two issue questions related to urban farming: Can urban farming meet the world's growing need for food? What are the most effective ways to encourage urban farming? Notice how each question can be answered with different claims that would lead to different arguments.

Issue Questions	Claims
Can urban farming meet the world's growing need for food?	Urban farming cannot contribute substantially to feeding the world's growing population.
	Urban farming can be a partial solution in feeding the world's growing population.
	Urban farming can be a main solution in feeding the world's growing population.
What are the most effective ways to encourage urban farming?	In order for urban farming to succeed, the rate of growth for cities must be slowed by helping people continue living in more rural areas.
	In order to promote urban gardening as a source of food, city planners and politicians must set aside land in cities for urban gardening.
	To encourage urban farming, all new city buildings should be designed for roof-top gardens.

To think about arguments rhetorically means to think in terms of who is arguing and who cares—in other words, who are the **stakeholders** or people who have investments in the answers to these questions. Issue questions become claims when people who care about them—stakeholders—decide to take a stand on them. The stakeholders in any argument include the people who are motivated to write about the issues and the people affected by the issues. The following stakeholders are people who have stakes in the arguments about urban farming:

- city dwellers who stand to benefit from growing their own food or buying locally produced food
- environmentalists who want to preserve the environment by using it wisely
- urban planners who could help make this farming possible

- businesses and city residents buying land and buildings in cities
- policymakers who influence politicians
- politicians who make city laws

For each argument you read, try to state the issue question behind the claim and identify the writer's stake and others' stake in the issue: To whom does this argument matter?

DISCUSSING AND WRITING ▰▰▰▰▰▰▰▰▰

Determining Issue Questions, Possible Claims, and Stakeholders

We frequently buy new electronic gadgets to replace broken or outdated ones. Where should we dispose of these old computers, televisions, cell phones, and other electronic items? Can these be recycled in environmentally friendly ways? Currently, some of this electronic trash (e-waste), much of it containing toxic chemicals, is dumped in poor developing countries. The reading that follows argues that disposal of e-waste plunges us into environmental, legal, economic, and human rights problems.

Read the following advocacy statement posted on the Web site for Basel Action Network (BAN), an environmental watchdog group dedicated to alerting American consumers about the problems of e-waste. After reading this campaign piece, follow these steps:

1. State at least five issue questions related to e-waste.

2. List at least five stakeholders, people involved in these issue questions in one way or another.

3. Formulate at least five possible claims, answers to these issue questions that stakeholders might want to argue.

Remember that an issue question should have at least two different answers, and a claim should be a controversial, arguable statement. (Later in this chapter, we will return to this article and these issues.)

The e-Waste Crisis
Basel Action Network

Every year, an estimated 400 million units of obsolete electronics are scrapped. Four billion pounds of electronic waste, or e-waste, was discarded in the United States in 2005, accounting for between 2% and 4% of the municipal solid waste stream. As much as 87.5% of this was incinerated or dumped in landfills. Of the remaining 12.5% collected for "recycling," industry sources claim that about 80% is exported to developing countries where it is processed in primitive conditions, severely endangering the environment, workers and communities. Pollution created by irresponsible e-waste processing can also come back to haunt those in the exporting countries as well in the form of air pollution fallout via long-range transport.

The world faces an e-waste crisis because of the following factors:

Huge volumes: The dual forces of rapid obsolescence of electronic gadgetry combined with astronomically burgeoning use have created mountains of e-waste—the largest growing waste stream our economy produces.

Toxic design: Electronic equipment contains some of the most toxic substances known: mercury, lead, cadmium, arsenic, beryllium, and brominated flame retardants, among others. Thus, when this equipment becomes waste, it is toxic waste. When burned, even worse toxins can be formed such as dioxins and polycyclic aromatic hydrocarbons that can cause cancer and birth defects. Until recently, far too little emphasis has been placed by manufacturers on eliminating toxic materials.

Poor design and complexity: E-waste is full of many different materials (such as multiple kinds of metals, plastics, and chemicals) that are mixed, bolted, screwed, snapped, glued, or soldered together. This makes separation for recycling difficult. Further, little attention has been paid to designing equipment for recycling. Therefore, recycling either requires intensive labor or sophisticated and costly technologies.

No financial incentive to recycle: There's usually not enough value in most electronic waste to cover the costs of responsibly managing it in developed countries unless laws require such management as a service industry. For this reason it is exported to countries where workers are paid low wages and the infrastructure and legal framework are too weak to protect the environment, workers and communities.

Reuse abuse: Sending equipment and parts for reuse—an important solution—can easily be abused by falsely labeling scrap as reusable or repairable equipment. Often this "reusable" equipment ends up getting dumped in countries lacking any infrastructure to properly manage it.

Policy of "free trade in toxic waste": In the U.S. and Canada, the laws governing export of trade in hazardous electronic waste are tragically inadequate, and thus these two countries are the primary sources of the global crisis. The U.S. is the only developed country in the world that has failed to ratify the 1989 Basel Convention, an international treaty controlling trade in hazardous waste from richer to poorer countries. In

1995, that treaty adopted a full ban on exports from rich to poorer countries. Both the U.S. and Canada actively oppose this prohibition. In Canada, the Basel Convention is not properly implemented, allowing almost all e-waste to flow abroad freely. In both countries, then, it is perfectly legal for businesses to maximize profit by exporting toxic electronics to developing countries, even when this export is a violation of the laws of importing countries. The export of toxic electronic waste to developing countries disproportionately burdens them with a toxic legacy and allows for externalization of real costs.

Prison laborers employed to process e-waste: Unlike other countries in the world, the U.S. sends much of its hazardous e-waste to U.S. prisons to process in less-regulated environments without the worker protections and rights afforded in the private sector. Moreover, such operations amount to government subsidies, undermining the development of responsible private-sector recycling infra-structure and distorting the economics of recycling.

Private data is imbedded in electronic devices: Computers, PDAs, mobile phones, and even printers and fax machines hold private data such as social security, bank account, and credit card numbers and private emails. These can be used by criminals involved in identity theft to hijack bank accounts and conduct blackmail and extortion if this data is not completely eradicated. Loss of confidential data is another form of liability and irresponsibility stemming from improper e-waste disposal.

Lack of regulation requiring proper management: U.S. regulations mostly exempt the electronic waste stream from environmental laws and active OSHA* oversight. Further, according to the laws of Canada and the U.S., most toxic electronic waste is still perfectly legal to dispose of in nonhazardous waste landfills and incinerators.

DOCUMENTED HARM

In 2002, the Basel Action Network (BAN) and the Silicon Valley Toxics Coalition released the ground-breaking report and film *Exporting Harm: The High Tech Trashing of Asia,* which exposed the toxic "recycling" of discarded electronics in China. A second film and report released in 2005 by BAN, *The Digital Dump: Exporting Reuse and Abuse to Africa,* showed similar tragic results happening in Africa, this time in the name of 'reuse' and 'bridging the digital divide.' Images of men, women, and children burning tons of toxic circuit boards, wires, and plastic parts

---

*OSHA is the Occupational Safety and Health Administration, part of the United States Department of Labor. It was created in 1971 to protect workers on the job.

exposed the fast-cheap-and-dirty side of our consumption of computers, televisions, faxes, printers, etc. Furthermore, BAN analyzed hard drives from exported computers collected in Africa and found massive amounts of private data freely available for criminal exploitation. We have also discovered that when U.S. prisoners are used as cheap labor, they are exposed to these poisons as well. The Federal Prison Industries' UNICOR, which processes much of the e-waste in the US, is now the focus of a Department of Justice investigation for the toxic exposures prisoners suffer. Finally as much as 87 percent of discarded toxic e-waste is simply dumped in municipal landfills or incinerators, ill equipped to contain or destroy such toxic waste.

Unfortunately this grossly irresponsible waste mismanagement and toxic trade is the norm in the North American recycling industry. It is still all too commonplace for recyclers and even electronics manufacturers, aided by the inadequate or non-existent policies of the Canadian and U.S. governments, to leave the dirty and dangerous work of managing our toxic waste to the poorest of the poor in developing countries. The resulting environmental hazards and social injustice ravage the land and people in these developing nations. Furthermore, these poisons come back to our shores and into our bodies via long-range air and ocean pollution, toxic imports and contaminated food.

GOVERNMENT FAILURE: EXTERNALIZING OUR TOXIC IMPACTS

To date, unlike the 27 member countries of the European Union, the United States and Canada have failed to create legislation providing a national system to finance and responsibly deal with toxic e-waste. Instead, an e-waste anarchy is sanctioned, where we can exploit the cheap and dirty 'solutions' that 'externalize' (or pass on) the real toxic impacts and their costs to others—poor communities in developing countries, disempowered prisoners in this country, or local municipalities and taxpayers who suffer from this material getting dumped in local landfills or incinerated, polluting soil, air and water. Further, the U.S. and Canada have failed to ratify or properly implement the Basel Convention that prescribes international rules to prevent such toxic waste trade.

U.S. Congress' watchdog agency, the Government Accountability Office (GAO) recently published a report entitled, "Electronic Waste: EPA Needs to Better Control Harmful U.S. Exports through Stronger Enforcement and More Comprehensive Regulation" [http: //www.gao .gov/new.items/d081044.pdf]. The GAO report describes, in no uncertain terms, the complete inadequacy of legislation to control e-waste exports and the lack of EPA enforcement of the minimal regulations that do exist, resulting in a flood of toxins to the developing world.

Instead of properly regulating electronic waste management and trade, the EPA has tried to bring interest groups together to create voluntary solutions. These efforts have ended in failure or have produced little more than minimalist, 'lowest-common denominator' standards, which seemingly please everyone, including waste exporters, but result in continued abuse to the environment and human health. One of these efforts is the recently released "R2" Standard for Responsible Recycling.

Meanwhile, in lieu of an appropriate federal response, states and municipalities must cope with the national failure by passing a variety of local laws and state laws. However, the U.S. Constitution forbids these local governments from legislating international trade, so states and municipalities are helpless to prohibit the flood of e-waste leaving our shores. It is in this unregulated landscape, that responsible electronics recycling companies are challenged to compete against unscrupulous brokers, and exporters and those who deceptively call themselves "recyclers." These bad actors simply load up seagoing containers and ship U.S. hazardous electronics to the highest bidders globally. Almost always, this results in the wastes shipped to a developing country to be processed by cheap, unprotected labor to maximize profits. These "low road" operators are thriving while the responsible companies, with their safer, more expensive methods, struggle. ∎

The Core of an Argument: A Claim with Reasons

To move from a claim to an argument, you need reasons to support the claim. We say that the core of an argument consists of a claim with **reasons.** A claim answers an issue question and becomes an argument when it is supported implicitly or explicitly by reasons. In reconstructing the core of arguments you read and in creating your own arguments, it is helpful to state reasons as *because* clauses. *Because* clauses help to show the logical and arguable reasons justifying the claim. In order for arguments to be persuasive, the claims and reasons that writers craft should be tailored to the values, assumptions, and interests of their chosen audience; in other words, they should be audience-based reasons. What reasons would make this audience consider this claim?

Let's take the example of the controversies over bottled water and its wide-spread consequences. People are arguing about how the corporate bottling of water—taking it from the ground and selling it in bottles—is exploiting sources of water in rural regions, including in developing countries like Kenya. They are also arguing about the production, recycling, and disposal of tons of plastic bottles. The following chart presents some examples of claims and audience-based reasons in response to this issue question: Should universities and college students continue to buy bottled water? Notice how the reasons change depending on the audience.

Issue question: Should universities and college students continue to buy bottled water?	
Audience and Stakeholders	**Argument Cores: Claim and Reasons**
Audience: University administration considering getting rid of vending machines with bottled water **Stakeholders:** The university administration, college students, and bottled water companies	**Claim:** Universities and college students should continue to purchase bottled water. **Reasons:** Because bottled water conveniently fits students' on-the-go schedules. Because students think bottled water tastes better than tap water.
Audience: University administration considering reducing the use of bottled water on campus **Stakeholders:** College athletic departments, college athletes, the university administration, and bottled water companies	**Claim:** College athletic departments should continue to purchase bottled water for athletic teams. **Reasons:** Because bottled water provides an ever-ready beverage that athletes especially need while engaged in strenuous physical activity. Because bottled water comes with good financial deals between the companies and universities purchasing bottled water in bulk.
Audience: Residence halls exploring ways to promote the university's commitment to global sustainability and healthy living **Stakeholders:** Student environmentalists, other college students, university administrations	**Claim:** College students should not continue to purchase bottled water. **Reasons:** Because the bottled water industry is producing tons of plastics that are damaging the environment world-wide. Because bottled water is often less healthful and safe than publicly regulated tap water.

These examples show a few of the argument cores that could be constructed in response to this issue question. Each argument core would lead to an entirely different argument with different reasons that would appeal to a different audience.

Assumptions in Argument

Besides claims and reasons, there are other parts of arguments to consider when thinking of arguments rhetorically. In addition to choosing audience-based reasons related to the beliefs, values, and interests of their intended audience, writers should think out the assumptions behind their reasons and determine if the audience shares these assumptions. You can think of **assumptions** as the principles behind the reasons. If these principles are acceptable to the audience, then the reasons will seem good and logical and will function as strong justification for the claim.

> **Example of a claim and reason:** We should have mandatory labeling stating the country of origin for all imported foods because such labeling would improve the monitoring of food safety in the global food system.

> **Assumption/principle:** Monitoring food safety in the global food system is important and beneficial.

Assumptions may be buried inside the argument or overtly discussed. Thinking out these assumptions and figuring out if they, too, need to be argued and supported often makes the difference between a successful argument and an unpersuasive one. In the following examples, the rationale explains possible problems with the argument that might emerge related to the assumptions behind the reasons.

> **Audience:** University administration considering getting rid of vending machines with bottled water.

> **Claim:** Universities and college students should continue to purchase bottled water.

Audience-Based Reasons	Thinking Out Assumptions
Because bottled water conveniently fits students' on-the-go schedules	**Assumption 1:** Convenience for busy students is a high priority for the university.
Because students think that bottled water tastes better than tap water	**Assumption 2:** Providing products that appeal to students' tastes is important to the university.
	Rationale: If the university administration does not value student convenience and satisfaction above other things, then the reasons will not be workable, or the writer will need to justify the assumptions as well as support the reasons.

Audience: University administration considering reducing the use of bottled water on campus.

Claim: College athletic departments should continue to purchase bottled water for athletic teams.

Audience-Based Reasons	Thinking Out Assumptions
Because bottled water provides an ever-ready beverage that athletes especially need while engaged in strenuous physical activity	**Assumption 1:** Conveniently meeting the physical needs of university athletes is important to the university.
Because bottled water comes with good financial deals between the companies and universities purchasing bottled water in bulk	**Assumption 2:** Saving money is important to the university.
	Rationale: If the needs of university athletes and the finances of the university are not top priorities, then other reasons would be more persuasive, or these reasons will require justification and supporting evidence.

Audience: Residence halls exploring ways to promote the university's commitment to global sustainability

Claim: College students should not continue to purchase bottled water.

Audience-Based Reasons	Thinking Out Assumptions
Because the bottled water industry is producing tons of plastics that are damaging the environment world-wide	**Assumption 1:** Producing tons of plastic and damaging the environment are bad consequences.
Because bottled water is often less healthful and safe than publicly regulated tap water	**Assumption 2:** Drinking unhealthful or unsafe water is something to be avoided.
	Rationale: Most likely the audience would agree that these consequences are negative. This argument, then, would concentrate on establishing exactly *how* bottled water's tons of plastic hurt the environment, and on *how* bottled water is unsafe and unhealthful, not on whether these effects and qualities are bad.

When you analyze an argument, determining the assumptions behind the reasons, which will often be implied and not stated, can help you understand how well an argument is constructed. Writers can build stronger arguments by adjusting their reasons and assumptions to their audience and in some cases, by defending and developing the assumptions as well as the reasons—in effect, carrying on a two-tier argument.

DISCUSSING AND WRITING ▐▬▬▬▬▬▬▬▬▬▬

Thinking Out Argument Cores and Assumptions

Working individually or in groups, take three of the claims that you formulated in the exercise on page17 in response to the e-waste article. For each of these claims, do the following tasks:

1. Develop at least two reasons that would support the claim.
2. For each reason, state what you think is the assumption, the principle behind the reason that an audience would have to accept to find the reason persuasive.

The Development of an Argument: Evidence

Another important part of an argument is the kind, amount, and quality of supporting evidence that writers use to make their arguments persuasive. **Evidence** can take the form of examples, facts, numerical data, testimonies and quotations, or further reasoning. Writers choose their evidence to meet the needs of their audience. What constitutes good evidence? Rhetorician Richard Fulkerson offers helpful criteria for evaluating the evidence in an argument, which he calls the **STAR criteria.***

STAR CRITERIA FOR EVALUATING EVIDENCE IN AN ARGUMENT
• **Sufficiency:** Is there enough evidence for this audience? • **Typicality**: Is the evidence typical or is it extreme and deceptively chosen? • **Accuracy**: Is the evidence accurate and current? • **Relevance**: Is the evidence related to the claim, reasons, and assumptions?

---

*Richard Fulkerson explains these criteria in more detail in his book *Teaching the Argument in Writing*. (Urbana, IL: NCTE, 1996), 44-50.

Applying the STAR criteria to evidence in the arguments you read and later to your own arguments will help you assess the effectiveness of the argument. The key rhetorical question, though, is "For whom is the evidence persuasive?" As with the other parts of an argument, evidence is also rhetorical in that what an audience considers persuasive evidence depends on its values, interests, and beliefs. Arguments that succeed with their audiences include appropriate audience-based evidence. As we saw in the charts on pages 23–24, writers may need to create additional subarguments to support their assumptions with evidence; in other words, other parts of the argument, besides the reasons, may call for evidence to make the whole argument persuasive.

Responses to Alternative Views

The final structural part of an argument is the writer's recognition of alternative or opposing views. Although not all arguments acknowledge opposing views, the presence or absence of these acknowledgments and responses to these views often makes the difference between a persuasive argument and a weak one. Because arguments are controversial and arguers most likely will be writing to an audience who is uninformed, undecided, or opposed, it is important for writers to show their awareness of alternative views and respond logically and authoritatively to them. Writers may either concede to those views by accepting their validity and then shift the focus back to their own case, or they may rebut them with counter-reasoning and counter-examples (see the chart on page 27). For example, if a writer is arguing the claim that her university should stop supplying bottled water in vending machines, she would need to anticipate objections that students and the university might make. She could either concede and admit that these objections do make sense and then shift back to her own views, or she could argue directly against these objections in a rebuttal, using her own reasons and examples. How much space a writer devotes in an argument to opposing views also depends directly on the audience.

Arguments Tailored to Audiences

The whole construction of an argument—its degree of edginess and development—is a function of the writer's relationship to his or her purpose, audience, and choice of the type of argument (flier, formal researched argument, editorial, and so forth). We can think of arguments as ranging on an argument continuum, with positions on the continuum representing the writer's specific purpose and relationship to the audience. On one end of the continuum, the arguer would have an exploratory purpose and would imagine a cooperative or collaborative relationship with

RESPONSES TO ALTERNATIVE OR OPPOSING VIEWS	
Claim: The university should stop selling bottled water in vending machines.	
Example of Concession	**Example of Rebuttal**
It is true that busy students are often racing around campus to classes and activities. I know that sometimes fountains are difficult to find, and when you do find one, it may be dirty. I also recognize that being thirsty can impair a student's ability to concentrate. One day when bad traffic made me late to campus and I had to run to class, all I could think about during my class was Gatorade, Pepsi, and water. Nevertheless, it is easy to carry aluminum reusable water bottles, which are inexpensive.	Although students get thirsty amidst their busy schedules, the university could try harder to maintain drinking fountains in clean, working order, and students could carry water in reusable aluminum containers, reducing their need to buy bottled water.

the audience. In effect this writer says, "Think this issue out with me." On the other end of the continuum, the arguer is basically writing propaganda with a hard-sell purpose that blasts the audience, denying any space or value to audience members. This writer says, "You have to see this issue my way, the only way." The more the writer engages in dialog with the audience and seeks to see the issue from this alternative perspective, the more the argument will convey a problem-solving, inquiry approach. When writers are assured of their audience's agreement, they may choose not to include alternative views.

The argument continuum shown on pages 28–29 demonstrates the range of possible purposes and relationships with the audience. All arguments fall somewhere on this continuum. When you are reading an argument, determine the purpose of the argument and the stance the writer is taking toward the audience. Is the writer trying to solve a problem of interest to the audience? Is the writer mostly in an inquiring mode, entertaining differing perspectives on the issue question; or is the writer shoving a view at the audience? How firmly and aggressively is the arguer asserting a claim? How does the engagement with alternative or opposing views enrich the argument?

Now that we have examined the structure of arguments in some detail, you may be wondering, "Does everyone who writes and publishes an argument plan the argument as systematically as this explanation suggests?" The answer is "No." However, writers who construct successful arguments for their audiences have most likely thought carefully about their issues in ways that reflect the deep structure of their arguments. You will have the greatest success with your own arguments if you think of planning them in terms of claims, reasons,

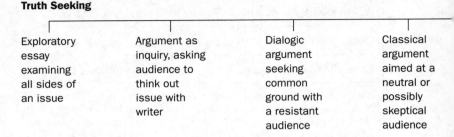

Truth Seeking

| Exploratory essay examining all sides of an issue | Argument as inquiry, asking audience to think out issue with writer | Dialogic argument seeking common ground with a resistant audience | Classical argument aimed at a neutral or possibly skeptical audience |

The Argument Continuum: From Truth-Seeking to Persuasion

assumptions, evidence, and acknowledgment of alternative views. (The last section of this chapter offers suggestions to help you with this planning.)

DISCUSSING AND WRITING

Analyzing an Argument's Structural Parts

The following argument presents a citizen's and consumer's perspective on the problem of sweatshop-made goods. The writer is addressing the issue questions, *Should we care whether our goods are made in sweatshops, and what can we do to reduce the use of sweatshops?* Sweatshops are highly exploitive factories with extremely long working hours and days, unsafe conditions, low and/or unreliable wages, and management control of workers. As you study this argument, you will see that the writer, Ed Finn, proposes that we change our buying habits for three main reasons.

Working individually or in groups, read the following example of a complete, well-crafted argument and analyze it by identifying these parts of the argument:

1. the claim
2. the reasons
3. the assumptions behind the reasons
4. several pieces of evidence used to support each reason
5. the alternative/opposing views; and the writer's response to these views.

This argument first appeared in June 2003 in the *Canadian Centre for Policy Alternatives Monitor,* a progressive monthly journal focusing on social and economic justice. According to its Web site, this organization's motto is "think again," and it seeks to inform people of alternatives "to the message that we have no choice about the policies that affect our lives" (www.policyalternatives.ca/aboutus/). Ed Finn is the senior editor of this publication.

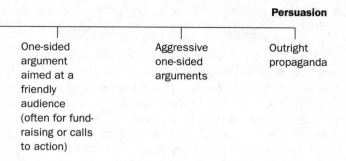

Persuasion

| One-sided argument aimed at a friendly audience (often for fund-raising or calls to action) | Aggressive one-sided arguments | Outright propaganda |

Harnessing Our Power as Consumers: Cost of Boycotting Sweatshop Goods Offset by the Benefits
Ed Finn

Being follicly challenged, I can't venture out in the noonday sun without a cap. So I went looking for one. My shopping foray took nearly two weeks. Not because headgear was hard to find in Ottawa, but because I wanted a cap made by workers who were fairly paid and well-treated—and that kind of headgear is hard to find.

Had I been content to buy a cap made in a sweatshop in China, Haiti, Malaysia, or some other Third World nation, it would have been easy. The stores were full of them. But I wanted a cap made preferably by a unionized worker in Canada, or, failing that, in another country with decent labour standards.

After visiting a score of clothing shops, I finally located such a cap. It was made in England. I had to pay nearly $40 for it, four or five times more than a comparable cap from an Asian sweatshop would have cost. But the Brit beanie was far more comfortable and durable. It comes out of the washing machine looking as good as new. I bought it four years ago and it still shows no sign of wearing out. So, even from an economic standpoint, I didn't suffer for sticking to my "buy non-sweatshop" principles.

Most Canadians, sad to say, don't make any effort to find domestic apparel. Or they give up after visiting their third or fourth clothing store, where the racks are crammed with shirts, pants, sweaters and jackets sewn by underpaid and abused workers in Asia or Latin America.

Imported outfits do cost less. They appeal to anyone looking for the cheapest item and indifferent to how and where it was made. Even when reminded that millions of children under the age of 14—the

UN estimates they number at least 25 million—are being inhumanly exploited in Third World sweatshops, most Canadians find the lure of a "bargain" irresistible.

They should be more concerned—not just because they want to help mistreated workers overseas, but because they want to help themselves. The exploitation of cheap foreign labour is part of a vast global strategy designed ultimately to force wages down in Canada and other Western nations. This strategy is already well advanced. Freed from national restrictions by free trade, deregulation, and instant global communications systems, the transnational corporations can now relocate production to countries and regions where wages, taxes, and environmental laws are the lowest.

This corporate mobility has eroded the power of Canadian workers and their unions to protect their jobs, benefits, and working conditions.

As consumers, however, we are far from powerless. We can refuse to buy the products of child labour, prison labour, and sweatshop labour in the Third World. In the short term, this will unavoidably increase our living expenses, but in the long term it could save our jobs and prevent our wages from plummeting further.

The corporations are counting on us to keep our needs as consumers entirely separate from our needs as workers. And, unfortunately, up to now, most of us have done just that—in the process unthinkingly worsening our own financial security. The more sweatshop goods we buy, the more we reward the corporations for their downsizing here and their cheap labour strategy abroad. And—contrary to some right-wing pundits—we aren't doing any favours to oppressed foreign workers, either. We are in effect perpetuating their serfdom.

Some politicians, business leaders and academics argue that, if we boycotted goods made by underpaid foreign workers, we would be depriving them of their livelihood, as meagre as it may be.

But this claim is as spurious today as it was in Victorian times, when it was advanced to rationalize the use of child labour. ("Take away these kids' jobs and they'll starve to death or turn to lives of crime.")

The same flawed reasoning was trotted out by conservatives to oppose the economic boycott of the apartheid regime in South Africa. Had their arguments been heeded, that country would still be ruled by a brutal and racist government, and Nelson Mandela would still be in prison.

The leaders of opposition movements in developing nations ruled by dictators know that boycotts of sweatshop goods would temporarily add to their people's woes. But they also know that, in the long run, such boycotts offer the best hope of toppling the dictators and thereby vastly improving their people's lives.

One such leader is Nobel Peace Prize winner Aung San Suu Kyi, who heads the National League for Democracy in Burma. Like Mandela, she too was jailed by that country's ruthless military rulers and still endures their harassment. She favours the same kind of economic sanctions that finally got rid of apartheid in South Africa, even if they temporarily cause more hardship for Burma's sweatshop workers.

"All profits from business enterprises in my country," she said recently, "go to a small privileged elite. Companies that continue to invest here only serve to prolong the agony of my country and its people by encouraging the military regime to persevere in its atrocities."

She could have said the same thing about consumers in Canada and other developed nations, who also prop up Burma's dictatorship when they buy made-in-Burma merchandise.

It's time for us to look at the labels of the goods we buy. If we stopped buying sweatshop products, we would accomplish three things: 1) we would be helping to slow down and eventually stop the export of jobs from Canada; 2) we would be helping the oppressed people in the Third World to throw off the yoke of military and corporate tyranny; and 3) we would be effectively challenging the corporations' global low-wage strategy.

Granted, such a change in our shopping habits would involve some additional costs to us as consumers. But these costs would eventually be offset by the gains we would derive as workers—and the gains that would be made by brutally mistreated workers in the Third World. ∎

A BRIEF INTRODUCTION TO RHETORICAL ANALYSIS

As you read in the introduction to this chapter, to rhetorically analyze a piece of writing—a verbal or a visual text— means to examine closely how the text is put together to create a specific effect. Although any text—a billboard, a course syllabus, a personal ad, a sermon, a travel brochure, a phone book— can be analyzed rhetorically, this section of the chapter will prepare you to analyze the arguments on global issues you will encounter in this book.

The Importance of Thinking and Reading Rhetorically

Before we look at how to read rhetorically, let's consider two important principles about rhetoric.

1. **Language plays an important part in constructing reality.** Language presents visions of what is real and shapes how we see the world. Taking a rhetorical approach to reading and writing emphasizes the knowledge-making, constructive potential of language and argument. As rhetorician James Berlin explains, "truth is dynamic and dialectical" and "truth is always truth for someone standing in relation to others" in a situation that is shaped by language.*

---

*James Berlin, "Contemporary Composition: The Major Pedagogical Theories," *College English* 44.8 (December 1982): 773.

2. **Every argument you read is actually a voice in a larger, ongoing public conversation.** No argument represents a complete answer or total view, and knowledge grows through these many contributions.

These two principles show that rhetoric is not decorative, static, or extraneous but part of our ongoing effort to make sense of the world. As contributions to larger conversations, arguments are moments of meaning-making in that effort. To take a rhetorical approach to arguments is to think about each argument as a part of an ongoing, situated conversation.

The rhetorical tools you will learn in this section will help you understand how arguments grow out of and contribute to these specific global conversations. These tools will help you evaluate the usefulness and value of these arguments for you and others. When rhetoricians talk about argument, they think, as rhetorician John T. Gage explains, in terms of "the sequence of moves which the writer has controlled for the purpose of leading the reader to assent."* Rhetorical reading, then, becomes a useful process for you as a citizen, student, and later a professional, of determining when an argument is well-constructed and when it deserves your "assent" because it has legitimately persuaded you. In addition, when reading and analyzing an argument, you will be able to determine when the writer is trying to solve a problem and when he or she is mostly selling his or her views, or even more, foisting them on you as if they were the only views.

In the next sections, you will learn how to apply your understanding of the structural parts of arguments and of some additional rhetorical principles to the analysis of arguments. For every argument you read, consider these key questions:

- For whom would this argument be persuasive? Or, put another way, what values, beliefs, and assumptions would an audience have to hold to find it persuasive?
- In what ways do you agree with that audience or differ from it? Why is (or is not) this argument persuasive for you?

Becoming adept at answering these questions for the arguments you read will spur your growth as a reader and writer. The following sections explain the foundational rhetorical concepts to help you examine the arguments you read. The examples of these concepts draw on the variety of stakeholders, views, and arguments on the problem of illegal immigration in the United States.

---

*John T. Gage, "Freshman English: In Whose Service?" *College English* 44.5 (September 1982): 472.

Identifying the Writer and the Writer's Angle of Vision

When you read an argument, you need to consider who is arguing. Begin with the writer of the argument. Figure out the writer's identity and background. In every argument, the writer expresses an **angle of vision,** which is the lens of values through which he or she is interpreting the issue.

CONSIDERING THE WRITER'S IDENTITY AND ANGLE OF VISION	
Rhetorical Concept and Working Definition	**Example Using the Illegal Immigration Issue**
Writer: Who is the writer or creator of the text? What is his/her background, profession? What knowledge or authority does he or she have?	Policymaker, immigration lawyer, Pulitzer-prize-winning journalist, Jesuit priest, film celebrity, advocacy organization in favor of immigrant rights
Angle of vision: All arguments have an angle of vision. Angle of vision refers to the selective seeing of the writer; the writer's angle of vision determines how the argument is framed and what is emphasized and what is omitted. The writer's stance on the subject is influenced by his/her values, beliefs, background (family history, education, gender, religion, age, class), ethnicity, political leanings. For every argument, we can ask, What is the writer's angle of vision, lens, filter, or perspective? How much does the angle of vision control or dominate the argument?	A Border Patrol agent "sees" illegal immigration differently from the way an economic analyst or the owner of a construction company sees it. A nativist organization wanting to restrict all immigration, especially illegal immigration, focuses on social problems such as crime rates and public costs and connects these to immigration. An environmental organization sees immigration through the lens of population growth and use of natural resources. For example, an environmental angle of vision might stress the damage to the desert plants and animals caused by the many people illegally crossing the deserts on the border.

Often, as in this book, introductory material for each argument provides information about the writer of the argument and helps you determine the writer's angle of vision. The writer's angle of vision can be perceived in every choice the writer has made in the argument: from the claim to the reasons and evidence; the way this evidence is presented to look positive or negative; the points emphasized; the consideration of alternative views; and the fairness or extremism of the language. Some arguments will never let you forget for a minute what the writer thinks of the issue and will make a conscious effort to shape your views at every point. Others will sequence and frame the evidence but also maintain a less insistent and aggressive presence. If the angle of vision of a writer does not coincide with your own values and views, you may find it more difficult to listen to the argument and find yourself talking back to the writer.

Identifying the Rhetorical Context

Another key part of thinking rhetorically is realizing that texts grow out of and operate in social contexts; therefore, we need to approach arguments as voices in controversial conversations. Arguers are moved to write by **motivating occasions;** they may be responding to a specific public event, private circumstance, or experience. Identifying the motivating occasion—the event, occasion, problem, or condition that prompts the arguer to speak out—can help you understand the argument. Related to the motivating occasion is the timeliness of the argument, what rhetoricians call the *kairos* or "why now" of the argument. You should also try to determine the specific **purpose** of the argument. Is the writer trying to change people's view of the issue, move them to action, or search for and work out an answer to a problem? Another part of the rhetorical context is the **audience** the writer has in mind, the people to whom he or she is directing the argument, sometimes called the target audience. Often, arguments have a primary and secondary audience, as in the genre of the open letter, which is written to a specific person although it will be read by a larger reading public. The audience—whether neutral, friendly, or antagonistic, uninformed or knowledgeable—influences the argument. Finally, the **genre** or type, kind, or category of argument also is related to the audience and purpose. Is this argument an editorial in a big city newspaper, a policy statement, a blog, an advocacy advertisement, a scholarly argument in a journal in a discipline, or is it a visual argument?

EXAMINING RHETORICAL CONTEXT	
Rhetorical Concept and Working Definition	**Example Using the Illegal Immigration Issue**
Audience. Who are the intended readers? What does the writer know about these readers' background knowledge, their interest in the subject, and their values, beliefs, and assumptions? Beyond the target audience, who might read this text?	Is the text directed toward a large, general audience of newspaper readers or toward scholars with years of background in the field? For example, does the audience already share the writer's belief that a strong, physical barrier at the border will not solve the illegal immigration problem?
Writer's motivating occasion and purpose. What is the occasion or event (exigency), the external or internal cause that compelled the author to write? What is the change the writer wants to bring about in the readers?	Is Congress voting on an immigration reform bill? Does the writer want to influence voters? What has the news reported on how many illegal immigrants have died recently crossing the border through the desert?

Kairos. *Kairos,* a term from classical rhetoric, refers to the "rightness" of the argument for the moment and the situation. What is the timing and appropriateness of a text? What is the kairotic moment for the argument? Why is this argument being written now for this audience?	Luis Alberto Urrea wrote his book *The Devil's Highway* after the incident of the Wellton 26, when fourteen "walkers" died hideous deaths trying to cross the border in the desert. He wanted to give readers a deeper understanding of the immigrants who risk their lives to enter the U.S. and of the Border Patrol whose job it is to intercept them.
Genre. Genre refers to the category/kind/form of the text (for example, news report, editorial, political cartoon, formal speech, and so forth). Genres have conventions (rules) that bring readers' expectations and that are intended to have social effects. Genre determines length, formality, treatment of sources, style and document design. What is the genre of an argument?	Is this text an op-ed piece (short, provocative, urgent) in the local newspaper about deported immigrants or shortages of workers? Or is it a policy proposal for a think tank (researched, thorough, supported by statistics and studies)? Is the genre personal or public, entertaining or motivational?

Examining the Use of Classical Appeals to *Logos*, *Ethos*, and *Pathos*

Some final basic concepts to consider when reading an argument are the arguer's use of the classical appeals to *logos, ethos,* and *pathos*. The Greek philosopher Aristotle outlined the importance of these appeals to the rhetorical effectiveness of arguments.

- **Appeals to *logos*** refer to the logical structure, consistency, and development of an argument.

- **Appeals to *ethos*** refer to the ethical character of the writer that comes across in the argument. For the writer to convey an ethical, positive *ethos,* he or she must be fair to opposing views, be credible and knowledgeable, and use evidence in a reliable manner.

- **Appeals to *pathos*** refer to how the writer engages the emotions and imaginations of the audience by evoking sympathy and how the writer taps into the audience's values. Writers can use case studies, extended examples, narratives, quotations, descriptions, figurative language, and images to make issues real and meaningful to the audience.

The role that these appeals play in particular arguments can vary enormously. For example, it is possible for an argument to be dominated by *logos* with few appeals to *pathos,* making the argument very intellectual, complex, or even dry or dull. Conversely, an argument can emphasize appeals to *pathos* and have little logical substance, trying only to work the audience's emotions. An argument can rest on the authority and reputation of the writer, relying on appeals to *ethos* and can gain persuasiveness through a writer's use of reliable evidence, or it can lose persuasiveness through a writer's unfair attack on opponents or use of scanty or unverifiable evidence.

The following chart summarizes the classical appeals and how they can be used to explore the effectiveness of an argument.

EXAMINING THE USE OF CLASSICAL APPEALS	
Rhetorical Concept and Working Definition	**Example Using the Illegal Immigration Issue**
Logos of the Argument (the logical appeal): What is the logical structure of the argument? What is the main claim? What reasons support this claim and how are they tailored to the audience? Is the evidence sufficient and accurate to make the claim and reasons persuasive? Are opposing views recognized and answered persuasively with counter-reasoning?	A policy analyst at a research institute might argue that only a thorough overhauling of U.S. hiring and labor practices will address the illegal immigration problem. She might cite studies and statistics.
Appeal to Ethos (the ethical appeal): The writer's *ethos* is shown in how he/she presents himself/herself as knowledgeable about the subject, treats alternative views responsibly, and reaches out to the audience by grounding the argument in shared values and assumptions. Has the writer given signs of having listened to other views? How well does the writer gain the readers' trust? How authoritative, credible, and fair is the writer?	If the writer is arguing about changes in policies at the border, has he lived or worked in Arizona or Texas on the border? Has the writer researched problems with illegal immigrants and quoted and cited verifiable sources?
Appeal to Pathos (emotional, imaginative appeal): How does the writer appeal to readers' emotions, imaginations, beliefs, and values? Has the writer used audience-based reasons? How prominent and effective is the writer's use of specific, vivid language; narratives and illustrations; humor? How much has the writer humanized the argument?	In the book *The Devil's Highway*, Urrea devotes fifteen pages to describing in detail what it is like to die of hyperthermia. He uses the pronoun "you" throughout to put the reader in place of the illegal immigrant whose blood is boiling and skin melting in the desert. The reader cannot remain detached. This scientifically accurate, graphic description evokes intense compassion for the immigrants risking their lives in the desert.

A Consideration of Style

Style is an elusive quality that is often noticed by readers but is difficult to describe in words. It is related to the writer's *ethos* and closely related to genre, which often dictates features of the style. The style of an argument can be very formal or very casual and conversational; it can be very intellectual and discipline-specific (suited to one field such as psychology or economics), using terminology from the field; or it can be very readable and suited to a popular audience. The following chart shows additional points that help to create and distinguish the style of a piece of writing.

Rhetorical Concept and Working Definition	Example Using the Illegal Immigration Issue
Style: Style refers to the level of formality of the writing, the complexity, the tone of the text (humorous, serious, mocking, ironic), and the use of language. It includes the length and complexity of sentence structure and the sophistication of the vocabulary. Style is closely related to genre because many genres dictate style: for example, the appealing readability of editorials in general circulation newspapers or the authoritative declarations of a policymaker in a white paper sketching out an organization's view of an issue.	Does the editorial writer attack opponents using colloquial language or use many Spanish words to convey the immigrants' culture? Is the policy statement packed with complicated statements in legal jargon, calling for a reform of the laws governing visas, or complex economic terms about remittances (the money immigrants send back to their communities and families in their countries of origin)?

Style can make an argument readable or tough going for readers. It can enhance the effectiveness of an argument, highlighting points in humorous, memorable, or powerful ways, or it can call attention to itself and distract readers.

Although you may not have time methodically to answer each of the questions about rhetorical features for each argument you read, the more attention you pay to these features, the more you will find yourself understanding the arguments and how they work. Furthermore, a sound rhetorical understanding of an argument will enable you to assess how much influence this argument should have over your own views—how much "assent" it merits. The following activity will give you an opportunity to practice what you have learned about the main features of arguments and rhetorical analysis.

DISCUSSING AND WRITING ▮▮▮▮▮▮▮▮▮

Conducting a Rhetorical Analysis

Working individually or in groups, return to the argument written by Ed Finn, "Harnessing Our Power as Consumers" on pages 29–31. Using the questions for rhetorical analysis in the charts on pages 33–37, take notes on how you think the writer's identity and angle of vision, the rhetorical context, argumentative strategies, and style are working in this text. Also, determine how well the appeals to *logos, ethos,* and *pathos* are working in this argument: How logical, well-structured, and well-supported is the argument? How ethical, responsible, and reliable is the writer? How does the writer appeal to readers' emotions and values? Sum up your rhetorical analysis by writing a paragraph explaining the appeal of this argument to its target audience. What specifically makes it persuasive? Then comment briefly on how persuasive this argument would be for other audiences.

WRITING A SUMMARY

You will find that writing summaries is a key part of writing both rhetorical analysis essays and arguments. In fact, summary writing is one of the most useful writing skills you can learn for academic and professional success. Many other academic and professional genres such as papers to be presented at conferences and proposals for grants or projects also draw on summary writing skills.

Using Summaries in Rhetorical Analyses

Before you can critique an argument to determine how well it is written and why it is persuasive for certain audiences, you need to have a sound understanding of the argument. This kind of understanding can be fostered through writing a summary of the argument. In writing a summary, you listen carefully to the argument, withholding your own views and judgments, simply trying to grasp what the argument is saying. In a rhetorical analysis essay, you can use your summary to ground readers in the argument, to build a base from which to launch your rhetorical critique. You usually include your summary, which can range from one or two sentences to a full paragraph, early in your essay to give readers a basic understanding of the argument so they will be able to follow and appreciate your analysis.

Using Summaries in Arguments

The process of summarizing and the summaries you produce also play a major role in writing arguments. Listening carefully and sympathetically to the arguments of others represents a critical step in entering argumentative conversations. Your understanding of multiple perspectives should inform the claims and reasons that you develop in your own arguments. Often, you will summarize views you are applying or enlisting in support of your position. You will also summarize opposing views that you are conceding to or refuting. In addition, incorporating a fair and accurate summary of a text into your own argument helps establish your positive *ethos*.

How to Write a Summary

As you are learning to write summaries, you should follow a deliberate and methodical process. Later you may develop your own effective shortcuts. The following chart proposes steps and strategies to write a summary of an argument.

STRATEGIES FOR WRITING A SUMMARY

- Read the article you are summarizing at least two times.
- Either in your head or on paper (writing your points is usually best), map out the shape or structure of the article by determining how each paragraph and section of the article functions.
  - How many paragraphs are introductory?
  - What is the thesis-claim—if it is stated?
  - Which paragraphs develop the writer's reasons?
  - Is there an alternative views section? Or are opposing points and objections woven throughout the article?
  - How many paragraphs make up the conclusion?
- Go back through the article, paragraph by paragraph or section by section, and translate the writer's ideas into your own words. Try to state in one sentence the main point of each section or paragraph.
- Take stock of the length of the summary you will be writing. Choose the drafting approach that works best for your needs.
  - To produce a summary of 200–350 words, draft your summary by combining your point statements from each paragraph. Once you have strung together these sentences, experiment with ways to combine and condense them into clearer, more concise and coherent statements.
  - For a one- to two-sentence summary, you can condense your paragraph summary down to the overall thesis-claim of the argument. Alternatively, you can try to identify, extract, and reformulate that main idea after achieving a good understanding of the article.
- Begin your summary by identifying the writer, the title of the article, and your own statement of the writer's overall thesis-claim.
- In revising your summary, be sure you have used **attributive tags** (Finn argues . . . , Finn asserts . . . , According to Finn, . . .) every few sentences to indicate that the ideas you are expressing belong to the writer, not to you.

(continued)

(continued)
- In revising your summary, check it for these features:
  - neutrality (you should keep your own views and judgments out of a summary)
  - fair and balanced coverage (your summary should be true to the importance of the ideas in the original article)
  - conciseness (you should use language economically—use the most direct and clear language with no wasted words)
  - coherence with smooth, logical movement from sentence to sentence
  - minimal or no quotations (only quote if you want to give the flavor of the article or if you can't do justice to the writer's ideas otherwise) and citation of page numbers using the documentation system your instructor specifies (Modern Language Association, American Psychological Association, or *Chicago Manual of Style*)

Test of a good summary: Would the writer of the article accept your summary as an accurate and fair abstract of his/her argument?

The following example is a summary of the article "The e-Waste Crisis." The annotations help to identify the features of an effective summary.

Example of a Summary

First sentence identifies the article and author and states the main idea. Attributive tag focuses on the author.	In the article "The e-Waste Crisis," Basel Action Network claims that the United States and Canada lead the world in the environmental destruction and social injustice caused by the dangerous dumping and exporting of toxic electronic waste. According to BAN, four billion pounds of e-waste, the largest single type of waste, were produced in 2005. Over 85% of it was burnt or deposited in landfill and 12% of what was recycled ended up in developing countries. The toxins in this waste endanger the environment and communities where it is dumped, the workers handling it, and even the rest of the
Attributive tag focuses on the author.	world through polluted air, water, and food. BAN asserts that many complex factors are compounding the e-waste crisis. First, electronic gadgetry is made up of highly toxic substances such as lead, mercury, and arsenic. This gadgetry, which rapidly
Transitions help to organize the summary.	goes out of date, is labor intensive to take apart to recycle parts, and the market for this equipment is growing, creating more e-waste. Second, lack of regulation also removes any incentive to recycle this waste and falsely labeled recycling hides the

disposal methods. The biggest problem, according to BAN, is that the U.S. is the only developed country that did not ratify the 1989 Basel Convention, controlling trade of e-waste and prohibiting the exporting of hazardous waste from rich to developing countries. The Basel Action Network and the Silicon Valley Toxics Coalition have documented on film the exporting of this waste to poorer countries in Southeast Asia and Africa where children and adults are exposed to dangerous toxins as they cheaply and primitively disassemble and burn this waste. BAN calls for legislation and a national system to confront this crisis. Finally, BAN argues that states, cities, U.S. prisons where the waste is often handled, poor countries around the world, and a few responsible companies, responding to the EPA's weak voluntary solutions, should not have to bear the brunt of the e-waste problem. (317 words)

> Additional transitions and attributive tags keep the focus on the main points.

> Concluding sentence wraps up the summary.

Example of a One-Sentence Summary

In its web article "The e-Waste Crisis," Basel Action Network claims that the United States, which has refused to adopt global regulations, leads the world in the discarding of toxic electronic waste in municipal dumps and the exporting of this toxic waste to poorer countries, and consequently contributes substantially to environmental destruction and social injustice.

DISCUSSING AND WRITING

Summarizing an Argument

Working individually or in groups, return to Ed Finn's argument "Harnessing Our Power as Consumers" on pages 29–31. Follow the steps and strategies for writing a summary explained in this section.

1. Write a 250–300 word summary.

2. Then write a one-sentence summary that captures the main claim of the article.

3. Finally, write a short reflective paragraph discussing the challenges you faced writing these summaries. What was difficult? How did you solve any problems?

WRITING A RHETORICAL ANALYSIS

This section discusses the main thinking and writing moves of a rhetorical analysis essay. Particularly, it explains how to find a focus and formulate a thesis statement for your essay. It concludes with an example of a student's rhetorical analysis, an essay by Tyler Bernard analyzing the rhetorical effectiveness of two advocacy films.

The Purpose and Audience of a Rhetorical Analysis

A rhetorical analysis is basically an interpretive argument. When writing a rhetorical analysis, you can usually assume that your audience is neutral or uninformed yet receptive, rather than hostile and antagonistic. Because a rhetorical analysis essay is an interpretation—your interpretation of someone else's argument—it has a persuasive purpose. Your main strategy is to make your interpretation persuasive by providing textual evidence and good discussions of all your points. Your goal is to make your audience see the argument you are analyzing your way. However, your essay may be as heavily analytical as it is persuasive.

Purpose. Your motivation and specific purpose for writing a rhetorical analysis may be described in three ways:

1. You may be writing as a citizen trying to make sense of the argument to develop your own views on the issue.
2. You may be writing as a student producing an academic essay critiquing an argument to show your understanding of the argument and of rhetorical analysis.
3. You may be writing as a citizen or student who is analyzing an argument in preparation for writing your own argument to join the public conversation on an issue.

Audience. The usual audience for a rhetorical analysis is other people who are interested in the issue explored in the argument and who want to know what it contributes to the public conversation on this controversy. Your audience might be other citizens and students who like yourself want to sort out the various public arguments to choose the most reasonable, informed view. Or occasionally, you may have a more specific audience in mind, such as a defined group of stakeholders (students who are considering volunteering time to help refugees; students considering becoming vegetarians; commuters who drive cars to campus, and so forth).

The Structure of a Rhetorical Analysis

In envisioning a structure for your rhetorical analysis, think of your essay as having these main parts:

- An **introduction** providing a brief context for the argument and perhaps for your analysis (a statement explaining your interest in the article and its timeliness and relevance)
- A **brief summary of the argument** to provide your readers with a foundation and basic understanding of the argument you are analyzing

- A **thesis statement** that indicates the focus of your analysis and perhaps maps out the points you will discuss
- A **well-developed main section** devoted to your analysis of the article and evaluation of the rhetorical strategies, perhaps considering the article's rhetorical context, purpose, and target audience.
- A **brief conclusion** that wraps up your analysis and possibly comments on the significance of the article's argument

Analyzing the Argument

A rhetorical analysis essay should reflect your close examination of an article. Give yourself time to think deeply about the article whose argument you are analyzing. Here are some strategies that will help you engage thoughtfully with an argument. Note how these strategies incorporate the summary writing strategies from the preceding section of this chapter.

STAGE 1: STRATEGIES FOR ANALYZING AN ARGUMENT

1. *Reach a thorough understanding of the article you are analyzing.* Familiarize yourself with the article and its argument by reading it several times.
2. *Follow the strategies for writing a summary on pages 39–40.* Map out the shape of the argument, and identify its main points. At the summary-writing stage, remember to put aside your own responses and try to get inside the argument and see the issue from the writer's perspective. Write a summary of the argument, perhaps both a longer summary of 150–250 words and a short one-sentence summary.
3. *Examine the argument the article is presenting.* Using your understanding of the main elements of an argument, ask yourself questions and jot down notes:
   - What is the question-at-issue? What is the writer's core argument? What reasons and evidence does the writer present?
   - Because all stakeholders are driven to present their views to change readers' perspectives, the question is not, "Is this writer biased or passionate?"(Of course, arguers are passionate!) Ask instead, "Is this writer arguing rationally with evidence to support reasons or only ranting and name calling, skewing evidence?" Is the writer aware of alternative views and fairly representing and refuting
   (continued)

(continued)
them? Is the writer addressing objections, or merely changing the topic and skating over the surface?

- How responsibly does the writer develop the *logos* of the argument and use appeals to *pathos*?

Your notes in response to questions like these can be either very thorough or rough, depending on how you work best and what your instructor requires.

4. ***Respond personally to the argument.*** Looking back through the argument and through your notes, identify spots or features of the argument that particularly catch your attention.

- What passages or features stand out by impressing you, disturbing you, or puzzling you?

- Where does your interest shift to a higher gear, or where do you disengage in frustration or disagreement?

- What will you remember about this argument? What leaves you thinking?

To generate ideas for your rhetorical analysis, you may find that freewriting in response to these questions helps you connect with the argument in an interesting, provocative way.

Now that you understand what argument the writer is making and have explored your response, you can dig deeper into its rhetorical construction.

Choosing a Focus for Your Rhetorical Analysis and Writing a Thesis Statement

You may find that you want to work with Stage 2 strategies at the same time as you grapple with the argument itself. With either process you choose, the goal is to reach a thorough understanding of this article and to discover some independent perceptions that you can share with your own readers. As you apply the rhetorical concepts and the questions presented in the charts in the section "A Brief Introduction to Rhetorical Analysis" (pages 31–38), try to refine your thinking about the argument you are analyzing and zero in on a focus. A typical focus for a rhetorical analysis essay is either (a) why and how an argument works for its target audience or (b) why and how the argument works for you or others who are not part of its target audience. Basically, how does this argument contribute to the public conversation on this issue?

STAGE 2: STRATEGIES FOR FOCUSING YOUR RHETORICAL ANALYSIS AND WRITING A THESIS STATEMENT

1. ***Think about the rhetorical context of the argument.*** Building on your working understanding of the argument, think specifically about the writer, the writer's angle of vision, the motivating occasion and writer's purpose, the *kairos* of the argument, and the target audience.

   - Analyze how rhetorically effective and persuasive the argument is. Most writing on global issues in the public sphere has a civic component, appealing to readers as citizens, voters, or consumers. Speculate about how the argument is working persuasively on them and how it might work for other readers.
   - Who are the stakeholders in this argument?
   - What values and assumptions would readers have to hold to be persuaded by this argument?
   - Think about how this argument fits in the larger public conversation on the issue. How is the writer framing the issue or articulating the problem? How does this argument intersect with other arguments you have read on the same issue?

2. ***Think about your relationship to the target audience and the argument's effectiveness for you.*** If you are not part of the target audience (for instance, not a supporter of the advocacy group, not a regular reader of the news commentary journal where the argument appears, or not a proponent of the view espoused by the article), ask yourself questions like these:

   - What features of the argument are persuasive to you?
   - What features of this argument make it a reliable, responsible view on this issue?
   - Where do the reasons, evidence, or argumentative strategies (for example, handling of alternative views) seem effective to you?
   - What questions or points would need more confirmation?

3. ***Choose several important features of the article that you want to discuss in depth in your essay.*** Identify points that grow out of your rhetorical thinking about the argument. These points should go beyond the obvious and should bring something fresh and insightful to your readers that will help them see this argument with new understanding. You may want to list your ideas and then look for ways to group them together around main points.

(continued)

(continued)

4. ***Write a thesis statement for your analysis.*** Given that you cannot discuss every rhetorical feature of the argument, from your notes and any freewriting you have done, identify the focus for your analysis.

   - For your audience, which features of this article's argument merit interpretation and discussion?

   - Which points do you think shed important light on the rhetorical effectiveness of the argument you are analyzing?

   In your thesis statement, you may choose to map out two or more points that you will explore in your essay. You may need two sentences to present these points.

Here are some examples of thesis statements for a rhetorical analysis essay.

Three Sample Thesis Statements

1. Ed Finn's editorial "Harnessing Our Power as Consumers" works beautifully to persuade an audience sympathetic to social justice issues by using Finn's personal experience to build a positive *ethos* and by making points about historical labor struggles, boycotts, and the causal link between cheap products and overseas labor.

2. Ed Finn's editorial "Harnessing our Power as Consumers" will not reach dissenting readers because he fails to acknowledge opposing views of sweatshops, relies heavily on his own experiences as a consumer, and does not address readers' real financial need for cheap products.

3. Although PETA's (People for the Ethical Treatment of Animals) YouTube video *Meet Your Meat* makes powerful verbal and visual appeals to *pathos,* the film fails to persuade meat eaters to change their ways because it distorts its evidence and disregards all other perspectives.

Drafting a Rhetorical Analysis

Once you have drafted a strong working thesis statement, you are ready to write a complete draft of your rhetorical analysis essay following the suggested structure on pages 42–43. The main writing moves that will make your rhetorical analysis essay persuasive as well as engaging are (1) setting up your points clearly and delivering on your readers' expectations by following through with lively explanations of them; and (2) using specific textual evidence, both examples and quotations, to give validity and credibility to your points.

An Example of a Rhetorical Analysis Essay

The following rhetorical analysis essay by student writer Tyler Bernard presents a comparative analysis of the two advocacy films *Meet Your Meat* and *VEGAN. For the People. For the Planet. For the Animals.* Tyler's rhetorical analysis grew out of his class's study of global food systems and factory farming, a system in which large businesses raise masses of animals in confinement, feeding them to promote rapid growth for slaughter. You can find these films at YouTube.com. Notice how the title sets up the focus of the rhetorical analysis. Other features and strategies of Tyler's analysis are identified by annotations.

 STUDENT VOICE: Responsibly Motivating the World? —A Rhetorical Analysis of Two Advocacy Films by Tyler Bernard

What does it mean to live responsibly in a globally connected world in which a growing population is making heavier demands on resources? According to the groups Nonviolence United and PETA (People for the Ethical Treatment of Animals), being a responsible person is closely correlated with what we choose to eat. These advocacy organizations emphasize different global problems such as global starvation, inefficient resource management, and global warming, yet come to the same conclusion: Avoid any and all food products related to animals. On its Web site, Nonviolence United's mission is building a better world "reflective of our shared values of justice, kindness and compassion for other people, for the planet and for animals" and it focuses on "need, not greed," as its film states. PETA, on the other hand, takes a much stronger stance in defense of animal rights by focusing on the four sites of long-term animal suffering: "on factory farms, in laboratories, in the clothing trade, and in the entertainment industry." Both advocacy organizations have created videos distributed through YouTube to communicate their goal to a general audience, but especially to meat eaters: to convince people to remove all forms of meat and animal products from their diets. However, whereas *Meet Your Meat*, PETA's film, falls short of successfully communicating the importance of living a vegan lifestyle, Nonviolence United's *VEGAN. For the People. For the Planet. For the Animals.* succeeds. *Meet Your Meat* lacks logical argument and factual evidence, over-emphasizes

> First sentence addresses the *kairos* or timeliness of the films.

> Introduction supplies important background information on the creators of the films.

> Three-sentence thesis statement sets up rhetorical analysis, contrasting the rhetorical effectiveness of each film

the emotional element, and creates a despairing tone. In contrast, the Nonviolence United film clearly outlines a logical argument, plays moderately on emotions, and takes a hopeful, optimistic tone towards its viewers and the future.

Both films are approximately twelve minutes long, use a series of separate images, and rely on narration. *Meet Your Meat* is composed of many horrifying video clips such as animals being beaten with clubs, living in extreme conditions (such as cramped cages) with other animals, and having their throats slit while fully conscious. These clips are intended to deeply disturb viewers. Titles are given to each horrific clip as it is shown, "Egg-Laying Hens," "Cattle," "Dairy Cows" and "Veal Calves," "Pigs," providing a logical structure to the footage of brutal killing that the narrator describes. In contrast, *VEGAN. For the People. For the Planet. For the Animals.* is a slideshow of images divided into three sections (the good of people, the good of the environment, and the good of animals). The cordial narrator's voice presents the message of "making choices connected with our values" over softly playing upbeat music. Beautiful scenes of forests and fields alternate with images of starving children, acres of forest cleared for cultivation of animal feed, and dolphins and sea turtles caught in fishing nets. Statistics are then given to support the extent of destruction and to inform viewers how their responsible actions can save the land, water, and other resources.

> Writer summarizes and describes the content of the films to give readers a foundational understanding for the analysis to follow.

Throughout PETA film's *Meet Your Meat*, the overall structure and organization of the film attempts to convey its logical, comprehensive content and evidence; however, this reasonableness is deceptive. The structure provides a logical basis for the flow of information, first part one, then part two, then part three, giving the film an appearance of being thorough, as though nothing had been left out, but this "whole story" is not the case. The film's evidence for why people should become vegan is the treatment of animals shown in the film. However, the film leaves viewers with many questions: In what country is this happening? How often and on what scale does this abuse take place? How long has this been happening? To my disappointment, none of these questions was answered. The film intends viewers to assume that the cruel butchering seen in the video takes place regularly in the United States as the normal treatment of livestock. The film also wants viewers to assume that all livestock live

> Writer discusses his first rhetorical point: the problem with the *logos* of *Meet Your Meat*.

a life of suffering and that this suffering will continue indefinitely until enough people have become vegan. Yet because these questions are never answered definitely, viewers can interpret the film in different ways. While some viewers may readily go along with PETA's intended assumptions, others like me may be highly skeptical about the content of this film.

In contrast, Nonviolence United does a much more genuinely thorough job of arguing the benefits of going vegan. The film logically progresses through arguments that eating meat contributes to the world's shortage of food, harms humans' health, damages forests, land, and water, contributes to global warming, and causes animal suffering. It supports statements such as "the fewer animal products we consume, the more people we can feed" with statistics. Although the film doesn't cite exact studies, it does mention studies and logically explains the relationship between eating animal products and heart disease, cancer, and the waste of water. At least, the legitimacy of these statements can be tested by viewers through independent research, enabling them to confirm these assertions on their own. The film also claims that the amount of water wasted throughout the production of a pound of meat totals 2,500 gallons, and the amount wasted in producing a gallon of milk is 750 gallons. According to Nonviolence United, one person eating meat and dairy will waste more water in twelve months than a person who let a shower run for an entire year. In addition, it asserts that a vegan will save an acre of trees per year, which is equivalent to recycling over one million pieces of paper per year. The math may be rough, but again, the entire film gives viewers something solid to be able to agree or disagree with.

> Writer explains how *VEGAN* offers a more logically developed argument with clearer claims, reasons, and evidence that can be checked.

Both films play on the emotions of viewers; however, PETA's film forces compassionate viewers to feel extremely guilty about consuming meat, and the key word here is "forces." Sensitive viewers may feel that they are responsible for the way the animals in *Meet Your Meat* are treated, and therefore believe that becoming vegan will help put an end to this mistreatment of livestock, but going vegan is not the only solution. Although PETA suggests that putting an end to meat consumption is essential for the betterment of the treatment of animals, it never addresses free range cows and chickens and the manner in which they are treated. It is quite possible for a compassionate person to continue eating meat while not supporting factory farms

> Writer contrasts the rhetorical effectiveness of the films' appeals to *pathos* and explains how *Meet Your Meat* uses deceptive appeals to *pathos* whereas *VEGAN* is more successful in its appeals.

that mistreat their livestock. In contrast, Nonviolence United's film does not claim that the primary issue with meat and dairy consumption is the treatment of animals, but broadens its appeal and asserts that only two billion people can be fed on a meat and dairy diet whereas the entire world can be fed if people choose to eat vegan. This appeal plays on the emotions of the viewers just as strongly as the images shown in *Meet Your Meat*. In *VEGAN*, images are shown of people starving in third world countries, and yet this point is supported with statistics, giving viewers' emotional responses validity. Nonviolence United's film includes other harsh images—of cleared forests and a dolphin and turtle caught in fishing nets— that evoke strong feelings and concern, but these images have a different rhetorical effect on viewers than those in *Meet Your Meat*.

The different manner in which each film presents its emotional and logical arguments also contributes to the contrasting tones and moods of these films. The tone and mood of PETA's film are sorrowful and despairing. They are conveyed by the voice of the narrator, the lack of music, the use of harsh, unedited sounds and noisy factories, and the images of suffering—all of which express the message that these poor creatures are living and dying in such conditons because we continue to eat meat. Intended to work on viewers' guilt, this message is somber and discouraging. Ironically, PETA's film undermines itself and fails to succeed for me—and, I imagine, most people—because it doesn't even seem to be hopeful of achieving its goal of ending the mistreatment of animals. The whole film is doom and horror.

> Writer explains his third main point, the weakness of *Meet Your Meat's* tone and how its tone contributes to its failure to achieve its purpose

Essential to understanding the difference between these two films is the impression that each ultimately communicates: PETA's dominant negativity makes its goal seem unattainable whereas Nonviolence United's film communicates the opposite impression. The hopeful tone of Nonviolence United's film, calling people to responsible, ethical choices, suggests its faith in its ability to move people toward its goal to end world hunger, diminish water consumption, and help create a healthier population. The film maintains this tone of hope through its upbeat music and mixture of both happy and sad images. The calm, pleasant-voiced narrator says that we can put an end to all these problems starting with our forks. This message is well supported and effectively

> Writer explains the contrasting, more positive appeal that *VEGAN* makes to viewers by conveying the positive impression that they can help solve the problem.

communicated to viewers, making this film a well-constructed argument in support of not just eating vegan, but living a vegan lifestyle. Judging by the reactions of my classmates watching the film, I believe I am not alone in thinking that Nonviolence United's film is a more effective rhetorical piece for a general audience than PETA's film.

> Writer decides to blend his final point into his concluding statement about the films' rhetorical effectiveness.

Works Cited

Nonviolence United. Nonviolence, n.d. Web. 1 Feb. 2009.

Nonviolence United. *VEGAN. For the People. For the Planet. For the Animals.* Nonviolence, n.d. *YouTube.* YouTube, 8 Aug. 2008. Web. 10 Feb. 2009.

People for the Ethical Treatment of Animals. "About PETA." *PETA.* People for the Ethical Treatment of Animals, n.d. Web. 1 Feb. 2009.

People for the Ethical Treatment of Animals. *Meet Your Meat.* People for the Ethical Treatment of Animals, n.d. *YouTube.* YouTube, 23 Feb. 2007. Web. 10 Feb. 2009.

> Writer includes a Works Cited list in MLA format to document his sources.

FOR DISCUSSING AND WRITING

Generating Ideas for a Rhetorical Analysis Essay

Choose one of the arguments in this chapter—"The e-Waste Crisis" or "Harnessing Our Power as Consumers: Cost of Boycotting Sweatshop Goods Offset by the Benefits"—or an argument specified by your instructor. Then using the Stage 1 and 2 Strategies charts on pages 43–46, do the following writing tasks in preparation for writing a rhetorical analysis essay:

1. Write your own 150-word summary of the article's argument.

2. Analyze the argument's parts based on the questions under number 3 in the Stage 1 chart on pages 43–44.

3. Freewrite—that is, write in rapid, nonstop, free associational, uncensored mode for a certain period of time, say fifteen or twenty minutes—in response to parts of the argument that impress or disturb you, using the suggestions in question number 4 on page 44.

4. Take notes about the rhetorical features of the argument using the Stage 2 questions on pages 45–46.

5. Then choose several analytical points about the argument and its rhetorical features that have emerged from your note taking and freewriting, and write the thesis statement you would develop in a rhetorical analysis essay if you were to write one on this article's argument.

WRITING AN ARGUMENT

In your academic career and very likely in your professional life, you will be called upon to construct arguments, some informal and some formal. In some situations, you may be writing an argument to support a cause you believe in or inventing a solution to a problem of interest to you. Sometimes you will be engaging in soul-searching and examination of your own values and experiences to figure out your stand on an issue. Other times, you will be researching an issue to develop your view and take an informed position on it. In all these cases, the thinking and writing moves explained in this section can help you write a rhetorically effective argument. This section will walk you through these strategies:

1. Posing a significant, perplexing issue question
2. Examining multiple perspectives on your issue by immersing yourself in the issue, by adopting different views, and by using brief informal and formal writing to think out your own views
3. Analyzing your audience, purpose, and genre
4. Constructing an argument core attuned to your audience's interests, values, and assumptions

After you have used these various approaches to discovering what argument you want to make and how you will make it, you will be better prepared to structure and draft your argument and then revise it. This section will briefly sketch some suggestions for these thinking and writing moves in writing an argument. It will show you examples of writing by student writer Lindsey Egan as she shapes and develops her policy proposal* argument on water usage in the American Southwest.

Posing a Significant, Perplexing Issue Question

Whether you are writing an argument to support a view that attracts you or pursuing a question or problem that genuinely puzzles you, your argument will achieve more depth and complexity if you approach it by posing a significant, perplexing issue question. The most successful, responsible arguments have developed through genuine inquiry—true engagement with the issue question and searching for an understanding of the issue. The question should be significant to you and other stakeholders so that the "Who cares?" "What are the stakes?" dimension is built into your argument from the beginning.

There are many ways to become engaged with an issue question. Throughout this text, you will encounter the premise that global and local

---

*A policy proposal—unlike a practical proposal that outlines an action to solve an immediate, local problem—presents a broad plan of action that tackles a big, public social, economic, or political problem.

issues are inevitably connected. Many of the discussion questions, after each reading and at the ends of chapters, and many of the writing assignments will spur you to find your own personal and local angles on global issues. Simply discovering how many of the products we use, from food to technology, are not made locally or domestically can lead you to vital issue questions. This text, your other courses, and casual reading, radio, television, the Web, and local events can also lead you to issues that matter to you.

In the following informal narrative, student writer Lindsey Egan uses her own experience to help her discover an issue question that interests her and that relates to her class's focus on environmental sustainability and water.

Example of a Student's Informal Writing to Discover Personal Investment in an Issue Question

Growing up, I spent early-summer weekends with my dad fly-fishing the Priest River at Binarch Creek. The small stretch of water is piercingly cold, clear as crystal, and loaded with deep, emerald pockets of water shaded by granite boulders—the seemingly perfect environment for sizeable cutthroat trout. I would tie on an elk hair caddis and cast my line, placing the fly right at the seam of the rapid, hoping to tempt hungry trout as my fly floated into the eddy downstream. Cast after cast, my line would drift, and I would wait . . . and wait . . . and wait. As a kid I wondered why I never caught a fish in that river.

My family discovered a few years later that the river is dammed upstream in order to regulate the flow of water into Priest Lake—where thousands of people spend their summers recreating at local resorts and privately owned cabins. Closing the dam in the summer lowers the water in the Priest River, diminishing it so far that bedrock is exposed by July, and in August a person can walk across the riverbed without ever touching water. The water temperature rises. Insects and fish eggs can't survive. The river can't sustain much life. Kayakers, rafters, people fly-fishing must share their source of recreation with those using the lake (and, all the while, the native plant, fish, and wildlife populations are displaced from *both* environments).

This early experience exposed me to the debate over water usage. Who should have the right to use our freshwater, and why? Why does our culture value water for private lawns and jet-skiing over sustaining natural habitats? Sure, relatively few people depend on the Priest River for water. On the other hand, my reading has shown me that the Colorado River is highly disputed and increasingly overused. I wonder if other parts of the world have similar problems with overused water sources and what we can learn from their problems. What should the American West do about its water policies?

In this informal narrative, Lindsey draws on her personal experience and her reading to ponder local, global, and national connections on the problem of water usage. Often, writing from personal experience and writing informally in response to reading you have done can lead you to find your own personal investment in issues that have local and global dimensions.

Examining Multiple Perspectives

Whether you are trying to deepen your view of an issue, determine where you stand on it, or come up with a solution to a problem, your argument will be stronger if you truly explore the issue by looking at it from multiple perspectives. There are a number of reasons for dwelling with your issue question—for leaving it open for awhile, for not taking a position on your issue early, and for letting your stand on your issue evolve before you try to formulate a claim. Here are some of those reasons: (1) seeing your issue from the vantage point of different stakeholders will help you question your values and assumptions, perhaps change or enlarge your view, and ultimately construct a more reasonable case; (2) seeing your issue through the eyes of different stakeholders will also enable you to construct an argument tailored to your audience's values and assumptions; (3) exploring an issue will enable you to recognize and answer alternative views effectively; (4) finally, thinking dialectically about an issue as you purposefully take on different perspectives restores to argument its ethical social function as a sincere search for the most valid solution to problems.

Because arguments gain depth when you approach your issue question with an open mind and a willingness to change views or let your views develop in unexpected ways, you should have a repertoire of strategies such as the following to help you encounter multiple perspectives.

STRATEGIES FOR EXPLORING AN ISSUE FROM MULTIPLE PERSPECTIVES

1. *Deliberately seek out different points of view on your issue*. Consult varied stakeholders and read sources by people who see your issue from different angles. Seek out different angles. (letters to the editor; editorials and op-ed pieces; articles in public affairs magazines, in scholarly journals, and in popular magazines; white papers produced by organizations; blogs; policy arguments and campaigns posted on advocacy Web sites; public affairs advocacy ads; speeches; even documentary films). Seek out sources from different political perspectives. Try to understand alternative and opposing views and see the issue from their frame of reference.

2. *Play rhetorician Peter Elbow's Believing and Doubting Game.** In this exercise, you deliberately adopt opposing perspectives on an issue and force yourself to dwell with a claim. As you believe the claim, you agree with it and seek to understand it by exploring it, supporting it, and applying it, adding your own examples. What would the world look like if you truly agreed with this claim? After freewriting for a certain length of time (usually fifteen or more minutes) from this assenting view, you then deliberately set out to doubt the claim and disagree with it. In your doubting freewrite, you challenge and question the claim, find holes in its view, and think of counter-reasoning and counter-examples. Try to freewrite for an equal amount of time believing and doubting. See what ideas and new insights about your issue emerge from this exercise.

3. *Use informal writing to respond to and interact with your sources.* Purposeful note taking (using your summary writing and rhetorical reading skills) can encourage you to track your evolving understanding of your issue. Novice writers and researchers tend to gather numerous sources and then try to wade through them hurriedly, often becoming overwhelmed and confused by the volume of material and the complexity of the different views on the issue. More experienced writers and researchers know the importance of processing their sources and responding in writing to them as they read. Freewriting, journaling, and summarizing of your sources as you read each one can help you enlarge and deepen your understanding of your issue. Some writers find double-entry journals helpful. In a double-entry journal, you divide your pages into two columns. In one column you write a quotation, idea, or fact (with the citation) that seems important to you. In the second column, you respond to that piece of information with your own thinking, as if you are talking back to your source or carrying on a conversation about it.

(continued)

---

*Rhetorician and compositionist Peter Elbow introduced his Believing and Doubting Game in his classic book *Writing Without Teachers* (Oxford University Press, 1973) in his appendix essay: "The Doubting Game and the Believing Game—An Analysis of the Intellectual Enterprise." In this essay and throughout his writing, he advocates resisting the urge to want immediate answers. He argues that only by trying to understand or "believe" views that clash with our own can we achieve an understanding of our own views and move toward the best solutions to problems.

(continued)

4. ***Use incremental formal writing such as annotated bibliographies or brief rhetorical analyses of sources to complicate and clarify your thinking on your issue.*** Brief formal writing can help you build your argument and also figure out what parts of your issue you still need to investigate. In an annotated bibliography, you formally cite each source, briefly summarize it, and then evaluate it, explaining how it has shaped your thinking and why it is valuable.

Analyzing Your Rhetorical Context

As you feel that you are moving closer to the claim and reasons you want to assert, you will probably want to firm up the rhetorical context for your argument—your target audience, specific purpose, and genre—and have this context consciously influence the development of the argument. Usually, audience, purpose, and genre are closely intertwined, with the genre itself holding certain reader expectations for depth and complexity of the argument, level of formality, and kinds of documentation. For example, an op-ed piece would target a general readership and would take a bold, appealing "broad-strokes" or a "small piece of the issue" approach and would not include extensive examples or formal documentation. The following questions can help you think out the rhetorical context that will shape your argument.

QUESTIONS TO HELP YOU TAILOR YOUR ARGUMENT TO YOUR AUDIENCE, PURPOSE, AND GENRE

1. What audience will you be targeting with this argument?

2. What is your audience's background knowledge of your issue?

3. What are your audience's values and beliefs that pertain to this issue?

4. What is your specific purpose; that is, what would you like your audience to think about your issue after reading your argument? What are you asking your audience to do?

5. What genre of argument is called for to reach this audience and carry out this purpose? Are you writing a formal scholarly argument, a policy proposal that might appear in a news commentary magazine or on an advocacy Web site, an op-ed piece or editorial for the local newspaper, a brochure advertising a campaign for an issue?

6. How agreeable or antagonistic is your audience? With what parts of your argument is your audience most likely to agree? To disagree?

7. How can you elicit your audience's agreement or support for your argument?

Constructing an Argument Core

Another strategy that can help you create a strong argument is constructing an argument core. Usually after you have consulted multiple perspectives, done some preliminary writing in response to your sources, and thought about your rhetorical context, you are ready to commit to a claim and to formulate reasons in support of it. Construct an argument core that is tailored to the audience you have in mind and the genre of argument you are writing. In your argument core, you should have a main claim and at least several audience-based reasons. To develop your argument core further, you could identify the assumptions or principles behind your reasons, sketch out the kinds of evidence and support you will need for those reasons, and even imagine the alternative views you will need to address. Creating an argument core can help you figure out exactly what you are arguing and what scope your argument will have. If you add assumptions and evidence to your argument core, you will be able to determine if you will need to provide support for your assumptions as well as for your reasons. In constructing your argument core, you can use the explanation of the parts of an argument at the beginning of this chapter, pages 15–18 to guide you in thinking of your argument as a persuasive structure.

Structuring and Drafting Your Argument

An argument core provides the deep structure, the essence of your argument; however, it does not outline your argument for you. It informs you what needs to be present in your argument for it to be persuasive for your audience, but it does not tell you where in the actual argument to put these parts. As you draft your argument, you will have to make a number of important decisions.

DECISIONS TO MAKE WHILE DRAFTING YOUR ARGUMENT

1. In what order will you develop your reasons? Which is the strongest reason from your audience's perspective?

2. If you have to provide support for your assumptions, where will you include these points?

3. How will you select evidence to meet the STAR criteria (that is, evidence that is sufficient, typical, accurate, and relevant for your audience)?

4. How will you incorporate material from sources so that it serves and does not control your argument? In other words, how will you frame your evidence and keep the focus on *your* points while strengthening your case with this material?

(continued)

(continued)

5. How will you introduce and give credit to your sources to meet the audience's expectations for documentation?

6. How will you appeal to your reader's imagination, emotions, and values? How will you make your argument come alive and make it memorable? How will you set up your claim in your introduction?

7. What alternative views do you need to consider, given your intended audience? Where in the argument will you address them? How will you respond to them to return the focus to your own argument?

8. How specifically will you build a positive *ethos*?

9. What title will introduce your issue and claim and will attract and appeal to your audience?

Reviewing and Revising Your Draft

As with any piece of formal writing, your argument will benefit from having several different readers, preferably members of your audience, at the complete draft stage. To elicit the most helpful responses, address some specific questions to your reviewers such as, where could the evidence for my reasons be more persuasive? where might I give more attention to alternative views? Once you have given your argument a test drive, so to speak, you can revise with your reviewers' suggestions in mind.

An Example of a Student's Researched Argument

Here is Lindsey Egan's researched argument about water use written for the general public, including her student peers. Her purpose is to persuade her audience to accept her view of the problem and to adopt the view she considers important. Note how the title suggests the focus and main claim of the argument. Annotations point out the way she has developed and structured this argument.

 STUDENT VOICE: American Privilege Dangerously Perpetuates Water Inefficiency by Lindsey Egan

Frequently, newspaper articles confront us with stories about food shortages. Pasta, bread, and meat become too expensive for many people, who are forced to change what and how much they eat. Often, these food shortages are the consequence of a lack of water to grow crops for human and animal consumption. For example, the recent food shortage in Egypt,

> Introduction makes the problem come alive in a global context.

driving people to stand in line for daily rations of bread, has been caused by this region's water scarcity. For decades, the ten countries sharing the Nile River Basin have diverted its waters to make farming possible in desert regions like the Sahara and Sinai. As a result of water overuse, the dry countries of Northern Africa and also the Middle East have to import much of their food. As the population here and around the world continues to grow, the combined problem of water and food increasingly becomes a global crisis.

What if a crisis like this happened right here in the United States? In a land where our freshwater seemingly flows freely, a food crisis may seem like a far-off implausibility, but the West's largest source of freshwater, the Colorado River, is also being overused and mismanaged to the point where it is nothing more than a trickle by the time it finds its way to the parched delta south of the U.S. border. Along with the Nile River in Egypt, the Colorado River has, as Marc Reisner, author of *Cadillac Desert*, notes, "more people, more industry, and a more significant economy dependent on it than any comparable river in the world" (120). Consequently, the American Southwest must make environmental sustainability its first priority in water usage for three main reasons: first, population growth is going to make increased demands on the river; second, changing climate patterns related to global warming are decreasing the water resources in this area; and third, the current emphasis on economic growth is leading the region on a course toward disaster.

> Thesis: policy proposal claim presents three causal reasons: (1) population growth will increase (2) climate change will affect the available water (3) current view of economic progress is dangerously dominating water use.

The Colorado River, the single-most disputed and legislated river on Earth, is inevitably a battle-site for cities, farmers, electric companies, environmentalists, and Native Americans—all of whom claim rights to the river and contest the amount to which they are entitled. As a result of the Colorado River Compact of 1922, the river was apportioned among seven states: Colorado, Utah, Wyoming, New Mexico, California, Nevada, and Arizona. It now generates electricity throughout many major cities in the West and irrigates the land used for much of America's agricultural production—just like the Nile. In fact, farmers claim around eighty percent of the river's entire water supply ("Water Use in the West" 1). While food is certainly a necessity, the water used for irrigation does not return to the river (Burness 115). Once the water is depleted, then, farming in such an arid region will become virtually impossible.

> Writer provides background on the demands on available water.

The current use of water resources in this area poses a major problem, particularly in light of the past and future population growth in this region. Government officials overestimated the river's capacity at the time the Colorado River Compact was signed. During that time, the region had experienced record precipitation for several years in a row, causing officials to overestimate the typical flow of the river. The region's urban populations, moreover, have since skyrocketed to levels no one living in 1922 could have predicted. The current population of California, for example, is around 36 million but is expected to rise to 60 million by 2050 (Gertner 3). When Californians in Los Angeles are using around 125 gallons of water per person per day (Gertner 4), the steady increase in population causes an immense increase in the amount of water needed for daily living. These miscalculations mean that today the river is unable to support all those who depend on it, and that population will inevitably increase, making the problem worse.

> Writer develops her first reason about the problem posed by increasing population growth.

Furthermore, related to the continuing population boom are the ever-worsening effects of global warming. Global warming currently causes more rain and snow to fall in regions near the poles, but areas closer to the equator are drying out—as is happening around the Colorado and Nile Rivers. In fact, recent scientific evidence suggests that "periodic long, severe droughts have become the norm in the Colorado River basin" (Archibold 2), thus worsening the water shortage and intensifying the need to solve disputes over rights.

> Writer develops her second reason about the problem posed by the changes in climate patterns due to global warming.

The most important reason that Americans need to change water policy in the American Southwest to value conservation and sustainability first is that the current emphasis on economic progress in terms of profit, luxury, and convenience is following a foolishly disastrous course. Water use in Las Vegas best exemplifies the dangers of prioritizing capital over sustainability. Located in the Mojave Desert—one of the hottest regions on Earth—Las Vegas is one of America's fastest growing cities. It requires tremendous amounts of energy generated from the Hoover Dam to keep its casinos and hotels brightly lit and air-conditioned and its fifty golf courses well-watered (each course soaking up millions of gallons of water each day). In an effort to bring life to the desert, the Venetian Hotel uses water to recreate the canals of Venice; Mandalay Bay fills live aquatic tanks; Treasure Island flaunts its pirate lagoon; Luxor runs

> Writer moves to her third and most important reason: the consequences of bad policies of economic growth.

an imitation Nile River; the Bellagio showcases an enormous choreographed fountain display every fifteen minutes; and the Mirage has an erupting volcano made entirely out of water. Residential housing developments are built around artificial lakes*, and residents also use about 100 gallons of water per day per person just to maintain their lawns and gardens (Revkin 2). In a region that receives a mere average of four inches of rain each year (Robbins 1), plants and animals struggle to survive in nature as it is—yet people continue to pump this scarcity *out* of nature and into homes and hotels so that people can enjoy life in the desert.

Water policy in this region is entirely wrong. With the Colorado River's water supply tapped out, however, Las Vegas looks to bring more water into the city—instead of looking to reduce the city's water usage. Patricia Mulroy, general manager of the Las Vegas Valley Water District since 1989, plans to tap 65 billion gallons of water a year through a 280-mile-long pipe drawing from a natural underground reservoir on the Nevada-Utah border—taking water away from both farmers and the natural environment. According to Howard Berkes of National Public Radio, Mulroy claimed in 1991 that "there is an *economic imperative* to taking water from rural counties largely dependent on ranching, and bringing it to the big city" (1, emphasis mine). Evidently, Mulroy disregards the need for water in nature and for agriculture in favor of economics—that is, making profit from tourists. Once again, progress is measured in terms of luxury and capital instead of sustainability.

> Writer continues to develop her third reason.

Conservationists warn that adding to the water capacity of Las Vegas will promote more growth in a region that cannot sustain it. The Pacific Institute and Western Resource Advocates contend that "if Las Vegas adopted more aggressive indoor and outdoor water conservation measures, it could, in essence, harvest some 28 billion gallons a year without laying a single costly pipeline" (Revkin 1). In fact, as Andrew Revkin of the *New York Times* reports, "the installation of water-efficient fixtures and appliances could cut indoor water use by 40 percent in single-family homes and 30 percent in hotels and casinos" (2).

> Writer continues to develop her third reason.

Granted, there have been some movements toward conservational water use. The MGM Mirage Company has

---

*One neighborhood known as "The Lakes" was constructed around three miles of synthetic shoreline (Robbins 2).

installed drip irrigation and low-flow bathroom fixtures in its eleven hotels (Robbins 2). The regional water agency in Las Vegas is also "removing the equivalent of a football field of grass every day from front lawns, playgrounds, and golf courses to save on outdoor watering" (Johnson "Drought" 3). Mulroy has even waged several water-conservation campaigns to combat the wasteful use of water on private lawns, and she implemented a "return-flow credits"* system to recycle the city's wastewater. Still, research shows that not enough is being done individually or collectively to avert the growing crisis. Even these practices are done in the name of economic growth—not sustainability. When enticing tourists (and their money) to Las Vegas is the primary objective in implementing "sustainable" practices, the actual conservation of water becomes secondary. Yes, the installation of water-efficient showerheads is a start. But lavish fountains still spew twenty-four hours a day, and fifty golf courses remain in operation (because tourists could not possibly choose from a mere twenty). If real solutions are to be found, revenue—although a practical concern—cannot motivate our reasons for conserving the environment. When the matter threatens the next generation's ability to enjoy clean drinking water, should not cutting back on our pirate lagoons and artificial volcanoes at least be an option?

> Writer addresses alternative views and refutes them with counter-reasoning and counter-examples.

Although Las Vegas is the most flagrant example of wastefulness and disregard for sustainability, this city is not the only culprit in the region. In 2001, for instance, a dispute emerged between the city of Los Angeles and Calpine Company (a giant energy corporation based in California) that exemplifies how America's prioritization of profit limits sustainable solutions. Despite opposition from environmentalists and a thirsty Los Angeles desperate for more drinking water, Calpine planned to pump fresh water from a Colorado River canal for the purpose of cooling a planned 530-megawatt power plant[†] in the

> Writer elaborates on the third reason, enlarging the scope of the problem.

---

*A system which allows the city's wastewater to be treated, returned to Lake Mead, and used again.

[†]California has laws that minimize the use of scarce water resources for power generation, but Calpine arranged to build this plant and two other facilities on Indian reservations where state regulations do not apply. Since water rights are a precious commodity, tribes—desperate for income—are selling their rights to companies like Calpine.

Palm Desert. According to Gerald Meral, the executive director of the Planning and Conservation League, an environmental group in Sacramento, there are other environmentally safe methods to cool power plants: Utilizing wastewater or dry-cooling technology, for example, uses ninety-five percent less water but is, admittedly, more expensive (Khan B.1). A substantial amount of Colorado River water could have been saved, but Calpine chose to save money instead. Once again, concern for the bottom line has taken precedence over environmental conservation, thus inhibiting real, sustainable solutions.

If the United States intends to avoid food and water crises, Americans ought to demand that governmental policies reflect these interests. The former Bush administration, though, certainly did not foster environmental sustainability when it passed policies to loosen the federal government's claim on rivers by ceding water rights to Western states in 2002. As Douglas Jehl of the *New York Times* writes, these policies "give the states more latitude to transfer water to their *cities* and away from national parks, forests, wildlife refuges, and other federal lands" (1, emphasis mine). When states have more control over where and how the water is apportioned, state officials typically draw water away from national parks and forests in order to support their cities—centers of profit and economic growth. Such losses of water threaten the natural beauty and environmental health of the parks. Certainly, more water is necessary in urban areas to sustain mass populations, but, when cities like Las Vegas and Los Angeles squander their resources in the name of luxury and convenience, Americans ought to ask themselves whether their casinos and private swimming pools are worth destroying our nation's last remaining natural sanctuaries.

Americans ultimately have a choice: We can use our privilege to solve the earth's freshwater crisis, or we can use it to perpetuate the problem. In choosing the latter, Americans have foolishly disregarded warnings around the globe and are headed toward disaster. When only 0.01 percent of the earth's total water supply is available for human consumption (Johnson *Global* 335), *no one* can afford to waste the one vital resource on which all life depends. The quest for profit—although inevitable and necessary in a capitalist society—is clearly

> Writer continues to elaborate on the third reason.

> Writer concludes the argument with a call for changes in attitude, practice, and policy.

useless if people will not have the resources to sustain future generations. The average American uses ninety gallons of water each day, while the European uses only fifty-three gallons, and people in sub-Saharan African use merely five gallons (Johnson *Global* 343). It is obviously possible, then, for humans to survive with a more modest use of water—without round-the-clock choreographed fountain displays. If Americans do not reconfigure social and economic development in terms of environmental sustainability, "progress" may send us, too, into breadlines.

Works Cited

Archibold, Randal C., and Kirk Johnson. "An Arid West No Longer Waits for Rain." *New York Times*. New York Times, 4 Apr. 2007. Web. 19 Jan. 2009.

Berkes, Howard. "Las Vegas Water Battle: 'Crops vs. Craps.'" *Morning Edition*.Natl. Public Radio, 12 June 2007. Web. 23 Jan. 2009.

Burness, H. Stuart, and James P. Quirk. "Water Law, Water Transfers, and Economic Efficiency: The Colorado River." *Journal of Law and Economics* 23.1 (1980): 111-34. Web. 21 Jan. 2009.

Gertner, Jon. "The Future Is Drying Up." *New York Times*. New York Times, 21 Oct. 2007. Web. 19 Jan. 2009.

Jehl, Douglas. "U.S. Eases Way for West to Control Big Volumes of Water." *New York Times*. New York Times, 13 Oct. 2002. Web.19 Jan. 2009.

Johnson, June. *Global Issues, Local Arguments: Readings for Writing*. New York: Pearson Longman, 2007. 333–345. Print.

Johnson, Kirk, and Dean E. Murphy. "Drought Settles In, Lake Shrinks and West's Worries Grow." *New York Times*. New York Times, 2 May 2004. Web.19 Jan. 2009.

Khan, Mahvish. "California's Needs for Water and Electricity Pit One Against the Other." *Wall Street Journal* 1 Aug. 2001: B1. Print.

Reisner, Marc. *Cadillac Desert*. New York: Penguin, 1993. Print.

Revkin, Andrew. "A 'Hidden Oasis' in Las Vegas' Water Waste." Dot Earth blog posting. *New York Times*, New York Times, 5 Nov. 2007. Web. 19 Jan. 2009.

Writer provides a Works Cited and complete documentation for this researched argument, using Modern Language Association citation style.

Robbins, Ted. "Stakes High for Las Vegas Water Czar." *Morning Edition.*Natl. Public Radio, 11 June 2007. Web. 23 Jan. 2009.

"Water Use in the West." *Issues & Controversies on File.* Facts on File, 23 Aug. 2004. Web. 23 Jan. 2009.

DISCUSSING AND WRITING

Creating an Argument Core and Shaping an Argument

This role-playing exercise asks you to try your hand at shaping an argument in the genre of a flier for a specific target audience. This genre calls for a concise, tightly structured argument that presents its case very clearly with several strong reasons and minimal but well-chosen evidence. This genre is visually appealing through the layout and use of images. A flier is also expected to change views and influence action. Working individually or in groups, choose one of the stakeholders and audience pairs below. Then follow the strategies on pages 54–58 for deepening your understanding of the issue and for shaping your argument for your audience. The underlying issue question is, What should be done to improve the United States' handling of e-waste?

STAKEHOLDERS AND TARGET AUDIENCE	
Stakeholders	**Target Audience**
You are a high-tech company that needs to charge more for your products to cover the costs of recycling.	Your audience is American consumers interested in buying high-tech products such as computers, monitors, DVD players, and so forth.
You are part of a group of environmentalists concerned about the pollution from high-tech products in third world countries.	Your audience is American consumers who regularly buy high-tech products such as computers, monitors, DVD players, and televisions.

1. To help you become familiar with the issue and think dialectically about it, you may want to reread the argument "The e-Waste Crisis," examine the following photos from the Basel Action Network carefully, and consult the Web sites listed here:
   - Basel Action Network www.ban.org
   - ReLectronics—Computer Reuse, Rebuilding, and Recycling in Bellingham, WA www.relectronics.org/eWaste.html
   - GreenBiz.com www.greenbiz.com
   - EuBusiness.com www.eubusiness.com/Environ/e-waste.01/

2. In response to these photos and the information and arguments you find on several of the Web sites, do a fifteen- or twenty-minute freewrite about two or three of these sources. What view of the e-waste problem does each photo and Web site present? How does each substantiate its view?

3. Briefly analyze your audience and decide on your purpose. What assumptions and values do you believe your audience holds on this issue?

4. Now construct an argument core for the argument you would present in your flier. Include a claim, at least two audience-based reasons, and a description of the kinds of evidence you would need to support your claim and reasons. If you need to support your unstated assumptions, how would you do it?

5. Decide how you would build a positive *ethos*, and explain how you would use appeals to *pathos*. Which, if any, of these photos would you consider using and why?

6. Your instructor may ask you to share your sketched out argument with the class or to flesh out and complete it as an actual short argument flier.

3

Trading Goods
Consumerism, Free Trade, and Sweatshops

Question to Ponder

We may find it difficult to comprehend that buying a latte at Starbucks is an action that makes us "players in the global economy" who "influence livelihoods and government policies around the world."* Coffee pickers in Latin America struggle to make a living wage as the price of coffee fluctuates under free trade conditions and agreements. However, Fair Trade Certification claims to guarantee coffee pickers $1.26 a pound, compared to the free trade price of as little as 10¢ a pound. As coffee drinkers, you and your friends are wondering if you should buy only fair trade coffee to help coffee workers. Should Americans and people in rich countries factor the working conditions under which products were grown or made into our consumer choices?

CONTEXT FOR A NETWORK OF ISSUES

Free trade affects us every day—what we eat, wear, and buy—and we hear the term "free trade" almost as frequently as we hear the term "globalization." Basically, **free trade** refers to the economic philosophy and practice of reducing barriers such as tariffs, taxes, subsidies, and quotas so that raw materials, goods, and services can move unhampered across national borders. Supporters of free trade point out that facilitating the movement of goods around the world enlarges the variety of available products, for example, bringing American consumers a choice of cars from South Korea, Japan, and Germany; a choice of wine from Australia, Italy, and

---

*Jake Baatsell, "Cup by Cup, Coffee Fuels World Market," *Seattle Times*, September 19, 2004.

France; and a choice of kiwis and apples from New Zealand when it is winter in the United States. Free trade also helps to lower the cost of goods so that consumers can buy more things and have a higher standard of living.

However, even as we enjoy bargains on DVDs, jeans, and household wares at nearby superdiscount stores, we are gradually becoming aware of some hidden costs of free trade. (One cost of free trade is the loss of American jobs to other countries, discussed in Chapter 4 on the global economic crisis and money.)* The media and advocacy groups are making us more conscious of the production processes that create the goods that make our lives comfortable. While advances in technology play a part in cheaper prices, we learn more about where our televisions, clothing, and toys are made when we look at the labels on these items: men's shirts from Cambodia and Taiwan, sheets from India, jeans from Mexico, women's sweaters from the Philippines, fleece jackets from Jordan, women's blouses from Sri Lanka, and athletic shoes from China. Even more important, news stories increasingly give us glimpses of the exploitation, injustices, and abuses experienced by workers in factories throughout Mexico, Central America, East Asia, the Middle East, and Southeast Asia: twelve- to eighteen-hour shifts; minimal or no overtime pay; housing in stark, barricaded dormitories; working amid poisonous chemical waste; dangerous, poorly maintained equipment; minimal or no compensation for occupational injuries; and firing in response to unionization efforts. These reports of **sweatshop** conditions in factories in developing countries raise questions for citizens and consumers in comfortable developed countries. How are we to interpret and respond to the contradictory views, experiences, and consequences of free trade?

Free Trade Theory in Brief. First we need a basic understanding of free trade as a philosophy and a global economic system. Free trade theory emphasizes continuous economic growth and believes that this growth is the solution to world poverty. In metaphoric terms, the "pie" of global wealth-earning potential needs to grow bigger so that more countries can have a piece, and the world needs to grow "flatter" so that all countries can share economic and technological benefits.†

---

*The readings in Chapter 3 and 4 complement each other by raising macro, global issues about free trade and the flow of capital along with more personal, local issues about consumer habits and responsibilities, the affordability of products, the availability of jobs, and the necessity of financial literacy.

†Thomas L. Friedman proclaims this equalized vision of global development in his book *The World Is Flat: A Brief History of the Twenty-First Century.* NY: Farrar, Straus, and Giroux, 2005.

Proponents of free trade regularly cite the theories of eighteenth-century Scottish economist Adam Smith (author of the 1776 book *The Wealth of Nations*) and David Ricardo, a nineteenth-century British economist. Smith argued that if government stays out of trade, then wealth created by private businesses and trade will benefit the public. Ricardo asserted that countries need to specialize in the goods that they can produce most efficiently and cheaply and that when countries trade their specialties, all will benefit (a principle called **comparative advantage**). Free trade theory claims that economic competition with minimal government intervention will lead to greater efficiency, productivity, and innovation; will reduce costs for consumers; and will free up more capital for further investment. Free trade's removal of **trade barriers** such as tariffs should promote economic growth, foster a cooperative spirit among nations, help developing nations become independent economies, and end poverty around the world.

Some Key Free Trade Agreements and Institutions. As citizens and consumers, we also need a basic understanding of how free trade has become the global trading system. In 1944, the global economic institutions and agreements that have implemented this theory of free trade—the **International Monetary Fund**, the **World Bank**, and the **General Agreement on Tariffs and Trade**—were launched. The International Monetary Fund and World Bank were intended to further economic progress in poorer countries by lending them money to help them through economic crises and help them build the systems (called "infrastructure") such as roads, power plants, ports, and education that provide the foundation for economic development. In 1947, the General Agreement on Tariffs and Trade (GATT), accepted by **developed countries** (also called "industrialized" or "first world" countries) and **developing countries** (also called "unindustrialized," or "third world" countries or emerging economies), sought to shape international trade by minimizing trade barriers, especially tariffs. In 1994, this agreement became an institution, the **World Trade Organization** (WTO). By removing barriers to trade, the WTO seeks to create "a level playing field"—that is, equal opportunity for businesses in all countries. Additionally, free trade agreements provide many benefits for large corporations, including the establishment of **Export Processing Zones** (EPZs) that are tax-free locations for factories producing goods for big retailers.

Besides the WTO, many other free trade agreements create free trade zones and regional partnerships among groups of countries. The **European Union** is a trading bloc among twenty-seven countries throughout Europe that was formed to coordinate these countries' political and economic affairs. Another trading bloc, the **North American Free Trade Agreement** among the United States, Canada, and Mexico, took effect in 1994.

STAKES AND STAKEHOLDERS

People throughout the world, businesses and multinational corporations, national and local governments, whole countries, and individual citizens and consumers have much to gain or lose from the way that conflicts over free trade's principles and practices are argued and resolved. Here are some of the significant issue questions that show how the interests of different global citizens are pitted against each other.

Is Free Trade a Universally Good Global Economic System? This major controversy over who benefits from free trade is complex partly because the information used to measure growth and success varies. Are South Korea, India, and now China really examples of unrestricted free trade? How should the wealth of nations be measured? Is wealth accumulating in the hands of a small group of privileged world-wide elites? Some political analysts and social activists representing workers and indigenous peoples around the world argue that free trade is creating winners (in particular, big corporations) and losers (indigenous peoples and poor workers in developing countries) because both the theory and practice of free trade are flawed. Environmentalists and social activists challenge free trade's goal of continuous economic growth with its drain on the earth's resources. Political analysts such as David Korten believe that free trade theory misinterprets and misapplies the theories of Adam Smith and David Ricardo. For instance, Korten asserts that Smith disliked corporations and believed in local investment and production so that business owners and managers would be responsible to the people most affected by industrial activity. Many critics contend that free trade enables powerful corporations called **transnationals** or **multinationals** to exploit poor developing countries' resources and workers. Furthermore, critics point out that much of the increased trade that appears to be among nations is actually intrafirm—one part of a corporation located in one country trading with another part of the same corporation located in another country.

Should Free Trade Be Freer? Some leaders and citizen groups in developing countries accept the model and goals of free trade but argue that the rules and agreements currently favor rich countries and large corporations. Farmers in developing countries protest that they cannot compete with U.S. and European farmers, whose governments give them tax cuts and financial support. Furthermore, rich countries put high tariffs on competing foreign goods (called **protectionism**) while at the same time demanding that developing countries lower their tariffs on American and European products. For small farmers and factories in developing countries such as Mexico, free trade can mean losing out to low-priced agricultural goods from the United States and Europe, going bankrupt, and falling into poverty. Since 2001 in what is called the Doha Round (from Doha, the capital of Qatar where the trade talks began), the developing countries led by India, China, Brazil and South Africa have struggled to compel developed countries represented by the United States, the European Union, and Japan to lower tariffs and remove agricultural subsidies. The developing countries want more trade advantages—more leveling of the economic playing field.

Should National, Regional, and Local Governments or Global Organizations Have More Power over Global Trade and Product Safety? Both supporters and opponents recognize that free trade agreements mean a loss of power and political control at the national, regional, and local levels of government. However, they disagree over whether dissolving national borders and powers is beneficial or detrimental. Should countries be able to make laws to meet their own needs? Opponents of free trade agreements argue that standardizing trade rules (in economic terms, "harmonizing" regulations) often leads to minimal protection of the environment, workers, and consumers. Many citizens want their government to be able to make laws covering inspection procedures, package and labeling requirements, and product content to protect consumers' health, a desire intensified in the United States by recent problems with poisoned pet food and toxic toys from China. In addition, in the harder economic times resulting from the global market crash of 2008, many citizens around the world want their governments to have more control over domestic production, exports, and imports, a move considered "protectionist" by free trade proponents and considered self-preserving and economically sensible by others.

Should Free Trade Agreements Be Extended or Reconceived? Around the world, politicians, economic leaders, and social activists are debating the expansion of free trade agreements. For example, should the North American Free Trade Agreement (NAFTA) linking the United States, Canada, and Mexico and the **Central America-Dominican Republic-United States Free Trade Agreement** (CAFTA-DR) expand to become the **Free Trade Agreement of the Americas**, linking thirty-four countries of the Western Hemisphere in a free trade bloc? Currently, Argentina, Brazil, and Venezuela—as well as labor unions, consumer groups, and the Catholic Church in Latin America—are protesting what they see as economic domination by largely U.S. transnational corporations. Recently, the United States' controversial free trade agreement with South Korea (KOR-US FTA) has met with protests from Korean farmers, workers, citizens, and students objecting to the process and effects of this agreement.

Does the Employment That Derives from the Current Free Trade System Benefit Global Workers? If we move from the big picture of free trade controversies to examine the well-being of workers, we find analysts, businesses, and activists arguing about sweatshops and foreign factories. Are grueling, low-paid jobs a necessary and inevitable road to economic progress? Or, as other analysts, social activists, and workers contend, are market competition and corporate greed creating sweatshop conditions in foreign factories? These people claim that free trade has enabled corporations to move their factories to the countries with the cheapest labor and fewest regulations on worker health and safety. Labor activists and workers argue that when transnational corporations like Wal-Mart pressure subcontracting factories to reduce costs or when they shift their manufacturing from Nicaragua to China, where workers will work longer hours for less pay, these corporations are forcing workers to compete against each other in a "race to the bottom." Furthermore, free trade has cost Americans jobs. As manufacturing has left the United States, where unions ensure fair wages, benefits, and conditions for workers, to go to developing countries with a much lower cost of living, few regulations, and no unions, some Americans have been left without comparable-paying jobs. (Chapter 4, "Trading Financial Risk and Jobs," examines these issues.) Anticorporate advocates view this worldwide competition among workers for jobs as a shift in the global distribution of wealth, dividing the workers everywhere from corporations, managers, owners, and stockholders.

What Role Do and Should Consumers Play in Free Trade? Advocates of the free market and corporations believe that consumers are *helping* workers in developing countries when they buy the products these workers make. Corporations argue that to meet the demands of their stockholders for profits and the demands of their customers for the lowest prices, they must seek the cheapest labor and the most favorable free trade agreements. Do the consumer habits of developed nations drive the global competition of corporations? Anticorporate activists and labor supporters say we need to use our consumer power to influence the improvement of factory conditions around the world. However, these human rights advocates, union supporters, worker organizations, and consumer groups disagree about *how* to use consumer power and *how* to change consumer habits: Should we boycott abusive companies, demand corporate accountability, buy only union-made goods, and/or be willing to pay higher prices for goods to ensure fair wages for workers?

What Are Alternatives to Free Trade? One alternative to free trade that is receiving much attention is **fair trade**, which seeks to connect farmers, artisans, and workers in developing regions more closely with markets in developed nations in long-term, transparent relationships. Proponents of fair trade want to establish dependable markets and a living wage and actively campaign to reduce poverty. Some of the main fair trade organizations and advocacy groups are SERRV International Fair Trade Association, the Fair Trade Federation, Global Exchange, and TransFair USA. In the last ten years, consumer awareness of fair trade has doubled. Even big chains such as Wal-Mart, McDonald's, and Dunkin' Donuts are selling fair trade coffee, and fair trade items have expanded to include cocoa, cotton, coffee, tea, cut flowers, bananas, and sugar, among others. Some critics believe that large companies are exploiting fair trade by trying to implement it on a large scale that by-passes groups of small farmers in favor of large plantations. Other critics of fair trade assert that fair trade standards designed to benefit small producers are not upheld, and workers are not receiving higher wages. Still other activists and businesses embrace **direct trade** over fair trade, especially for coffee. Direct trade restores control to individual sellers and growers through respectful, private price-setting agreements, which yield more financial benefits for both. However, skeptics argue that fair trade networks and direct trade cannot realistically compete with the scope, capital, and efficiency of free trade.

The three sections that follow—"Student Voice," "International Voices," and "Global Hot Spot"—help you explore ways that your life and other people's lives are being touched by consumerism, free trade, and factory production.

 ### STUDENT VOICE: Thinking Beyond My American Consumerism by Tiffany Anderson

Some Americans, as Tiffany Anderson shows, are beginning to question our participation in the unequally distributed benefits of free trade.

> I spent the summer of my sophomore year of college working stock at the Gap Outlet in the nearby mall. Although I complained of the early morning hours, the stifling heat of the back room, and the physical labor it required, I was secretly proud to be a part of our all-girl stock team. We worked hard, but our shifts resembled the ambiance of sleepovers; we gossiped, joked around, and blasted the top-40 station as we unpacked boxes of clothing and accessories. On days when shipments of new products came in, we each took turns passing snap judgments on the cuteness of the new items. On this particular day, I knew it was going to be rough because we were getting one of the biggest shipments for the Back to School season. I pulled on my black apron and searched for my exacto-knife, eyeing the seemingly endless stacks of boxes. There was nothing to do but start.
>
> I hummed along to the new Christina Aguilera song as I pulled corduroy pants from their protective plastic wrapping, wrinkling my nose at the sour smell of newness that clung to them. I finished unpacking the box, broke it down, threw it onto the garbage heap, and ripped open the next box on my stack. I tore off the lid and froze as a numbing chill enveloped my perspiring body, and I yelled, "Oh, you guys. Look."

My coworkers gathered around, anticipating my horror at an atrocious sweater or some ill-advised pants. Instead, I pointed to a few lines scrawled across the inside lid of my box in navy blue pen and in a foreign language that I couldn't translate or decipher. The language looked Thai, or maybe Vietnamese . . . something Asian, I was sure. The tags on the clothing were of little help. In the one box alone, there were tags from Indonesia, China, Vietnam, and Thailand.

"What do you think it says?" asked Amy.

Each of us knew The Gap had been cited repeatedly as a major employer of sweatshop labor, although we rarely acknowledged this fact to each other.

"Do you think it's a cry for help?" I sensed the author's presence, as if the sight of the blue right-slanting writing had freed the author from her prison, like the rubbing of a lamp releases a genie. I pictured a woman, my age but skinny, with sunken eyes and black hair, locked into a blindingly hot factory until she met her daily quota. I thought about her family of five she had to feed on a skimpy wage, children raised by a mother who was practically absent as she tried to provide for them. We went through the possible scenarios, embarrassed by our frequent references to our own jobs as "sweatshop labor." An unsettling silence descended on the room, and all you could hear was the tearing of plastic and cardboard. Before I recycled the box, however, I tore off the piece with the message and put it in my locker, hoping to find a translation, although I never did.

As the day progressed, I couldn't shake the feeling that I had been chosen to open that box, that I now had a responsibility to my friend overseas, trapped in a situation she couldn't free herself from. Maybe I was being melodramatic, but the problem was I had very little information on the actual working conditions of the people who made my clothes. Now I could no longer ignore the fact that I didn't know.

As an American, I realized that I had the privilege to listen to the radio at work and chatter with my coworkers. My biggest complaints consisted of feeling tired after a six- or seven-hour day, or of having to drive home sweaty and dust-covered. I worked to make money so I could go out dancing during the school year and get a discount on Gap jeans. I now felt guilty that my $30 pair of jeans paid a marginal fraction of the profit to the person who had made them. It slowly began to occur to me that I had a choice of which companies to support and that I had a responsibility as a consumer to know what sort of practices my money supported. While research only complicated these issues further for me, I at least think now that consumer consciousness is encouraging. Nothing will change if I continue to ignore the problem, unwrapping khakis and singing along with the radio, as if I'm the only person in the world.

INTERNATIONAL VOICES

One problem American consumers have in trying to understand how free trade competition affects foreign workers is the contradictory messages we receive from workers. To investigate the workers' situation, we could focus on any of the Export Processing Zones (also called Export Trade Zones) in Central America and Southeast Asia or any place where multinational corporations have subcontracted their manufacturing work. While some workers would agree with Candida Rosa Lopez, an employee in a Nicaraguan garment factory, who told a *Miami Herald* reporter, "I wish more Americans would buy the clothes we make,"* others convey their distress over the exploitive factory conditions. For example, Isabel Reyes, a worker in Honduras, reported her experience of the pressure to produce more goods at lower prices. This passage comes from an article entitled "Wal-Mart Wrings Efficiency from Third World Factories" by Nancy Cleeland, Evelyn Iritani, and Tyler Marshall that appeared on November 28, 2003, in the *Seattle Times*:

Comments from a Factory Worker Producing Clothing for Wal-Mart

San Pedro Sula, Honduras—When Wal-Mart Stores demands a lower price for the shirts and shorts it sells by the millions, the consequences are felt in a remote Chinese industrial town, at a port in Bangladesh and in Honduras, under the corrugated metal roof of the Cosmos clothing factory.

Isabel Reyes, who has worked at the plant for 11 years, pushes fabric through her sewing machine 10 hours a day, struggling to meet the latest quota scrawled on a blackboard.

She now sews sleeves onto shirts at the rate of 1,200 garments a day. That's two shirts a minute, one sleeve every 15 seconds.

"There is always an 'acceleration,'" said Reyes, 37, who can't lift a cooking pot or hold her infant daughter without the anti-inflammatory pills she gulps down every few hours. "The goals are always increasing, but the pay stays the same."

Reyes, who earns the equivalent of $35 a week, says her bosses blame the long hours and low wages on big U.S. companies and their demands for ever-cheaper merchandise. Wal-Mart, the biggest company of them all, is the Cosmos factory's main customer.

Reyes is skeptical. Why, she asked, would a company in the richest country in the world care about a few pennies on a pair of shorts?

---

*David R. Henderson, "The Case for Sweatshops," *Miami Herald*, February 7, 2000.

The answer: Wal-Mart has built its empire on bargains.

The company's size and obsession with shaving costs have made it a global economic force. Its decisions affect wages, working conditions and manufacturing practices—even the price of a yard of denim—around the world.

GLOBAL HOT SPOT: China

The news about China's rapid industrialization is also full of contradictions. Recently, China has been the recipient of many factories relocated from Mexico and has become the largest exporter of goods to the United States. On the one hand, China exemplifies substantial growth toward market capitalism, modernization, and economic prosperity. The following passage from an article titled "Factory Labor Runs Short in China" by Peter S. Goodman from the *Seattle Times*, September 26, 2004, supports the positive picture of free trade economic development:

> Dongguan, China—. . . . Where once a paycheck, even under harsh conditions, was enough to entice tens of millions of people to leave their villages in China's interior and flock to factories on the coast, workers are beginning to turn their backs on the prospect of laboring in 100-degree heat, living in rat-infested dormitories and being cheated out of their earnings.
>
> They are instead staying in their home villages to take advantage of rising farm wages—up from 15 to 40 percent in the past year as the government streamlines taxes and as growing domestic spending power raises the price of vegetables and meat.
>
> Or they are finding jobs closer to home in inland cities along China's expanding road and rail networks.
>
> At bus and train stations here, migrant workers carry belongings in plastic sacks, headed back to villages in the interior. "The wages are too low and the work is too hard," said a 21-year-old man from Guangxi province as he waited to board an all-night bus home. "It's a waste of time."
>
> "Manufacturing wages are going up, and they are going to keep going up," said Jonathan Anderson, a former International Monetary Fund official and now chief economist at UBS Investment Research in Hong Kong.
>
> That refutes a theory that as more of the world's manufacturing shifts to this country of 1.3 billion people, China's peasant-labor force would force global wages lower for decades, particularly given that independent labor unions are banned and even the threat of organization meets with stiff prison sentences.

On the other hand, China also illustrates the economic dependence and exploitation found in developing countries. The pressures of global free trade to cut costs and to treat workers as dispensable parts of the production process have made economic progress costly to many workers. The following excerpt from a *Detroit Free Press* article titled "Savage Form of Capitalism: Chinese Factory Workers Risk Limbs to Hold Jobs" by Tim Johnson, published on April 17, 2004, reveals some of these costs:

> Shenzhen, China—. . . . In a grim replay of the industrial revolution in the United States and other countries, industrial machinery will crush or sever the arms, hands and fingers of some 40,000 Chinese workers this year, government-controlled news media report. Some experts privately say the true number is higher.
>
> A majority of accidents occurs in metalworking and electronics plants with heavy stamping equipment, shoe and handbag factories with leather-cutting equipment, toy factories and industrial plastics plants with blazing hot machinery.
>
> In Shenzhen's hospital wards, maimed factory workers nurse mangled hands and forearm stumps. They tell of factory managers who've removed machine safety guards that slowed output and of working on decrepit, unsafe machinery. Workers toiling 100 hours a week grow dazed from fatigue, then lose their fingers to machines.
>
> Local officials routinely overlook appalling safety conditions, worried that factory owners will relocate. They send mutilated migrant workers back to distant rural villages, shunting the burden of workplace injuries onto poorer inland provinces.
>
> . . . But labor monitors say that foreign companies that relentlessly demand lower prices and U.S. consumers who gobble up low-cost goods contribute to the problem.
>
> Zhou Litai, a lawyer who represents hundreds of workers maimed or killed on the job, said foreign consumers should be aware that some "Made in China" products are "tainted with blood from cut-off fingers or hands."

As these news stories suggest, free trade, global factory production, and consumerism meet in complex economic and ethical ways. As you study the following readings on the benefits and drawbacks of free trade, on consumers' responsibility to the workers who make our goods, and on locating responsibility for product safety in a global economy, examine not only what arguments the writers are making but *how* they are making them.

READINGS

Poor Man's Hero
[Interview with Johan Norberg]
Nick Gillespie

This article appeared in the December 2003 issue of *Reasononline*, the Web version of *Reason*, a monthly magazine dedicated to "free minds and free markets." *Reason* states its libertarian perspective and purpose: to provide "a refreshing alternative to right-wing and left-wing opinion magazines by making a principled case for liberty and individual choice in all areas of human activity" (http:reason.com/aboutreason.shtml). Nick Gillespie is editor-in-chief of the online and television editions of this libertarian publication, a widely published journalist who has written for the *New York Times*, the *Washington Post*, *Slate*, and *Salon*, and a frequent commentator on radio and television news networks. Johan Norberg, the focus of this interview, is a Swedish political writer and activist best known for his 2001 book *In Defense of Global Capitalism*.

> How does Norberg try to make his libertarian pro–free trade views under-
> standable and persuasive in this interview? What view of protectionism
> versus open borders do libertarians hold?

If there is any moral certainty underpinning today's antiglobalization movement, it's that desperate actions—from sometimes violent street demonstrations to public crop burnings to dressing up as giant sea turtles—are needed to protect the traditions, forests, and human rights of the Third World against the rapacious greed of the First. The anti-globo left has little doubt that anyone who favors international free trade, open markets, and the cultural mongrelization they foster must be a greedy corporate bastard hellbent on plundering the world's poor and chopping down the last tree left on the planet. On the right, if George W. Bush is any indication, a different sort of blindness is at work: It's OK to pass nakedly protectionist legislation as long as you talk a good game about favoring free trade.

This is why Johan Norberg, a 30-year-old Swede with roots in the anarchist left, is so important. He is the author of *In Defense of Global Capitalism*, which makes a powerful moral and economic case for globalization. Norberg throws rhetorical Molotov cocktails both at left-wing critics who would condemn developing countries to poverty by insisting on First World workplace and environmental standards as a prerequisite for trade and at Western governments whose free market rhetoric is shamefully undercut by draconian tariffs on textiles and agriculture, the two areas in which the developing world can actually compete.

Norberg focuses on the human dimension of globalization, how increased and freer trade is the best way to help the wretched of the earth. A bestseller in Sweden when it appeared there in 2001, *In Defense of Global Capitalism* is a richly detailed and nuanced brief in favor of globalization. It was translated for British audiences by the influential London free market think tank the Institute of Economic Affairs. The Cato Institute has just released a new and updated American translation by Roger Tanner (with help from Reason Associate Editor Julian Sanchez, who previously worked at Cato).

A fellow at the Stockholm think tank Timbro, Norberg is the author of several previous books, including *State, Individual, and Market* (2000), *A History of Swedish Liberalism* (1998), and *The Resistance Man* (1997), a study of the Swedish writer Vilhelm Moberg.

In Defense of Global Capitalism is a compelling book on what is arguably the major economic issue of our time. In Johan Norberg, globalization has found a persuasive and passionate spokesman who may well reshape the terms of debate. If he succeeds in doing so, it won't be his first such success. In the early 1990s, as part of a libertarian group called the Freedom Front, Norberg helped to organize speakeasies that illegally sold liquor to protest Sweden's restrictive licensing laws. After the group grew to 30,000 members—and after more than a dozen raids by the police—Swedish politicians realized they couldn't contain what was becoming a broad-based social movement. Instead, they liberalized their laws, allowing drinking establishments to maintain longer hours. "That's my biggest political success to date," jokes Norberg.

Editor-in-Chief Nick Gillespie interviewed Norberg in Washington, D.C., in early September.

REASON: Your book is titled *In Defense of Global Capitalism*. Can you summarize your case?

JOHAN NORBERG: The core is that capitalism and globalization—by which I basically mean free and open markets and the liberal political, economic, and social institutions that support them—bring freedom of choice to people in countries that have never experienced this before. If we want to defend globalization—and we should—our focus must be on developing countries, not our own Western countries. Global capitalism means that people are no longer confined by the decisions of national elites. These could be the local monopolies, the local powers, politicians, and so on.

By making local powers compete or by bypassing them altogether, globalization gives people more freedom to decide over their own consumption, to buy things from abroad, to get the cultural influences they want, to travel, to meet friends, and to cross borders.

REASON: What's the evidence that global capitalism benefits people in poor countries?

NORBERG: Take just about any statistic, any indicator of living standards in the world, and you can see the progress that has been made over the exact period that worries globalization critics. In the last 30 years we've seen chronic hunger and the extent of child labor being halved. In the last 40 years, we've seen life expectancy going up to 64 years in developing countries. We've seen literacy levels approaching the maximum in most countries in the world. According to World Bank statistics, 200 million people have left absolute poverty—defined as living on the equivalent of less than $1 a day—over the past 20 years. What's more, the most progress is found in the countries that increased trade and contacts with the outside world.

Globalization has also helped extend rights to women that had long been confined to men. These include being able to go into business, get an education, inherit money, and so on. One reason for this is simple economics. In a globalized, competitive economy, women are a potential resource. They are able to have new ideas, to produce, and to work. If you discriminate against women—or anyone else—you lose opportunities as a society or as an employer. Take the discussion that's going on now in Saudi Arabia about whether women should be allowed to drive, which they can't legally do now. While it's unlikely the situation there will change anytime soon, it's progress just to have the discussion. People are saying it's extremely costly to hire drivers, often from other countries, to drive women around. You can see how basic economics, basic capitalism, creates the incentive to give women more rights.

A second reason is that all the goods, ideas, and people that cross borders under globalization allow people to see more alternatives, to see other ways of living. When women and other oppressed groups in poor countries see how their counterparts in Western societies are treated, they begin to have ideas about how they want to be treated. Globalization is a great influence because people everywhere get all sorts of new ideas. They say, "Wow, things can be very different than I'm used to."

This isn't to say everything is rosy. Most things are getting better in the developing world, but there are new problems, including AIDS. Yet we can see the old scourges, the old diseases, being abolished. Life expectancy wouldn't be getting longer if things were getting worse in terms of health, hunger, and the environment. We have the few exceptions in sub-Saharan Africa, which also happens to consist of the very countries that are the least globalized. They have the least foreign investment and, generally speaking, the least political and economic liberty. More than anything, they need the sort of economic growth that will allow them to buy not simply relatively expensive AIDS drugs but penicillin and vaccines for more basic sorts of illnesses.

REASON: Can you give a specific example of a developing nation that has benefited from globalization?

NORBERG: Look at Vietnam, which I visited recently. It had the benefit that when the Communists took power there, they actually implemented their ideas. They collectivized agriculture and they destroyed private property, which meant that in the mid-1980s people were starving there. The Communists' own ideas managed to do what the American bombs never did: destroy communism. In the wake of such failure, the government began to look for other examples, and they saw that Taiwan had succeeded by globalizing. The Communists in China were liberalizing trade and ownership laws and were seeing fast progress. The contrast is especially clear on the Korean peninsula. It's the same population, with the same culture, just having two very different political and economic systems. In 50 years, one of them went from hunger and poverty to Southern European living standards. The other one is still starving.

Looking at all this, the Vietnamese chose to go global. They began to price land and they began to open up for investments and for trade, which led to quick results. Agricultural production took off and has made them one of the world's biggest exporters of rice. But they also took in investments for manufacturing production. They've received tons of foreign investments and factories that gave people new opportunities and new resources that have increased their standard of living.

REASON: Critics would say that what Vietnam really imported were sweatshops.

NORBERG: Sweatshops are a natural stage of development. We had sweatshops in Sweden in the late 19th century. We complained about Japanese sweatshops 40 years ago. You had them here. In fact, you still do in some places. One mistake that Western critics of globalization make is that they compare their current working standards to those in the developing world: "Look, I'm sitting in a nice, air-conditioned office. Why should people in Vietnam really have to work in those terrible factories?" But you've got to compare things with the alternatives that people actually have in their own countries. The reason why their workplace standards and wages are generally lower is the lack of productivity, the lack of infrastructure, the lack of machinery, and so on. If workers were paid U.S. wages in Vietnam, employers wouldn't be able to hire them. The alternative for most workers would be to go back to agriculture, where they could work longer hours and get irregular and much lower wages.

Sweatshops are the way poor countries tap into their competitive advantage, which is cheap labor. Multinational corporations bring in more modern technology, including things like training and management systems, that actually increase productivity. When workers are more productive, they tend to earn more. That's why in a typical developing nation, if you're able to work for an American multinational, you make eight times the average wage. That's why people are lining up to get these jobs. When I was in Vietnam, I interviewed workers about their dreams and aspirations. The most common wish was that Nike, one of the major targets of the anti-globalization movement, would expand so that a worker's relatives could get a job with the company.

When unions, when protectionists, when uncompetitive corporations in the U.S. say that we shouldn't buy from countries like Vietnam because of its labor standards, they've got it all wrong. They're saying" Look, you are too poor to trade with us. And that means that we won't trade with you. We won't buy your goods until you're as rich as we are." That's totally backwards. These countries won't get rich without being able to export goods. . . .

REASON: If the benefits of globalization are so obvious, why is there so much opposition to it, especially in the West? Vietnamese workers may be clamoring for more Nike factories, but protesters in Europe and North America are tossing bricks through the windows of McDonald's and Starbucks.

NORBERG: The further you get from the West, the more positive people are toward globalization, toward more business and trade ties with the rest of the world. The most vocal opponents of globalization in poor countries are often funded by critics from wealthier countries. For instance, Vandana Shiva [director of the New Delhi-based Research Foundation for Science, Technology, and Ecology] is a very vocal opponent of economic liberalization and biotechnology, and she's funded by a lot of different Western groups. Actual farmers in the developing world mostly would like these new crops to actually get something done.

There are the old groups that have always been scared of foreign competition. Corporations that wouldn't be able to beat competition from other countries are one of them. In the U.S., that includes the textile industry, which has funded a lot of the anti-sweatshop propaganda. You see the same thing when it comes to unions that are trying to educate people against free trade, trying to block the NAFTA agreements, the World Trade Organization negotiations, and similar things. But there are newer pressure groups too. These include nongovernmental organizations that have been mostly interested in domestic issues, which could be anything from workplace safety to opposing privatization and outsourcing. In a globalized world, it makes sense for these groups to make their case in front of international bodies. Probably more than most, environmental groups understood that they have an interest in challenging the new globalization forces. They are used to being able to lobby their own governments to stop certain substances, to stop genetically modified crops and the like. They understand that they have to take their issues to the WTO and to be able to fight for them there.

All these groups may have different agendas—the unions are interested in domestic jobs and the greens in air quality—but they're willing to collaborate. They don't have the same views, and they don't have the same goals. But they do have the same enemy.

REASON: Let's talk about the environmental groups a bit. In your book, you convincingly demonstrate that economic development is a boon to the environment because richer countries tend to pollute less. You point to research suggesting that economic growth correlates positively with cleaner air and water once countries reach around $10,000 per capita GDP—the level of South Korea, Argentina, and Slovenia. You argue that the best way to clean the environment is to get the developing world to move as quickly as possible from a pre-industrial to a post-industrial economy. Why would environmental groups not buy that argument?

NORBERG: I think that there are two basic reasons that lead environmentalists to oppose globalization and the industrial development that goes along with it. The first is a real concern about the environment. Many environmentalists care about green forests, clean air, clean water, and so on. What they don't appreciate is that attitude is itself a result of industrial development. In our countries, people didn't care about these things 100 years ago. Preferences shift when you can feed your children and give them an education. That's when you begin to care about these sorts of things. Environmentalists in this camp merely project a contemporary sense of these issues onto developing countries that are at the place where the West was a century ago. It's an intellectually honest mistake, one that new information and data can change. So can talking with people in developing countries.

But there's another motivation at work among some environmentalists. I don't think this viewpoint represents the majority, but it often includes the intellectual leaders of environmental groups. These are people who are bothered not by environmental degradation per se. Rather, they reject the modern project altogether. They are skeptical of the lifestyles and societies that we have created. They think we are alienated from nature compared to the past and that it is wrong to see nature as a tool that human beings can use for their own convenience and benefit. It's a fundamentally aesthetic understanding of the world that is reminiscent of early 19th century German romanticism. It paints a very distorted view of the pre-industrial world as a utopia. In reality, that world was a place in which starvation was the rule and not the exception.

I was extremely skeptical towards modern industrial society for a long time, so I understand these sentiments. If you live in an urban, developed area and your main experience of rural areas is secondhand, they're quite understandable. You feel very sad about countries that are modernizing and building factories, and about people who will be buying espresso machines that make loud noises instead of, I don't know, sitting around listening to the birds singing.

My attitude changed as I began to read history and understood what kind of circumstances my ancestors lived in. The world they lived in was far from ideal. It was starvation, it was children dying in the first year of their lives. And of course, backbreaking labor, including child labor, was everywhere. I think the best way to rebut this romantic, aesthetic challenge to globalization, to our modern project, is by actually looking at the circumstances of pre-industrial society.

REASON: In your book, you really lay into Western governments, many of which talk out of both sides of their mouths when it comes to liberalizing trade. They want unfettered access to new markets, but they routinely employ protectionist tariffs against developing countries. You call this "the white man's shame" and point out that "Western duties on export commodities from the developing world are 30 percent above the global average."

NORBERG: Since the end of the Second World War, we've liberalized trade in most areas. Ironically, the main places where we haven't done so are textiles and agriculture—the very two areas where poor countries can compete.

In the developed world, the textile and agricultural sectors are very strong special interest groups with a lot of political resources. They can make a lot of noise in the public debate. We know that if we open these markets to competition, we'll have to restructure those parts of our economies. People will have to change jobs and go into something else. That would be painful, of course, but it's outrageous, since those are precisely where poor countries would be able to do well.

REASON: This opens up a larger question about increasing globalization. If trade laws come down to special interest politics, how do you defeat those interests? How do we get to a point where the U.S. and the European Union finally give up on protectionism for textiles and agriculture?

NORBERG: I think the first thing that is necessary is moral outrage. We need to explain what's on the line, what the cost is to poor people in the least developed countries. People are *dying* because we in the

West are unwilling to change and to actually live by the free market rhetoric we often spout. We also have to explain to the public that it's not merely developing countries that lose out by these policies. We do too.

REASON: How do we lose out?

NORBERG: We deny ourselves access to better goods at cheaper prices from other countries. We lose out because we have to pay billions in tax-funded subsidies to these special interest groups so that they don't have to face competition. Agricultural subsidies cost something on the order of $1 billion a day in Western countries. We have to explain to people, "Look, if we have real free trade, we'll make another $1 billion every day, simply because we abolished our agricultural subsidies." One study I cite in the book estimates that the world would gain about $70 billion annually from a 40 percent tariff reduction on manufactures—and that 75 percent of that gain would go to developing nations.

REASON: The WTO is meeting in Cancun as we're talking. What do you think of the WTO, which is a major target both of anti-globalizers and many free market advocates?

NORBERG: It's a good thing that it exists, but it's rightly been called the free traders' deal with the devil. The best solution for all of us would be unilateral free trade: Just open our borders. We don't need *protection* from cheap goods; they're exactly what we want!

Unfortunately, we don't live in a perfect world, and in that case I think that the WTO is important for two reasons. One is that it's hard to combat the special interests that are against opening up market access for other countries. But if we do it in multilateral negotiations, we can face the special interests and say: "OK, we might lose jobs in those sectors that we open up to competition. But in exchange we get access to new markets over here." That helps convince people in the export business. It helps get, say, unions on our side for free trade, and that's a good thing. The other reason that the WTO is important is that [it] helps create a rule of law in the international trade system. We lock in free trade reform so that politicians can't backtrack every time there's a failure or a downturn in their national or local economy.

Those are reasons the WTO is important, but it really is a deal with the devil, if only because it gives the impression constantly that when we open up markets, when we give ourselves the opportunity to buy a wider variety of goods at better prices, we are giving up something. I think that's one of the reasons why we have a backlash against free trade. The president of the U.S. and everybody else always act as if free trade is some sort of concession.

REASON: In the wake of the 9/11 attacks and the rationale offered for them by bin Laden, many observers in the West suggested that there was something intrinsic to the Arab world and Islam that makes them particularly uncomfortable with the creative destruction that accompanies what you've called "global capitalism." What do you think?

NORBERG: . . . Although I'm glad Saddam has been toppled—it's a good day whenever a tyrant is dethroned—I don't think that war and occupation are the way to do this. The best way is through globalization, through the introduction of new ideas, of Western influences, into these countries. You can see that happening even in Iran. You can see it happening in Jordan and Qatar and in many other countries that have more access to Western goods and media.

Because of globalization, it's easier for people to watch and read about Western societies, and more and more do. As we mentioned, Arab women see that Western women have the same rights and opportunities as men. That sort of contact is a great source of inspiration. The same thing happens when they see that we can express our own beliefs in a general way, in culture and in music. That's the big hope, I think, for the region. But we have to be very patient because it's going to take a long time. It took a long time for Japan to turn into a peaceful, productive country; it took nearly 50 years for South Korea to become something like a liberal democracy.

But I see the rise of fundamentalist forces in the Middle East not as a sign of the strength of their ideas. It's more a sign that they are terrified of the globalization that is already occurring. The fundamentalists can see that there's a new middle class growing in these countries and that these people are interested more in living the good life, in choosing their own lives, and not in following the literal teachings of the Koran. Critics of globalization worry about the Disneyfication or McDonaldization of culture, of standardization replacing "authentic" traditions. But it's more correct to say that no single culture is becoming dominant. Instead, it's pluralism, the freedom to choose among many different paths and destinations, that is gaining ground due to globalization and greater exchange.

For Class Discussion

1. This interview has two "writers" in that Nick Gillespie introduces Johan Norberg, and then Norberg presents his argument as answers to Gillespie's questions. In his introduction, how does Gillespie identify different groups and their views on globalization? How does he characterize the

antiglobalization movement? How does Gillespie's choice of words contribute to readers' sense of his authority on the subject and to the persuasiveness of his views?

2. What claims does Johan Norberg make about the advantages of global capitalism for developing countries?

3. What is Norberg's view of sweatshops and how does he justify this view?

4. Which of Norberg's points about the benefits of global free trade or the problems of global free trade as it is currently conducted do you think he most effectively supports with evidence? How could you confirm or dispute his use of numerical evidence?

5. *Reason* is a widely read and well-respected nonpartisan publication that often discusses the libertarian case for free trade. What audience besides libertarians do you think would find Norberg's argument persuasive and why? ■

Twelve Reasons to Oppose the World Trade Organization
Global Exchange

This policy statement is taken from the Web site for Global Exchange, an international human rights organization that works toward a "people centered globalization that values the rights of workers and the health of the planet; that prioritizes international collaboration as central to ensuring peace; and that aims to create a local, green economy designed to embrace the diversity of our communities" (www.globalexchange.org/about). Global Exchange seeks to stir up public awareness about injustices and elicit support for fair trade. This campaign policy flier was downloaded April 30, 2009.

> This flier lays out a case against the World Trade Organization in broad, sweeping points. For what purpose and for what audience would it be particularly effective?

For Class Discussion

1. What goals and principles of free trade policy does Global Exchange challenge in this flier? Or to put it another way, what alternative views does it articulate and rebut?

2. The authors of this flier and Johan Norberg are both critical of the WTO. How do their positions on the WTO and free trade differ?

3. What policies and course of action does this piece advocate?

TOP TWELVE REASONS TO OPPOSE
THE WORLD TRADE ORGANIZATION

The World Trade Organization is writing a constitution for the entire globe. The trade ministers and corporate CEOs who control the WTO would like you to believe that its purpose is to inspire growth and prosperity for all. In reality, the WTO has been the greatest tool for taking democratic control of resources out of our communities and putting it into the hands of corporations. But an international movement is growing to oppose the corporate rule of the WTO and replace it with a democratic global economy that benefits people and sustains the communities in which we live. And importantly, we are winning!

1. The WTO Is Fundamentally Undemocratic

The policies of the WTO impact all aspects of society and the planet, but it is not a democratic, transparent institution. The WTO's rules are written by and for corporations with inside access to the negotiations. For example, the US Trade Representative gets heavy input for negotiations from 17 "Industry Sector Advisory Committees." Citizen input by consumer, environmental, human rights and labor organizations is consistently ignored. Even simple requests for information are denied, and the proceedings are held in secret. Who elected this secret global government?

2. The WTO Will Not Make Us Safer

The WTO would like you to believe that creating a world of "free trade" will promote global understanding and peace. On the contrary, the domination of international trade by rich countries for the benefit of their individual interests fuels anger and resentment that make us less safe. To build real global security, we need international agreements that respect people's rights to democracy and trade systems that promote global justice.

3. The WTO Tramples Labor and Human Rights

WTO rules put the "rights" of corporations to profit over human and labor rights. The WTO encourages a 'race to the bottom' in wages by pitting workers against each other rather than promoting internationally recognized labor standards. The WTO has ruled that it is illegal for a government to ban a product based on the way it it produced, such as goods produced with child labor. It has also ruled that governments cannot take into account "non commercial values" such as human rights, or the behavior of companies that do business with vicious dictatorships such as Burma when making purchasing decisions. The WTO has more power to punish countries that violate its rules than the United Nations has to sanction violators of international human rights standards.

4. The WTO Would Privatize Essential Services

The WTO is seeking to force national governments to privatize essential public services such as education, health care, energy and water, so that these sectors are open to multinational corporations. The WTO's General Agreement on Trade in Services, or GATS, includes a list of about 160 threatened services including elder and child care, sewage, garbage, park maintenance, telecommunications, construction, banking, insurance, transportation, shipping, postal services, and tourism. When free trade and corporate globalization turn public services over to private for-profit corporations, those least able to pay for vital services—working class communities and communities of color—are the ones who suffer the most.

5. The WTO Is Destroying the Environment

The WTO is being used by corporations to dismantle hard-won local and national environmental protections, by attacking them as "barriers to trade." The very first WTO panel ruled that a provision of the U.S. Clean Air Act, requiring both domestic and foreign producers alike to produce cleaner gasoline, was WTO-illegal. The WTO also declared illegal a provision of the Endangered Species Act requiring shrimp sold in the United States to be caught with an inexpensive device allowing endangered sea turtles to escape. The WTO is now attempting to deregulate service industries such as logging, fishing, water utilities, and energy distribution, leading to further exploitation of natural resources.

6. The WTO Is Killing People

The WTO's fierce defense of 'Trade Related Intellectual Property rights (TRIPs)—patents, copyrights and trademarks—comes at the expense of health and human lives. The WTO has protected pharmaceutical companies' 'right to profit' against governments seeking to protect their people's health by providing life-saving medicines in countries in areas like sub-saharan Africa, where thousands die every day from HIV/AIDS. Developing countries won an important victory in 2001 when they affirmed the right to produce generic drugs (or import them if they lacked production capacity), so that they could provide essential lifesaving medicines to their populations less expensively. Unfortunately, in 2003, many new conditions were agreed to that will make it more difficult for countries to produce those drugs. Once again, the WTO demonstrates that it favors corporate profit over saving human lives.

7. The WTO Is Increasing Inequality

Free trade is not working for the majority of the world. During the most recent period of rapid growth in global trade and investment (1960 to 1998) inequality worsened both internationally and within countries. The United Nations Development Program reports that the richest 20 percent of the world's population consume 86 percent of the world's resources while the poorest 80 percent consume just 14 percent. WTO rules have hastened these trends by opening up countries to foreign investment and thereby making it easier for production to go where the labor is cheapest and most easily exploited and evironmental costs are low.

8. The WTO Is Increasing Hunger

Farmers produce enough food in the world to feed everyone—yet because of corporate control of food distribution, as many as 800 million people worldwide suffer from chronic malnutrition. According to the Universal Declaration of Human Rights, food is a human right. In developing countries, as many as four out of every five people make their living from the land. But the leading principle in the WTO's Agreement on Agriculture is that market forces should control agricultural policies—rather than a national commitment to guarantee food security and maintain decent family farmer incomes. WTO policies have allowed dumping of heavily subsidized industrially produced food into poor countries, undermining local production and increasing hunger.

9. The WTO Hurts Poor, Small Countries in Favor of Rich Powerful Nations

The WTO supposedly operates on a consensus basis, with equal decision-making power for all. In reality, many important decisions get made in a process whereby poor countries' negotiators are not even invited to closed-door meetings—and then 'agreements' are announced that poor countries didn't know were being discussed. Many countries do not have enough trade personnel to participate in all the negotiations or to even have a permanent representative at the WTO. This severely disadvantages poor countries from representing their interests. Likewise, many countries are too poor to defend themselves from WTO challenges from the rich countries, and are forced to change their laws rather than pay for their own defense.

10. The WTO Undermines Local Level Decision-Making and National Sovereignty

The WTO's "most favored nation" provision requires all WTO member countries to treat each other equally and to treat all corporations from these countries equally regardless of their track record. Local policies aimed at rewarding companies who hire local residents, use domestic materials, or adopt environmentally sound practices are essentially illegal under the WTO. Developing countries are prohibited from creating local laws that developed countries once pursued, such as protecting new, domestic industries until they can be internationally competitive. California's Former Governor Gray Davis vetoed a "Buy California" bill that would have granted a small preference to local businesses because it was WTO-illegal. When the WTO was created in 1995, entire sections of U.S. laws were rewritten. Many countries are even changing their laws and constitutions in anticipation of potential future WTO rulings and negotiations.

11. There Are Alternatives to the WTO

Citizen organizations have developed alternatives to the corporate-dominated system of global economic governance. Together we can build the political space that nurtures a democratic global economy that promotes jobs, ensures that every person is guaranteed their human rights to food, water, education, and health care, promotes freedom and security, and preserves our shared environment for future generations. Check out the International Forum on Globalization's Alternatives to Economic Globalization: A Better World is Possible (available on the Global Exchange online store).

12. The Tide Is Turning Against Free Trade and the WTO!

International opposition to the WTO is growing. Massive protests in Seattle of the 1999 WTO Ministerial brought over 50,000 people together to oppose the WTO—and succeeded in shutting the meeting down. In 2001, the WTO had to go to Qatar—a country that effectively lacks freedom of speech rights—to launch a new round of negotiations. The WTO met in Cancún, Mexico in September of 2003, and met thousands of activists in protest. Developing contries refused to give in to the rich countries' agenda of WTO expansion and the talks collapsed! Find out how you can help Stop the WTO!

GET INVOLVED!!

EDUCATE your community and connect with local corporate issues through bringing speakers, videos, and books like GX's *Globalize This! The Battle Against the World Trade Organization and Corporate Rule*, available on our website.

***SPEAK OUT** to your Member of Congress about the WTO and other trade issues. Urge him or her to reject the expansion of the WTO and other Free trade agreements. Find helpful resources for these and more ideas at www.globalexchange.org.

***LEARN MORE** at www.globalexchange.org.

4. What effect do the enumerated reasons in bold type have on readers? What are the strengths and limitations of this genre of argument?

5. How effective is this piece in influencing your view of free trade?

Wal-Mart Failed America
Associated Press

This Associated Press photo depicts a protest organized by WakeUpWalMart.com. As one of the largest global corporations, Wal-Mart has frequently come under fire for its supplier relations and employment practices.

> In order to sympathize with these protestors in this photo or refute them, what cultural knowledge about Wal-Mart's corporate identity do viewers need?

Ric Francis/AP

For Class Discussion

1. Think about Wal-Mart's advertising campaigns. How do the messages and images on the signs speak back to this advertising?

2. What free trade issues do the signs ask viewers to consider?

3. What values would the audience have to hold to agree with the people represented in this photo?

4. The introduction to this chapter quotes a news story describing a worker's experience sewing in a factory that produces clothes sold in Wal-Mart. In addition to Wal-Mart's association with sweatshops abroad, what questions about Wal-Mart's connection to free trade and consumerism does this photo prompt?

My Six-Year-Old Son Should Get a Job: Is Free Trade Always the Answer?

Ha-Joon Chang

Ha-Joon Chang was born in the Republic of Korea, and he holds a doctorate in economics from Cambridge University, where he also works as a Reader in the Political Economy of Development. He has served on the editorial board of the *Cambridge Journal of Economics* and as a consultant to the World Bank, the Asian Development Bank, and the European Investment Bank as well as to Oxfam and various United Nations agencies. He is also a fellow at the Center for Economic and Policy Research in Washington, D.C. This excerpt is from Chang's book *Bad Samaritans: The Myth of Free Trade and the Secret History of Capitalism* (2008), which refutes the neoliberal claim that the United States and Britain became powerful in the nineteenth century through unrestricted free trade. He argues that wealthy countries who preach free trade and free markets to developing countries are acting as "Bad Samaritans." Their real goal, he asserts, is to capture larger market shares in these developing countries and preempt competition rather than to nurture these countries' economic development.

> What is surprising, shocking, or appealing about Chang's opening to his argument? How effective is it in launching his argument?

I have a six-year-old son. His name is Jin-Gyu. He lives off me, yet he is quite capable of making a living. I pay for his lodging, food, education and health care. But millions of children of his age already have jobs. Daniel Defoe, in the 18th century, thought that children could earn a living from the age of four.

Moreover, working might do Jin-Gyu's character a world of good. Right now he lives in an economic bubble with no sense of the value of money. He has zero appreciation of the efforts his mother and I make on his behalf, subsidizing his idle existence and cocooning him from harsh reality. He is over-protected and needs to be exposed to competition, so that he can become a more productive person. Thinking about it, the more competition he is exposed to and the sooner this is done; the better it will be for his future development. It will whip him into a mentality that is ready for hard work. I should make him quit school and get a job. Perhaps I could move to a country where child labour is still tolerated, if not legal, to give him more choice in employment.

I can hear you say I must be mad. Myopic. Cruel. You tell me that I need to protect and nurture the child. If I drive Jin-Gyu into the labour market at the age of six, he may become a savvy shoeshine boy or even a prosperous street hawker, but he will never become a brain surgeon or a nuclear physicist—that would require at least another dozen years of my protection and investment. You argue that, even from a purely materialistic viewpoint, I would be wiser to invest in my son's education than gloat over the money I save by not sending him to school. After all, if I were right, Oliver Twist would have been better off pick-pocketing for Fagin, rather than being rescued by the misguided Good Samaritan Mr. Brownlow, who deprived the boy of his chance to remain competitive in the labour market.

Yet this absurd line of argument is in essence how free-trade economists justify rapid, large-scale trade liberalization in developing countries. They claim that developing country producers need to be exposed to as much competition as possible right now, so that they have the incentive to raise their productivity in order to survive. Protection, by constrast, only creates complacency and sloth. The earlier the exposure, the argument goes, the better it is for economic development.

Incentives, however, are only half the story. The other is capability. Even if Jin-Gyu were to be offered a £20m reward or, alternatively, threatened with a bullet in his head, he would not be able to rise to the challenge of brain surgery had he quit school at the age of six. Likewise, industries in developing countries will not survive if they are exposed to international competition too early. They need time to improve their capabilities by mastering advanced technologies and building effective organizations. This is the essence of the infant industry argument, first theorized by Alexander Hamilton, first treasury secretary of the US, and used by generations of policy-makers before and after him, as I have just shown in the previous chapter.

Naturally, the protection I provide to Jin-Gyu (as the infant industry argument itself says) should not be used to shelter him from competition forever. Making him work at the age of six is wrong, but so is subsidizing him at the age of 40. Eventually he should go out into the big wide world, get a job and live an independent life. He only needs protection while he is accumulating the capabilities to take on a satisfying and well-paid job.

Of course, as happens with parents bringing up their children, infant industry protection can go wrong. Just as some parents are over-protective, governments can cosset infant industries too much. Some children are unwilling to prepare themselves for adult life, just as infant industry support is wasted on some firms. In the way that some children manipulate their parents into supporting them beyond childhood, there are industries that prolong government protection through clever lobbying. But the existence of dysfunctional families is hardly an argument against parenting itself. Likewise, cases of failures in infant industry protection cannot discredit the strategy *per se*. The examples of bad protectionism merely tell us that the policy needs to be used wisely.

FREE TRADE ISN'T WORKING

Free trade is good—this is the doctrine at the heart of the neo-liberal orthodoxy. To the neo-liberals, there cannot be a more self-evident proposition than this. Professor Willem Buiter, my distinguished former colleague at Cambridge and a former chief economist of the EBRD (European Bank for Reconstruction and Development), once expressed this succinctly: 'Remember: unilateral trade liberalization is not a "concession" or a "sacrifice" that one should be compensated for. It is an act of enlightened self-interest. Reciprocal trade liberalization enhances the gains but is not necessary for gains to be present. The economics is all there.' Belief in the virtue of free trade is so central to the neo-liberal orthodoxy that it is effectively what defines a neo-liberal economist. You may question (if not totally reject) any other element of the neo-liberal agenda—open capital markets, strong patents or even privatisation and still stay in the neo-liberal church. However, once you object to free trade, you are effectively inviting ex-communication.

Based on such convictions, the Bad Samaritans have done their utmost to push developing countries into free trade—or, at least, much freer trade. During the past quarter of a century, most developing countries have liberalized trade to a huge degree. They were first pushed by the IMF and the World Bank in the aftermath of the Third World debt crisis of 1982. There was a further decisive impetus towards trade liberalization following the launch of the WTO in 1995. During the last decade or so, bilateral and regional free trade agreements (FTAs) have also proliferated. Unfortunately, during this period, developing countries have not done well at all, despite (or because of, in my view) massive trade liberalization, as I showed in Chapter 1.

The story of Mexico—poster boy of the free-trade camp—is particularly telling. If any developing country can succeed with free trade, it should be Mexico. It borders on the largest market in the world (the US) and has had a free Trade Agreement with it since 1995 (the North American Free Trade Agreement or NAFTA). It also has a large diaspora living in the US, which can provide important informal business links. Unlike many other poorer developing countries, it has a decent pool of skilled workers, competent managers and relatively developed physical infrastructure (roads, ports and so on).

Free trade economists argue that free trade benefited Mexico by accelerating growth. Indeed, following NAFTA, between 1994 and 2002, Mexico's *per capita* GDP grew at 1.8% per year, a big improvement over the 0.1% rate recorded between 1985 and 1995. But the decade before NAFTA was also a decade of extensive trade liberalisation for Mexico, following its conversion to neo-liberalism in the mid-1980s. So trade liberalization was also responsible for the 0.1% growth rate.

Wide-ranging trade liberalization in the 1980s and the 1990s wiped out whole swathes of Mexican industry that had been painstakingly built up during the period of import substitution industrialization (ISI). The result was, predictably, a slowdown in economic growth, lost jobs and falls in wages (as better-paying manufacturing jobs disappeared). Its agricultural sector was also hard hit by subsidized US products, especially corn, the staple diet of most Mexicans. On top of that, NAFTA's positive impact (in terms of increasing exports to the US market) has run out of steam in the last few years. During 2001–2005, Mexico's growth performance has been miserable, with an annual growth rate of *per capita* income at 0.3% (or a paltry 1.7% increase in total over five years). By contrast, during the 'bad old days' of ISI (1955–82), Mexico's *per capita* income had grown much faster than during the NAFTA period—at an average of 3.1% per year.

Mexico is a particularly striking example of the failure of premature wholesale trade liberalization, but there are other examples. In Ivory Coast, following tariff cuts of 40% in 1986, the chemical, textile, shoe and automobile industries virtually collapsed. Unemployment soared. In Zimbabwe, following trade liberalization in 1990, the unemployment rate jumped from 10% to 20%. It had been hoped that the capital and labour resources released from the enterprises that went bankrupt due to trade liberalization would be absorbed by new businesses. This simply did not happen on a sufficient scale. It is not surprising that growth evaporated and unemployment soared.

Trade liberalization has created other problems, too. It has increased the pressures on government budgets, as it reduced tariff revenues. This has been a particularly serious problem for the poorer countries. Because they lack tax collection capabilities and because tariffs are the easiest tax to collect, they rely heavily on tariffs (which sometimes account for over 50% of total government revenue). As a result, the fiscal adjustment that has had to be made following large-scale trade liberalization has been huge in many developing countries—even a recent IMF study shows that, in low-income countries that have limited abilities to collect other taxes, *less than* 30% of the revenue lost due to trade liberalization over the last 25 years has been made up by other taxes. Moreover, lower levels of business activity and higher unemployment resulting from trade liberalization have also reduced income tax revenue. When countries were already under considerable pressure from the IMF to reduce their budget deficits, falling revenue meant severe cuts in spending, often eating into vital areas like education, health and physical infrastructure, damaging long-term growth.

It is perfectly possible that *some* degree of *gradual* trade liberalization may have been beneficial, and even necessary, for certain developing countries in the 1980s—India and China come to mind. But what has happened during the past quarter of a century has been a rapid, unplanned and blanket trade liberalization. Just to remind the reader, during the 'bad old days' of protectionist import substitution industrialization (ISI), developing countries used to grow, on average, at double the rate that they are doing today under free trade. Free trade simply isn't working for developing countries.

For Class Discussion

1. Ha-Joon Chang creates an extended analogy between his six-year-old son and developing countries, claiming that for both, rapid growth is harmful. What are the advantages of this analogy? What are the analogy's limitations or difficulties?

2. How does Chang refute the claims of free trade proponents (for example, Norberg) that trade liberalization accelerates growth in developing nations? What examples does he employ to measure or quantify growth and support his own argument?

3. What economic terms does Chang use in his argument? What assumptions do these terms suggest about his readers?

4. Chang, an economist, is well known for his approach of placing sociopolitical and moral issues at the center of discussions regarding economics and policy. How does this approach influence his authority, credibility, and impact on readers?

5. How has this argument influenced your views on free trade? ∎

Yes, Globalization Passed Its Peak
Rawi Abdelal and Adam Segal

Rawi Abdelal is the Joseph C. Wilson Professor of Business Administration at Harvard Business School. His research focuses on the politics of globalization and the political economy of Eurasia, and his books include *National Purpose in the World's Economy* (2002) and *Capital Rules* (2007). Adam Segal is the Maurice R. Greenberg Senior Fellow for China Studies at the Council on Foreign Relations. His work focuses on technology and development in China and India, and Chinese domestic and foreign policy. This essay, published in the online version of *Foreign Affairs* on March 17, 2009, follows up on an earlier article by Abdelal and Segal titled, "Has Globalization Passed Its Peak?" (in *Foreign Affairs* in 2007). *Foreign Affairs*, published by the Council on Foreign Relations since 1922, describes itself as "America's most influential publication on international affairs and foreign policy" and "the international forum of choice for the most important new ideas, analysis, and debate on the most significant issues in the world" (www.foreignaffairs.org).

> This article is Abdelal and Segal's response to their own earlier argument about the slowdown of globalization's economic integration. How does the opening paragraph both summarize that earlier article and set up the focus for their response?*

Two years ago, in an article in the January/February issue of *Foreign Affairs*, we argued that the process of worldwide economic integration was likely to continue but that political support for globalization was rapidly weakening. Without political and institutional underpinnings, we feared, the single global economic space could disintegrate, just as it had during the 1930s. Politicians and mass publics in the United States, Europe, and Asia were not only skeptical that the benefits of globalization outweighed the costs, they also seemed intent on raising new barriers to the movement of people, capital, goods, and services across borders. The future looked muddled, driven by strong technological forces pushing global commercial and financial integration forward and equally potent political forces pushing in the opposite direction.

At the time, many people considered us overly pessimistic. Now it looks like we might have been too sanguine. The IMF predicts that global economic activity will expand by only 0.5 percent in 2009—down from 3.4 percent in 2008 and 5.2 percent in 2007. Global trade is expected to fall by more than 2.1 percent this year, and no major exporting country has escaped: China exported nearly 18 percent less in January 2008 than it did just one year earlier; for Korea, the drop was 33 percent; for Taiwan, 42 percent; and for Japan, 46 percent. According to the Institute of International Finance, private investment in developing economies has collapsed, falling more than 80 percent from its 2007 level. Whereas the worry two years ago was about the renaissance of state capitalism in energy and finance, it now appears that the banking sector in the United States, and almost every other major developed economy, will end up wholly or partially owned by the state.

Our description of the future as "muddled" turns out to have been an understatement. Today many are pessimistic about the future of the

---

*For a complete understanding of their declarative title, "Yes, Globalization Passed Its Peak," you might locate and read their longer, earlier article, which thoroughly maps out their analysis of the status of globalization in 2007.

international system for the same reasons we were two years ago. In January, the World Trade Organization hopefully reported that most states were resisting the lure of protectionism. Although many were offering subsidies to their banks and auto manufacturers, it noted, "to date, most WTO Members appear to have successfully kept domestic protectionist pressures under control." A month later, the organization was no longer so certain, and optimism about the future was more difficult to locate. In the last several months, Brazil has raised tariffs on manufactured goods, the European Union has barred Chinese bolts and resumed subsidies on dairy products, and India has considered tariffs on steel imports.

The uproar among U.S. trade partners over the "buy American" principle initially embedded in the stimulus package—companies would have been required to use U.S. steel and other goods in projects—is a clear reflection of the concern that the economic crisis might kill globalization in its current form. Speaking out against the "buy America" provisions, President Barack Obama warned that the United States could not afford to send a protectionist message or "trigger a trade war." While this particular Smoot-Hawley-like bullet was ultimately dodged, protectionist temptations will not disappear and the political struggle for openness is likely to become ever more contentious.

The current crisis has caused the destruction of value, the contraction of capital, a decline in consumption, and an increase in unemployment. But its ultimate impact may be even more pervasive, because the crisis has further undermined the political legitimacy of the free movement of capital, goods, and services.

The legitimacy problem existed beforehand, of course, but the current downturn is making it much, much worse. When we wrote our article in 2007, for example, the U.S. public was wondering about how much globalization benefited them and whether some Americans—say, bankers and CEOs of large corporations—had benefited too much. Try asking the question now. The Chinese, meanwhile, were already working hard to keep all their plates spinning, ensuring continued rapid growth while addressing rising inequality and social protests. Soon the floor might be full of broken crockery.

As one of the most prolific exporters and important investors in U.S. dollar-denominated assets, China must play an important role in saving the global economy from which it has benefited so much. Beijing gamely talks about the need to "rebalance," shifting to a more domestic demand-driven model of growth, but has found it hard to abandon incentives for even more exports. Premier Wen Jiabao told the *Financial Times*, "Running our own affairs well is our biggest contribution to mankind." Perhaps. But the world will also need reassurances that Beijing's appetite for Treasury securities will outlast a crisis that, in the medium term, will threaten the value of the U.S. dollar.

Our message two years ago was that policy leaders needed to manage expectations at home as they worked together internationally. In particular, we argued that the United States needed to reinforce the global institutions that supported international trade while getting its own domestic house in order. Following through on these prescriptions is now even more necessary. In order to avoid disaster, all of the major economic players are going to have to resist pressure to protect home markets through subsidies or tariffs. Individual governments need to tackle the downturn through macroeconomic and financial policies; unemployment and worker retraining should be addressed through expanding and strengthening the social safety net. The United States in particular needs to absorb one of the most important lessons of European social democracy—that a generous, well-designed welfare state is not the antithesis of capitalist globalization but rather its savior.

Amid all this gloom and doom, however, there is also a glimmer of optimism. Over the past 15 years, American capitalism lost its way, abetted by a world much too ready to lend it vast amounts of capital. The U.S. economy—its households and companies—essentially squandered those borrowed funds, saving and investing less, building and consuming more. The debate about the sustainability of those global imbalances has lost any charm it might once have had. Now, some $11 trillion of losses later, the answer is clear. And if the crisis proves to be a catharsis that persuades the United States to change its profligate ways, the legitimacy and promise of globalization may eventually be restored.

For Class Discussion

1. What stance do Abdelal and Segal take toward free trade and globalization? What evidence do they provide that globalization is a desirable goal?

2. What threat do they say the global economic crisis, which exploded in 2008, represents for free trade? According to Abdelal and Segal, what changes has this crisis brought about in global trade?

3. What proposal for salvaging U.S. participation in free trade do they present in the latter part of their argument?

4. What are the indicators that this essay is written for a knowledgeable audience who shares Abdelal and Segal's values? What points might need more development for an audience who does not necessarily share their views?

5. How does this argument contribute to your understanding of the current state of globalization and of free trade's role in the world economy?

When Americans No Longer Own America

Thom Hartmann

Thom Hartmann is an author, a political commentator, and the host of a progressive daily talk radio show that is broadcast on over fifty radio stations nationwide. His recent books—*We the People: A Call to Take America Back* (2004) and *Screwed: The Undeclared War against the Middle Class* (2006)—show his commitment to the principle that "all true and lasting cultural change begins with new insights propagating through enough people to reach a critical mass. History demonstrates that when stories change, the world changes" (www. thomhartmann.com). This essay was posted on February 27, 2006, on common dreams.org, a nonprofit Web site established as a news source and news commentary community for progressive writers and activists.

> Many of the essays in this chapter focus on the effects of free trade on people in developing nations. What effects does Hartmann claim that free trade has on Americans?

The Dubai Ports World deal is waking Americans up to a painful reality: So-called "conservatives" and "flat world" globalists have bankrupted our nation for their own bag of silver, and in the process are selling off America.

Through a combination of the "Fast Track" authority pushed for by Reagan and GHW Bush, sweetheart trade deals involving "most favored nation status" for dictatorships like China, and Clinton pushing us into NAFTA and the WTO (via GATT), we've abandoned the principles of tariff-based trade that built American industry and kept us strong for over 200 years.

The old concept was that if there was a dollar's worth of labor in a pair of shoes made in the USA, and somebody wanted to import shoes from China where there may only be ten cents worth of labor in those shoes, we'd level the playing field for labor by putting a 90-cent import tariff on each pair of shoes. Companies could choose to make their products here or overseas, but the ultimate cost of labor would be the same.

Then came the flat-worlders, led by misguided true believers and promoted by multinational corporations. Do away with those tariffs, they said, because they "restrain trade." Let everything in, and tax nothing. The result has been an explosion of cheap goods coming into our nation, and the loss of millions of good manufacturing jobs and thousands of manufacturing companies. Entire industry sectors have been wiped out.

These policies have kneecapped the American middle class. Our nation's largest employer has gone from being the unionized General

Motors to the poverty-wages Wal-Mart. Americans have gone from having a net savings rate around 10 percent in the 1970s to a minus .5 percent in 2005—meaning that they're going into debt or selling off their assets just to maintain their lifestyle.

At the same time, federal policy has been to do the same thing at a national level. Because our so-called "free trade" policies have left us with an over $700 billion annual trade deficit, other countries are sitting on huge piles of the dollars we gave them to buy their stuff (via Wal-Mart and other "low cost" retailers). But we no longer manufacture anything they want to buy with those dollars.

So instead of buying our manufactured goods, they are doing what we used to do with Third World nations—they are buying us, the USA, chunk by chunk. In particular, they want to buy things in America that will continue to produce profits, and then to take those profits overseas where they're invested to make other nations strong. The "things" they're buying are, by and large, corporations, utilities, and natural resources.

Back in the pre-Reagan days, American companies made profits that were distributed among Americans. They used their profits to build more factories, or diversify into other businesses. The profits stayed in America.

Today, foreigners awash with our consumer dollars are on a two-decades-long buying spree. The UK's BP bought Amoco for $48 billion—now Amoco's profits go to England. Deutsche Telekom bought VoiceStream Wireless, so their profits go to Germany, which is where most of the profits from Random House, Allied Signal, Chrysler, Doubleday, Cyprus Amax's US Coal Mining Operations, GTE/Sylvania, and Westinghouse's Power Generation profits go as well. Ralston Purina's profits go to Switzerland, along with Gerber's; TransAmerica's profits go to The Netherlands, while John Hancock Insurance's profits go to Canada. Even American Bankers Insurance Group is owned now by Fortis AG in Belgium.

Foreign companies are buying up our water systems, our power generating systems, our mines, and our few remaining factories. All because "flat world" so-called "free trade" policies have turned us from a nation of wealthy producers into a nation of indebted consumers, leaving the world awash in dollars that are most easily used to buy off big chunks of America. As www.economyincrisis.com notes, US Government statistics indicate the following percentages of foreign ownership of American industry:

- Sound recording industries—97%
- Commodity contracts dealing and brokerage—79%
- Motion picture and sound recording industries—75%
- Metal ore mining—65%
- Motion picture and video industries—64%

- Wineries and distilleries—64%
- Database, directory, and other publishers—63%
- Book publishers—63%
- Cement, concrete, lime, and gypsum product—62%
- Engine, turbine and power transmission equipment—57%
- Rubber product—53%
- Nonmetallic mineral product manufacturing—53%
- Plastics and rubber products manufacturing—52%
- Plastics product—51%
- Other insurance related activities—51%
- Boiler, tank, and shipping container—50%
- Glass and glass product—48%
- Coal mining—48%
- Sugar and confectionery product—48%
- Nonmetallic mineral mining and quarrying—47%
- Advertising and related services—41%
- Pharmaceutical and medicine—40%
- Clay, refractory, and other nonmetallic mineral products—40%
- Securities brokerage—38%
- Other general purpose machinery—37%
- Audio and video equipment manufacturing and reproducing magnetic and optical media—36%
- Support activities for mining—36%
- Soap, cleaning compound, and toilet preparation—32%
- Chemical manufacturing—30%
- Industrial machinery—30%
- Securities, commodity contracts, and other financial investments and related activities—30%
- Other food—29%
- Motor vehicles and parts—29%
- Machinery manufacturing—28%
- Other electrical equipment and component—28%
- Securities and commodity exchanges and other financial investment activities—27%
- Architectural, engineering, and related services—26%
- Credit card issuing and other consumer credit—26%
- Petroleum refineries (including integrated)—25%
- Navigational, measuring, electromedical, and control instruments—25%
- Petroleum and coal products manufacturing—25%
- Transportation equipment manufacturing—25%
- Commercial and service industry machinery—25%
- Basic chemical—24%
- Investment banking and securities dealing—24%
- Semiconductor and other electronic component—23%
- Paint, coating, and adhesive—22%

- Printing and related support activities—21%
- Chemical product and preparation—20%
- Iron, steel mills, and steel products—20%
- Agriculture, construction, and mining machinery—20%
- Publishing industries—20%
- Medical equipment and supplies—20%

Thus it shouldn't surprise us that the cons have sold off our ports as well, and will defend it to the bitter end. They truly believe that a "New World Order" with multinational corporations in charge instead of sovereign governments will be the answer to the problem of world instability. And therefore they must do away with quaint things like unions, a healthy middle class, and, ultimately, democracy.

The "security" implications of turning our ports over to the UAE are just the latest nail in what the cons hope will be the coffin of American democracy and the American middle class. Today's conservatives believe in rule by inherited wealth and an internationalist corporate elite, and things like a politically aroused citizenry and a healthy democracy are pesky distractions.

Everything today is driven by profits for multinationals, supported by the lawmaking power of the WTO. Thus, parts for our missiles are now made in China, a country that last year threatened us with nuclear weapons. Our oil comes from a country that birthed a Wahabist movement that ultimately led to 14 Saudi citizens flying jetliners into the World Trade buildings and the Pentagon. Germans now own the Chrysler auto assembly lines that turned out tanks to use against Germany in WWII. And the price of labor in America is being held down by over ten million illegal workers, a situation that was impossible twenty-five years ago when unions were the first bulwark against dilution of the American labor force.

When Thomas Jefferson wrote of King George III in the Declaration of Independence, "He has combined with others to subject us to a jurisdiction foreign to our constitutions and unacknowledged by our laws, giving his assent to their acts of pretended legislation . . ." he just as easily could have been writing of the World Trade Organization, which now has the legal authority to force the United States to overturn laws passed at both local, state, and federal levels with dictates devised by tribunals made up of representatives of multinational corporations. If Dubai loses in the American Congress, their next stop will almost certainly be the WTO.

As Simon Romero and Heather Timmons noted in *The New York Times* on 24 February 2006, "the international shipping business has evolved in recent years to include many more containers with consumer goods, in addition to old-fashioned bulk commodities, and that has helped lift profit margins to 30 percent, from the single digits. These smartly managed foreign operators now manage about 80 percent of port terminals in the United States."

And those 30 percent profits from American port operations now going to Great Britain will probably soon go to the United Arab Emirates, a nation with tight interconnections to both the Bush administration and the Bush family.

Ultimately, it's not about security—it's about money. In the multinational corporatocracy's "flat world," money trumps the national good, community concerns, labor interests, and the environment. NAFTA, CAFTA, and WTO tribunals can—and regularly do—strike down local and national laws. Thomas Paine's "Rights of Man" are replaced by Antonin Scalia's "Rights of Corporate Persons."

Profits even trump the desire for good enough port security to avoid disasters that may lead to war. After all, as Judith Miller wrote in *The New York Times* on January 30, 1991, quoting a local in Saudi Arabia: "War is good for business."

For Class Discussion

1. According to Hartmann, what are the main, but lesser known, costs of the United States' commitment to free trade?

2. What different methods does Hartmann employ to present evidence of his claims? How effective are they in convincing his audience?

3. Hartman adopts a bold, "I won't mince words" stance and tone in this argument in his overall approach and his language, including in his title. How do these choices work for his intended audience? How might they be risky for other audiences?

4. Where does Hartmann acknowledge and respond to alternative views?

5. Though Hartmann claims that the issue is ultimately "not about security," how does he link the flow of goods into, and money out of, the United States to security concerns? What effect does this have on his audience?

6. How has Hartmann's argument affected your thinking as a consumer and as a potential member of the American middle class?

Buy American, Buy Union
Rebecca Cook, Reuters

Rebecca Cook is a Detroit-based photographer who has been photographing Detroit area news events and major league sporting events for Reuters global-news service since 1990. Her freelance work has appeared in *USA Today,* the *New York Times,* and *Time* magazine. This photo was taken in early June 2009 and accompanied an article titled "Canadians Angered over 'Buy American'

Rule" in the *NewsDaily* on June 6, 2009. The person whose arm is pictured in this photo is Don Skidmore, president of United Auto Workers union local 594. Variations of this image appeared in June 2009 alongside stories about a provision in a U.S. economic stimulus package passed in February that requires public works projects to use iron, steel, and other goods made in the United States. The provision has engendered controversy with U.S. trade partners, particularly Canada.

What are your first impressions of this image?

Rebecca Cook/Reuters/Corbis

For Class Discussion

1. How do the image of the tattoo and the appearance of the arm in the photo influence your idea of Skidmore's beliefs and values?

2. In this photo, only Skidmore's forearm is shown. At the *Detroit News* Web site (www.detnews.com), Skidmore and his tattoo are pictured more fully in other photos, often next to stories about the shutdown of General Motors' plants and the maintenance or opening of plants abroad. What rhetorical effect does this photo of Skidmore's arm have? Does this effect differ from that of more complete photos of him? How do different contexts for this image affect your interpretation of it?

3. Many of the readings in this chapter deal with issues of production and consumption on a global scale. How does this photo ask the individual American consumer to participate in the debate?

4. What arguments about free trade would this photo support? Refute? ∎

Going Downhill: Forget GDP, Americans' Quality of Life Has Been in a Recession Since 1975

Robert Costanza

Robert Costanza is the Gund Professor of Ecological Economics and Director of the Gund Institute for Ecological Economics at the University of Vermont. He is cofounder and past president of the International Society for Ecological Economics, and he has served on the U.S. EPA National Advisory Council for Environmental Policy and Technology. His work focuses on the connections between ecological and economic systems, and he is the author or coauthor of more than 300 scientific papers and 20 books, the most recent of which is a coedited collection (with Lisa Graumlich and Will Steffen), *Sustainability or Collapse? An Integrated History and Future of People on Earth* (2007). This opinion piece appeared in the *Los Angeles Times* on March 10, 2008.

> How does Robert Costanza reframe the idea of progress, national economic success, and "recession" in this argument?

The news media and the government are fixated on the fact that the U.S. economy may be headed into a recession—defined as two or more successive quarters of declining gross domestic product. The situation is actually much worse. By some measures of economic performance, the United States has been in a recession since 1975—a recession in quality of life, or well-being.

How can this be? One first needs to understand what GDP measures to see why it is not an appropriate gauge of our national well-being.

GDP measures the total market value of all goods and services produced in a country in a given period. But it includes only those goods and services traded for money. It also adds everything together, without discerning desirable, well-being-enhancing economic activity from undesirable, well-being-reducing activity. An oil spill, for example, increases GDP because someone has to clean it up, but it obviously detracts from well-being. More crime, more sickness, more war, more pollution, more fires, storms and pestilence are all potentially positives for the GDP because they can spur an increase in economic activity.

GDP also ignores activity that may enhance well-being but is outside the market. The unpaid work of parents caring for their children at home doesn't show up in GDP, but if they decide to work outside the home and pay for child care, GDP suddenly increases. And even though $1 in income means a lot more to the poor than to the rich, GDP takes no account of income distribution.

In short, GDP was never intended to be a measure of citizens' welfare—and it functions poorly as such. Yet it is used as a surrogate appraisal of national well-being in far too many circumstances.

The shortcomings of GDP are well known, and several researchers have proposed alternatives that address them, including William Nordhauss' and James Tobin's Measure of Economic Welfare, developed in 1972; Herman Daly's and John Cobb's Index of Sustainable Economic Welfare, developed in 1989; and the Redefining Progress think tank's more recent variation, the Genuine Progress Indicator. Although these alternatives—which, like GDP, are measured in monetary terms—are not perfect and need more research and refinement, they are much better approximations to a measure of true national well-being.

The formula for calculating GPI, for instance, starts with personal consumption expenditures, a major component of GDP, but makes several crucial adjustments. First, it accounts for income distribution. It then adds positive contributions that GDP ignores, such as the value of household and volunteer work. Finally, it subtracts things that are well-being-reducing, such as the loss of leisure time and the costs of crime, commuting and pollution.

While the U.S. GDP has steadily increased since 1950 (with the occasional recession), GPI peaked about 1975 and has been relatively flat or declining ever since. That's consistent with life-satisfaction surveys, which also show flat or dropping scores over the last several decades.

This is a very different picture of the economy from the one we normally read about, and it requires different policy responses. We are now in a period of what Daly—a former World Bank economist now at the University of Maryland—has called "uneconomic growth," in which further growth in economic activity (that is, GDP) is actually reducing national well-being.

How can we get out of this 33-year downturn in quality of life? Several policies have been suggested that might be thought of as a national quality-of-life stimulus package.

To start, the U.S. needs to make national well-being—not increased GDP—its primary policy goal, funding efforts to better measure and report it. There's already been some movement in this direction around the world. Bhutan, for example, recently made "gross national happiness" its explicit policy goal. Canada is developing an Index of Well-being, and the Australian Treasury considers increasing "real well-being," rather than mere GDP, its primary goal.

Once Americans' well-being becomes the basis for measuring our success, other reforms should follow. We should tax bads (carbon emissions, depletion of natural resources) rather than goods (labor, savings, investment). We should recognize the negative effects of growing income disparities and take steps to address them.

International trade also will have to be reformed so that environmental protection, labor rights and democratic self-determination are not subjugated to the blind pursuit of increased GDP.

But the most important step may be the first one: Recognizing that the U.S. is mired in a 33-year-old quality-of life recession and that our continued national focus on growing GDP is blinding us to the way out.

For Class Discussion

1. In this argument, what environmental and ethical principles does Robert Costanza apply to questions of labor and economics?

2. While free trade proponents point to the gross national product (GDP) as proof of free trade's success, Costanza challenges this standard. How does he support the legitimacy and practicality of establishing a measure of "national well being"?

3. Both Hartmann and Costanza address the influence of global economic policy on American citizens. On what points might they agree? On what points would they likely differ?

4. How does Costanza's argument relate to the peoples' search for alternatives to corporate-driven free trade such as fair or direct trade? ∎

Bangladesh: On the Ladder of Development
Jeffrey D. Sachs

Jeffrey D. Sachs is the director of The Earth Institute, Quetelet Professor of Sustainable Development, and Professor of Health Policy and Management at Columbia University. He is also Special Advisor to United Nations Secretary-General Ban Ki-moon. From 2002 to 2006, he was Director of the UN Millennium Project and Special Advisor to United Nations Secretary-General Kofi Annan on the Millennium Development Goals. A leading voice for combining economic development with environmental sustainability, Professor Sachs was named one of the one hundred most influential leaders in the world by *Time* magazine in both 2004 and 2005. His books include *Common Wealth* (2008) and *The End of Poverty* (2005), from which this excerpt is taken. The book, intended for a general audience, presents Sachs's plan to eliminate extreme poverty around the world by 2025 and outlines the roles of globalization, the United Nations, the International Monetary Fund (IMF), the World Bank, and both wealthy and developing nations in achieving that goal. In the chapter from which this excerpt is taken, Sachs presents Bangladesh as a case study of the second rung on his well-known ladder of economic development. The African country, Malawi, represents extreme poverty at the bottom of the ladder; both India and China represents stages of greater economic progress.

How does Sachs hook your interest in Bangladesh?

A few thousand miles away from this perfect storm is another scene of poverty. This is poverty in retreat, where the fight for survival is gradually being won, although still with horrendous risks and huge unmet needs. This struggle is being waged in Bangladesh, one of the most populous countries in the world, with 140 million people living in the flood plains of the deltas of the two great rivers, the Brahmaputra and the Ganges, that flow through Bangladesh on their way to the Indian Ocean.

Bangladesh was born in a war for independence against Pakistan in 1971. That year, it experienced massive famine and disarray, leading an official in Henry Kissinger's State Department to famously label it an "international basket case." Bangladesh today is far from a basket case. Per capita income has approximately doubled since independence. Life expectancy has risen from forty-four years to sixty-two years. The infant mortality rate (the number of children who die before their first birthday for every 1,000 born) has declined from 145 in 1970 to 48 in 2002. Bangladesh shows us that even in circumstances that seem the most hopeless there are ways forward if the right strategies are applied, and if the right combination of investments is made.

Still, Bangladesh is not out of the grip of extreme poverty. Although it has escaped the worst of the ravages of famine and disease in the past generation, it faces some profound challenges today. A few months after my visit to Malawi, I was up at dawn one morning in Dhaka, Bangladesh, to see a remarkable sight; thousands of people walking to work in long lines stretching from the outskirts of Dhaka and from some of its poorest neighborhoods. Looking more closely, I noticed that these workers were almost all young women, perhaps between the ages of eighteen and twenty-five. These are the workers of a burgeoning garment industry in Dhaka who cut, stitch, and package millions of pieces of apparel each month for shipment to the United States and Europe.

Over the years, I have visited garment factories all over the developing world. I have grown familiar with the cavernous halls where hundreds of young women sit at sewing machines, and men at cutting tables, where the fabrics move along production lines and the familiar labels of Gap, Polo, Yves Saint Laurent, Wal-Mart, J.C. Penney, and others are attached as the clothing reaches the final stages of production. There is nothing glamorous about this work. The women often walk two hours each morning in long quiet files to get to work. Arriving at seven or seven-thirty, they may be in their seats for most of the following twelve hours. They often work with almost no break at all or perhaps a very short lunch break, with little chance to go to the lavatory. Leering bosses lean over them, posing a threat of sexual harassment. After a long, difficult, tedious day, the young women trudge back home, when they are again sometimes threatened with physical assault.

These sweatshop jobs are the targets of public protest in developed countries; those protests have helped to improve the safety and quality of the working conditions. The rich-world protesters, however, should support increased numbers of such jobs, albeit under safer working conditions, by protesting the trade protectionism in their own countries that keeps out garment exports from countries such as Bangladesh. These young women already have a foothold in the modern economy that is a critical, measurable step up from the villages of Malawi (and more relevant for the women, a step up from the villages of Bangladesh where most of them were born). The sweatshops are the first rung on the ladder out of extreme poverty. They give lie to the Kissinger state department's forecast that Bangladesh is condemned to extreme poverty.

On one visit to Bangladesh, I picked up an English-language morning newspaper, where I found an extensive insert of interviews with young women working in the garment sector. These stories were poignant, fascinating, and eye-opening. One by one, they recounted the arduous hours, the lack of labor rights, and the harassment. What was most striking and unexpected about the stories was the repeated affirmation that this work was the greatest opportunity that these women could ever have imagined, and that their employment had changed their lives for the better.

Nearly all of the women interviewed had grown up in the country side, extraordinarily poor, illiterate and unschooled, and vulnerable to chronic hunger and hardship in a domineering, patriarchal society. Had they (and their forebearers of the 1970s and 1980s) stayed in the villages, they would have been forced into a marriage arranged by their fathers, and by seventeen or eighteen, forced to conceive a child. Their trek to the cities to take jobs has given these young women a chance for personal liberation of unprecedented dimension and opportunity.

The Bangladeshi women told how they were able to save some small surplus from their meager pay, manage their own income, have their own rooms, choose when and whom to date and marry, choose to have children when they felt ready, and use their savings to improve their living conditions and especially to go back to school to enhance their literacy and job-market skills. As hard as it is, this life is a step on the way to economic opportunity that was unimaginable in the countryside in generations past.

Some rich-country protesters have argued that Dhaka's apparel firms should either pay far higher wage rates or be closed, but closing such factories as a result of wages forced above worker productivity would be little more than a ticket for these women back to rural misery. For these young women, these factories offer not only opportunities for personal freedom, but also the first rung on the ladder of rising skills and income for themselves and, within a few years, for their children. Virtually every poor country that has developed successfully has gone through these first stages of industrialization. These Bangladeshi women share the experience of many generations of immigrants to New York City's garment district and a hundred other places where their migration to toil in garment factories was a step on the path to a future of urban affluence in succeeding generations.

Not only is the garment sector fueling Bangladesh's economic growth of more than 5 percent per year in recent years, but it is also raising the consciousness and power of women in a society that was long brazenly biased against women's chances in life. As part of a more general and dramatic process of change throughout Bangladeshi society, this change and others give Bangladesh the opportunity in the next few years to put itself on a secure path of long-term economic growth. The countryside that these women have left is also changing quickly, in part because of the income remittances and ideas that the young women send back to their rural communities, and in part because of the increased travel and temporary migration between rural agriculture and urban manufactures and services.

In 2003, my colleagues at Columbia and I visited a village near Dhaka with one of the leaders of an inspiring nongovernmental organization, the Bangladeshi Rural Advancement Committee, now known universally as BRAC, There we met representatives from a village association, which BRAC had helped to organize, in which women living about an hour outside the city were engaged in small-scale commercial activities—food processing and trade—within the village and on the roads between the village and Dhaka itself. These women presented a picture of change every bit as dramatic as that of the burgeoning apparel sector.

Wearing beautiful saris, the women sat on the ground in six rows, each with six women, to greet us and answer questions. Each row represented a subgroup of the local "microfinance" unit. The woman in the front of the row was in charge of the borrowing of the whole group behind her. The group in each line was mutually responsible for repayments of the loans taken by any member within the line. BRAC and its famed counterpart, Grameen Bank, pioneered this kind of group lending, in which impoverished recipients (usually women) are given small loans of a few hundred dollars as working capital for microbusiness activities. Such women were long considered unbankable, simply not credit-worthy enough to bear the transaction costs to receive loans. Group lending changed the repayment dynamics: default rates are extremely low, and BRAC and Grameen have figured out how to keep other transaction costs to a minimum as well.

Perhaps more amazing than the stories of how microfinance was fueling small-scale businesses were the women's attitudes to child rearing. When Dr. Allan Rosenfield, dean of Columbia University's Mailman School of Public Health and one of the world's leading experts on reproductive health, asked the women how many had five children, no hands went up. Four? Still no hands. Three? One nervous woman, looking around, reluctantly put her hand in the air. Two? About 40 percent of the women. One? Perhaps another 25 percent. None? The remainder of the women. Here was a group where the average number of children for these mothers was between one and two children.

Rosenfield then asked them how many they wanted in total. He again started at five—no hands, Four? No hands. Three? No hands. Two? Almost all the hands went up. This social norm was new, a demonstration of a change of outlook and possibility so dramatic that Rosenfield dwelt on it throughout the rest of our visit. He had been visiting Bangladesh and other parts of Asia since the 1960s, and he remembered vividly the days when Bangladeshi rural women would typically have had six or seven children.

The jobs for women in the cities and in rural off-farm microenterprises; a new spirit of women's rights and independence and empowerment; dramatically reduced rates of child mortality; rising literacy of girls and young women; and, crucially, the availability of family planning and contraception have made all the difference for these women. There is no single explanation for the dramatic, indeed historic, reduction in desired rates of fertility: it is the combination of new ideas, better public health for mothers and children, and improved economic opportunities for women. The reduced fertility rates, in turn, will fuel Bangladesh's rising incomes. With fewer children, a poor household can invest more in the health and education of each child, thereby equipping the next generation with the health, nutrition, and education that can lift Bangladesh's living standards in future years.

Bangladesh has managed to place its foot on the first rung of the ladder of development, and has achieved economic growth and improvements of health and education partly through its own heroic efforts, partly through the ingenuity of NGOs like BRAC and Grameen Bank, and partly through investments that have been made, often at significant scale, by various donor governments that rightly viewed

Bangladesh not as a hopeless basket case but as a country worthy of attention, care and development assistance.

For Class Discussion

1. What is Jeffrey Sachs's main claim in this excerpt from his book? How does he defend the existence of "sweatshops" even as he critiques them?

2. In this excerpt, Sachs blends vivid narrative with detailed presentation of evidence. What examples of this strategy can you cite? How does this argumentative strategy affect readers? How persuasive is it?

3. What assumptions does Sachs make about his audience's position on the existence of sweatshops, and how does he address these concerns?

4. How does he link developing countries' labor issues to other issues such as women's rights and economic futures?

5. This excerpt participates in the controversy over the responsibility of the developed world to the developing world. Sachs concludes his case study with an assertion of the real responsibility of "rich-world protestors" to the poor of Bangladesh. How might these protestors respond to his ideas?

6. How has this reading influenced your view of free trade, sweatshops, and American consumerism?

Garment Factory in Saipan

The photo on page 114, taken in 2004, shows workers in a garment factory in Saipan, part of the U.S. Commonwealth of the Northern Mariana Islands in the Pacific Ocean and an Export Processing Zone. Workers come from China, Thailand, the Philippines, Vietnam, and other Asian countries to make garments in some thirty factories for big-name retailers such as Abercrombie & Fitch, Calvin Klein, Gap, J. Crew, The Limited, Liz Claiborne, and Tommy Hilfiger. Recent lawsuits have yielded improvements in the sweatshop conditions in these factories: better dormitories, improved water and food, overtime pay for work over forty hours a week, protection from sexual abuse, and payment of back wages.

What are your first impressions of the scene depicted in this photo?

For Class Discussion

1. How would a journalist who wanted to use this photo in an article criticizing the treatment of workers in factories in Export Processing Zones (EPZs) interpret this photo? What features of the scene would lend themselves rhetorically to an antisweatshop article?

© June Johnson

Garment Factory in Saipan

2. Imagine a different rhetorical use of this photo. What do you think a journalist who wanted to praise improved conditions in foreign factories would emphasize?

3. Consult these Web sites to investigate the lawsuits brought against companies' exploitation of factory workers: Global Exchange (www.globalexchange.org) and Clean Clothes Campaign (www.cleanclothes.org). With this background information, examine the photo again. What features of the scene draw your attention now? ∎

Sweat, Fire and Ethics
Bob Jeffcott

Bob Jeffcott works with Maquila Solidarity Network, a labor and women's rights organization, based in Toronto, Canada, that "supports the efforts of workers in global supply chains to win improved wages and working conditions and a better quality of life"(en.maquilasolidarity.org).This editorial appeared in the April 2007 issue of *New Internationalist*, a progressive British publication with a focus on issues of world poverty and inequality.

How does Jeffcott use recaps of the history of clothing manufacturing and recent developments in sweatshops and trade as part of his persuasive strategy in this argument?

AT THE MAQUILA SOLIDARITY NETWORK, WE GET PHONE CALLS and emails almost every day of the week from people wanting to know where they can buy clothes that are Fairtrade-certified or sweatshop-free. Alternative retail outlets even contact us to ask whether we have a list of 'sweatfree' manufacturers. So, what are we to tell them? Unfortunately, there are no easy answers.

First, there's the cotton used to make the clothes. If you live in Canada, you may soon be able to buy a T-shirt at your local Cotton Ginny store that is both organic and Fairtrade Cotton certified. If you live in Britain, you can already purchase T-shirts and other apparel products bearing the Fairtrade Cotton label, not only through alternative fairtrade companies, but also at your local Marks & Spencer shop.

This is all to the good, isn't it? Growing organic cotton is better for the environment, and farmers are no longer exposed to dangerous chemicals. Fairtrade certified cotton goes a step further—a better price and a social dividend to small farmers in the global South.

But what happens when cotton goes downstream? What does the Fairtrade Cotton label tell us about the working lives of the young women and men who spin the cotton into yarn in China, or those who cut the cloth and sew the T-shirt in a Bangladeshi factory before it's shipped to my local Cotton Ginny store in Toronto?

Unfortunately, very little. The Fairtrade Cotton certification is about the conditions under which the cotton was grown, not how the T-shirt was sewn.

To use the Fairtrade Cotton label, a company does have to provide evidence that factory conditions downstream from the cotton farms are being monitored by a third party; but the kind of factory audits currently being carried out by commercial social-auditing firms are notoriously unreliable. In other words, my organic, Fairtrade Cotton certified T-shirt could have been sewn in a sweatshop by a 15-year-old girl who's forced to work up to 18 hours a day for poverty wages under dangerous working conditions. So what's a consumer to do?

Well, maybe we could start by admitting the limitations of ethical shopping. Isn't it a little presumptuous of us to think that we can end sweatshop abuses by just changing our individual buying habits? After all, such abuses are endemic to the garment industry and almost as old as the rag trade itself.

The term 'sweatshop' was coined in the United States in the late 1800s to describe the harsh discipline and inhuman treatment employed by factory managers, often in subcontract facilities, to sweat as much profit from their workers' labour as was humanly possible.

Sweatshop became a household word at the beginning of the 20th century when the tragic death of over a hundred garment workers became headline news in the tabloid press across the US. On 25 March 1911, a fire broke out on the ninth floor of the Asch Building in New York City, owned by the Triangle Shirtwaist Company. Unable to escape through the narrow aisles between crowded sewing machines and down the building's only stairway, 146 young workers burned to death, suffocated, or leapt to their doom on to the pavement below. Firefighters and bystanders who tried to catch the young women and girls in safety nets were crushed against the pavement by the falling bodies.

GLOBALIZATION AND FREE TRADE

In the decades that followed, government regulation and union organizing drives—particularly in the post-World War Two period—resulted in significant improvements in factory conditions. This period, in which many—but not all—garment workers in North America enjoyed stable, secure employment with relatively decent working conditions, was short-lived.

Globalization and free trade changed all that. To lower production costs, garment companies began to outsource the manufacture of their products to subcontract factories owned by Asian manufacturers in Hong Kong, Korea and Taiwan. Companies like Nike became 'hollow manufacturers' whose only business was designing fashionable sportswear and marketing their brands. Other retailers and discount chains followed Nike's lead, outsourcing to offshore factories. Competition heightened. Asian suppliers began to shift their production to even lower-wage countries in Asia, Latin America and Africa. A race to the bottom for the lowest wages and worst working conditions went into high gear.

Today, countries like Mexico and Thailand are facing massive worker layoffs because production costs are considered too high. While most production is shifting to China and India, other poor countries like Bangladesh attract orders due to bargain-basement labour costs.

On 11 April 2005, at one o'clock in the morning, a nine storey building that housed the Spectrum Sweater and Shahriar Fabrics factories in Savar, Dhaka, Bangladesh, collapsed, killing 64 workers, injuring dozens and leaving hundreds unemployed. Just 16 hours before the building crumbled, workers complained that there were cracks in the structure's supporting columns. Despite the lack of an adequate foundation and the apparent lack of building permits, five additional storeys had been added. To make matters worse, heavy machinery had been placed on the fourth and seventh floors.

The Spectrum factory produced clothes for a number of major European retailers, all of whose monitoring programmes failed to identify the structural and health-and-safety problems.

'Negligence was the cause of the 11 April tragedy,' said Shirin Akhter, president of the Bangladeshi women workers' organization, Karmojibi Nari. 'This was a killing, not an accident.'

In February and March 2006 there were four more factory disasters in Bangladesh, in which an estimated 88 young women and girls were killed and more than 250 were injured. Most of the victims died in factory fires, reminiscent of the Triangle Shirtwaist fire, in which factory exits were either locked and blocked.

Twelve years ago, when we started the Maquila Solidarity Network, the word 'sweatshop' had fallen out of common usage. When we spoke to high school and university assemblies, students were shocked to learn that their favourite brand-name clothes were made by teenagers like themselves, forced to work up to 18 hours a day for poverty wages in unsafe workplaces.

BADLY TARNISHED BRANDS

Students who had proudly worn the Nike swoosh wrote angry letters to Nike CEO Phil Knight declaring they would never again wear clothes made in Nike sweatshops. But the big brands weren't the only villains: the clothes of lesser-known companies were often made in the same factories or under even worse conditions.

Twelve years later, the Nike swoosh and other well-known brands are badly tarnished, and the word 'sweatshop' no longer needs explaining to young consumers. Companies like Nike and Gap Inc are publishing corporate social responsibility reports, acknowledging that serious abuses of worker rights are a persistent problem throughout their global supply chain.

Today some major brands have 'company code of conduct compliance staff' who answer abuse complaints almost immediately, promising to investigate the situation and report back on what they are willing to do to 'remediate' the problems.

Yet, despite such advances, not much really changes at the workplace. On the one hand, a little less child labour, fewer forced pregnancy tests or health-and-safety violations in the larger factories used by the major brands. But, on the other hand, poverty wages, long hours of forced overtime and mass firings of workers who try to

organize for better wages and conditions remain the norm throughout the industry.

Recent changes in global trade rules (the end of the import quota
system) are once again speeding up the race to the bottom. The same
companies pressuring suppliers to meet code-of-conduct standards are
also demanding their products be made faster and cheaper, threatening to
shift orders to factories in other countries. Conflicting pressures make
suppliers hide abuses or subcontract to sewing workshops and home-
workers. The name of the game remains the same: more work for less pay.

Targeting the big-name brands is no longer a sufficient answer.
Given how endemic sweatshop abuses are throughout the industry, selective shopping isn't the answer either.

We need to start by remembering that we are not just consumers:
we are also citizens of countries and of the world. We can lobby our
school boards, municipal governments and universities to adopt ethical purchasing policies that require apparel suppliers to disclose factory
locations and evidence that there are serious efforts to improve conditions. We can write letters to companies when workers' rights are violated and in support of worker's efforts to organize. And we can put
pressure on our governments to adopt policies and regulations that
make companies accountable when they fail to address flagrant and
persistent violations of workers' rights.

We should worry a little less about our shopping decisions, and
a bit more about what we can do to support the young women
and girls who labour behind the labels that adorn our clothes and
sports shoes.

For Class Discussion

1. What is Jeffcott's main claim in this piece?

2. How does Jeffcott establish a connection with his audience? How does he
   then employ this connection to make the audience members question
   their own values and motivations?

3. What conflicts of interest does he identify for brands that have established
   "codes of conduct" for their manufacturing facilities?

4. How does Jeffcott both seek to enlighten readers and complicate their
   understanding of free trade, sweatshops, and consumer responsibility?
   How does his use of examples enhance his credibility and authority?

5. This article concludes with a different kind of call to activism than is usually
   made in arguments about sweatshops. What does Jeffcott propose that
   consumers do to address the issue?

6. How does this piece add context to the photo of garment workers in
   Saipan?

STUDENT VOICE: Is There Blood on These Diamonds? by Patrick Scholze

Patrick Scholze is an international business major who hopes to have a career in a foreign country. He wrote this researched exploratory essay for a writing course entitled "Global Exchanges and Civic Stewardship." An exploratory essay begins with a writer's genuine perplexity about a question that should also be important and complex to other people. The essay represents the writer's true quest to create an answer to the question. Unlike an argument, an exploratory essay is driven by a question in its introduction, not a thesis-claim, and takes a narrative form that can be informal. Also, unlike an argument, an exploratory essay tracks the evolution of the writer's deepening understanding of the question as he/she reads a variety of sources to sample multiple perspectives. In this essay, as Patrick moves from source to source, he summarizes key ideas from each source and interacts with them. As Patrick demonstrates, an exploratory essay focuses on the writer's thinking about the subject as much as on the subject itself. Often the understanding a writer achieves through this process of exploration leads to an argument in which the writer takes a position on the issue.

How does Patrick establish his sincere interest in his research question?

This last summer I worked in Juneau, Alaska, for the jewelry company Diamonds International, a large jewelry chain with over 120 stores in Mexico, the Caribbean, and Alaska (where the cruise ships sail). The store where I worked mainly sold diamonds and tanzanite. Multiple times a week customers asked me if the diamonds we sold were "blood diamonds." All these people had seen the 2006 motion picture *Blood Diamond* about the horrors of the diamond-funded wars of Sierra Leone in 1999. This question annoyed me. I replied that our company does not deal with blood or "conflict" diamonds and added that we could offer a certificate as verification. However, how could I be sure that we were not selling conflict diamonds? I never saw one of the certificates we promised that stated how the diamonds were conflict free; I was going on my manager's word that Diamonds International does not trade in blood diamonds. Throughout the summer, the question had little importance to me, but as I became aware of the importance of social injustices in the world, I asked myself the same question that those annoying customers had asked me: Were the diamonds I sold conflict diamonds? If so, was I then responsible for the encouragement of these gruesome wars funded by conflict diamonds?

Using the database *Academic Search Complete,* I began my research with the article "Dying for a Diamond?" by Rory E. Anderson, from *Sojourners Magazine,* a publication devoted to social justice issues. This article offered extensive information on the wars in Sierra Leone and Angola in the 1990s, which were financed by conflict diamonds. It clarified for me that the diamonds were not causing the wars but rather were used to fund the major rebel force in Sierra Leone, the RUF (Revolutionary United Front), which was known for amputating civilians' hands and forcing children to fight in their army. According to Anderson, although we talk as if blood diamonds are not in circulation anymore, there is still a "widespread humanitarian crisis in the Democratic Republic of Congo" and, as of 2007, around one percent of diamonds on the market were conflict diamonds. Anderson explains that "[o]ne percent of the annual $60 billion diamond retail market means $600 million worth of cheap weapons killing thousands every year in the Congo and elsewhere." In addition to giving me basic information about conflict diamonds, this article introduced me to the Kimberley Process Certification Scheme of 2002, a topic for further investigation. Anderson mentions how "58 percent of diamond retailers in the U.S. and the U.K. do not have policies on conflict diamonds." Could Diamonds International be one of these retailers? After reading this article, I e-mailed my sister's boyfriend, Avi, who has worked for Diamonds International for over ten years and is the general manager in Grand Cayman, and I asked him about the certificate that guarantees that the diamonds sold by Diamonds International are not conflict diamonds. I also wanted to know whether Diamonds International had ever been accused of selling conflict diamonds. Avi's response reached me later, as I mention.

I turned to another article found through my database search, Linda Stern's "More Bling for Your Buck," from the general news magazine *Newsweek.* This article gave tips for diamond shoppers looking for diamonds for Valentine's Day. It claimed that shoppers can be sure that diamonds are conflict free if they are certified by the Kimberley Process, which tracks the diamonds to confirm that they were not obtained to fund the wars in Africa. I wondered how well this process really regulates the sales of conflict diamonds and decided to follow up Stern's lead, the Web site globalwitness.org, which proved to be a goldmine of information on the Kimberley Process.

The Web site *Global Witness* offered useful information on conflict diamonds and the Kimberley Process Certification Scheme. The NGO (nongovernmental organization) Global Witness began its campaign against conflict diamonds in 1998. Its efforts and that of other NGOs led to meetings with representatives from the diamond industry in Kimberley, South Africa, in May of 2000 to discuss the problem of conflict diamonds.

After three years of negotiation, the Kimberley Process Certification Scheme was ratified in an effort to end the sale of blood diamonds in the global market. I also learned from this site that the Kimberley Process has not yet stopped the conflict diamond trade. Global Witness explains that the needed strict government regulations are often absent or are circumvented, as in the smuggling of blood diamonds out of Cote d'Ivoire, where "poor controls are allowing significant volumes of blood diamonds to enter the legitimate trade through Ghana, where they are being certified as conflict free, and through Mali" ("Conflict Diamonds"). Global Witness is calling for standards each country should be required to meet for the control over their diamonds, increased policing in these countries to ensure that there are no blood diamonds leaking through, statements of statistics of diamond trading, and funding for the Kimberley Process "to better coordinate and strengthen" the process ("Conflict Diamonds").

This informative Web site confirmed my suspicions about holes in the Kimberley Process Scheme and shocked me with facts about Africans' suffering caused by conflict diamonds. According to Global Witness, conflict diamonds have left at least 500,000 dead in Angola, 3 million dead in the Democratic Republic of the Congo, 50,000 dead in Sierra Leone, 200,000 dead in Liberia, and 1 million displaced in Liberia also. This organization also estimates that 15 percent of diamonds traded in the mid 1990s were conflict diamonds. It distresses me to think how many lives have been lost and how long it has taken for the global community to confront this enormous problem.

Returning to my database search, I decided to explore further the heated controversy over blood diamonds. T.L. Stanley's article "Gem Sellers Launch Blitz against *Blood Diamond*" from the business magazine *Advertising Age* discussed the release of the motion picture *Blood Diamond* in 2006 and states that "[t]he World Diamond Council trade group has launched an estimated $15 million public-relations and education campaign to combat the movie's images of diamond smuggling from war-torn African countries." According to Stanley, "South Africa-based De Beers, which markets more than 40 percent of the world's diamonds, has been front and center of the PR efforts." This article prompted me to find out more about the De Beers Corporation, their policies about conflict diamonds, and their relationship with Diamonds International.

At this point, I thought Tom Nevin's article "De Beers Moves to Clean Up Dirty Diamonds?", published in another business magazine *African Business,* might give me more insight concerning this major diamond corporation. Nevin explained that increased media attention (even before the film *Blood Diamond* was released) and public scrutiny led De Beers to take a more active stand against conflict diamonds and to "guarantee the origin of the diamonds it sells to sightholders" as of 2000. The company I worked for, Diamonds International, is a sightholder at the mines that De Beers owns. Although this article reassured me about diamonds purchased after 2000, I wondered about diamonds bought before 2000.

For my last article, I consulted another article from *African Business,* "Diamond Trade Funding," which provided evidence that De Beers stopped buying diamonds from Angola, but they did so "only days after a group of European organizations launched a campaign to alert the public to the fact that the diamond trade has been funding wars." This information revealed that during the mid 1990s De Beers was buying diamonds from Angola, where 60 to 70 percent of the diamond mines were controlled by rebel forces. I realized that if I had worked for Diamonds International ten to fifteen years ago, there is a good chance I could have been selling conflict diamonds that supported killing and destruction.

By this time in my research, I received e-mailed answers to my questions from my sister's boyfriend, who affirmed Diamond's International use of the Kimberley Process Certification Scheme and the observation of strict standards regarding tampering with the diamonds. I concluded that it is most unlikely that the diamonds I sold during the summer were conflict diamonds.

My research on conflict diamonds answered some but not all of my questions. I still plan to investigate recently published articles to give me further knowledge about blood diamonds currently in circulation, the continuing effects of the blood diamond trade on the war torn countries in Africa, and the progress toward reform. I now want to know, What steps should we as global citizens take to ensure that our purchases are not used to fund rebel forces?

Works Cited

Anderson, Rory E. "Dying for a Diamond?" *Sojourners Magazine*
    36.3 (2007). *Academic Search Complete.* Web. 16 Nov. 2008.
"Conflict Diamonds." *Global Witness.* Global Witness, n.d.
    Web. 17 Nov. 2008.
"Diamond Trade Funding Wars." *African Business* Nov. 1999.
    Research Library Complete. Web. 17 Nov. 2008.
Nevin, Tom. "De Beers Moves to Clean Up Dirty Diamonds?"
    African Business Jul./Aug. 2000. *Research Library Complete.*
    Web. 17 Nov. 2008.
Stern, Linda. "More Bling for Your Buck." *Newsweek* 12 Feb.
    2007. *Academic Search Complete.* Web. 16 Nov. 2008.
Stanley, T. L. "Gem Sellers Blitz Against *Blood Diamond.*"
    Advertising Age 11 Dec. 2006. *Academic Search Complete.*
    Web. 16 Nov. 2008.

For Class Discussion

1. How would you trace the development of Patrick's ideas about his initial question?

2. Where does he question his knowledge and his sources? Where might he challenge his sources more?

3. In this exploratory essay genre, how does Patrick seek to maintain and guide his readers' attention?

4. By the conclusion of this essay, what position on the global diamond trade has Patrick reached?

5. What view of consumer responsibility and the complexity of global trade have you gained from this essay?

Low Prices Come at a High Cost
Froma Harrop

Froma Harrop writes regularly for the *Providence Journal*, and her twice-a-week syndicated column appears in about 200 newspapers including the *Seattle Times, Philadelphia Inquirer, Denver Post, Dallas Morning News, Houston Chronicle, Detroit News,*and *Newsday*. She is well-known for her liberal bent and lively, forthright style. Harrop has also been a guest on PBS, Fox News, MSNBC, and NPR, among other broadcast and cable media. This op-ed piece appeared in the *Seattle Times* on September 19, 2007, during a recall of lead-painted toys from China.

> Froma Harrop participates in the ongoing controversy over the inadequate regulation of manufacturing allowed by the U.S. government and corporations committed to free trade. How does Harrop immediately signal readers that her focus encompasses and exceeds the product safety issue?

China' factories are pretty soulless affairs. Into one end are fed sweatshop workers and the world's raw materials. Through their stacks pour smog and greenhouse gases. The local environment is hideous, and the industrial pollution is so thick that plumes of dust and aerosol particles are making their way to California. The products of this manufacture get stamped with familiar American brand names.

None of these realities has aroused U.S. consumers as much as news that lead paint has been found on made-in-China toys bearing the Mattel label. Now the matter is personal—that is, about the health of people's children. And, suddenly, parents are checking dolls and toy cars for country-of-origin labels.

But let's back up. The story isn't simply about Chinese suppliers using lead paint, which was against Mattel's rules. It is about Amercian society's obsession with low prices.

Consider the whole picture. Big-box stores fight every penny increase in manufacturers' prices. That immediately knocks the American worker out of the game. Wal-Mart has actually told its U.S. suppliers to move their factories to China. This price mania has also cost jobs in Mexico, where workers are still better-paid than in Asia.

So Mattel now makes two-thirds of its toys in China. (It closed its last U.S. plant in 2002.) But there's still more price-scraping to do. Even the Chinese factories have to undercut each other.

Mattel owns 12 Chinese plants, which make about half its toys from that country. The rest are produced by outside vendors. These other suppliers were responsible for the lead paint in Barbie's accessories, Pixar cars and other toys. These factories cut corners because labor and material costs had recently risen. Rather than just charge more for the toys, the factories used lead paint, which was cheaper, if hazardous to children.

Why didn't Mattel produce all its Chinese toys in company-owned factories, where it had maximum quality control? Because the subcontractors did the job for less money. Wall Street had even been urging Mattel to sell its 12 factories and subcontract all the work.

And so what are the remedies here?

Politicians in Washington demand stiffer penalties for companies that sell dangerous products, but is that really necessary? Mattel can face no greater torture than having its CEO testify before Congress on the nightly news, following recalls of its Elmo Light Up Musical Pal—and all in time for the launch of the holiday shopping season.

We can go after China, but why bother? Seeing its giant American market in jeopardy, China just signed an agreement to ban lead paint in the toys it exports. But China also has "laws" mandating a 40-hour week and paid vacation for all workers.

"It's a game. It's a joke," says Charles Kernaghan, executive director of the National Labor Committee in Support of Human and Worker Rights.

Reports on China's globe threatening environmental degradation haven't moved the public. Chinese exports to the United States have nearly tripled over five years to $288 billion. Stories of abused labor in Asia and the collapse of factory employment here haven't changed the buying habits of flag-waving Americans who fill the big-box parking lots.

Perhaps the specter of dangerous toys will make the difference. Even Wal Mart's customers worry about the safety of the toys, according to the retailing giant.

The solution, ultimately, is for Americans to vote with their credit cards against a production system that trolls the Earth for the most downtrodden labor force and lowest environmental standards.

Rather than zero in on one country or company, let's zero in on ourselves. American consumers must understand that low prices come with a price.

For Class Discussion

1. What is Froma Harrop's purpose in this op-ed piece, and what is her central claim?

2. What are her main rhetorical strategies for achieving that purpose? How does she illustrate the futility of depending on alternate solutions to the problem?

3. Harrop's piece both criticizes American consumers and makes a strong appeal to them. How does she try to make her tone engaging despite her urgent message?

4. How effectively has Harrop argued the causal links among American consumer habits, foreign working conditions, and global environmental issues?

5. How does Harrop's solution for consumers to "vote with their credit cards" differ from Jeffcott's message regarding consumers and trade issues? How has this argument influenced your view of bargains?   ∎

Supermarket Tennis Shoes
Henry Payne

Henry Payne is a well-known conservative cartoonist and journalist. The cartoon on page 126 appeared on the Reasononline Web site (http://www.reason.com/news/show/32433.html) on September 19, 2003. Reasononline is a libertarian publication, forthrightly promoting free trade.

What are the key economic ideas behind the scenario that this cartoon portrays?

For Class Discussion

1. What dimension of the pro–free trade perspective does this cartoon draw on?

2. How does the cartoon employ exaggeration to convey its claim?

3. How could you find out how much tennis shoes would cost if they were made in the United States?

"THANK GOODNESS CONGRESS PASSED LEGISLATION PREVENTING MANUFACTURING JOBS FROM GOING TO CHEAP, OVERSEAS LABOR.... THAT'LL BE $1,599.99 FOR THE TENNIS SHOES."

Henry Payne: © DetroitNews/Dist. By United Feature Syndicate, Inc.

4. Would you say that this cartoon appeals the most to an audience who agrees with the economic views underlying it, a neutral audience, or a resisting audience? Why?

5. Which of the readings in this chapter does this cartoon support? Which does it rebut?

Toxic Toys: Is This Just China Bashing?
Madelaine Drohan

Madelaine Drohan is the Ottawa correspondent for the *Economist* and an award-winning author and journalist who has covered business, economics, and politics in Canada, Europe, and Africa. This News Commentary analysis was published on August 18, 2007, on the Canadian Broadcasting Corporation's news Web site (http://www.cbc.ca/news).

What cultural, social, and economic context does Drohan provide for the term "China bashing"?

Ever since China joined the World Trade Organization in 2001 and began its spectacular transformation into a trade superpower, the chorus of complaints about its low-priced goods has been swelling. China has been blamed for the massive loss of manufacturing jobs in countries such as Canada and the U.S., and it has also been accused of using unfair trade practices to capture an ever-increasing share of the world market. Governments with hard-hit industries have attempted to shut out, or at the very least limit, low-priced imports from China. The tiff between China and the European Union over lingerie imports, dubbed "The Bra War," was just one of numerous instances where China was accused of flooding markets with everything from auto parts to shoes.

It is tempting to assume that the current uproar about toxic toys, sparked by the massive recall of Chinese-made Barbie dolls, Polly Pockets, and other playthings, is part of this broader agenda. Certainly the time is ripe for China bashing south of the border. China's trade surplus with the U.S. has soared to record levels in recent months, just as the political campaign to be the presidential candidate is heating up in both the Republican and Democratic parties. In the 2008 U.S. election, the presidency, vice-presidency, a third of the seats in the Senate, and all of the seats in the House of Representatives are up for grabs. Standing up for America against a foreign foe is a time-tested way to win political support.

CHINA NOT ALONE IN PRODUCING UNSAFE GOODS

Lending credence to the argument that China is being unfairly targeted is the fact that China is hardly alone in producing unsafe products. Remember the spinach infected with E. coli last year? The toxic bottled carrot juice? How about the arthritis drug that appeared to cause heart attacks? Or the contact lens cleaner that appeared to cause temporary blindness? As far as I know, there was no link to China in any of these cases. They were all products, or produce in the case of the spinach, made in North America and Europe by western manufacturers.

The toxic toy affair is undoubtedly being exploited for trade reasons. However, there is more to it than that. Coming as it did on the heels on tainted seafood, poisonous toothpaste, unsafe car tires, and wheat gluten laced with plastic, the latest health scare has helped expose a raft of more fundamental problems that need to be addressed, not just in China, but also in the countries that buy Chinese-produced goods. Some of them are so entrenched, however, that it would take an optimist to assume they will be resolved any time soon.

Regulation is a good place to start. Every country has its share of cowboy producers who cut corners and use inferior goods in order to make a buck. The difference between Canada and China, however, is that we have a well-established system of product safety regulations, which, while not perfect, manages to catch problem products and force manufacturers to recall items. We also have environmental and labour regulations, again, hardly perfect, but capable of limiting the worst excesses.

LOCAL GOVERNMENTS IGNORE CENTRAL DIRECTIVES

Now, China apparently has a good set of regulations covering both quality control and the environment. The only problem is that these are set by the central government and largely ignored by lower levels of governments because they stand in the way of economic growth. The central government is moving to take away some authority from local governments, but this won't happen overnight. And as long as China continues to make economic growth its key priority, local governments, not to mention some companies, still have a powerful incentive to ignore regulations.

Here in Canada, the business community often talks about regulation as if it is a uniformly bad thing. Getting rid of red tape is practically a mantra for some business leaders. While overregulation is admittedly a bad thing, no regulation at all would lead to the situation you now see in some parts of China, where rules exist but are not enforced. Some red tape is necessary to keep society safe.

Which brings us to the situation on this side of the Pacific Ocean. The toxic toys were made in China for a respected U.S. company, Mattel Inc., one of thousands of western companies who have outsourced production to China to take advantage of cheaper prices (possibly in part because of the lack of concern for environmental damage or labour standards). The company has moved swiftly to recall the suspect toys and has been lauded for its actions. But questions are also being asked about its responsibility to ensure that quality standards are met at every step of its supply chain. Clearly, if lead-painted goods for children made it into shops in Canada and the U.S., there is something wrong with the company's internal system of quality control. Fixing internal controls is the responsibility of western companies, not the Chinese government.

SHOULD THE CANADIAN GOVERNMENT DO MORE?

The finger pointing related to the latest health scare has also extended to government checks on imported goods. If Chinese regulations were followed to the letter and companies had effective internal quality control systems, import inspections would be superfluous. Unfortunately, we live in a world where you cannot count on the first two, so the government must play a role in ensuring the health and welfare of its citizens, not just with foreign goods but also with those made in Canada.

As with regulations, there is a fine balance between too much inspection and not enough. However, effective and efficient inspections cost money and governments are under pressure to reduce spending and cut taxes. It takes a very brave politician to stand up to business and announce new rules that might slow the flow of trade and cost more money, even if it is done in the interest of consumer safety. It is easier to claim the problem lies elsewhere.

Those who support totally free markets contend that "buyer beware" should be the operating principle. But how can consumers judge the safety of a product if they are given incomplete information? Inadequate labelling in this era of globalized production makes it impossible to determine, not just where your car comes from, but also the ingredients of much of the food you put on your table. Business could fix this problem, with labels that spell out the source of various parts and ingredients. This would be costly.

These, then, are the complicated problems that the toxic toy scare has helped expose. Some of them could be resolved right here in North America. But it is easier to distract consumers and politicians here by pointing the finger at China. Does China deserve to be bashed? Undoubtedly. But so do a host of others much closer to home.

For Class Discussion

1. What is Madelaine Drohan's position on quality control, product safety, and regulatory responsibility? How does her claim seek to highlight the complications in the controversies over national control of free trade?

2. Drohan writes from the Canadian perspective. What differences does she assert between Canada's approach to free trade and the United States' approach?

3. According to Drohan, where do politics and economics intersect?

4. What evidence does Drohan provide in this brief commentary? Why do you think a general news audience would or would not find this evidence compelling?

5. Where do you as a consumer and citizen draw the line between regulation and responsibility?

Low Prices Have Consequences
Eric Devericks

Eric Devericks was a blogger and editorial cartoonist for the *Seattle Times* from 2001 to 2008. In his Web blog and cartoon archives, Devericks included a note about the origin of the idea for the cartoon on page 130. He wrote, "I'll be the first to admit that I'm a Wal-Mart shopper. I love low prices. Hell, I need low prices. This cartoon idea came from a note I wrote in my sketchbook a couple days ago. 'Maybe low prices have consequences?'" (http://blogseattletimes.nwsource/com/antatonisticink/archives/2007/08). This cartoon first appeared in the *Times* on August 16, 2007.

What are your initial reactions to this cartoon?

For Class Discussion

1. What is the emotional appeal made by this cartoon?

Eric Devericks

2. This cartoon draws on cultural knowledge. When in history and literature have children been ritually sacrificed? How does contextual knowledge shed light on and deepen the claim of this cartoon?

3. How does Devericks' statement from his sketchbook affect your view of him and the cartoon?

4. With which readings in this chapter is the argument of this cartoon most closely aligned? Which arguments does it most strongly oppose? ■

 STUDENT VOICE: Uncove[RED] by Nicole Cesmat

Student writer Nicole Cesmat is interested in the medical field. She developed her concern for social justice and public health in Africa on a summer service trip to Uganda. She wrote this argument for a writing assignment that called for a personal response to the role of American college students in global trade, basically answering the question, "Where should we shop?" This op-ed piece, imagined as a newspaper article written for the university community, drew on personal experience, fieldwork, reading, and research.

How does Nicole establish the motivating occasion for writing, and how does she build a bridge to her audience with the opening of her op-ed piece?

Like so many other Americans who occasionally turn on the Oprah show, I was incredibly excited when my mom wanted to show me the episode about the (RED) campaign, pioneered by Bono and supported by Oprah and a number of corporations. The participating businesses are Dell and Microsoft, Hallmark, Motorola, Armani, American Express, Apple, Converse, and Gap. Each company involved gives a percentage of its sales of certain designated (RED) products to AIDS medication for Africa. The percentage varies product to product, but Gap usually gives about 50 percent whereas Armani gives 40 percent and Converse gives 15 percent, etc. Because not all people need a new credit card or can afford to buy a new Razr cell phone or iPod or shop at Armani, Gap has received the most publicity with its consumer participation.

In addition to being the most affordable of the (RED) product stores, Gap also sells products that make it easiest for consumers to wear the cause on their sleeves. Their t-shirts bearing phrases such as "Inspi(red)" and "Empowe(red)" can easily be recognized anywhere. Wearing products that support charitable causes has become trendy and popular in recent years, such as the army of people in yellow rubber Livestrong bracelets that could be found in numerous U.S. cities a few years ago. The recent popularity of products like these makes Gap's (RED) t-shirts especially appealing. To enhance the popularity even more, all the models used to display the products in Gap's advertising are huge celebrities such as Dakota Fanning, Penelope Cruz, and Chris Rock, to name a few.

I can't help wondering, though, if Gap is in it for the publicity or is really changing its ways and becoming more involved in social justice issues. I believe we as consumers must question corporate practices and think about what we are buying into.

Undoubtedly, the (RED) campaign has benevolent and inspirational goals. In a world of consumerism, what better way to raise money for countries in need of aid than to sell people popular items that donate part of the profits to charity? I am not questioning the intentions of product (RED) itself. However, past accusations regarding Gap's manufacturing practices (and those of its related companies, Old Navy and Banana Republic) have made me increasingly suspicious of the company's motives for their involvement in the (RED) campaign.

Gap's involvement has benefited its business a great deal and there has been little if any sacrifice involved. I know that when I first went to check out the products that Gap had supporting product (RED), I became frustrated that in a store of $20 T-shirts and $60-to $70 jeans, the (RED) brand t-shirts were $30 and the jeans were $98. Why should we have to pay more for these products? I'm sure that the company can afford to keep the price down and still make the donation to the Global Fund that product (RED) supports. It seemed to me that all Gap was really doing was tacking on a built-in donation for each customer. I worry that these more expensive prices may deter numerous customers from purchasing the (RED) products and send them over to the sales racks where their money will support nothing but the business of the Gap Corporation. How do we as consumers know that Gap is a company we should be supporting? Even if a portion of the sales does go to a good cause for these limited products, do the rest of the profits from each purchase go back to supporting Gap's sweatshops, its exploitation of laborers, and its abuse of the environment? What is it that we are accomplishing by spending an extra $10 on our T-shirts? I wondered if it would be better to purchase my clothes somewhere else and donate some money directly to the Global Fund.

Now it is true that while Gap engages in sketchy manufacturing practices and is far from ideal, in the corporate world it is not the worst of evils. It is turning in the right direction. *Coopamerica.org* says that Gap has shown interest in addressing labor issues (key word here is *interest*) and has become an EPA climate leader, taking steps to make environmentally sound practices a top priority. Both of these accomplishments are very promising, considering the corporation's history.

As consumers we have a lot of power in the corporate world. It is our job to keep Gap heading in this right direction. If these issues are important to consumers, they become important to the company. If Gap, a huge corporation, changes its practices, it may lead other companies to do so as well. One way you can help is to write to Gap and say that this progress is important to you as a customer. An easy way to do this is to visit *organicconsumers.com* on its Clothes for Change page to find information on how to contact current Gap executives.

I'm not going to tell you that purchasing (RED) designated products at the Gap, or anywhere else for that matter, is wrong. I hope, though, that you might begin to question corporate actions such as Gap's involvement in charity fundraisers. What are you willing to support with the second 50 percent of the money you hand over for a T-shirt just to say that the first 50 percent went to Africa to fight AIDS? Think about that.

For Class Discussion

1. What is Nicole's main claim in this argument?

2. How does she convey her personal investment in and knowledge of the subject? How does she win readers' consideration of her view?

3. Nicole uses questions as a rhetorical strategy to get her readers to engage with the issue. If you consider yourself a member of her target audience, how effective is this strategy in drawing you in? What does she gain by taking a reflective, rather than a hard sell, tone in this piece?

4. What concessions does she make in analyzing the Gap Corporation's motives?

5. What contribution does Nicole, like Sachs, Jeffcott, Scholze, and Harrop, make to the larger conversations about the influence consumers in developed countries may wield in shaping the ethics of buying in this global economy?

CHAPTER QUESTIONS FOR REFLECTION AND DISCUSSION

1.   Some of the arguments in this chapter explore the big issue of free trade as a global economic system—its benefits, costs, successes, and problems. Now that you have read these arguments, how many specific ways can you identify in which free trade affects your life? Try to list five to ten specific ways.

2. Student writers Tiffany Anderson, Patrick Scholze, and Nicole Cesmat were all inspired to write about issues regarding free trade, consumerism, and sweatshops based on their own work experiences, shopping habits, and academic interests. Using the list you generated from question 1, decide which connection you might be inspired to investigate.

3. A number of the arguments in this chapter make different assumptions about global trade and its benefits and interpret the economic facts differently. Choose two writers from each group and list what are the major differences in the way they frame the issues—in their claims, reasons, and assumptions. Where do they look for evidence to support their claims? What counterarguments, reasons, and evidence would each enlist to refute the other's points?

   - Nick Gillespie/Johan Norberg and Ha-Joon Chang, Bob Jeffcott, or Global Exchange
   - Nick Gillespie/Johan Norberg and Thom Hartmann, Froma Harrop, or Madelaine Drohan
   - Rawi Abdelal/Adam Segal and Thom Hartmann or Ha-Joon Chang
   - Jeffrey Sachs and Thom Hartmann or Global Exchange

4. Johan Norberg, Ed Finn ("Harnessing Our Power as Consumers" in Chapter 2), Jeffrey Sachs, and Bob Jeffcott share a concern for the economic and social injustice that foreign workers are experiencing. How do their proposals for action differ?

5. Thom Hartmann and Robert Costanza both challenge visions of American economic progress and social well-being, yet they frame their arguments differently and make different rhetorical appeals to their audiences. Where do their arguments coincide and where do they diverge?

6. The following readings and visuals in this chapter all speak to consumer responsibility and the web of connection among consumers' values, the national economy, and social justice: Ed Finn's piece in Chapter 2, the photo "Buy American, Buy Union," the Devericks cartoon "Low Prices Have

Consequences," the Payne cartoon "Supermarket Tennis Shoes," Bob Jeffcott's argument, Froma Harrop's argument, Patrick Scholze's exploratory essay, and Nicole Cesmat's op-ed piece. Summarize and outline the argument in several of these readings. Which of the readings and visuals in this list make the strongest case for consumer responsibility?

7. In groups or individually, conduct research on one of the following questions related to this chapter's readings. Prepare to present your findings to the class. You might want to use a table, chart, or visual to explain your findings.

   - What are the top three countries that produce most of your clothing? What is the approximate dollar amount of these countries' garment production for the United States?

   - What items of clothing or food that you regularly buy could you buy as fair trade products? As union-made products? As American-made products? Where would you buy them?

   - What food or consumer products have recently been questioned for safety and where did they originate?

   - What popular toys are produced in the United States?

8. Controversies over free trade, consumerism, and sweatshops intersect with issues presented in other chapters of this text, such as the trading of financial risk and outsourcing of jobs (Chapter 4), immigration (Chapter 5), environmental resources (Chapter 6), food for the world (Chapter 7), and human rights (Chapter 9). For instance, global trade and fears of protectionism are definitely related to the collapse of the global money market. Identify an issue or subissue in this chapter and pursue it in a related chapter. What do you see as the main connections?

WRITING ASSIGNMENTS

Brief Writing Assignments

1. Write a brief narrative in which you describe a moment that made you think in a new way about your consumer habits. You could describe a personal experience (1) when you became aware of the consumer benefits of free trade; (2) when you realized some of the production problems of free trade; (3) when you discovered your consumer role in the global economy; or (4) when you discovered the danger of some globally traded and unregulated product.

2. Choose one of the following controversial claims and write informally for twenty minutes, supporting or contesting this claim. Use examples from your reading, personal experience, and knowledge to provide evidence to support your views. As a variation on this assignment, your instructor might ask you to write a short response in favor of the claim and then a short response arguing against it.

   A. The free trade global system is inherently flawed and favors rich nations.

B. All corporations should be required to give information about country of origin and manufacturing practices for their products.

C. The rewards and benefits of free trade will eventually be more evenly distributed among nations.

D. The wealth and well-being of countries should not be measured in only economic terms such as Gross Domestic Product.

E. Buying American products will ensure our country's prosperity and reduce the exploitation of workers in other countries.

3. Write a short response to these questions: How have the readings in this chapter affected the way you think about the connection between your buying habits and global economic justice? Which reading in this chapter made the strongest impression on you—in terms of bringing you a new perspective, creating a memorable argument, or changing your views on the global exchange of goods?

Writing Projects

1. Choose one of the following claims about free trade, sweatshops, and consumerism and construct a well-developed argument in favor of or against this claim. Write for a neutral or indifferent audience of your peers who have not thought much about this issue.

A. Free trade benefits developing countries.

B. Encouraging free trade agreements helps the United States economically and geopolitically.

C. Consumers in rich nations hold responsibility for the exploitation and social injustices experienced by workers and people in developing countries.

D. Americans should think beyond themselves and the pursuit of bargain prices when they shop.

E. Consumers and citizens should demand government and corporate quality control of domestic and foreign manufactured goods instead of expecting quality control by the manufacturing countries.

F. Protecting American industries and agriculture with tariffs and quotas on imports is economically sound.

2. Role-play this situation. Suppose a friend says to you, "I really feel bad that workers are laboring under life-threatening conditions to produce the jeans (or sneakers, sweaters, CD player) I buy. However, practically, I don't have time right now to figure out how to be a college student, prepare for a career, work at my part-time job, *and* change my consumer habits." Write an argumentative response to your friend in which you either agree and elaborate on the difficulties of changing our consumer habits, or disagree and propose some concrete ways to learn about manufacturing processes and the treatment of workers. For evidence to build your argument, you might use these sources: the affordable prices of superdiscount stores;

the good sales at local malls; the convenience of retail catalogs; personal experience; the readings in this chapter; other research you have done; and the following Web sites, which explore the ways that goods are produced:

Responsible Shopper (www.greenamericatoday.org)
American Apparel (www.americanapparel.net)
No Sweat Apparel (www.nosweatapparel.com)
Ethical Threads (www.ethicalthreads.co.uk)
Clean Clothes Campaign (www.cleanclothes.org)

3. Formulate a question about free trade, fair trade, protectionism, or consumer responsibility that fascinates and puzzles you, like the question about blood diamonds with which student writer Patrick Scholze began his research and his essay. Then, write a short exploratory paper in which you investigate your thinking about this question as you examine a variety of sources. Interviews, fieldwork, and specific experiences could also be sources. Write your essay for your class in an informal narrative format as you recount the development of your thinking on your question. Go source by source, and be sure to document your sources.

4. **Analyzing Arguments Rhetorically.** Thinking about the contribution one of the writers in this chapter has made to the general public's understanding of the issue, write an essay in which you analyze the argumentative strategies of one of the following: Ha-Joon Chang, Thom Hartmann, Jeffrey Sachs, or Froma Harrop. In your analysis, you might focus on the writer's use of analogy, evidence, description and narrative, or personal experience as support for his/her claim and reasons; the writer's credibility and authority; or the match between the genre of the argument, the audience for the argument, and the writer's word choice and level of formality. You may want to include a short summary of the argument in your introduction. Write to attract readers like yourself to this writer's argument or discourage them from reading it.

5. Fair trade as a movement and a trading system has sought to avoid exploiting growers, producers, and workers. Some coffee companies have adopted direct trade practices. As fair trade and direct trade have gained momentum, critics have become more outspoken in exposing the faults in these alternative trade systems. Research the controversy over fair trade and direct trade as improvements over free trade. Write an argument addressed to consumers in which you promote or critique one of these trade systems. You might focus on problems with certification, enforcement of labor standards and wages, transparency, and scale of business. You might choose to target specific foods or products (coffee, tea, cotton, cut flowers, etc.) or specific businesses (coffee sellers, Wal-Mart, etc.) that are carrying fair trade or direct trade products.

6. After conducting research, write a letter to your U.S. representative or senator expressing the stand you would like him or her to take on one of

the following issues. Use your research to help you construct a letter that is an informed, well-supported, clear argument:

- Should the United States adopt the same toy safety regulations that countries and companies in Canada or the European Union must meet?

- Should the United States promote "buying American" to strengthen the American economy?

- Should the United States enact legislation that would require U.S. companies to monitor working conditions and observation of human rights at their overseas manufacturing facilities?

7. A number of the readings in this chapter (as well as Ed Finn's "Harnessing Our Consumer Power" in Chapter 2) put pressure on the link between consumers in rich nations and the condition of workers in sweatshops around the world. However, some analysts and journalists argue that sweatshops greatly benefit workers in developing countries and that consumers can help these workers most by continuing to buy the goods they produce. Considering these views and consumer responsibility, write a policy proposal for a consumer group, expressing your informed view of sweatshops and consumerism. Argue your case for boycotting irresponsible companies, for pressuring companies to make their manufacturing practices transparent, for rewarding socially responsible companies with your business, or for political action to encourage economic development in poor countries.

8. After doing field and Web research, write an op-ed piece for your university newspaper. (Nicole Cesmat's argument, "Uncove(RED)" was written for this assignment.) In this short argument, assert your vision of responsible consumerism in your community and propose a course of action for your fellow students. Within your argument, you will need to address what responsible consumerism means to you. To prepare to write this op-ed piece, you might visit local thrift stores, your favorite clothing or food store, fair trade shops, farmers markets, or big box stores. A typical successful op-ed piece will have these features: a compelling opening; a tight, clear argument; a lively, authentic voice; vivid details; and a memorable conclusion, perhaps including a challenge to your audience. For background on company practices, you may want to consult these Web sites:

No Sweat (www.nosweatapparel.org)
Responsible Shopper (www.greenamericatoday.org)
United Students Against Sweatshops (www.studentsagainstsweatshops.org)
Maquila Solidarity Network (www.maquilasolidarity.org)
Corporation Watch (www.corpwatch.org)
Clean Clothes Campaign: Improving Working Conditions in the Garment Industry (www.cleanclothes.org)

4

Trading Financial Risk and Jobs
The Global Economic Crisis

QUESTION TO PONDER

You have been reading news stories about the serious economic problems around the world. For example, in Iceland, whose financial institutions were linked to those in the United States, currency has been devalued, inflation has soared, salaries have dropped, unemployment has risen to 10 percent, retirement savings have shrunk by 25 percent, and Iceland has urgently sought aid from the International Monetary Fund (IMF) and the European Union to hold up its crumbling economy. Meanwhile, as consumers in America and Europe have bought less, China's textile and apparel industry, centered in Shaoxing, has experienced a 33 to 80 percent cut in orders. This region's industry, which formerly employed over 20 million workers and generated over half of China's $300 billion trade surplus, is facing threats of mass unemployment.* You are wondering: How has the global economy been so vulnerable? What roles do the financial decisions of American consumers and Wall Street institutions play in the global economy?

CONTEXT FOR A NETWORK OF ISSUES

The crash of the global financial market in fall 2008 swept up average citizens around the world, seriously disrupting jobs, the cost of living, the availability of credit, and the economic stability of countries. The daily news remains packed with heated discussions of the interlinked and ongoing effects of the economic crash. For example, when a large number of homeowners in the United States

---

*David Barboza, "A Textile Capital of China Is Hobbled by a Downturn Gone Global," *New York Times* 28 February 2009.

defaulted on their mortgages, some of the biggest financial institutions that held these mortgages, like Washington Mutual and Countrywide, failed; the resulting stock market decline wiped out many people's savings and retirement funds, and the value of homes dropped nationwide. In response, the U.S. government and governments in other wealthy countries, hoping to prevent further destabilizing of their economies, voted hundreds of billions in bailouts to prop up these financial institutions. However, soaring national debt, reduced consumer spending, and the downsizing of companies as big as Microsoft, Boeing, Starbucks, and General Motors has caused the unemployment rate in the United States to rise to 9.5 percent as of June 2009.* Meanwhile, as General Motors has closed its European factories and consumer demand for manufactured goods has dropped, unemployment in many European Union countries has reached comparable rates. Around the world, the economies of developing countries have been substantially weakened by a decline in trade and financial aid.

The Crisis of the Global Financial System in Brief. So how did some of the world's largest financial institutions, such as Lehman Brothers, Bear Stearns, the American International Group (AIG), and Citigroup, come to the brink of failure, and in some cases collapse?

Part of the answer lies in a change in financial institutions' transactions, which have become more complex and risky—often involving billions of dollars. In the past, banking involved depositors and small but reliable promises of return. Banks retained a percentage of the money or assets entrusted to them and invested the rest at a modest interest rate. (Some small local banks in the United States and most Canadian banks still follow this model.) In addition to depositing money in banks, people could invest in mutual funds, bonds, and stocks that were more volatile and offered opportunities to bring greater financial returns.

However, in the last twenty years, banks and financial investors have increasingly traded in risk. Financial investors on Wall Street created a system of **structured finance**† that involved lending without using capital (money), enabling a small amount of money to **leverage** (control) bigger and bigger investments. Investors also embraced **securitization:** Banks would sell car loans, credit card debt, mortgages, music royalties, and other assets— all involving regular payments—by packaging them in trusts that pay bondholders principal and interest. Investors could opt for low risk and low returns or greater risk, potentially yielding the largest profits. **Derivatives,** contracts based on a stock, bond, or commodity and specifying the selling of future cash flows, became another means to buy and sell risk. Derivatives and securitizations have been sold and resold around the world.

---

*The Bureau of Labor Statistics (www.bls.gov) gives the latest figures on unemployment.
†The terms in bold type pertaining to the global financial crisis are defined in the Glossary at the end of this text.

Financial institutions have also grown and flourished outside public and governmental oversight. **Deregulation** of the financial system enabled banks and investment institutions to buy up companies and grow very large—as in the popular phrase "too big to fail." Deregulation also helped create a complicated system that minimized disclosure so that banks and investors buying and selling securitizations did not know what they held. When these large, consolidated financial institutions such as AIG and Citigroup engaged in the sale of securitizations, the scale and volume of transactions increased dramatically and became difficult to track.

In the last twenty years, the financial market has become a major contributor to the Gross Domestic Product (GDP) of the United States and of many other countries. In fact, securitization has functioned as "a shadow banking system that funds most of the world's credit cards, car purchases, leveraged buyouts, and subprime mortgages."[*] This financial system has made credit more available and increased borrowing and consumer spending, causing the U.S. consumer debt to triple since 1988. The United States has exported its "debt culture"[†] along with its most lucrative export business of the twenty-first century: securitization.[‡] The importance of this trade in financial investments is shown by the fact that five financial institutions have been listed on the Dow Jones Industrial Index: AIG (removed in September 2008), Citigroup (removed in June 2009), Bank of America, American Express, and JP Morgan Chase. The wealth-generating potential of the financial market has enticed other countries to participate and to adopt these methods for themselves. For example, banks in Iceland, Germany, and Japan, to name a few other countries, bought billions of dollars in securitizations.

Securitization has thrived on the subprime mortgage market, which has been fueled by investors looking for new opportunities to make money and consumers welcoming credit. In the past, to qualify for a mortgage, home buyers needed to have their credit approved, showing they could afford the mortgage, and to provide a down payment, usually about 10 percent to 20 percent of the value of the house. However, banks and lending institutions such as Countrywide, Washington Mutual, Fannie Mae, and Freddie Mac adopted the idea of giving **subprime mortgages** to people who had no down payments, poor credit, or inadequate regular income. These subprime mortgages often started off with low interest rates. Banks happily packaged these risky mortgages with less risky ones (securitization) for investors who then sold and resold them around the world. Because the worth of houses had been rising for several years, this gambling on the housing market seemed to be a good idea, and was definitely a profitable one.

---

[*]Mark Pittman, "Wall Street Toxic Exports." *Seattle Times* 7 December 2009.
[†]Pittman.
[‡]Pittman.

However, the subprime market in the United States and the whole system of securitization, based on explosive consumption, debt, and investment, was bound to blow up at some point.* Accumulating credit card debt, tapping equity in their houses, and overconsuming have become habits for many Americans: "Household debt hit a record 133 percent of disposable personal income by the end of 2007."[†] When the poor-risk buyers could not make their payments on their subprime mortgages, banks and institutions around the world were left holding assets they could not liquidate (turn into cash). The over-spent financial market, held up in large part by investors' confidence and mood, collapsed.[‡] In the United States, the economic crisis has engulfed many people: "Americans have lost one-quarter of their net worth in just a year and a half, since June 30, 2007."[§]

The bleak picture in the United States and in the European Union, where banks held a higher percentage of bad mortgages, is even more dismal for developing countries with their fragile economies dependent on trade and global income. The financial trouble in industrialized countries means that the International Monetary Fund (IMF) will have less money to lend, and credit will diminish as stricter lending standards are imposed. In addition, developed countries now have a strong impulse to protect their own jobs and industries, further stranding developing countries.

Offshore Outsourcing in Brief. Outsourcing, the movement of jobs from the United States and the rich EU countries to developing countries and the poorer EU countries, has only become more controversial with the global financial crisis.

Since the 1980s when corporations began to move manufacturing jobs and whole auto plants and clothing factories to developing countries with inexpensive labor and minimal government regulations, outsourcing has continued to increase. However, **offshore outsourcing,** the movement of white-collar jobs to other countries, has been gaining momentum and publicity in the last ten years. Substantial advances in the Internet, technology, and communication have made it possible for all kinds of work to be conducted in real time from the other side of the world. In the late 1980s and 1990s, call centers (customer service departments of companies such as help desks for computer software that are accessed by phone) and business processing also moved to other countries with lower wages. More recently,

---

*Mark Pittman, "Wall Street's Toxic Exports." *Seattle Times.* 7 December 2008.

[†]Stephen Roach, "Dying of Consumption." *New York Times.* 28 Nov. 2008.

[‡]For one of the most accessible and useful explanations of the subprime mortgage collapse, using animated figures and a straightforward definition of terms, see the short YouTube video by Jonathan Jarvis titled *The Crisis of Credit Visualized.* This video is also available at www.globalissues.org

[§]R. Altman, "The Great Crash, 2008: A Geopolitical Setback for the West." *Foreign Affairs.* 88(1). January 2009.

corporations, especially high-tech companies, have transferred departments and whole stages of their businesses to developing countries such as
India, the Philippines, Hong Kong, Taiwan, South Korea, and Singapore,
where a qualified labor force can do the same work for much lower wages
than American workers. This outsourcing draws increasing public scrutiny
as the competition for jobs world-wide becomes more intense with the
global financial crisis.

With the unemployment rate rising in the United States and the European
Union and with jobs disappearing every month, another aspect of the international flow of jobs has come under increased scrutiny: the U.S. H-1B visa. This
main work visa is given to skilled international professionals and/or international students in specialty areas such as accounting, advertising, architecture,
banking, business, computing, engineering, health care/medical, hospitality,
law, management, public relations, sales, scientific research, and teaching. This
visa entitles a person to work in the United States for up to six years, to bring a
spouse and family, and to apply for a Green Card (legal permanent residency).
High-tech, healthcare, and other scientific companies like Microsoft particularly favor the H-1B visa program as a means to diversify, invigorate, and
prestigiously staff their companies with the most educated and qualified
professionals. Because these visas are job-dependent, if workers lose their jobs,
they must either find another one quickly or they and their families will have
to leave the country.*

STAKES AND STAKEHOLDERS

The financial crisis has kicked off debates about the condition of the U.S.
economy, jobs, and corporate responsibility. Because everyone has stakes
in these issues, journalists, economists, corporate and political leaders,
financial experts, workers, taxpayers, and citizens everywhere are speaking
out on the causes of the global economic crisis and the precedents and
proposals for fixing the problems. Here are some of the major issue questions shaping the controversies.

Who Is to Blame for This Global Economic Crash? The economic crash
has been blamed to varying degrees on the U.S. government, the financial
system, and the American people.

- **The extent of government responsibility.** Many financial leaders believe
  the U.S. government contributed to the problem by lowering interest
  rates too much after 9/11, at a time when foreign investors had large
  amounts of money available to invest and were looking for investments

---

*The Travel.State.Gov link of the U.S. Department of State Web site provides informa-
tion on employment visas.

that paid more. Other political and economic analysts, including financial leaders in India, blame the U.S. government for deregulating the financial sector and failing to exercise oversight. These critics fault the United States for allowing companies to merge, grow, and develop financial methods that jeopardized the whole economy, treating the world as a vast "gambling casino" and exporting a "culture of corporate irresponsibility."*

- **Deeper systemic problems.** Economist Joseph Stiglitz asserts that "free market theories were not originally intended to be applied to finance".† Other critics of unregulated capitalism cite the failure of the financial markets as a confirmation that free trade ideology doesn't work.‡ These critics also argue that corporate globalization has continuously elevated profits for a corporate and Wall Street elite above the well being of people and the good of the country. For others, the financial crisis has fueled the fear that globalization itself has become too complex, unpredictable, and unfathomable. Economic analyst Naseem Taleb, author of the book *The Black Swan* (2007), believes the creation of megabanks is disastrous because the "fragile [global] banking system is too complicated for our traditional economic structure." Taleb and his colleague Benoit Mandelbrot call the banking system "a monstrous giant built on feet of clay."§

- **The extent of Americans' responsibility.** Many people fault average Americans for irresponsibly and wholeheartedly swallowing the growth model of the economy based on spending. These critics and worried citizens argue that now all taxpayers must pay for the ignorance, negligence, and unrealistic expectations of people who have foolishly run up huge credit card debts or let themselves be gulled into subprime mortgages. Taking a different view, others sympathize with those who have been victims of greedy and unscrupulous business practices.

What Are the Most Promising Economic Recovery Strategies? There is considerable disagreement about how best to help the economy recover.

- **Assistance for financial institutions or struggling homeowners and unemployed citizens.** Many investors and political leaders in the United States, Britain, and other parts of the European Union believe that financial institutions are vital to economic stability. Consequently, the U.S. Congress appropriated $1.5 trillion in 2008 and 2009 for the U.S. Treasury Department's **Troubled Assets Relief Program** (TARP) to bolster weakened banks and financial institutions. However, many

---

*Stiglitz. "Let's Throw Away the Rule Book," *The Guardian.* 6 Nov. 2008 guardian.co.uk
†Stiglitz. "The Fruit of Hypocrisy," *The Guardian.* 16 Sept. 2008 www.globalissues.org
‡See the arguments in Chapter 3: Trading Goods that examine this controversy.
§Naseem Taleb and Benoit Mandelbrot. "Benoit Mandelbrot Thinks We're All Screwed" http:// www.youtube.com

economic policymakers and citizens argue that helping financial institutions shifts the burden of the problem to the taxpayers. Instead, they say, as unemployment and home foreclosures rise, the federal government should improve the economy overall by directing money to people who *really* need it, by slowing the loss of savings and homes and creating jobs. These critics and citizen advocates are campaigning for help for small businesses and the modification of mortgages (reduced principals and lower mortgage payments).

- **The extent of government control.** Some proponents of free market ideology, corporate leaders, and conservative politicians argue that financial reform with more governmental oversight will cripple business innovation. However, other people call for more government intervention to prevent stockholders and executives from recovering at the expense of taxpayers. This debate also turns on political views and the use of rhetoric. Corporations and their political advocates protest that government intervention such as nationalizing banks means "socialism," a step on the road to communism, whereas more moderate policymakers and analysts counter that there are different national models of capitalism: for example, Norway, Sweden, the European Union, and Japan, where government plays a bigger role in monitoring capitalistic forces.

- **Other ways to stimulate recovery.** Economists are debating whether the usual government tools to stimulate the economy—lowering interest rates, stimulating production and consumption, and lowering taxes—will work to pull the country out of recession. Arguing that President Obama's $789 million stimulus package is not enough, some economists, policymakers, taxpayers, and workers demand more investment in unemployment insurance, worker retraining, education, and universal healthcare. Controversies also focus on whether federal policies, programs, and assistance employed during the Great Depression would work today. The balance between national and global interest is being hotly debated, with some policymakers and workers asserting the need to "Buy American" and rebuild American industries while other leaders warn that adopting "protectionist" measures will jeopardize international relations and vital trade with developing countries.* The European Union has also experienced serious tensions as individual countries have put their national interests above the EU market as a whole.

What Responsibility Does the Ordinary American Citizen Have for Financial Self-protection and Economic Recovery? Some debate centers on whether ordinary citizens can and should do more to safeguard their personal finances and contribute to economic recovery.

---

*Chapter 3 approaches this controversy over protectionism and buying American-made goods from the perspective of free trade.

- **The importance of financial literacy.** Educators, financial experts, and ordinary Americans are arguing that citizens should acquire financial literacy in order to understand the multiple and cumulative ways global financial institutions and personal financial choices affect them and others around the world. These people also maintain that government itself should simplify laws, regulations, and forms as well as establish programs to teach financial literacy. However, some legal and financial experts disagree, saying that the laws of finance today will always change rapidly and be too complicated for average citizens, and instead the solution lies in more government regulation and better financial advising.

- **Individual contributions to economic recovery.** Economic advisors and policymakers disagree about whether people should be spending money to promote business or saving for their own financial security.

How Extensively Should Global Financial Institutions Be Reformed?
While some analysts and policymakers vote simply to rein in the United States' free market capitalism and economic leadership, citizens around the world are opposing their own governments' alignment with U.S. economic policies. These social activists and citizens object to the decision to give massive aid to financial institutions, a policy they say is a repeat of the IMF and U.S. Treasury bailouts of countries such as Argentina in the 1990s, when ordinary taxpayers in these countries paid for corporate and governmental policies. Developing countries—and China and India, two countries that have maintained their own financial stability through more state-run markets and investment regulations—are arguing for decision-making power in global economic organizations such as the International Monetary Fund. Instead of the Group of Eight (G-8: the United States, Canada, France, Germany, Italy, Japan, Russia, the United Kingdom, and the nonvoting European Union), the countries in the Group of Twenty,* a forum to bring together the leading industrialized nations with emerging-market nations, are also demanding a bigger role in global economic issues. Other progressive thinkers believe we need to dismantle Wall Street: "We must reboot the economy with a new, values-based operating system designed to support social and environmental balance and the creation of real, living wealth."[†]

---

*Nineteen countries: Argentina, Australia, Brazil, Canada, China, France, Germany, India, Indonesia, Italy, Japan, Mexico, Russia, Saudi Arabia, South Africa, South Korea, Turkey, the United Kingdom, and the United States. www.g20.org/
[†]David Korten, "The New Economy and Why This Crisis May Be Our Best Chance." *YES!* Summer 2009, 20.

How Do Current Practices of Global Employment Influence the United States and the Global Economy? Jobs and workers tend to follow multinational corporations, and nations may or may not benefit from the global trends in employment.

- **Corporations versus American workers.** Corporate leaders along with some economists claim that offshore outsourcing will spur innovation in business, prompt the creation of new jobs, and enable corporations to lower costs for consumers and raise profits for stockholders. They also insist that to be competitive, companies need the expertise of international workers with H-1B visas. However, critics argue that outsourcing and the use of H-1B visas elevate short-term corporate gain over long-term benefits for the country and contribute to high unemployment in the United States. Critics, questioning the motives of some international applicants and U.S. businesses, point to the finding that 20 percent of the applications for H-1B visas in 2008 involved fraud.* In opposition, immigrant lawyers offer the perspective of international professionals who have contributed to their American employers but recently lost their jobs. Workers and labor advocates underscore the ongoing problem with the loss of U.S. jobs in manufacturing, most recently the closing of General Motors plants while auto manufacturing continues in Mexico, and challenge the claim that new jobs are being created. Some advocacy groups and workers' organizations also claim that moving businesses, especially factories, abroad has enabled corporations to lower the standards of working conditions, increasing profits at the expense of foreign workers, with no guarantee of long-term employment.

- **National versus global interest.** Proponents of free trade and supporters of offshore outsourcing argue that outsourcing jobs to other countries helps the United States by creating new markets for goods from developed countries, substantially enhancing the economic development and political stability of those countries, and promoting peaceful global relations. Yet critics, while acknowledging these benefits, point to the erosion of local, state, and federal tax bases when businesses are relocated abroad. With the outsourcing of increasingly diverse and sophisticated jobs—technical support for computer companies, software and data management, medical transcription, reading X-rays and CAT scans, and now product design—and with the growing number of educated global workers whose economies enable them to work for less than Americans do, some people are wondering if any jobs in the United States are secure.

---

*Lornet Turner, "Report Finds Fraud in 20% of H-1B Applications." *Seattle Times.* 15 February 2009.

STUDENT VOICE: Thanking the Poor Economy by Rahel Tesfahun

In this personal narrative, student writer Rahel Tesfahun shares how the financial crisis has affected her everyday financial decisions.

Up until September 2008, I used to be a "consumption whore." I automatically pulled out my trusty, handy credit card for everything, from a latte at Starbucks to a sale at Macy's. Shopping was a therapeutic addiction that helped curb my anxiety in dealing with school, work, family, and friends. My life revolved around the power of product. Buying a five-dollar latté every morning or wearing a new outfit and eating out became a personal ritual that gave me a false sense of temporary escape from the stresses of school work and my personal life. I didn't question how the consequences of my spending would impact my future.

But then, the sour reality of our current blundering economy and my negative bank account hit. I had trouble finding a job, was piling on school debt, and was left with a closet full of outdated clothes that didn't help me buy dinner or pay rent. Seeing graduation looming, I grasped that I was without a stable bank account and any monetary conservation skills. I had no choice but to start making changes in my lifestyle toward minimal consumption. With regular news of our failing global financial system flooding in, I found myself in a depressing situation but a strangely inspiring one, too.

The bad economy has profoundly changed my life. Cash, not credit, now guides my purchases. As I have curbed my spending, I have found myself happier and healthier, with an increasing admiration for the parts of my life not based on monotonous clothing trends or ritzy bars. I have discovered my community, neighbors, and fellow students. Within my neighborhood block, people are interacting more with house parties and homemade meals as a means of creating pastimes that don't hit their bank accounts. The result: I believe that people are learning more and becoming increasingly aware and tolerant of different cultures and lifestyles.

I now host themed dinners for roommates and friends such as Mexican Fiesta, complete with cheese quesadillas and Coronas, or Chinese Food Potluck dinners. These nights are filled with Scrabble tournaments (now held weekly) and good conversation as opposed to stale nights of overpriced movie tickets, swanky overrated bars full of impersonal conversation and over-glorified, expensive low-calorie salads. My roommates and I are exploring cooking options at home, having fun with new recipes, buying more local food, and becoming more aware of what and how we eat. These changes and time together have improved the quality of our friendships. I've become more social and authentic, comforted by the lack of pressure to justify my new simpler lifestyle.

Another plus is that I have become less dependent on credit, experiencing what it feels like to save rather than *spend, spend, spend*. In the past six months alone, I have managed to cut my coffee consumption habits by about half and open up a free savings account. I have improved my health and paid off my credit cards. Living debt free has reduced my stress and encouraged me to keep saving.

At this time when jobs are limited, bank account balances are low, and personal debts are at an all time high, many graduating students find themselves perplexed about how they will function in a society that seems to have no room for them. However, I've become less obsessed with seeking a big income and am thinking more locally. I am finding fulfillment in giving back to my community through tutoring and am contemplating a career in education.

The repercussions of the economy offer me and many others an opportunity to try a different direction: making a better community by shifting toward an intellectual and more social way of life. With the failing economy and precarious job market, now is a better time than ever for students to embrace this new social culture. I am not much of an optimist, but the benefits of this crisis are something I can't overlook. In a society where the political and social habits of Americans are drastically changing, so are the ideas of those who understand the revolution happening in our society. Perhaps this bad economy is a good thing for my generation.

INTERNATIONAL VOICES

The effects of recession and diminished consumer spending are threatening industries and jobs around the world, even in the European Union countries where unions hold substantial sway with governments. Unlike the United States where losing a job usually means losing health insurance, in EU countries, government safety nets (social services such as unemployment insurance and health insurance) also lessen the damage of job loss while the practice of reducing work hours to avoid layoffs provides an alternative to cost-cutting through shedding of jobs. This excerpt from the article titled "Shadows Grow Longer in Germany's Golden City as Unemployment Surges," by Nicholas Kulish, published in the *New York Times* on April 14, 2009, shows the impact of the global economic crisis.

Workers in a German Town Comment on Losing Their Jobs

According to economists here, German consumers have been one of the few pillars of strength for the global economy, not having felt the effects of the recession as directly as have Americans. There was no real estate bubble here and relatively few rely on equities for their retirements or have credit-card debts, and job protections are much stronger. But as declining exports lead to ever more layoffs, the brunt of the crisis is expected to cause pain throughout Germany, Europe's largest economy, the way it already has in Pforzheim.

This town on the northern edge of the Black Forest traces its heritage as a jewelry center to 1767, when its overlord founded a factory for watches and jewelry at the local orphanage. In recent decades, as the production of lower-end necklaces, rings and bracelets migrated to cheaper labor markets in Asia, the highly trained metal workers here turned to making precision parts for the automobile industry.

But the combination of luxury goods and automobile parts proved a poor one in this economic downturn, leaving the town of around 120,000 exposed to the clampdown on spending by consumers, particularly in the United States. . . .

Locals say that the worsening economy is a constant topic of discussion. "I still get up every day at 5 o'clock in the morning," said Helmut Frey, 57, a goldsmith who lost his job at the end of December. Mr. Frey, who began learning the trade in 1965, said he had sent out some 18 job applications without getting a single interview. "For me, it's basically over," he said, waving away questions about his future. . . .

In February exports fell 23 percent compared with the previous year. Industrial output shrank 20.6 percent for the month compared to the year before. . . .

What has astounded even older people, who have lived through recessions and restructurings in the past, was the speed with which business ground to a halt. "At factories that last summer were running seven days a week orders simply collapsed, and now they're running just two or three days a week, " said Marin Kunzmann, a local representative for the union IG Metall.

Ralf Scheithauer, 49, lost his job at an electronics factory where he worked for 15 years, but was lucky enough to find an internship in occupational therapy that could lead to a full-time position. "People don't like to talk about it. You just find yourself thinking, 'What's he doing working in his garden during the day?'" Mr. Scheithauer said, "There's this sense that, if someone doesn't have work, they must somehow be to blame."

GLOBAL HOTSPOT: The United States

Newspapers and magazines have tellingly probed both the lenders and the buyers in the subprime mortgage market. According to Peter S. Goodman and Gretchen Morgenson, in their expose of Washington Mutual, this bank's mortgage department aggressively pursued predatory lending practices:

> WaMu gave mortgage brokers handsome commissions for selling the riskiest loans, which carried higher fees, bolstering profits and ultimately compensation of the bank's executives. WaMu pressured appraisers to provide inflated property values that made loans appear less risky, enabling Wall Street to bundle them more easily for sale to investors.
>
> "It was the Wild West," said Steven M. Knobel, a funder of an appraisal company, Mitchell, Maxwell & Jackson, that did business with WaMu until 2007. "If you were alive, they would give you a loan. Actually, I think if you were dead, they would still give you a loan."*

Those people who were already stretched by home ownership have been particularly vulnerable to the subprime mortgage market crisis, as shown in this excerpt from an article "Subprimes Pave the Road to Neighborhood Ruin" by Carrie Teegardin and John Perry from *The Atlanta Journal-Constitution* (May 31, 2009).

> . . . . John Bussie, 74, and his wife Lillie, 80, bought their first house a decade ago. Bussie, who said he left school in the fifth grade, worked until retirement for the city of Atlanta. Lillie worked as a nanny and housekeeper. Their two-bedroom, one-bath dwelling on a quiet street off I-20 is a cheery house filled with floral arrangements and brightly-painted walls. There's a cactus garden in the front.
>
> "It was my dream house when I saw it," Lillie Bussie said.
>
> The couple refinanced their fixed-rate mortgage in 2005 and thought they had replaced it with a new fixed-rate loan. What they got was much more complicated: the first mortgage had a fixed rate for two years and was adjustable thereafter, with a ceiling of 12.15 percent; the second mortgage as part of the deal was a 15-year balloon note at a fixed rate of 10.5 percent.
>
> "These exotic mortgage products didn't make any sense for them at all," said Sarah Bolling, an attorney with Atlanta Legal Aid now representing the couple. Atlanta Legal Aid helps low-income borrowers take on mortgage lenders.
>
> The couple says they can't remember exactly how they got involved in the refinance. The transaction paid off $1,897 in tax

---

*"Saying Yes to Anyone, WaMu Built an Empire on Shaky Loans." *New York Times* 28 December 2008.

liens, but was otherwise a straight refinance of their existing loan with no cash out. The Bussies said they were rushed through the closing and told to sign without much explanation.

The loan included features that Congress may soon ban: a prepayment penalty and a "yield spread premium," a bonus usually paid to a mortgage broker by a lender for putting a borrower in a loan that is more expensive than what they could have qualified for.

The Bussies soon realized the mortgage wasn't what they thought it was.

"I just wondered why my mortgage kept going up," Johnnie Bussie said. "I got to where I couldn't buy groceries."

The couple got so far behind that loan servicer EMC Mortgage planned to auction the house last March before the process was delayed.

When the experts say that subprime lenders threw out the underwriting rules, they are talking about loans made to people like the Bussies—senior citizens on a fixed income who plan to spend the rest of their lives in the house. The loan wasn't affordable on the Bussies' gross income of about $2,400 a month.

"They didn't get any benefit at all from the transaction," said Bolling, their attorney. "It had everything to do with the investment banks filling up the pools with the kinds of mortgages they wanted on that day." . . .

The first group of readings in this chapter explores controversies over what caused the crash of the global financial system, how it is affecting the world, and what solutions look the most promising. The second group examines the arguments over offshore outsourcing and the importation of high-tech workers and professionals. The last group argues about the need for individuals to understand these financial issues and to take responsibility for their own financial decisions.

READINGS

The G-20 Summit: Time to Renew Commitment to Economic Freedom
Anthony B. Kim

Anthony B. Kim holds a masters degree in international trade and investment policy. Since 2001 he has worked as a policy analyst for the Heritage Foundation's Center for International Trade and Economics (CITE). At CITE he is responsible for the research for the *Index of Economic Freedom* (produced jointly with the *Wall Street Journal*). The Heritage Foundation is a very large public policy research institute with the mission "to formulate and promote conservative public policies based on the principles of free enterprise, limited government, individual freedom, traditional American values, and a strong national defense" (www.heritage.org/about). This WebMemo was posted on its Web site on March 31, 2009.

What large, ongoing conflicts of globalization underlie this policy analysis argument?

In his recent op-ed on the upcoming G-20 meeting in London, President Obama stated that "now is the time to work together to restore the sustained growth that can only come from open and stable markets that harness innovation, support entrepreneurship and advance opportunity."[1]

In light of the ongoing worldwide economic turmoil, there may be no distinct formula through which to quickly reinstate the unrelenting growth. However, President Obama and other leaders of the G-20 should be reminded that as a fundamental linking element between economic opportunity and lasting prosperity, economic freedom is indispensable in amplifying and cascading the benefits of any plans that may come out of the summit.

THE CONTINUING STRUGGLE BETWEEN THE STATE AND THE FREE MARKET

As G-20 leaders prepare to meet in London on April 2, they face an unprecedented challenge: The global economy is likely to shrink this year for the first time since the Second World War. The World Bank predicts that during 2009 world trade is likely to record its largest decline since the Great Depression.[2]

In light of this challenge, the current state of the world economy is a vivid reminder of the continuing struggle between the state and the free market. There is little global demand for a shift to central planning or extensive state ownership of private businesses in the name of recovery and stability. Rather, states' interventionist measures have been inching up at an increasing pace, thereby eroding economic freedom—the backbone of the world economy.

In a time of economic calamity, it is expected that people look to their governments for answers. However, plausible solutions to the current economic crisis do not lie in more direct government intervention, which will prolong the crisis by adding more risk and uncertainty. Furthermore, governments' stimulus packages should not be based on handing out cash or shortsighted populism. Nor should they target one group or industry: Such packages should benefit the whole economy. To achieve maximum impact, the state should guarantee market rules and reassure market confidence.

In doing so, as President of the European Central Bank Jean-Claude Trichet pointed out, governments will have to "reassure [their] own people that [they] have an exit strategy, to reassure households that [they] are not putting in jeopardy the situation of the children, and to reassure businesses that what is done today is not done to the detriment of their own taxation in the years to come."[3]

NO MORE LIP SERVICE

For many decades, the world has reaped the economic benefits of gradual liberalization in trade and investment. Today, however, the place of free trade in policymaking is far from secure. Despite repeated pledges by world leaders not to disrupt the international flow of goods and services with more barriers, protectionism is on the march, undermining efforts to lay out a coordinated and credible response to the current global economic downturn. As in all trade wars, the collateral damage is too costly.

The Declaration of the Summit on Financial Markets and the World Economy issued by the G-20 in November 2008, stated that within the next 12 months, "we will refrain from raising new barriers to investment or to trade in goods and services, imposing new export restrictions, or implementing World Trade Organization inconsistent measures to stimulate exports."[4] However, this pledge has been broken. According to a recent study by the World Bank, since G-20 leaders signed the declaration to avoid protectionism, 17 of them have implemented measures that restrict trade at the expense of other countries.[5]

CYNICISM DRIVING PROTECTIONISM: A PERILOUS RECIPE FOR THE WORLD ECONOMY

A key driver of economic prosperity is a high level of flexibility and resilience founded on economic freedom. This has been continuously protected by keeping levels of regulation and government intervention low while emphasizing great transparency and strongly protected property rights. The powerful force of economic freedom has fostered the spirit of entrepreneurship and innovation that creates new products and more jobs, spreading the benefits of a dynamic economy around the globe.

Indeed, today's economic development and lasting prosperity depend on maintaining and improving an environment in which entrepreneurial activities and innovation can flourish. Investment capital and entrepreneurial talent flow toward economies with lower taxes, secure property rights, sound money, and sensible regulatory policies. Countries with higher degrees of openness and flexibility benefit from the free exchange of commerce and ideas—and, consequently, citizens of those countries—enjoy more opportunities and greater prosperity.

Yet economic freedom, like other freedoms, is always vulnerable. History demonstrates that this is never more so than when politicians espouse populist rhetoric, playing to people's fears and calling for more government interventions that promise a quick fix to whatever is deemed faulty in a complex economy. Politicians and leaders increasingly disparage free markets and push for counterproductive regulatory rules, increase costs on investment, or, worse, pursue protectionist policies that curtail global economic growth.

SUSTAINING ECONOMIC FREEDOM: KEY TO ECONOMIC RECOVERY

Today's cynicism and doubts about the benefits of globalization and the free market system should not abruptly halt America's long-standing commitment to openness and economic freedom.[6] Economic freedom is not a dogmatic ideology. It is not the only way—nor a perfect way—to put an economy in order. However, it is a far better way than other systems that have been tested. As the direct opposite of government interference and control, economic freedom is a threat only to those who want special privileges by pressuring societies to expand the size and weight of government intervention.

The world must not be discouraged from pursuing greater economic freedom. The G-20 should take this week's summit as an opportunity to renew their commitment to economic freedom.

Notes

1. President Barack Obama, "A Time for Global Action," *The Chicago Tribune*, March 23, 2009, at *http://www.chicagotribune.com/news/ chi-oped0324obamamar24,0,103411.story* (March 30, 2009).
2. CNN, "World Bank: Economy Worst Since Depression," March 9, 2009, at *http://money.cnn.com/2009/03/09/news/international/global_ economy_world_bank* (March 30, 2009).
3. Jean-Claude Trichet, interview with *Wall Street Journal*, March 23, 2009, at *http://www.ecb.europa.eu/press/key/date/2009/html/sp090323. en.html* (March 30, 2009).
4. Press release, "Declaration of Summit on Financial Markets and the World Economy," The White House, November 17, 2008, at *http:// www.america.gov/st/texttrans-english/2008/November/20081117173241 xjsnommis0.4479639.html* (March 30, 2009).

5. Elisa Gamberoni and Richard Newfarmer, "Trade Protection: Incipient but Worrisome Trends," The World Bank, March 2, 2009, at *http://siteresources.worldbank.org/NEWS/Resources/Trade_Note_37.pdf* (March 30, 2009).
6. See Terry Miller, "Freedom Is Still the Winning Formula," *The Wall Street Journal*, January 13, 2009, at *http://online.wsj.com/article/ SB123180425194675361.html* (March 30, 2009).

For Class Discussion

1. What specific economic and political events are motivating Kim to write this piece?

2. How does Kim employ the following two sets of terms to frame his argument: on the one hand, "economic freedom," "market rules,' and "market confidence"; on the other, "export restrictions," "protectionism," "government intervention," and "populist rhetoric"?

3. How are the values of the Heritage Foundation reflected in this policy argument? What, for instance, does Kim mean by "economic freedom"?

4. How does Kim use evidence from research to support his claim and reasons?

5. Why would (or would not) this argument influence the views of readers whose values are not aligned with those of the Heritage Foundation? In other words, how well does Kim reach a neutral or dissenting audience?

Markets Can't Rule Themselves
Joseph E. Stiglitz

Joseph E. Stiglitz, one of the most well-known and respected liberal economists in the world, won the Nobel Prize in Economics in 2001. He served as a member of President Clinton's Council of Economic Advisors and as chief economist of the World Bank. A distinguished professor, he has taught at Yale, Princeton, Stanford, MIT, and, most recently, Columbia University's Graduate School of Business and Department of Economics. He has published both textbooks on economics and books on global economic issues for a larger educated public audience. Among his books are *Globalization and Its Discontents* (2001), *Fair Trade for All* (2005) with Andrew Charlton, *Making Globalization Work* (2006), and *The Three Trillion Dollar War: The True Cost of the Iraq Conflict* with Linda Bilmes (2008). Stiglitz's columns and analyses appear regularly in news commentary forums in Britain and the United States. This policy argument was published in *Newsweek*'s international edition on December 31, 2008.

In your own words, how would you describe the problem Stiglitz is addressing in this argument?

For years, there has been an ongoing discussion among world leaders and thinkers about deficiencies in the international financial architecture and about economic imbalances, including the widening U.S. trade deficit. Many worried about a disorderly unwinding of these imbalances. Nothing was done.

We are now paying the price for our failure to act. Ten years ago, the fear was that financial turmoil in the developing world might spill over to the advanced industrialized countries. Today, we are in the middle of a "made in the U.S.A." crisis that is threatening the entire world.

If we are going to address this worldwide crisis and prevent a recurrence, we must reform and reconfigure the global financial system. There are simply too many interdependencies to allow each country to go its own way. For example, the United States benefited from its export of toxic mortgages; had it not sent some of them to Europe via complex securitization, its downturn would have been far worse. But the resulting weaknesses in Europe's banks are now ricocheting back to the United States.

Better regulation would have helped prevent such a situation. But the reform of the global financial system must go much further. For example, there must be better monetary-policy coordination around the world. Europe's current slowdown is due in part to the fact that while the European Central Bank spent the past year focusing on inflation, the United States was (rightly) focusing on the impending recession. The resulting difference in interest rates led to a strong euro and weak exports. That hurt Europe. But a weak Europe eventually hurts the United States, as Europe is forced to reduce its imports of American goods. With better coordination, perhaps America would have been able to convince Europe of the risks of recession, and that would have led to moderation of Europe's interest rates.

There is also a need for internationally coordinated stimulus programs to help jump-start growth. It is good news that China, the United States and Japan have now all instigated major programs of fiscal expansion. But they are of vastly different sizes, and so far, Europe's is lagging behind. Its growth and stability pact imposes constraints that may have global consequences.

Beyond this, confidence in financial markets will not be fully restored unless governments take a stronger role in regulating financial institutions, financial products and movements of capital. Banks have shown that they can't manage their own risk, and the consequences for others have been disastrous. Even former Fed chairman Alan Greenspan, the high priest of deregulation, admits he went too far.

What we need now is a global financial regulatory body to help monitor and gauge systemic risk. If financial rules are allowed to vary too widely from nation to nation, there is a risk of a race to the bottom—some nations will move toward more lax regulation to capture financial business at the expense of their competitors. The financial system will be weakened, with consequences that are now all too apparent.

What should this new set of global financial rules encompass? For starters, it should ensure that managerial incentive schemes are transparent and do not provide perverse encouragement for bad accounting, myopic behavior and excessive risk taking. Compensation should be based on returns not from a single year but over a longer time period. At the very least, we should require greater transparency in stock options, including making sure that they receive appropriate accounting treatment. And we need to restrict the scope for conflicts of interest—whether among rating agencies being paid by those they are rating, or mortgage companies owning the companies that appraise the properties on which they issue mortgages. We need to restrict excessive leverage, and other very risky behavior. Standardization of financial products would enhance transparency. And financial-product safety and stability commissions could help decide which products were safe for institutions to use, and for what purposes. We have seen what happens if we rely on bankers to regulate banking.

> **What should this new set of global financial rules encompass?**

Beyond better global coordination of macroeconomic policy and regulation, there are at least two other actions governments should take. First, we need a reform of the global reserve system. More than 75 years ago, John Maynard Keynes, the greatest economist of his generation, wrote that a global reserve system was necessary for financial stability and prosperity; since then the need has become much more dire.

Keynes's hope was that the International Monetary Fund would create a new global reserve currency that countries would hold instead of sterling (the reserve of the time). Today, such a currency could be used to replace the dollar as the de facto reserve currency. Because it would not depend on the fortunes of any one country, it would be more stable. Supply could be increased on a regular basis, ensuring that reserves kept up with countries' needs. Issuance could be done on the basis of simple rules—including punishment for countries that caused global weaknesses by having persistent surpluses. This is an idea whose time may have finally come.

The other major reform should be a new system of handling cross-border bankruptcies (including debt defaults by sovereign states). Today, when a bank or firm in one country defaults, it can have global ramifications. With various national legal systems involved, the tangle may take years to unwind. For example, the problems arising from Argentina's 2001 default are still not resolved, and bankruptcy complications plagued

South Korea and Indonesia during their crises a decade ago, slowing down the process of recovery. The world may soon be littered with defaults, and we need a better way of handling them than we have had in the past.

This crisis has highlighted not only the extent of our interdependencies but the deficiencies in existing institutions. The IMF, for instance, has done little but talk about global imbalances. And as the world has focused on problems of governance as an impediment to development, deficiencies in the IMF's own governance meant its lectures had little credibility. Its advice, especially that encouraging deregulation, seems particularly hollow today. Many critics in Asia and the Middle East, where pools of liquid capital dwarf the IMF's own, are wondering why they should turn over their money to an institution in which the United States, the source of the problem, still has veto power, and in which they have so little voting power.

This is a Bretton Woods moment—a time for dramatic reforms of existing institutions or, as was done at the end of World War II, the creation of new ones.

Until now, Washington has consistently blocked efforts to create a multilateral global financial system that is stable and fair. It exported the deregulatory philosophy that has proved so costly, both to itself and to the world. President Obama has an opportunity to change all this. Much depends—now and for decades to come—on his response.

For Class Discussion

1. What are the main changes in global financial institutions and policies that Stiglitz puts forth in this proposal argument? What reforms is he advocating?

2. This policy proposal, written for a news commentary source for a general audience, nevertheless presupposes some background knowledge of both the causes of the economic crash and global economic institutions such as the International Monetary Fund. What events, institutions, and economic terms would you find helpful to learn more about?

3. Both Stiglitz and Anthony B. Kim address the global dimension of the economic crisis. How does Stiglitz's argument contrast with and refute Kim's?

4. Stiglitz frequently writes for *The Guardian* and the *New York Times*. How does knowing something about Stiglitz's reputation and authority contribute to the persuasiveness of his argument?

5. This argument uses rational and logical strategies. What emotional and imaginative appeals might increase readers' enthusiasm for Stiglitz's views?

G-20 Protest
Julie Sell

Julie Sell is a graduate of Mount Hollyoke College. She has worked for *The Asian Wall Street Journal* in Hong Kong, *The International Herald Tribune* in Paris, and recently, *The Economist* in London. She authored a book, *Whispers at the Pagoda: Portraits of Modern Burma* (1999) and writes on international financial topics. This photo appeared in the *Seattle Times* on April 2, 2009, accompanying an editorial titled "President Obama Vs. the G20."

Descriptions of this photo mentioned the anticapitalists, environmentalists, and anarchists demonstrating outside the G-20 meeting in London in April 2009. What impressions does the photo give you?

For Class Discussion

1. Based on the people's clothing and expressions, the background and their placard, how would you describe their values and purpose?

2. Journalists reported the frustration, anger, and even violence of protestors. Research the newspaper coverage of this event and contrast the photos you find with the scene shown in this photo. What differences do you see in the image of the protestors depicted in several photos? What argument from the people's perspective does the photo shown here support?

Julie Sell/MCT/Landov

3. What does this photo contribute to readers' understanding of the response in Europe to the global financial crisis and the leaders who convened to explore solutions to it?

4. What arguments in this chapter might this photo support? What arguments might it challenge? ∎

A Stimulus Package for the World
Robert B. Zoellick

Robert B. Zoellick, who has a law degree from Harvard Law School and a masters degree in public policy from the Kennedy School of Government, has alternated between political and economic leadership positions in government and the private sector. In the periods of 1985–1993 and 2001–2006, he served as U.S. Trade Representative and Deputy Secretary of the U.S. State Department. In these capacities, he promoted regional and global bilateral free trade agreements between the United States and over fourteen countries. He has worked to expand the membership of the World Trade Organization and has helped initiate the Doha Development Agenda of the WTO. The goal of this negotiation is to make free trade more equitable for developing countries by removing the trade barriers of developed countries. In the private sector, Zoellick has been Executive Vice President of Fannie Mae and Vice Chairman, International, of the Goldman Sachs Group. In 2007, Zoellick became the president of the World Bank, one of the main institutions of global financial governance with a membership of 185 countries. He frequently conducts press conferences and delivers policy statements. This op-ed piece appeared in the *New York Times* on January 23, 2009.

How would you describe the motivating occasion and Zoellick's purpose in this op-ed piece?

Within his first 100 days, President Obama will attend his inaugural global summit meeting: an April gathering of the Group of 20 industrialized and developing nations in London. The president, with bipartisan backing in Congress, should send an audacious signal of hope. Starting with the United States, Mr. Obama should call for each developed country to pledge 0.7 percent of its stimulus package to a vulnerability fund for assisting developing countries that can't afford bailouts and deficits.

The United States could begin by pledging some $6 billion of its own $825 billion stimulus package—just 4 percent of what was provided to American International Group. With this modest step, the United States would speed up global recovery, help the world's poor and bolster its foreign policy influence.

There is no time to waste. The economic crisis has already pushed an estimated 100 million people back into poverty. Slumping exports have helped imperil the jobs of workers around the world. In many places foreign and domestic investment is frozen. So far we have avoided the currency collapses of 1997 and 1998, but 2009 will be a dangerous year.

The good news is that if Mr. Obama sends the right signal, many countries are likely to contribute to a vulnerability fund. British Prime Minister Gordon Brown has expressed interest in the idea. Last year President Nicolas Sarkozy of France called for an increase in aid, and has taken a particular interest in Africa. Chancellor Angela Merkel of Germany wants to help finance construction projects in poor countries.

Japan has already pledged to help the World Bank recapitalize banks in poor countries. Australia and Russia have supported a food vulnerability fund that we created last year. Canada has been increasing its aid; the European Commission has been debating over contributing more assistance. Last year, Saudi Arabia gave an emergency $500 million grant to the World Food Program.

Italy, as the host of the Group of 8 industrialized nations finance ministers' meeting next month, should pave the way for the Group of 20 meeting by making the drive for a vulnerability fund a priority. The World Bank, with the United Nations and regional development banks, could then manage the fund to facilitate fast and flexible aid delivery, backed by safeguards to ensure that the money is well spent.

There are three priorities for vulnerability fund investments. First, we need safety net programs that are aligned with the developing country's ability to put them to good use. Over the past year as food and fuel prices soared, the World Bank worked with United Nations agencies to increase food-for-work programs, seed and fertilizer projects, maternal and child nutrition programs and other assistance. We have committed nearly $1.2 billion for projects like a school meals program for more than 30,000 children in Haiti, a cash-for-work program in Sierra Leone for road work and drainage, and grants for farmers in Rwanda to buy fertilizer. These investments in health, education and nutrition are more than just temporary poverty relief. They are investments in human capital. The vulnerability fund would help expand these modest shock absorbers for the poor.

Second, investments in infrastructure can yield huge benefits. Just look at China, which demonstrated 10 years ago that wisely chosen infrastructure projects can create jobs while building a foundation for productivity and growth. The World Bank is increasing support for such projects to $15 billion a year over the next three years. This includes financing for low-carbon technology projects as well as public-private partnerships that will create jobs while improving the delivery of basic services.

Third, the vulnerability fund would help support small and medium-sized enterprises and microfinance institutions. Small businesses are the most dynamic and flexible employers, and the best safety net is a job. Small businesses operate where Wall Street, and even Main Street, give way to villages with no streets. The credit contraction squeezes out small businesses and their lenders, while state-owned enterprises and big companies get bailed out. The World Bank has already responded to the global crisis with plans to recapitalize small banks in developing countries, as well as by providing credit lines for microfinance institutions that serve the poorest people. The vulnerability fund would continue these initiatives.

The conventional wisdom is that Congress can't be bothered with foreign assistance. In reality, prodded by churches, schools and community groups, both Democrats and Republicans have generously backed well-run programs to improve nutrition and fight hunger, AIDS, malaria and tuberculosis. Congress has supported microfinance and small business development worldwide. There is an additional incentive for America to help: building projects abroad are likely to increase demand for American-made equipment.

Poor people in Africa should not pay the price for a crisis that originated in America. The total aid from developed countries is about $100 billion a year, a modest sum in light of developing countries' needs. The United Nations target for aid is 0.7 percent of an economy. The United States contribution is about 0.2 percent, although polls consistently show the American public is willing to contribute much more.

Support for a vulnerability fund can help limit the depth and length of the international downturn, prevent the contagion of social unrest and help save a generation from a new poverty trap. For less than 1 percent of America's stimulus package, President Obama can lead the G-20 in London and reintroduce America to the world.

For Class Discussion

1. What is the core of Zoellick's proposal argument?

2. What resistance does he anticipate and seek to overcome?

3. How do Zoellick's tone and approach in this argument suit the *New York Times* readership? Start with what he assumes that his readers know and what values he shares with them. Where does he appeal to the self-interest of his readers?

4. What are Zoellick's strongest rhetorical strategies in this short piece? Where did you find his reasoning persuasive?

5. What global dimensions of the financial crisis does Zoellick inspire you to investigate further?

How Capitalism Will Save Us
Steve Forbes

Steve Forbes, one of the most prominent leaders in the U.S. and global business community, is president and CEO of Forbes and editor-in-chief of *Forbes* magazine, the nation's foremost business magazine with a circulation close to a million. Forbes now has other publications, including *Forbes Global* and *ForbesLife Executive Woman*, *Gilder Technology Report* and the online media source Forbes.com. As an undergraduate at Princeton University, Steve Forbes launched *Business Today*, the largest circulating student-oriented business magazine. In 1996 and 2000, Forbes challenged contenders Bob Dole and George Bush for the Republican nomination for the Presidency. Forbes is highly regarded in the conservative business community for his economic predictions in his "Fact and Comment" editorials like this one, which appeared in the November 10, 2008, edition of *Forbes*.

> Steve Forbes' editorial makes several nested causal and proposal arguments. What causal explanation of the global economic crisis does Steve Forbes offer in this editorial, and how does it shape the solution he proposes?

We are experiencing the devastating consequences of a chain of major economic policy errors, which, to use a current cliché, created the perfect storm. These government blunders temporarily paralyzed the global credit system and are now sending the U.S. and Europe into recession, while sharply cutting back Asia's growth rates.

Left to its own devices, the credit crisis, which began in August 2007, would have crushed economies as severely as did the Great Depression.

Belatedly, but thankfully, governments recognized that the only way to get credit flowing again was for them to make quick and direct massive infusions of new equity into beleaguered banks, as well as commit to other emergency measures hitherto unimaginable.

If sensible rescue efforts continue—and they will—the immediate crisis will quickly pass. Shell-shocked businesses and consumers won't recover rapidly from the trauma of recent months, especially as we now cope with recession. But the downturn shouldn't be prolonged: The economy here and those overseas should start to pick up no later than next spring.

That soon? Despite the crisis, the global economy still retains enormous strengths. Between the early 1980s and 2007 we lived in an economic Golden Age. Never before have so many people advanced so far economically in so short a period of time as they have during the last 25 years. Until the credit crisis, 70 million people a year were joining the middle class. The U.S. kicked off this long boom with the economic reforms of Ronald Reagan, particularly his enormous income tax cuts. We burst from the economic stagnation of the 1970s into a dynamic, innovative, high-tech-oriented economy. Even in recent years the much-maligned U.S. did well. Between year-end 2002 and year-end 2007 U.S. growth exceeded the entire size of China's economy. Obviously China's growth rates were higher, but China was coming off a much smaller base.

The world is flush with cash. It's frozen because of fear, but the cash is there. Productivity gains are burgeoning.

So, will this global boom resume next year, slowly at first and then with increasing momentum? It should. Whether that happens, however, depends on the next, highly dangerous phase: the political aftermath.

Will we and other countries pursue policies that hinder growth and retard or abort a full-blown recovery, e.g., regulations that stifle innovation and taxes that harm the creation and deployment of capital? Washington politicians are asking: If the federal government can bail out banks, why not other battered businesses? Congress recently voted for $25 billion in loan guarantees aimed at helping Detroit automakers. (This money is to be used not only to aid Detroit but also to prevent another flare-up of the credit crisis. If the Big Three defaulted on their debts, holders of credit default swaps—which in recent years have grown like toxic weeds—would demand payment from those who wrote the insurance on the automakers' bonds. This would create another wave of losses for financial institutions.)

Some liberal political activists are advocating using Washington's new powers to pursue other agendas, such as forcing tighter emissions curbs or mandating costly health insurance coverage. New attempts to restrict corporate pay, at least in some sectors, is a given—overlooking the unintended side effects of Bill Clinton's attempt to limit CEO pay packages back in 1993. (The deductibility of CEOs' salaries was capped, which led companies to use stock options as never before.) Protectionists are renewing calls for trade restrictions in the name of consumer safety and promoting "better" labor and environmental standards. Politically resurgent labor unions and other activists will push for rules on who sits on corporate boards to "better represent consumers and investors." They want an implicit veto power over the policies of publicly held companies. They're also ready to remove barriers, such as the secret ballot, in order to coerce workers into joining unions.

The financial sector will certainly face new rules and regulations. Will these be sensible, such as rationalizing our myriad, overlapping financial regulatory structures and pushing for the creation of exchanges and clearinghouses for exotic instruments, such as credit default swaps, so we have transparency and standardization? Or will they be punitive and costly like the Sarbanes-Oxley Act? Washington's new powers over banks may make our capital markets more hostile to entrepreneurs— savings bonds won't give you high returns, but they will protect you from political fallout. Or, as happened with Fannie Mae and Freddie Mac, will they make banks do things for political not economic reasons?

A chilling result of the crisis will be furthering the deadly process of criminalizing business failures. In the old days when an enterprise failed, the proprietors often ended up in debtors' prison. One of the significant advances of civilization and economic progress was the idea of limited liability, which took hold in the 19th century: Investors would be liable only for the money they actually put into a corporation; their other assets would be safe. If an enterprise failed, they lost only what they had invested. Limited liability thereby set off a positive explosion of risk taking. Our standard of living today would be where it was in the 1850s were it not for the wide use of limited liability.

> **A chilling result of the crisis will be furthering the criminalizing of business failures.**

But in recent years, particularly after the Enron/WorldCom corporate scandals, federal and local prosecutors began actively pursuing evidence of fraud whenever a big business went bust. Yes, there has been corporate wrongdoing, and miscreants have been tried and jailed. But many noncriminal individuals have been pursued.

One notorious case was the IRS's attempt to prosecute KPMG and a number of its partners and employees for alleged tax fraud. The shelters KPMG sold in the 1990s were not illegal. The IRS still determined, however, that they weren't valid. That kind of tax dispute would normally be settled in civil court. Instead, prosecutors threatened KPMG with annihilation: Settle on our terms or we will hit you with an enterprise-killing indictment. Arthur Andersen had recently been destroyed by such an indictment, even though the courts subsequently threw the charges out. The feds even pressured KPMG not to pay the legal bills of the targeted individuals—which would have forced these people to settle, as they couldn't afford the massive legal costs of defending themselves. Thankfully, a courageous federal judge stopped this abuse.

But the itch to indict remains. No sooner had Bear Stearns, Lehman Brothers and AIG gone bust than criminal investigators swarmed in. They will find evidence of "fraud"—why didn't you more aggressively mark down the value of suspect paper even if there wasn't a market for it? Why the expressions of confidence in the soundness of your businesses when the rumors of trouble were surfacing? Lost in all this will be the fact that Lehman and AIG didn't know they were in mortal peril until almost the very end. There will be indictments. The chilling lesson: Unsuccessful risk taking or failing in business can send you to prison.

So what *should* our responses be now? To answer that, we must first understand the crisis' causes.

What started in August 2007 was not the failure of free markets but the outcome of bad government actions. Greed and recklessness always run rampant during bubbles, and the mania that engulfed housing and much of the financial sector was no exception. The behavior of mortgage bankers and of Wall Street packagers of subprime mortgages, as well as the excesses and misuses of exotic instruments, will be grist for investigators and writers for decades to come. But all this came about because of government errors—regulatory and monetary.

In 2004 the Federal Reserve made a fateful miscalculation. It thought the U.S. economy was much weaker than it was and therefore pumped out excessive liquidity and kept interest rates artificially low. When too much money is printed, the first area to feel it is commodities. Thus the Fed begat a global commodities boom. The price of oil, copper, steel, international shipping—even mud—shot up. The price of gold roared above its average of the previous 12 years. For nearly 4 years the dollar sank against the euro, yen and pound. Domestically the already booming housing market went on steroids. Housing was experiencing above-average price rises because of a favorable change in the tax law in 1998 that virtually eliminated capital gains taxes on the sale of most primary residences. Now with money easy, a bubble mentality took hold. The reasoning was that housing prices always go up; therefore, lending standards could be safely lowered. If a dodgy borrower defaulted, it didn't matter— the value of the house would always be higher. Wall Street's appetite for these fee-generating packages of subprime mortgages became gluttonous. Rating agencies also drank the Kool-Aid and gave AAA ratings to this stuff, which, thanks to securitization, was spread all around the world. The Fed and other bank regulators stood by as the bubble ballooned.

Why didn't the Treasury Department—behind the scenes—tell the Fed to strengthen the enfeebled greenback? Because the Bush Administration likes a weak dollar, feeling that it will improve our trade balance by artificially making our exports cheaper. Not since Jimmy Carter has the U.S. had such a weak-dollar Administration. This mania would never have reached the proportions it did had the Fed and Treasury had a strong-dollar policy.

The housing bubble burst in 2007, and banks and investors began to be fearful—who had this junk, and how much did they hold? The credit system showed the first signs of panic. The Federal Reserve responded with another round of easy money, thus creating yet another commodities bubble. Finally, this summer, the Fed ceased spraying money like a fire hose. Dollars that had been lent out through the Fed's various borrowing facilities were then soaked up in its open-market operations. That's why, when the panic reached a peak this fall, gold prices didn't go through the roof as everyone sought safety. In fact, gold never reached the level it had in July.

Maybe, just maybe, Ben Bernanke has learned a lesson about the need for stable money that his predecessor, Alan Greenspan, never did.

Another factor fanning the housing bubble was Fannie Mae and Freddie Mac. They were smarting from studies (including a couple from the Federal Reserve) concluding that these two "government-sponsored enterprises" had little or no positive impact on helping the housing market. And they were also reeling politically from egregious accounting scandals. The companies, therefore, decided they could justify their existence by becoming champions of "affordable housing." They guaranteed $1 trillion of less-than-prime mortgages and kept more than $100 billion of this suspect paper on their balance sheets. Mortgage banks and Wall Street packagers of securities knew that Fannie and Freddie were there to buy whatever questionable stuff they offered up.

Over the years efforts by a handful of senators and representatives to rein in these two monsters were easily brushed off, as were those of the Fed to have them shrink their mammoth sizes. (Of course, now that the bubble has burst, what was once dubbed as promoting affordable housing is being portrayed as "predatory lending.")

> **What was once promoting affordable housing is now "predatory lending."**

Even with Fannie and Freddie inflating the bubble and the Fed and the rest of the Bush Administration weakening the dollar, the crisis never would have become so unprecedentedly destructive but for a seemingly arcane accounting principle called mark-to-market, or fair value, accounting. The idea seems harmless: Financial institutions should adjust their balance sheets and their capital accounts when the market value of the financial assets they hold goes up or down. That works when you have very liquid securities, such as Treasurys or the common stock of IBM or GE. But when the credit crisis hit there was *no* market for subprime securities. Yet regulators and lawsuit-fearful auditors pressed banks and other financial firms to relentlessly knock down the book value of this subprime paper, even in cases where these obligations were being serviced in the payment of principal and interest. Mark-to-market became *the* weapon of mass destruction.

When banks wrote down the value of these assets they had to get new capital. The need for new capital was a signal to ratings agencies that these outfits might be in need of a credit-rating reduction. This forced financial firms to increase collateral for credit default swaps— which meant more calls for new capital.

Result: Investment banks that still had positive cash flows found themselves in a death spiral. Of the $600-plus billion that financial institutions have written off, almost all of it has been *book* writedowns, not actual *cash* losses. This accounting madness sank Fannie and Freddie this summer when the government effectively took them over and provided them with a $200 billion loan facility. The two entities are still cash positive and haven't drawn down a dime of this new line of credit.

Rigid mark-to-market accounting is similar to a highway that has a speed limit and a speed minimum. When snow appears on the road, bad road conditions cause drivers to go slowly. Under a mark-to-market concept, police would be ticketing these slow drivers for going below the minimum speed.

If this accounting asininity had been in effect during the banking trouble in the early 1990s, almost every major commercial bank in the U.S. would have collapsed. We would have had a second Great Depression.

Congress has made it clear that it wants mark-to-market suspended or abolished, but the SEC and the Treasury Department still refuse to meaningfully modify it. This is the one big piece of business left undone in ending the credit crisis.

The final factor in this perfect storm was short-sellers. They quickly saw how mark-to-market made seemingly impregnable companies vulnerable to destruction. They picked their targets and relentlessly sold financial stocks short. The SEC helped them out. In the summer of 2007 the commission abolished the uptick rule, which held that a stock couldn't be shorted unless it had gone up in price. It's no surprise to anyone but the SEC that market volatility exploded after the uptick rule ceased. There were no speed bumps left when shorts went after a stock.

Compounding this lunacy was the SEC's inexplicable failure to enforce the rule against "naked" short-selling. Before an investor can short a stock, he is supposed to borrow the shares and pay a broker or stockholder a fee. What sellers soon realized was that the SEC was turning a blind eye to naked short-selling, thus adding even more pressures to beleaguered bank equities.

As the crisis progressed, Treasury errors didn't help, particularly its policy of virtually wiping out the value of Bear Stearns's common stock. With that precedent set, shareholders knew that at the merest whiff of a bad rumor they'd better bail out of a bank or insurance company, or their money could be obliterated. That's why Fannie's and Freddie's stocks collapsed so quickly, not to mention those of Lehman Brothers, AIG and Wachovia.

Letting Lehman Brothers fail was also a blunder. The fallout vastly exceeded what would have come down if Bear Stearns had filed for bankruptcy. Had the Treasury not announced in mid-September that it would seek a $700 billion bailout facility, Morgan Stanley and Goldman Sachs would have been destroyed as well.

BLAME THE VICTIM

Not surprisingly, despite government's big, basic blunders in this debacle, politicos and much of the media are blaming "excessive deregulation." "A free-market failure," they call it.

We've been here before. The experiences of the two big economic disasters of the 20th century—the Great Depression in the 1930s and the great inflation of the 1970s—dramatically demonstrate how government mistakes can lead to economic stagnation or impoverishment and geopolitical disaster. Both of these economic horrors were blamed on greedy corporations and "economic royalists."

The Depression was actually triggered by the Smoot-Hawley Tariff of 1929–30, which imposed massive taxes on countless imports. Other countries retaliated in kind. The global trading system collapsed. International capital flows dried up. The legislative history of Smoot-Hawley is instructive. When it first surfaced in Congress during the fall of 1929, the stock market cratered. When near the end of 1929 it appeared that Smoot-Hawley was being sidetracked, stocks rallied, ending the year almost where they had begun. But then in early 1930 Smoot-Hawley resurfaced, and stocks resumed their slide, which continued after Smoot-Hawley was signed into law that June. A devastating global contraction ensued.

Compounding that error was the U.S.'s giant tax increase in 1932. President Herbert Hoover thought a balanced budget would restore confidence. The top income tax rate was raised from 25% to 63%. Hoover even legislated an excise tax on checks—you had to pay Uncle Sam a fee every time you wrote a check. Not surprisingly, strapped consumers withdrew massive amounts of cash from banks in order to conduct their business, which put even more stress on troubled banks. This check tax was one of the factors leading to the bank closures of 1933. The huge tax increase deepened the U.S. economic slump.

If not for the Depression, Hitler would never have come to power—the Nazis had carried only 2% of the vote in 1928.

The 1970s were a decade of stagnation. The U.S. cut the dollar loose from gold, and other central banks gleefully followed suit. The results were three massive bouts of inflation, each more severe than the one before. The U.S. turned inward. Communism seemed ascendant. Nicaragua fell to a pro-Soviet dictatorship, and its neighbors looked likely to follow. Islamic fanatics seized power in Iran.

By the time Ronald Reagan took office, our military was in a shambles, with the U.S. seen as fatally weak. Our economy was in dreadful shape, with short-term interest rates reaching nearly 21%. But Reagan pursued the right policies. The American economy came booming back, and the U.S. won the Cold War, signaled by the fall of the Berlin Wall.

Okay, now that we are finally effectively dealing with the crisis, what should be done going forward?

A formal strong-dollar policy is essential. Economists gag at the thought, but the best barometer of monetary disturbances is gold. The Fed should tie the dollar to a gold price range of, say, $500 to $550. Though the dollar is stronger today, markets rightly fear that monetary blunders will happen again.

Which brings us to the Fed's enormous new powers, not to mention its current ones. Our central bank is now the U.S.'s de facto commercial bank *and* our commercial paper market. It is bailing out private firms. The necessary change here is simple: After the crisis, the Fed must undergo a dramatic downsizing and be given a *focused* mission. Otherwise, it'll be a dinosaur-size beast that will severely hurt our country. The Fed is politically unaccountable. Yes, its chairman makes periodic appearances before Congress, but the Fed is not dependent on congressional appropriations. It literally prints its own budget. It pays for its operations out of the interest it receives on all the securities it holds and then remits the rest to Uncle Sam. Talk about the ATM that keeps on giving. In a democracy this is an intolerable situation for an agency that now has such enormous power over the American economy.

The big change—the Federal Reserve should have only two missions. They are: keeping the dollar as good as gold and dealing with financial panics. If it does the dollar part right, a panic should be a once-in-a-century occurrence.

Years ago Congress mandated that the Fed do its part to keep unemployment low and the economy growing. But it is truly preposterous to think this bureaucracy can direct a $13 trillion economy. Look at how impotent the Fed has been in resolving the financial troubles of the past 14 months.

Regulating banks? Clearing checks for banks (which the Fed still does)? Leave those tasks to other agencies.

The dollar must be a fixed measure of value. Changing its value is disruptive, similar to repeatedly changing the number of minutes in an hour or inches in a foot. Since the dollar was cut off from gold nearly 40 years ago, the U.S. and the world have had repeated monetary disruptions. Thanks to the ingenuity of free markets we've still achieved enormous progress. But the pernicious idea that manipulating money is a sound economic tool has repeatedly wrought havoc: the great inflation of the 1970s; the stock market crash of 1987 (which was triggered when the U.S. threatened to let the dollar go into a free fall); the 1994 Mexican peso crisis; the 1997 Asian "contagion," which gratuitously battered the entire Pacific Rim; and the 1998 Russian financial collapse.

Cutting tax rates is also a necessity. Political cultures have a hard time understanding that taxes don't just raise revenue, they are also a price and a burden. The tax you pay on income is the price you pay for working, just as the tax on capital gains is the price you pay for taking risks that work out and the tax on profits is the price you pay for success. If you make it more worthwhile for people to work productively and take risks, they will do so. Rebates are useless—they don't change incentives the way lower tax rates do. Ideally, we should enact a simple flat tax. Twenty-five countries have adopted some form of a flat tax, all successfully.

Economic growth will help prevent another financial time bomb—credit default swaps, a form of debt insurance—from exploding. The nominal amount peaked at $62 trillion and is now down to $55 trillion. Renewed prosperity will enable big companies to service their debts, thus nullifying the need to ever collect on the insurance. Most of these swaps will expire within five years.

Sensible, not punitive, regulations in the financial sector are needed, such as standardization of new financial products so that there is more transparency.

Fannie and Freddie should be broken up into a number of new, recapitalized companies that have no ties to Uncle Sam.

If we have the kind of policies that marked the 1980s and not the kind that marked the 1930s and 1970s, we will be in for a dazzling era of innovation and economic advances. Free-market capitalism will save us—if we let it.

For Class Discussion

1. Where specifically does Forbes assume his audience's familiarity with the language of finance and investment? Using two major Web resources, www.Investorwords.com and BusinessDictionary.com, create a working definition of "limited liability," "liquidity," "mark-to-market," and other unfamiliar terms.

2. On its Web site, the U.S. Securities and Exchange Commission voices its mission "to protect investors, maintain fair, orderly, and efficient markets, and facilitate capital formation." For an audience outside the business community, how does Forbes try to make his claim—that businesses should not be punished for deals that damage the public—persuasive?

3. How does Forbes negotiate a position between pushing for a different kind of role for government in business than we have had in the last ten years and advocating freedom for capitalism? How does he support his claim that the crisis was caused by "government errors—regulatory and monetary"?

4. How effectively does Forbes use arguing from precedent—that is, using historical reasoning about the Smoot-Hawley Tariff of 1929–1930? How

does he intend his reference to the rise of Hitler before World War II to work in his argument? What political-economic moves does he oppose?

5. How would you argue against Forbes's view? What interpretation of facts about the measurement of economic growth, the growth of the middle class, and the effectiveness of free-market capitalism might opponents offer to counter Forbes' argument?   ▮

All of Them Must Go
Naomi Klein

Naomi Klein is an internationally known Canadian social activist, feminist, journalist, and author of popular controversial books exposing the damaging effects of free trade ideology and corporate globalization: *No Logo: Taking Aim at the Brand Bullies* (2000); *Fences and Windows: Dispatches from the Front Line of the Globalization Debate* (2002); and *The Shock Doctrine: The Rise of Disaster Capitalism* (2007). She has written for *The Globe and Mail* of Canada; she now writes regular columns for the liberal U.S. news commentary magazine *The Nation* and Britain's liberal publication *The Guardian.* This editorial appeared in *The Nation* on February 23, 2009.

> How does Klein display her knowledge of the global scope of the conflict between, on the one hand, political and corporate decision makers, and on the other, the mass of global citizens who have to live with the results of their decisions?

Watching the crowds in Iceland banging pots and pans until their government fell reminded me of a chant popular in anti-capitalist circles back in 2002: "You are Enron. We are Argentina."

Its message was simple enough. You—politicians and CEOs huddled at some trade summit—are like the reckless scamming execs at Enron (of course, we didn't know the half of it). We—the rabble outside—are like the people of Argentina, who, in the midst of an economic crisis eerily similar to our own, took to the street banging pots and pans. They shouted, *"¡Que se vayan todos!"* ("All of them must go!") and forced out a procession of four presidents in less than three weeks. What made Argentina's 2001–02 uprising unique was that it wasn't directed at a particular political party or even at corruption in the abstract. The target was the dominant economic model—this was the first national revolt against contemporary deregulated capitalism.

It's taken a while, but from Iceland to Latvia, South Korea to Greece, the rest of the world is finally having its *¡Que se vayan todos!* moment.

The stoic Icelandic matriarchs beating their pots flat even as their kids ransack the fridge for projectiles (eggs, sure, but *yogurt*?) echo the tactics made famous in Buenos Aires. So does the collective rage at elites who trashed a once thriving country and thought they could get away with it. As Gudrun Jonsdottir, a 36-year-old Icelandic office worker, put it: "I've just had enough of this whole thing. I don't trust the government, I don't trust the banks, I don't trust the political parties and I don't trust the IMF. We had a good country, and they ruined it."

Another echo: in Reykjavik, the protesters clearly won't be bought off by a mere change of face at the top (even if the new PM *is* a lesbian). They want aid for people, not just banks; criminal investigations into the debacle; and deep electoral reform.

Similar demands can be heard these days in Latvia, whose economy has contracted more sharply than any country in the EU, and where the government is teetering on the brink. For weeks the capital has been rocked by protests, including a full-blown, cobblestone-hurling riot on January 13. As in Iceland, Latvians are appalled by their leaders' refusal to take any responsibility for the mess. Asked by Bloomberg TV what caused the crisis, Latvia's finance minister shrugged: "Nothing special."

But Latvia's troubles are indeed special: the very policies that allowed the "Baltic Tiger" to grow at a rate of 12 percent in 2006 are also causing it to contract violently by a projected 10 percent this year: money, freed of all barriers, flows out as quickly as it flows in, with plenty being diverted to political pockets. (It is no coincidence that many of today's basket cases are yesterday's "miracles": Ireland, Estonia, Iceland, Latvia.)

Something else Argentina-esque is in the air. In 2001 Argentina's leaders responded to the crisis with a brutal International Monetary Fund-prescribed austerity package: $9 billion in spending cuts, much of it hitting health and education. This proved to be a fatal mistake. Unions staged a general strike, teachers moved their classes to the streets and the protests never stopped.

This same bottom-up refusal to bear the brunt of the crisis unites many of today's protests. In Latvia, much of the popular rage has focused on government austerity measures—mass layoffs, reduced social services and slashed public sector salaries—all to qualify for an IMF emergency loan (no, nothing has changed). In Greece, December's riots followed a police shooting of a 15-year-old. But what's kept them going, with farmers taking the lead from students, is widespread rage at the government's crisis response: banks got a $36 billion bailout while workers got their pensions cut and farmers received next to nothing. Despite the inconvenience caused by tractors blocking roads, 78 percent of Greeks say the farmers' demands are reasonable. Similarly, in France the recent general strike—triggered in part by President Sarkozy's plans to reduce the number of teachers dramatically—inspired the support of 70 percent of the population.

Perhaps the sturdiest thread connecting this global backlash is a rejection of the logic of "extraordinary politics"—the phrase coined by Polish politician Leszek Balcerowicz to describe how, in a crisis, politicians can ignore legislative rules and rush through unpopular "reforms." That trick is getting tired, as South Korea's government recently discovered. In December, the ruling party tried to use the crisis to ram through a highly controversial free trade agreement with the United States. Taking closed-door politics to new extremes, legislators locked themselves in the chamber so they could vote in private, barricading the door with desks, chairs and couches.

Opposition politicians were having none of it: with sledgehammers and an electric saw, they broke in and staged a twelve-day sit-in of Parliament. The vote was delayed, allowing for more debate—a victory for a new kind of "extraordinary politics."

Here in Canada, politics is markedly less YouTube-friendly—but it has still been surprisingly eventful. In October the Conservative Party won national elections on an unambitious platform. Six weeks later, our Tory prime minister found his inner ideologue, presenting a budget bill that stripped public sector workers of the right to strike, canceled public funding for political parties and contained no economic stimulus. Opposition parties responded by forming a historic coalition that was only prevented from taking power by an abrupt suspension of Parliament. The Tories have just come back with a revised budget: the pet right-wing policies have disappeared, and it is packed with economic stimulus.

The pattern is clear: governments that respond to a crisis created by free-market ideology with an acceleration of that same discredited agenda will not survive to tell the tale. As Italy's students have taken to shouting in the streets: "We won't pay for your crisis!"

For Class Discussion

1. What is Klein's main claim in this argument?

2. How does she use historical precedent and numerous examples to support her claim in this piece? How persuasive is this evidence?

3. What clues in Klein's writing reveal that she is writing for an audience sympathetic to her views?

4. What gives this piece the tone of a political rally? What would Klein like her audience to do after reading her argument?

5. What events and issues does Klein inspire you to explore further?   ■

The Open-Door Bailout
Thomas L. Friedman

Thomas L. Friedman, a Pulitzer-prize winning journalist, is the foreign affairs writer for the *New York Times* and a nationally syndicated columnist. He has authored three major popular books that are influencing the public's view of globalization: *The Lexus and the Olive Tree: Understanding Globalization* (1999), *The World Is Flat: A Brief History of the Twenty-first Century* (2005); and *Hot, Flat, and Crowded: Why We Need a Green Revolution—and How It Can Renew America* (2008). Friedman analyzes globalization as a new phenomenon: ". . . what is new today is the degree and intensity with which the world is being tied together into a single globalized marketplace and village. What is also new is the sheer number of people and countries able to partake of today's globalized economy and information networks, and to be affected by them."* This op-ed piece appeared in the *New York Times* on February 11, 2009, and was reprinted in other national newspapers.

What argument does Friedman make in favor of more H-1B visas?

Bangalore, India—Leave it to a brainy Indian to come up with the cheapest and surest way to stimulate our economy: immigration.

"All you need to do is grant visas to two million Indians, Chinese and Koreans," said Shekhar Gupta, editor of *The Indian Express* newspaper. "We will buy up all the subprime homes. We will work 18 hours a day to pay for them. We will immediately improve your savings rate— no Indian bank today has more than 2 percent nonperforming loans because not paying your mortgage is considered shameful here. And we will start new companies to create our own jobs and jobs for more Americans."

While his tongue was slightly in cheek, Gupta and many other Indian business people I spoke to this week were trying to make a point that sometimes non-Americans can make best: "Dear America, please remember how you got to be the wealthiest country in history. It wasn't through protectionism, or state-owned banks or fearing free trade. No, the formula was very simple: build this really flexible, really open economy, tolerate creative destruction so dead capital is quickly redeployed to better ideas and companies, pour into it the most diverse, smart and energetic immigrants from every corner of the world and then stir and repeat, stir and repeat, stir and repeat, stir and repeat."

While I think President Obama has been doing his best to keep the worst protectionist impulses in Congress out of his stimulus plan, the U.S. Senate unfortunately voted on Feb. 6 to restrict banks and other

---

The Lexus and the Olive Tree: Understanding Globalization (New York: Random House, 1999), xvii.

financial institutions that receive taxpayer bailout money from hiring high-skilled immigrants on temporary work permits known as H-1B visas.

Bad signal. In an age when attracting the first-round intellectual draft choices from around the world is the most important competitive advantage a knowledge economy can have, why would we add barriers against such brainpower—anywhere? That's called "Old Europe." That's spelled: S-T-U-P-I-D.

"If you do this, it will be one of the best things for India and one of the worst for Americans, [because] Indians will be forced to innovate at home," said Subhash B. Dhar, a member of the executive council that runs Infosys, the well-known Indian technology company that sends Indian workers to the U.S. to support a wide range of firms. "We protected our jobs for many years and look where it got us. Do you know that for an Indian company, it is still easier to do business with a company in the U.S. than it is to do business today with another Indian state?"

Each Indian state tries to protect its little economy with its own rules. America should not be trying to copy that. "Your attitude," said Dhar, should be "'whoever can make us competitive and dominant, let's bring them in.'"

If there is one thing we know for absolute certain, it's this: Protectionism did not cause the Great Depression, but it sure helped to make it "Great." From 1929 to 1934, world trade plunged by more than 60 percent—and we were all worse off.

We live in a technological age where every study shows that the more knowledge you have as a worker and the more knowledge workers you have as an economy, the faster your incomes will rise. Therefore, the centerpiece of our stimulus, the core driving principle, should be to stimulate everything that makes us smarter and attracts more smart people to our shores. That is the best way to create good jobs.

According to research by Vivek Wadhwa, a senior research associate at the Labor and Worklife Program at Harvard Law School, more than half of Silicon Valley start-ups were founded by immigrants over the last decade. These immigrant-founded tech companies employed 450,000 workers and had sales of $52 billion in 2005, said Wadhwa in an essay published this week on BusinessWeek.com.

He also cited a recent study by William R. Kerr of Harvard Business School and William F. Lincoln of the University of Michigan that "found that in periods when H-1B visa numbers went down, so did patent applications filed by immigrants [in the U.S.]. And when H-1B visa numbers went up, patent applications followed suit."

We don't want to come out of this crisis with just inflation, a mountain of debt and more shovel-ready jobs. We want to—we have to—come out of it with a new Intel, Google, Microsoft and Apple. I would have loved to have seen the stimulus package include a government-funded venture capital bank to help finance all the start-ups that are clearly not starting up today—in the clean-energy space they're dying like flies—because of a lack of liquidity from traditional lending sources.

Newsweek had an essay this week that began: "Could Silicon Valley become another Detroit?" Well, yes, it could. When the best brains in the world are on sale, you don't shut them out. You open your doors wider. We need to attack this financial crisis with green cards not just greenbacks, and with start-ups not just bailouts. One Detroit is enough.

For Class Discussion

1. The first quotation from *The Indian Express* ironically exaggerates and criticizes the United States. In what ways does Gupta suggest that Indians, Chinese, and Koreans are wiser than Americans?

2. What evidence does Friedman offer to support a claim about increasing rather than decreasing H-1B visas? What "authorities" does Friedman appeal to?

3. What assumptions would readers have to hold about business and economic growth to find this argument persuasive?

4. This op-ed piece appeared in U.S. newspapers under various names: "The Open-Door Bailout," "Make Greenbacks with Green Cards," and "Immigration Is the Surest Way to Stimulate the Economy." Which title do you think is most helpful in attracting a general newspaper readership to this piece and preparing readers to understand and be persuaded by the argument?

Job Fair
Mike Siegel

This photo appeared on the front page of the *Seattle Times* on February 5, 2009, accompanying a brief article titled "Job Fair Jammed: Caught in the Crunch: Living through Tough Economic Times." Mike Siegel is a *Seattle Times* staff photographer.

What are your immediate impressions of the job fair line in this photo?

For Class Discussion

1. What visual details stand out in this photo?

2. What emotional impact, rhetorical effect, timeliness, and urgency does this realistic photo have?

3. Since the fall of 2008 when the global economic crash began dominating the news, newspapers have featured articles and photos from the

Mike Siegel/The Seattle Times

Great Depression when unemployment reached 20 percent. How does this photo conjure up scenes from that economic crisis? You may want to research photos from the 1930s and compare them with this one.

4. What connections do you see between this photo and other articles in this chapter? What arguments could you see this photo supporting?

Testimony Before the Committee on Science and Technology, U.S. House of Representatives
Ralph E. Gomory

Ralph E. Gomory holds a PhD in mathematics from Princeton University. From 1959 to 1989, Gomory held various leadership positions at IBM: director of the mathematical sciences department; director of research; and vice president and senior vice president for science and technology. With eminent economist William J. Baumol, he authored the book *Global Trade and Conflicting National Interest* (2001), which is gaining traction in political circles. In addition to being president of the Albert P. Sloan Foundation—a grant-giving research organization devoted to science, technology, and the economy, he is a part of the eleven-member Horizon Project, whose mission is "to provide the new Congress with a legislative agenda to ensure that America continues to be the preeminent economic power in an era of globalization" and to prompt action in order "to stave off the erosion of our competitive advantages and the loss of the nation's middle class base" (www.horizonproject.us). This testimony before the United States House of Representatives, given on May 22, 2008, is part of that ongoing project.

What is Gomory's main claim about corporate responsibility in this argument?

Thank you for the opportunity to take part in this hearing. . . .

Some of you may remember that I testified to the full Science and Technology Committee on June 12 of last year on the subject of the globalization of R&D. At that time I stated:

> The effect on the United States of the internationalization of the scientific and technical enterprise can only be understood as one part of the revolutionary process of globalization, which is fundamentally revising the relation of companies to the countries from which they have originated. In this new era of globalization, the interests of companies and countries have diverged. *What is good for America's global corporations is no longer necessarily good for the American economy.*

My testimony today will bear on this same question, viewed in the broader context of the evolving relation of countries and companies. I will address the impact of these events on the overall ability of this country to produce a large GDP (value of the total national product), as well as on the rapidly growing problem of extreme inequality in the distribution of that national product. Nonetheless, my conclusion will be exactly the same:

> What is good for America's global corporations is no longer necessarily good for the American economy.

To see why this is so, let us review the fundamental social role that the corporation fulfills in this country and in other developed countries.

THE BASIC SOCIAL FUNCTION OF THE CORPORATION

For a very long time most of the work of the world was done on farms or in small shops. An individual could learn the printing trade or shoe-making and graduate to his own shop; a family could run a farm. In both cases an individual or very small groups of people could grow crops or make shoes that could be sold to others and thus have the money to supply what was not made at home.

But today the goods we consume cannot be made at home; they are complex and require large organizations to create them. You cannot manufacture a car in your garage; it takes a large-scale organization to do it. . . .

The same is true of services: There is no way to build your own telephone service. And even medicine, one of the last strongholds of the individual practitioner, is rapidly agglomerating into large-scale enterprises.

A person must now be part of an organization that makes or distributes the complex goods and services that people buy today. Being part of an organization is what people must do to earn a living and support themselves and their families. The fundamental social role of corporations and other businesses is to enable people to participate in the production of the goods and services that are consumed in the modern world; the corporation enables them to earn a share of the value produced for themselves and their families.

My testimony bears on the question of how well America's global corporations are fulfilling that fundamental purpose today. The whole thrust of my testimony is that in the last few decades the shift in corporate motivation toward emphasizing profits above everything else has had a deleterious effect on the way they are fulfilling that role. That deleterious effect is now being enormously accelerated through globalization.

THE ROLE OF PROFITS AND COMPETITION

Business organizations today do not proclaim the social mission that I have just described; rather, they make clear that they are there to make profits for their shareholders.

But while it is true that profit can be a creative force it is also true that emphasizing profit above everything else can be bad for the nation. Profit under the right circumstances can be an energizing force that creates GDP. But we should remember that from a national point of view, profit is a means to the end of creating GDP, not an end in itself.

THE DIVERGENCE OF THE PROFIT MOTIVE AND THE FUNDAMENTAL ROLE

Globalization has now made it possible for global corporations to pursue their profits by building capabilities abroad. *Instead of investing alongside U.S. workers and using their investment and R&D to increase their productivity, corporations today can produce goods and services abroad using low-cost labor and import those goods and services into the United States.* But in creating their profits this way, they are building up the GDP of other countries while breaking their once tight links with America's own GDP.

Economists will sometimes argue that this development of capabilities abroad is good for the U.S. economy as a whole. For one thing, we get cheaper goods. That is certainly true, but it is also true that if we lose our superior capabilities in many areas and are less competitive, we have less to trade for those goods, so that eventually the cheaper goods become expensive in real terms. I do not intend to repeat today the arguments that I have already outlined to the full committee in my earlier testimony and that are spelled out in the book on global trade and its consequences that I coauthored with Professor Will Baumol.

I would like to point out, however, that the view that the industrial development in your trading partner can be harmful to your total GDP is not new. There is a long history of well-known economists making that observation, most recently Paul Samuelson.[1] What Professor Baumol and I have added to that long history in our book *Global Trade and Conflicting National Interests* is the realization that the benefits of your trading partner's economic development occur in the early stages of its development, and as your partner becomes more fully industrialized and is no longer confined to low value-added industries, further development is harmful to your GDP.

This result, which we derive rigorously from the most standard economic models, corresponds to the intuitive notion that we do well when we lose low-wage jobs and not well when we start losing high-wage or high-tech jobs. And that is what we are seeing today. And as I said in my previous testimony, in agreeing with my co-panelist Professor Alan Blinder, there are many reasons to believe that the impact on the United States will be severe.

IN ADDITION TO THE IMPACT ON GDP, THE EFFECT OF GLOBALIZATION ON INEQUALITY

Globalization was not the beginning of the divorce between corporate profits and the economic welfare of the American people. It is rather a very large next step down a long road already traveled. To see how far we have come, let us look back 35 years.

Reginald Jones became CEO of General Electric in 1972, and shortly thereafter made two remarkable speeches to the Business Roundtable and the National Press Club.[2]

Mr. Jones said that with his appointment as CEO, he would henceforth view his responsibilities as being equally split among the company and its shareholders, employees, American industry, and the nation. This sense of broad responsibility became pervasive in American industry. In

---

[1]See References 1–6.
[2]This is summarized from Reference 7.

fact, urged on by Jones, the Business Roundtable—the organization of major company CEOs intended to look after the interests of business in the public policy arena—formally endorsed in 1981 the policy that shareholder returns had to be balanced against other considerations.

In the intervening years that view of corporate leadership has waned, largely replaced by the idea that the business of business is solely to make profits for shareholders, and that in the pursuit of profits, or shareholder value, all other values can be sacrificed.

In the decades from 1973 to now, GDP increased steadily as new technologies were introduced that increased productivity. If the gains in productivity had been reflected evenly in incomes, a typical worker would get 35% more today than in 1973. In fact, the typical worker saw a far smaller gain. Median *household* income grew about 16 percent since 1973, much of that gain being due to the fact that many households became two-earner households. So, instead of looking at households, if we look instead at individual workers—for example, men in the 35–40 age bracket—their inflation-adjusted wages have in fact decreased in real terms since 1973.

In fact the gains from productivity growth have been going to the rich—and even among the rich, primarily to the very rich—while most Americans have seen little or no growth in real wages.[3] While details can be disputed, as is the case with much economic data, the general trend toward a sharply increasing degree of inequality in incomes and wealth cannot be disputed; and we are seeing today a concentration of wealth at the very top, unmatched since the days of the so-called "robber barons" at the close of the 19th century.

And just to remove any ambiguity about what is going on, in 2004 the Business Roundtable revised its earlier position on CEO responsibility and publicly asserted that the obligation of business is only to maximize shareholder wealth.[4]

While many explanations have been brought forward for this divergence of the richer and the poorer in our country, one very simple one has received remarkably little discussion. Companies today are aimed primarily at maximizing shareholder gains, and their shares are held overwhelmingly by those who are already wealth[5] or by those, like top executives, who will become wealthy if share values go up. Corporations today are motivated to cut wages and benefits whenever they can to increase profits and shareholder value. The money saved from wages and benefits comes out of the middle and lower income groups; the gain in profits goes to the wealthy.

---

[3]This is discussed in much greater detail in Reference 8 Chapter 1, especially pages 22 and 23 and in Reference 9 Chapter 7. See also Reference 7.

[4]From Reference 7.

[5]Reference 8, page 23, states that almost 90% of shares are held by the top 20% of stock owners and has further data.

As we remarked above, important American corporations have found that the easiest way to maximize shareholder wealth today is to take their technology, know-how and capital overseas to wherever labor is cheapest and subsidies are the greatest. The capital, know-how and technology that once made American workers the most productive in the world are being transferred overseas to other workers who will do the same job for a fraction of the wage. This makes for good corporate profits, but it leaves American workers far behind. Corporate goals, as they are now being stated, have been diverging for a long time from what is good for the country. Now, however, that decades-long history of workers and more generally the middle class losing share in the productivity gains is being accelerated by globalization. In globalization, jobs leave the country altogether and only the corporate profits remain.

We need to realize that the interests of the American global corporation, whose interest is profit, and the interests of most Americans, who want a higher standard of living, have been diverging. Globalization is causing that divergence to occur faster and further than ever before.

CAN ANYTHING BE DONE?

This testimony does not pretend to take on in any systematic way the task of answering the question, "What is to be done?" I will be content if I can contribute to the clarification of some of the issues.

While the United States has no stated national strategy aimed at the goal of greater GDP, there is no lack of individual suggestions about ways to improve the U.S. economic situation vis-a-vis the more rapidly developing nations. This often translates into asking for improved K–12 education, especially in science and technology. While improved education can only do good, education improvement is hard to come by and it is hard to imagine an improvement in education so profound that it turns out Americans who are so productive that they are worth hiring in place of the four or five Asians who can be hired for the same wage.

Another emphasis is the quest for innovation, usually innovation that is closely linked to R&D [research and development]. More R&D can only help. But the role of science and technology in globalization needs to be understood. R&D does not contribute to a nation's wealth directly by employing large numbers of people in high value-added or high-wage jobs. It contributes by supporting a small number of people whose work is intended to give a competitive edge to the end product, whether that is goods or services. It is these end products, whether they are cars or computers or medical services that make up the bulk of a corporation's revenues and support the wages of its employees.

If in the process of globalization the production (or delivery in the case of services) of the good moves overseas, so do the wages. Even if R&D remains behind, the vast bulk of value creation has moved to another country, and it is there that it supports the wages of employees.

It is also hard to envision a significant industrial advantage vis-á-vis other countries derived from more university research, when a large fraction of graduate students in science are from Asian countries and return home after obtaining their advanced degrees. Understand, too, that the great global companies Intel and Microsoft have research centers in leading universities and are well positioned to spread the latest research to their labs and development sites in other countries around the world.

Proposals of this sort about education and R&D can be helpful. But they can also be harmful if they create the mistaken belief that these measures alone can deal with the problem.

Another class of suggestions points to the U.S. infrastructure, correctly observing the crumbling bridges, crowded airports, and inadequate broadband, which restricts the bit traffic of the future.* Again, addressing these domestic needs is worth doing as it does add to U.S. productivity across the board.

The main thrust of this testimony, however, points to the divergence of company goals, focused almost exclusively on profit, and the broader goals of greater GDP and less inequality in the United States. Therefore, we need to turn our attention not only to the familiar suggestions I have just listed, but also to the issue of better aligning corporate and national goals.

ALIGNING COUNTRY AND COMPANY

Some Asian countries, for example Singapore and China, have national strategies aimed at the rapid increase of their GDP. As part of that strategy they align corporate goals with their national goals. They have made it profitable for foreign (often U.S.) corporations to create high value-added jobs in their countries. They do this by offering tax and other incentives that make it *profitable* for corporations to locate high value-added jobs in their countries.

We need to consider a U.S. national economic strategy that includes incentives for companies to have high value-added jobs in the United States. If we want high value-added jobs, let us reward our companies for producing such jobs—whether they do that through R&D and advanced technology, or by just plain American ingenuity applied in any setting whatsoever.

---

*All computer information is stored as bits.

The Asian countries have done this usually by individual deals with individual companies. We have neither the tradition nor the knowledge nor the inclination in the U.S. government to do that. An approach that is better suited to what the United States can do would be to use the corporate income tax. We have already used the corporate income tax to spur R&D, so why not apply it to directly reward what we are aiming at—high value-added jobs?

For example, the corporate tax rate could be scaled by the value added per fulltime employee, by the workers of corporations operating in the United States. A company with high value-add per U.S. employee would get a low rate, a company with low value-add per U.S. employee would get a high rate. . . .

Critics may say that our national economic strategy is, in fact, to leave markets alone and take whatever free markets produce. They may also suggest that this is the best possible economic strategy. But "free market" is not a single, simple concept. Do we mean free markets with or without antitrust laws, with or without child-labor laws or with or without the ability for labor to organize? Do we mean free markets that do or don't have access to government sponsored research, etc., etc? The presence or absence or degree of these restrictions or abilities will produce very different results, all coming from "free markets"; as will different tax policies or special loans for special industries, and so on and so on.

On the subject of government incentives, a present day General Electric CEO Jeffrey Immelt recently stated[6]:

If the U.S. government "wants to fix the trade deficit, it's got to be pushed," he said. "GE wants to be an exporter. We want to be a good citizen. Do we want to make a lot of money? Sure we do. But I think at the end of the day we've got to have a tax system or a set of incentives that promote what the government wants to do."

ON INEQUALITY

In this part of my testimony I have discussed mainly total GDP. But we have seen that who benefits from GDP is important too and that globalization affects the distribution of GDP wealth as well as the total GDP.

So far I have discussed mainly increasing GDP. But there is also the question of extreme inequality, the concentration of wealth and power, and the influence over government that goes with it.

To reduce the natural forces working toward extreme inequality we should obviously consider what can be done through taxes,

---

[6]See Interview in Reference 10.

individual or corporate, but also consider charters for corporations that require consideration of other factors than profit maximization. Today in the United States, a Delaware-chartered corporation gives nothing in return for its charter. It is interesting that Theodore Roosevelt saw the role of corporations quite differently from the current Delaware perspective. Roosevelt's agenda was to control and regulate corporations in the public interest. "Great corporations exist only because they are created and safeguarded by our institutions," he stated in his 1901 State of the Union Message. "And it is therefore our right and our duty to see that they work in harmony with these institutions."

We have an interesting mild precedent for broadening the goals of corporations in the British Corporations Law of 2006. This law is explicit in allowing directors to consider employees, the community and many other factors in their decisions. Many U.S. states have in recent years passed similar statutes, but they have had little impact so far on the actions of corporations. . . .

CONCLUSION

We live in a world of rapid technological change. That change has made possible a degree of globalism in economic development that was previously not possible. In so doing it has strongly accelerated the emerging gap between the goals of global corporations and the aspirations of the people of individual countries. This is true not only in the United States but also in less developed countries. Even when globalization increases a country's wealth, which it does not always do, most of the gains are going to a thin upper crust, and the bulk of the people do not participate.

We need to change this and better align the goals of corporations and the aspirations of the people of our country. This is not an idle dream, the growth we had in America in the decades after WWII and before 1970 was both rapid and well distributed. Americans of almost every stripe benefited.

To do this we must realign the interests of global corporations with those of the country. We have given a few examples of changes that could push in that direction. However, much more thought is needed in that direction. If we look we will find more and better ways to do this.

In addition, in a globalizing world where nations pursue their own interests with mercantilist policies, we must balance trade if we are to control our own destiny. . . .

There are many things we can work on to make the United States a stronger nation. Let us clear our vision and start now.

References

1. Hicks, J.R. 1953. *An Inaugural Lecture*. Oxford Economic Papers 5: 117–35.
2. Dornbush, Rudiger W., Stanley Fisher, and Paul A. Samuelson, 1977. "Comparative advantage, trade and payments in a Ricardo model with a continuum of goods." *American Economic Review* 67 pp. 823–829.
3. Krugman, Paul R. 1985. "A Technology Gap' Model of International Trade" in K. Jungenfelt and D. Hague eds. *Structural Adjustment in Developed Open Economies*, New York, St. Martin's Press pp. 39–45.
4. George E. Johnson and Frank P. Stafford. "International Competition and Real Wages" *The American Economic Review*, Vol. 83, No. 2, Papers and Proceedings of the Hundred and Fifth Annual Meeting of the American Economic Association (May, 1993), pp. 127–130.
5. Samuelson, Paul A. 2004. "Where Ricardo and Mill Rebut and Confirm Arguments of Mainstream Economists Supporting Globalization." *Journal of Economic Perspectives*, Volume 18, Number 3, pp. 135–146.
6. Ralph E. Gomory and William J. Baumol. 2001. *Global Trade and Conflicting National Interests*, MIT Press.
7. Barron's On Line Monday. August 13, 2007. "A Plea for Corporate Conscience," by Leo Hindery Jr.
8. Robert Kuttner. 2007. *The Squandering of America*. Alfred A. Knopf Publisher.
9. Paul Krugman. 2007. *The Conscience of a Liberal*. W.W. Norton & Co. Publisher.
10. Jeffrey Immelt. 2007. Interview in *Manufacturing and Technology News*, November 30. Volume 14, No. 21.

For Class Discussion

1. According to Gomory, what effect have corporate values and practices had on the condition of American workers and the United States' economy?

2. What role does he argue that corporations should play?

3. Where and how does Gomory's methodical, explanatory tone contribute to his purpose of "clarification of some of the issues"?

4. Where does Gomory address alternative views? How would Gomory refute the charge of protectionism? How does Gomory's vision of the connections among science education, foreign workers, and economic prosperity differ from Bill Gates's vision in his testimony before Congress (see page 189)?

5. Gomory, a trained mathematician, has worked as a high-level researcher in the sciences and as a top business executive. How does his background lend authority and credibility to his argument? Where do you see evidence of his background in mathematics and business? Why do you think he has chosen not to use numerical data in his testimony? How might he have used it?

Outsourcing
Clay Bennett

Clay Bennett is a nationally known editorial cartoonist for the *Chattanooga Times Free Press*. He is a graduate of the University of North Alabama and holds degrees in art and history. He has worked for the *Pittsburgh Post-Gazette*, the *St. Petersburg Times*, and the *Christian Science Monitor*. In 2002, he won a Pulitzer Prize for editorial cartooning. This cartoon is archived on his Web site www.claybennett.com.

Very simply, what do you see in this cartoon?

Clay Bennett

For Class Discussion

1. What background information does Bennett assume that readers have?

2. Why might the parallel behavior of the two groups of people be depicted similarly?

3. What subtle argument is Bennett making? How does this cartoon contribute to your views on the financial crisis and U.S. management of jobs? ∎

Testimony Before the Committee on Science and Technology, U.S. House of Representatives
Bill Gates

In 1975, Bill Gates cofounded (with Paul Allen) Microsoft Corporation, the world's leading software company. For years, he served as the chairman and chief software architect of Microsoft before retiring to focus on the philanthropic Bill and

Melinda Gates Foundation, which donates hundreds of millions of dollars to global health and education projects. Gates frequently delivers addresses around the world, speaking on global health issues, science education, and the role of high-tech industry in the economy. He gave this testimony to the United States House of Representatives on March 12, 2008.

> In this proposal argument, how does Gates describe the problems in U.S. innovation, economic leadership, and education that he is addressing?

Thank you. It's a privilege to be here. Chairman Gordon, ranking member Hall, members of the Committee, I'm Bill Gates and I'm the chairman of Microsoft. With my wife, Melinda, I'm also the founder of the Bill & Melinda Gates Foundation. And it's an honor to be here to commemorate your 50th anniversary.

During these 50 years incredible advances in science and technology have revolutionized the way people around the world communicate, run business, find information and much more. I'm optimistic that over the decades ahead, information technology will continue to transform business productivity and have a profound positive impact on our day-to-day lives. It will also help us address important global challenges related to education, healthcare, energy, and other issues.

Many of the key advances of these 50 years were pioneered by researchers working in U.S. universities and for U.S. companies. U.S. preeminence in science and technology and this nation's unmatched ability to turn innovation into thriving business have long been the engine of job creation and the source of our global economic leadership.

I know we all want the U.S. to continue to be the world's center for innovation. But our position is at risk. There are many reasons for this but two stand out. First, U.S. companies face a severe shortfall of scientists and engineers with expertise to develop the next generation of breakthroughs. Second, we don't invest enough as a nation in the basic research needed to drive long-term innovation.

If we don't reverse these trends, our competitive advantage will erode. Our ability to create new high-paying jobs will suffer.

Addressing these issues will take commitment, leadership, and partnership on the part of government, private, and nonprofit sectors.

Let me start by saying that business has a critical role to play. The private sector must contribute to building a workforce that has the skills to innovate and compete. That's why Microsoft is committed to improving educational quality and encouraging young people to study math and science through programs like Partners in Learning, which has reached more than 80,000 teachers and 3 million students.

Nonprofit organizations also have an important role to play. The Bill and Melinda Gates Foundation, for its part, has invested almost $2 billion to help establish or improve nearly 2,000 U.S. high schools, and provided over $1.7 billion for college scholarship programs.

But organizations like these cannot address the issues alone. Only government has the resources to effect change on a broad scale. If this nation is to continue to be the global center of innovation, Congress, the current administration, and the next president must act decisively.

It starts with education. Today, graduation rates for our high school students and their level of achievement in math and science rank at the bottom among industrialized nations. Thirty percent of ninth-graders and nearly half of African-Americans and Hispanic ninth-graders do not graduate on time. Fewer than 40 percent of high school students graduate ready to attend college.

As a nation, we must have a fundamental goal that every child in the U.S. should graduate from high school prepared for college, career and life. To achieve this, we need metrics that reflect what students learn and the progress they make. Such metrics may be difficult to develop, but they provide the essential foundation for deciding which programs best improve outcomes in our public schools. Better data will also help us identify the most effective teachers, and adopt better policies for recruiting, training and retaining these teachers for our public schools.

If the problem with high schools is one of quality, the issue at our universities is quantity. Our higher education system doesn't produce enough top scientists and engineers to meet the needs of the U.S. economy. According to the Bureau of Labor Statistics, we are adding over 100,000 new computer-related jobs each year. But only 15,000 students earned bachelor's degrees in computer science and engineering in 2006 and that number continues to drop.

One of the most important steps Congress can take to address this problem is to fully fund the America COMPETES Act. Introduced by this Committee, this act would significantly increase funding for the National Science Foundation's Graduate Fellowship and Traineeship programs.

As bad as the disparity between supply and demand looks, these numbers understate the severity of the problem. Today, our university computer science and engineering programs include large numbers of foreign students. In fact the science and engineering indicators report showed that 59 percent of doctoral degrees and 43 percent of all higher ed degrees in engineering and computer science are awarded to temporary residents. But our current immigration policies make it increasingly difficult for these students to remain in the United States. At a time when talent is the key to economic success, it makes no sense to educate people in our universities, often subsidized by U.S. taxpayers, and then insist that they return home.

U.S. innovation has always been based, in part, on the contributions of foreign-born scientists and researchers. For example, a recent survey conducted by several universities showed that between 1995 and 2005, firms with at least one foreign-born founder created 450,000 new U.S. jobs. Moreover, as a recent study shows for every H-1B holder that technology companies hire, five additional jobs are created around that person.

But as you know, our immigration system makes it very difficult for U.S. firms to hire highly skilled foreign workers. Last year, at Microsoft, we were unable to obtain H-1B visas for over a third of our foreign-born candidates.

An example is the story of our Arpit Guglani, a talented young man who graduated from the University of Toronto. He graduated in 2006 and we offered him a job, but he has not been able to obtain an H-1B visa for two straight years and we were forced to rescind his job offer. He's exactly the type of science and engineering graduate that we need to continue to add jobs and drive innovation.

Our immigration system makes it very difficult to hire highly skilled foreign workers.

There are a number of steps that Congress and the White House should take to address this problem, including extending the period that foreign students can work here after graduation, increasing the current cap on H-1B visas, clearing a path to permanent residency for high-skilled foreign-born employees, eliminating per-country green card limits, and significantly increasing the annual number of green cards.

I want to emphasize that to address the shortage of scientists and engineers, we must do both—reform our education system and our immigration policies. If we don't, American companies simply will not have the talent they need to innovate and compete.

Finally, we must increase our investment in basic scientific research.

In the past, federally funded research helped spark industries that today provide hundreds of thousands of jobs. Even though we know that basic research drives economic progress, real federal spending on research has fallen since 2005. I urge Congress to increase funding for basic research by 10 percent annually for the next seven years. I fully support Congress's efforts to fund basic research through the America COMPETES Act.

I believe the country is at a crossroads. For decades innovation has been our engine of prosperity. Now economic progress depends more than ever on innovation. Without leadership from Congress and the President to implement policies like those I've outlined today and the commitment of the private sector to do its part, the center of progress can shift to other nations that are more committed to the pursuit of innovation.

I'm going to conclude by again congratulating the Committee on its 50th anniversary, and to thank you for this opportunity to share my perspective. I'd be happy to respond to any questions you may have on these topics.

For Class Discussion

1. What multiprong proposal is Bill Gates arguing for in this testimony before Congress?

2. What evidence does Gates supply to back up his reasoning? How does Gates's reputation in the business world contribute to the credibility and weight of his argument?

3. In the question and discussion section of this testimony, Mr. Rohrabacher, a U.S. Representative from California, raises a counterargument to Gates's proposal, touching on the competition to Americans created by H-1B visas. How effectively does Gates anticipate this counterargument? Think about other dimensions of the issue: for example, the question, What are the possible long-term drawbacks of hiring foreigners? How might some readers claim that Gates oversimplifies a complex issue?

4. How does the genre of this argument limit its depth and development?

5. What did you find particularly persuasive about this argument? What would you question or challenge? ∎

Cover of *Wired* Magazine

Wired magazine is a mainstream publication that offers wide coverage of popular Internet, science, and technology topics and in-depth analyses as well as brief news reports and reviews. Its features and advertisements are known for their slick, attractive design. The February 2004 cover of *Wired* magazine provoked enormous controversy, especially within the information technology community in the United States and in India. The editor of *Wired*, Chris Anderson (who also wrote an article in the February 2004 edition titled "Why Coders and Call Centers Are Just the Beginning"), described readers' powerful response to the February cover and articles saying, "Of the record 1,000-plus letters we received, 80 percent expressed 'concern' about outsourcing," and "February may have been our best newsstand issue ever. . . . I am happy that we stimulated debate, and this will continue" (from the March 15, 2004 *Media Industry Newsletter*).

How do the image and writing on this magazine cover differ from the way you might expect the issue of outsourcing computer technology jobs to India to be presented? What contradictory messages does this cover send?

For Class Discussion

1. What stands out the most about the image of the woman? What appears on her hand and what is the intended cultural reference? What is the type style of the phrase "Kiss Your Cubicle Good-Bye"? What 1960s associations does that type style have?

2. Some commentators have called the woman who appears on this cover "a Bollywood image"; in other words, she looks like an Indian movie star and

Ian White/Wired, © Conde Nast Publications

not a computer programmer. What other conflicting or problematic messages does this cover send?

3. Some Indians writing on DialogNow, an online discussion community founded as a forum for conversations in South Asia, accused this cover of being "deliberately grabby," of being racist and fanning prejudice, and of "scapegoating Indians." One person wrote, "I think it's very troubling that people are getting away with blaming an entire country when it is the decisions of top managers that are the cause." What visual features of this cover support these criticisms? How does this cover promote global competition for jobs?

4. Many American information technology professionals responded angrily to this cover and the articles, some even canceling their subscriptions to *Wired*. What makes the text on this cover offensive to Americans?

5. How does this cover suggest that American workers should respond to off-shore outsourcing?

6. Do you agree with *Wired* editor Chris Anderson that this cover makes a worthwhile contribution to the public dialogue about outsourcing? ■

Watching Greed Murder the Economy

Paul Craig Roberts

Paul Craig Roberts, who holds a PhD from the University of Virginia, has been prominent in academic scholarship, public journalism, politics, and research for major think tanks. A leader in formulating economic policy, he served as assistant secretary of the Treasury for economic policy under President Reagan. He has held prestigious research positions at the Center for Strategic and International Studies (1982–1993); the Cato Institute (1993–1996); and, currently, the Institute for Political Economy, Stanford University's Hoover Institute, and the Independent Institute. He has written numerous academic articles for economic, finance, and law scholarly journals. Author of the *The Tyranny of Good Intentions* (2000) with Lawrence Stratton, among other books, he is a syndicated columnist, winner of the Warren Brookes Award for Excellence in Journalism in 1993, among other awards, and a regular contributor to the *Wall Street Journal, Business Week, Investor's Business Daily*, and *National Review*. Roberts is a conservative who is known as a critic of both Republicans and Democrats and an initiator of bipartisan economic policies. This editorial was posted on the Web site for *Counterpunch* (www.counterpunch.org), on July 10, 2008. *Counterpunch* bills itself as "a bi-weekly muckraking newsletter" that offers "readers the stories that the corporate press never prints" (www.counterpunch.org/aboutus.html).

> Although Roberts's affiliations include conservative and libertarian think tanks, how does he criticize free trade ideology's policies on offshore outsourcing in this piece?

The collapse of world socialism, the rise of the high speed Internet, a bought-and-paid-for US government, and a million dollar cap on executive pay that is not performance related are permitting greedy and disloyal corporate executives, Wall Street, and large retailers to dismantle the ladders of upward mobility that made America an "opportunity society." In the 21st century the US economy has been able to create net new jobs only in nontradable domestic services, such as waitresses, bartenders, government workers, hospital orderlies, and retail clerks. (Nontradable services are "hands on" services that cannot be sold as exports, such as haircuts, waiting a table, fixing a drink.)

Corporations can boost their bottom lines, shareholder returns, and executive performance bonuses by arbitraging labor across national boundaries. High value- added jobs in manufacturing and in tradable services can be relocated from developed countries to developing countries where wages and salaries are much lower. In the United States, the high value-added jobs that remain are increasingly filled by lower paid foreigners brought in on work visas.

When manufacturing jobs began leaving the US, no-think economists gave their assurances that this was a good thing. Grimy jobs that required little education would be replaced with new high tech service jobs requiring university degrees. The American work force would be elevated. The US would do the innovating, design, engineering, financing and marketing, and poor countries such as China would manufacture the goods that Americans invented. High-tech services were touted as the new source of value-added that would keep the American economy preeminent in the world.

The assurances that economists gave made no sense. If it pays corporations to ship out high value-added manufacturing jobs, it pays them to ship out high value-added service jobs. And that is exactly what US corporations have done.

Automobile magazine (August 2008) reports that last March Chrysler closed its Pacifica Advance Product Design Center in Southern California. Pacifica's demise followed closings and downsizings of Southern California design studios by Italdesign, ASC, Porsche, Nissan, and Volvo. Only three of GM's eleven design studios remain in the US.

According to Eric Noble, president of The Car Lab, an automotive consultancy, "Advanced studios want to be where the new frontier is. So in China, studios are popping up like rabbits."

The idea is nonsensical that the US can remain the font of research, innovation, design, and engineering while the country ceases to make things. Research and product development invariably follow manufacturing. Now even business schools that were cheerleaders for offshoring of US jobs are beginning to wise up. In a recent report, "Next Generation Offshoring: The Globalization of Innovation," Duke University's Fuqua School of Business finds that product development is moving to China to support the manufacturing operations that have located there.

The study, reported in *Manufacturing & Technology News*, acknowledges that "labor arbitrage strategies continue to be key drivers of offshoring," a conclusion that I reached a number of years ago. Moreover, the study concludes, jobs offshoring is no longer mainly associated with locating IT services and call centers in low wage countries. Jobs offshoring has reached maturity, "and now the growth is centered around product and process innovation."

According to the Fuqua School of Business report, in just one year, from 2005 to 2006, offshoring of product development jobs increased from an already significant base by 40 to 50 percent. Over the next one and one-half to three years, "growth in offshoring of product development projects is forecast to increase by 65 percent for R&D and by more than 80 percent for engineering services and product design-projects."

More than half of US companies are now engaged in jobs offshoring, and the practice is no longer confined to large corporations. Small companies have discovered that "offshoring of innovation projects can significantly leverage limited investment dollars."

It turns out that product development, which was to be America's replacement for manufacturing jobs, is the second largest business function that is offshored.

According to the report, the offshoring of finance, accounting, and human resource jobs is increasing at a 35 percent annual rate. The study observes that "the high growth rates for the offshoring of core functions of value creation is a remarkable development."

In brief, the United States is losing its economy. However, a business school cannot go so far as to admit that, because its financing is dependent on outside sources that engage in offshoring. Instead, the study claims, absurdly, that the massive movement of jobs abroad that the study reports are causing no job loss in the US: "Contrary to various claims, fears about loss of high-skill jobs in engineering and science are unfounded." The study then contradicts this claim by reporting that as more scientists and engineers are hired abroad, "fewer jobs are being eliminated onshore." Since 2005, the study reports, there has been a 48 percent drop in the onshore job losses caused by offshore projects.

One wonders at the competence of the Fuqua School of Business. If a 40–50 percent increase in offshored product development jobs, a 65 percent increase in offshored R&D jobs, and a more than 80 percent increase in offshored engineering services and product design-projects jobs do not constitute US job loss, what does?

Academia's lack of independent financing means that its researchers can only tell the facts by denying them.

The study adds more cover for corporate America's rear end by repeating the false assertion that US firms are moving jobs offshore because of a shortage of scientists and engineers in America. A correct statement would be that the offshoring of science, engineering and professional service jobs is causing fewer American students to pursue these occupations, which formerly comprised broad ladders of upward mobility. The Bureau of Labor Statistics' nonfarm payroll jobs statistics show no sign of job growth in these careers. The best that can be surmised is that there are replacement jobs as people retire.

The offshoring of the US economy is destroying the dollar's role as reserve currency, a role that is the source of American power and influence. The US trade deficit resulting from offshored US goods and services is too massive to be sustainable. Already the once all-mighty dollar has lost enormous purchasing power against oil, gold, and other currencies. In the 21st century, the American people have been placed on a path that can only end in a substantial reduction in US living standards for every American except the corporate elite, who earn tens of millions of dollars in bonuses by excluding Americans from the production of the goods and services that they consume.

What can be done? The US economy has been seriously undermined by offshoring. The damage might not be reparable. Possibly, the American market and living standards could be rescued by tariffs that offset the lower labor and compliance costs abroad.

Another alternative, suggested by Ralph Gomory, would be to tax US corporations on the basis of the percentage of their value added that occurs in the US. The greater the value added to a company's product in America, the lower the tax rate on the profits.

These sensible suggestions will be demonized by ideological "free market" economists and opposed by the offshoring corporations, whose swollen profits allow them to hire "free market" economists as shills and to elect representatives to serve their interests.

The current recession with its layoffs will mask the continuing deterioration in employment and career outlooks for American university graduates. The highly skilled US work force is being gradually transformed into the domestic service workforce characteristic of third world economies.

For Class Discussion

1. In the third paragraph, Roberts rehearses the classic rationale for offshore outsourcing jobs. What points does he include?

2. What counterclaim to the value of outsourcing does Roberts assert in this editorial? How would you articulate what Roberts values in the United States economy?

3. What evidence does Roberts muster to rebut the policy of offshore outsourcing endorsed by the American business community and academic economists?

4. Roberts uses a vehement and bleak tone in this piece. How does it suit the publication? How rhetorically effective do you think it is for both its target audience and a wider general audience?

5. How has this argument influenced your understanding of U.S. corporations' policies on jobs?

STUDENT VOICE: The United States Needs to Nationalize Now by Matthew Brady

Matthew Brady is a double major in English/Creative Writing and Fine Arts/Photography from Montana with an interest in the outdoors, volunteer work, and marketing. He wrote this researched argument for his peers in a course on argumentation. The class had explored the global financial crisis from multiple perspectives.

How does Matthew Brady use personal experience to establish the problem his proposal argument addresses?

I grew up in a family of six people, living off a single teacher salary that started off below the poverty line. Like so many other poor Americans, my parents saved what they could. They protected a portion of their earnings with both a tax-sheltered annuity for schoolteachers and an individual retirement account. They saved and saved, but when the financial crisis hit in 2008, years of saving disappeared in a flash. My parents lost 35 percent of every penny they had put away for retirement in eighteen years of teaching public school. They never bought a second house, or rolled the dice on shady investments, but they still suffered. This example is obviously localized, but it is an integral part of the larger picture. With unemployment rates climbing and savings vanishing, the United States needs a solution that will protect vulnerable Americans from further catastrophe.

Currently, the United States government is spending enormous amounts of money to patch up and reinflate our ailing financial system, but that money is being wasted when we refuse to utilize the most effective solutions available. The government needs to step in with intelligent public policy that will put our economy back on track. In February 2009, major national and international news sources such as the *New York Times*, *Business Week*, and the *Irish Times* were debating the pros and cons of bank nationalization. Then on February 23, 2009, the Federal Reserve issued a statement saying that any nationalization of the American financial system was impossible (United States Department of the Treasury). However, shouldn't we consider every option to fix the economy? If nationalization has so many problems, why does it have so many advocates? Why do people, such as former chairman of the Federal Reserve and frequent opponent of government regulation, Alan Greenspan, believe that we should temporarily nationalize the banks (Guha and Luce)? Indeed, a significant portion of the banking system desperately needs to be nationalized now for a short period in order for the United States to ascend from our deepening economic crisis before the situation gets any worse. Although many people distrust nationalization, I will show why temporary nationalization should be our guide on the path out of our economic darkness.

Temporary nationalization would bring an enormous boom for the United States economy. Banks would have enough money to begin normal lending, and our stalled economy would burst into life once again. Beyond that, nationalization would provide the economy with much needed stability. The federal government's backing of your money causes that money to be far safer than it was before nationalization. Investors should be clamoring to have the backing of the country with the world's largest GDP. The security and stability that nationalization would bring to the financial system is critical for restoring consumer and investor confidence. Since our economy is strongly rooted in consumer and investor confidence, stabilizing it and halting its plummet into distrust is important for economic health.

Temporary nationalization would also bring stability and confidence through accountability and transparency. Currently, billions in bailout money (read: taxpayer dollars) is being injected into failing financial institutions, but not all of that money is being used for its intended purposes. For example, significant amounts of the Troubled Asset Relief Program (TARP) funds were given as bonuses to employees and CEOs of failing financial institutions: $18 billion in bonuses in 2008 alone (Brown). Failing companies took government money and then celebrated their success; all the while regulatory action was failing to protect Americans from the people who created the crisis! That should be a signal that more accountability and transparency are necessary in order to stem the crisis; both of which are nearly impossible if institutions remain under private ownership. However, if we nationalize, we will have full access to bonus records, past business deals, bad assets, and all the other reasons why financial institutions are barely operating. Without the openness and knowledge that nationalization would provide we are covering our eyes and giving money to the first hand that taps our shoulder. And the collective American shoulder is being tapped by many hands. We need to know where our money is going and how it is being used, or we are going to be completely ineffective at reviving our financial system. Nationalization will give us that oversight.

Also, nationalization would mean that the people most responsible for bad financial management would be removed and replaced with more competent and discerning private sector business people. How can I trust a bank that lost 35 percent of my parent's retirement investments when the CEO who makes $40 million a year still runs the company? I can't, and I doubt I am alone. CEOs and board members that presided over this mess need to be replaced in order for new managers to craft rational and measured approaches to finance. Currently, bad managers are profiting from their own failure. Stopping that profiting is instrumental in restoring confidence in ailing financial institutions.

Now we know why to nationalize, but *how* should we nationalize? The precedents of other countries that have nationalized parts of their financial systems offer guidance. The Japanese allowed bad banks to flounder for ten years before nationalizing in 2003. John H. Makin of the American Enterprise Institute, a conservative think-tank, claims, "The lesson from Japan in the 1990s was that they should have stepped up and nationalized the banks" (qtd. in Tabuchi).

Although Princeton professor of economics and public affairs Alan S. Blinder opposes nationalization by pointing out dissimilarities between the United States and other countries, I think we can profit from Sweden's 1990s example. In his op-ed piece, "Nationalize? Hey, Not So Fast," Blinder argues that Sweden had far fewer and much smaller banks than the United States and that "nationalization runs counter to deeply ingrained American traditions and attitudes" and so would hurt confidence in the banks. However, Swedish economist Anders Aslund providers insight into how nationalization worked in Sweden. "[Sweden] had outside, mainly foreign, consultants . . . scrutinize all bank debts and establish objectively which were nonperforming. The banks were forced to write off their bad debts and transfer them to bad banks." Once the bad was split from the good, the government gave banks capital to resume normal lending in return for stock. With banks lending and making money, the government began to sell its stock back to private investors. Banks were left in private hands the entire time and never run by the government. That is the kind of nationalization that I am suggesting.

But how much did all of this cost? Carter Dougherty of the *New York Times* writes, "the final cost to Sweden ended up being less than 2 percent of its G.D.P. Some officials say they believe it was closer to zero, depending on how certain rates of return are calculated." By April 2009, the TARP funds that the United States government allocated for financial relief had been whittled down by almost $600 billion without any hope of return. We need to nationalize instead of throwing our money away. Since we are already spending the money, shouldn't we at least try to get our money back? This kind of nationalization is not socialism, as opponents like to call it to whip up negative emotions, but rather intelligent capitalism with limited governmental intervention. Let's use Sweden as our guide.

If we follow Sweden, nationalization would be administered so that supported financial institutions would still be private companies, and so that in acting in their own self-interest they would achieve stability. I am rarely an advocate of complete *laissez faire* capitalism, but financial institutions must be mostly unfettered in order to revitalize themselves. The best form of nationalization would mean government backing and stock ownership, and not government management. Such nationalization places politics aside and allows financial institutions to make the best decisions for themselves in a highly competitive business environment. Only one Swedish bank was nationalized in the traditional sense of the word (Aslund). In this version of nationalization the government gives the following small number of directives: Hire new management and split mostly worthless assets off from the larger bank. That's it. Sweden purchased stock from stockholders, much as the United States has already done with Citigroup, but in the United States, we bought stock, and then allowed banks to operate exactly as before. We cannot continue that sort of ignorance if our goal is to revitalize our economy.

Another key to the nationalization solution is that all government intervention should be temporary, so that financial institution stock will be held for as short a time as possible. No, we cannot know how long that will be, but we can use examples in our own country, as well as the Swedish example, to hint at how long nationalization might last. In 1984, the Continental Illinois National Bank and Trust Company was nationalized by President Reagan. That bank was sold back into the market ten years later. Even Reagan called upon nationalization when it was necessary. Ideally, our period of nationalization would more closely resemble the three-year Swedish model, but that may be far too optimistic for a system as complex as ours. Whichever becomes our reality, our emphasis needs to be on giving financial institutions all the tools to improve themselves so that we can sell their stock back into the private sector and prevent extensive government ownership.

Still, many people argue that we should not wipe out shareholders because they are an invaluable resource who pay taxes on their dividends and financially support financial institutions. But,

Sweden did not wipe out shareholders; why should we? In exchange for capital, the Swedish government received shares from the bank or bought shareholder stock, but did not clean out all the existing shareholders. If banks fall deeper into crisis and it becomes necessary to take over all company shares, then the unfortunate loss of shareholders would be balanced by the upswing of the United States economy. The priority needs to be on making financial institutions solvent again so that they can lend money securely and hopefully intelligently. If that means sacrificing shareholders' already almost worthless shares in order to promote stability, then that is a necessary evil.

Another problem, as economist Gerald O'Driscoll sees it, is that "from the beginning, the handling of the U.S. crisis has been politicized." The government, as in Sweden's case, will have the task of hiring new management. When they do, the American people need to speak up in order to keep this hiring process from becoming even more politicized. Furthermore, we need President Obama to follow through on his campaign promises and make tough decisions that defy partisanship and support economic growth. Our future depends on our collective resolve, so let us not take such a responsibility lightly.

The biggest benefit of nationalization, besides a healthy economy, is that we as American taxpayers will make our money back when we reprivatize. The problem with the current bailout bucks is that no money will ever be given back to the government. Although companies need capital and we give it to them, we treat this as if it is free, donated money. In late February the entire market capitalization (or the total market worth of all of the shares of each company) of Bank of America and Citigroup was $34.6 billion combined. This is despite the fact that the two received a total of almost $90 billion in the previous few months (*"BAC: Summary for BK of America CP"* and *"C: Summary for CITI GROUP INC"*). Why are we giving companies *three times as much money* as they are worth? If we are using that money, we should use it to support financial institutions in exchange for stock. We will get some of our money back once we sell our shares back to private investors. We did this under Reagan. Sweden did this in the 1990s. Japan is working toward full reprivatization. Reprivatization would wash the money spent right back into the great American coffers.

I advocate that financial institutions be nationalized, their management be replaced, their books be combed, and then we slowly work towards reprivatization. Temporary nationalization would replace bad management and prevent further losses with new management and more accountability. It would allow full transparency and an eventual return on investment. It would stabilize consumer and investor confidence, and prevent those that created this mess from reaping any benefits from government intervention. We need nationalization so that we can get our economy booming again now and not later. We need nationalization so that hardworking taxpayers like my parents won't lose the money they spent a lifetime to save. We need nationalization because it works and it is the most cost-effective solution. We need to look to the long term in order to avoid wasting our valuable money now. Scared to nationalize? For the sake of all of your past, present, and future investments, pray to nationalize.

Works Cited

Aslund, Anders. "Lessons for the US from the Swedish Bank Crisis." *Peter G. Peterson Institute for International Economics.* Peterson Institute for International Economics, 24 Feb. 2009. Web. 11 Mar. 2009.

"BAC: Summary for BK OF AMERICA CP." *Yahoo! Finance.* Yahoo! 11 Mar. 2009. Web. 11 March 2009.

Blinder, Alan S. "Nationalize? Hey, Not So Fast." *New York Times.* New York Times, 7 Mar. 2009. Web. 18 May 2009.

Brown, Campbell. "Commentary: Outraged by Wall Street Bonuses." *CNN.com.* Cable News Network, 2 Feb 2009. Web. 11 Mar. 2009.

"C: Summary for CITIGROUP INC." *Yahoo! Finance.* Yahoo!, 11 Mar. 2009. Web. 11 Mar. 2009.

Dougherty, Carter. "Stopping a Financial Crisis, the Swedish Way." *New York Times.* New York Times, 22 Sept. 2008. Web. 10 Mar. 2009.

Guha, Krishna, and Luce, Edward. "Greenspan Backs Bank Nationalization." *Financial Times.* Financial Times, 18 Feb. 2009. Web. 19 May 2009.

O'Driscoll, Gerald. "The Problem with Nationalization." *Wall Street Journal.* Dow Jones, 23 Feb. 2009. Web. 23 Feb. 2009.

Tabuchi, Hiroko. "In Japan's Stagnant Decade, Cautionary Tales for America." *New York Times.* New York Times, 12 Feb. 2009. Web. 10 Mar. 2009.

United States. Dept. of the Treasury. *Joint Statement by the Treasury, FDIC, OCC, OTS and the Federal Reserve. US Department of the Treasury Press Room.* US Dept. of the Treasury, 23 Feb. 2009. Web. 10 Mar. 2009. http://treasury.gov/press/releases/tg38.htm.

For Class Discussion

1. Summarize the core of Matthew Brady's argument in two or three sentences.

2. "Nationalization" is an emotionally and politically loaded word. How does Matthew handle the controversy over this word itself?

3. How does he use precedent arguments to support his claim and reasons?

4. What features of this argument help readers form a positive impression of Matthew and his personal and civic investment in this issue? For instance, how does he use material from his sources to make a rational case for his view? How does he engage with objections to nationalizing the banks?

5. In what ways has this argument influenced your thinking about the widespread repercussions of the failure of U.S. financial institutions and of the federal government's corrective policies?   ∎

Apocalypse Now
Daniel Kurtzman

Daniel Kurtzman is a political cartoonist, humorist, and journalist with a degree in political science. He is known for his books of political humor: *How to Win a Fight with a Conservative* and *How to Win a Fight with a Liberal* (2007). After working as a Washington correspondent, he began publishing satirical commentaries in the *New York Times*, the *Huffington Post*, and the *Funny Times*. Exemplifying his style and perspective, Kurtzman writes that he seeks "to provide a witty and irreverent look at all the bizarre political antics inside, outside and below the Beltway" (About.com Political Humor). This cartoon was posted on Cagle Cartoons for the week of March 1–7, 2009.

> What background knowledge about the financial crisis and the U.S. economy does Kurtzman expect readers to bring to this cartoon?

For Class Discussion

1. Who are the characters in this cartoon and what story does it tell?

2. Scott McCloud, who has theorized extensively about how cartooon images affect viewers and convey meaning, describes "cartooning as a form of amplification through simplification."* In this cartoon, how has Kurtzman both simplified the American economy and amplified or exaggerated the scene? What icons—"any image used to represent a person, place, thing, or idea"—does Kurtzman employ?

---

*Scott McCloud, *Understanding Comics: The Invisible Art.* New York: HarperCollins, 1993, 27.

"SO ALL THIS IS BECAUSE WE TOOK OUT A HOME EQUITY LOAN TO REDO THE BATHROOM?"

3. What is Kurtman satirizing in this cartoon?

4. How would you articulate Kurtzman's argument? For whom would this argument carry weight?

Prudence or Profligacy?
Hamish McRae

Hamish McRae holds a masters degree in economics and politics from Trinity College in Dublin. He has been an editor of various British publications, including *The Banker* and *Euromoney*, financial editor of *The Guardian*, and now associate editor of *The Independent*. As an economic journalist who theorizes about the economic future, he has written a number of books, among them, *The World in 2020: Power, Culture and Prosperity* (1994). In financial journalism he won the Periodical Publisher's Award for Columnist of the Year in 1996 and the British Press Award Business and Finance Journalist of the Year in 2006. This editorial was published in *New Statesman*, a British magazine known for its independent political thinking and lack of attachment to a party, on December 4, 2006.

How does McRae define "financial literacy" and "financial numeracy"?

I was talking to some international executives a few months ago about pensions and asked them whether they intuitively preferred to trust governments or their employers to provide their own pensions.

"You're missing something," one said. "There is a third option. I would only trust myself."

She was right, of course. But it is not just those people who stand a fair way up the income ladder who will have to become more self-reliant in handling their finances. For a host of reasons, just about everyone in the developed world will need to take greater control of their financial destiny.

The plain truth is that a number of global trends are sufficiently embedded to run on for another generation at least. All of these demand greater financial competence, although there will be different views as to whether these are desirable or otherwise.

> **Just about everyone will need to take greater control of their financial destiny.**

Most obvious are the changes in the labour market. These include greater job mobility, but also greater insecurity. People have more fluid working patterns, including more part-time work and more self-employment. Some 12 percent of the workforce in London and the South East are teleworkers, working either from home or from a variety of locations using home as a base, and of these people more than two-thirds are self-employed.

People at all income levels move between different jurisdictions much more freely; witness the arrival of people from the new EU member states seeking jobs in the UK. The rise of entrepreneurship creates opportunities for many people, but inevitably increases the risks. So while people have much greater financial opportunity, they also have more complex needs.

On the other side is the increasing inability of both private and public sectors to provide either security of employment or a reasonable pension. The problem is more obvious in the private sector, with the legacy of mistrust left by Robert Maxwell and Equitable Life. But the arithmetic of public-sector pension liabilities, both for the government's workers and for the public at large, looks very difficult. People who have relied solely on the public sector will almost certainly, a generation from now, be disappointed.

There is a third element. Finance has become more complicated. Obviously, many more financial products are available, pushed at us by an enthusiastic financial services industry. To have credit cards offering six months free credit landing on the doormat would have seemed odd a generation ago. But the scale of both the financial opportunities people have available and the pitfalls in store are much greater. For example, some 5 percent of consumption in Britain is financed by equity take-out—people borrowing against the increased value of their homes. If those loans are used to build an extension and increase the value of the house that might make sense; if it is to pay for a holiday in the south of France, maybe less so, particularly if house prices subsequently go down.

So how well are we coping? My intuitive answer is that, with three specific reservations, we are not doing too badly, but that we will need to do much better in the future if we are to avoid misery for many. It is hard to come by data on financial literacy and harder still on financial numeracy, which actually matters more. (You don't need to know what APR stands for when you are seeking a loan; you do need to know that if it is 15.9 percent then it is too high.) I did see a survey some years back that suggested Britons were more literate about economic matters than people in other developed countries: more of us could explain in general terms what the balance of payments or Gross Domestic Product actually meant.

That is probably right and may well be a function of the vigorous financial press in the UK, in particular the substantial personal finance sections in the national newspapers. Whether we are more numerate is another matter. Witness the extent to which people fret about buying foreign currency for a holiday: is the pound likely to go up against the euro or the dollar, should they rely on credit cards or should they buy currency in advance and so on? Contrast that with the lack of attention most people give to their pension. Yet the first has really minimal impact on people's finances, whereas the latter matters as much as or more than what they do about buying a home.

What is surely beyond dispute is that financial competence is unevenly distributed, and that is my first reservation to the cautiously optimistic judgement above. This is partly an education issue: people who have suffered from poor schooling are more likely to find it tough to cope with financial problems. But it is not just that. Plenty of clever people are bad with money. One of the oddities of British life is that it is socially acceptable to tell people that you are not interested in finance. Substitute the word history or literature and you can see how odd that sounds. Yet to understand the modern world it is as important to have some grasp of finance as it is to have a working knowledge of those other subjects.

Nor is it an income or a wealth issue. Some people manage to live well on quite low incomes and others run through inherited fortunes. There is nothing new there, as Hogarth's "A Rake's Progress" reminds us. But it may be that two generations of successful extension of government-funded welfare systems have shaded people's sense of personal opportunity and responsibility. Do people realise the financial implications of the choices they are making when they decide on their career, their home or their pension provision? And is there something that can be done to help people make somewhat more informed decisions?

That leads to the second reservation. We are uneven in terms of our financial outcomes, partly because we are not well informed about the specifics of finance and economics and also because we do not understand the huge consequences of our lifestyle choices.

I can cite a couple of examples. Just this month a survey by Alliance & Leicester showed how damaging divorce was to people's finances: specifically that people whose partnerships broke up often spent the whole of the rest of their lives suffering financially as a result of that decision.

Another was a conversation I had with an economics professor. She was furious at how badly she was paid compared with economists working in the City. But surely you realised that when you made the decision to teach the subject, I asked?

"Yes," came the reply, "but I didn't realise that I would have to work as hard as I do now."

Her particular concern was that the rules of the game had changed; and indeed they have for academics. But then they have changed for everyone in the labour market, and they will continue to change. True financial literacy is not just about understanding the importance of building financial capital; it is equally about the need to build one's own human capital so that one can adapt to changes in demand for skills.

My final reservation is that we have lived through good times and may find it hard to adapt to somewhat tougher ones. The Chancellor of the Exchequer frequently points out, correctly, that the UK has had the longest period of uninterrupted growth since records began.

Most other developed countries, by contrast, experienced recession or stagnation during the past decade, just as Britain had quite a long recession in the early 1990s. There is still an identifiable global economic cycle. Though some evidence indicates that the amplitude of these cycles is diminishing, the present expansion is quite mature and the world should be due for some sort of downturn within three or four years.

It may be that the UK will come through this coming cycle in relatively good order. Even so, the British population as a whole is heavily borrowed. Debts are high relative to income both historically and when compared with those in other developed countries. Many people will find themselves squeezed if and when tougher times come along.

There is a broader point here. The function of financial and economic education is not just to enable people to make better decisions about their life choices. If people can be nudged towards making what for them are the right decisions about their own financial futures then they will be happier and more fulfilled, which is not only helpful for them but is also greatly beneficial for society as a whole. We become more content, sure, but we also release resources that can be devoted to helping people who aren't coping so well. Those resources can come from the state but also from the voluntary sector and, indeed, from commerce. Fewer bad debts means a lower cost of loans for all.

But the purpose of financial education—as with all education—is not just the utilitarian one of helping individuals make better decisions about their pensions. It is also to help them understand how and why the world economy is changing.

Why are China and India success stories now whereas a generation ago they were failing? Why are there strong economic arguments for energy conservation? How might having an ageing population be turned into an economic advantage? Why does YouTube matter?

We are living in an astoundingly interesting time and we are fortunate in that. But to understand it, you do need to know about finance and economics.

For Class Discussion

1. What case does McRae build for financial literacy for everyone? What reasons does he provide to bolster his claim?

2. What obstacles does McRae recognize to peoples' acquisition of knowledge about financial matters?

3. What indications are there in this article that McRae is writing for a British audience? Would he have to take a different approach or write differently for an American audience?

4. How does McRae's tone, including his choice of title, contribute to the persuasiveness of his argument? How successful is McRae's concluding challenge and encouragement to readers?

5. How has this argument affected your understanding of financial literacy? ■

Forget Commercialism! The New Realities of Consumption and the Economy
Juliet Schor

Juliet Schor is an internationally known sociologist and economist, scholar, and author who has taught at Harvard University and Boston College, consulted with the United Nations, lectured around the world, and spoken often on television and radio. She writes prolifically for both academic economics journals and magazines and newspapers, such as the *Wall Street Journal* and *Newsweek*, for a general readership. As a public intellectual, she has written best-selling, nationally recognized books: *The Overworked American: The Unexpected Decline of Leisure* (1991); *The Overspent American: Why We Want What We Don't Need* (1998); and *Born to Buy: The Commercialized Child and the New Consumer Culture* (2004). In 1997, she cofounded the advocacy organization The Center for the New American Dream, which states its mission as helping "Americans consume responsibly to protect the environment, enhance the quality of life, and promote social justice" (www.newdream.org). This piece appeared on the New Dream Blog for November 18, 2008.

What common and widespread belief about consumerism is Juliet Schor rebutting in this editorial blog?

Spending our way to prosperity? Not this time around.

As a "New Dream" economist, I am asked all the time: won't consuming less hurt the economy? When there's less spending, people get laid off, their incomes fall and businesses, especially small ones, go bankrupt. This question is especially urgent today, given that the recession is deepening and spreading. George Bush was widely (and rightly) criticized for suggesting shopping as the patriotic response to 9/11. Would Barack Obama be wrong if he suggested the same?

Short answer: Yes. But with this topic, there's rarely a short answer. So here's the longer one.

Let's remember, first, that the economic crisis wasn't caused by a decline in consumer spending. It was triggered by the bursting of the housing bubble, Wall Street excesses, and some other factors. Consumers are cutting back now, but the decline in spending is one of a series of falling dominos—more an effect of recession than a cause.

Even if she didn't cause the problem, can the heroic consumer still save the day, as she has in recent recessions? Not this time around. Consumers can't afford to be the engine of growth because they've suffered traumatic losses of jobs, incomes, creditworthiness, homes, and wealth, far beyond the experiences of other recessions. If the government were to give another tax rebate, it would most likely be saved, not spent. And if it were spent, a lot of that money would flow right out of the country, because so much of consumer spending is for imports. That's especially true at the holiday season, when people buy apparel, footwear, toys, games, household items, and other so-called durable goods. A huge fraction of those items (in the 90% range for some of the categories) are now manufactured abroad.

In a stunning reversal of the reigning "free market" or "neo-liberal" paradigm, economists across the political spectrum have recognized this and are saying that the government needs to step in with big expenditures to put people back to work. They recognize that jobs, not consumer spending, are the key. Action on foreclosures, debt, and some other issues is also needed. But the system needs bold action from its biggest player, the Federal government, to instill confidence, stabilize demand and provide leadership.

So we're getting a lot of calls that harken back to the 1930s. But old-style Depression-economics isn't the answer either. Because the planet is telling us, loud and clear, that it can't cope with business as usual (BAU).

People who are following the news on climate, bio-diversity and other ecological issues also understand that the standard remedy of getting consumers and/or government, to spend more can't work this time around. We've lost the ability to profitably or responsibly grow our way out of recession. The usual kinds of consumer spending (cars, electronics, furniture, apparel, travel) degrade vital eco-systems and have an economic cost. BAU puts us deeper into an economic hole, because every dollar of GNP creates new and unacceptable damage to the planet. A government program which mainly goes to shoring up a failing automotive infrastructure (roads and bridges) suffers from the same problem. It's throwing good money after bad. The latest findings about climate are that we need to stabilize greenhouse gases in the atmosphere immediately. Whatever government and consumers spend on needs to reflect that reality.

So where does that leave us? We need to do more sharing—job sharing, property and income re-distributing, and sharing of access and know-how. This time the economic pain needs to be assuaged by deeper structural changes that re-introduce fairness into our system. That's not just moral, it's also good economic sense. The deepest, underlying structures of inequality are ultimately at the root of why we got into this mess. Reversing the dramatic growth in inequality will help us get out of it.

And yes, there are opportunities for spending. But they are for purchases that enhance and re-generate the planet and its people, such as buying from local food systems, hiring the unemployed to provide services (especially green ones), and supporting non-profits that are solving, rather than creating problems. It's good to spend on businesses that are truly sustainable, especially those that are expanding the green economy. Those patterns of spending, which new dreamers are in the forefront of, are key to the structural transformation toward more equality, fairness and sustainability. So here's to a local, frugal, just, and fun holiday season. More music, less wrapping paper!

For Class Discussion

1. What is Schor's main proposal claim about solutions to the economic crisis and individual consumers? How does she reason out and support her argument?

2. What alternative and historical proposals does Schor address and reject?

3. What intersection between economics and environmentalism does Schor tap in her argument?

4. Thinking of the site of publication and the genre of this piece, what audience do you think Schor would reach? How would she have to reshape her argument for a less sympathetic audience?

5. How does Schor's argument affect your attitude toward consumer responsibility at this historical moment? ∎

CHAPTER QUESTIONS FOR REFLECTION AND DISCUSSION

1. Thinking about the chapter readings, the news, and your personal experience, list five to ten direct ways that the global financial crisis has touched your life in the last year. For instance, you might consider credit card terms, availability of student loans or jobs, the closing of local stores or restaurants, changes in a relative's retirement funds or housing, or budget cuts for local public education. Be as specific as you can.

2. Many of the arguments in this chapter make different assumptions about the relationship between free trade and the global economic crisis; the value and effectiveness of capitalism; corporate responsibility and the needs of citizens and taxpayers; the government and the market; and individual financial responsibility. Choose two sets of contrasting writers from the list below. Describe the major differences in the way they frame the issues: that is, differences in their claims, reasons, and assumptions. Where do they look for evidence to support their claims? What counterarguments, reasons, and evidence would each enlist to refute the other's points? (For example, how does Gomory's vision of science education, foreign workers, and economic prosperity differ from Gates's?)

   Anthony Kim and Joseph Stiglitz
   Joseph Stiglitz and Steve Forbes
   Steve Forbes and Naomi Klein
   Steve Forbes and Julie Schor
   Thomas Friedman or Bill Gates and Ralph Gomory or Paul Craig Roberts

3. A number of the arguments in Chapter 3 examine problems with free trade and consumerism that intersect with the arguments in Chapter 4. Select a pair of articles from the list below, and identify and summarize common assumptions, reasons, or evidence.

   Nick Gillespie or Rawi Abdelal/Adam Segal (Ch. 3) and Anthony Kim or Joseph Stiglitz (Ch. 4)
   Thom Hartmann, Froma Harrop, or Madelaine Drohan (Ch. 3) and Joseph Stiglitz, Ralph Gomory, or Paul Craig Roberts (Ch. 4)
   Jeffrey Sachs or Bob Jeffcott (Ch. 3) and Thomas Friedman, Bill Gates, or Paul Craig Roberts (Ch. 4)

4. Take one of the many financial literacy quizzes, which you can find on the Web, and then write a short reflection, exploring why you did or did not know the answers and how you feel about the importance of this knowledge.

5. Examine one of the visuals in this chapter or investigate one of the videos mentioned in the chapter (at YouTube.com, CnnMoney.com, or www.globalissues.org). For example, both *The Crisis of Credit Visualized* by Jonathan Jarvis and interview with Naseem Taleb and Benoit Mandelbrot are available at YouTube.com. Write a brief summary of the visual argument and list three or four ideas from this visual that clarify the current global financial problems or raise questions about them.

6. Working individually or in a group, research one of the following economic problems related to this chapter's readings and prepare a short presentation in which you teach your class about your findings. Think in terms of the last three to six months and consider using a graph, chart, or other numeric display of data.

   • Layoffs and unemployment rates in your home region or your university's region, or job creation figures in your home or university region

   • Numbers of delinquencies on mortgages, housing foreclosures or houses for auction, and short sales of houses (houses sold for less than the value of the owners' mortgages)

   • Numbers of businesses closed in your home or university region

   • Banks in your region that have received TARP funds

   • H-1B visas issued to people in your state or region, or jobs outsourced from your state

   • Job losses and unemployment rates in European Union countries

WRITING ASSIGNMENTS

Brief Writing Assignments

1. Write a brief reflective letter to yourself—a letter you might open and read in five years—describing your biggest fears or hopes about your present financial situation or the country's. Why are you fearful or hopeful? Make this reflection lively and probing by including specifics.

2. Research photos that depict some aspect of the global financial crisis and choose one that you find particularly striking and memorable. Write a brief persuasive presentation for the class in which you make a case for the power of this photo to make an argument or support an argument. You might look for depictions of U.S. workers, protestors in Europe, houses up for auction or foreclosure, or families in difficult financial circumstances.

3. Choose one of the arguments in this chapter with which you disagree and write a fair, accurate summary of it, one that the writer would accept. Then list several assumptions about free trade, corporate business, or the location of jobs that you share with the writer and at least one point you could agree on. Finally, offer two or three reasons against the writer's views and briefly elaborate on your reasons with examples.

4. **Analyzing Arguments Rhetorically.** The following pairs of writers share similar perspectives on one of the issues covered in this chapter, yet their arguments differ in prominent ways. Choose a pair of writers and contrast their arguments in terms of genre, audience, and use of rhetorical appeals. (For example, how do their different audiences shape Gomory's and Roberts's claims, use of evidence, and tone?) Briefly list and explain your points in preparation for discussion or formal writing.

   Thomas Friedman and Bill Gates
   Ralph Gomory and Paul Craig Roberts
   The job line photo and Daniel Kurtzman's cartoon "Apocalypse Now"
   Hamish McRae and Julie Schor

5. Choose one of the following controversial claims and write informally for twenty minutes, supporting or contesting this claim. Use evidence from your reading, personal experience, or knowledge to support your points. As a variation on this assignment, your instructor might ask you to write a short response in favor of the claim and then a short response arguing against it.

   A. The U.S. government should give money to struggling homeowners, the unemployed, and people filing for bankruptcy (Main Street), not financial institutions and banks (Wall Street).

   B. The U.S. government should grant more H-1B visas to international professionals.

   C. Individuals have the primary responsibility for their financial contracts and commitments.

Writing Projects

1. Using Rahel Teshafun's personal narrative as an inspiration, write an editorial in a personal voice for your university newspaper encouraging a new affordable lifestyle, perhaps including managing finances, avoiding debt, finding bargains.

2. **Analyzing Arguments Rhetorically.** In this chapter, several writers and artists use a dominating, overtly insistent approach, making their arguments edgy or heavy handed. In contrast, several others try to win supporters by being calm, low key, and highly rational. Write a rhetorical analysis of one of the following pairs of arguments as an interpretive argument for a general news commentary magazine. Analyze the differences and

rhetorical risks and successes of these texts for their target audiences and for other readers:

Naomi Klein and Joseph Stiglitz
Anthony Kim and Robert Zoellick
Thomas Friedman and Bill Gates
the cover of *Wired* and Clay Bennett's cartoon
Paul Craig Roberts and Ralph Gomory

3. Choose one of the articles in this chapter written for a highly educated audience knowledgeable about financial matters or global economic institutions. Rewrite its argument shaping it for one of the following new rhetorical situations:

   A. an op-ed piece for a local newspaper audience

   B. a presentation for a junior high or high school history class

   C. a newsletter for a retirement community

For the option you choose, you will need to (1) analyze the values, knowledge, and interest of your audience; (2) consider features of the genre; (3) find definitions for the useful terms (online business dictionaries might help); (4) formulate a statement of your specific purpose; (5) construct the core of your argument; and (6) identify ways you will appeal to your audience.

The following writing projects involve research on databases and the free access Web.

4. Pretend you are a junior researcher assigned to write a policy analysis that could be posted on a think tank Web site. Choose one of the following issues to research and investigate it by consulting a range of sources and views.

   A. When General Motors filed for bankruptcy in 2009 and the U.S. government became the owner of 60 percent of the company, about 20,000 union auto workers lost their jobs in Michigan, Indiana, Wisconsin, and Ohio. The bankruptcy of General Motors has left you—a taxpayer and consumer—wondering, Should U.S. citizens, now part-owners of G.M., pressure the federal government to compel G.M. to make new smaller, more fuel-efficient cars in U.S. plants rather than overseas?

   B. The countries in the European Union are also struggling with escalating economic problems. Research one of the twenty-seven EU countries to learn about its specific economic challenges, recovery strategy, and success to date. Should the United States adopt this strategy? It might help you to focus on one industry (green technology) or institution (education) or economic sector (jobs, unemployment insurance, or housing).

5. Write an exploratory essay on a controversial issue posed as a problem or question. Follow the assignment and model of student writer Patrick Scholze's researched exploratory essay in Chapter 3, pages 119–122.

6. Choose one of the following problems, research it, and write a policy proposal in the form of a letter to your U.S. senator or representative or an editorial for an online news commentary site such as CommonDreams.org. Write as a concerned, informed citizen with the purpose of compelling your audience to support your proposal.

   A. How should the federal government stimulate the American economy? Should it encourage American production and promote "buying American"?

   B. Many small, local banks did not follow the money-making practices of the larger banks. What can the government and the financial system learn from these small banks?

   C. What safety nets—universal healthcare, unemployment insurance, or more protection for pensions and retirement funds—would most strengthen American society and economy?

   D. For global stability and fairness, should the membership of the IMF be expanded and should it cancel the debts of developing countries? Should the G-20 replace the G-8 in exercising global economic power?

   You might find these think tanks useful in your research: Center for Economic and Policy Research; Economic Policy Institute; Pew Research Institute; Brookings Institute; Center for American Progress; Horizon Project; Heritage Foundation; the World Bank; the International Monetary Fund.

7. Research the challenges of teaching financial literacy, including basic economic principles and money management, and investigate what courses and programs already exist. You may choose to explore elementary and middle school, high school, college, or outside-school programs. Write a proposal argument addressed to a group of decision makers, arguing for or against the adoption of a financial literacy program. Include a response to objections to your proposal.

8. Research some question of interest to you related to the financial crisis (for example, What did flipping houses contribute to the housing market collapse? Is renting housing better than buying in times of economic downturn? Is going back to school for retraining or graduate degrees advisable during economic downturns? What can we learn from the Great Depression?). Then write an argument directed to an audience that shares your interest.

Crossing Borders
Immigration

QUESTION TO PONDER

One of the many editorials written in the ongoing debate over immigration reform asserted that Americans "pay the lowest prices for agricultural products in any industrialized nation in the world" because our produce is "subsidized by the poorest wage earners in America," many of whom are illegal immigrants from Mexico.* If you investigated the supermarket prices of fresh fruit grown and picked in the United States, you would find low prices like these: apples for $1.99 a pound; oranges for 99¢ a pound; grapefruit for $1.49 a pound; pears for $1.29 a pound. Realizing that this fruit was most likely picked by immigrant laborers, you are asking, "How do average Americans benefit from legal and illegal immigrants and what global forces are driving the growing immigrant population?"

CONTEXT FOR A NETWORK OF ISSUES

In some communities on Long Island, New York, tension has been building over the last few years as homeowners, politicians, and advocacy groups wrangle over what to do about the growing influx of Latino immigrants. In these long-established suburban communities with few rental properties, immigrants are crowding into houses, causing concern over health, sanitation, and residential codes. Each morning, immigrants cluster on corners waiting to be hired by contractors for a day's wages negotiated between the parties. Upset residents of these communities are embroiled in civic debates over these questions: Should communities designate town halls as hiring locations for day laborers? Should landlords be allowed to rent one-family homes to large groups of immigrants? If not, where should these people live? What can be done about businesses employing illegal immigrants and

---

*Ricardo Sanchez, letter to the editor, *Seattle Post-Intelligencer*, January 30, 2004, http://seattlepi.nwsource.com/opinion/158609_ricardo30.html

undercutting competitors who have higher labor costs because they pay their legal immigrant workers good wages and provide medical insurance and benefits? And should the presence of large groups of immigrants be allowed to change the "character" of these communities? Like the towns on Long Island, many cities and communities around the country are wrestling with these questions.

Sites of social conflict such as these communities on Long Island are a symptom of larger U.S. issues with immigration. Known as a nation of immigrants, the United States now has a population of whom 11 percent are foreign-born, according to the 2000 census. The decades 1901–1910 and 1981–1990 were peak periods of immigration, with the greatest number of immigrants arriving between 1991 and 2000: roughly nine million.* The *Statistical Yearbook of the Immigration and Naturalization Service* reports that Mexico, India, the Philippines, China, and El Salvador—developing countries with great economic needs and large, growing populations—contributed 39 percent of the legal immigrants in 2008. The trend toward increasing numbers of immigrants raises questions about the future of U.S. immigration.

Efforts by the U.S. government to control immigration through legislation and physical restraint have proved problematic. The McCarran-Walter Act of 1952 repealed the 1924 Immigration Act and ended the ban on Asian immigration, but it established a quota system by which immigrants were limited by national origin, race, and ancestry. Then in 1965, the Immigration and Nationality Act Amendments ended the discriminatory national origins quota system. This was replaced with a first-come, first-served system, giving preference to uniting families and establishing numerical restrictions according to the Eastern and Western Hemispheres. Another significant piece of legislation was the Immigration Reform and Control Act of 1986, which attempted to fix the problem of the large number of illegal immigrants by granting permanent resident status to those who had lived and worked in the United States since 1982.

More recent governmental efforts to control the volume of immigration have been ineffective. In 1990, the Immigration Act increased the number of new immigrants allowed into the country to 700,000 a year. However, both the total number and the rate of legal and illegal immigration continue to increase. The number of illegal immigrants residing in the United States is now somewhere between eleven and twelve million, 80 percent of whom are from Latin America, according to estimates by the Pew Hispanic Centers.† That number grows by hundreds of thousands each year. Furthermore, governmental strategies to restrain immigration physically along the 1,951-mile U.S.–Mexican border—a concern that has become a heightened national security issue—have

---

*Figures for the 2001–2010 period will become available following the 2010 census.

†Haeyoun Park, "Recession's Toll on Hispanic Immigrants," the *New York Times*, updated March 24, 2009.

also proved unsuccessful. The millions of dollars spent on fences, helicopters, and border patrols have failed to deter illegal immigrants. Instead, because of tighter surveillance in border cities such as El Paso and Laredo, Texas, and San Diego, California, people now take more dangerous routes through the Sonora Desert, where many die of thirst, hunger, and heat.

Once in the United States, immigrants face discrimination and exploitation. Immigrants, particularly undocumented Mexicans, work under the most dangerous conditions in construction jobs and agriculture. In 2004, Mexicans represented one in twenty-four workers in the United States but one in fourteen deaths on the job. According to the Occupational Safety and Health Administration, these largely preventable deaths occurred because of lack of safety equipment and job training.* More recently, journalists and policymakers have been drawing attention to the huge subclass of undocumented workers who work for low wages at some of the most necessary but least appreciated jobs in manufacturing, agriculture, and the service sector. Indeed, businesses, hospitals, restaurants, and other parts of American society including American households that hire gardeners, nannies, and housecleaners have come to depend on this inexpensive labor. For example, estimates suggest that between 50 and 85 percent of agricultural workers are in the United States illegally.†

U.S. immigration issues are part of the larger global picture of political, economic, and social forces driving immigration and of the global economic and social problems of regulating and humanely treating immigrants. The movement of masses of people across national borders continues to increase in our globally connected world. According to Susan F. Martin, director of the Institute for the Study of International Migration at Georgetown University, "150 million people or 2.5% of the world's population live outside their country of birth," a figure that has "doubled since 1965."‡ Some are refugees fleeing political or ethnic persecution and extreme danger, leaving countries such as Haiti, Bosnia, Kosovo, Sudan, Myanmar, Iraq, and Bhutan, which have had political upheavals and ethnic clashes. However, most immigrants move for economic reasons. Some college-educated persons and professionals choose to leave their poorer countries for developed countries, where they can use their training and education under better conditions for substantially higher pay, a phenomenon called the "brain drain." The main pattern of migration is from developing countries to richer, more economically stable, and prosperous developed countries. The United States, Canada, and the countries of the European Union are receiving, or destination, countries for many immigrants from sender countries, usually poorer countries.

---

*Justin Pritchard, "Lethal Labor," *Seattle Times*, March 27, 2004.

†Suzanne Gamboa, "Q&A," *Seattle Times*, August 1, 2004.

‡Susan F. Martin, "Heavy Traffic: International Migration in an Era of Globalization." *Brookings Review* 19, no. 4 (Fall 2001): 41.

STAKES AND STAKEHOLDERS

Citizens of developed countries as well as citizens of developing countries hold stakes in the potential gains and costs of global immigration. Policymakers, analysts, and citizens around the world are speculating about the reasons that so many people are leaving their countries of origin and are arguing about the most effective ways to manage immigration. Here are some key issue questions and some of the positions arguers are taking.

How Is Globalization Fueling Immigration? Some analysts emphasize "pull" factors such as the enticing lifestyle of the world's wealthiest nations that is broadcast globally by television and other media, and that insidiously suggests the superiority of these values, customs, and opportunities to live the "good life." Other analysts, such as former U.S. Ambassador to Mexico Jeffrey Davidow, posit the dominance of "push" factors—the conditions compelling people to move from developing countries to developed countries. Davidow asserts that emigration from Mexico "will continue at high rates until the Mexican economy can provide sufficient work opportunities and decent standards of living for a far greater percentage of its population."* Some activists and citizens of developing countries fault global institutions such as the International Monetary Fund (IMF) and the North American Free Trade Agreement (NAFTA) for pressuring developing countries to pay their debts and criticize large multinational corporations for displacing the poor. For example, when giant agribusinesses buy up small subsistence farms in Mexico, they force these farmers to seek food, work, and dignity in the United States. Analysts and politicians from Latin America note that their developing nations depend on remittances— money earned by their citizens abroad and sent back to their own countries in the form of money orders, personal checks, or electronic transfers—as a key percentage of their gross domestic product. Although the global economic downturn has reduced the money sent to home countries, remittances to Latin America and the Caribbean in 2008 still totaled $69.2 billion.

How Much Should Receiving Countries Focus on Their National Interest and How Can Immigrants Be Integrated for the Economic and Social Benefit of All? Citizens and politicians of the rich European Union (EU) nations are debating whether to impose restrictions on immigration from the ten new EU members from Eastern Europe, who, like Slovakia and the Czech Republic, have high unemployment rates. Many British citizens, journalists, U.S. citizens, policymakers, and activists are debating how and to what degree they should restrict immigrants' access to social benefits, such as the dole (welfare) and housing in Britain and driver's licenses,

---

*"Immigration, the United States, and Mexico," Mexidata.Info, http://www.mexidata. info/id350.html.

welfare, food stamps, Medicaid, and financial support for higher education in the United States. In the United States, some environmental groups such as the Sierra Club are concerned about the need to limit immigration in order to reduce U.S. population growth and the drain on natural resources, whereas some European analysts and politicians are arguing that immigrants are beneficial, even necessary, to supply labor to offset Western Europe's aging population and low birthrate.

To What Extent Are the Most Urgent Problems of Immigration Economic Problems and to What Extent Are They Cultural Problems? Some analysts, politicians, and groups of citizens see immigration problems as religious and cultural differences affecting national identity and cultural integrity. For example, confronted with increasing numbers of Muslim immigrants from Turkey, Southeast Asia, North Africa, and the Middle East, some Europeans are speaking out in favor of preserving traditional European values. Some voices in this controversy, such as political scientist Samuel Huntington in the United States and France's president, Nicolas Sarkozy, believe that large immigrant groups need to assimilate into the dominant culture of their receiving countries. In opposition, some immigrants, such as members of the Muslim community in Europe, have labeled these attitudes as racist and are protesting. The recent furor in France over whether Muslim girls should be allowed to wear headscarves (hijabs) in school is an example of these complex clashes over culture and religion. The killing of Dutch filmmaker Theo van Gogh by a Moroccan man because van Gogh had made a controversial film about abused Muslim women and the recent fires and riots in France reveal the potential for violence in these cultural conflicts.

What Would Be a Fair and Effective Way to Manage Legal and Illegal Immigration Involving Workers? Part of the immigration reform that President George W. Bush proposed in January 2004 was a "guest worker plan" that would have enabled immigrants to apply for renewable three-year worker visas. Businesses and employers would have been required to give evidence that they couldn't fill their jobs with American workers and thus had a need for these immigrant workers. The plan also proposed offering worker protection, retirement benefits, and tax savings accounts to immigrant workers, as well as temporary visas allowing workers to come and go across the U.S. border. The Bush plan died in Congress in 2007 after opposition steadily mounted across the country, but the debate over what approach to take to the treatment of immigrant workers continues.

In April 2009, the two leading labor federations in the United States (the AFL-CIO and Change to Win) joined in a campaign to give illegal workers already in the country legal status, but they also strongly opposed any new program that would allow employers to bring in new workers on a temporary basis, a practice many labor advocates have claimed benefits employers much more than workers. The U.S. Chamber of Commerce, representing businesses, promptly came out in favor of a temporary worker program to meet business needs and thus ensured that the legislative struggle over this aspect of immigration reform would continue.

President Barack Obama's approach to immigration reform has stressed the strengthening of border security; encouraging legal immigration to meet employment needs but cracking down on those who employ illegal immigrants; promoting Mexican economic development as a way to reduce illegal immigration; and establishing a system for "undocumented immigrants in good standing to pay a fine, learn English, and go to the back of the line for the opportunity to become citizens."*

Some citizens and anti-immigration groups are unhappy with any program that, like both the Bush and Obama plans, seems to them to reward illegal immigrants with visas or a path to citizenship and thus amounts to what they call a "backdoor amnesty." More extreme anti-immigration groups such as the Federation for American Immigration Reform (FAIR) want to preserve Anglo-American values and racial priorities and call for tighter control of U.S. borders and strict penalties for employers who hire illegal immigrants. In opposition, Latin American politicians and immigrant advocacy groups argue that years of work in the United States should be a qualification for applying for citizenship.

The debate over how to manage immigration involving both legal and illegal workers is a crucial part of efforts at overall immigration reform, and the number of parties to that debate indicates both the stakes involved and the challenges facing those seeking an agreement on the best way to proceed.

What Are Some Alternatives to a Guest Worker Program? Some politicians, analysts, and policymakers believe that the way to solve U.S. immigration problems with Mexico and other Latin American countries, to stop the further erosion of the U.S. workers' economic base, and to bring political stability and prosperity to these countries is to tackle the income disparity between the United States and these developing countries. Free trade proponents argue that more emphasis on free trade will bring economic improvement and greater economic equality to these countries. However, other activists contend that free trade dominated by corporations has been a major source of economic disruption—even devastation—in these Latin American countries, and are working instead for more independence and social justice in these countries.

What Existing and New Global Institutions Could Help to Guide and Regulate Immigration on a Global Level? Some analysts and policymakers do not think immigration can be controlled or restricted, while other leaders are campaigning for regional and international organizations and multilateral approaches with new policies and new laws to help deal with the patterns of global immigration. They propose that global organizations beyond the United Nations should govern the movement of both refugees and economic migrants.

---

*http://www.whitehouse.gov/agenda/immigration/, April 20, 2009.

STUDENT VOICE: La Migra by Esperanza Borboa

In the narrative that follows, student writer Esperanza Borboa shares her experience of the exploitation of illegal immigrants in the United States.

I'm from Los Angeles, California, and in 1976, I worked in the garment industry in the heart of downtown where small and large cutting rooms employed anywhere from 5 to 100 people. Gender roles were clearly marked in this industry. Men were cutters, spreaders and pattern makers. Women were seamstresses. Salaries were oftentimes below minimum wage with no benefits, and women sat at the bottom of that pay scale. I worked in the office as an assistant bookkeeper for minimum wage and no benefits. Most of the workers at our shop were Mexicans with a few Cubans. Everyone, including the boss, knew there were some who were undocumented, but we never talked about it. I was slowly becoming aware of how these people were exploited with no protection or recourse. Working and getting to know these men and women, I was learning what they were willing to risk and suffer just for the opportunity to work and provide for themselves and their children, something they couldn't do in their home countries. One day an experience made me feel the pain of their situation.

On that day I walked out to the cutting room to double-check some tickets with numbers I couldn't read. A young man came running by me, and all at once people were running in all directions. I asked Carmen, one of the lead workers, what was going on and she said the Migra (Immigration) was outside. There was a black passenger van in the alley half filled with workers from our shop and the one across the alley. One of the women being led to the van was crying and shouting to her co-worker "Vaya a mi casa y escoge a mis hijos y te llamo por teléfono!" ("Go to my house and get my children and I'll phone you!")

Although I knew they couldn't take me, a U.S. citizen, in that van, I was scared and stunned. I had known that raids were common, but this was my first experience of one. I asked Carmen what would happen to these people. She said, "They'll be deported to Mexico, and some of them will be back here by next week if they can come up with the money to pay a Coyote to cross them over the border. Their kids will stay here with friends till their mother or another family member can get here." As we watched the van pull away, my furious boss was ranting that he needed our help finding replacement workers and that we should let our friends know he was hiring. The Immigration official said they had received an anonymous call about illegal aliens working in this area. We all knew that someone always benefited from these raids, perhaps a competitor or the boss himself. Sometimes the raids would conveniently come the day before payday, enabling the boss not to have to pay "illegal" workers, even if they managed to come back.

That day my heart ached for all those picked up, and I felt powerless, voiceless and guilty for working there, but as a young single mother I needed to work. I quit that job shortly after the raid and found another job with a company in the same industry only to see it happen again, but this time, most of us were pretty sure the boss had something to do with it because it was too close to a pay period. I quit that job too.

Many years later, I moved to Washington state, and while working with farmworkers, I found out that the same practices were taking place in fields all across the country. The Migra would show up when the fields were almost completely cleared. The growers would deny they had anything to do with it just as the company owners did in Los Angeles, but we all knew better.

INTERNATIONAL VOICES

Along with a number of Latin American countries, Mexico is experiencing dramatic social and economic changes bound up with immigration. Immigration can mean economic survival, improving individuals' lives and enabling immigrants to send home money, which is then used to build up those communities. However, immigration can also cause emotional distress and major social disruption for individuals, families, communities, and regions. The following article, "Town's Fate Lies in Immigration Reform" by Mark Stevenson from the March 27, 2004, *Seattle Times*, reveals some of the repercussions of immigration: economic and social instability and importation of negative cultural influences from the United States.

Residents of a Small Town in Mexico Responding to Immigration

Santa Ana Del Valle, Mexico—

. . . Teacher Eleazar Pedro Santiago says that elsewhere in the mountains of Oaxaca state, he has seen several "ghost towns" with just a few old people and farm animals. . . .

"Everybody has the same idea—to earn money up there and start a business back here," says Aquino, the weaver. "What they don't think about is: What are they going to sell and who are they going to sell to?"

Most residents agree things can't go on as they are. The dual existence the town has led since the 1960s—one foot here, one foot in the north—has not been good for Santa Ana.

"Many of the people came back corrupted by the U.S. lifestyle," Aquino says. "They import all these fantasies from up north: the good life, total freedom, not having to answer to anyone."

The habits of U.S. inner cities have already begun to invade. Boys greet each other with a street gang-style handshake, drugs are a problem, and graffiti has begun to appear on the town's adobe walls.

Many say the town's salvation doesn't involve the United States at all.

"What we need here are more job opportunities, so people won't have to go," says Abelardo Gonzalez, the school director. "Now, there's just farmwork, and that's only when there's rain."

GLOBAL HOT SPOT: Mexico

As the United States has increased its surveillance of the border and its pressure on cities such as San Diego and El Paso, the risks of immigrating have increased substantially. This excerpt from the article "Mexican Biologist's Desperate Dream Leads to Doom in Desert" by Richard Boudreaux from the October 20, 2004, edition of the *Seattle Times* reveals both Mexico's social acceptance of illegal immigration as a route to economic survival and the desperation and persistence of Mexican immigrants. It also points out some of the physical dangers of crossing the border illegally: the possibility of dying of heat, cold, thirst, exhaustion, and abandonment.

Sasabe, Mexico—. . . The border's busiest migration corridor has become the 57-mile dirt road from Altar to Sasabe in the Mexican state of Sonora. Altar's 7,000 residents run guest houses, sell backpacks and work as drivers for migrants, who gather by the hundreds in the town square each day to meet with smugglers and ride north to foot trails that cross the border.

Within 25 minutes on a recent afternoon, eight vans crammed with migrants out of Altar passed a checkpoint just south of Sasabe run by Grupo Beta, the humanitarian arm of Mexico's National Migration Institute. Many of the occupants were from tropical lowlands in southern Mexico, getting their first blast of desert heat.

They looked bored by Julio Mallen's words of caution.

"It's important to go with enough water for at least two or three days," the Beta agent emphasized, peering into each van. "Wear long sleeves to protect yourself from the sun. If anyone feels tired and cannot continue, tell your companions so they can help you find a road and get help."

Grupo Beta defines its mission as minimizing harm to U.S.-bound migrants without explicitly discouraging their exodus. "Have a safe trip and God bless you," Mallen said at the end of his lecture.

The readings in this chapter will help you think about globalization and immigration from different national and global perspectives as you try to formulate your own views on how receiving and sender nations should respond to these global migration issues.

READINGS

Borders Beyond Control
Jagdish Bhagwati

Jagdish Bhagwati has been a prolific contributor to the field of migration and immigration policy over the last three decades. He holds the title University Professor (in economics and law) at Columbia University and is a senior fellow in International Economics at the Council on Foreign Relations. Bhagwati has published numerous books, among them his *In Defense of Globalization* (2004), which has been translated into sixteen languages. Bhagwati is currently at work on a book titled *An Unfinished Agenda: Managing International Migration*. His work is also published regularly in the *Financial Times*, the *Wall Street Journal*, and the *New Republic*. This piece appeared in the January–February 2003 issue of *Foreign Affairs*. Published by the Council on Foreign Relations since 1922, the journal describes itself as "America's most influential publication on international affairs and foreign policy" and "the international forum of choice for the most important new ideas, analysis, and debate on the most significant issues in the world" (www.foreignaffairs.org/about/).

> Jagdish Bhagwati's target audience for this piece is readers who are well informed about and engaged in global issues. How does he try to make his views on immigration accessible to other readers seeking insights into global immigration problems?

A DOOR THAT WILL NOT CLOSE

International migration lies close to the center of global problems that now seize the attention of politicians and intellectuals across the world. Take just a few recent examples.—Prime Ministers Tony Blair of the United Kingdom and Jose Mará Aznar of Spain proposed at last year's European Council meeting in Seville that the European Union withdraw aid from countries that did not take effective steps to stem the flow of illegal emigrants to the EU. Blair's outspoken minister for development, Clare Short, described the proposal as "morally repugnant" and it died amid a storm of other protests.—Australia received severe condemnation worldwide last summer when a special envoy of the UN high commissioner for human rights exposed the deplorable conditions in detention camps that held Afghan, Iranian, Iraqi, and Palestinian asylum seekers who had landed in Australia.

—Following the September 11 attacks in New York City and Washington, D.C., U.S. Attorney General John Ashcroft announced several new policies that rolled back protections enjoyed by immigrants. The American Civil Liberties Union (ACLU) and Human Rights Watch fought back. So did Islamic and Arab ethnic organizations. These groups employed lawsuits, public dissent, and congressional lobbying to secure a reversal of the worst excesses.

—The *Economist* ran in just six weeks two major stories describing the growing outflow of skilled citizens from less developed countries to developed countries seeking to attract such immigrants. The "brain drain" of the 1960s is striking again with enhanced vigor.

These examples and numerous others do not just underline the importance of migration issues today. More important, they show governments attempting to stem migration only to be forced into retreat and accommodation by factors such as civil-society activism and the politics of ethnicity. Paradoxically, the ability to control migration has shrunk as the desire to do so has increased. The reality is that borders are beyond control and little can be done to really cut down on immigration. The societies of developed countries will simply not allow it. The less developed countries also seem overwhelmed by forces propelling emigration. Thus, there must be a seismic shift in the way migration is addressed: governments must reorient their policies from attempting to curtail migration to coping and working with it to seek benefits for all.

To demonstrate effectively why and how this must be done, however, requires isolating key migration questions from the many other issues that attend the flows of humanity across national borders. Although some migrants move strictly between rich countries or between poor ones, the most compelling problems result from emigration from less developed to more developed countries. They arise in three areas. First, skilled workers are legally emigrating, temporarily or permanently, to rich countries. This phenomenon predominantly concerns the less developed countries that are losing skilled labor. Second, largely unskilled migrants are entering developed countries illegally and looking for work. Finally, there is the "involuntary" movement of people, whether skilled or unskilled, across borders to seek asylum. These latter two trends mostly concern the developed countries that want to bar illegal entry by the unskilled.

All three problems raise issues that derive from the fact that the flows cannot be effectively constrained and must instead be creatively accommodated. In designing such accommodation, it must be kept in mind that the illegal entry of asylum seekers and economic migrants often cannot be entirely separated. Frustrated economic migrants are known to turn occasionally to asylum as a way of getting in. The effective tightening of one form of immigrant entry will put pressure on another.

SOFTWARE ENGINEERS, NOT HUDDLED MASSES*

Looking at the first problem, it appears that developed countries' appetite for skilled migrants has grown—just look at Silicon Valley's large supply of successful Indian and Taiwanese computer scientists and venture capitalists. The enhanced appetite for such professionals reflects the shift to a globalized economy in which countries compete for markets by creating and attracting technically skilled talent. Governments also perceive these workers to be more likely to assimilate quickly into their new societies. This heightened demand is matched by a supply that is augmented for old reasons that have intensified over time. Less developed countries cannot offer modern professionals the economic rewards or the social conditions that they seek. Europe and the United States also offer opportunities for immigrant children's education and career prospects that are nonexistent at home. These asymmetries of opportunity reveal themselves not just through cinema and television, but through the immediacy of experience. Increasingly, emigration occurs after study abroad. The number of foreign students at U.S. universities, for example, has grown dramatically; so has the number who stay on. In 1990, 62 percent of engineering doctorates in the United States were given to foreign-born students, mainly Asians. The figures are almost as high in mathematics, computer science, and the physical sciences. In economics, which at the graduate level is a fairly math-intensive subject, 54 percent of the Ph.D.'s awarded went to foreign students, according to a 1990 report of the American Economic Association.

Many of these students come from India, China, and South Korea. For example, India produces about 25,000 engineers annually. Of these, about 2,000 come from the Indian Institutes of Technology (IITS), which are modeled on MIT and the California Institute of Technology. Graduates of IITS accounted for 78 percent of U.S. engineering Ph.D.'s granted to Indians in 1990. And almost half of all Taiwanese awarded similar Ph.D.'s had previously attended two prestigious institutions: the National Taiwan University and the National Cheng Kung University. Even more telling, 65 percent of the Korean students who received science and engineering Ph.D.'s in the United States were graduates of Seoul National University. The numbers were almost as high for Beijing University and Tsinghua University, elite schools of the People's Republic of China.

These students, once graduated from American universities, often stay on in the United States. Not only is U.S. graduate education ranked

---

*Readings in Chapter 4 (by Bill Gates, Ralph Gomory, and Paul Craig Roberts) explore the controversy over the globalizing of high-tech jobs and the importation of international professionals.

highest in the world, but it also offers an easy way of immigrating. In fact, it has been estimated that more than 70 percent of newly minted, foreign-born Ph.D.'s remain in the United States, many becoming citizens eventually. Less developed countries can do little to restrict the numbers of those who stay on as immigrants. They will, particularly in a situation of high demand for their skills, find ways to escape any dragnet that their home country may devise. And the same difficulty applies, only a little less starkly, to countries trying to hold on to those citizens who have only domestic training but are offered better jobs abroad.

A realistic response requires abandoning the "brain drain" approach of trying to keep the highly skilled at home. More likely to succeed is a "diaspora" model, which integrates present and past citizens into a web of rights and obligations in the extended community defined with the home country as the center. The diaspora approach is superior from a human rights viewpoint because it builds on the right to emigrate, rather than trying to restrict it. And dual loyalty is increasingly judged to be acceptable rather than reprehensible. This option is also increasingly feasible. Nearly 30 countries now offer dual citizenship. Others are inching their way to similar options. Many less developed countries, such as Mexico and India, are in the process of granting citizens living abroad hitherto denied benefits such as the right to hold property and to vote via absentee ballot.

However, the diaspora approach is incomplete unless the benefits are balanced by some obligations, such as the taxation of citizens living abroad. The United States already employs this practice. This author first recommended this approach for developing countries during the 1960s, and the proposal has been revived today. Estimates made by the scholars Mihir Desai, Devesh Kapur, and John McHale demonstrate that even a slight tax on Indian nationals abroad would substantially raise Indian government revenues. The revenue potential is vast because the aggregate income of Indian-born residents in the United States is 10 percent of India's national income, even though such residents account for just 0.1 percent of the American population.

UNSTOPPABLE

The more developed countries need to go through a similar dramatic shift in the way they respond to the influx of illegal economic immigrants and asylum seekers. Inducements or punishments for immigrants' countries of origin are not working to stem the flows, nor are stiffer border-control measures, sanctions on employers, or harsher penalties for the illegals themselves.

Three sets of factors are behind this. First, civil-society organizations, such as Human Rights Watch, the ACLU, and the International Rescue Committee, have proliferated and gained in prominence and influence. They provide a serious constraint on all forms of restrictive action. For example, it is impossible to incarcerate migrants caught crossing borders illegally without raising an outcry over humane treatment. So authorities generally send these people back across the border, with the result that they cross again and again until they finally get in. More than 50 percent of illegals, however, now enter not by crossing the Rio Grande but by legal means, such as tourist visas, and then stay on illegally. Thus, enforcement has become more difficult without invading privacy through such measures as identity cards, which continue to draw strong protests from civil liberties groups. A notable example of both ineffectual policy and successful civil resistance is the 1986 Sanctuary movement that surfaced in response to evidence that U.S. authorities were returning desperate refugees from war-torn El Salvador and Guatemala to virtually certain death in their home countries. (They were turned back because they did not meet the internationally agreed upon definition for a refugee.) Sanctuary members, with the aid of hundreds of church groups, took the law into their own hands and organized an underground railroad to spirit endangered refugees to safe havens. Federal indictments and convictions followed, with five Sanctuary members given three- to five-year sentences. Yet, in response to a public outcry and an appeal from Senator Dennis DeConcini (D-Ariz.), the trial judge merely placed the defendants on probation.

Sanctions on employers, such as fines, do not fully work either. The General Accounting Office, during the debate over the 1986 immigration legislation that introduced employer sanctions, studied how they had worked in Switzerland and Germany. The measures there failed. Judges could not bring themselves to punish severely those employers whose violation consisted solely of giving jobs to illegal workers. The U.S. experience with employer sanctions has not been much different.

Finally, the sociology and politics of ethnicity also undercut enforcement efforts. Ethnic groups can provide protective cover to their members and allow illegals to disappear into their midst. The ultimate constraint, however, is political and results from expanding numbers. Fellow ethnics who are U.S. citizens, legal immigrants, or amnesty beneficiaries bring to bear growing political clout that precludes tough action against illegal immigrants. Nothing matters more than the vote in democratic societies. Thus the Bush administration, anxious to gain Hispanic votes, has embraced an amnesty confined solely to Mexican illegal immigrants, thereby discarding the principle of nondiscrimination enshrined in the 1965 Immigration and Nationality Act.

MINDING THE OPEN DOOR

If it is not possible to effectively restrict illegal immigration, then governments in the developed countries must turn to policies that will integrate migrants into their new homes in ways that will minimize the social costs and maximize the economic benefits. These policies should include children's education and grants of limited civic rights such as participation in school-board elections and parent-teacher associations. Governments should also assist immigrants in settling throughout a country, to avoid depressing wages in any one region. Greater development support should be extended to the illegal migrants' countries of origin to alleviate the poor economic conditions that propel emigration. And for the less developed countries, there is really no option but to shift toward a diaspora model.

Some nations will grasp this reality and creatively work with migrants and migration. Others will lag behind, still seeking restrictive measures to control and cut the level of migration. The future certainly belongs to the former. But to accelerate the progress of the laggards, new institutional architecture is needed at the international level. Because immigration restrictions are the flip side of sovereignty, there is no international organization today to oversee and monitor each nation's policies toward migrants, whether inward or outward bound.

The world badly needs enlightened immigration policies and best practices to be spread and codified. A World Migration Organization would begin to do that by juxtaposing each nation's entry, exit, and residence policies toward migrants, whether legal or illegal, economic or political, skilled or unskilled. Such a project is well worth putting at the center of policymakers' concerns.

For Class Discussion

1. How would you summarize the three main global immigration patterns that Jagdish Bhagwati describes?

2. How—and how well—does Bhagwati support his claim that the migration of masses of people cannot be stopped in a globalized economy?

3. What does Bhagwati mean by the terms "brain drain," "civil-society organizations," "the politics of ethnicity," "economic immigrants," and "asylum seekers"?

4. Bhagwati proposes two solutions to the immigration problems facing the world today: (1) a "diaspora" model and (2) a World Migration Organization. How does he support and justify these proposed solutions?

5. What views of "enlightened immigration policies" does he assume his readers will share? How does he handle opposing views?

6. What strengths and weaknesses in Bhagwati's argument might general readers identify?

■

Lecture on International Flows of Humanity

Kofi Annan

Born in Ghana, and educated both internationally and in the United States, Kofi Annan became Secretary-General of the United Nations (UN) in 1997 after having held various leadership positions there. He served two terms as Secretary-General, and was awarded the Nobel Peace Prize in 2001. Annan remains a constant advocate for both human rights and the rule of law in his role on the board of directors for the United Nations Foundation. He is also Chancellor for the University of Ghana. Annan delivered this speech at Columbia University on November 21, 2003, as the Emma Lazarus Lecture. (Emma Lazarus [1849–1883] was a well-known Jewish-American poet and political activist. Her famous sonnet "The New Colossus" was engraved on a plaque on the Statue of Liberty's pedestal in 1903. This poem helped to enhance the Statue's role as a symbol of the United States as a welcoming place of freedom and opportunity for immigrants. Copies of this poem are readily available on the Web.)

> How does Kofi Annan make use of the specific rhetorical context of this speech, and how does he try to connect with his audience in his introductory remarks?

There could be no place more fitting for a lecture on international flows of humanity than this great university, located as it is in a city which has been the archetypal success story of international migration.

And you could not have chosen a better person to name it after than Emma Lazarus, whose unforgettable lines are inscribed on the base of the Statue of Liberty, the Mother of Exiles. Just in case you have forgotten them, they are printed in your programme!

While Emma Lazarus's immortal words promised welcome to the tired, the poor, the wretched, and the huddled masses yearning to be free, another American poet, Walt Whitman, spoke of the vibrancy and vitality that migrants brought to the new world. He called New York the "city of the world" because, he said, "all races are here, all lands of the earth make contributions here".

How right he was—and still is. Today, more than one in three inhabitants of New York City was born outside the United States. The city boasts communities of 188 different national origins—only three fewer than there are Member States in the United Nations—and 47 per cent of them speak a second language at home.

New York, in other words, is a brilliant success story of migration, as are many other cities all around the world today. In fact, in the year 2000, some 175 million people, about 3 per cent of the world's population, lived outside their country of birth—more than at any other time in history.

Of these, around 16 million were recognized refugees—people who did not choose to leave home but were forced to. Another 1 million were asylum seekers—people who claimed to be refugees, but whose claims were in the process of being verified. The remainder, some 158 million, were deemed international migrants—that is, people who have chosen to move.

So much mobility and diversity should be cause for celebration. But migration also gives rise to many problems, leading people to ask: Can we absorb large numbers of new people? Will they take our jobs or absorb our social services? Are they a threat to our security, our way of life or our national identity?

These are understandable concerns, and they must be answered. The answers are not easy. But I have come here today to say that they do not lie in halting migration—a policy that is bound to fail. I say the answer must lie in managing migration—rationally, creatively, compassionately and cooperatively. This is the only approach that can ensure that the interests of both migrant and host communities will be looked after and their rights upheld.

It is the only approach that can effectively address the complex issues surrounding migration—issues of human rights and economic opportunity, of labour shortages and unemployment, of brain drain and brain gain, of xenophobia and integration, of refugee crises and asylum seekers, of law enforcement and human trafficking, of human security and national security. And it is the only approach that can, if we get it right, bring advantages to all parties—sender countries, countries of transit, host countries, and migrants themselves.

Many migrants, while not literally forced to move, choose to do so under duress. They see no opportunity at home to improve themselves, or perhaps even to earn a living at all. Their departure may be a source of sadness for themselves and their families, and also a loss for their home countries—often poor ones, which could have benefited from their talents. They are usually not free riders looking for an easy life, but courageous men and women who make great sacrifices in search of a better future for themselves or their families.

Nor are their lives always to be envied once they have left home. They often face as many risks and unknowns as they do hopes and opportunities. Many fall prey to smugglers and traffickers on their journey, and many more face a surly welcome of exploitation, discrimination and prejudice once they arrive. Many have little choice but to do dirty, dangerous and difficult jobs.

Undoubtedly more needs to be done to create opportunities in poor countries for individual self-improvement. This is yet another reason why we must strive harder to achieve the Millennium Development Goals, including by forging a global partnership for development which, among other things, gives poor countries a fair chance to compete in the global market.

But migration itself can also be part of that global partnership—part of the solution to economic problems, not only in sender countries, but also in receiving ones. Sender countries benefit enormously from migrant remittances. They bring not only vital sustenance to the migrants' families. They also bring much-needed stimulus to the national economy. Last year alone, migrant workers in developed countries sent at least $88 billion back to their countries of origin—more than those same developing countries received in official development aid. These amounts are growing fast.

Emigration also relieves the pressures of overpopulation and unemployment, and in time endows sender countries with an educated diaspora who often bring or send home new skills, products, ideas and knowledge.

In short, migration is one of the tools we have to help put more of the world's people on the right side of—and ultimately, to eliminate—the vast divides that exist today between poor and rich, and between fettered and free.

Host country economies, too, can reap benefits. After all, the main reason any country attracts immigrants is its need for their labour. They perform many services that the host population is eager to consume, but is either unwilling or unable to provide for itself—from highly skilled work in research or information technology to less skilled jobs tending fields, nursing the sick and elderly, working on construction sites, running corner shops that stay open all night, or looking after children and doing housework while parents are out pursuing careers.

Increasingly, as birth rates in many developed countries fall, and populations age, immigrant labour, taxes and spending are becoming a demographic and economic necessity. Without them, pension schemes and health-care systems will be in danger of collapse. While immigration may not by itself be the answer to all these challenges, there is no answer to them that does not include immigration.

So migration has a demand as well as a supply side. Migrants are rational human beings who make economic choices. Up to now, rich countries have been far too comfortable with a policy framework that allows them to benefit from immigrant labour, while denying immigrants the dignity and rights of a legal status.

That is not good enough. Let us remember from the start that migrants are not merely units of labour. They are human beings. They have human emotions, human families, and above all, human rights—human rights which must be at the very heart of debates and policies on migration. Among those rights is the right to family unity—and in fact families reuniting form by far the largest stream of immigration into North America and Europe.

The more we try to deal with migration simply by clamping down on it with tighter border controls, the more we find that human rights are sacrificed—on the journey, at the border, and inside host countries.

Few, if any, States have actually succeeded in cutting migrant numbers by imposing such controls. The laws of supply and demand are too strong for that. Instead, immigrants are driven to enter the country clandestinely, to overstay their visas, or to resort to the one legal route still open to them, namely the asylum system. This experience shows that stronger borders are not necessarily smarter ones. And it shows that they can create new problems of law enforcement and lead almost inevitably to human rights violations.

The gravest violations come at the hands of smugglers and traffickers. Smuggling occurs with the complicity of migrants, usually because they can see no legal route to migrate. Trafficking is a modern form of slavery in which migrants are coerced and exploited. All too often, people who initially collaborate with smugglers later find themselves in the hands of traffickers.

Asylum processes, meanwhile, become clogged with doubtful cases, with the result that bona fide refugees are often detained for long periods. They are often denied the rights accorded to accused or convicted criminals—and, when free, they are objects of suspicion and hostility. This, in turn, undermines support for migration in host countries—despite the fact that many of them need migrants.

> **Let us remember from the start that migrants are not merely units of labor.**

Those who manage to get in, or stay, illegally become acutely vulnerable to exploitation. If they attempt to assert their rights, they can be met with a threat of exposure and deportation. Migrant women and unaccompanied children are especially vulnerable to physical, psychological, and sexual abuse, sometimes involving the risk of infection with HIV/AIDS.

I am not suggesting that all these problems could be solved at a stroke simply by lifting all restrictions on migration. It is vital for States to harmonize their policies and maintain networks of cooperation and information sharing on smuggling and trafficking routes and trends, and on effective practices in prevention and assistance.

Nor do I suggest that a society can be expected to forego any process for deciding which immigrants it will accept, and how many at a time. But I do say that those decisions need to be positive as well as negative. And I say here, in the United States, that while I understand this nation's need to ensure that those who come here are not a threat to homeland security, it would be a tragedy if this diverse country were to deprive itself of the enrichment of many students and workers and family members from particular parts of the world, or if the human rights of those who would migrate here were compromised.

I also believe that States need carefully thought-out policies for integrating immigrants who are allowed in. Since both migrants and host societies stand to benefit from successful integration, both must play their part in making it happen. It is reasonable for societies to expect those who would become citizens to share certain basic values, to respect the law of the land, and to develop fluency in the local language, with assistance if they need it.

For their part, host societies must have effective anti-discrimination legislation and procedures, reflecting international standards and obligations, and should also take measures to promote appreciation of cultural diversity among all their citizens and residents.

But laws and policies are not enough. Leadership is vital too. All national leaders should be conscious that any form of discrimination against immigrants is a regression from the standards for a just society enshrined in the Universal Declaration of Human Rights and the binding treaties that derive from it.

Many people, in government and academia, in the private sector and in civil society as a whole, are showing the leadership that is needed to combat xenophobia and stigma. I salute them for it. But I am also disturbed by the vilification, in some quarters, of migrants—particularly of asylum seekers—often in an effort to achieve political gain.

Many of those vilified have fled their homelands in fear of their lives. States have a legal obligation not to return them to danger. They must establish fair procedures to determine the legitimacy of asylum claims. If, in extreme circumstances, asylum seekers must be detained, certain minimal standards must be provided, and enforced, to ensure respect for their human dignity and human rights.

The international regime for protecting migrant workers, set out in a host of human rights conventions that are either regional in scope or confined to particular categories of workers, should be made applicable to all categories of migrants, both regular and irregular, and to members of their families. Many States have recognized this need.

Recently, a step forward was taken with the entry into force of the International Convention on the Protection of the Rights of All Migrant Workers and Members of their Families—the bill of rights for migrant workers and their families in their new home countries. This step was important. But it was not enough. So far, only sender States have ratified the Convention, which means that it will have little practical effect. I call on all States, and in particular receiving States, to ratify the Convention, so that the human rights of migrant workers are protected by law.

The Migrant Workers Convention is but one instance of the efforts that are being made to address the issue of migration at the global level. But despite these efforts, consensus is lacking on many of the principles and policies which should be applied to the governance of international migration.

Internationally, we are not well organized to forge that consensus.

The United Nations does play an important role in dealing with many aspects of migration, and a leading role in helping refugees through the office of the High Commissioner. The International Labour Organization gives a voice to organized labour, and sets standards for fair labour practices, in conjunction with governments and the private sector. Outside the

United Nations system, the International Organization for Migration (IOM) facilitates the movement of people, at the request of member States. United Nations agencies and the IOM have come together in the Geneva Migration Group to work more closely on this issue.

But we still lack a comprehensive institutional focus at the international level that could protect the rights of migrants and promote the shared interest of emigration, immigration and transit. No single agency works systematically across the whole spectrum of migration issues, and there is no complete legal framework in place to deal with this quintessentially global phenomenon.

I do not pretend that we can achieve such a framework overnight. And we should not await it before increasing bilateral and regional efforts. I am heartened by the efforts of some States—particularly those of the European Union—to find ways of coordinating their actions and harmonizing their policies.

Yet more and more people are coming to the conclusion that we also have to address this issue globally. Doing it regionally or bilaterally is not enough. I particularly welcome the decision taken by a core group of Member States from both North and South to form a Global Commission on International Migration to deepen our understanding of this issue and to make recommendations for improving international cooperation.

The Commission will have two distinguished co-Chairs in Jan Karlsson of Sweden and Mamphela Ramphele of South Africa. It has my full backing, and I hope it will receive support from States in all parts of the world and from institutions like yours. Most of all, I hope it will help us approach this issue creatively and cooperatively.

As the Commission's work proceeds, there are many questions I believe it should be asking, and that the rest of us should be asking too. For instance:

- Can greater cooperation be built between sender and receiver countries?
- Have the benefits of short-term and long-term temporary immigration been fully explored?
- Could more be done to work with the laws of supply and demand rather than against them?
- Might financial methods of discouraging illegal migration be more effective and more humane than some current practices?
- What are the best ways to speed up the integration of immigrants into host societies?
- Could more be done to harness the potential of migration as a force for development?
- Can developing countries do more to maintain contact with their emigrants?

No doubt there are numerous other equally important issues to be addressed as well.

Above all, I believe we must approach this issue with a strong ethical compass. The basic fairness and decency of any society can best be measured by its treatment of the weak and vulnerable. The principle of nondiscrimination has become an integral part of the universal moral code, one on which the defence of all other universal values depends. We should keep a firm hold upon it.

The willingness of rich countries to welcome migrants, and the way that they treat them, will be a measure of their commitment to human equality and human dignity. Their preparedness to adjust to the changes that migration brings will be an indicator of their readiness to accept the obligations as well as the opportunities of globalization, and of their conception of global citizenship. And their attitude to the issue will also be a test of their awareness of the lessons, and obligations, of history. After all, many migrants today are seeking to enter countries which not so long ago conquered and exploited their own. And many countries that are now attracting immigrants were until recently major exporters of emigrants.

Along with other countries, the United States falls into a third category—a nation built by immigration, a land where constant renewal and regeneration are essential elements of the national character. That character must never be lost.

And the hope and reality of a new future for those who would migrate must glow brighter today than ever before.

As Emma Lazarus wrote: "Send these, the homeless, tempest-tost to me, I lift my lamp beside the golden door."

For Class Discussion

1. Kofi Annan identifies the global stakeholders in immigration issues as "sender countries, countries of transit, host countries, and migrants themselves." According to Annan, what does each group lose and gain through migration? What are the responsibilities he identifies for each group?

2. What does Annan claim are the main problems with immigration that are facing receiving countries? What role in regulating immigration does Annan advocate for global institutions?

3. One argumentative strategy that Annan adopts in this speech is to change his audience's idea of immigrants and to reframe immigration in terms of the problem of poverty. How does he work on his audience members' emotions and imaginations to recast the identity of immigrants and the nature of the immigration problem?

4. How does remembering that this argument was delivered as a speech affect your response to it?

5. What features of this piece contribute to making it a persuasive argument in favor of global migration? ∎

From *Guide for the Mexican Migrant*
Mexico's Ministry of Foreign Relations

In January 2005, Mexico's Ministry of Foreign Relations issued a pamphlet titled *Guide for the Mexican Migrant*. This publication was produced as a supplement to *El Libro Vaquero*, an adult comic book romanticizing cowboy life and frequently read by uneducated male workers. In this pamphlet, the Mexican government addresses the reality of steady illegal migration and tries to protect its citizens who are seeking a new life in the United States. Soon after its publication, translations of the *Guide* began appearing in U.S. newspapers. *American Renaissance*, a monthly magazine that bills itself as "a literate, undeceived journal of race, immigration and the decline of civility," printed a version of the *Guide* in English, from which this excerpt is taken (www.amren.com/). To see the entire text of the *Guide*, go to this site or others on the Web.

> As its title indicates, this pamphlet falls in the genre of guidebooks. How are the function and purpose of this guidebook like and unlike those of guidebooks you have used?

INTRODUCTION

Esteemed Countryman:

The purpose of this guide is to provide you with practical advice that may prove useful to you in case you have made the difficult decision to search for employment opportunities outside of your country.

The sure way to enter another country is by getting your passport from the Ministry of Foreign Affairs, and the visa, which you may apply for at the embassy or consulate of the country you wish to travel to.

However, in practice we see many Mexicans who try to cross the Northern Border without the necessary documents, through high risk zones that involve grave dangers, particularly in desert areas or rivers with strong, and not always obvious, currents.

Reading this guide will make you aware of some basic questions about the legal consequences of your stay in the United States of America without the appropriate migratory documents, as well as about the rights you have in that country, once you are there, independent of your migratory status.

Keep in mind always that there exist legal mechanisms to enter the United States of America legally.

In any case, if you encounter problems or run into difficulties, remember that Mexico has 45 consulates in that country whose locations you can find listed in this publication.

Familiarize yourself with the closest consulate and make use of it.

DANGERS IN CROSSING HIGH RISK ZONES

To cross the river can be very risky, above all if you cross alone and at night.

Heavy clothing increases in weight when wet and this makes swimming and floating difficult.

If you cross by desert, try to walk at times when the heat will not be too intense.

Highways and population centers are far apart, which means you will spend several days looking for roads, and you will not be able to carry foodstuffs or water for long periods of time. Also, you can get lost.

Salt water helps keep liquids in your body. Although you may feel more thirst if you drink salt water, the risk of dehydration is much less.

The symptoms of dehydration are:

- Little or no sweat.
- Dryness in the eyes and in the mouth.
- Headache.
- Tiredness and excessive exhaustion.
- Difficulty in walking and thinking.
- Hallucinations and visions.

If you get lost, guide yourself by [telephone poles], train tracks, or dirt roads.

BEWARE OF HUMAN TRAFFICKERS (COYOTES, POLLEROS)

They can deceive you with assurances of crossing in a few hours through the mountains and deserts. This is simply not so!

They can risk your life taking you across rivers, drainage canals, desert areas, train tracks, or highways. This has caused the death of hundreds of persons.

If you decide to hire people traffickers to cross the border, consider the following precautions:

Do not let them out of your sight. Remember that they are the only ones who know the lay of the land, and therefore the only ones who can get you out of that place.

Do not trust those who offer to take you to "the other side" and ask you to drive a car or to take or carry a package for them. Normally, those packages contain drugs or other prohibited substances. For this reason, many people have ended up in jail.

For Class Discussion

1. How is this guide designed to appeal to its target audience?

2. What does the use of comic book illustrations contribute to the rhetorical effect of this pamphlet? (If you find this *Guide* on the Web, you will see the numerous illustrations in color.) What do the illustrations suggest about the target audience?

3. How do you think the genre and appearance of the *Guide* have contributed to the strong emotional responses it has evoked, especially from some advocacy groups and politicians in the United States?

4. The *Guide* includes this disclaimer by the Mexican government: "This Consular Protection Guide does not promote crossing by Mexicans without legal documentation required by the government of the United States. Its purpose is to make known the risks, and to inform the migrants about their rights, whether they are legal residents or not." What features of the content, tone, and style of this pamphlet support this declaration? What features, if any, suggest an ambivalent attitude toward illegal migration?

5. Do a brief investigation of the *Guide* on the Web. What have people in Mexico and in the United States said about this pamphlet? What is at stake for those who take the strongest stances?   ◼

The Special Case of Mexican Immigration
Samuel P. Huntington

Samuel P. Huntington (1927–2008) was a major scholarly voice on issues of national security and strategy, democratization and development of less-developed countries, cultural factors in world politics, and American national identity. He was the chair of Harvard Department of Government and its Academy for International and Area Studies, the cofounder of *Foreign Policy* magazine, a vocal neoconservative, and a prolific writer. His famous book *The Clash of Civilizations and the Remaking of the World Order* (1996) posits the thesis that the main conflicts of our global age will not be economic, political, or environmental; instead they will center on the values of groups of people (civilizations) and will involve their history, culture, and religion. Huntington sparked even more controversy with his argument about the threat and challenge of Mexican immigration to U.S. national identity. He advanced this position both in an article titled "The Hispanic Challenge" and in the more recent book *Who Are We? The Challenges to America's National Identity* (2004). "The Special Case of Mexican Immigration" is an adaptation of these longer writings. It appeared in 2000 in the *American Enterprise*, the online publication of the American Enterprise Institute, a conservative think tank. This publication says it seeks to appeal to a wide range of readers and to promote informed, independent thinking by offering well-reasoned and highly readable arguments.

> Many of the articles in this chapter focus on economic issues related to immigration. In contrast, where does Samuel Huntington think the main U.S. problems with immigration lie?

America is often described as a country defined by commitment to a creed formulated in the writings of our Founders. But American identity is only partly a matter of creed. For much of our history we also defined ourselves in racial, religious, ethnic, and cultural terms.

Before the Revolution we thought of ourselves in religious terms: 98 percent of Americans were Protestants, and Catholic Spain and France were our enemies. We also thought of ourselves in racial and ethnic terms: 80 percent of Americans at the time of the Revolution were from the British Isles. The other 20 percent were largely German and Dutch.

America is also often described as a nation of immigrants. We should distinguish immigrants, however, from settlers. Immigrants are people who leave one society and move to a recipient society. Early Americans did not immigrate to an existing society; they established new societies, in some cases for commercial reasons, more often for religious reasons. It was the new societies they created, basically defined by Anglo-Protestant culture, that attracted subsequent generations of immigrants to this country.

Demographer Campbell Gibson has done a very interesting analysis of the evolution of the United States' population. He argues that if no immigrants had come to this country after 1790, the population of the United States in 1990 would have been just about half of what it actually was. Thus, the American people are literally only half an immigrant people.

There have been great efforts in our history to limit immigration. In only one decade in the nineteenth century did the annual intake of immigrants amount to more than 1 percent of the population each year. In three other decades it was slightly over eight-tenths of 1 percent, while in six decades it was less than four-tenths of 1 percent. Obviously immigration has been tremendously important to this country, but the foreign-born population has exceeded 10 percent of our total population only in the seven census years from 1860 to 1930. (When the 2000 census results come out we will be back above the 10 percent level again.)

As I began to investigate the question of immigration, I came to the conclusion that our real problem is not so much immigration as assimilation. Seventy-five or 100 years ago there were great pressures to ensure that immigrants assimilated to the Anglo-Protestant culture, work ethic, and principles of the American creed. Now we are uncertain what immigrants should assimilate to. And that is a serious problem.

As I went further in my research, I concluded there was a still more significant problem, a problem that encompasses immigration, assimilation, and other things, too—what I will refer to as the Mexican problem. Much of what we now consider to be problems concerning immigration and assimilation really concern Mexican immigration and assimilation. Mexican immigration poses challenges to our policies and to our identity in a way nothing else has in the past.

There are five distinctive characteristics of the Mexican question which make it special. First, Mexican immigration is different because of contiguity. We have thought of immigration as being symbolized by Ellis Island, and perhaps now by Kennedy Airport. But Mexicans do not come across 2,000 miles of ocean. They come, often easily, across 2,000 miles of land border.

Our relationship with Mexico in this regard is in many respects unique in the world. No other First World country has a land frontier with a Third World country—much less one of 2,000 miles. The significance of this border is enhanced by the economic differences between the two countries. The income gap between Mexico and us is the largest between any two contiguous countries in the world.

The second distinctive aspect of today's Mexican immigration concerns numbers. Mexican immigration during the past several decades has been very substantial. In 1998 Mexican immigrants constituted 27 percent of the total foreign-born population in this country; the next largest two contingents, Filipinos and Chinese, each amounted to only 4 percent. Mexicans constituted two-thirds of Spanish-speaking immigrants, who in turn were over half of all new arrivals between 1970 and 1996. Our post-1965 wave of immigration differs from previous waves in having a majority from a single non-English language group.

A third distinguishing characteristic of this Mexican immigration is illegality. Illegal immigration is overwhelmingly a post-1965 and Mexican phenomenon. In 1995, according to one report, Mexicans made up 62 percent of the immigrants who entered the United States illegally. In 1997, the Immigration and Naturalization Service estimated Mexican illegals were nine times as numerous as the next largest contingent, from El Salvador.

The next important characteristic of Mexican immigration has been its concentration in a particular region. Mexican immigrants are heavily concentrated in the Southwest and particularly in southern California. This has very real consequences. Our Founders emphasized that immigrants would have to be dispersed among what they described as the English population in this country. To the extent that we have a large regional concentration of immigrants, it is a departure from our usual pattern.

Now obviously we have previously had high concentrations of immigrants in particular areas, such as the Irish in Boston, but by and large the immigrants have dispersed to different cities, and those cities have simultaneously hosted many different immigrant groups. This is the case still in New York, where there are many immigrants today, but no group that dominates. In Southern California, though, two-thirds or more of all the children in school are Spanish speaking. As Abe Lowenthal and Katrina Burgess write in *The California-Mexico Connection,* "No school system in a major U.S. city has ever experienced such a large influx of students from a single foreign country. The schools of Los Angeles are becoming Mexican."

Finally, there is the matter of the persistence of Mexico's large immigration. Previous waves of immigration fairly soon came to an end. The huge 1840s and '50s influxes from Ireland and Germany were drastically reduced by the Civil War and the easing of the Irish potato famine. The big wave at the turn of the century came to an end with World War I and the restrictive legislation in 1924.

These breaks greatly helped to facilitate the assimilation of the newcomers. In contrast, there does not seem to be any prospect of the current wave, begun over three decades ago, coming to an end soon. Mexican immigration may eventually subside as the Mexican birth rate slows, and possibly as a result of long-term economic development in Mexico. But those effects will only occur over a very long term. For the time being we are faced with substantial continued immigration from Mexico.

Sustained high levels of immigration build on themselves. After the first immigrants come from a country, it is easier for others from that country to come. Immigration is not a self-limiting process, it is a self-enhancing one.

And the longer immigration continues, the more difficult politically it is to stop. Leaders of immigrant organizations and interest groups develop a vested interest in expanding their own constituency. Immigration develops political support, and becomes more difficult to limit or reshape.

For all these reasons Mexican immigration is unique. What are the implications of this for assimilation?

The answer appears uncertain. In education and economic activity, Mexicans rate much lower than other immigrant groups. The rate of intermarriage between Hispanics and other Americans appears to be decreasing rather than increasing. (In 1977, 31 percent of all Hispanic marriages were interethnic; in 1994, 25.5 percent were.) With respect to language, I suspect Mexicans will in large part follow the pattern of earlier immigrants, with the third generation being fluent in English, but quite possibly, unlike previous third generations, also fluent in their ancestral language.

All of the characteristics I have mentioned lead to the possibility of a cultural community evolving in the Southwest in which people could pursue their lives within an overwhelmingly Mexican community, without ever having to speak English. This has already happened with the Cubans in Miami, and it could be reproduced on a larger and more significant scale in the Southwest. We know in the coming decades people of Hispanic origin will be a majority of the people in California and eventually in other southwestern states. America is moving in the direction of becoming a bilingual and bicultural society.

Without Mexican immigration, the overall level of immigration to this country would be perhaps two-thirds of what it has been—near the levels recommended by Barbara Jordan's immigration commission a few years ago. Illegal entries would be relatively minor. The average skill and education level of immigrants would be the highest in American history, and the much-debated balance of economic benefits versus costs of immigration would tilt heavily toward the positive side. The bilingual education issue would fade from our agenda. A major potential challenge to the cultural, and conceivably political, integrity of the United States would disappear.

Mexico and Mexican immigration, however, will not disappear, and learning to live with both may become more and more difficult. President-elect Vicente Fox wants to remove all restrictions on the movement of Mexicans into the United States.

In almost every recent year the Border Patrol has stopped about 1 million people attempting to enter the U.S. illegally from Mexico. It is generally estimated that about 300,000 make it across illegally. If over 1 million Mexican soldiers crossed the border, Americans would treat it as a major threat to their national security and react accordingly. The invasion of over 1 million Mexican civilians is a comparable threat to American societal security, and Americans should react against it with comparable vigor.

Mexican immigration looms as a unique and disturbing challenge to our cultural integrity, our national identity, and potentially to our future as a country.

For Class Discussion

1. What key points would you include in a summary of Samuel Huntington's ideas in this article?

2. The American Enterprise Institute is a conservative think tank. What features of this article's structure, depth of material, main points, and kinds of

evidence indicate that its publication, the *American Enterprise*, seeks to reach a broad audience?

3. Many people responding to Huntington's book *Who Are We?* and his article "The Hispanic Challenge," which develop the views presented in this piece, have criticized Huntington for fostering racism and nativism (privileging native-born residents over immigrants). What ideas in this article could fuel those attitudes toward immigrants?

4. Huntington's values and views dominate this argument in its approach and points. What points about immigration, especially Mexican immigration, is Huntington *not* factoring into his argument? In your view, how would including those points affect the logic and credibility of his argument?

5. Carefully describe the assumptions about Mexican immigration and immigrants an audience would have to hold in order to agree with Huntington's main points. What points would a rebuttal challenging those assumptions need to include?   ■

MALDEF and LULAC Rebuke Samuel Huntington's Theories on Latino Immigrants and Call on America to Reaffirm Its Commitment to Equal Opportunity and Democracy

Mexican American Legal Defense and Educational Fund (MALDEF) and League of United Latin American Citizens (LULAC)

This policy statement, dated April 23, 2004, is a formal response to Samuel P. Huntington's publications on Mexican immigration. The Mexican American Legal Defense and Educational Fund is a national, nonprofit, nonpartisan organization headquartered in Washington, D.C. Also centered there, the League of United Latin American Citizens is the oldest grassroots organization committed to the education, civil rights, and employment of Latinos. Both of these organizations are large, well established, and highly reputable. On the "About Us" page of its Web site, MALDEF states its mission: "to bring Latinos into the mainstream of American political and socioeconomic life, providing better educational opportunities, encouraging participation in all aspects of society, and offering a positive vision for the future" (www.maldef.org/about).

How does the mission of MALDEF itself refute Samuel Huntington's underlying thesis? What impression of the Latino community does this refutation of Huntington's views convey?

On May 27th, Samuel P. Huntington will publish his new book, alleging that Latino immigration threatens "Anglo-Protestant values" which are the "creed" of American culture. Since the release of his article announcing his new theory in *Foreign Policy* magazine in March,[1] Huntington's methodology and conclusions have been proven wrong by experts across the board.[2] As national Latino civil rights groups, we further believe that Huntington's writing is dangerously biased against Latinos and goes against fundamental American values.

Huntington's biases are un-American. The United States is a nation of immigrants from around the world. In the U.S., individual accomplishment is valued. The very foundation of American democracy is the Bill of Rights, respecting and even guaranteeing individual rights. By passing various civil rights laws in the 1960's, Congress re-established that our Constitution also means that not one race, religion or ethnicity should dominate another. The American dream is built upon the hard work of immigrants and the fundamental value of equal opportunity. We must not go back to a system where one's race, class or religion determines one's fate, regardless of one's intellect or willingness to work hard.

Huntington has made astonishing and unsupported generalizations about Latinos. His generalizations about Latinos being "persistent" in immigrating to the U.S., being exceedingly fertile, having less interest in education and not wanting to learn English are not based on fact and appear to emanate from a prejudice against Latinos. He has no proof that every Latino/a, or even the majority of Latinos/as and their families, fall into these stereotypes, nor any proof that Latinos are very different from other ethnic groups. This kind of analysis harkens back to

---

[1] S. Huntington, "José, Can You See?" Samuel Huntington on how Hispanic immigrants threaten America's identity, values, and way of life (*Foreign Policy*, March/April 2004) (cover story).

[2] *See*, e.g., D. Glenn, "Critics Assail Scholar's Article Arguing that Hispanic Immigration Threatens U.S.," *Chronicle of Higher Education* (Feb. 24, 2004)(disproving methodology/ citations); D. Brooks, "The Americano Dream," *New York Times* (Editorial, Feb. 24, 2004); A. Oppenheimer, "Racists Will Love New 'Hispanic Threat' Book," *Miami Herald* (Feb. 26, 2004)(assimilation trend); R. Navarrette, "Professor Huntington Has Short Memory of Past Immigrants," *Dallas Morning News* (Mar. 3, 2004) (immigration facts wrong); Lexington, "A Question of Identity—Despite new arguments to the contrary, Latino immigration is still good for America," *The Economist* (Mar. 6th–12th, 2004 issue); F. de Ortego y Gasca, "Something About Harvard-Dreaming in English," *Hispanic Vista* (Mar. 14, 2004); M. Casillas, D. Rocha & M. Hernandez, "The Hispanic Contribution," *Harvard Crimson* (Mar. 18, 2004); C. Fuentes, "Looking for Enemies in the Wrong Places," *Miami Herald* (Mar. 28, 2004); A. Lanier, "Stigmatization of Hispanics is Unwarranted," *Chicago Tribune* (Editorial Board Member)(April 4, 2004); M. Elliott, "New Patriots In Our Midst—A forthcoming book says Mexican Americans won't assimilate. It's wrong," *TIME Magazine* (April 12, 2004)(citations wrong and do not prove conclusions).

the justifications for legal segregation and discriminatory policies that were commonplace prior to the civil rights laws of the 1960's.[3]

Mexican-Americans and Latino immigrants are not inferior to white Anglo-Protestants. A recent *New York Times* poll found that Latino immigrants are hard-working, have strong family values, do not take public benefits, and generally epitomize the American dream.[4] Latino immigrants are contributing billions of dollars to the economy and even creating jobs for U.S. citizens.[5] Studies consistently find that immigrants contribute far more in taxes to the government than they use in government services.[6]

Latina/o parents value education and encourage their children to do well in school at the same rates as Anglo parents, with more than 90 percent of Latina/o children reporting that their parents want them to go to college.[7] Moreover, studies demonstrate that Mexican Americans support American core values at least as much as Anglos.[8]

Huntington alleges that Latinos do not want to become American, despite the fact that Latino immigrants consciously choose to leave

---

[3]V. Ruiz, "We Always Tell Our Children They Are Americans" *Méndez v. Westminster* and the California Road to Brown v. Board of Education, Review No. 200, Fiftieth Anniversary of the Supreme Court Ruling (College Board, Fall 2003), at p. 20–23 (Detailing history of Latino school segregation, along with other forms of segregation, "justified" by racial myths alleging Mexican Americans [are] not like "Americans"; social scientists were needed to disprove these myths in a 1944 *Méndez v. Westminster* school desegregation case.)

[4]S. Romero & J. Elder, "Hispanics in U.S. Report Optimism," *New York Times* (Aug. 6, 2003).

[5]D'Vera Cohn, "Immigrants Account for Half of New Workers—Report Calls Them Increasingly Needed for Economic Growth" *New York Times* (Dec. 2, 2003)(analyzing Center for Labor Market Studies report). *See also* R. Hinojosa-Ojeda, "Comprehensive Migration Policy Reform in North America: The Key to Sustainable and Equitable Economic Integration." North American Integration and Development Center, University of California, Los Angeles (2001).

[6]*See*, e.g., M. Fix & J. Passel, "Immigration and Immigrants. Setting the Record Straight." Urban Institute (1994) at [p.] 6 ("Overall, annual taxes paid by immigrants to all levels of government more than offset the costs of services received, generating a net annual surplus of $25 billion to $30 billion.").

[7]A. Ginorio & M. Huston, *¡Sí Se Puede! Yes We Can! Latinas in School,* Values, Expectations and Norms (American Assn. of Univ. Women, 2001), at 22–24.

[8]R. de la Garza, A. Falcon & F. C. Garcia, "Will the Real Americans Please Stand Up: Anglo and Mexican-American Support of Core American Political Values," Vol. 40, No. 2 *American Journal of Political Science* (May 1996), pp. 335–51 (Results were that: "At all levels of acculturation, Mexican-Americans are no less likely and often more likely to endorse values of individualism and patriotism than are Anglos."). Also, 9 out of 10 Latinos new to the U.S. believe it is important to change so they can fit into American society. R. Pastor, *Toward a North American Community; Lessons from the Old World for the New World* (Wash, D.C., Institute for International Economics, 2001), pp. 164–166 (*citing* Washington Post, Kaiser Foundation and Harvard Univ. comprehensive poll).

their home countries and migrate to the U.S. in order to become American and live the American dream, especially for their children. Everything that is traditionally thought of as "American," Latinos live out fully. They are family-oriented, religious, hard-working and loyal to the U.S. In fact, Latinos have won more medals of honor for their service in the U.S. military than any other ethnic group.

Huntington fails to take into account that the significant accomplishments of Latinos have occurred in spite of the long and shameful history of discrimination specifically directed against Latinos in the U.S. When Huntington alleges that Latinos have not achieved as much as whites in education, he neglects to acknowledge the history of segregation against Latinos, and Mexican Americans in particular, especially in the Southwest. Even today, when legal segregation is outlawed, Huntington does not take into account that Latinos are attending the most segregated schools in the country, which are providing a lesser quality of education as compared to majority white schools.[9] Predominantly minority schools have less-qualified teachers, more overcrowding, worse educational facilities, and less access to advanced curricula. Despite all these barriers, children of Latino immigrants are succeeding at a very high rate.

It is ironic that Huntington blames Latinos for segregation.[10] Latinos and other people of color know from tough experience that such segregation is not voluntary, as it [is] still difficult for Latinos to gain equality in white communities, and there is still discrimination in jobs and housing. However, like African-Americans, Latinos have been segregated and mythologized as "different," and subject to unfair criticism, because of their ethnicity.

Huntington criticizes Latinos' use of Spanish and falsely alleges that Latinos do not want to learn English. The majority of Latinos speak English. Among Spanish-speaking Latinos, poll after poll shows that Latinos want to learn English.[11] Their ability to learn English is

---

[9]Associated Press, "Latinos Segregated 50 Years After Brown v. Board of Ed" (April 6, 2004)(also reporting that no national policies specifically address Latino school education).

[10]"Majority of Americans Prefer to Live in Mixed Neighborhoods," *Diversity.com* (April 9, 2004)("According to the 'Civil Rights and Race Relations' survey conducted by Gallup, 68 percent of African Americans, 61 percent of Latinos and 57 percent of whites prefer to live in mixed neighborhoods.").

[11]Moreover, comprehensive studies demonstrate that the rate of linguistic assimilation of immigrants is just as rapid as it has been in previous generations. *See* S. Nicolan & R. Valdivieso, "The Veltman Report: What it Says, What it Means," Intro, C. Veltman, *The Future of Spanish Language in the United States* (New York, Wash. D.C.: Hispanic Policy Dev. Project, 1988) at i–x. Among first-generation native born Mexican Americans, 95% are proficient in English. K. McCarthy & R. Burciaga Valdez, *Current and Future Effects of Mexican Immigration in California* (The Rand Corp. 1985).

sometimes limited if they entered the U.S. at an older age and when they do not have access to English classes because they are working more than one job and there are limited English classes offered. As far as the ability to speak Spanish, Huntington portrays it as a negative, whereas in the global economy, many see such language capabilities are a positive.

Huntington mischaracterizes the history between the U.S. and Mexico and the causes for migration patterns between the two countries. Huntington characterizes Mexican immigration as "persistent" and a "massive influx" post-1960's civil rights laws. This characterization fails to recognize the unique, historical relationship between the two countries. In 1848, the U.S. acquired a significant portion of Mexico, which became what is now known as the Southwest in the U.S. Those people living in that region were Mexican citizens prior to the acquisition. When the U.S. experienced severe labor shortages while its soldiers were fighting in the world wars, the U.S. entered into several agreements with Mexico to bring temporary migrant laborers from Mexico who worked under abusive conditions in the agricultural fields for decades. Most of these workers did not have the opportunity to become citizens, making it difficult to exercise full political participation. During the Great Depression, the U.S. government and a number of state and local governments forced repatriation of one-third of the Mexican American population to impoverished conditions in Mexico. Shockingly, most of those who were deported were U.S. citizens who happened to be of Mexican ethnicity.[12] Despite this checkered past, Mexican immigrants continued to come to the U.S. to fill U.S. economic needs and to pursue economic opportunities not available in Mexico.[13]

Characterizing past non-Mexican immigration as "legal" and current Mexican immigration as "illegal" is false and misleading. Prior to 1939, it was not illegal to enter the U.S. without the U.S. government's permission. Millions of immigrants, mostly from Western Europe, entered the U.S. without proper visas.[14] Currently, many Mexicans enter the U.S legally. The U.S. legal immigration system, however, is in need of serious overhaul. The current system is not meeting the economic or family reunification principles it was designed to meet. The backlogs in legal visa processing for the spouses and children of Mexican legal immigrants living in the U.S.

---

[12]F. Balderrama & R. Rodríguez, *Decade of Betrayal: Mexican Repatriation in the 1930's* (1995).

[13]*See*, e.g., "The Hispanic Challenge? What We Know About Latino Immigration," Woodrow Wilson International Center/Migration Policy Institute Panel of Experts (R. Suro, E. Grieco, D. Gutierrez, M. Jones-Correa, R. Stanton-Salazar)(Mar. 29, 2004).

[14]D. Weissbrodt, *Immigration Law and Procedure*, Ch. 1. History of U.S. Immigration Law and Policy (West 1998).

are causing families to be separated for 13 years. In order to reunite with their families, some Mexican citizens do enter without proper documentation.

Present high levels of migration between the U.S. and Mexico are based on geographic proximity and economic interdependence of the two countries. Many Mexicans come here because Mexico is our close neighbor and trading partner. Mexico is closer than Europe so the voyage to America is more natural. The U.S. and Mexican fate and economies are inextricably intertwined. That is, the U.S. is just as dependent on Mexico and Mexican migration as the opposite is true.

For Class Discussion

1. Which segments of this policy statement seem to respond most directly to Samuel P. Huntington's points?

2. What is the rhetorical effect of the extensive documentation (by way of footnotes) in this argument?

3. In your mind, does this article incorporate key points about immigration that Huntington omits? How does MALDEF seek to reframe the controversy over cultural integration?

4. Where or how could this argument acknowledge alternative views? Do you think a more balanced approach woud better serve the two organizations' rhetorical and political goals?

5. This is a bare-bones argument, a policy statement structured as a rebuttal to Huntington's articles and book on Mexican immigration. What reasoning and evidence are persuasive? What points would need more development in order to be persuasive to a general neutral or dissenting audience?

It's Time to End Worker Exploitation
Linda Chavez-Thompson

Linda Chavez-Thompson was for many years the highest-ranking woman, and Latina, in the U.S. labor movement. Beginning in 1967 as union secretary and local union representative, she rose swiftly through the ranks, ultimately becoming the executive vice-president of the AFL-CIO (the largest union federation in the country, representing ten million men and women), a post she held until her retirement in 2007. She has been a continuous advocate for closer ties between the unions and women and minorities. This commentary was published May 5, 2007, in the Opinions section of *Forbes*, a conservative business and financial news publication.

How does Linda Chavez-Thompson seek to establish her credibility and authority in the eyes of the conservative, business-oriented readers of *Forbes?*

Growing up in western Texas as the daughter of cotton sharecroppers, I spent my summers weeding cotton, five days a week, 10 hours a day, in 95-degree heat. As grueling as this workload was, others had it even worse.

For foreign workers toiling as "guest workers" (or "braceros") alongside us in the cotton fields, the five-day work week was an impossible luxury. They were often stiffed on wages, and health care was simply nonexistent. Viewing them as units of production, employers worked them to their limit, knowing that the following season a fresh unsuspecting batch would arrive.

The horrific abuses suffered by workers in programs such as the bracero program are well documented and indisputable. And although most people like to think of bracero programs as a phenomenon of the past, the reality is that their legacy of exploitation and abuse continues to thrive in contemporary American society through modern guest worker programs such as the H-2A and H-2B.

Like undocumented workers, "guest workers" in this country face enormous obstacles in enforcing their labor rights.

The H-2 guest worker programs bring in agricultural and other seasonal workers to pick crops, do construction and work in the seafood industry, among other jobs. Workers typically borrow large amounts of money to pay travel expenses, fees and even bribes to recruiters. That means that before they even begin to work, they are indebted.

According to a new study published by the Southern Poverty Law Center, it is not unusual for a Guatemalan worker to pay more than $2,500 in fees to obtain a seasonal guest worker position, about a year's worth of income in Guatemala. And Thai workers have been known to pay as much as $10,000 for the chance to harvest crops in the orchards of the Pacific Northwest. Interest rates on the loans are sometimes as high as 20% a month. Homes and vehicles are required collateral.

Handcuffed by their debt and bound to employers who can send them home on a whim, the "guests" are forced to remain and work for employers even when their pay and working conditions are second-rate, hazardous or abusive. Hungry children inevitably trump protest. Technically, these programs include some legal protections, but in reality, those protections exist mostly on paper. Government enforcement is almost nonexistent. Private attorneys refuse to take cases, and language barriers make it virtually impossible for workers to speak out.

Undocumented immigrants face similar obstacles at work. Because they are under the constant threat of deportation, they cannot effectively assert their rights at the workplace, and employers routinely take advantage of them.

The result is that both guest workers and undocumented workers end up working the most dangerous and most exploitative jobs in our country.

It's getting worse, not better. Among foreign-born workers, workplace fatalities increased by an alarming 46% between 1992 and 2002. Since 1992, fatalities among Hispanic workers have increased by 65%.

When immigrant workers try to correct such injustices by forming unions, they are cruelly harassed, intimidated and even terminated for their actions. When all else fails to break a union drive, employers simply call in the immigration authorities and everyone gets deported for standing up for basic rights.

For years, the AFL-CIO has campaigned for an end to the exploitation and abuse of immigrant workers who are here working hard and contributing to our economy. The best way to guarantee the rights and wages of all workers in this country is to give every immigrant the opportunity to become a citizen, with all the rights and duties that entails.

The exploitation of immigrant workers hurts us all. When standards are driven down for some workers, they are driven down for all workers. For this same reason, guest worker programs must be squarely rejected. Because workers in these programs are always dependent on their host employers for both their livelihoods and legal status, these programs create a disenfranchised underclass of workers.

History, economics and common sense dictate that exploitation of workers will continue as long as it makes economic sense for employers to do so. We must step outside of the status quo and revise the current immigration law in a way that guarantees full labor rights for future foreign workers and reflects real labor market conditions by restructuring the current permanent employment visa category. That is, future foreign workers should be welcomed as permanent residents with full rights at the onset—not as disposable "guests." This is the only way to guarantee that foreign workers enjoy the same rights and protections as all other U.S. workers, including the freedom to form unions and bargain for a better life.

As a nation that prides itself on fair treatment and equality, how can we possibly settle for anything less?

For Class Discussion

1. What are some of the key problems with guest worker programs that Linda Chavez-Thompson identifies?

2. Chavez-Thompson offers a way to reduce the problems encountered by immigrant workers. What is she arguing for?

3. What would be some of the benefits of her proposal? What possible drawbacks might opponents see in it?

4. How does Chivez-Thompson appeal to her readers' emotions and values? What is the intended rhetorical effect of her word choices, such as "grueling workload," "horrific abuses," and "cruelly harassed"? How might readers of *Forbes* react to this tactic?

5. Near the end of her commentary, Chavez-Thompson attempts to broaden the stakes of her argument by asserting that "the exploitation of immigrant workers hurts us all." What unspoken assumptions underlie this reasoning? How persuasive is she in supporting it? ∎

Transnational Labor Citizenship
Jennifer Gordon

Jennifer Gordon is an Associate Professor at Fordham University's School of Law, where she teaches courses on immigration and labor law, advanced public interest, and workers in a changing economy. In 1998 she was named Outstanding Public Interest Lawyer by the National Association for Public Interest Law to recognize her contributions as executive director of the Workplace Project in New York, a nonprofit organization that organizes immigrant workers to fight exploitation on the job through advocacy, negotiation, and community education. In 1999, Gordon was awarded a MacArthur prize and fellowship ("genius grant"). (Among the MacArthur Foundation's core goals is defending human rights.) Reprinted here is the introduction to Gordon's much longer policy analysis and proposal, which was published in the March 2007 issue of the *Southern California Law Review*.

> What specific problems with immigration, the treatment of immigrant labor, and the effect of immigrants on the national workforce is Gordon addressing in her proposal?

On the parched plaza outside the U.S. Consulate in Monterrey, Mexico, hundreds of men and women lean against tree trunks or press their backs into the consulate wall, seeking any sliver of shade. They wait to be fingerprinted, interviewed, and—with luck—approved as one of the 175,000 guest workers admitted to the United States each year. An ordinary day in May 2005—or perhaps not quite. Under one tree, a meeting is underway. At the center of a circle stands a labor organizer, copy of a contract in hand. *Asegúrense que sus derechos sean respetados,* he urges the crowd, all of whom are bound for North Carolina. "Make sure that your rights are respected." Another man, his crisp shirt and spotless jeans belying the previous sixteen hours spent on a bus from his hometown, stands up and offers advice to the others. *Cuidado con el patrón en Ranch Farm.* "Careful with the boss at Ranch Farm." He continues: "He's still trying to get away with piece rate when he's supposed to be paying us by the hour. Call the union's North Carolina office if it happens to you." Others nod assent. After half an hour of sharing information and reestablishing bonds, the group disperses. Before the week's end, they will be thinning tobacco plants in the hot Carolina fields. For the first time in history, guest workers are about to cross the border into the United States as union members.

Over one million new immigrants arrive in the United States each year.[1] This spring, Americans saw several times that number pour into the streets, protesting proposed changes in U.S. immigration and guest work policies.[2] As the signs they carried indicated, most migrants come to work, and it is in the workplace that the impact of large numbers of newcomers is most keenly felt. For those who see both the free movement of people and the preservation of decent working conditions as essential to social justice, this presents a seemingly unresolvable dilemma. In a situation of massive inequality among countries, to prevent people from moving in search of work is to curtail their chance to build a decent life for themselves and their families. But from the perspective of workers in the country that receives them, the more immigrants, the more competition, and the worse work becomes.

As an advocate for immigrant workers for over twenty years, I have often spoken from the heart of that dilemma.[3] This Article proposes a way out. In it, I develop the idea of "transnational labor citizenship," a new approach to structuring cross-border labor migration that draws on, but goes beyond, current theories of transnational political citizenship. Transnational *labor* citizenship reconceptualizes the relationship among the governments of immigrant sending and receiving countries, civil society labor institutions, such as unions and worker centers, and private actors. Inspired by recent efforts to organize workers as they move across borders, transnational labor citizenship would link permission to enter the United States in search of work to membership in cross-border worker organizations, rather than to the current requirement of a job offer from an employer. It would facilitate the enforcement of baseline labor rights and allow migrants to carry benefits and services with them as they move. Its goal, heretofore elusive, is to facilitate the free movement of people while preventing the erosion of working conditions in the countries that receive them.

---

[1]Jeffrey S. Passel & Roberto Suro, *Rise, Peak, and Decline: Trends in U.S. Immigration 1992–2004*, at i–ii (2005), *available at* http://pewhispanic.org/reports/report.php?Report ID=53.

[2]Luis Andres Henao, *After the Amnesty: 20 Years Later*, Christian Sci. Monitor, Nov. 13, 2006, at A3.

[3]*See, e.g.*, Jennifer Gordon, *Suburban Sweatshops: The Fight for Immigrant Rights* (2005) [hereinafter Gordon, Suburban Sweatshops]; Jennifer Gordon, *We Make the Road by Walking: Immigrant Workers, the Workplace Project, and the Struggle for Social Change*, 30 Harv. C.R.-C.L.L. Rev. 407 (1995); Jennifer Gordon, *Immigrants Fight the Power—Worker Centers Are One Path to Labor Organizing and Political Participation*, Nation, Jan. 3, 2000, at 16.

Labor organizations are central to this proposal. Historically, unions have been restrictionist in their approach to immigration, but today most unions in the United States welcome immigrants already present in the industries they organize, including the undocumented.[4] While this Article applauds this pro-immigrant position, it argues that to move forward on the immigration question from a social justice perspective, *and* to succeed in their goal of improving working conditions, unions must refashion themselves so they can accommodate an ongoing influx of new migrants. Simultaneously, the United States must reconfigure its approach to labor migration so that it sees workers' organizations as allies in the process.

This Article offers the new concept of "labor citizenship" as a lens for understanding the challenges unions face in taking the leap to an open attitude toward the future flow of migrants. By labor citizenship I mean the ways in which workers' organizations create membership regimes, set and enforce rules for those who belong, and approach their goal of improving wages and working conditions. Labor citizenship also encompasses the normative expectation of solidarity among workers and active participation by them in the democratic governance of their own institutions.

Strikingly, aspects of labor citizenship implemented by unions in the United States parallel the conventional national citizenship framework. Like countries, which apportion privileges based on national citizenship, unions offer a special set of benefits to their members alone.[5] At a minimum, union boundaries separate those eligible to claim the higher wages guaranteed by union contracts from those beyond the

---

[4]I use the term "undocumented" to refer to noncitizens with no legal immigration statue because it avoids the pejorative inherent in phrases like "illegal immigrant" or "illegal alien." The word also highlights a fairly recent emphasis on documentation at the intersection of U.S. labor and immigration law. It was not until 1986, with the passage of the Immigration Reform and Control Act and its employer sanctions provisions, that all job seekers in the United States were required to present "documents" providing their authorization to work before being hired.

[5]For an accounting of the way nonunion workers also benefit from the efforts of unions, see *infra* note 50 and accompanying text. In this Article, I use the word "members" when referring to workers who are represented by a union. This should be qualified. First, in states that have passed so-called "Right to Work" legislation, workers are released from the obligation to join or pay dues to the union that represents them. For a typical "Right to Work" Law, see IDAHO CODE ANN. §§ 44-2003 (2003). In such states— currently numbering twenty-three—employees in a unionized workplace who do not wish to offer the union their financial support do not have to do so, although under the doctrinal duty of fair representation the union must always represent the interests of *all* workers in the bargaining unit. Steele v. Louisville & Nashville R.R., 323 U.S. 192, 204 (1944); U.S. Dep't of Labor, State Right-to-Work Laws and Constitutional Amendments in Effect as of January 1, 2007, with Year of Passage, http://www.dol.gov/esa/programs/whd/state/righttowork.htm (last visited Jan. 27, 2007). Furthermore, after the

(continued)

contract's scope. In some organizing models, particularly in the building trades, there have been times when labor citizenship is treated as a limited commodity, denied to some workers in order to increase the share of those within the circle. This model echoes the way that nation-states circumscribe those who will be admitted to citizenship to facilitate the amassing and distribution of limited resources. As nations do, unions assert that this line drawing is normatively important, in addition to its instrumental value. From the union perspective, bounded citizenship aids in the development of democracy and solidarity within the union, and enhances the capacity of union members to realize full and equal citizenship outside the workplace as well. From the perspective of the nation-state, it is often said to be a precondition for the creation of community and the flourishing of democracy.

In the past decade, much has been written about the ways that political participation, once seen as a single-state phenomenon, has transformed into a transnational experience under pressure from massive migration around the globe.[6] Transnational scholarship describes immigrant remittances as the driving force behind many of these

---

(*continued*)

passage of the Taft-Hartley Act, although unions in non-"Right to Work" states can negotiate "agency shop" or "union shop" contracts that require that all workers in the bargaining unit pay dues, it is illegal to require workers to formally affiliate as members with the unions that represent them. *See, e.g.,* Int'l Union of Elec., Elec., Salaried, Mach. & Furniture Workers Local 444, 311 N.L.R.B. 1031, 1041 (1993) (invalidating a clause in a collective bargaining agreement requiring all employees to become "members of the Union in good standing" because such a clause "fails to apprise employees of the lawful limits of their obligation" to the union and "would lead an employee unversed in labor law to believe that employees were obliged to join the Union and satisfy all of the requirements for membership as a condition of employment"). Thus, even in a "union shop" there may be workers represented by the union who are not technically members.

[6]The literature on transnational citizenship is vast. Foundational works include *towards A Transnational Perspective on Migration: Race, Class, Ethnicity, and Nationalism Reconsidered* (Nina Glick-Schiller et al. eds., 1992) and Yasemin Nuhoglu Soysal, *Limits of Citizenship: Migrants and Postnational Membership in Europe* (1994). Linda Bosniak's article, *Citizenship Denationalized,* 7 Ind. J. Global Legal Stud. 447 (2000), offers an empirical and theoretical exploration of whether citizenship is an inherently national project, or whether it can and should be expanded across national borders. Roger Waldinger, David Fitzgerald, and Jonathan Fox, among others, have recently offered critiques of the argument that transnational citizenship represents a meaningful shift in the citizenship paradigm. *See* Jonathan Fox, *Unpacking "Transnational Citizenship,"* 8 Ann. Rev. Pol. Sci. 171 (2005); Roger Waldinger & David Fitzgerald, *Transnationalism in Question,* 109 Am. J. Soc. 1177 (2004). A recent volume of the *N.Y.U. Law Review* explores this phenomenon in detail including Anupam Chander's useful taxonomy of the emerging institutions of transnational economic and political citizenship. Anupam Chander, *Homeward Bound,* 81 N.Y.U.L. Rev. 60 (2006).

changes but is curiously silent on the conditions of the work that produces remittance income.[7] Such scholars have also been reluctant to
take the leap from description of transnational activities to normative
exploration of how the transnational framework might be reshaped so
that it serves the ends of a more just labor and immigration system.[8] In
exploring the potential for transnational labor citizenship, this Article
take on both tasks.

The same forces shifting the practice and structure of citizenship
on the national level are also bearing down on unions. Yet the transna-
tionalization of political citizenship emerging on the national level
does not yet have a clear parallel in labor citizenship. I argue that
unions' legitimate concerns about the effect of an oversupply of workers on working conditions has hampered their ability to reshape labor
citizenship to respond effectively to ongoing immigration. To be sure,
as of the late 1990s unions in the United States became much more
open to organizing new immigrants, including the undocumented.[9]

---

[7]There are a few exceptions, including the work of David Fitzgerald and Lynn Stephen,
who have explored the links between labor unions and transnational political behavior.
See David Fitzgerald, *Beyond "Transnationalism": Mexican Hometown Politics at an
American Labour Union*, 27 Ethnic & Racial Stud. 228 (2004); Lynn Stephen, *Mixtec
Farmworkers in Oregon: Linking Labor and Ethnicity Through Farmworker Unions and
Hometown Associations*, in *Indigenous Mexican Migrants in the United States* 179
(Jonathan Fox & Gaspar Rivera-Salgado eds., 2004).

[8]It is also important to challenge the idea that the shift from nationalism or transnationalism has been linear, universal, or complete. Borders are still tremendously important sites
for the exercise of real and symbolic national power, as the 2006 congressional mandate
for the construction of a 700-mile wall along the southern U.S. border illustrates. Secure
Fence Act of 2006, H.R. 6061, 109th Cong. §3 (2006). Within the United States, the state's
capacity to exclude and deport immigrants increased over the course of the 1990s and
2000s. Changing laws drastically increased the facility with which legal permanent residents convicted of crimes could be stripped of their green cards, and ramped up surveillance and enforcement against those whose religion, ethnicity, or nationality placed
them within the state's rubric of "suspected terrorists." *See generally* Muneer Ahmad,
Homeland Insecurities: Racial Violence the Day After September 11, 20 Soc. Text 72 (2002);
Leti Volpp, *The Citizen and the Terrorist*, 49 UCLA L. Rev. 1575 (2002); E-mail from
Sameer M. Ashar, Assistant Professor, City University of New York School of Law, to author (Aug. 2, 2006) (on file with author)("[T]he post-9/11 reinforcement of national borders and immigration enforcement and the 1996 targeting of LPR's with criminal convictions seem to suggest a tiered system in which some populations are allowed to
transnationalize, while others are targeted and put outside of our national borders.") In
these ways, transnationalism is best understood as a phenomenon that is permitted for
"desirable aliens" by some receiving country governments, but forbidden by them to a
large swath of would-be migrants (some of whom nonetheless migrate or remain illegally,
and create transnational forms of participation from the bottom up).

[9]*See infra* Part III. B.1.c.

And, in the context of the global movement of capital, a number of unions have initiated cross-border efforts to support workers and unions in other countries.[10] But the core model of labor citizenship has remained reliant on efforts to curtail the number of workers entering the labor market. In bringing undocumented immigrants into the fold of labor citizenship, most unions did not forgo the idea of boundaries. They merely extended their borders to include the reach a new group. The idea that the future flow of migrants remain outside the reach of labor citizenship—and that union borders must be defended against them, or they will undermine the viability of that citizenship—remains essential to the vision of much of the labor movement today. And yet, new migrants continue to arrive.

Surprising many, Service Employees International Union ("SEIU") and UNITE HERE, two leading members of the Change to Win Coalition made up of unions that withdrew from the American Federation of Labor and Congress of Industrial Organizations ("AFL-CIO") in 2005, recently endorsed a new "guest work" program.[11] After the 1964 demise of the *bracero* program, which brought over 4 million Mexicans to U.S. fields over the two decades of its existence, the idea of addressing large-scale labor needs through guest work fell into disfavor.[12] But the idea of an expanded temporary worker program was revived by President George W. Bush in 2004[13] and has gained currency in some unexpected quarters, including

---

[10]For a historical overview of labor's *cross*-border efforts, see Beverly J. Silver, *Forces of Labor: Workers' Movements and Globalization Since 1870* (2003). Examples of concrete campaigns are set out in Terry Davis, *Cross-border Organizing Comes Home: UE & FAT in Mexico & Milwanikee,* 23 Lab. Res. Rev. 23 (1995); Andrew Herod, *Organizing Globally, Organizing Locally: Union Spatial Strategy in a Global Economy,* in *Global Unions? Theory and Strategies of Organized Labour in the Global Political Economy* 83 (Jeffrey Harrod & Robert O'Brien eds., 2002); Kenneth Zinn, *Labor Solidarity in the New World Order: The UMWA Program in Columbia,* 23 Lab. Res. Rev. 35 (1995)

[11]*See infra* Part IV.B. The ironies of using the term "guest" to describe workers brought in on a temporary basis to take a country's most undesirable jobs under conditions of extreme exploitation are inescapable. However, because the phrase "guest worker" enjoys universal recognition and its potential synonyms—temporary worker, nonimmigrant worker—have multiple meanings, I will refer to "guest workers" throughout this piece.

[12]For overviews of the *bracero* program, see generally Kitty Calavita, *Inside the State: The Bracero Program, Immigration, and the I.N.S.* (1992); Ernesto Galarza, *Merchants of Labor: The Mexican Bracero Story* (1964) [hereinafter Galarza, *Merchants of Labor*]; Ernesto Galarza, *Spiders in the House and Workers in the Field* (1970) [hereinafter Galarza, *Spiders in the House*]; Mae Ngai, *Impossible Subjects: Illegal Aliens and the Making of Modern America* (2004).

[13]President George W. Bush's first guest worker speech was delivered on January 7, 2004. *Bush on Immigration; Excerpts from Bush's Address on Allowing Immigrants to Fill Some Jobs,* N.Y. Times, Jan. 8, 2004, at A28.

some immigrant advocacy groups that had previously considered permanent legalization the only acceptable solution to the problems of the
undocumented.[14] SEIU and UNITE HERE have joined that camp.
Meanwhile, the AFL-CIO contends that a new guest work program would
undercut every effort to organize low wage workers. In truth, as long as a
guest worker program positions "guests" outside the paradigm of labor
citizenship, such a program is doomed to undermine the quality of work
despite whatever protections it technically provides for its participants.[15]

It is the central contention of this Article that the hard-bordered
model of labor citizenship is untenable in the face of an increasingly
global market for labor. Instead, I ask how we might productively
reconceive of the relationship between labor citizenship and nation-
state citizenship in a context of ongoing labor migration. Could a
different *form* of labor citizenship better achieve the *norms* that the
concept embodies? What approach to labor organization makes sense
in a globally interconnected world, if the goal is to create good work—
at a bare minimum, work that can support a family, does not endanger
the worker's health, and provides adequate time off for other pursuits—
in this country no matter who the worker is?[16]

In response, I call for a thought experiment in the transnationaliza-
tion of labor citizenship.[17] I propose an opening up of the fortress of labor
and of the nation-state to accommodate a constant flow of new migrants
through a model that would tie immigration status to membership in organizations of transnational workers rather than to a particular employer.
These memberships would entitle migrants to services, benefits, and
rights that cross borders just as the workers do. In exchange for the authorization to work that they would receive as members, migrant workers
would commit to the core value of labor citizenship: solidarity with other
workers in the United States, expressed as a commitment to refuse to
work under conditions that violate the law or labor agreements.

The premise behind this proposal is that in the face of enormous
inequality between countries, immigration controls will not stop the
movement of workers from the South to the North. But recognizing
that migrants will continue to arrive in the United States regardless of
our policy does not require abdicating wages and working conditions
to employers who would set them as low as the market permits.
Advocates have long stated that the government must actively enforce
basic workplace standards in immigrant-heavy workplaces to set a floor

---

[14]For a full exploration of the guest work issue, see Part IV, *infra.*

[15]*See infra* Part IV.C (discussing the problems posed by even the best-designed guest
worker programs).

[16]Despite the transnational focus of my proposal, the central concern of this Article
remains addressing conditions of work within the United States.

[17]*See infra* Part V.

for all workers. Such a step is necessary but insufficient. The state does not have the political will, the staffing, or the mechanisms to enforce those laws consistently, and even if it did, the minimums are set too low to assure workers a decent standard of living. To engage the state more fully in enforcement, and to go beyond inadequate existing levels of protection, workers themselves must organize. Transnational labor citizenship would shift the enforcement of a floor on working conditions from the arena of immigration policy in employer hands, where it currently lies, to the arena of labor solidarity in worker hands, where it belongs. In this way, I argue, we can create structures that respond at once to the desires of migrants for jobs and to the aspirations of labor citizenship to preserve decent working conditions in this country.

For Class Discussion

1. According to Susan Gordon, what is the basic dilemma or conflict at the heart of public efforts to address the movement of labor across borders?

2. What is the core of Gordon's proposal? How does she reason out and support her proposal? What benefits does she say it will have for all the various stakeholders?

3. Some key definitional arguments lie at the heart of this proposal. For example, how does she define and argue for the concepts of "transnational," "labor citizenship," and "transnational labor citizenship"?

4. Gordon also identifies a gap in transnational scholarship that prompts and justifies her article as a contribution to such scholarship. How does she establish her knowledge, authority on these issues, and professional experience?

5. This policy analysis is largely intellectual. What is the value of the scene she describes at the beginning of this piece?

6. Gordon's argument could be read as a response to Kofi Annan's call for new thinking about immigration. How does her proposal for transnational labor citizenship seem promising in effecting reform of immigration policy as Annan advocated? Who might object and what refutation would they offer?

One of America's Best-Selling Vehicles
America's Leadership Team for Long Range Population-Immigration-Resource Planning

America's Leadership Team for Long Range Population-Immigration-Resource Planning is a coalition formed in 2008 from five groups: the Federation for American Immigration Reform, the American Immigration Control Foundation, Californians for Population Stabilization, Numbers USA, and Social Contract Press.

The Leadership Team has been criticized for furthering an anti-immigrant ideology, but its members contend that their goal is to raise public awareness of population growth problems and their source. This advocacy ad ran in the *New York Times* and *The Nation*, a liberal magazine of news and opinion, in June 2008.

One of America's Best Selling Vehicles.

Bulldozer sales in America have been booming. Road builders need them to level rolling hills into concrete interchanges and bypasses. Developers need them to turn farmland into housing developments and shopping malls. You can find big earthmoving equipment throughout America, turning our most picturesque land into suburban sprawl, while adding to some of the worst traffic problems in the world. But traffic is just one of the problems facing America as a result of population growth wildly out of control. Schools and emergency rooms are bursting at the seams, and public infrastructure is under great stress. Property taxes are on the rise. Yet the bulldozers keep on coming, ripping up some of the most beautiful farms and forests in the world and turning them into concrete and asphalt suburbs. But with U.S. census projections indicating our population will explode from 300 million today to 400 million in thirty years and 600 million before 2100*, bulldozer sales should keep on booming. Unless we take action today. The Pew Hispanic Research Center projects 82% of the country's massive population increase, between 2005 and 2050, will result from immigration. And with every new U.S. resident, whether from births or immigration, comes further degradation of America's natural treasures. There's not much we can do to reclaim the hundreds of millions of acres already destroyed. But we can do something about what's left. Visit our websites to find out how you can help.

America's Leadership Team for Long Range Population-Immigration-Resource Planning

300 million people today, 600 million tomorrow. Think about it.

American Immigration Control Foundation   www.aicfoundation.com
Californians for Population Stabilization   www.capsweb.org
Federation for American Immigration Reform   www.fairus.org
NumbersUSA   www.numbersusa.org
Social Contract Press   www.thesocialcontract.com

*Based on 2000 census projections. **Paid for by America's Leadership Team for Long Range Population-Immigration-Resource Planning**

Californians for Population Stabilization/Davis & Company Advertising

If you were flipping through a magazine and saw this advocacy advertisement, what would you notice about the image and text?

For Class Discussion

1. What connotations of "bulldozer" might come into play when a reader first
   sees this ad? How are the elements of the image calculated to create a
   certain feeling in readers? How does the visual effect of the photo carry
   over to the first few sentences of the text, leading to the main points of
   the argument?

2. What role does the name of the coalition responsible for the ad play in
   terms of audience appeal and in terms of seeking to influence the way
   people think about issues that they normally might not connect?

3. This advocacy ad sets up a chain of consequences as it leads readers to its
   call to action. What connections does it make among resource planning,
   population, and immigration? How logical are these connections?

4. How does the effectiveness of this ad depend on readers' values? What
   emotional responses does it seek to evoke?

5. How are the stakes of immigration changed by the argument presented in
   this ad?

6. The entire ad campaign funded by America's Leadership Team for Long
   Range Population-Immigration-Resource Planning was met with a
   firestorm of criticism from such groups as the Anti-Defamation League and
   the Southern Poverty Law Center, which went so far as to call the
   Leadership Team an antiimmigrant hate group. Which elements of the ad
   would you say these groups were reacting to, and would you agree with
   their accusation?

Assimilation Nation
Peter D. Salins

Peter D. Salins holds the title University Professor in Political Science at the
State University of New York Stony Brook. He has served in numerous leadership positions for the university as well as for organizations such as the
Citizens Housing and Planning Council of New York and the American Institute
of Certified Planners. His book *Assimilation, American Style* (1996) provoca-
tively defends assimilation on the grounds that, historically, immigrants to the
United States assimilated by embracing the Protestant work ethic, sending
their children to (English only) public schools, and valuing "new beginnings."
Salins has published widely in a variety of newspapers, periodicals, and
scholarly journals. This opinion piece appeared on May 11, 2006, in the *New
York Times*, during a time when debate over immigration policy was raging in
the U.S. Congress.

How does Peter Salins recast the debate about immigration policy reform?

In the debate over the redesign of this country's immigration policies, Americans often lose sight of the project's overriding objective. Immigration reform is urgently needed not to fill gaps in our labor force, or to accommodate pro- or anti-immigrant voters, but to ensure that all immigrants, present and future, are integrated into American civic and social life—or, to use an unfashionable phrase, assimilated.

The failure to absorb immigrants is the bane of most nations with large immigrant populations, as exemplified by France's recent turmoil. The key to assimilation in the United States has been our openness to large-scale immigration and tolerance of ethnic and religious differences. But it has also depended heavily on laws and policies that have allowed legal immigrants to become American in every sense.

Clearly, the 11 million to 12 million undocumented immigrants now here can never assimilate, whether they want to or not. Their illegal status will keep them from being accepted by their American neighbors, regardless of their virtue or utility. Thus, legalizing their status is essential.

The more problematic issue is the status of future immigrants, and that is where several proposals for immigration reform go awry. The most troublesome of these ideas, heavily promoted by immigration proponents, would allow in a large cohort of guest workers. Guest workers (a group that would soon grow into the millions), by definition, will never become Americans. Like the Turks in Germany and guest workers in other European nations, many will not return to their native countries once their work permits are up, thus inevitably becoming the next generation of illegal aliens. Yet, the favored solution of immigration hard-liners, sealing the border, is untenable unless we also expand legal immigration pathways.

Thus, a successful immigration reform package must consist of three components. First, as the bill stalled in the Senate envisions, we must put the illegal immigrants already here on a secure path to legal residency and ultimate citizenship. Second, we must enlarge the quota of legal new entrants, but not through the kind of guest worker program being proposed. Instead, we should allow an equivalent number of immigrants (300,000 to 400,000) to enter annually with permanent resident visas, but under a different set of rules.

As it stands, there are only four major eligibility criteria for immigrants: family ties, sponsored employment in a few skill areas, documented persecution or selection in a visa lottery. But the majority of those wanting to come here do not have close American relatives, the right skills or proof of persecution. And the lottery offers slim odds.

A fairer approach, and one that offers future immigrants enough hope of success to discourage border-jumping, would award entry on a first-come basis, placing all potential immigrants (with clean records) on a waiting list, possibly giving favorable weighting to applicants from the Western Hemisphere, or those with desirable characteristics like proficiency in English.

Opening up a better pathway for legal immigrants that paves the way for their full acceptance and citizenship would allow us to deal more forcefully with the third component of a reformed immigration policy: stanching illegal immigration. The logistical challenges to border control will remain formidable, but with an enlarged quota in place and more effective enforcement (including deportation and employer sanctions), the motivation for immigrants to enter illegally and for American employers to hire them should lessen considerably.

This three-pronged approach will allow the United States to remain both a beacon for immigrants and a unified society, all of whose residents eventually become Americans in self-conception as well as legal fact. Advocates of liberalization are wrong to justify immigration primarily as a way to recruit workers for our most difficult or poorly paid occupations; labor unions and other restrictionists are wrong to oppose it primarily because it might depress wages or raise social welfare costs. Not only are these arguments empirically dubious, they are also beside the point.

Any immigration policy that focuses on the labor market or national and state budgets can generate only transitory benefits, if any, while its failure to assure the assimilation of the millions of immigrants among us will surely cause permanent harm.

For Class Discussion

1. What is the core of Salins proposal? What reasons does he offer in support of it?

2. What assumptions about a "unified society" with a codifiable "American civic ad social life" underlie this op-ed piece?

3. What opposing views does Salins introduce, and how does he deal with each one?

4. How does Salins structure the support for his own position? How convincing do you find his logic and use of evidence? In what ways would the "fairer approach" that Salins proposes for dealing with future immigrants differ from how visas are issued at present? Would you agree that it is fairer?

5. What similarities and differences do you see between Huntington's argument and Salins' proposal?

Europe as a Walled Fortress
Karsten Schley

Reclusive German cartoonist Karsten Schley is a prolific creator of political, news, and gag-style single-frame cartoons on a range of topics and is also a coauthor of several book-length collections of cartoons in German.

> What is the first thing that you notice about the cartoon? Does that impression change or grow stronger as you examine it more closely?

EUROPE A FORTRESS? WHAT ARE YOU TALKING ABOUT?!
CAN'T YOU SEE - THE DOOR IS OPEN WIDE!

For Class Discussion

1. Explain the rhetorical effect of the contradiction between the caption and the dominant image that helps the reader interpret the cartoon.

2. What implied argument is made by the sign the would-be immigrants are carrying?

3. How does the posted notice "Welcome to Europe! No climbing. No flying! Don't use ladders!!!" function to reveal the artist's perception of existing official immigration policy in Europe? Beyond that, where does one often see public signs prohibiting certain behavior, and what might this association suggest about Europe's view of itself as a certain type of place?

4. Continue a "close reading" of the visual rhetoric of the cartoon, listing as many details as you notice that contribute to a complex argument (for example, you might notice that the would-be immigrants are empty-handed and speculate about what that implies as part of a larger argument about key issues in European immigration).

5. High walls can imprison as well as exclude. What historical European wall designed to isolate people might be related to the criticism being offered in the cartoon, and what might that additional criticism be? ∎

A Year of Living Dangerously
Francis Fukuyama

Francis Fukuyama is a professor of international political economy at the Paul H. Nitze School of Advanced International Studies at Johns Hopkins University. He is the author of numerous books on politics, democracy, the international political economy, and culture's effect on the economy. He is widely recognized for his award-winning book *The End of History and the Last Man* (1992); among his most recent books are *State-Building: Governance and World Order in the 21st Century* (2004) and *America at the Crossroads: Democracy, Power, and the Neoconservative Legacy* (2006). This editorial was published November 2, 2005, in the *Wall Street Journal*, one of the largest-circulation newspapers in the United States.

> What common view of jihadist terrorism and the European Union's problem with its immigrant population does Fukuyama seek to change in this editorial?

One year ago today, the Dutch filmmaker Theo van Gogh had his throat ritually slit by Mohamed Bouyeri, a Muslim born in Holland who spoke fluent Dutch. This event has totally transformed Dutch politics, leading to stepped-up police controls that have now virtually shut off new immigration there. Together with the July 7 bombings in London (also perpetrated by second generation Muslims who were British citizens), this event should also change dramatically our view of the nature of the threat from radical Islamism.

We have tended to see jihadist terrorism as something produced in dysfunctional parts of the world, such as Afghanistan, Pakistan or the Middle East, and exported to Western countries. Protecting ourselves is a matter either of walling ourselves off, or, for the Bush administration, going "over there" and trying to fix the problem at its source by promoting democracy.

There is good reason for thinking, however, that a critical source of contemporary radical Islamism lies not in the Middle East, but in Western Europe. In addition to Bouyeri and the London bombers, the

March 11 Madrid bombers and ringleaders of the September 11 attacks such as Mohamed Atta were radicalized in Europe. In the Netherlands, where upwards of 6% of the population is Muslim, there is plenty of radicalism despite the fact that Holland is both modern and democratic. And there exists no option for walling the Netherlands off from this problem.

We profoundly misunderstand contemporary Islamist ideology when we see it as an assertion of traditional Muslim values or culture. In a traditional Muslim country, your religious identity is not a matter of choice; you receive it, along with your social status, customs and habits, even your future marriage partner, from your social environment. In such a society there is no confusion as to who you are, since your identity is given to you and sanctioned by all of the society's institutions, from the family to the mosque to the state.

The same is not true for a Muslim who lives as an immigrant in a suburb of Amsterdam or Paris. All of a sudden, your identity is up for grabs; you have seemingly infinite choices in deciding how far you want to try to integrate into the surrounding, non-Muslim society. In his book *Globalized Islam* (2004), the French scholar Olivier Roy argues persuasively that contemporary radicalism is precisely the product of the "deterritorialization" of Islam, which strips Muslim identity of all of the social supports it receives in a traditional Muslim society.

The identity problem is particularly severe for second- and third-generation children of immigrants. They grow up outside the traditional culture of their parents, but unlike most newcomers to the United States, few feel truly accepted by the surrounding society.

Contemporary Europeans downplay national identity in favor of an open, tolerant, "post-national" Europeanness. But the Dutch, Germans, French and others all retain a strong sense of their national identity, and, to differing degrees, it is one that is not accessible to people coming from Turkey, Morocco or Pakistan. Integration is further inhibited by the fact that rigid European labor laws have made low-skill jobs hard to find for recent immigrants or their children. A significant proportion of immigrants are on welfare, meaning that they do not have the dignity of contributing through their labor to the surrounding society. They and their children understand themselves as outsiders.

It is in this context that someone like Osama bin Laden appears, offering young converts a universalistic, pure version of Islam that has been stripped of its local saints, customs and traditions. Radical Islamism tells them exactly who they are—respected members of a global Muslim umma to which they can belong despite their lives in lands of unbelief. Religion is no longer supported, as in a true Muslim society, through conformity to a host of external social customs and observances; rather it is more a question of inward belief. Hence Mr. Roy's comparison of modern Islamism to the Protestant Reformation, which similarly turned religion inward and stripped it of its external rituals and social supports.

If this is in fact an accurate description of an important source of radicalism, several conclusions follow. First, the challenge that Islamism represents is not a strange and unfamiliar one. Rapid transition to modernity has long spawned radicalization; we have seen the exact same forms of alienation among those young people who in earlier generations became anarchists, Bolsheviks, fascists or members of the Bader-Meinhof gang. The ideology changes but the underlying psychology does not.

Further, radical Islamism is as much a product of modernization and globalization as it is a religious phenomenon; it would not be nearly as intense if Muslims could not travel, surf the Web, or become otherwise disconnected from their culture. This means that "fixing" the Middle East by bringing modernization and democracy to countries like Egypt and Saudi Arabia will not solve the terrorism problem, but may in the short run make the problem worse. Democracy and modernization in the Muslim world are desirable for their own sake, but we will continue to have a big problem with terrorism in Europe regardless of what happens there.

> The challenge that Islamism represents is not a strange and unfamiliar one.

The real challenge for democracy lies in Europe, where the problem is an internal one of integrating large numbers of angry young Muslims and doing so in a way that does not provoke an even angrier backlash from right-wing populists. Two things need to happen: First, countries like Holland and Britain need to reverse the counterproductive multiculturalist policies that sheltered radicalism, and crack down on extremists. But second, they also need to reformulate their definitions of national identity to be more accepting of people from non-Western backgrounds.

The first has already begun to happen. In recent months, both the Dutch and British have in fact come to an overdue recognition that the old version of multiculturalism they formerly practiced was dangerous and counterproductive. Liberal tolerance was interpreted as respect not for the rights of individuals, but of groups, some of whom were themselves intolerant (by, for example, dictating whom their daughters could befriend or marry). Out of a misplaced sense of respect for other cultures, Muslim minorities were left to regulate their own behavior, an attitude which dovetailed with a traditional European corporatist approaches to social organization. In Holland, where the state supports separate Catholic, Protestant and socialist schools, it was easy enough to add a Muslim "pillar" that quickly turned into a ghetto disconnected from the surrounding society.

New policies to reduce the separateness of the Muslim community, like laws discouraging the importation of brides from the Middle

East, have been put in place in the Netherlands. The Dutch and British police have been given new powers to monitor, detain and expel inflammatory clerics. But the much more difficult problem remains of fashioning a national identity that will connect citizens of all religions and ethnicities in a common democratic culture, as the American creed has served to unite new immigrants to the United States.

Since van Gogh's murder, the Dutch have embarked on a vigorous and often impolitic debate on what it means to be Dutch, with some demanding of immigrants not just an ability to speak Dutch, but a detailed knowledge of Dutch history and culture that many Dutch people do not have themselves. But national identity has to be a source of inclusion, not exclusion; nor can it be based, contrary to the assertion of the gay Dutch politician Pym Fortuyn who was assassinated in 2003, on endless tolerance and valuelessness. The Dutch have at least broken through the stifling barrier of political correctness that has prevented most other European countries from even beginning a discussion of the interconnected issues of identity, culture and immigration. But getting the national identity question right is a delicate and elusive task.

Many Europeans assert that the American melting pot cannot be transported to European soil. Identity there remains rooted in blood, soil and ancient shared memory. This may be true, but if so, democracy in Europe will be in big trouble in the future as Muslims become an ever larger percentage of the population. And since Europe is today one of the main battlegrounds of the war on terrorism, this reality will matter for the rest of us as well.

For Class Discussion

1. What are the main events (motivating occasion) that are prompting Fukuyama's writing of this editorial? How does he use both shock and familiarity to launch his argument?

2. Summarize Fukuyama's central argument about the EU's current unsuccessful treatment of its immigrant. What proposal is he making for a new kind of national identity and how does it differ from past attempts (including multiculturalism)? How does he connect his proposal with security issues?

3. What contradiction in European attitudes toward national identity does Fukuyama believe contributes to the sense of alienation experienced by many young Muslims there?

4. Describe how Fukuyama draws on the work of French scholar Olivier Roy to bolster his own argument about Islam in Europe. What does Fukuyama

do to make Roy's concept of "deterritorialization" more accessible to his *Wall Street Journal* readers?

5. What parallels might be drawn between Fukuyama's argument and the "Fortress Europe" cartoon? Between the European experience with national identity and immigration and the American experience? ■

Muslim Riots in Europe: Wasn't This Part of the Programme?
Farish A. Noor

Dr. Farish A. Noor is a Malaysian political scientist and human rights activist who has taught at the Centre for Civilisational Dialogue, University of Malaya, the Institute for Islamic Studies, and the Free University of Berlin, and has been an associate fellow at the Institute for Strategic and International Studies (ISIS), Malaysia. He has written extensively on how Islamic history and identity get taken up in political discourses. This piece was posted on the July/August edition of the Future Islam site (www.futureislam.com), which bills itself as "a journal of future ideology that shapes today the world of tomorrow" and is published in Urdu and Arabic as well as English versions. "In a nutshell," the editors say, "Future Islam is intended to emerge as a global forum where best minds of the world will participate in shaping a better future."

Who is Noor's primary audience for this argument? For what other groups might he also be writing?

Across Europe today Islam and Muslims are being put to question. In early May the British National Party (BNP) contested local elections across the country calling the elections a 'referendum on Islam'. In France similar questions were posed by the Front National on 1st May. Likewise in Denmark and the Netherlands. All across Western Europe, European citizens are being asked if they are willing to 'put up' with the presence of Islam and Muslims in their midst. Europe's universalist dreams and pretentions have been laid bare and rendered hollow by the parochialism that now masks itself as patriotism and nationalism. These countries look, sound and feel more like rural villages in the outback, with the villagers scared of the first black or brown face they see.

To make things worse, the political mainstream has also shifted to the right thanks to the vociferous campaigning by the extreme right-wing. In Britain, France, Netherlands, Germany and Italy not a day passes without yet another flaccid editorial piece about 'European identity being under threat' and the 'failure of multiculturalism'. Western Europe bemoans the end of cosmopolitan pluralism and yet cannot grapple with the very real structural-economic reasons for the failure of nation-building.

Rather than deal with concrete issues of class, power relations and power differentials between the majority and migrant communities, we have passed onto the more ambiguous and abstract register of cultural difference instead. If Europe cannot deal with Islam and Muslims, so we are told, it is because Muslims are 'culturally different' from other Europeans. (Little is said about the millions of 'Others' who reside in Europe, including the millions of Jews, Hindus and Buddhists who are there as well. . .)

The starting point of this spurious non-debate is the question of violence and instability. The right-wing Islamophobes point to the recent instances of riots by young Muslims in the ghettos and suburbs of London, Paris and other major cities of Western Europe. These instances of civil disobedience and conflict are, for many right-wingers, 'proof' that Muslims are generally a burden and trouble-makers who ought to be pacified, integrated or repatriated to their home countries. Muslims are presented as a 'problem' that needs to be pathologised, analysed, solved. But the obvious question follows: Was this not part of the programme in the first place?

The 'programme' here refers to the Liberal-Capitalist project of Western Europe itself. Let us remember that all these countries that are facing the 'problem' of failed integration and failed multiculturalism happen to be developed capitalist states. And as any good political scientist and historian will remind us, capitalist states have always thrived on civil dispute, precariousness, instability and the politics of divide-and-rule.

Capitalism requires there to be a surplus working class that can be played against itself and exploited at will. It requires a surplus of work-ers who can be domesticated, disciplined and co-opted when the needs of the market arise. Throughout the history of capitalism, the ruling commercial and political elite have sought to keep the workers divided along lines of race and communalism so that they would not unite and stir up a revolution. In the late 19th century the poor workers of England were pit against the poor migrants of Ireland. The Irishman was cast as the poor white parasite who had descended upon the shores of England to steal the jobs of honest English working men. Irishmen were contemptuously referred to as the 'white niggers' of Europe who were savage drunkards and hooligans best kept at bay by the police baton (and later rubber bullets and tear gas). The history of migration to countries like America, the United Kingdom, Netherlands, France and Germany is a record of successive ways of poor migrants being abused, demonised, exploited and turned against other equally poor communities.

Today the debate in Europe about 'violent Muslims' strikes a resonant chord with this older narrative of mistrust and alienation. Europe's Muslims are cast in culturalist terms as backward, violent, anti-social and untrustworthy; in the same way that earlier migrants from Ireland, Greece, the Jews etc. were portrayed. In all these cases the discussion of cultural difference is a convenient way to avoid the discussion of class, power differentials, institutionalised discrimination and exploitation by Capital.

The net effect is also the same: As was the case during the anti-Irish campaigns of the 19th and early 20th century, what is happening today is the division of the poor working classes of Europe along racial, ethnic and also religious lines. Yet we often forget that the plight of poor Muslims in Europe is similar to the plight of poor Europeans as well. All these minority communities suffer from unequal mediatic and political representation, less access to education and the tools of governance, less legal protection (and too much policing instead).

How can the problem be solved? One way out would be for Muslims in Europe to emphasise their class and political identities more and their religio-cultural identity less. The issue is not Islam or being Muslims; but rather racial and class discrimination which is not limited exclusively to Muslims themselves. As long as the poor working class Muslims of Europe do not realise this, and do not try to bridge the gap with other poor working class communities, they will remain a culturally-defined minority that will remain perpetually on the margins and treated like outsiders. For too long Europe's Muslims have blindly walked into the right-wingers' trap of sectarian communal-religious identification and allowed themselves to be cast and seen exclusively as members of a religious community. Now they need to emphasise the universality of their class condition and see themselves for what they are: the poor and exploited of Europe, who are no different than the poor Irish of the past.

For Class Discussion

1. Noor structures his argument in response to opposing views. What views have galvanized his writing and motivated his rebuttal?

2. What are the main points of Noor's rebuttal argument? How do his political-economic views shape and position this argument in a larger historical context? What does he mean by the "programme"?

3. Noor's argument has a passionate, urgent tone. What words, phrases such as "Islamaphobes," "failed integration," and "failed multiculturalism," and argumentative strategies contribute to that tone?

4. What is the rhetorical purpose of Noor's introduction of the historical case of Ireland? Do you find it an effective move?

5. How has Noor's argument influenced your thinking about immigration problems in the European Union?

This Carry-On About Muslim Dress

Yasmin Qureshi

A Pakistani-born criminal lawyer, former Chair of the Human Rights and Civil Liberties Working Group of the Association of Muslim Lawyers, Yasmin Qureshi became Great Britain's first woman Muslim MP in 2007. Before that she served as a human rights advisor to the mayor of London, a post in which she stood in opposition to racism and anti-Semitism, tackled domestic violence, opposed homophobia and bullying in schools, and worked to stamp out hate crimes. One of her key tasks was to address issues of Islamophobia, especially in the British media. This letter to the editor was published October 18, 2006, in the liberal British newspaper *The Guardian* in response to an October 16 article by Martin Newland about the pigeonholing and "separateness" of Muslim women (to see that original article, go to http://www.guardian.co.uk).

In this short letter to the editor, what are some of the primary ways in which Yasmin Qureshi defines "being British"?

It was refreshing to read the article by Martin Newland (G2, October 16). He is the only commentator who seems to understand that women choose to wear the Niqab as an expression of their faith and that you can still be a "regular person", albeit religious. I am a Muslim woman, as well as a practising barrister, past Labour parliamentary candidate, human-rights adviser to the mayor of London and past worker for the UN mission in Kosovo. But I fast, give zakat (alms), have performed Haj, say the slaat (prayers), do not drink, and am proud to call myself Muslim, will never wear a short dress or a bikini etc.

At the same time, I love, like many of my Muslim friends and family, watching *Carry On* films, Benny Hill, Rory Bremner, *Have I Got News for You*, love fish and chips, and have friends from all religions, cultures and backgrounds. Go and talk to and get to know a Muslim. Then you will know they are no different than anyone else.

I always thought the best thing about being British was that as long as you obeyed the laws, you could lead your life as you wanted. And yet we are all being pushed into one straightjacket. Just as people who want to "take their kit off" have the right to do so, so should people who want to "keep their kit on". This debate has already got some nasty undertones to it—and a lot of underlying ignorance.

For Class Discussion

1. How does the genre of a letter to the editor influence the way in which Yasmin Qureshi presents her argument? What challenges does the genre offer, but also what freedoms does it grant her?

2. What does Qureshi's rhetorical strategy of mixing her professional credentials with her private and religious practices accomplish in terms of establishing her relationship with her readers?

3. At the end of her first paragraph, Qureshi addresses the reader directly. How does this move contribute to the point she is trying to make about identity as well as shift a reader's relationship to the argument being made?

4. What contribution does this letter make to ongoing arguments about national identity? Does it raise points that other selections like Fancis Fukuyama's piece might miss?

CHAPTER QUESTIONS FOR REFLECTION AND DISCUSSION

1. How has immigration affected your local community, city, or region? Describe some of the political, economic, or social and cultural effects and influences of immigration in your area.

2. Where do Jagdish Bhagwati's and Kofi Annan's acceptance and praise of global migration intersect? Where do their arguments differ in rhetorical features and in content? For example, you might take a moment to freewrite on what difference the greater emphasis on "compassion" and "cooperation" makes to Annan's persuasiveness.

3. **For Rhetorical Analysis.** A number of the readings in this chapter address ways to reform the United States' immigration policy toward the goals of justice, reduction of poverty, shared global economic prosperity, and preservation of human rights. Where do the arguments of Kofi Annan, Susan Gordon, Linda Chavez-Thompson, and Peter Salins intersect? How do they differ in terms of their proposals, argumentative strategies, audiences, and appeals?

4. Many visual arguments—political cartoons, posters, ads, and even bumper stickers—make strong emotional arguments on immigration issues. Find either a political cartoon to contrast with "Europe as a Walled Fortress" or an ad, poster, or bumper sticker to contrast with the "One of America's Best-Selling Vehicles" advocacy ad. How do the arguments made by these visual texts differ? In both, how does the use of symbols, relationship of image to text, abbreviated argument, and shock, irony, or humor work? What insights do these texts contribute to the public conversation about immigration issues?

5. Linda Chavez-Thompson and Jennifer Gordon's proposed solutions to problems of immigrant labor seem to rely on collective action or unionization, but even they admit that the relationship between organized labor and immigrants hasn't always been perfectly congenial. Investigate and discuss

how a large immigrant labor force influences wages and working conditions for native workers. Possible sources might include the following:

a. Bureau of Labor Statistics (www.bls.gov)—search for the effect of immigrant labor on the earnings of unskilled American workers

b. The Urban Institute on economic and social policy research (www.urban.org)–search for trends in the low-wage immigrant labor force

c. American Federation of Labor (www.afl-cio.org)—search for their policies and testimony on immigrants

6. Samuel Huntington, MALDEF and LULAC, Peter Salins, Francis Fukuyama, and Yasmin Qureshi all concern themselves with the relationship between immigration, assimilation, and national identity. What are some points on which they seem close in their thinking, and where do their views diverge? With which ideas might you agree and with which might you disagree?

7. Farish A. Noor claims that to make the immigration argument an argument about cultural difference is to avoid "deal[ing] with concrete issues of class, power relations and power differentials between the majority and migrant communities, [. . .] institutionalized discrimination, and exploitation." How would you respond? How might scholars like Samuel Huntington and Francis Fukuyama respond?

8. There is considerable debate right now about how patterns of economic migration to the United States are being influenced by a turn toward economic hard times and significant U.S. unemployment. There is even evidence of a new phenomenon: the *Gran Salida* (loose translation: "mass exodus") of Latino workers from the United States as work becomes increasingly difficult to find. How might trends like this (in receiving countries) change the whole tenor of arguments about global migration?

9. Which authors suggest connections between immigration's economic and cultural repercussions? In other words, which authors' views provide the most complex and informed approach to immigration issues?

WRITING ASSIGNMENTS

Brief Writing Assignments

1. Write a short narrative recounting (a) part of your family's immigration story; (b) part of the immigration experiences of a friend; or (c) an experience of acceptance or alienation you had while living in another country. Be prepared to comment on how these experiences support and complicate arguments put forward by authors in this chapter.

2. In a recent opinion piece in the *New York Times*, lawyer and activist Jennifer Gordon again advocates for transnational labor, even in the face of the severe downturn in the U.S. economy that has been especially marked by job losses in all sectors. Sketch an outline of an argument responding to

critics who say that "American jobs should go to American workers." Then see what Gordon had to say: http://www.nytimes.com/2009/03/10/opinion/10gordon.html.

3. Francis Fukuyama's argument about the need for unified European national identities relies in part on the premise that the United States' approach to assimilating immigrants has been a successful one. Write a response supporting and/or contesting this premise based on both your own personal experiences and other texts you've read.

4. Choose one of the following controversial claims and write for twenty minutes supporting or rebutting the claim. Use examples from the readings, your own background knowledge, and your experiences as evidence to develop your view.

   A. Illegal immigation to the United States cannot be stopped.

   B. Immigrants—even undocumented ones—are beneficial to Americans and to the United States.

   C. U.S. policy toward immigration, especially illegal immigration, is contradictory and hypocritical.

   D. Immigration problems can be solved only by international institutions and policies.

   E. In the United States (and/or Europe), the effects of immigration on national identity and culture are more urgent and important than immigration's effect on the economy.

5. Write a short response to this question: How have the readings in this chapter helped you understand the complexity of immigration issues in a globalized world?

Writing Projects

1. Sometimes the citizens of a country that is experiencing a heavy influx of immigrants feel overwhelmed, irritated, or threatened by foreigners. Imagine that you have a friend who is wrestling with these feelings toward immigrants. Write an argument with this person as your audience. Drawing on what you've learned from your reading, try to enlarge your friend's understanding of immigration and arouse sympathy for immigrants as struggling human beings seeking jobs and dignity, and/or as small pieces in a vast, global political and economic system.

2. **Analyzing Arguments Rhetorically.** Choose an article in this chapter that you think is very effective for a general audience, and writing for a general news magazine readership, analyze this piece and argue for its persuasiveness. In what ways does it make a valuable contribution to the public debates on global immigration? Include a short summary of the piece and an analysis of several of its rhetorical features (for example, the clarity of its claim, the strength of its evidence, its emotional impact, the author's credibility). How has this article changed your views of immigration?

3. From your understanding of U.S. immigration issues, write a letter to your U.S. senator or representative in which you present a case for what sort of national policies on immigration you would like him or her to support and why.

4. Imagine that you work with a group like the Anti-Defamation League or the Southern Poverty Law Center, and you have been given the task of designing an ad (to be run on the facing page of the *New York Times*) that directly responds to the issues raised in the series of ads run by America's Leadership Team for Long Range Population-Immigration-Resource Planning. Create an argument that combines text and visual elements.

5. Choose one of the arguments in this chapter with which you disagree. Write an open letter to the author in which you (1) summarize the author's argument fairly and accurately; (2) discuss values and goals that you share with the author; (3) argue your own view of the issue, which could include pointing out the problems you see in the author's argument. Write your open letter with the idea of working with the author toward solving a problem related to immigration.

The following research suggestions can lead to the creation of visual or verbal arguments.

6. Research the patterns of immigration in your own region of the country, or more locally, your city or community, and write a description of these patterns. If your region is experiencing an influx or outflow of immigrants, you could develop your research into an argument in which you first describe those patterns and then make a claim about why immigration is or is not an issue in your community. Based on your research, you might (a) argue for measures that are successfully integrating immigrants into your community; (b) argue against current unsuccessful measures for integrating immigrants; or (c) propose alternative measures that you think would be helpful. Your audience for this piece could be the residents of your community or its decision makers and political representatives.

7. After doing field research about local (often nonprofit) organizations that seek to support immigrants in your community or region, create a brochure or series of ads informing the general public about how individuals can facilitate the work of one or several of these organizations.

8. This chapter has dealt primarily with U.S. immigrants from Mexico and Latin America. Investigate the varied current concerns of another U.S. immigrant group, such as Irish, Asian, or Middle Eastern immigrants, and propose a way that U.S. policy and practices could most successfully integrate them into American life while still being responsive to their cultural differences and heritage. You might consider the following organizations and sites:

Irish Radio Network in New York
Philadelphia's Irish Immigration and Pastoral Center
Emerald Isle Immigration Center in Queens

Asian Nation
Seattle's Chinese Information and Service Center (CISC)
Asian Counseling and Referral Service (ACRS)
Council on American-Islamic Relations (CAIR)
American Muslim Alliance
You might create a policy argument or a flier or brochure promoting an organization or policy. Choose an appropriate civic audience for your argument.

9. A number of Latino organizations and advocacy groups are working for the well-being of legal and illegal immigrants. After researching some of these groups' programs and proposals, write an argument for your classmates in which you support/defend a program, proposal, or piece of legislation as "the best solution" to a particular problem related to Latino immigrants. The following is a list of organizations you might want to consider:

National Council of La Raza
Workplace Project
Hispanic Alliance for Progress (Prosperity)
Latino Coalition for Faith and Community Initiative
Pew Hispanic Center
Labor Council for Latin American Advancement
Justice for Janitors campaign (out of the Service Employees International Union)
California Coalition for Immigration Reform
United Farm Workers Union

6

Protecting the Environment

Water Issues and Emerging Energy Technologies

QUESTION TO PONDER

You have recently read an article that claimed that the world spends around thirty billion dollars a year on bottled water and that many of these consumers reside in developed countries that have good, safe tap water. Furthermore, you've heard that bottling water wastes water, energy, and plastic and that bottled water is not necessarily more pure than tap water. You are wondering if you and your friends should promote the use of tap water over bottled water and spend your money instead on environmental causes or on helping global organizations provide safe water in developing countries.*

CONTEXT FOR A NETWORK OF ISSUES

The global community is wrestling with conflicting views of the earth's natural resources. These are classified as **renewable resources,** which includes renewable energy (solar, wind, and geothermal power), and **nonrenewable resources** such as minerals and **fossil fuels** (coal, oil, and natural gas). Whereas some corporations envision the earth as an expansive space with vast, lucrative resources to be tapped and marketed, other groups see the earth as our life-support system that has finite resources that need careful management. Recently, scientists have been wondering whether some renewable resources—trees, fertile soil,

---

*Tom Standage argues for this course of action in his article "Bad to the Last Drop," *New York Times* (August 1, 2005).

and water—are being depleted or contaminated at a rate that exceeds their replenishment and have been warning that the world's population growth over the next fifty years will only increase this threat to the environment. In addition, greenhouse gas emissions and changes in climate may very well be affecting the availability of resources.

Two concepts that regularly appear in controversies over natural resources, human dependence on the environment, and global interdependence are **sustainable development** and the **commons**. In 1987, the World Commission on Environment and Development (often called the "Brundtland Commission" after its chairwoman Gro Harlem Brundtland) articulated this now widely accepted definition of "sustainable development" as "development that meets the needs of the present without compromising the ability of future generations to meet their own needs."[*] The concept of "the commons" asks people to think of the earth's resources as belonging equally to all nations and peoples of the world. The commons include "the air we breathe, the freshwater we drink, the oceans and the diverse wildlife and plant biodiversity of the world, . . . and among indigenous peoples, communal lands that have been worked cooperatively for thousands of years."[†] Clearly, the ideas of sharing environmental resources with future generations and with all peoples directly oppose the practices of environmental overuse and competition.

Freshwater is a prime example of a finite natural resource that is subject to global competition. The award-winning musical *Urinetown* depicts a fictional city where one company owns the water system and manipulates accessibility and cost according to its own whims. The poor must pay a fee to use the restrooms, and it is illegal *not* to use the facilities. The penalty for breaking the law is banishment to Urinetown, a death sentence. Although *Urinetown* is a melodramatic postmodern self-parody, its main conflict between "the people" and a powerful corporation that controls the water imitates real-world conflicts over water. For example, recently in Cochabamba, Bolivia, hundreds of thousands of poor people protested against a group of corporations (among them, the Bechtel Corporation) that controlled the city's water distribution system. Rallying behind the slogans "Water is God's gift and not merchandise" and "Water is life," the Citizen Alliance compelled the government to regain control of the water system. The Bolivian crisis and the musical raise serious environmental, political, and economic questions about the scarcity of usable water; the privatizing of water supplies; the money and technology required to manage water systems; and the consequences of corporate control of environmental resources.

---

[*]1987: Brundtland Report, (an easy-to-read version of the report is available at http://www.worldinbalance.net/agreements/1987-brundtland.php).

[†]The International Forum on Globalization, *Alternatives to Economic Globalization: A Better World Is Possible* (San Francisco: Berrett-Koehler Publishers, Inc., 2002), 81.

What is the global status of water? The following facts give some idea of global problems with water:

Water: A Limited Resource

- 97.5 percent of earth's water is saltwater and undrinkable.
- Polar snow and ice hold most of the freshwater.
- Less than 1 percent of freshwater is usable, amounting to only 0.01 percent of the earth's total water.
- 70 percent of water goes to agricultural use; 22 percent to industrial use; 8 percent to domestic use.[*]
- "Across the world, 1.1 billion people have no access to clean drinking water. More than 2.6 billion people lack basic sanitation."
- "Each year, diseases related to inadequate water and sanitation kill between 2 and 5 million people and cause an estimated 80 percent of all sicknesses in the developing world."[†]
- Water is wasted through misuse, inefficiency, leakage, evaporation, and allocation of pure water to tasks that don't need it.
- It is projected that in twenty years, the demand for water will increase by 50 percent and two-thirds of the world population will be water-stressed.[‡]

Clearly, water is a precious global resource that requires efficient, equitable management worldwide.

Present and future equitable treatment of the environment is also at issue in the global controversies over atmospheric pollution and climate change. **Climate change** is affecting rainfall patterns, the intensity and frequency of storms, and the longevity of droughts. Many scientists think that pollution from greenhouse gases (mostly carbon dioxide caused by the burning of fossil fuels), which trap the earth's heat like a greenhouse, is playing a role in raising average surface temperatures and that changes in temperatures are causing changes in the earth's climate. According to scientists, "[c]arbon **emissions** from burning fossil fuel now stand at 6.5 billion tons a year (four times 1950 levels), resulting in atmospheric carbon dioxide concentrations 33 percent greater than preindustrial levels."[§] Furthermore, countries have unequally contributed to this atmospheric pollution: Each American emits about 5.99 tons of carbon dioxide a year compared with 0.31 ton emitted by each resident of India and 0.05 ton by

---

[*]"Water the Facts," *New Internationalist* (March 2003).

[†]"I Thirst," Water Advocates Advertisement, *New York Times* (March 22, 2005).

[‡]Richard Steiner, "The Real Clear and Present Danger," *Seattle Post-Intelligencer* (May 30, 2004).

[§]Ibid.

each Bangladeshi.* Most climatologists believe that the growing population and industrialization of third world countries will magnify problems with greenhouse gases and their effect on the earth's atmosphere and climate.

As a result of global concern over atmospheric pollution and climate change, scientists, corporations, and governments have begun to seek out environmentally friendly **alternative energy** such as biofuels, solar power, and wind energy, in order to provide for the world's continuing energy needs. Other factors that contribute to this search include the increasing scarcity of fossil fuels (which are nonrenewable resources), the difficulty of accessing the remaining untapped deposits of fossil fuels, and the instability of the price of oil, coal, and natural gas in global markets, as the world saw when the price of oil hit record highs in 2008.† Another discussion centers around questions of energy security and energy independence. Fossil fuel deposits are not evenly distributed around the globe, and political instability in some of the major oil-producing countries including Nigeria, Iran, and Brazil have prompted the United States, among other nations, to pass legislation urging the development of alternative fuels to lessen the country's dependence on foreign sources.‡

This chapter explores water scarcity and the development of alternative energy as global environmental issues.

STAKES AND STAKEHOLDERS

Because all humans need fresh air, safe water, and predictable weather, and because of our dependence on energy to light our homes, produce our food and goods, and fuel our vehicles, we are all prime stakeholders in global environmental issues. We are stakeholders along with governments and corporations, who often control citizens' consumers' access to natural resources, and scientists, who analyze environmental conditions and make predictions and recommendations about human impacts. These and other stakeholders are debating issues related to the following key questions.

What Are Some of the World's Major Problems with Environmental Resources? As stakeholders battle over defining the problems, many scientists are now saying that the amount of resources humans consume (as well as the damage to the earth we do—our "ecological footprint") is 20 percent over Earth's carrying capacity; we are overusing Earth's resources at too

---

*Maria Woolf and Colin Brown, "Beckett Exposes G8 Rift on Global Warming" and "Global Warming: The U.S. Contribution in Figures," *Independent* (June 13, 2005).

†"Oil Prices Top 147 U.S. Dollars per Barrel," *The Sydney Morning Herald* (July 12, 2008).

‡John M. Broder, "Bush Signs Broad Energy Bill," *New York Times* (December 19, 2007).

great a rate. Conservation specialist Richard Steiner, a professor at the University of Alaska–Fairbanks, describes the overuse in these terms:

> Conspicuous consumption has become a homogenizing force across the developed world. Just since 1950, we have consumed more goods and services than all previous generations combined. The consumption of energy, steel, and timber more than doubled; fossil fuel use and car ownership increased four-fold; meat production and fish catch increased five-fold; paper use increased six-fold, and air travel increased one hundred-fold.*

Furthermore, ecologists point out that developed countries, roughly 20 percent of the world's population, consume between 70 and 80 percent of the planet's resources, a level of use that cannot continue.† Considering the excessive consumption of developed countries, environmentalists and social justice activists are now worried about the increasing drain on environmental resources as giants China and India as well as third world countries adopt the developmental pattern of Europe and the United States in their effort to industrialize and advance economically. Studies have projected that if people in the developing world were to take on the American lifestyle, the world would need the resources of five or six Earths to maintain that level of consumption. In contrast, many political leaders, policymakers, economists, and businesses acknowledge the increasing pressures on the environment caused by population growth and the economic development of third world countries, but they disagree about the severity and urgency of the problem.

Perhaps the fiercest battles raging over environmental issues involve global warming and climate change. Stakeholders disagree about the extent and causes of global warming. Are natural causes creating global warming or are human-produced high emissions of carbon dioxide from the burning of fossil fuels (for industry, agriculture, energy, and cars) a major contributor to rising temperatures on Earth? Or are both natural and human causes involved? The reputable Intergovernmental Panel on Climate Change‡ thinks of global warming in terms of climate change and is focusing on critical temperature changes such as those that cause the warming of the

---

*"The Real and Clear Present Danger," *Seattle Post-Intelligencer* (March 30, 2004).

†Thomas Pugh and Erik Assadourian, "What Is Sustainability, Anyway?" *World-Watch* (September–October, 2003): 17.

‡The Intergovernmental Panel on Climate Change, established in 1988 by the World Meteorological Organization (WMO) and the United Nations Environment Programme (UNEP), focuses on evaluating "scientific, technical and socioeconomic information relevant for the understanding of climate change, its potential impacts, and options for adaptation and mitigation." The IPCC issues regular reports (1990, 1995, 2001, and 2007) to provide an assessment of the state of knowledge on climate change (www.ipcc.ch/about/index.htm).

oceans and the melting of the polar ice caps. These scientists cite erratic weather, more intense storms, earlier blooming of plants, changes in animals' seasonal ranges, and cooling of the Northern Hemisphere as signs of climate change. They also speak in terms of the complex, cumulative interplay among many factors (such as ocean currents, ocean warming, snowfall, etc.) and regard climate change as not fully understood or calculable. For many, climate change is a human rights and social justice issue because rising sea levels and coastal flooding as well as changes in rainfall and violent storms hit hardest the most vulnerable, climate-dependent people—the poor.

In opposition, a small number of scientists, the fossil fuel industry, some corporate leaders, some American political leaders, and some outspoken public figures such as the late novelist Michael Crichton (in his novel on global warming and ecoterrorism, *State of Fear* [2004]), maintain that human influence on the global climate is insignificant, that we are seeing mostly natural climate fluctuations and changes, and that computer climate models are inaccurate.

Questions about environmental problems and climate change also involve conflicts among scientists, politics, and the way the media represent environmental issues to the public. Both environmentalists and global warming skeptics accuse the other side of violating principles of science, of oversimplifying causes and effects, and of pursuing a political agenda; both groups claim the media are biased. Arguments about what science can deliver in the way of certainty and predictions are entangled with scientists' government funding and affiliations with the fossil fuel industry and environmental organizations.

As Third World Countries Develop and the Global Population Increases, How Can Environmental Resources Be Conserved and Fairly and Wisely Managed? Many nongovernmental organizations (NGOs), governments, indigenous peoples, and activist groups call for respect for the environmental commons and an environmental ethic of sustainable development. They advocate immediate changes in consumption patterns and the adoption of alternative clean energy sources, such as wind and solar power and hybrid and hydrogen-fueled cars. These stakeholders want voluntary limits on the production of greenhouse gases through international controls like the **Kyoto Protocol.** This global agreement, which went into effect in February 2005 and has been signed and ratified by 181 states as of February 2009, compels thirty-five developed nations, by 2008–2012, to reduce their greenhouse gas emissions by 5.2 percent compared to 1990. Some people see the Kyoto Protocol as more symbolic than instrumental and argue for much more radical changes and reductions in emissions, beyond 50 percent and even 70 percent over the next few years in order to return to preindustrial levels of greenhouse gas emissions.

In contrast, some economists, corporate leaders, and politicians claim that major shifts in energy use would be too economically disruptive and damaging. Contending that climate changes are natural and cyclical over millennia and that global warming is not human-induced, these people argue that reducing greenhouse gas emissions, especially as called for by the Kyoto Protocol's proposal, will have no positive impact on the earth's atmosphere and will be excessively costly to industries, consumers, and workers.*

What Is the Role of Economics and the Market in Managing Environmental Resources? Many environmental and anticorporate advocates argue that multinational corporations' pursuit of short-term profits leads to the exploitation of natural resources with little concern for the long-term good of the environment or for the lives of the local people most affected by these corporations' use of resources. For example, advocates maintain that when water is privatized, the public loses access to information about its quality. Social justice advocates emphasize that free trade agreements and institutions like the World Trade Organization, the World Bank, and the International Monetary Fund grant corporations the freedom to act without accountability, promote the privatization of resources, and enable corporations to override national governments' efforts to protect resources. The biggest water corporations, Vivendi Environment and Suez-Lyonnaise des Eaux, hold water interests in 120 countries. Vandana Shiva, an Indian physicist and environmental and political activist, claims that big corporations in India can easily take advantage of the scarcity of environmental resources:

> Privatization will aggravate the water crisis, because . . . water markets will take the water from the poor to the rich, from impoverished rural areas to affluent urban enclaves. It will also lead to overexploitation of water, because when access to water is determined by the market and not by limits of renewability, the water cycle will be systematically violated and the water crisis will deepen. Local community management is a precondition for both consumption and equitable use.†

Arguing that these resources are the commons belonging to everyone, environmental advocates insist that governments should regulate and protect these resources for the public interest. Many social justice activists believe that access to safe water should be declared a human right so that water cannot be sold for profit.

In contrast, many corporate leaders and economists think that *more* market involvement in natural resources will foster good stewardship.

---

*S. Fred Singer, atmospheric physicist and president of the Science and Environmental Policy Project, is a strong spokesperson for this view.
†Vandana Shiva, "World Bank, WTO, and Corporate Control over Water," *International Socialist Review* (August–September 2001).

They claim that government subsidies encourage waste and that the task of managing environmental resources is so huge and expensive that only capital-rich companies can take on the job. Richard L. Sandor, chairman and CEO of Chicago Climate Exchange, which enables companies to trade, sell, or buy credits in carbon dioxide emissions, explains his view of markets:

> Nobody owns the atmosphere, so nobody takes account. Respectfully treating it as the limited resource it really is requires limiting consumption, and instituting a process for treating it responsibly. The zero price now being charged for its use means there is no direct reward for those who might . . . [try to conserve]. Private capital is not being mobilized. The market is missing.*

One other view of how the market can tackle environmental issues is addressed by Thomas L. Friedman, a Pulitzer Prize-winning columnist for the *New York Times* and a longtime advocate of the free market, in his book *Hot, Flat, and Crowded* (2008). The book argues that energy technology will be the next great global industry and that if both the U.S. government and U.S. corporations take the initiative to develop alternative energy, it will lead to greater economic security and a greener world.†

In the absence of a clear governmental policy for environmental protection, some businesses have decided that embracing limits on their own is shrewd. Anticipating the need to meet European Union emissions standards, companies such as Dupont, IBM, General Electric, United Technologies, Baxter International, and International Paper are embracing the Kyoto restrictions on their own. Some American companies, along with EU and Chinese companies, are using these restrictions to spur innovation with low-carbon technologies and clean energy. Policymakers and analysts point to Brazil as an example of how fruitful collaboration between government and the market can help the environment *and* the economy. After the oil crisis in the 1970s, the Brazilian government financially encouraged its new ethanol industry (ethanol is a clean burning fuel consisting of alcohol from sugarcane, among other crops), which has been thriving since the 1980s.

---

*Richard L. Sandor. "Climate and Action: Trading Gases," *Our Planet Magazine* 9.6 (November 1998), http://www.ourplanet.com/imgversn/96/sandor.html.
†Thomas L. Friedman, *Hot, Flat, and Crowded: Why We Need a Green Revolution—and How It Can Renew America* (New York: Farrar, Straus, and Giroux, 2008).

What International Organizations Should Regulate Conflicts Between Nations over Natural Resources and Encourage Global Cooperation in Establishing Sustainable Practices? In the 1970s, when scientists began to understand that most environmental problems are global and interrelated (for example, weather patterns, rainfall, and growing seasons), the need for global institutions to tackle these problems became apparent. Conflicts over resources can be politically destabilizing, weakening poor countries and making them vulnerable to terrorists and dangerous political forces; indeed, environmental problems are security problems requiring global solutions. Still, people disagree about how to measure sustainability and what goals and timetables to establish.

Nations are also realizing that dependence on foreign countries for natural resources can lead to political instability. To prevent takeover by multinational companies and to ensure that domestic businesses stay competitive with foreign businesses, many analysts, policymakers, and businesses are calling for strong, clear national water and energy policies.

In particular, many developing nations are turning to the United Nations and its various programs and agencies to help them protect the environmental rights of their people. By designating water a human right, the United Nations could further encourage global cooperation and help ward off water wars. Because approximately 260 rivers flow through two or more countries and numerous bodies of water are bounded by multiple countries, intergovernmental organizations are needed to regulate the rights to and use of this water. On the global warming issue, advocates of global cooperation such as Europe and Japan are pleased that industrialized nations have accepted the Kyoto Protocol's legal restraint and have established a mutually beneficial exchange, the first "international trading system allowing countries to earn credits toward their treaty targets by investing in emissions cleanups outside their borders."* Some people are arguing that countries should have legal recourse when they suffer from global warming damages and water exploitation. For example, developing countries should be able to seek reparations from multinationals in world courts; perhaps the International Court of Justice should mandate that rich polluting countries pay poorer developing countries for damages to their environment.

Finally, many NGOs and policymakers are calling for global strategies for water conservation, reclamation, and efficiency and for equitable,

---

*Larry Rohter and Andrew C. Revkin. "Cheers, and Concern, for New Climate Pact," *New York Times* (December 13, 2004).

sustainable environmental practices to prepare for the world's population growth.

What Can Technology Contribute to Encouraging Sustainability and to Solving Problems with Environmental Resources? Some more radical ecologists (deep ecologists) would argue that humans have created environmental problems by interfering with nature and that more technology represents more interference. Some ecofeminists like Vandana Shiva argue that we must consider power relationships: Who owns the technology? Who decides how it will be used? Will it harm nature? Many environmentalists would say that wise investment in technology—for example, to find renewable energy alternatives—should supplement a drastic reprogramming of our habits. Some environmentalists call for completely new designs for energy systems, cars, insulation, lighting, household appliances, and water systems. Many corporate leaders believe in technology and have embraced environmental problems as incentives and business opportunities. They cite the improvement in car fuel economy from 1977 through 1985, the advancement in energy-efficient refrigerators and air conditioners, and the current work with desalination of water. And on the far protechnology extreme, some people assume that technology will be able to solve our environmental problems, remedy all our mistakes, and renew the environment; therefore, they see no need for new habits of consumption or energy use.

The three sections that follow—"Student Voice," "International Voices," and "Global Hot Spot"—take you deeper into the network of environmental issues connected to water resources and climate change that we as global citizens need to address.

 STUDENT VOICE: Changing Lives with Water by Malia Burns-Rozycki

For some Americans like Malia Burns-Rozycki, experiencing the great need for water elsewhere in the world—in this case, in rural Benin, West Africa—has led to a deeper awareness of how Americans take water for granted.

> The dash board read 43 degrees Centigrade. Reaching for my second bottle of water I calculated the temperature to be around 110 Fahrenheit. It was almost unbearable, even inside the air-conditioned SUV. It was during times like these that I questioned what I was doing in Benin, West Africa. Why hadn't I found an internship in Washington DC like all my other friends? And yet here I was, camera in hand, bumping over winding dirt roads, miles from the nearest flushing toilet.

Stepping out of the car, I was blasted in the face by the heat. The sun seared the barren landscape, preventing grass from growing. A few brave trees seemed to stand in defiance of the elements saying "look at me, I can survive the heat." I was amazed at how flat and monochromatic everything was. Even the huts in the village were made out of red dirt, making them disappear into the horizon.

Fifty people were gazing intently at a large piece of machinery. I cannot imagine what this kind of technology would have looked like to a community where not one person owns a car, women walk miles to sell their goods at market, and few speak the national language. For a brief moment all villagers had put down their work to witness this momentous event, the drilling of a community well.

The project coordinator explained to me that the nearest well was in the next village, more than two hours on foot, I estimated. Each morning women from the village set out with large metal bowls on their heads, returning in time to prepare the morning meal. Four hours a day are spent on this commute. Village life is not easy. Indicators can be seen everywhere, on the weathered faces, in the tired eyes, the muscular arms. A little girl who barely reached my hip carried an infant on her back and twigs on her head, proving that literally everyone who was capable worked.

I wondered how Catholic Relief Services even found this village, when so many of these northern communities need water. In Benin only 23 percent of the population has access to improved sanitation and only 63 percent have sustainable access to an improved water source. Catholic Relief Services funded the drilling as part of its education program, conceptualizing water as a prerequisite for formal education. The village is in no way unique; it is one of many that need water, though I never found out why this one had been chosen.

The drilling had already been going for a few hours and the drillers were not yet pleased with their soil samples; they were still too dry. Yet with their superior technology and expertise, they had no doubt that water would soon be reached.

It wasn't until I got home and looked at the photos that I really understood. Looking through the lens I missed the magic of the moment, the marvel on their faces, and the true importance of what was taking place. I am constantly humbled by how much I take for granted. The showers, the laundry, the dishes—all the water—this valuable resource goes down the drain without a second thought. And yet this hole in the ground will fundamentally alter the way of life in the village. For most of the women there will be more hours in the day. The crops will have a much larger chance of survival during the two dry seasons. Hygiene could improve dramatically if people are able to wash their hands after they use the latrine. Sanitation in food preparation can prevent the spread of illness-causing bacteria. Life will change because the village now has water.

INTERNATIONAL VOICES

The disparity between developed and developing countries' access to safe water is pronounced: "The average American uses 90 gallons of water a day, says the EPA. A European uses only 53 gallons; a sub-Saharan African, 5 gallons."* Recognizing these disparities and the centrality of water in sustaining and improving life, the United Nations General Assembly in 2003 declared that 2005–2015 would be the International Decade for Action, "Water for Life," and it targeted Africa as a special focus. The **Millennium Development Goals** for water include halving the "proportion of people without access to safe drinking water," halting "unsustainable exploitation of water resources," and creating "integrated water resource management and efficiency plans."[†] Africa, which has some 288 million people without access to safe drinking water and 36 percent of the population without access to basic sanitation,[‡] is particularly in need of water. However, Africans' problems with water are entangled in complex economic, political, and environmental conditions as shown in the news story "Swaziland: Coping with Diminishing Water Resources" from *Africa News*, March 22, 2005. (Swaziland is a tiny country surrounded by South Africa and Mozambique.)

Comments from Water Authorities in Swaziland

Rivers that were once perennial have now begun to run dry during the winter months, from June to September, when little or no rain falls. Dams throughout the country were below their usual level for this time of year. The largest of

---

*Micah Morrison, "Will We Run Dry?" *Parade* (August 24, 2005): 4.

[†]"International Decade for Action: Water for Life, 2005–2015," http://www0.un.org/waterforlifedecade/.

[‡]Inter Press Service, "PanAfrica; Water, Water Everywhere . . . ," *Africa News* (August 23, 2005). "The eight Millennium Development Goals include a 50 percent reduction in poverty and hunger; universal primary education; reduction of child mortality by two-thirds; cutbacks in maternal mortality by three-quarters; the promotion of gender equality; the reversal of the spread of HIV/AIDS, malaria, and other diseases; environmental sustainability, including access to safe drinking water; and a North-South global partnership for development."

these, the Maguga dam in the mountainous northern Hhohho region, a joint venture between Swaziland and South Africa, had not reached even half its capacity since it opened two years ago.

Melvin Mayisela, senior water engineer in the rural water supply department, said, "We encourage communities to use boreholes and streams instead of rivers—if a river is used, it would mean qualified technicians would have to monitor the project to ensure a safe water supply."

He recently denied the residents of rural Hosea community permission to use water from the Ngwavuma river in southern Swaziland, due to its high level of toxic pollutants. River pollution is a lethal byproduct of Swaziland's push for industrialization, and has further compromised the nation's water supply.

GLOBAL HOT SPOT: Africa

African countries are engaged in numerous strategies to solve their water problems. These countries are seeking both big solutions involving large investments of foreign capital and technological equipment and small, community-based solutions that nurture independence and sustainable development. In the following excerpt from the news article "PanAfrica: Water, Water Everywhere . . . " from the August 23, 2005, issue of *Africa News*, South Africa's minister of water affairs and forestry gives a big-picture sketch of Africa's water problems and reaches toward solutions.

. . . ."In spite of a few large rivers like the Congo and the Nile, twenty-one of the world's most arid countries, in terms of water per person, are located in Africa," South Africa's minister of Water Affairs and Forestry told a symposium marking "World Water Week" in the Swedish capital.

The Nile and its tributaries flow through nine countries: Egypt, Uganda, Sudan, Ethiopia, Democratic Republic of Congo (DRC), Kenya, Tanzania, Rwanda, and Burundi. The Congo, the world's fifth longest river, flows primarily through DRC, People's Republic of Congo, Central African Republic, and partially through Zambia, Angola, Cameroon, and Tanzania.

Addressing over 1,400 water experts and representatives of nongovernmental organizations, Buyelwa Sonjica said that in arid and semi-arid countries, rivers only flow for short periods in the rainy season, "and you need dams to store water for dry periods."

"The need for water resource infrastructure in Africa is clear. The same arguments are also applicable to many countries in the developing world," she added.

But she warned that the construction of dams should be conditioned on two factors: first, people affected or displaced by a dam should be guaranteed benefits of some nature— "and they should also be better off after the construction of the dam than they were before." Secondly, she said, the impacts on aquatic and terrestrial ecosystems should be mitigated. . . .

The state of Jigawa, Nigeria, in West Africa has achieved success through the government's commitment to the "Water for All" project, involving boreholes (open wells) and hand pumps. To supply water for households and irrigation, the government has constructed 1,420 open wells. Appreciative citizens of Jigawa have supported the governor for his follow-through on his promises, and international organizations and other countries are hoping to imitate Jigawa's success. The following excerpt from the news story "Nigeria; Jigawa: When Governance Overrides Politics" from the August 18, 2005, issue of *Africa News* recounts this achievement.

Nigeria—[The State Commissioner for Water Resources Alhaji Yusuf Shitu] Galambi said to ensure a more organized approach to the provision of water, the state government set up the State Water Initiative Committee (SWIC), at a time [when] about thirty-eight wild cart drilling rigs purchased from Texas, USA, had just arrived [in] the state. According to him, "the committee was inaugurated on August 22, 2003, to drill 900 boreholes in a month in the thirty constituencies of the state. . . ."

Galambi said his ministry had introduced a proven medium, tagged the "Peoples Forum," of sensitizing the local communities on water hygiene and standard practices with respect to water treatment in the state. He explained that the programme involved the selection of qualified community leaders to oversee the monitoring of government water projects in the state. . . .

As you read the articles in this chapter, think about the interconnection of environmental, political, and economic issues, and note how assumptions about the environment, science, and technology operate in these arguments' interpretations of problems and proposed solutions.

READINGS

Private Water Saves Lives
Fredrik Segerfeldt

Fredrik Segerfeldt researches and writes for the Swedish think tank Timbro, founded in 1978 and committed to "an agenda of reform based on our core values—individual liberty, economic freedom, and an open society" (from www.timbro.com). Timbro shares perspectives with its American free market counterpart, the Cato Institute. Segerfeldt authored *Water for Sale: How Business and the Market Can Resolve the World's Water Crisis* (2005), which has been translated and published by the Cato Institute. The following policy proposal was originally published by the *Financial Times* on August 25, 2005, and was posted on the Cato Institute Web site on August 29, 2005.

> How has Segerfeldt written this argument, identified with a free market philosophy, to appeal to a wider audience than fellow libertarians?

Worldwide, 1.1 billion people, mainly in poor countries, do not have access to clean, safe water. The shortage of water helps to perpetuate poverty, disease and early death. However, there is no shortage of water, at least not globally. We use a mere 8 percent of the water available for human consumption. Instead, bad policies are the main problem. Even Cherrapunji, India, the wettest place on earth, suffers from recurrent water shortages.

Ninety-seven percent of all water distribution in poor countries is managed by the public sector, which is largely responsible for more than a billion people being without water. Some governments of impoverished nations have turned to business for help, usually with good results. In poor countries with private investments in the water sector, more people have access to water than in those without such investments. Moreover, there are many examples of local businesses improving water distribution. Superior competence, better incentives and better access to capital for investment have allowed private distributors to enhance both the quality of the water and the scope of its distribution. Millions of people who lacked water mains within reach are now getting clean and safe water delivered within a convenient distance.

The privatization of water distribution has stirred up strong feelings and met with resistance. There have been violent protests and demonstrations against water privatization all over the world. Western antibusiness nongovernmental organizations and public employee unions, sometimes together with local protesters, have formed antiprivatization coalitions. However, the movement's criticisms are off base.

The main argument of the antiprivatization movement is that privatization increases prices, making water unaffordable for millions of poor people. In some cases, it is true that prices have gone up after privatization; in others not. But the price of water for those already connected to a mains network should not be the immediate concern. Instead, we should focus on those who lack access to mains water, usually the poorest in poor countries. It is primarily those people who die, suffer from disease and are trapped in poverty.

They usually purchase their lower-quality water from small-time vendors, paying on average 12 times more than for water from regular mains, and often more than that. When the price of water for those already connected goes up, the distributor gets both the resources to enlarge the network and the incentives to reach as many new customers as possible. When prices are too low to cover the costs of laying new pipes, each new customer entails a loss rather than a profit, which makes the distributor unwilling to extend the network. Therefore, even a doubling of the price of mains water could actually give poor people access to cheaper water than before.

There is another, less serious, argument put forward by the antiprivatization movement. Since water is considered a human right and since we die if we do not drink, its distribution must be handled democratically; that is, remain in the hands of the government and not be handed over to private, profit-seeking interests. Here we must allow for a degree of pragmatism. Access to food is also a human right. People also die if they do not eat. And in countries where food is produced and distributed "democratically", there tends to be neither food nor democracy. No one can seriously argue that all food should be produced and distributed by governments.

The resistance to giving enterprise and the market a larger scope in water distribution in poor countries has had the effect desired by the protesters. The pace of privatization has slowed. It is therefore vital that we have a serious discussion based on facts and analysis, rather than on anecdotes and dogmas.

True, many privatizations have been troublesome. Proper supervision has been missing. Regulatory bodies charged with enforcing contracts have been non-existent, incompetent or too weak. Contracts have been badly designed and bidding processes sloppy. But these mistakes do not make strong arguments against privatizations as such, but against bad privatizations. Let us, therefore, have a discussion on how to make them work better, instead of rejecting the idea altogether. Greater scope for businesses and the market has already saved many lives in Chile and

Argentina, in Cambodia and the Philippines, in Guinea and Gabon. There are millions more to be saved.

For Class Discussion

1. What are Segerfeldt's main reasons in support of his claim?

2. Many countries worldwide are trying to determine who can most efficiently and fairly manage their access to water—the government, private corporations, or public-private partnerships. How does Segerfeldt acknowledge that he is entering a very heated controversy? How does he avoid emotionalism?

3. In this rebuttal-based argument, how does Segerfeldt accommodate and respond to opposing views?

4. What do you see as the strongest points or features of this argument? How has this piece influenced your view of water privatization?

5. In what ways do the Web sites for big water corporations such as Veolia Environnement (www.veolia.com) and Suez (www.suez.com) echo Segerfeldt's defense of privatization?   ■

Where Has All the Water Gone?
Maude Barlow

Maude Barlow is National Chairperson of the Council of Canadians and Senior Advisor on Water to the President of the United Nations General Assembly. She also founded the Blue Planet Project, chairs the board of Washington-based Food and Water Watch, and is a Councillor with the Hamburg-based World Future Council. Her books include *Blue Covenant: The Global Water Crisis and the Coming Battle for the Right to Water* (2007) and, with Tony Clarke, *Blue Gold: The Battle Against Corporate Theft of the World's Water* (2002), which has been published in seventeen languages and forty-seven countries. This position statement was first published as part of a forum titled "The Global Freshwater Crisis and the Quest for Solutions" in the June 2008 issue of *The American Prospect*, a magazine committed to "a just society, an enriched democracy, and effective liberal politics" (www.prospect.org).

How effective are Barlow's opening scenarios in capturing her readers' attention?

Three scenarios collude toward disaster. Scenario one: The world is running out of freshwater. It is not just a question of finding the money to hook up the 2 billion people living in water-stressed regions of our world. Humanity is polluting, diverting, and depleting the Earth's finite water resources at a dangerous and steadily increasing rate. The abuse and displacement of water is the ground-level equivalent of greenhouse-gas emissions and likely as great a cause of climate change.

AP Images

Women and children in Bhopal, India, wait in a line for drinking water.

Scenario two: Every day more and more people are living without access to clean water. As the ecological crisis deepens, so too does the human crisis. More children are killed by dirty water than by war, malaria, HIV/AIDS, and traffic accidents combined. The global water crisis has become a powerful symbol of the growing inequality in our world. While the wealthy enjoy boutique water at any time, millions of poor people have access only to contaminated water from local rivers and wells.

Scenario three: A powerful corporate water cartel has emerged to seize control of every aspect of water for its own profit. Corporations deliver drinking water and take away wastewater; corporations put massive amounts of water in plastic bottles and sell it to us at exorbitant prices; corporations are building sophisticated new technologies to recycle our dirty water and sell it back to us; corporations extract and move water by huge pipelines from watersheds and aquifers to sell to big cities and industries; corporations buy, store, and trade water on the open market, like running shoes. Most important, corporations want governments to deregulate the water sector and allow the market to set water policy. Every day, they get closer to that goal. Scenario three deepens the crises now unfolding in scenarios one and two.

Imagine a world in 20 years in which no substantive progress has been made to provide basic water services in the Third World; or to create laws to protect source water and force industry and industrial agriculture to stop polluting water systems; or to curb the mass movement of water by pipeline, tanker, and other diversions, which will have created huge new swaths of desert.

Desalination plants will ring the world's oceans, many of them run by nuclear power; corporate-controlled nanotechnology will clean up sewage water and sell it to private utilities, which will in turn sell it back to us at a huge profit; the rich will drink only bottled water found in the few remaining uncontaminated parts of the world or sucked from the clouds by corporate-controlled machines, while the poor will die in increasing numbers from a lack of water.

This is not science fiction. This is where the world is headed unless we change course—a moral and ecological imperative. But first we must come to terms with the dimension of the crisis.

WE ARE RUNNING OUT OF FRESHWATER

In the first seven years of the new millennium, more studies, reports, and books on the global water crisis have been published than in all of the preceding century. Almost every country has undertaken research to ascertain its water wealth and the threats to its aquatic systems. Universities around the world are setting up departments or cross-departmental disciplines to study the effects of water shortages. The Worldwatch Institute has declared: "Water scarcity may be the most underappreciated global environmental challenge of our time."

From these undertakings, the verdict is in and irrefutable: The world is facing a water crisis due to pollution, climate change, and surging population growth of unprecedented magnitude. Unless we change our ways, by the year 2025 two-thirds of the world's population will face water scarcity. The global population tripled in the 20th century, but water consumption went up sevenfold. By 2050, after we add another 3 billion to the population, humans will need an 80 percent increase in water supplies just to feed ourselves. No one knows where this water is going to come from.

Scientists call them "hot stains"—the parts of the Earth now running out of potable water. They include northern China, large areas of Asia and Africa, the Middle East, Australia, the Midwestern United States, and sections of South America and Mexico.

The worst effects on people are, of course, in those areas of the world with large populations and insufficient resources to provide sanitation. Two-fifths of the world's people lack access to proper sanitation, which has led to massive outbreaks of waterborne diseases. Half of the world's hospital beds are occupied by people with an easily preventable waterborne disease, and the World Health Organization reports that environmental factors, including contaminated water, are implicated in 80 percent of all sickness and disease worldwide. In the last decade, the number of children killed by diarrhea exceeded the number of people killed in all armed conflicts since World War II. Every eight seconds, a child dies from drinking dirty water.

Meanwhile, some wealthier countries are just beginning to understand the depth of their own crises. Many parts of the United States are experiencing severe water shortages. Pressure is mounting on the governors in the Great Lakes region to open up access to the lakes to the burgeoning mega-cities around the basin. In 2007, Lake Superior, the world's largest freshwater lake, dropped to its lowest level in 80 years. Florida is in trouble, trying to keep its fast-spreading lawns and golf courses green. California has a 20-year supply of freshwater left. New Mexico has only 10. And Arizona is out: It now imports all of its drinking water. Experts assert that this is more than a cyclical "drought": Major parts of the United States are running out of water. In fact, the Environmental Protection Agency warns that if current water use continues unchecked, 36 states will suffer water shortages within the next five years.

HOW DID WE GET HERE?

We were all taught certain fundamentals about the Earth's hydrologic cycle in grade school. There is, we learned, a finite amount of available freshwater on the planet, and it makes its way through a cycle that ensures its safe return to us for our perpetual use. In the hydrologic cycle, water vapor condenses to form clouds. Winds move the clouds across the globe, spreading the water vapor. When the clouds cannot hold the moisture, they release it in the form of rain or snow, which either seeps into the ground to replenish groundwater or runs off into lakes, streams, and rivers. As these processes happen, the power of the sun causes evaporation, changing liquid water into vapor to renew the cycle. In this scenario, the planet could never "run out" of water.

But this cycle, true for so many millennia, did not take into account modern humans' collective capacity for destruction. In the last half-century, the human species has polluted surface waters at an alarming rate. The world may not exactly be running out of water, but it is running out of clean water. Ninety percent of wastewater produced in the Third World is discharged, untreated, into local rivers, streams, and coastal waters. As well, humans are now using more than half of accessible runoff water, leaving little for the ecosystem or other species.

OUR POLITICAL LEADERS ARE FAILING US

The freshwater crisis is easily as great a threat to the Earth and humans as climate change (to which it is deeply linked) but has had very little attention paid to it in comparison. It is like a comet poised to hit the Earth. If a comet really did threaten the entire world, it is likely that our politicians would suddenly find that religious and ethnic differences had lost much of their meaning. Political leaders would quickly come together to find a solution to this common threat.

However, with rare exceptions, average people do not know that the world is facing a comet called the global water crisis. And they are not being served by their political leaders, who are in some kind of inexplicable denial. The crisis is not reported enough in the mainstream media, and when it is, it is usually reported as a regional or local problem, not an international one.

Every day, the failure of our political leaders to address the global water crisis becomes more evident. Every day, the need for a comprehensive water-crisis plan becomes more urgent. If ever there were a moment for all governments and international institutions to come together to find a collective solution to this emergency, it is now. If ever there were a time for a plan of conservation and water justice to deal with the twin water crises of scarcity and inequity, it is now. The world does not lack the knowledge about how to build a water-secure future; it lacks the political will.

This, then, is the task: nothing less than reclaiming water as a commons for the Earth and all people that must be wisely and sustainably shared and managed if we are to survive. This will not happen unless we are prepared to reject the basic tenets of market-based globalization. The current imperatives of competition, unlimited growth, and private ownership when it comes to water must be replaced by new imperatives—those of cooperation, sustainability, and public stewardship.

For Class Discussion

1. Maude Barlow asserts that average people do not know that there is a world water crisis. How familiar were you with this issue before reading her essay?

2. What reasons does she give to establish the urgency of the issue?

3. What types of evidence does Barlow provide to convince her readers of the global water crisis?

4. The audience for this publication is likely to be sympathetic to Barlow's views. How would the inclusion of alternative or opposing views affect the persuasiveness of her argument?

5. This essay connects a global issue with local water supplies in many regions of the United States. How could you find out more about water issues in your area? You might begin with your state's Department of Ecology or Department of Natural Resources, your city's water department, or the Environmental Protection Agency (www.epa.gov).   ∎

The Missing Piece: A Water Ethic
Sandra Postel

Sandra Postel directs the Global Water Policy Project, which "fosters ideas and inspiration for redirecting society's use and management of fresh water toward conservation and ecosystem health" (www.globalwaterpolicy.org). A leading authority and prolific author on international water issues, Postel's books include *Last Oasis: Facing Water Scarcity* (1993), *Rivers for Life: Managing Water for People and Nature* (coauthored with Brian Richter [2003]), and *Liquid Assets: The Critical Need to Safeguard Freshwater Ecosystems* (2005). Like Barlow's piece, this policy proposal first appeared in "The Global Freshwater Crisis and the Quest for Solutions" in the June 2008 issue of the *American Prospect*.

> Many authors, including those in this chapter, have proposed technological solutions to environmental problems. How does Postel's approach to the freshwater crisis differ?

Now for the million-dollar questions: Why has so much of modern water management gone awry? Why is it that ever greater amounts of money and ever more sophisticated engineering have not solved the world's water problems? Why, in so many places on this planet, are rivers drying up, lakes shrinking, and water tables falling?

The answer, in part, is simple: We have been trying to meet insatiable demands by continuously expanding a finite water supply. In the long run, of course, that is a losing proposition: It is impossible to expand a finite supply indefinitely, and in many parts of the world the "long run" has arrived.

For sure, measures to conserve, recycle, and more efficiently use water have enabled many places to contain their water demands and to avoid or at least delay an ecological reckoning. Such tried-and-true measures as thrifty irrigation techniques, water-saving plumbing fixtures, native landscaping, and wastewater recycling can cost-effectively reduce the amount of water required to grow food, produce material goods, and meet household needs. The conservation potential of these measures has barely been tapped.

Yet something is missing from this prescription, something less tangible than drip irrigation lines and low-flow showerheads, but, in the final analysis, more important. It has to do with modern society's disconnection from nature's web of life and from water's most fundamental role as the basis of that life. In our technologically sophisticated world, we no longer grasp the need for the wild river, the blackwater swamp, or even the diversity of species collectively performing nature's work. By and large, society views water in a utilitarian fashion—as a "resource" valued only when it is extracted from nature and put to use on a farm, in a factory, or in a home.

Overall, we have been quick to assume rights to use water but slow to recognize obligations to preserve and protect it. Better pricing and more open markets will assign water a higher value in its economic functions, and breed healthy competition that weeds out wasteful and unproductive uses. But this will not solve the deeper problem. What is needed is a set of guidelines and principles that stops us from chipping away at natural systems until nothing is left of their life-sustaining functions, which the marketplace fails to value adequately, if at all. In short, we need a water ethic—a guide to right conduct in the face of complex decisions about natural systems that we do not and cannot fully understand.

The essence of such an ethic is to make the protection of freshwater ecosystems a central goal in all that we do. This may sound idealistic, yet it is no more radical a notion than suggesting that a building be given a solid foundation before adding 30 stories to it. Water is the foundation of every human enterprise, and if that foundation is insecure, everything built upon it will be insecure, too. As such, our stewardship of water will determine not only the quality but the staying power of human societies.

The adoption of such a water ethic would represent a historic shift away from the strictly utilitarian approach to water management and toward an integrated, holistic approach that views people and water as interconnected parts of a greater whole. Instead of asking how we can further control and manipulate rivers, lakes, and streams to meet our ever-growing demands, we would ask instead how we can best satisfy human needs while accommodating the ecological requirements of freshwater ecosystems. It would lead us, as well, to deeper questions of human values, in particular how to narrow the wide gap between the haves and have-nots within a healthy ecosystem.

Embedded within this water ethic is a fundamental question: Do rivers and the life within them have a right to water? In his famous essay, "Should Trees Have Standing? Toward Legal Rights for Natural Objects," legal scholar Christopher D. Stone argued more than 35 years ago that yes, rivers and trees and other objects of nature do have rights, and these should be protected by granting legal standing to guardians of the voiceless entities of nature, much as the rights of children are protected by legal guardians. Stone's arguments struck a chord with U.S. Supreme Court Justice William O. Douglas, who wrote in a famous dissent in the 1972 case Sierra Club v. Morton that "contemporary public concern for protecting nature's ecological equilibrium should lead to the conferral of standing upon environmental objects to sue for their own preservation. . . . The river, for example, is the living symbol of all the life it sustains or nourishes—the fish, aquatic insects, water ouzels, otter, fisher, deer, elk, bear, and all other animals, including man, who are dependent on it or who enjoy it for its sight, its sound, or its life. The river as plaintiff speaks for the ecological unit of life that is part of it."

During the next three decades, U.S. courts heard cases brought by environmental groups and other legal entities on behalf of nature and its constituents. In water allocation, concepts such as "instream flow rights" began to take hold, although these rights often received too low a priority to offer meaningful protection of river health. With freshwater life being extinguished at record rates, a more fundamental change is needed. An ethical society can no longer ignore the fact that water-management decisions have life-or-death consequences for other species. An ethically grounded water policy must begin with the premise that all people and all living things should be given access to enough water to secure their survival before some get more than enough.

On paper, at least one government has grounded its water policy in precisely such an ethic. South Africa's 1998 water law establishes a water reserve consisting of two parts. The first is a non-negotiable water allocation to meet the basic drinking, cooking, and sanitary needs of all South Africans. (When the African National Congress came to power, some 14 million poor South Africans lacked water for these basic needs.) The second part of the reserve is an allocation of water to support the long-term sustainability of the nation's aquatic and associated ecosystems. The water determined to constitute this two-part reserve has priority over licensed uses, such as irrigation, and only this water is guaranteed as a right.

Do rivers and the life within them have a right to water?

At the core of South Africa's policy is an affirmation of the "public trust," a legal principle that traces back to the Roman Empire, that says governments hold certain rights and entitlements in trust for the people and are obliged to protect them for the common good. In addition to the public trust, another rule fast becoming essential for freshwater ecosystem protection is the "precautionary principle," which essentially says that given the rapid pace of ecosystem decline, the irreversible nature of many of the resulting losses, and the high value of freshwater ecosystems to human societies, it is wise to err on the side of protecting too much rather than too little of the remaining freshwater habitat.

The utilitarian code that continues to guide most water management may fit with prevailing market-based socioeconomic paradigms, but it is neither universal nor unchanging. The American conservationist Aldo Leopold viewed the extension of ethics to the natural environment as "an evolutionary possibility and an ecological necessity." More recently, Harvard biologist Edward O. Wilson noted in his book, *Consilience,* that ethical codes historically have arisen through the interplay of biology and culture. "Ethics, in the empiricist view," Wilson observes, "is conduct favored consistently enough throughout a society to be expressed as a code of principles."

In other words, ethics are not static; they evolve with social consciousness. But that evolution is not automatic. The extension of freedom to slaves and voting rights to women required leaders, movements, advocates, and activists that collectively pulled society onto higher moral ground. So it will be with the extension of rights to rivers, plants, fish, birds, and the ecosystems of which they are a part. As societies wrap their collective minds around the consequences of global environmental change—rising temperatures, prolonged droughts, chronic water shortages, disappearing species—it may well be that a new ethic will emerge, one that says it is not only right and good but necessary that all living things get enough water before some get more than enough. Because in the end, we're all in this together.

For Class Discussion

1. What is Sandra Postel's main claim in this policy proposal? What reasons does she provide for her position?

2. How does Postel express a set of shared values with her audience? Where and how does she anticipate skepticism toward her claims?

3. How does Postel use precedents, expert opinions, and analogies as evidence to support her claim and convey her authority on this issue?

4. According to Postel, how is a water ethic connected to other ethical concerns such as human rights and human values?

5. Postel rejects the business model exemplified by "utilitarian" approaches to water management. In what ways it is useful or dangerous to talk about nature in business terms? ■

Health and Environment
United Nations Environment Programme

This poster is one of a series sponsored by the United Nations Environment Programme for an exhibition at the World Summit on Sustainable Development, held August 26–September 3, 2002, in Johannesburg, South Africa. The United Nations Environment Programme's mission is "to provide leadership and encourage partnership in caring for the environment by inspiring, informing, and enabling nations and peoples to improve their quality of life without compromising that of future generations" ("About UNEP," www.unep.org). The posters in this series have a dual educational and persuasive aim.

If you look only at the title of the poster, "Health and Environment," and the photo, what connections between environmental, economic, and social problems can you see? What background knowledge does it expect of its audience?

United Nations Environment Programme Poster (*This poster has been reproduced by kind permission of the United Nations Environment Programme. This poster on "poverty and the environment" can be found at* www.unep.org/wssd/Pictures/Posters/HEALTH.2.jpg.)

For Class Discussion

1. What are the impressions and ideas that this poster conveys?

2. In your own words, how would you state the main claim of this poster? What evidence does it offer in support of its claim?

3. What ideas about water, sanitation, and health does this poster convey?

4. What is the rhetorical effectiveness of using a photo of children? How does this poster appeal to the emotions and values of a global audience, especially people living in developed countries?

5. In what ways does this poster argue causes and consequences? In what way does it make a proposal and support it? How effective is it in communicating its argument? ∎

Acceptance Speech for the Nobel Peace Prize for 2004
Wangari Muta Maathai

Wangari Muta Maathai of Kenya is an internationally known political and environmental leader and one of the foremost women of our time. She holds a doctorate in veterinary anatomy and served as chair of the department of veterinary anatomy at the University of Nairobi, the first woman in East and Central Africa to attain this professional stature. In 1977, she founded the Green Belt Movement (GBM), a grassroots NGO involved in "planting trees with women groups in order to conserve the environment and improve their quality of life." The GBM describes its values as "volunteerism, love for environmental conservation, proaction for self-betterment, accountability, transparency, and empowerment" (www.greenbeltmovement.org). In 1986, this movement developed a Pan African Green Belt Network. Maathai has won numerous prestigious awards for her activism; she also served in the Kenyan parliament from 2002 to 2007 and as the assistant minister for environment, natural resources, and wildlife from 2003 to 2005. She is currently the Goodwill Ambassador for the Congo Basin Forest Initiative. She delivered this acceptance speech for her Nobel Peace Prize on December 10, 2004, in Oslo, Norway.

How does Wangari Muta Maathai use the convention of award acceptance speeches—the traditional tributes and acknowledgments—to reach out to her larger audience (fellow Africans and global citizens) and build community?

Your Majesties
Your Royal Highnesses
Honourable Members of the Norwegian Nobel Committee
Excellencies
Ladies and Gentlemen

I stand before you and the world humbled by this recognition and uplifted by the honour of being the 2004 Nobel Peace Laureate.

As the first African woman to receive this prize, I accept it on behalf of the people of Kenya and Africa, and indeed the world. I am especially mindful of women and the girl child. I hope it will encourage them to raise their voices and take more space for leadership. I know the honour also gives a deep sense of pride to our men, both old and young. As a mother, I appreciate the inspiration this brings to the youth and urge them to use it to pursue their dreams.

Although this prize comes to me, it acknowledges the work of countless individuals and groups across the globe. They work quietly and often without recognition to protect the environment, promote democracy, defend human rights and ensure equality between women and men. By so doing, they plant seeds of peace. I know they, too, are proud today. To all who feel represented by this prize I say use it to advance your mission and meet the high expectations the world will place on us.

This honour is also for my family, friends, partners and supporters throughout the world. All of them helped shape the vision and sustain our work, which was often accomplished under hostile conditions. I am also grateful to the people of Kenya—who remained stubbornly hopeful that democracy could be realized and their environment managed sustainably. Because of this support, I am here today to accept this great honour.

I am immensely privileged to join my fellow African Peace laureates, Presidents Nelson Mandela and F.W. de Klerk, Archbishop Desmond Tutu, the late Chief Albert Luthuli, the late Anwar el-Sadat and the UN Secretary General, Kofi Annan.

I know that African people everywhere are encouraged by this news. My fellow Africans, as we embrace this recognition, let us use it to intensify our commitment to our people, to reduce conflicts and poverty and thereby improve their quality of life. Let us embrace democratic governance, protect human rights and protect our environment. I am confident that we shall rise to the occasion. I have always believed that solutions to most of our problems must come from us.

In this year's prize, the Norwegian Nobel Committee has placed the critical issue of environment and its linkage to democracy and peace before the world. For their visionary action, I am profoundly grateful. Recognizing that sustainable development, democracy and peace are indivisible is an idea whose time has come. Our work over the past 30 years has always appreciated and engaged these linkages.

My inspiration partly comes from my childhood experiences and observations of Nature in rural Kenya. It has been influenced and nurtured by the formal education I was privileged to receive in Kenya, the United States and Germany. As I was growing up, I witnessed forests being cleared and replaced by commercial plantations, which destroyed local biodiversity and the capacity of the forests to conserve water.

Excellencies, ladies and gentlemen,

In 1977, when we started the Green Belt Movement, I was partly responding to needs identified by rural women, namely lack of firewood, clean drinking water, balanced diets, shelter and income.

Throughout Africa, women are the primary caretakers, holding significant responsibility for tilling the land and feeding their families. As a result, they are often the first to become aware of environmental damage as resources become scarce and incapable of sustaining their families.

The women we worked with recounted that unlike in the past, they were unable to meet their basic needs. This was due to the degradation of their immediate environment as well as the introduction of commercial farming, which replaced the growing of household food crops. But international trade controlled the price of the exports from these small-scale farmers and a reasonable and just income could not be guaranteed. I came to understand that when the environment is destroyed, plundered or mismanaged, we undermine our quality of life and that of future generations.

Tree planting became a natural choice to address some of the initial basic needs identified by women. Also, tree planting is simple, attainable and guarantees quick, successful results within a reasonable amount [of] time. This sustains interest and commitment.

So, together, we have planted over 30 million trees that provide fuel, food, shelter, and income to support their children's education and household needs. The activity also creates employment and improves soils and watersheds. Through their involvement, women gain some degree of power over their lives, especially their social and economic position and relevance in the family. This work continues.

Initially, the work was difficult because historically our people have been persuaded to believe that because they are poor, they lack not only capital, but also knowledge and skills to address their challenges. Instead they are conditioned to believe that solutions to their problems must come from outside. Further, women did not realize that meeting their needs depended on their environment being healthy and well managed. They were also unaware that a degraded environment leads to a scramble for scarce resources and may culminate in poverty and even conflict. They were also unaware of the injustices of international economic arrangements.

In order to assist communities to understand these linkages, we developed a citizen education program, during which people identify their problems, the causes and possible solutions. They then make connections between their own personal actions and the problems they witness in the environment and in society. They learn that our world is confronted with a litany of woes: corruption, violence against women and children, disruption and breakdown of families, and disintegration of cultures and communities. They also identify the abuse of drugs and chemical substances, especially among young people. There are also devastating diseases that are defying cures or occurring in epidemic proportions. Of particular concern are HIV/AIDS, malaria and diseases associated with malnutrition.

On the environment front, they are exposed to many human activities that are devastating to the environment and societies. These include widespread destruction of ecosystems, especially through deforestation, climatic instability, and contamination in the soils and waters that all contribute to excruciating poverty.

In the process, the participants discover that they must be part of the solutions. They realize their hidden potential and are empowered to overcome inertia and take action. They come to recognize that they are the primary custodians and beneficiaries of the environment that sustains them.

Entire communities also come to understand that while it is necessary to hold their governments accountable, it is equally important that in their own relationships with each other, they exemplify the leadership values they wish to see in their own leaders, namely justice integrity and trust.

The tree became a symbol for the democratic struggle in Kenya.

Although initially the Green Belt Movement's tree planting activities did not address issues of democracy and peace, it soon became clear that responsible governance of the environment was impossible without democratic space. Therefore, the tree became a symbol for the democratic struggle in Kenya. Citizens were mobilised to challenge widespread abuses of power, corruption and environmental mismanagement. In Nairobi's Uhuru Park, at Freedom Corner, and in many parts of the country, trees of peace were planted to demand the release of prisoners of conscience and a peaceful transition to democracy.

Through the Green Belt Movement, thousands of ordinary citizens were mobilised and empowered to take action and effect change. They learned to overcome fear and a sense of helplessness and moved to defend democratic rights.

In time, the tree also became a symbol for peace and conflict resolution, especially during ethnic conflicts in Kenya when the Green Belt Movement used peace trees to reconcile disputing communities. During the ongoing rewriting of the Kenyan constitution, similar trees of peace were planted in many parts of the country to promote a culture of peace. Using trees as a symbol of peace is in keeping with a widespread African tradition. For example, the elders of the Kikuyu carried a staff from the thigi tree that, when placed between two disputing sides, caused them to stop fighting and seek reconciliation. Many communities in Africa have these traditions.

Such practices are part of an extensive cultural heritage, which contributes both to the conservation of habitats and to cultures of peace. With the destruction of these cultures and the introduction of new values, local biodiversity is no longer valued or protected and as a result, it is quickly degraded and disappears. For this reason, The Green Belt Movement explores the concept of cultural biodiversity, especially with respect to indigenous seeds and medicinal plants.

As we progressively understood the causes of environmental degradation, we saw the need for good governance. Indeed, the state of any country's environment is a reflection of the kind of governance in place, and without good governance there can be no peace. Many countries, which have poor governance systems, are also likely to have conflicts and poor laws protecting the environment.

In 2002, the courage, resilience, patience and commitment of members of the Green Belt Movement, other civil society organizations, and the Kenyan public culminated in the peaceful transition to a democratic government and laid the foundation for a more stable society.

Excellencies, friends, ladies and gentlemen,

It is 30 years since we started this work. Activities that devastate the environment and societies continue unabated. Today we are faced with a challenge that calls for a shift in our thinking, so that humanity stops threatening its life-support system. We are called to assist the earth to heal her wounds and in the process heal our own—indeed, to embrace the whole creation in all its diversity, beauty and wonder. This will happen if we see the need to revive our sense of belonging to a larger family of life, with which we have shared our evolutionary process.

In the course of history, there comes a time when humanity is called to shift to a new level of consciousness, to reach a higher moral ground. A time when we have to shed our fear and give hope to each other.

That time is now.

The Norwegian Nobel Committee has challenged the world to broaden the understanding of peace: there can be no peace without equitable development; and there can be no development without sustainable management of the environment in a democratic and peaceful space. This shift is an idea whose time has come.

I call on leaders, especially from Africa, to expand democratic space and build fair and just societies that allow the creativity and energy of their citizens to flourish. Those of us who have been privileged to receive education, skills, and experiences and even power must be role models for the next generation of leadership. In this regard, I would also like to appeal for the freedom of my fellow laureate Aung San Suu Kyi so that she can continue her work for peace and democracy for the people of Burma and the world at large.

Culture plays a central role in the political, economic and social life of communities. Indeed, culture may be the missing link in the development of Africa. Culture is dynamic and evolves over time, consciously discarding retrogressive traditions, like female genital mutilation (FGM), and embracing aspects that are good and useful.

Africans, especially, should rediscover positive aspects of their culture. In accepting them, they would give themselves a sense of belonging, identity and self-confidence.

Ladies and Gentlemen,

There is also need to galvanize civil society and grassroots movements to catalyse change. I call upon governments to recognize the role of these social movements in building a critical mass of responsible citizens, who help maintain checks and balances in society. On their part, civil society should embrace not only their rights but also their responsibilities.

Further, industry and global institutions must appreciate that ensuring economic justice, equity and ecological integrity are of greater value than profits at any cost. The extreme global inequities and prevailing consumption patterns continue at the expense of the environment and peaceful co-existence. The choice is ours.

I would like to call on young people to commit themselves to activities that contribute toward achieving their long-term dreams. They have the energy and creativity to shape a sustainable future. To the young people I say, you are a gift to your communities and indeed the world. You are our hope and our future.

> **There is a need to galvanize civil society and grassroots movements to catalyse change.**

The holistic approach to development, as exemplified by the Green Belt Movement, could be embraced and replicated in more parts of Africa and beyond. It is for this reason that I have established the Wangari Maathai Foundation to ensure the continuation and expansion of these activities. Although a lot has been achieved, much remains to be done.

Excellencies, ladies and gentlemen,

As I conclude I reflect on my childhood experience when I would visit a stream next to our home to fetch water for my mother. I would drink water straight from the stream. Playing among the arrowroot leaves I tried in vain to pick up the strands of frogs' eggs, believing they were beads. But every time I put my little fingers under them they would break. Later, I saw thousands of tadpoles: black, energetic and wriggling through the clear water against the background of the brown earth. This is the world I inherited from my parents.

Today, over 50 years later, the stream has dried up, women walk long distances for water, which is not always clean, and children will never know what they have lost. The challenge is to restore the home of the tadpoles and give back to our children a world of beauty and wonder.

Thank you very much.

For Class Discussion

1. Wangari Muta Maathai articulates a philosophy of environmental and political activism as much as she outlines a proposed course of action. What are the main points of her philosophy and how does she underscore the connections among "sustainable development, democracy, and peace"?

2. What global organizations and people constitute the larger audience for this talk? How does Maathai seek to inspire and move her audience through appeals to their values, imaginations, and emotions? What actions is she calling on them to take?

3. What many meanings and values do trees have for Maathai?

4. How does this speech convey her authority and credibility?

5. What important connections does Maathai establish between women and the environment?

6. How has this speech affected your view of Africa, environmental resources, and successful environmental practices? ■

Big Dams Are Not Sustainable but They Continue to Be Built
Khadija Sharife

Khadija Sharife is a journalist and musician based in South Africa. She is a Visiting Scholar at the Center for Civil Society and is currently at work on a book titled *Africa—Policy Profiteering and the Washington Consensus*. She also blogs on politics, human rights, and the environment in Africa, specifically relating to the intersection of conflict and exploitation of natural resources. This op-ed piece appeared in the March 6, 2009, edition of *Business Day* (businessday.co.za), a South African daily newspaper covering economics, commerce, and industry.

> How does Sharife link the development of hydropower to other environmental issues such as climate change and freshwater supply?

Thanks to NASA and its famous "image of the Earth at night" snapshot, we know what Africa looks like from space: largely unlit, almost entirely devoid of the city lights that characterise an important aspect of modern "civilisation"—night time electricity consumption.

According to the International Monetary Fund, less than 25% of sub-Saharan Africa has access to electricity, with nearly two-thirds of the region experiencing acute energy shortages, caused by factors such as drought and erratic rainfall.

The latter, made worse by climate change, has caused crippling shortages in recent years in hydro-dependent countries from Tanzania to Uganda and Ghana. Though 60% of the continent already depends on grid-based hydropower, the United Nations Intergovernmental Panel on Climate Change has declared Africa "the continent most vulnerable to the impacts of projected climate change," threatening food and water security, stability, development and survival. Yet "development" experts don't seem to be listening, identifying hydropower as a "sustainable" model for electrifying the continent.

Reynold Duncan, an energy specialist at the World Bank, urged Africa to consider "riskier" assets like hydropower, saying that just 5% of the continent's hydroelectric potential had been explored. SA's Climate Change Policy Framework promotes solving SA's energy crisis using "imported hydroelectricity from neighbours" including Mozambique and the Congo. Mozambique, touted by development banks as a prime example of successful hydropower development, produces enough energy to power the country. But the bulk is exported to regions such as SA and used by industry. Less than 9% of Mozambicans have access to electricity, with costly transmission lines—often 50% or more of the expense—bypassing the majority.

Silt build-up behind dams, estimated at 1% a year renders large dams useless in the long term, specifically concerning the Boot (Build-Own-Operate-Transfer) development model, allowing corporations to own dams for a period of 20–25 years.

Globally, 80-million to 100-million people have been displaced by dams; 400-million "downstreamers" have been affected by the loss of fisheries (estuaries are habitats for 80% of the world's fish catch), fertile land and coastal erosion. Mega-dams endanger freshwater biodiversity and wetlands, increase soil salinisation and salt-water intrusion, and release the highest volume of human-engineered methane emissions, all while burdening underdeveloped nations with billion-dollar projects designed to develop Africa.

"There is nothing sustainable about large dams at all," says Professor Thayer Scudder, a leading dam expert, formerly the World Bank's principal resettlement consultant, and one of 12 commissioners on the World Commission on Dams. "Millions in Africa depend on the rivers for sustenance—they are the losers when rivers are dammed up. The World Bank ignores impacts; they want to stay in the game. This development is driven by hydro-politics—the multinationals, the African governments, the development banks. The people who need electricity do not benefit; distribution is controlled by political elites."

A study by University of Cape Town geologists, assessing data from 21 of the best climate change models, revealed that 25% of the continent would soon experience a decrease in water availability, with 75%

of the continent—that is, regions experiencing 400mm-1000mm of rainfall—most vulnerable to climate change.

But from the World Bank-backed Bujagali (Uganda) to the Chinese-backed Mphanda Nkuwa (Mozambique), the race is on to dam(n) Africa, no matter the consequence.

For Class Discussion

1. Who are the stakeholders for this issue? How does Sharife represent the conflicting voices in this debate?

2. What does Sharife claim would happen to Africa's already limited freshwater supplies if these dams were built?

3. Sharife posits a similar point of view to other authors in this book by contending that people and organizations in developed countries do not fully understand the issues faced by developing nations. What evidence does she provide to illustrate that those in need would not benefit from the development of hydropower?

4. What organizations or terms would you need to learn more about in order to assess Sharife's argument more fully?

5. How does Sharife's argument extend or change the understanding of water issues in Africa that you had after reading the Student Voice, International Voices, and Global Hot Spot sections of this chapter?

Wind versus Tidal Energy
Adrian Raeside

Adrian Raeside, born in New Zealand, has been an editorial cartoonist for the *Victoria Times Colonist* (Canada) for thirty years. His editorial cartoons appear in over 250 magazines and newspapers worldwide. This cartoon is from his comic strip, The Other Coast, which appears in over 350 newspapers worldwide.

What does the perspective in each of these cartoon panels suggest about the value and attention afforded to different environmental issues?

Used with the permission of Adrian Raeside and Creators Syndicate. All rights reserved.

For Class Discussion

1. How does this cartoon employ humor and the element of surprise to convey its argument?

2. In your own words, how would you describe this cartoon to a friend? What additional context might you need to provide to help your friend understand the issues?

3. Who is the intended audience for this cartoon? How might different audiences interpret its argument?

4. In what ways does this cartoon present the tradeoffs inherent in adopting one form of energy production over another?   ■

Nuke Power Is Earth's Friend
William Sweet

William Sweet is senior news editor at *IEEE Spectrum*, the flagship publication of the Institute of Electrical and Electronic Engineers. His work has appeared in several newspapers and magazines, including the *Los Angeles Times*, The *New Republic*, and MIT's *Technology Review*. He is also the author of the book *Kicking the Carbon Habit: Global Warming and the Case for Renewable and Nuclear Energy* (2006). This policy proposal appeared in the August 2007 issue of *Discover* magazine, whose tagline is "Science, Technology, and the Future" (discovermagazine.com).

> How does Sweet anticipate and address his readers' assumptions and fears about nuclear energy?

ExxonMobil has thrown in the towel, terminating its campaign to convince the public that global warming is a hoax concocted by some pointy-headed intellectuals. All three major Democratic candidates for president, and some of the top Republican contenders as well, have promised serious action. Leading members of Congress have introduced a half dozen bills that would impose some kind of carbon regulation, and even the president now concedes that climate change is important.

Using coal to make electricity accounts for about a third of America's carbon emissions. As a result, tackling emissions from coal-fired power plants represents our best opportunity to make sharp reductions in greenhouse gases.

Fortunately, we already have the technology to do that. Unfortunately, right now the United States is addicted to coal, a cheap, abundant power source. Burning coal produces more than half the country's electricity, despite its immense human and environmental costs. Particulates and other air pollutants from coal-fired power plants cause somewhere between 20,000 and 30,000 premature deaths in the United States each year. Fifty tons of mercury—one-third of all domestic mercury emissions—are pumped into the atmosphere annually from coal plants. In addition, the extraction of coal, from West Virginia to Wyoming, devastates the physical environment, and its processing and combustion produce gigantic volumes of waste.

For the last decade, coal-burning utilities have been fighting a rearguard action, resisting costly antipollution measures required by environmental legislation. At the same time, they have been holding out the prospect of "clean coal"—in which carbon is captured and stored as coal is burned. But clean-coal technologies have yet to be demonstrated on a large scale commercially, and by the admission of even the president's own climate-technology task force, clean coal doesn't have any prospect of making a big dent in the climate problem in the next 15 to 20 years.

By comparison, nuclear and wind power are proven technologies that emit no carbon and whose environmental risks and costs are thoroughly understood and which can make an immediate difference for the better.

The first thing to be appreciated about reactors in the United States is that they are essentially immune to the type of accident that occurred at Chernobyl in April 1986. Put simply, because of fundamental design differences, U.S. reactors cannot experience a sudden and drastic power surge, as happened at Chernobyl's Unit Number 4, causing it to explode and catch fire. In addition, the reliability of U.S. nuclear plants has been constantly improving. In 1980, American nuclear power plants were generating electricity only 56 percent of the time because they frequently needed special maintenance or repair. By 2004, reactor performance had improved to the point of generating electricity over 90 percent of the time.

Our regulatory regime, which was enormously strengthened in the wake of the 1979 Three Mile Island accident (during which no one was hurt, by the way), is indisputably much better than the Soviet system, which bred endemic incompetence. Management of U.S. nuclear power plants has improved dramatically since Three Mile Island, and security has been tightened significantly since 9/11 (though more remains to be done). By comparison with other tempting terrorist targets like petrochemical complexes, reactors are well fortified.

What about the problem of storing radioactive waste? It is overrated from an engineering standpoint and pales in comparison with the challenges associated with the permanent sequestration of immense quantities of carbon, as required by clean-coal systems. Though the wastes from nuclear power plants are highly toxic, their physical quantity is surprisingly small—barely more than 2,000 tons a year in the United States. The amount of carbon dioxide emitted by our coal plants? Nearly 2 billion tons.

Let us say it plainly: today coal-fired power plants routinely kill tens of thousands of people in the United States each year by way of lung cancer, bronchitis and other ailments; the U.S. nuclear economy kills virtually no one in a normal year.

Perhaps the most serious concern about increasing our reliance on nuclear power is whether it might lead to an international proliferation of atomic bombs. Contrary to a stubborn myth, however, countries do not decide to build nuclear weapons because they happen to get nuclear reactors first; they acquire nuclear reactors because they want to build nuclear weapons. This was true of France and China in the 1950s, of Israel and India in the '60s and '70s, and it's true of Korea and Iran today. Does anybody honestly think that whether Tehran or Pyongyang produces atomic bombs depends on how many reactors the United States decides to build in the next 10 to 20 years?

Ultimately, the replacement of old, highly polluting coal-fired power plants by nuclear reactors is essentially no different from deciding, after putting sentimental considerations aside, to replace your inexpensive and reliable—but obsolete—1983 Olds Omega with a 2007 Toyota Camry or BMW 3 Series sedan.

All that said, it's important to be clear about nuclear energy's limits. It's likely that the construction of at least one new nuclear power plant will be initiated by the end of this year, ending a two-decade drought in new nuclear plant construction. But by its own estimates, the U.S. nuclear industry can handle only about two new nuclear reactor projects annually at its present-day capacity.

> All that said, it's important to be clear about nuclear energy's limits.

Obviously, given these limits, a lot of new wind generation, conservation, and improvements in energy use will also be needed. Wind is especially important because, despite the hopes of many, solar power just isn't going to cut it on a large scale in the foreseeable future. Right now, on a dollar per megawatt basis, solar installations are six or seven times as expensive as wind.

Wind turbines already generate electricity almost as inexpensively as fossil fuels. Thanks to a two cents per kilowatt-hour production incentive from the U.S. government, they are being built at a rate that will increase the amount of wind-generated electricity by nearly three gigawatts a year. Taking into account that wind turbines produce electricity only about a third of the time, that's roughly the equivalent of building one standard one-gigawatt nuclear power plant a year.

Currently, nuclear and wind energy (as well as clean coal) are between 25 and 75 percent more expensive than old-fashioned coal at current prices (not including all the hidden health and environmental costs of coal), and so it will take a stiff charge on coal to induce rapid replacement of obsolete plants. A tax or equivalent trading scheme that increases the cost of coal-generated electricity by, say, 50 percent would stimulate conservation and adoption of more efficient technologies throughout the economy and prompt replacement of coal by some combination of wind, nuclear, and natural gas. Proceeds from the tax or auctioned credits could (and should) be used to compensate regions and individuals most adversely affected by the higher costs, like the poor.

For the last six years, the U.S. government, with well-orchestrated support from industry, has told the American people that we can't afford to attack global warming aggressively. That's nonsense. We're the world's richest country, and we use energy about twice as extravagantly as Europe and Japan. It's no surprise that we account for a quarter of the globe's greenhouse-gas emissions.

What the United States needs to do is get in step with the Kyoto Protocol, both to establish its bona fides with the other advanced industrial countries and to give countries like India and China an incentive to accept mandatory carbon limits. That implies cutting U.S. carbon emissions by 25 percent as soon as possible.

The United States could do that by simply making the dirtiest and most inefficient coal plants prohibitively expensive by means of the carbon tax or trading systems mentioned above.

All we need to move decisively on carbon reduction is a different kind of political leadership at the very top. Surprisingly, it's the muscle-bound action-movie star who runs California who has best captured the spirit of what's needed. Last September, the day Arnold Schwarzenegger signed a bill committing his state to a program of sharp greenhouse-gas reductions, he told an ABC interviewer that climate change kind of "creeps up on you. And then all of a sudden it is too late to do something about it. We don't want to go there."

For Class Discussion

1. How do Sweet's examples and choice of wording indicate that he is writing to a more general rather than technical audience?

2. How does Sweet support his claim that coal is more dangerous than nuclear power production?

3. This policy proposal was written in the months leading up to the 2008 presidential election. Which aspects of Sweet's argument are tied to its political context, and which aspects transcend its motivating occasion?

4. What solutions does Sweet provide to refute readers' objections to the cost of new wind and nuclear power development?

5. As this argument illustrates, there are many conflicting points of view on what forms of alternative energy should be pursued. How does Sweet prioritize the available options? Why is (or is not) Sweet's argument compelling for you?

The Energy Shortage
National Review

This short opinion piece appeared in the *National Review* on June 30, 2008. According to the magazine's Web site, the *National Review* is America's "most widely read and influential magazine" for "Republican/conservative news, commentary, and opinion" (www.nationalreview.com). This piece appeared at the height of the oil crisis in 2008, when many consumers were facing gasoline prices topping four or even five dollars per gallon. The effects of the crisis were far-reaching, with the prices of food and other goods also rising due to the costs of manufacturing and shipping.

What values does the author of this brief editorial assume are shared by readers of the *National Review*?

The U.S. Commodity Futures Trading Commission announced that it has opened an investigation into whether futures traders conspired to drive up oil prices. We doubt the investigation is necessary; when one considers breakneck economic development in India and China, the weak U.S. dollar, and the Organization of the Petroleum Exporting Countries (OPEC), one hardly needs the services of the CFTC to solve the mystery of the oil-price spike.

But there is a group of people conspiring to make energy more expensive for Americans. That group is the U.S. Congress. By refusing to open domestic lands and coastal waters for energy exploration, Congress is keeping billions of barrels of oil off the market. OPEC would be proud, and must be pleased.

Critics of proposals to open these areas for business argue that it would take up to ten years to bring any new supplies online. Of course, they were using this same argument ten years ago, and if they hadn't prevailed then the U.S. would be less dependent on foreign oil today.

They also argue that Congress should be encouraging renewable energy sources such as solar power, wind power, and biofuels rather than opening the spigots on new sources of petroleum. But the simple fact of the matter is that solar power and wind cannot take the place of nonrenewables in the U.S. economy. As for biofuels such as corn ethanol, the 2007 mandate requiring the production of 36 billion gallons by 2022 has exacerbated an increase in world food prices without doing anything to lessen the pain at the pump.

Superior U.S. technology has made it possible to drill in the environmentally sensitive areas off our coasts with minimal disturbance to the surrounding ecosystem. It is better to increase production in the U.S. than to allow high prices to spur increased production in countries with worse environmental track records. With oil nearing $140 a barrel, there are no good arguments for keeping this supply off the market.

Nor are there any good arguments for artificially making energy more expensive, though congressional Democrats (and a few Republicans) recently attempted to do just that. First, the Senate tried to pass a cap-and-trade bill. By rationing the use of fossil fuels, the bill would have led to higher coal, natural-gas, and petroleum prices, even though the prices of those commodities are already at historic highs. Fortunately, an adequate number of GOP senators banded together to kill the bill. Even some Senate Democrats reportedly began to wonder about the political wisdom of pushing through higher energy prices.

Undaunted, Senate Democrats proposed a windfall-profits tax on U.S. oil companies. The Congressional Research Service found that the last time Congress imposed one, it reduced domestic production.

Republican senators stymied the windfall-profits tax, also, but with several Senate seats in danger and a presidential nominee who supports energy rationing, whether the GOP can continue to fight effectively for a cheap-energy agenda remains an open question. The CFTC is investigating oil-price fixing, but where is the agency that will protect Americans from Congress?

For Class Discussion

1. What is the motivating occasion for this commentary? To what extent is it ultimately related to the claims put forth in the argument?

2. What assumptions and values underlie the criticism of those who oppose domestic oil drilling?

3. How might the presentation of evidence need to be expanded or altered for a different audience?

4. What is this editorial's position on alternative energy options? How does it engage with these opposing views? Does it envision a role for energy sources other than oil? ■

 ### STUDENT VOICE: A Letter to Ken Salazar by Tine Sommer

Tine Sommer is originally from Denmark where she earned a master's degree in engineering and where she has worked as a bridge planner and designer. She is currently residing in Seattle with her partner, Morten, an engineer working with wind turbines, and is now pursuing a post-baccalaureate degree in English due to her interest in literature, American culture, and the English language. For this paper, she chose to address her argument to Ken Salazar, the secretary of the United States Department of the Interior in the Obama administration. As secretary, he oversees federal agencies including the National Park Service, the Bureau of Land Management, the Fish and Wildlife Service, and the United States Geological Survey.

How does Sommer establish her credibility in this argument?

Dear Mr. Secretary:

I am writing in response to your February 10, 2009, speech "Statement on Offshore Energy Strategy" (Salazar). In your speech, you called for more public opinions on offshore energy, and I am hereby offering you mine. As you will see, I am suggesting an approach to offshore energy that will benefit America's suffering economy as well as the environment, help the United States gain more independence from foreign oil markets, and achieve the same benefits from wind power that Denmark has gained. The financial crisis is affecting the development of wind power as an alternative source of energy; however, contrary to inclinations, the U.S. government needs actually to increase its investment in wind energy. A U.S. resident, originally from Denmark where wind turbines are widespread, I have a background in engineering and a knowledge of wind energy. My suggestions could be useful to you, as secretary of the U.S. Department of the Interior, and I hope you will consider them. The United States should contribute to the solution of a crisis that is affecting us all.

In this time of serious financial crisis, the United States needs to boost the economy by supporting projects that will benefit the country financially now and in the future. If you, in the Obama government, would support investments in new wind turbine projects, offshore and onshore, the United States could be helped out of this financial crisis. The main reason that the economy would benefit is that building wind farms would create new jobs for both highly skilled and unskilled workers. The Global Wind Energy Council, which represents wind energy companies and organizations, has in cooperation with Greenpeace published the report *Global Wind Energy Outlook 2008*. The Council finds that, based on experience from Europe, every additional megawatt of energy produced from wind turbines creates 15 new jobs a year. If growth in the wind energy industry continues at the current rate in North America, the United States will increase its yearly production of wind energy from 18,664 megawatts in 2007 to 92,000 megawatts in 2020, creating 84,000 new jobs in thirteen years. If we continue to increase our production of wind energy even more with the help of government incentives, in the most optimistic scenario, the United States would create 270,000 new jobs by 2020. The annual increase in new jobs would be highest in the beginning of the period, yielding an immediate effect on the number of employed Americans, increasing consumption and tax revenues. By supporting the wind energy industry you will therefore be supporting the American economy.

Another huge benefit of supporting the wind energy industry is that environmentally it is right thing to do. Since global warming is increasing, we cannot wait any longer to reduce our carbon dioxide emissions from fossil fuels, recession or not. As Mark Hertsgaard, environment correspondent for the *Nation*, explains: "You wouldn't know it from our politicians or TV shows, but the climate crisis is even more serious than the financial crisis. The financial crisis, while painful and severe, can be resolved, given time and wise policies. The climate crisis, not so." Wind energy benefits the environment by allowing us to lower the amount of electricity we derive from coal and natural gas and thereby lower our carbon dioxide emissions. (Carbon dioxide builds up in the atmosphere, causing higher temperatures, rising sea-levels, melting of the inland ice, and extermination of certain animal and plant species.) Furthermore, coal mining and drilling for natural gas have bigger impacts on the environment than building wind turbines. For example, coal mining affects larger areas of land and causes air and water pollution. Compared to offshore production of natural gas, offshore wind farms are less harmful to the marine ecosystem. Wind farms only have an impact on the sea while they are being built, while natural gas production has a continuing impact on the marine environment. In their recent objections to drilling off the coast of Virginia, the Southern Environmental Law Center (SELC) ". . . compared the meager amount of recoverable oil and gas with the potentially drastic impacts of drilling to important marine species, including the endangered northern right whale and humpback whale, dolphins, sea turtles, and many migratory birds. . . . [SELC] also asks the agency to integrate offshore wind power into its 5-year plan." Offshore wind power is far more attractive than offshore drilling and offers a way to benefit the environment in the short and long term.

In addition to creating new jobs and benefiting the environment, supporting wind energy would also address the problem of dependence on foreign oil. In the very near future the world oil supply will decrease drastically and this, in combination with increasing costs of extracting less accessible oil, will increase oil prices. By investing in wind energy we can support the United States with electricity generated in our own country and thereby decrease our dependence on increasingly expensive foreign oil. Although wind energy will never be able to replace oil, in the long run it can help ensure that our society can keep on developing even when oil resources shrink. Being economically, dependent on foreign oil is not wise; the geopolitical balance of power would drastically change if the U.S. found itself at the mercy of oil-producing countries who chose to use their power corruptly and dangerously.

Finally, other countries, especially Denmark, offer a model of successful governmental investment in wind energy. In Denmark the government provides an economic supplement for companies that sell electricity from wind turbines, so the cost difference between producing electricity from oil, gas, or coal and producing electricity from wind decreases. Wind energy has created many jobs in design, manufacturing, and operations. According to the Danish Wind Industry Association, by the end of 2007, 23,500 Danes were employed in the wind energy business. Denmark's knowledge and experience with wind turbines have increased the demand for Danish engineering services and wind turbine parts, boosting Denmark's exports and reducing the impact of the financial crisis. Supporting the wind energy industry in America would have the same beneficial effects on the U.S. economy.

Despite the compelling case for the government's support of wind energy, a number of people have opposing views on the subject. If we invest in wind energy, some people argue, we could not "buy American" as Louis Uchitelle explains in his article "'Buy American' in Stimulus (But Good Luck With That)" in the *New York Times*, because 70% of wind turbines in America are imported. Even though some money will leave the country, we would be creating American jobs for those who design and plan wind farms (highly skilled workers) and for the people who build and operate them (unskilled and skilled workers). In the long term, the United States would build its experience with wind turbines so there would be a basis for manufacturing them here. Eventually, we could "buy American."

Another objection to supporting wind energy is fluctuating oil prices. When oil prices are low, some ask why we should use money on developing wind energy. The underlying assumption is that if people can afford to buy oil there is no reason to invest in alternative forms of energy such as wind turbines. However, we should realize that oil prices will rise again as soon as the recession turns and the demand for oil rises. When oil prices start rising we will be prepared by having other energy sources.

Perhaps the most consistent argument against supporting investment in wind energy is that it is very expensive to build and use wind turbines, especially when money is scarce. Although it is a problem to obtain money in a financial crisis, I advise that we have to think long term. Consider that once a wind turbine is built it uses a source of energy that is free and unlimited, the wind. Even though wind energy is more expensive to harvest and transport than traditionally obtained electricity, the price gap is closing. The difference in the cost of energy from coal-produced electricity and from wind power is down to about $10 per megawatt hour. According to the Energy Information Administration, an average home in America uses around 11 megawatt hours per year (2007), so the difference in the price the consumer has to pay is minimal. With further development of wind technologies, this gap will continue to decrease. Since this is a time when banks are hesitant to lend, the government should guarantee repayment of loans for investments in wind energy instead of providing a tax credit. The problem these days is that many companies don't have a high positive income to take advantage of a tax credit. I therefore suggest that we alter the tax credit system: Instead of having to apply the tax credit on income the same year that a company invests in wind energy, it should be able to postpone using the credit to future profitable years.

However, some conservative opponents of wind energy say that we shouldn't use taxpayers' money to support an industry that can't make it on its own; the market should regulate itself. The Heritage Foundation, for example, suggests that we should instead allow offshore oil and gas drilling because it is privately financed (Lieberman). Even though drilling for offshore oil and gas was encouraged by the previous administration, it is an inefficient solution as it will not significantly increase the supply of oil. It would be a drop in the ocean so to speak. Because this oil would be sold on the free global markets, it would neither lower the price of oil for the United States nor would it significantly decrease our dependence on foreign oil. Drilling for offshore oil and gas would probably benefit the companies that invest in it, but it will have no impact on oil prices and therefore have no advantages for the average American. Besides, do we really want to increase our harmful impact on the environment by burning more oil when there are alternatives? Furthermore, the recent financial crisis has refuted the theory that the market can regulate itself. By regulating some minor areas, we would be using the taxpayers' money in a beneficial way that will eventually create jobs and lower the cost of energy in the long term.

For all these reasons, I am asking you, Mr. Secretary, to support a government guarantee on loans for investments in wind energy and the postponement of tax credits on income from these investments. By doing so, you would help the U.S.'s suffering economy, reduce the destruction of the environment, as well as take steps toward national independence from foreign oil. Let the U.S. take advantage of the experiences of other countries who have shown that these measures work and embrace this avenue of economic prosperity and growth.

Sincerely,
Tine Sommer

Works Cited

Danish Wind Industry Association. "Sector Statistics 2008." *Windpower.org.* Danish Wind Energy Association, 2008. Web. 23 Mar. 2009.

Energy Information Administration. Office of Coal, Nuclear, Electricity, and Alternative Fuels. "U.S. Average Monthly Bill by Sector, Census Division and State 2007." Dept. of Energy, Jan. 2009. Web. 13 Feb. 2009.

Global Wind Energy Council. *Global Wind Energy Outlook 2008.* Global Wind Energy Council and Greenpeace International, Oct. 2008. Web. 23 Mar. 2009.

Hertsgaard, Mark. "Wanted: A Climate Bailout." *Nation.* Nation, 17 Nov. 2008. Web. 21 Mar. 2009.

Lieberman, Ben. "The Obama Administration Should Not Delay Offshore Oil and Gas Leasing." *Heritage Foundation.* Heritage Foundation, 19 Feb. 2009. Web. 22 Feb. 2009.

Salazar, Ken. "Statement on Offshore Energy Strategy." Speech. Dept. of the Interior, 10 Feb. 2009. Web. 11 Feb. 2009.

Southern Environmental Law Center. "Environmental Groups Call for Withdrawal of Offshore Drilling Proposal for Virginia." Press release. Southern Environmental Law Center, 13 Jan. 2009. Web. 9 Feb. 2009.

Uchitelle, Louis. "'Buy American' in Stimulus (But Good Luck With That)." *New York Times.* New York Times, 21 Feb. 2009. Web. 23 Feb. 2009.

For Class Discussion

1. What aspects of the issue make Ken Salazar a good choice as the audience for Sommer's letter?

2. What are Sommer's main claim and reasons?

3. How does Sommer establish the impetus for her argument? How does this motivation influence her claim and choice of evidence?

4. What assumptions does Sommer make about her audience's knowledge of the problems with oil? What information might she need to add to draw in a broader audience?

5. How effectively does she anticipate and address potential objections to her recommendations?

6. On what ideas do Tine Sommer and William Sweet agree? Where might their positions on the future of alternative energy differ?

The Ethanol Delusion

Kenneth P. Green

Kenneth P. Green is a resident scholar at the American Enterprise Institute for Public Policy Research, a conservative think tank dedicated to "limited government, private enterprise, individual liberty and responsibility . . . political accountability, and open debate" (www.aei.org). He holds a doctorate in environmental science and engineering from UCLA, and in 2001 served as an expert reviewer for the United Nations' Intergovernmental Panel on Climate Change (IPCC). Green, in his capacity with AEI, is a widely recognized skeptic of the IPCC's findings. He is also the author of a textbook for middle-school students titled *Global Warming: Understanding the Debate*. This opinion piece appeared in the *Pittsburgh Post-Gazette* on August 10, 2008.

> Kenneth P. Green devotes most of his article to rejecting common arguments for ethanol. What is his rhetorical strategy and what effect does he want it to have on his readers?

Ethanol—the chemical that gives your booze its kick—has been used by mankind for a very long time, 8,000 years or so. Even Stone Age people recognized the value of a good tipple. Of late, ethanol has been touted as the super-fuel that will reduce global warming, bring down gas prices, relieve our dependence on foreign oil, starve terrorists of funding, restore the family farm, create jobs and basically Save The Planet!

Contrary to popular belief, vastly expanding our use of ethanol fuel would do few, if any, of these things. But it almost certainly would increase food prices, greenhouse gas emissions and local air and water pollution while decreasing our supply of fresh water, consuming more of our land and destroying more of our ecosystems.

• • •

First, the lack of benefits.

While nature spent millions of years concentrating solar energy in the forms of peat, coal, oil and natural gas, ethanol relies on the sunlight that strikes living plants in a single growing season. Because solar energy is diffuse, the scale of land consumption and the labor required to gather massive quantities of vegetation quickly leads to diminishing returns. As Rockefeller University researcher Jesse Ausubel points out, it would take 1,000 square miles of prime Iowa farm land to produce as much electricity from biomass as from a single nuclear power plant.

The highly touted cellulosic ethanol, made from such plants as switch grass, is no solution, either. Professor John Deutch of the Massachusetts Institute of Technology recently showed that we might conceivably produce enough ethanol from cellulose to displace 1 million to 2 million barrels of oil per day in the next couple of decades. But we currently use 20 million barrels a day and have a growing population, so it's clear we're not going to seriously influence world oil markets, become energy independent, impoverish oil-rich enemy regimes, or de-fund terrorists by making ethanol.

• • •

Now, let's address ethanol's many drawbacks.

• Ethanol increases greenhouse gas emissions in two ways—by raising the output of the most potent greenhouse gases and by requiring land-clearance, which releases carbon dioxide into the air.

• In 1997, the U.S. Government Accountability Office found that the ethanol production process produces more nitrous oxide and other powerful greenhouse gases than does gasoline production. A decade later, Colorado scientists Jan Kreider and Peter Curtiss concluded that carbon dioxide emissions in the production cycle are about 50 percent higher for ethanol than for traditional fossil fuels.

• Making ethanol from cellulosic plants such as switch grass, briefly touted by President Bush a couple of years ago, won't help. In February, researcher Timothy Searchinger and colleagues calculated that ethanol from switch grass, if grown on U.S. corn lands, would increase greenhouse gas emissions by 50 percent compared to using regular gasoline.

• Then there's local air pollution. The Environmental Protection Agency says using more ethanol fuel would increase ozone-producing chemicals. Mark Jacobson, a researcher at Stanford University, recently estimated that widespread switching to a blend of 85 percent ethanol and 15 percent gasoline might increase ozone-related mortality, hospitalization and asthma by about 9 percent in Los Angeles and 4 percent in the United States as a whole.

• Now, let's talk about water consumption. Messrs. Kreider and Curtiss estimate that growing and refining corn for a gallon of corn ethanol today requires about 140 gallons of water. That would mean the 5.4 million gallons of corn ethanol used in America in 2006 required the use of 756 million gallons of fresh water.

• Things do not look much better for ethanol made from cellulose crops, which require between 146 and 149 gallons of water per gallon of ethanol fuel, depending on the scale of production. To meet the Bush administration's target of 35 billion gallons of renewable and alternative fuels production in the United States by 2017 with cellulosic ethanol would require as much water as flows in the Colorado River every year.

• There's a water pollution issue, as well. The National Academy of Sciences points out that expanding corn-based ethanol production without new environmental protection policies would pose a "considerable" threat to water quality. Corn requires more fertilizers and pesticides than other food or biofuel crops. Pesticide contamination is already highest in the corn belt, and nitrogen fertilizer runoff from corn already produces the most serious agricultural impact on the Mississippi River.

- Fertilizer runoff does not just pollute local waters. Each summer, the nitrogen fertilizers in the Mississippi hit the Gulf of Mexico, creating a large dead zone—a region of oxygen-deprived waters unable to support sea life that extends for more than 10,000 square kilometers. The same phenomenon occurs in Chesapeake Bay.

- A recent study by researchers at the University of British Columbia shows that if the United States were to meet its proposed ethanol production goals of 15 billion to 36 billion gallons of corn and cellulosic ethanol by 2022, nitrogen flows to the Gulf of Mexico would increase by 10 percent to 34 percent.

- Finally, there's land consumption and food prices to consider. In a February *Science* article, researchers calculated that projected corn ethanol production in 2016 would require 43 percent of the land harvested for corn in 2004 that otherwise was used to feed livestock. This represents an enormous change in land use—to either replace the grain lost to food production by vastly expanding corn fields—or a significant increase in food prices of the sort we've already seen due to scarcity of grain raised for human and livestock consumption.

● ● ●

There is little question that high gasoline and oil prices damage the national economy and the personal economies of individual Americans. But putting our hope in ethanol (whether from corn, switch grass or other cellulosic crops) is not a rational policy response, however attractive it might be to the corn lobby.

Although it is rare for anyone to recommend that lawmakers hit the bottle, in the case of ethanol, the balance of virtue and vice is fairly clear. America's motto should not be "Ethanol for Energy Independence." It should be "Ethanol: Drink It, Don't Drive It."

For Class Discussion

1. How does Green structure his argument? Is this pattern effective in presenting the reasons for his claim?

2. Ethanol enjoys considerable public support. What issues does Green raise that may not have been previously addressed? What stakeholders stand to benefit through the widespread adoption of ethanol?

3. How do you think Green's intended audience would respond to the tone and style he adopts?

4. Is it sufficient that Green addresses why ethanol is not a solution, or would his argument be strengthened by presenting an alternative to ethanol?

5. Where does this argument fit within the range of energy viewpoints expressed in this chapter?

■

The White House Goes Green
Matt Wuerker

Matt Wuerker is a political cartoonist and illustrator based in Washington D.C., where he is the staff cartoonist and in-house illustrator for the newspaper/website, *Politico* (http://www.politico.com). Two collections of his cartoons have been published: *Standing Tall in Deep Doo Doo: A Cartoon Chronicle of the Bush Quayle Years* (1991) and *Meanwhile in Other News: A Graphic Look at Politics in the Empire of Money, Sex and Scandal* (1998). This cartoon first appeared on December 3, 2008.

> The audience for political cartoons can vary widely, depending on the publication and the context. How might different audiences interpret the message behind this image?

For Class Discussion

1. How would you describe the tone of this cartoon? What details of the drawing influenced your interpretation?

2. This cartoon was published shortly after Barack Obama was elected as president. What claim does the image support?

3. Cartoons often employ exaggeration or humor to make their point. What or whom does this cartoon appear to be satirizing?

4. What readings in this chapter would this cartoon agree with or support?

Aiming for Energy Security, Not Independence

Tony Hayward

Tony Hayward holds a Ph.D. in geology from the University of Edinburgh and is the chief executive of BP Group. Primarily an oil and gas company, BP employs over 96,000 people and operates in over 100 countries worldwide. The company has recently invested in alternative energy "to help meet the world's demand for energy that emits little or no carbon—such as biofuels, solar, wind, hydrogen, and gas-fired power" (www.bp.com). This brief position statement is from the February 26, 2009, issue of the *Wall Street Journal Europe* (www.wsj.com), a daily newspaper focusing on U.S. and international business and finance. According to the Web site, the newspaper includes among its readership "influential business and financial decision makers, top opinion leaders, and the affluent set."

> How does Hayward establish himself as a credible and reasonable voice in this debate?

Every U.S. president since Richard Nixon has expressed concern about America's growing dependence on imported oil. But effective action has proved elusive: Oil imports have more than doubled in the past 35 years—from 30% at the time of the first oil shock in 1973 to around 65% today.

Yet the collapse in world energy demand and the fall of energy prices present a rare, once-in-a-generation opportunity. Congress and the Obama administration can work with energy producers to craft an energy policy that creates jobs, expands and diversifies the nation's energy supply, generates government revenue, and protects the environment.

Reaching those goals begins with rejecting the false choice between "drill, baby, drill" and a near-exclusive focus on alternative energies and conservation. An "all-of-the-above" approach holds far more promise.

President Barack Obama seems to recognize this. In his address to Congress this week, he spoke forthrightly about the need to tackle climate change—while acknowledging the role of hydrocarbons in the overall energy mix, and emphasizing the need for energy security and efficiency. At BP we welcome his commitment to "invest $15 billion, a year to develop technologies like wind power and solar power, advanced biofuels, clean coal and more efficient cars and trucks built right here in America."

BP has already demonstrated its commitment to a diverse energy portfolio. We're the largest producer of oil and gas in the U.S. We're also investing more than $8 billion over 10 years to develop solar, wind, hydrogen power and biofuels. We support energy conservation and efficiency, as well as addressing climate change via a cap-and-trade system to harness the power of the market to reduce CO_2 emissions.

But if the country is to gain full value from the technology, knowledge and expertise possessed by BP and its major competitors, I'd like to offer policy makers a few suggestions.

First, energy providers and governments must have confidence in one another. An adversarial stance does nothing to increase the supply of energy. Regulatory policies need to be sensible, stable and right the first time.

Second, energy security can only be built on a solid foundation of free markets and free trade. Two-thirds of the world's oil is traded across international borders. This huge and agile market makes it possible to respond quickly to supply disruptions, such as hurricanes or political unrest. Tariffs, heavy taxes, or restrictions on the free movement of petroleum products interfere with that process.

Third, transitional incentives are needed to make low-carbon energy competitive with other energy sources, and to kick-start technologies for large-scale carbon abatement, such as carbon capture and storage. But these incentives should taper away over time, so costs are driven down and the market can take over as quickly as possible.

Finally, America must stop looking to others for the oil it needs and actively develop its own hydrocarbon endowment. Even with the rapid growth of alternatives, fossil fuels will continue providing most of the energy Americans consume for decades into the future.

The search for new sources of domestic crude has been constrained by a lack of access to promising areas, notably the Outer Continental Shelf (OCS). Resource estimates for closed areas exceed 100 billion barrels of oil, with 30 billion recoverable with today's technology and at today's prices.

Opening up the OCS would enhance America's energy security. Moreover, a new study by ICF International estimates that it could create as many as 76,000 new jobs and generate a total of nearly $1.4 trillion in new government revenue by 2030.

No one in the energy business thinks America can drill its way to energy security. But a policy based exclusively or even primarily on conservation and efficiency is a recipe for ongoing scarcity and economic decline.

The prize is great and the time is right. When the world economy begins to recover—and it will—demand for energy will rise and the moment will likely have passed. We are extending our hand. We hope Washington policy makers will grasp it.

For Class Discussion

1. What is Tony Hayward's main claim and specific lens (background and investment) on this issue?

2. What has inspired Hayward to write this argument? What global events does he reference?

3. Several of the authors in this chapter argue for a particular form of alternative energy, while others, like Hayward, advocate a "mixed approach." On what points might Hayward agree with other writers? On what points might he disagree?

4. Both Hayward's piece and the editorial from the *National Review* advocate domestic oil drilling, at least in part. How do their tone and their approaches to convincing their audiences differ? ◼

Pedaling Our Way to Energy Independence
Jonathan Facelli

Jonathan Facelli is a corporate attorney in Cambridge, Massachusetts. This essay is from the March/April 2009 edition of the *Humanist*, a magazine that describes itself as applying "humanism—a naturalistic and democratic outlook informed by science, inspired by art, and motivated by compassion" and specifies its goal of providing "alternative ideas" (www.thehumanist.org). This column originally appeared under the heading "Satirically Speaking." In satire, the author employs wit in order to attack a folly or vice with the aim of exposing or correcting it. The target may be people, institutions, ideas, or things, and the methods include exaggeration, distortion, humor, ridicule, and irony.

How does Facelli apply the formal principles of argument to his humorous proposal?

During the 2008 U.S. presidential campaign the buzzword "energy independence" reemerged atop the nation's political agenda. U.S. policymakers and talking heads have increasingly declared the need for energy self-sufficiency. According to economist Daniel Yergin, writing for the *Wall Street Journal*, the United States is presently over 70 percent self-sufficient, a higher percentage than many Americans realize. But the pundits insist we must do better. How can we achieve that additional 30 percent without sending billions of U.S. dollars to OPEC nations and that big pink country to the north?

If you listen to the John McCains and the Sarah Palins, we should start by drilling in Alaska and building nuclear power plants. If Barack Obama and Al Gore are more to your tastes, the answers are in hybrid cars, clean coal technology, and investment in renewable energy sources such as wind and hydroelectric power. But maybe there's another option, one our pundits and political leaders have overlooked.

Wind, water, and steam turbines generate energy by using natural kinetic sources to rotate drive shafts connected to electric generators. At work are basic principles of physics, which instruct that an electric current is generated by cranking a loop of wire between stationary magnets. A massive steel windmill generates electricity the same way as a science experiment with two magnets and a coil of wire; the wire and magnets are merely larger in the windmill.

That got me thinking—how else might we crank generators to produce electrical energy? How do we gain that final 30 percent of energy we currently import? Maybe the question we should be asking is, how can we do more cranking? It's not an energy deficit we're dealing with—it's a cranking deficit.

Once the question is properly posed, the answer becomes obvious—foot pedals.

Tens of millions of students and white-collar employees in the United States spend their days seated at a desk. Instead of idling all day, these people could be pedaling. Accountants, attorneys, and academics could be winding their legs under the desk as they work. Students could be pedaling away while they listen and learn. If every cubicle desk, office chair, and board room were equipped with pedals, we could harness millions of kilowatt hours of electricity per day. Consider the possibilities in exercise facilities. Treadmills, stationary bikes, circuit trainers—all could be harnessing energy if equipped with a small generator.

An esteemed physics professor, who wishes to remain anonymous, conservatively estimates that an office worker could generate one kilowatt hour of electricity per day pedaling a small sub-desk generator. When we consider the total number of workers and work days in a year, we're talking about the potential for billions of kWhs generated annually from human movement alone. That's a big number. Then take into account the international possibilities—India's call centers alone could power the world if equipped with pedals. Let's get those telemarketers winding.

To be sure, there will be skeptics. The infrastructure required to install all those pedals and generators would be staggering, opponents will surely suggest. Granted, it will take some time and a bit of R&D, but leave that to the engineers and smart people like Bill Gates and Al Gore—if they can figure out how to make the Clapper, the Segway, and an iPod the size of a credit card, I'm sure they can whip up the portable pedal generator (or PPG) in no time. Other skeptics will argue that, with all of that churning and spinning, people will require greater food intake, which would offset the harnessed energy. This argument fails to consider the substitution effect: by churning away all day, students and office workers will have less need to exercise independently. Instead of running or biking after work, people will simultaneously stay fit and solve the energy crisis. On account of the obesity epidemic, we're already carrying around colossal amounts of excess energy in our guts and upper thighs; the PPGs will enable us to convert that blubber into a more usable form.

It's almost too simple. In fact, I'm surprised efforts haven't already been taken to install PPGs in office spaces and public classrooms. There's a lot of work to do, and there's no time like the present to get started.

We can install pedals on everything: restaurant booths, airplane seats, subway trains, toddler car seats, and church pews. Let's make it fun— employer-sponsored prizes, private office pools for energy production, bragging rights for best pedaler and most improved. The sky's the limit.

Who needs more windmills and oil rigs when we can collectively crank our way to energy independence? Call your local representative; write a letter to the Department of Energy. No more dependence on foreign oil—let's get cranking!

For Class Discussion

1. Though this argument is meant to be humorous, the technology for human-powered generators exists. What features of Facelli's writing help readers identify his tongue-in-cheek tone?

2. What is Facelli's main claim, and how does he use evidence to support it? Could his audience find the argument reasonably convincing?

3. What other problems faced by Americans does Facelli argue would be solved through his proposal?

4. Facelli ties certain alternative energy options to different political points of view. Based upon the readings in this chapter, do you agree with how he categorizes technologies such as nuclear, wind, and hydroelectric power? ■

CHAPTER QUESTIONS FOR REFLECTION AND DISCUSSION

1. What are your perceptions of bottled water and how often do you drink it? How have the articles in this chapter influenced your views on bottled water?

2. What reasons have you encountered in these articles that support the argument that water should be a human right? A good or service?

3. According to environmentalists, what attitudes about water need to be examined or changed in order to meet our needs in the future?

4. Choose a pair of writers from the following list and analyze where they agree and disagree about effective and ethical approaches to natural resources. Specifically examine their assumptions, reasoning, and interpretation of facts. Identify where their use of language reveals their values and challenges alternative views.

   A. Fredrik Segerfeldt and Maude Barlow

   B. Fredrik Segerfeldt and Khadija Sharife

   C. Maude Barlow and Sandra Postel

   D. Tony Hayward and "The Energy Shortage" or William Sweet

   E. "The Energy Shortage" and Tine Sommer or William Sweet

   F. "Health and Environment" poster and Wangari Muta Maathai

5. Choose one of the readings in this chapter that argues for important connections between economics and environmental problems. What connections does the reading make and how persuasive is its approach or solution?

6. Increased awareness of global warming informs many of the readings in this chapter. How do authors acknowledge the role of global warming in their arguments?

7. Having read the articles on alternative energy, what would you say is the most reasonable and compelling approach to solving our energy problems and why?

8. Working in groups or individually, investigate and take the environmental quiz "The Good Stuff? Quiz" posted on the Worldwatch Institute site (www.worldwatch.org/pubs/goodstuff/quiz/). What has this quiz shown you about your use of environmental resources?

9. Research and report to your class on one of the following topics:

   A. China, in its rapid industrialization, is experiencing serious problems with water pollution, growing energy needs, and conflicts over damming its major rivers. Research the recent crises related to these problems. How is China dealing with these problems? What is the response of the global community?

   B. If you wanted to invest ten thousand dollars in an ecofriendly, socially responsible company known for its commitment to sustainable development, which companies would you consider?

   C. A number of the world's rivers cross national borders. For example, in Africa, the Nile and Congo Rivers are potential sites of international conflict, as are the Mekong River in South Asia and the Colorado River in North America. What countries and government are competing for the water from these rivers? What intergovernmental agreements for equitable use of this water exist?

   D. Indigenous peoples, citizens of developing countries, and the poor everywhere are the most vulnerable to environmental disasters. Research the concept of "environmental refugees." What events like the December 2004 tsunami, Hurricane Katrina in August 2005, drought in the Darfur region of the Sudan, and other floods or droughts have exposed this vulnerability?

   E. Utility companies in many U.S. cities are providing financial incentives for individuals and companies who invest in renewable energy technologies for their homes or buildings. What options are available in your area?

F. Different energy options are more feasible for some regions of the United States than for others. Some of the options are discussed in this chapter, including wind, nuclear, and hydropower; other options include solar, geothermal, tidal, and clean coal energies. What alternative energy sources are being discussed in your region? Are there any controversies attached to potential development of these resources?

G. Much water is wasted. What are ways that individuals, agriculture, and industry can use water more efficiently? What methods hold promise for global use?

H. Though not explicitly addressed in this chapter, one of the ways that individuals influence energy policy is through their choice of vehicle. Automakers have invested considerable resources in the production of alternative energy vehicles and thus strive to attract potential "green" buyers with their advertising. Research print, Web, or television ads for these vehicles and, using the rhetorical analysis guidelines in Chapter Two, pages 33–38, evaluate how effective these automakers are in reaching their target audience. (On the Web, you might begin with automakers' Web sites, youtube.com, or spinitgreen.org.)

WRITING ASSIGNMENTS

Brief Writing Assignments

1. Briefly describe how the readings in this chapter have influenced your thinking about your own use of water and energy.

2. Which article in this chapter about environmental problems did you find the most eye-opening, disturbing, or inspirational? What features of the argument affected you?

3. **Analyzing Arguments Rhetorically.** A number of the writers in this chapter (Maude Barlow, Wangari Muta Maathai, Sandra Postel, and Kenneth P. Green) have international reputations as spokespersons for particular stances in global environmental debates. Select one of these writers' arguments and examine it rhetorically. How directly and explicitly does the writer present his or her claim? How specific, relevant, and effective is his or her evidence? How does this writer use emotional and imaginative appeals to the audience and treat alternative views? How well do these features confirm the writer's knowledge and expertise?

4. As with most controversial issues, discussions of environmental problems are often serious in tone. Briefly explain how arguments such as Jonathan Facelli's and political cartoons by Matt Wuerker and Adrian Raeside serve to lighten the mood while still addressing real concerns. In fact, what specific insights does their lighter approach offer?

5. Freewrite for twenty or more minutes on one of these propositions using ideas and examples from the readings in this chapter. To force yourself to think from different perspectives, you might try writing in agreement with the statement and then writing against it:

A. Water should be a human right, not a commodity for sale.

B. Technology is more important than conservation in finding solutions to water shortages and energy needs.

C. Governments, not businesses, should control and manage environmental resources.

D. We should invest in alternative energy technologies rather than track down the remaining deposits of fossil fuels across the globe.

E. Developing countries need corporations with their capital and technological know-how to help solve their water problems.

F. The United States should focus on energy independence in order to protect the nation from global price fluctuations and international conflicts over natural resources.

6. In her 2004 Nobel Prize acceptance speech, Wangari Muta Maathai writes, ". . . there can be no peace without equitable development; and there can be no development without sustainable management of the environment in a democratic and peaceful space." Using ideas from the readings in this chapter, write in support of this claim by briefly discussing the connections among equitable and sustainable management of environmental resources, social well-being, and political stability.

Writing Projects

1. Write a synthesis paper for your peers in which you explain how the readings in this chapter have shaped your view of problems related to water or energy. You might sketch out your view (for example, on the need for more government or business control of water in Africa or on the need for people to encourage investment in alternative energy technologies) or simply present your view as a series of key questions you think individuals and countries need to address. Use ideas from the arguments in this chapter to support your view or questions, and document these sources.

2. Make an advocacy poster for your residence, community, or university similar to the United Nations Environment Programme poster on page 305 supporting use of the environment that aids the poor. Your poster might urge people to use water or energy more efficiently. Think in terms of a powerful main image/photo and a small amount of text that reinforces or interprets the image and that calls people to action.

3. Using fieldwork and research, investigate the water or electricity system in your area: What is the source of this resource? Who owns it? Are the records regarding the quality of water or the safety of the electrical

production system available to the public? Who sets the standards? How efficient and sustainable is this system? Then write an argument addressed to your community in which you either (a) support or criticize this system or (b) propose strategies for individual and communal conservation of water or energy.

4. The role of corporations and businesses in managing environmental resources is a key controversy that many writers in this chapter address. In addition, corporate leaders such as Richard Sandor (chapter introduction), Frederick Segerfeldt, and Tony Hayward, and environmentalists such as Vandana Shiva (chapter introduction), Maude Barlow, and Sandra Postel write and speak extensively about the topic. Based on this chapter's introduction and readings, take your own stand on this controversy over privatizing water or greater engagement of corporations in environmental problems. Write your argument as a policy proposal for your region or state. You might want to research these relevant global issues: the Friends of the Earth's campaign to stop the privatization of water in Bolivia; Chile's recent water management successes; or engineering advances in Africa such as water purifiers, nonelectrical water pumps, and desalinization procedures.

5. Imagine that your friend, who has recently graduated from college and has begun his or her first career job requiring a commute, has received a $15,000 graduation present from a rich relative who is committed to a green lifestyle. Your friend is deciding how to use this gift (1) to solve his/her transportation problems and (2) to uphold the green values of this generous relative. Write a letter to this friend in the form of an informal but well-reasoned argument that proposes an environmentally sound way to meet these two objectives. Should your friend buy an eco-friendly vehicle—a hybrid, an electric car, a hydrogen car, or a SmartCar? In your letter to your friend, argue either that he/she should or should not buy one of these vehicles. Build a strong case for your view: think about your friend and his/her values and needs and try to be as persuasive and lively as you can. Consider how you will address alternative views, establish yourself as a credible source, and appeal to your friend's emotions. If you consult sources for information, be sure you give credit to these sources.

6. Argue that water management or energy efficiency is a political issue that calls for political solutions in the form of national policies that promote government–business collaboration. You might research one of the following examples: France has had good results through taxing gasoline, encouraging industries to shift from oil to other fuels, and promoting diesel-powered cars. In the 1970s, Brazil financially motivated farmers, investors in distilleries, and automakers to develop a domestic ethanol fuel industry. Responding to the 1970s oil embargo, the United States supported

the building of a clean coal-burning plant in Tampa, Florida, lowered the speed limit to 55 miles per hour, and promoted the manufacture of small cars with high gas mileage. South Africa has instituted a two-tier pricing system for water that provides 25 liters per day free but charges users beyond that amount. Australia has instigated a new system of government ownership of water and of pricing and trading. Make the case, directed toward a political representative, that political power can help solve environmental problems.

7. In an op-ed piece "The Last Row of the Plane," David Sirota uses the analogy of people tilting their seats back on an airplane and privileging their personal comfort over the comfort of others as a way of talking about our use of finite environmental resources to satisfy selfish needs (full text available at davidsirota.com). Write an analogy argument as an op-ed piece for your university newspaper. Help your audience understand the need for water conservation, the development of alternative energy, or some other change using a dominant analogy. Remember that a good analogy need not correspond exactly to the situation you wish to shed light upon, but it does help readers see a situation in a creative and interesting way.

8. Suppose a friend says to you, "Okay, I recycle all my plastics, newspapers, and cans. I carpool once a week to campus and take a bus once a week; I keep the heater in the apartment at sixty-two degrees; and I turn off all lights and electrical appliances when I am not using them. But some analysts, both liberals and conservatives, tell me that these individual efforts are pretty useless in saving energy and affecting environmental issues like global warming." What argument would you make to your friend, affirming or rebutting this claim that individual efforts to change energy consumption are insignificant?

9. **Analyzing Arguments Rhetorically.** Environmental advocacy organizations are often thought of as appealing to a very specific audience, often white, middle- to upperclass Americans or Europeans with liberal political views. Using three or four of the following criteria, write a rhetorical analysis of an organization's Web site or one of its Web campaigns directed to the organization that created it. Identify the target audience for the organization, explain the strengths of the site's rhetorical features, and propose a set of recommendations for the organization to help it reach its target audience more effectively or broaden its outreach. You might consider these criteria:

A. Visual appeal and functionality of the site

B. Clear explanation of the problem and sufficient evidence to support the organization's position

C. Strong appeal to readers' emotions, sympathies, and values, including how specific language choices might affect the site's appeal

D. Good credibility or currency of the information presented

E. Clear requests and directives indicating what the organization wants its audience to do

Natural Resource Defense Council

Global Water Policy Project

UN Global Alliance for Water Security

International Rivers Network

Water Aid

Water for People

Global Strategy Institute

Water Partners International

Center for Global Safe Water

New Economics Foundation

World Wind Energy Association

The Energy and Resources Institute

African Rural Energy Enterprise Development

World Energy Council

International Network for Sustainable Energy

World Renewable Energy Network

American Energy Initiative

Feeding the World
Biotechnology, Culture, and Local Food

QUESTION TO PONDER

You have seen the photos of gaunt African children with stick-thin limbs in countries such as Sudan, Niger, and Malawi, which have experienced devastating famines recently. According to Sophia Murphy, director of the Trade Program at the Institute for Agriculture and Trade Policy in Minneapolis, when droughts and shortages add to the inadequate food production in these countries, the death rate for children under age five threatens to rise above one in four.* Murphy claims that U.S. food aid is not substantially helping these starving people. You are wondering, Should developed countries give aid in the form of money, not food, as Murphy suggests? And how can individuals contribute to finding solutions to the problem of world hunger—through changes in our eating habits, voting, donations?

CONTEXT FOR A NETWORK OF ISSUES

Between the 1940s and 1970s, the **Green Revolution** transformed agriculture, industrializing it in part by applying scientific and technological advances such as pesticides, herbicides, chemical fertilizers, hybrid seeds, and animal antibiotics. These new approaches dramatically increased crop yields of rice, wheat, and other basic foods. Favoring **agribusiness,** or corporate farming, over smaller farmers who were less likely to be able to afford them, these capital-intensive changes led to a reduction in the number of small farms. At the same time, agribusinesses, growing single crops for export, came to dominate the global food system and global trade. More recently, a second Green Revolution—scientific advances with gene splicing or bioengineering of crops—has offered possibilities for increased food production.

How have these technological advances in agriculture affected the world's hunger problems? According to a UN study in 2004, although the portion of

---

*"Feeding More for Less in Niger," *New York Times* (August 19, 2005).

the world's population that is hungry or undernourished has dropped from one-fifth to one-sixth, this one-sixth involves 852 million people. According to UN figures, 221 million people in India, 204 million in sub-Saharan Africa, 156 million in Asia and the Pacific, 142 million in China, 53 million in Latin America and the Caribbean, 39 million in the Near East and North Africa, and 37 million in industrialized countries are undernourished.[*] In a statement of its **Millennium Development Goals,** the United Nations reports these facts: "Extreme poverty remains a daily reality for more than 1 billion people who subsist on less than $1 a day"; "every year, almost 11 million children die—that is, 30,000 children a day—before their fifth birthday"; and "malnutrition contributes to over half these deaths."[†] While famines, droughts, environmental disasters such as the tsunami of December 2004, and political strife create hunger crises that contribute to starvation and malnutrition, chronic hunger is a systemic problem related to what food is grown, who grows it, and how it is priced, sold, and traded. A UN report from 2004 shows that 50 percent of the people suffering from hunger are people working the land who should have direct access to nourishing food, while 20 percent are the landless poor. These numerical data suggest that we need to look beyond population growth to understand the complex relationship among global trade, poverty, and hunger to figure out how the global standard of living and advances in agriculture have left one-sixth of the world underfed. To focus on this hunger and poverty problem, the United Nations has chosen as the first of its Millennium Development Goals to call the global community to "[e]radicate extreme poverty and hunger"; "reduce by half the proportion of people living on less than a dollar a day"; and "reduce by half the proportion of people who suffer from hunger."[‡]

Other parts of the global food picture reflect problematic benefits. Global food trade is prospering, having tripled in the last forty years. Although some of this food travels from rural agricultural areas to cities, some trade involves countries importing food they produce themselves, raising questions about fossil fuel use, its costs, and its eventual impact on food prices. Furthermore, the Green Revolution's emphasis on industrialized farming and the production of single crops (**monocultures**) for export has left many countries dependent on other parts of the world for their food. This dependence weakens **food security,** or the ability of countries independently to provide regular, adequate, and reliable food at a reasonable cost

---

[*]These numerical data appear in a pie chart in *UN Millennium Project 2005. Halving Hunger: It Can Be Done*, produced by the Task Force on Hunger. The lead authors are Pedro Sanchez, M. S. Swaminathan, Philip Dobie, and Nalan Yuksel.

[†]*The United Nations Millennium Development Report 2005*; the 191 member states of the United Nations have pledged to meet the Millennium Development Goals by 2015. This document is posted on the UN Millennium Development Goal Web site, http://www.un.org/millenniumgoals/reports.shtml.

[‡]http://www.un.org/millenniumgoals/reports.shtml.

for their own people. In addition, tests of soil and water and even of animal and human blood indicate an accumulation of pesticides and chemical residues from industrialized farming. Finally, although supermarkets in rich countries display a good assortment of fruits and vegetables year-round and have low prices, the freshness of these fruits and vegetables is questionable when they have traveled over 1,000 miles to the store. Also, ten multinational food and beverage companies control the production of about half of the 300,000 or so items in our supermarkets.* These troubling points are motivating more people to explore the connections among this consolidated, long-distance, global food system, overabundance in developed countries, starvation and malnutrition for millions in developing countries, and the environment. This chapter investigates issues of available, affordable, sustainable, safe, and healthy food for both developed and developing countries.

STAKES AND STAKEHOLDERS

All of us are immediate stakeholders in world food issues. Also, governments, multinationals, global trade organizations, scientific research institutes, indigenous peoples, **nongovernmental organizations** (NGOs), environmental and human rights activists, and many civil society groups are invested in the production and distribution of food. To understand what economic, political, and environmental conflicts these stakeholders are arguing about, we can start with the following major issue questions.

What Is Causing World Hunger? Some people claim that the world simply isn't producing enough food: In other words, low and inefficient production causes shortages. Corporate leaders, proponents of free trade, economists, and some political leaders and scientists cite lack of financial resources and technology and ineffective farming methods coupled with poor or exhausted soil, poor irrigation, weak crops that can't resist harsh weather or pests, and unstable, often corrupt, governments as the root causes of cycles of poverty and starvation.

In contrast, many social justice activists, NGOs, indigenous peoples, and civil society groups maintain that economic and political control of food production and trade, not food shortage, is the primary contributor to poverty and starvation around the world. These people contend that together, the Green Revolution and the global free trade system† have favored agribusiness and multinationals. This global free trade system has forced small farmers in developing countries to grow export crops such as

---

*Brian Halweil, "The Argument for Local Food," *Worldwatch* (May–June 2003): 22.
†For a discussion of the history and main principles of free trade, see the introduction in Chapter 3: "Trading Goods: Consumerism, Free Trade, and Sweatshops."

bananas, cotton, coffee, and sugar that have to compete in volatile global markets. To produce these crops in this volume, small farmers in developing countries have turned to expensive Green Revolution technology such as tractors, special fertilizers, pesticides, and, now, genetically modified seeds that have made these farmers increasingly debt-ridden and dependent on the prosperous corporations that make these products. As world-renowned economist Amartya Sen asserts, "Hunger has increased . . . because the poor's entitlement to food has been eroded by technological developments that displaced farmers and reduced the production of staple foods . . . ."* When displaced small farmers try to survive by farming marginal lands, by becoming landless workers, or by moving to cities, they are often left with little means to produce or buy food.

Some people say that global institutions, rich countries, and corporate domination are contributing to world hunger in other ways as well. These activists and analysts emphasize that when the World Bank forces third world countries to pay off their debts, these countries have to reduce their financial help to their own farmers. When wealthy countries "dump" their surplus crops in third world markets, selling their food far below the prices that farmers in developing countries can meet, these low-cost surpluses weaken the domestic markets of developing countries and often drive small farmers out of business. In addition, these analysts and activists protest the way that global free trade agreements have constrained national governments' abilities to protect the interests of their own people from the will of multinational corporations and the fluctuations in trade.

Some environmentalists and ecologists are framing problems with food production as a large-scale environmental crisis. They believe exhaustion of the earth's ecosystem threatens the earth's ability to continue to feed its growing population. According to Lester Brown of the Earth First Institute, "mega-threats" to the earth's potential to support adequate food production include (1) overuse of the world's underground water supplies (aquifers); (2) erosion of soil and desertification; (3) depletion of fisheries; and (4) climate changes bringing extremes such as heat waves.† Brown and others believe that the earth will not be able to sustain production for a larger world population of meat eaters and that the collapsing environment will have a domino effect, creating economic conflicts and eventually political conflicts over food.‡

---

*Quoted in Robert K. Schaeffer, *Understanding Globalization: The Social Consequences of Political, Economic, and Environmental Change* (Oxford, Rowman & Littlefield Publishers, Inc., 1997), 168.

†Lester Brown, "Rescuing a Planet Under Stress," *Humanist* (November–December 2003).

‡The readings in Chapter 6: "Protecting the Environment: Water Issues and Emerging Energy Technologies" discuss problems with water shortages.

How Can We End World Hunger Now and Meet the World's Food Needs in the Future? Most stakeholders emphasize that sustainable agricultural practices and environmental conservation are their goals. Green Revolution supporters believe that science and technology hold answers for continued high-yield production and for environmental preservation. These agriculturalists, economists, and researchers like the Consultative Group on International Agricultural Research (CGIAR) advocate the following solutions to increase agricultural efficiency and productivity: better food policies; investment in roads, communication, and management of resources like water; more strategic investment in technology to develop new farming methods; and the application of innovative science, particularly biotechnology. Some corporations, research groups, and scientists believe that **biotechnology**—the genetic modification of plants (also called "gene splicing" and **"transgenic crops"**)—offers the best solution to the world's food needs. They claim that biotech crops will cut soil erosion, reduce the use of pesticides, enable crops to grow in poor or dry soil, and provide important nutrients and vitamins. However, some environmentalists warn that biotech crops could destroy the valuable genetic diversity inherent in wild and traditional plants. Anticorporate advocates, indigenous peoples, and civil society groups believe that multinationals such as Monsanto and Syngenta are largely economically motivated and are fostering small farmers' dependence on these large corporations' patented, genetically modified seeds. Other moderate voices in the biotech crop controversy also object to corporate control of this technology but believe that some research into plant genetics holds promise for bigger and better crop yields.

In opposition to agribusinesses' use of biotech seeds, chemicals, and large one-crop farms, many people are proposing an organic small-farm model of food production to maximize a sustainable food supply and environmental preservation. Environmental activist Vandana Shiva asserts that agribusiness calculates crop yields in terms of volume of individual crops produced instead of in terms of "total output of food" and that "small biodiverse farms can produce thousands of times more food than large, industrial monocultures": "In Java, small farmers cultivate 607 species in their home gardens. In sub-Saharan Africa, women cultivate as many as 120 different plants in the spaces left alongside the cash crops."* Proponents of **organic food** argue that pests, weeds, soil quality, fertility, and productivity can be managed with intercropping (planting mixed crops together), crop rotation, and human care for the land.

Focusing on the big picture of saving the earth and preventing further environmental deterioration, environmentalists and ecologists are calling

---

*Vandana Shiva, "Globalization and Poverty," *Resurgence* 202, http://www.resurgence .gn.apc.org/issues/shiva202.htm.

for population reduction, a change in countries' diets away from meat and processed junk food, and global regulation of damaging practices such as fossil fuel emissions and polluting of water.

Can Global Free Trade Help Solve World Hunger? **Free trade** proponents say that developing countries will become more prosperous and advanced when they participate more fully in free trade through such agreements as the **Central America–Dominican Republic–United States Free Trade Agreement** (CAFTA-DR), voted into law in 2005 by the U.S. Congress. At the 2005 meeting of the World Trade Organization in Hong Kong, developing countries fought for and won more access to markets in rich countries. To help developing countries compete, rich countries finally agreed to phase out their agricultural export subsidies and their tariffs and quotas on agricultural imports—all of which have hurt small farmers in poor countries.[*] Meanwhile, **fair trade** advocates want a different model of agricultural trade that places the farmer-producer in more direct contact with consumers and restores power to these farmers through fair, guaranteed prices.[†]

In contrast, some stakeholders insist that food be removed from the global free trade system and are campaigning for **food sovereignty** with **land reform** as the first major step to returning control of food to citizens everywhere. Agricultural ecologist Peter Rosset defines food sovereignty as "being able to feed yourself as a people or nation," free from the economic and political power of other countries; "[f]ood sovereignty says that every nation and people should have the right to define their own kind of agriculture with their own culinary and historic and agrarian traditions."[‡] Groups around the world—particularly in Brazil, Bolivia, Venezuela, and Mexico—have embraced the cause of food sovereignty and land reform to redistribute land and return to family farms. Among the most active are Via Campesina, the global alliance of peasant organizations representing roughly 200 million people; the Land Research Action Network; the Landless Social Movement; and the Center for the Study of Change in the Mexican Countryside. These groups also call for national governments to provide realistic, fair subsidies to support domestic agriculture through roads, credit, or regulation of market prices. In addition, they are campaigning for agroecology that involves preservation of local varieties of plants and farmers' control of native seeds. A number of NGOs and other

---

[*]For more information on these negotiations between developed and developing countries, see the "Doha Development Agenda" on the World Trade Center site at http://www.wto.org/english/tratop/e_dda_e/dda/htm.

[†]See the discussion of fair trade in Chapter 3: "Trading Goods: Consumerism, Free Trade, and Sweatshops."

[‡]"Interview with Peter Rosset of CECCAM and Land Research Action Network, San Felipe, Yaracuy, Venezuela," *In Motion Magazine* (July 4, 2005), http://www.inmotionmagazine.com/global/p_rosset_int.html.

groups see hope in working directly with third world governments, the landless, and small farmers by making it possible through microcredit loans and microplots of home and garden land for the poor to be able to grow their own food and support themselves.

Would a Return to a Local Food System Be a Good Global Food Policy?
Multinationals and large supermarket chains continue to emphasize their ability to supply food cheaply. Supporters of global free trade stress the magnitude of the global food system and the logistical and financial unfeasibility of returning to dismantled local food systems. They challenge the idea that local agriculture could produce the volume and crop diversity needed to feed regional cities and surrounding areas. These skeptics point out that many communities and regions also no longer have food processing systems such as dairies, slaughterhouses, canneries, and mills for grain as well as marketing systems.

Still, many people argue that reconstructing local food systems would enhance regional and national security, boost local economies, and encourage direct ties between farmers and consumers. Supporters of **local food** are actively promoting farmers markets, food delivery subscription schemes, farmers' marketing cooperatives, and connections among local farmers and school cafeterias.

The local food movement intersects with the advocates for food sovereignty, small farmers, and cultural rights by pushing for developing countries' independence from global markets. Nonprofit organizations such as the International Society for Ecology and Culture work to preserve ancestral diets and the uniqueness of regions and cultures.

How Can Food Be Made Safer to Eat, Less Contaminated with Chemicals, and Less Destructive of the Environment? Environmentalists point out that returning to a local food system would help the environment by reducing the amount of fossil fuel expended on transporting food and would foster more accountability from food producers who would be less likely to use toxic chemicals. In addition, ecologists claim that rebuilding local food systems would counteract the soil-depleting overcultivation of single crops and encourage biodiversity. Groups like Via Campesina want to replace large-scale, chemical-intensive farming with agroecology—organic farming, native wisdom, and traditional environmentally friendly practices.

Health advocates argue that a return to local food systems would enable people to regain control over what they eat. Other countries may have lower environmental standards for chemical toxins; and food that travels long distances has more potential for bacterial contamination and more need for preservatives. Nutritionists point out that people's health suffers when they abandon local diets and begin eating imported foods, as seen in developing countries where consumption of Western food has led to Western illnesses such as heart disease and diabetes.

The three sections that follow—"Student Voice," "International Voices," and "Global Hot Spot"—take a closer look at problems with hunger and food.

 ## STUDENT VOICE: Nurturing the Land or Poisoning It by Kevin Uhl

In the following narrative, student writer Kevin Uhl contrasts his experience with organic farming in the United States with his experience observing the consequences of industrial agriculture in Nicaragua.

The best food I have ever tasted is the food I grew myself on an organic farm in Carnation, Washington, where I worked for a season. This farm, part of community supported agriculture, raised potatoes of all colors including purple, apples, lettuce, cabbage, carrots, tomatoes, and the craziest melons, which for some reason grew incredibly well next to the river. All these crops grew without synthetic chemicals, and when I ate a plump tomato or purple potato, it tasted delicious and "pure."

The environment abounded with trees, animals, and birds. The land itself was full of life. Sometimes I would stop and watch the birds fly by or close my eyes and simply listen to the symphonies of the returning birds in spring. After rainstorms, the farm breathed, and I felt more alive.

This cooperative farm ran on volunteer labor with participants receiving fresh fruits and vegetables. There were always at least four of us working together, talking and building our own little community. We put our hands in the rich soil and it gave us life. I felt a connection with these people and the earth.

When I visited Nicaragua, however, I saw a different world of farming. In Managua, coffee workers and banana farmers were camping out in front of the government building because they had no money and nothing to eat. They were farmers with no land and no access to unused portions. Many were sick from the chemicals they used while farming and hungry because the crops they grew, mostly nonfood, were for export. The market had failed them.

In Chinandega, Nicaragua, I noticed the farmland itself—deforested and stripped to grow bananas and cotton. The land was dying. Growing one crop drains the land while growing many crops restores and nurtures it. Here to pressure the land to keep producing, many synthetic fertilizers were used and many poisons employed to fight weeds and pests. I was warned about chemical residues, soil contamination, and poisoned water. This land could kill as it was dying.

Indeed, this farming system seemed to be promoting death. I saw many people drinking water from visibly contaminated places and eating foods that would make them sick later. Almost all of the dogs were mangy, and they were definitely not pets. Burning garbage left a foul smell and toxic air. Everything seemed to be poisoned and poisonous.

Despite all this pain, I did see hope. People worked together cooperatively and generously. They wanted a better life through participation, not pity. I took these impressions back to the United States.

I have seen two farming styles. The deadly one prevails, not just in Nicaragua, but throughout this country and the world. The terms of land tenure leave a few with much and many with so little. If more people could participate in farming and growing their own food, working with the land, not against it, this understanding of ecology would nurture healthful, tasty food, singing birds, and living land.

INTERNATIONAL VOICES

As the UN data on page 342 show, there are many global sites of hunger and malnutrition. India's agricultural and hunger problems are particularly controversial. India has experienced both the Green Revolution and the current biotech crop revolution. Yet recently thousands of farmers, burdened by drought and debts from the cost of fertilizers and high interest rates, have committed suicide, especially in the state of Andhra Pradesh. Shamed by their debts, these small farmers—growers of rice, sunflowers, peanuts, and cotton—have resorted to swallowing pesticides to escape despair.

The Oral Testimony Programme of the Panos Institute believes that the global community should consult disadvantaged and marginalized people, who are often the ones most affected by development policies in which they have little say. This organization has collected over three hundred interviews with poor farmers in rural mountain communities throughout the world. The following excerpts from interviews with farmers in the Himalayas, the mountainous regions of northern India, reveal how these small farmers have struggled with Green Revolution technology.

Excerpts from Interviews with Farmers and Activists in Northern India

Sudesha, a fifty-year-old woman, farmer, and activist:

"Yes, in the first year, I thought [chemical fertilizer] was really wonderful. But in the second year the yield began to fall, and in the third year it fell even lower. In the fourth year it was exactly where it was before I started using fertilizer. The money that I spent on buying the fertilizer is a separate matter. Our land was harmed in exactly the same way that a man's body [is] harmed when he drinks liquor. That was the effect the fertilizer had upon my land. . . ."

Vijay, a forty-one-year-old man, farmer, and activist:

"Our traditional agriculture was fully self-reliant. The seeds, the manure, and the bullock, everything was personal. Only seeds were exchanged by farmers. But the farmer today is totally dependent on the government machinery. It would not be an exaggeration to say that he has become a slave to multinational seeds and fertilizer.

". . . the government and the scientists are telling us not to grow [the traditional crops of] mandua and jhangora, but to grow soya bean, as oil and milk can be produced from it, and it is rich in proteins. But who can extract oil and milk out of it? It is not possible for local men to do this. Earlier, when people cultivated mandua and jhangora, they had enough food grain for the cattle. Soya bean is useless for fodder but good only for big factories.*

GLOBAL HOT SPOT: India

India has the largest population of hungry, malnourished people; however, India is also the site of a variety of efforts to solve these problems. The Rural Development Institute (RDI) is an American legal institution committed to using its knowledge of international land law to combat "one of the chief structural causes of global poverty—rural landlessness." For the last thirty-six years, this institute has worked with over forty governments of developing countries and foreign aid agencies to create microcredit loans to enable poor people to buy microplots to grow food. This case study from the RDI Web site reveals how help of this kind leads to better nutrition and health, self-sufficiency, and economic and social progress.

Forty-two teak trees on one-tenth of an acre plus twelve mango, eight neem, four bamboo, one sandalwood, two jambu, pomegranate, gooseberry, custard apple, guava, papaya, date palm, lime, almond, areca, field beans, bitter gourds, onions, curry leaf, ginger, greens, sweet potatoes, eggplant, passion fruit, roses, jasmine, and chrysanthemums are the trees, fruits, nuts, vegetables, herbs, and medicinals grown by Jiyappa and his family on a 5,400-square-foot house-and-garden plot they have owned since 1993 in the Indian state of Andhra Pradesh.

Jiyappa is a former "bonded laborer"—an indentured servant who lived and worked in his master's house and farm fields in exchange for basic food, a primitive shelter, and 700 Rupees (US $16) per year. That was before he was hired by the Deccan Development Society (DDS), a local NGO working to economically empower the

---

*http://www.mountainvoices.org.

poorest of the rural poor. In 1993, the DDS employee's association helped Jiyappa and fellow DDS workers purchase small house-and-garden plots of about one-tenth of an acre.

Today, Jiyappa, his wife Sukkammaa, and three of their six children live in a small house they have constructed on the plot. The plot is producing 90 percent of the family's annual vegetable and fruit needs, plus 6,000 Rupees (US $133) a year from the sale of what they can't eat themselves. The twenty chickens they keep on the plot are used for family consumption, plus provide 3,000 Rupees (US $67) a year from the sale of poultry and eggs. And ten years from now, when the teak trees begin to reach maturity, the wood from each tree will fetch at least 25,000 Rupees (US $556), giving the forty-two trees a total value of roughly 1,050,000 Rupees (US $23,333) in today's Rupees/dollars—an enormous sum for a poor rural family in India.*

Despite some hopeful movements to restore land to the landless, India's farmers are struggling to grow export crops using genetically modified seeds. Crop failures point to flaws in the system and are fueling poverty and suicide. The following news story, "Approval for New Modified Cotton Planting Stirs Alarm" by Ranjit Devraj, published in New Delhi on April 22, 2005, shows how decisions influenced by corporations, politics, and global trade affect farmers' lives.

Environmentalists are alarmed that the Indian government has given approval for more areas to be planted with new varieties of genetically modified Bt cotton, despite farmers suffering huge losses in the past from growing the transgenic crop.

Bt cotton is genetically modified to include a pest-killing gene borrowed from a soil bacterium called "bacillus thuringiensis." While Bt cotton is sold as pest resistant seed in India, it has proved to be more vulnerable to pests and diseases than the traditional and conventional varieties. . . .

Approvals of three cotton hybrids developed by Mahyco-Monsanto Biotech Ltd. expired in March but the Genetic Engineering Approval Committee could not grant extensions on their licenses because of adverse reports coming in not only from leading voluntary agencies but also from the state government of Andhra Pradesh.

In fact, local authorities in the Warangal district of Andhra Pradesh have been demanding that Mahyco-Monsanto compensate the Andhra Pradesh farmers after crop losses last year drove scores of them to commit suicide.

---

*"Rural Development Institute—Lives Changed," http://www.rdiland.org/OURWORK/OurWork_LivesChanged03.html.

"The problems of the peasants started with rampant supply of spurious seeds and pesticides which continued with every stage of crop production up to the marketing stage," wrote the *Deccan Herald* newspaper. . . .

The main idea behind approving genetically engineered Bt cotton as a commercial crop was that this would increase farmers' income by reducing expenditure on chemical pesticides. However, studies indicate that in the past few years the amounts spent on pesticides by Indian farmers growing the crop have actually increased by two-to-three fold, because of the growing resistance of pests—especially the bollworm—to chemical pesticides.

The articles in this chapter will help you further explore the complexities of global food production, hunger, and poverty.

READINGS

Why You Can't Sit Down to Eat Without Making a Statement
Scott Canon

Scott Canon is a national correspondent for Knight Ridder Newspapers, which publishes over thirty daily newspapers including the *Kansas City Star*, where this article first appeared. He has covered conflicts involving food and markets, including food aid to Africa and Anheuser-Busch's rejection of biotech crops. This piece was reprinted in the *Seattle Times* on June 25, 2005.

> Written for a general newspaper audience, this loose argument seeks to sketch out the main conflicts among the parties involved in the global food market. Who are these stakeholders and how do they wield power?

Whether consumers care or not, just about everything they eat is spiked with implications for the environment, international trade, health and the American economy.

Some people talk of how buying some foods undermines the world's rain forests or coastlines. Others campaign to save the American family farm or improve conditions for foreign laborers. Some call for the American system of big farms and companies to get bigger and deliver ever-cheaper food. Box labels and grocery shelves don't mention the federal fights over tariffs and subsidies, but they're there.

In the global village of twenty-first-century food production, what you eat makes a political statement.

BIG AG

For many, purchasing McNuggets is a tacit endorsement of Big Agriculture—from genetically engineered crops that make for cheaper feed, to concentrated poultry barns where manure can spoil the local groundwater, to a system of production that leaves little room for smaller farms.

At the same time, however, McDonald's has responded to public pressure. The fast-food chain uses its substantial buying power to insist that suppliers not dose their chickens with antibiotics to promote growth. The company has also been commended by animal-rights groups for pressuring slaughterhouses into using more humane methods—imposing its standards by surprise audits at packing houses.

Granola stands as the iconic organic snack—that healthful mix of grains and dried fruit. When certified organic, the nibbler can chow down knowing the food was grown without pesticides.

But most oats in this country are imported—new short-season varieties of more heavily subsidized soybeans have elbowed oats out of acres in the upper Midwest. So if that granola isn't certified organic, its oats were probably grown in countries with less stringent labor standards and are more likely to carry traces of pesticides outlawed in the U.S.

IMPORTS JUMP

In fact, there's hardly a meal that doesn't relate in some way to legislative food fights in Washington pitting home-grown lobbies against foreign-interest groups, one region opposite another, or crop-versus-crop. Even as America ships its meat and grain around the planet, the country imports 13 percent of its food—56 percent more than two decades ago.

As food crosses borders, so do trade squabbles such as those between the United States and Europe over wine and cheese.

Still, picky eaters are every bit as influential in such matters as politicians.

Consumer pressure changed fishing practices so now countries that don't properly monitor dolphin-free tuna catches face U.S. import restrictions. Starbucks and others hold on to consumers by making their suppliers deliver "shade-grown" coffee raised below the rain-forest canopy rather than on land razed to make way for farming. A generation ago boycotts of grapes gave bargaining leverage to California farmworkers.

Today the debate over the best way to stock pantries churns on.

"This global food system has been a great benefit to agribusiness, but it has not been a benefit at all for farmers," said Ben Lilliston of the Institute for Agriculture and Trade Policy, a group that sees itself as the champion of small family farms. "Both here and in the developing world, there are fewer farmers every day."

THE VIRTUES OF YIELD

Go organic if you want, say others, but big-scale farming feeds the world.

"We haven't given high-yield farming enough credit for the high yield," said Dennis Avery, director of the agribusiness-supported Center for Global Food Issues and author of *Saving the Planet with Pesticides and Plastic.*

Avery and other defenders of conventional large-scale agriculture say it makes food cheap. Government research shows that in 1930 Americans spent an average of 21.2 percent of their family income on food. Today, that portion is 6.1 percent—the lowest in the world.

What's more, American food is typically safer than that consumed by the rest of the developed world. And incidences of food-borne illness caused by listeria, salmonella and E. coli continue to decline.

"We spend less than anyone else," said American Meat Institute spokeswoman Janet Riley, "and we get the safest food."

Even as the market explodes for fresh and organic foods, the amount of processed food consumed by Americans continues to grow—a market eating up $500 billion of the national annual grocery bill.

"American consumers are concerned about what they're eating, but they put a priority on making it work with their lifestyle," said Stephanie Childs of the Grocery Manufacturers of America. "They want to know: How convenient is it? Will it fit into their family's budget? Will their kids even eat it?"

Still, advocates for various trade, environmental or labor standards say food's path to market matters.

THE SALMON DEBATE

Consider salmon, chock full of heart-healthy omega 3 fatty acids. Demand is up, but natural fisheries are dwindling.

"Farm-raised" salmon has grown popular as depleted fisheries have made wild salmon harder to find and even harder to afford. But farmed salmon have been found in repeated studies to contain higher levels of PCBs, contaminants that pregnant women and nursing mothers have been advised to avoid. Critics also complain about the excessive use of antibiotics with aquaculture.

The author of *Dwellers in the Land,* environmentalist Kirkpatrick Sale, is a fierce advocate for buying seasonally and regionally. He said that when people attempt to bring global variety to their diet, they end up supporting the reckless use of natural resources and corporations he says have little financial incentive to protect the environment.

Yet the federal government and the Food and Agricultural Organization of the United Nations estimate that fishing open waters can meet only half the global demand for seafood as commercial fish stocks decline worldwide.

"Aquaculture is a sustainable alternative," said Stacey Felzenberg, a spokeswoman for the National Fisheries Institute, which represents fishermen, processors and restaurants.

BIG ON SHRIMP

Americans have yet to develop much farm-raised shrimp, but they eat plenty of it. The environmental group Worldwatch Institute estimates that as much as 35 percent of the world's coastal mangrove forests have been destroyed in the past 20 years, mostly for shrimp farms. Even with tariffs used to discourage dumping—importing below cost to capture the market—more than 85 percent of the shrimp consumed in the United States is imported, chiefly from Thailand and China. Meantime, the number of American shrimpers trawling the Gulf of Mexico has fallen by half in the past five years.

"We can compete on taste," said Ewell Smith of the Louisiana Seafood Promotion and Marketing Board. "We can't compete on price."

The global market of vegetables doesn't offer such a price break, but rather cherries and pineapples in the Midwest in winter. Much of America's whole fruits and vegetables are harvested green in another country and ripen on the way to market.

That gives Americans a variety of food once unimagined. But those who advocate buying locally say such imports reduce the incentive of U.S. farmers to grow produce and encourage them to turn to more subsidized commodity grains.

In 1997, an outbreak of potentially fatal hepatitis A from frozen strawberries shipped from Mexico sickened 270 people in five states, 130 Michigan schoolchildren among them. The U.S. Food and Drug Administration says imported food is three times more likely than U.S.-grown food to be contaminated with illegal pesticide residues.

The Environmental Working Group found those chemicals on 18.4 percent of strawberries, 15.6 percent of head lettuce and 12.3 percent of carrots imported from Mexico. Whether that poses a health risk is controversial.

FDA inspections of imported food dropped from about 8 percent before the 1994 North American Free Trade Agreement to less than 2 percent five years later as import volume ballooned.

Now comes the Central American Free Trade Agreement, or CAFTA, pending before Congress. This country's sugar industry, in which strict quotas limiting production prop up U.S. sugar costs to nearly three times the world market, fears the agreement.

Government farm subsidies in the United States and Europe draw criticism from groups who say such policies keep crop prices artificially low. That, in turn, discourages farmers in poor countries from trying to compete.

Buy chocolate and you risk supporting Ivory Coast plantations notorious for using child slave labor to grow and harvest cocoa. Drink java, and unless it's shade-grown, you could be accused of encouraging destruction of South American rain forests to make room for your coffee beans. Even your table's floral centerpiece carries implications. Half the cut flowers sold in the United States are grown in Colombia, where human-rights groups say farmworkers are exposed to dangerous amounts of pesticides.

Kate Van Ummersen, who sells cheese made by dairies that shun antibiotics and hormones, tried briefly and largely in vain to peddle organic flowers in the Pacific Northwest. She touted them as more people- and planet-friendly than imported flowers.

"People would say, 'Why should I care? I don't eat flowers,'" she said. "They just weren't willing to pay a premium for organic flowers."

For Class Discussion

1. What is Scott Canon's main purpose in this loosely structured argument?

2. Canon quotes a number of stakeholders as authoritative representatives of their respective groups. How well do these quotations contribute to the ideas and persuasiveness of this piece?

3. How has this article influenced the way that you view global food production and the food you eat?

Technology That Will Save Billions from Starvation
C. S. Prakash and Gregory Conko

Gregory Conko is vice president of the AgBioWorld Foundation and a senior fellow and director of food safety policy at the Competitive Enterprise Institute, a policy think tank devoted to "free enterprise and limited government" ("About CEI," www.cei.org). He has published extensively on the safety of pharmaceutical drugs and bioengineered foods, including the book *The Frankenfood Myth: How Protest and Politics Threaten the Biotech Revolution* (2004, coauthored with Henry I. Miller). C. S. Prakash started AgBioWorld Foundation, a nonprofit organization that does not accept financial support from biotech corporations and that seeks to "provide information to teachers, journalists, policymakers, and the general public about developments in plant science biotechnology, and sustainable agriculture" (www.agbioworld.org). Prakash is a world-renowned scientific researcher, professor, scholar, and director of the Center for Plant

Biotechnology Research at Tuskegee University, Alabama. Known for promoting biotechnology research in developing countries and training students and scholars from these countries, he has written prolifically to gain the public's acceptance of plant biotechnology. This policy argument was published by *The American Enterprise* on March 1, 2004, and posted on the AgBioWorld Foundation site.

> How do this argument's claim, structure, treatment of scientific ideas and terms indicate that it is intended to reach both people well-versed in biotechnology and a less-informed general public?

Today, most people around the world have access to a greater variety of nutritious and affordable foods than ever before, thanks mainly to developments in agricultural science and technology. The average human life span—arguably the most important indicator of quality of life—has increased steadily in the past century in almost every country. Even in many less developed countries, life spans have doubled over the past few decades. Despite massive population growth, from 3 billion to more than 6 billion people since 1950, the global malnutrition rate decreased in that period from 38 percent to 18 percent. India and China, two of the world's most populous and rapidly industrializing countries, have quadrupled their grain production.

The record of agricultural progress during the past century speaks for itself. Countries that embraced superior agricultural technologies have brought unprecedented prosperity to their people, made food vastly more affordable and abundant, helped stabilize farm yields, and reduced the destruction of wild lands. The productivity gains from G.M. crops, as well as improved use of synthetic fertilizers and pesticides, allowed the world's farmers to double global food output during the last 50 years, on roughly the same amount of land, at a time when global population rose more than 80 percent. Without these improvements in plant and animal genetics and other scientific developments, known as the Green Revolution, we would today be farming on every square inch of arable land to produce the same amount of food, destroying hundreds of millions of acres of pristine wilderness in the process.

Many less developed countries in Latin America and Asia benefited tremendously from the Green Revolution. But due to a variety of reasons, both natural and human, agricultural technologies were not spread equally across the globe. Many people in sub-Saharan Africa and parts of South Asia continue to suffer from abject rural poverty driven by poor farm productivity. Some 740 million people go to bed daily on an empty stomach, and nearly 40,000 people—half of them children—die every day of starvation or malnutrition. Unless trends change soon, the number of undernourished could well surpass 1 billion by 2020.

The U.N. Food and Agriculture Organization (FAO) expects the world's population to grow to more than 8 billion by 2030. The FAO projects that global food production must increase by 60 percent to accommodate the estimated population growth, close nutrition gaps, and allow for dietary changes over the next three decades. Food charity alone simply cannot eradicate hunger. Increased supply—with the help of tools like bioengineering—is crucial.

Although better farm machinery and development of fertilizers, insecticides, and herbicides have been extremely useful, an improved understanding of genetic principles has been the most important factor in improving food production. Every crop is a product of repeated genetic editing by humans over the past few millennia. Our ancestors chose a few once-wild plants and gradually modified them simply by selecting those with the largest, tastiest, or most robust offspring for propagation. Organisms have been altered over the millennia so greatly that traits present in existing populations of cultivated rice, wheat, corn, soy, potatoes, tomatoes and many others have very little in common with their ancestors. Wild tomatoes and potatoes contain very potent toxins, for example. Today's cultivated varieties have been modified to produce healthy and nutritious food.

Hybridization, the mating of different plants of the same species, has helped us assimilate desirable traits from several varieties into elite specimens. And when desired characteristics were unavailable in cultivated plants, genes were liberally borrowed from wild relatives and introduced into crop varieties, often of different but related species. Wheat, rye, and barley are regularly mated with wild grass species to introduce new traits. Commercial tomato plants are commonly bred with wild tomatoes to introduce improved resistance to pathogens, nematodes, and fungi. Successive generations then have to be carefully backcrossed into the commercial cultivars to eliminate any unwanted traits accidentally transferred from the wild plants, such as toxins common in the wild species.

Even when crop and wild varieties refuse to mate, various tricks can be used to produce "wide crosses" between two plants that are otherwise sexually incompatible. Often, though, the embryos created by wide crosses die before they mature, so they must be "rescued" and cultured in a laboratory. Even then, the rescued embryos typically produce sterile offspring. They can only be made fertile again by using chemicals that cause the plants to mutate and produce a duplicate set of chromosomes. The plant triticale, an artificial hybrid of wheat and rye, is one such example of a wide-cross hybrid made possible solely by the existence of embryo rescue and chromosome doubling techniques. Triticale is now grown on over 3 million acres worldwide, and dozens of other products of wide-cross hybridization are common.

When a desired trait cannot be found within the existing gene pool, breeders can create new variants by intentionally mutating plants with radiation, with chemicals, or simply by culturing clumps of cells in a Petri dish and leaving them to mutate spontaneously during cell division. Mutation breeding has been in common use since the 1950s, and more than 2,250 known mutant varieties have been bred in at least 50 countries, including France, Germany, Italy, the United Kingdom, and the United States. A relatively new mutant wheat variety, made to be resistant to a commercial herbicide, was put on the market in the U.S. as recently as July 2003.

Recombinant DNA (rDNA) methods are a recent extension of the myriad techniques that have been employed to modify and improve crops. The primary difference is that modern bioengineered crops involve a precise transfer of one or two known genes into plant DNA—a surgical alteration of a tiny part of the crop's genome compared to the traditional sledgehammer approaches, which bring about gross genetic changes, many of which are unknown and unpredictable.

Crops enhanced through modern biotechnology are now grown in 16 countries.

Leading scientists around the world have attested to the health and environmental safety of agricultural biotechnology, and they have called for bioengineered crops to be extended to those who need them most— hungry people in the developing world. Dozens of scientific and health associations, including the U.S. National Academy of Sciences, the American Medical Association, the U.K.'s Royal Society, and the United Nations Development Programme, have endorsed the technology. Nearly 3,500 eminent scientists from all around the world, including 24 Nobel laureates, have signed a declaration supporting the use of agricultural biotechnology. And a review of 81 separate research projects conducted over 15 years—all funded by the European Union—found that bioengineered crops and foods are at least as safe for the environment and for human consumption as conventional crops, and in some cases even safer.

Crops enhanced through modern biotechnology are now grown on nearly 143 million acres in 16 countries. More important, more than three quarters of the 5.5 million growers who benefit from bioengineered crops are resource-poor farmers in the developing world. Unremarkably, most commercially available biotech plants were designed for farmers in the industrialized world. They include varieties of corn, soybean, potato, and cotton modified to resist insect pests, [to resist] plant diseases, and to make weed control easier. However, the increasing adoption of bioengineered varieties by farmers in developing countries over the past few years has shown that they can benefit at least as much as, if not more than, their industrialized counterparts. The productivity of farmers everywhere is limited by crop pests and diseases—and these are often far worse in tropical and subtropical regions than the temperate zones.

About 20 percent of plant productivity in the industrialized world, and up to 40 percent in Africa and Asia, is lost to insects and pathogens, despite the ongoing use of copious amounts of pesticides. The European corn borer destroys approximately 7 percent, or 40 million tons, of the world's corn crop each year—equivalent to the annual food supply for 60 million people. So it comes as no surprise that, when they are permitted to grow bioengineered varieties, poor farmers in less developed nations have eagerly snapped them up. According to the International Service for the Acquisition of Agri-Biotech Applications, farmers in less developed countries now grow nearly one quarter of the world's bioengineered crops on more than 26 million acres.

Bioengineered plants have also had other important benefits for farmers in less developed countries. In China, where pesticides are typically sprayed on crops by hand, some 400 to 500 cotton farmers die every year from acute pesticide poisoning. Researchers at Rutgers University and the Chinese Academy of Sciences found that using bioengineered cotton in China has lowered the amount of pesticides by more than 75 percent and reduced the number of pesticide poisonings by an equivalent amount. Another study by economists at the University of Reading in Britain found that South African cotton farmers have seen similar benefits.

The reduction in pesticide spraying also means that fewer natural resources are consumed to manufacture and transport the chemicals. In 2000 alone, U.S. farmers growing bioengineered cotton used 2.4 million fewer gallons of fuel and 93 million fewer gallons of water, and were spared some 41,000 ten-hour days needed to apply pesticide.

Soon, many bioengineered varieties that have been created specifically for use in underdeveloped countries will be ready for commercialization. Examples include insect-resistant rice for Asia, virus-resistant sweet potato for Africa, and virus-resistant papaya for Caribbean nations. The next generation of bioengineered crops now in research labs around the world is poised to bring even further improvements for the poor soils and harsh climates that are characteristic of impoverished regions. Scientists have already identified genes resistant to environmental stresses common in tropical nations, including tolerance to soils with high salinity and to those that are particularly acidic or alkaline.

The primary reason why Africa never benefited from the Green Revolution is that plant breeders focused on improving crops such as rice, wheat, and corn, which are not widely grown in Africa. Also, much of the African dry lands have little rainfall and no potential for irrigation, both of which played essential roles in the success stories for crops such as Asian rice. Furthermore, the remoteness of many African villages and the poor transportation infrastructure in landlocked African countries make it difficult for African farmers to obtain agricultural chemical inputs such as fertilizers, insecticides, and herbicides—even if they could be donated by charities, or if they had the money to purchase them. But, by packaging technological inputs within seeds, biotechnology can provide the same, or better, productivity advantage as chemical or mechanical inputs, and in a much more user-friendly manner. Farmers would be able to control insects, viral or bacterial pathogens, extremes of heat or drought, and poor soil quality, just by planting these crops.

Still, anti-biotechnology activists like Vandana Shiva of the New Delhi-based Research Foundation for Science, Technology and Ecology, and Miguel Altieri of the University of California at Berkeley, argue that poor farmers in less developed nations will never benefit from biotechnology because it is controlled by multinational corporations. According to Altieri, "Most innovations in agricultural biotechnology have been profit-driven rather than need-driven. The real thrust of the genetic engineering industry is not to make Third World agriculture more productive, but rather to generate profits."

That sentiment is not shared by the thousands of academic and public sector researchers actually working on biotech applications in those countries. Cyrus Ndiritu, former director of the Kenyan Agricultural Research Institute, argues, "It is not the multinationals that have a stranglehold on Africa. It is hunger, poverty and deprivation. And if Africa is going to get out of that, it has got to embrace" biotechnology.

Biotechnology also offers hope of improving the nutritional benefits of many foods. The next generation of bioengineered products now in development is poised to bring direct health benefits to consumers through enhanced nutritive qualities that include more and higher-quality protein, lower levels of saturated fat, increased vitamins and minerals, and many others. Bioengineering can also reduce the level of natural toxins (such as in cassava and kidney beans) and eliminate certain allergens from foods like peanuts, wheat, and milk. Many of these products are being developed primarily or even exclusively for subsistence farmers and consumers in poor countries.

> **Biotechnology also offers hope of improving the nutritional benefits of many foods.**

Among the most well known is Golden Rice—genetically enhanced with added beta carotene, which is converted to Vitamin A in the human body. Another variety developed by the same research team has elevated levels of digestible iron. The diet of more than 3 billion people worldwide includes inadequate levels of essential vitamins and minerals, such as Vitamin A and iron. Deficiency in just these two micronutrients can result in severe anemia, impaired intellectual development, blindness, and even death. Even though charities and aid agencies such as the United Nations Children's Fund and the World Health Organization have made important strides in reducing Vitamin A and iron deficiency, success has been fleeting. No permanent effective strategy has yet been devised, but Golden Rice may finally provide one.

The Golden Rice project is a prime example of the value of extensive public sector and charitable research. The rice's development was funded mainly by the New York-based Rockefeller Foundation, which has promised to make the rice available to poor farmers at little or no cost. Scientists at public universities in Switzerland and Germany created it with assistance from the Philippines-based International Rice Research Institute and from several multinational corporations. Scientists at publicly funded, charitable, and corporate research centers are developing many other similar crops. Indian scientists, for example, have recently announced that they would soon make a new high-protein potato variety available for commercial cultivation.

Research is already under way on fruits and vegetables that could one day deliver life-saving vaccines—such as a banana with the vaccine for Hepatitis B, and a potato that provides immunization against diarrheal diseases.

It is true that certain aspects of modern farming have had a negative impact on biodiversity and on air, soil, and water quality. But biotechnology has proven safer for the environment than anything since the invention of the plow. The risk of cross-pollination from crops to wild relatives has always existed, and such "gene flow" occurs whenever crops grow in close proximity to sexually compatible wild relatives. Yet, breeders have continuously introduced genes for disease and pest resistance through conventional breeding into all of our crops. Traits, such as stress tolerance and herbicide resistance, have also been introduced in some crops with conventional techniques, and the growth habits of every crop have been altered. Thus, not only is gene modification a common phenomenon, but so are many of the specific kinds of changes made with rDNA techniques.

Naturally, with both conventional and rDNA-enhanced breeding, we must be vigilant to ensure that newly introduced plants do not become invasive and that weeds do not become noxious because of genetic modification. Similarly, we must ensure that target genes are safe for human and animal consumption before they are transferred. But, while modern genetic modification expands the range of new traits that can be added to crop plants, it also ensures that more will be known about those traits and that the behavior of the modified plants will be, in many ways, easier to predict.

The biggest threats that hungry populations currently face are restrictive policies stemming from unwarranted public fears. Although most Americans tend to support agricultural biotechnology, many Europeans and Asians have been far more cautious. Anti-biotechnology campaigners in both industrialized and less developed nations are feeding this ambivalence with scare stories that have led to the adoption of restrictive policies. Those fears are simply not supported by the scores of peer reviewed scientific reports or the data from tens of thousands of individual field trials.

In the end, over-cautious rules result in hyper-inflated research and development costs and make it harder for poorer countries to share in the benefits of biotechnology. No one argues that we should not proceed with caution, but needless restrictions on agricultural biotechnology could dramatically slow the pace of progress and keep important advances out of the hands of people who need them. This is the tragic side effect of unwarranted concern.

In 2002, Zambian President Levy Mwanawasa rejected some 23,000 metric tons of food aid in the midst of a two-year-long drought that threatened the lives of over 2 million Zambians. President Mwanawasa's public explanation was that the bioengineered corn from the United States was "poisonous." Other Zambian government officials conceded that the bigger concern was for future corn exports to the European Union, which observes a moratorium on new G.M. foods.

Zambia is not unique. European biotechnology restrictions have had other, similar consequences throughout the developing world. Thai government officials have been reluctant to authorize any bioengineered rice varieties, even though it has spent heavily on biotechnology research. Uganda has stopped research on bioengineered bananas and postponed their introduction indefinitely. Argentina has limited its approvals to the two bioengineered crop varieties that are already permitted in European markets.

Even China, which has spent hundreds of millions of dollars funding advanced biotechnology research, has refused to authorize any new bioengineered food crops since the European Union's moratorium on bioengineered crop approvals began in 1998. More recently, the International Rice Research Institute, which has been assigned the task of field-testing Golden Rice, has indefinitely postponed its plans for environmental release in the Philippines, fearing backlash from European-funded NGO protestors. Still, the E.U. moratorium continues to persist after five long years, despite copious evidence, including from the E.U.'s own researchers, that biotech modification does not pose any risks that aren't also present in other crop-breeding methods.

> Of course, hunger and malnutrition are not solely caused by a shortage of food.

Of course, hunger and malnutrition are not solely caused by a shortage of food. The primary causes of hunger in some countries have been political unrest and corrupt governments, poor transportation and infrastructure and, of course, poverty. All of these problems must be addressed if we are to ensure real, worldwide food security.

But during the next 50 years, the global population is expected to rise by 50 percent—to 9 billion people, almost entirely in the poorest regions of the world. And producing enough to feed these people will require the use of the invaluable gift of biotechnology.

For Class Discussion

1. What is the core claim of Prakash and Conko's case in favor of food biotechnology? What are their reasons?

2. What assumptions have Prakash and Conko made about the world's food problem and the process and products of plant bioengineering? How do the assumptions of their opponents differ?

3. Prakash and Conko are very conscious of arguing against opponents of plant biotechnology. How do they summarize these views? How do they seek to refute them? Where do Prakash and Conko make concessions?

4. Golden rice is a favorite example of biotech proponents. How do Prakash and Conko use golden rice in this argument? How do they use their professional backgrounds to bolster their argument?

5. What are this piece's strongest points? How has it influenced your understanding of biotechnology's potential to combat world hunger? ∎

Biotech Snake Oil: A Quack Cure for Hunger
Bill Freese

Bill Freese is a science policy analyst at the Center for Food Safety, a nonprofit public interest and environmental advocacy organization established for the purpose of "curtailing industrial agricultural production methods that harm human health and the environment, and promoting sustainable alternatives" ("What We Do," www.centerforfoodsafety.org). He has authored numerous reports on the science and regulation of genetically engineered crops. His recent work addresses genetically engineered (GE) crops, industrial biotechnology, and cost-effective alternatives to genetic engineering. This policy analysis argument was published in the September/October 2008 issue of the *Multinational Monitor*, a journal that tracks corporate activity with a particular focus on third world business and the environment.

> What attracts or intrigues readers about Bill Freese's choice of title? What cultural and historical knowledge is it helpful to have to experience its full rhetorical effect?

Rising global food prices reached a flash point this spring, sparking food riots in over a dozen countries. Mexican tortillas have quadrupled in price; Haiti's prime minister was ousted amid rice riots; African countries were especially hard hit. According to the World Bank, global food prices have risen a shocking 83 percent over the past three years. And for the world's poor, high prices mean hunger.

The global food crisis has many causes, but according to the biotechnology industry, there's a simple solution—genetically modified, or biotech, crops. Biotech multinationals have been in media blitz mode ever since the food crisis first made headlines, touting miracle crops that will purportedly increase yields, tolerate droughts, grow in saline soils, and be chockfull of nutrients, to boot.

"If we are to achieve the Millennium Development Goals of cutting hunger and poverty in half by 2015," says Clive James, founder of the International Service for the Acquisition of Agri-biotech Applications (ISAAA), an organization whose funders include all the major biotech companies, "biotech crops must play an even bigger role in the next decade."

Not everyone is convinced. In fact, the UN and World Bank recently completed an unprecedentedly broad scientific assessment of world agriculture, the International Assessment of Agricultural Knowledge, Science and Technology for Development (IAASTD), which concluded that biotech crops have very little potential to alleviate poverty and hunger. This four-year effort, which engaged some 400 experts from multiple disciplines, originally included industry representatives. Just three months before the final report was released, however, Monsanto, Syngenta and chemical giant BASF pulled out of the process, miffed by the poor marks given their favorite technology. This withdrawal upset even the industry-friendly journal *Nature,* which chided the companies in an editorial entitled, "Deserting the Hungry?"

SERVING THE WEALTHY

Genetic engineering involves the laboratory-based transfer of DNA derived from bacteria, viruses or virtually any living organism into plants to endow them with a desired trait. As implemented by biotechnology firms, critics say genetic engineering has trod the well-worn path of previous innovations of industrial agriculture—serving wealthier farmers growing commodity crops in huge monocultures by saving labor through the use of expensive inputs.

Biotech proponents insist genetically modified (GM) seeds are delivering results for farmers. "Already in its first 12 years, this technology has made a significant impact by lifting the incomes of farmers," says James.

But genetically modified crops are heavily concentrated in a handful of countries with industrialized, export-oriented agricultural sectors. Nearly 90 percent of biotech acres in 2007 were found in just six countries of North and South America, with the United States, Argentina, and Brazil accounting for 80 percent. For most other countries, including India and China, biotech crops account for 3 percent or less of total harvested crop area.

Commercialized GM crops are confined to soybeans, corn, cotton, and canola. Soybeans and corn predominate, and are used mainly to feed animals or fuel cars in rich nations. For instance, Argentina and Brazil export the great majority of their soybeans as livestock feed, mainly to Europe and Japan, while more than three fourths of the U.S. corn crop is either fed to animals or used to generate ethanol for automobiles. Expanding soybean monocultures in South America are displacing small farmers, who grow food crops for local consumption, and thus contribute to food insecurity, especially in Argentina and Paraguay. The only other commercial GM crops are papaya and squash, both grown on miniscule acreage.

Most revealing, however, is what the biotech industry has engineered these crops for. Hype and promises of future innovations notwithstanding, there is not a single commercial GM crop with increased yield, drought-tolerance, salt-tolerance, enhanced nutrition or other attractive-sounding traits touted by the industry. Disease-resistant GM crops are practically non-existent.

"We have yet to see genetically modified food that is cheaper, more nutritious or tastes better," says Hope Shand, research director for the Ontario-based ETC Group. "Biotech seeds have not been shown to be scientifically or socially useful."

The industry's own figures reveal that GM crops incorporate one or both of just two "traits"—herbicide tolerance and insect resistance. Insect-resistant cotton and corn produce their own "built-in" insecticide to protect against certain, but far from all, insect pests. Herbicide-tolerant crops are engineered to withstand direct application of an herbicide to kill nearby weeds. These crops predominate, with 82 percent of global biotech crop acreage.

Herbicide-tolerant crops (mainly soybeans) are popular with larger farmers because they simplify and reduce labor needs for weed control. They have thus helped facilitate the worldwide trend of consolidating farmland into fewer, ever bigger farms, like Argentina's huge soybean plantations. According to a 2004 study by Charles Benbrook, former executive director of the Board on Agriculture of the National Academy of Sciences, herbicide-tolerant crops have also led to a substantial increase in pesticide use. Benbrook's study found that adoption of herbicide-tolerant crops in the United States increased weed-killer use by 138 million pounds from 1996 to 2004 (while insect-resistant crops reduced insecticide use by just 16 million pounds over the same period).

The vast majority of herbicide-tolerant crops are Monsanto's "Roundup Ready" varieties, tolerant to the herbicide glyphosate, which is sold under the brand-name Roundup. The dramatic rise in glyphosate use associated with Roundup Ready crops has spawned an epidemic of glyphosate-resistant weeds, just as bacteria evolve resistance to an overused antibiotic. Farmers respond to resistant weeds by upping the dose of glyphosate and by using greater quantities of other herbicides, such as the probable carcinogen 2,4-D (a component of Agent Orange) and the endocrine-disrupting weed killer atrazine, recently banned in the European Union. Glyphosate-resistant weeds and rising herbicide use are becoming serious problems in the United States, Argentina and Brazil.

"Roundup continues to be the cornerstone of weed management for farms today and provides a lot of value to farmers," responds Darren Wallis, a Monsanto spokesperson. "We have some online tools to help farmers manage any weed control issues that they might have. There have been some documented cases of weed resistance, but Roundup continues to control hundreds of weeds very effectively."

Critics retort that resistant weeds are spreading despite Monsanto's efforts, and that a technology often promoted as moving agriculture beyond the era of chemicals has in fact increased chemical dependency and accelerated the pesticide treadmill of industrial agriculture. And, of course, expensive inputs like herbicides (the price of glyphosate has doubled over the past year) are beyond the means of most poor farmers.

What about yield and profitability? The most widely cultivated biotech crop, Roundup Ready soybeans, actually suffers from a 5 to 10 percent lower yield versus conventional varieties, according to a University of Nebraska study, due to both adverse effects of glyphosate on the soybean's nutrient uptakes, as well as unintended effects of the genetic engineering process used to create the plant. Unintended, yield-lowering effects are a serious though little-acknowledged technical obstacle of genetic engineering, and are one of several factors foiling efforts to develop viable GM crops with drought-tolerance, disease-resistance and other traits.

> **Critics retort that resistant weeds are spreading despite Monsanto's efforts...**

Monsanto says yield problems occurred only in the first year Roundup Ready soy was introduced, and that initial problems have been cured. "The first year we came out with Roundup Ready soybeans, there was a slight yield drag, but we improved the [seed] in subsequent years," says Brad Mitchell, Monsanto spokesperson.

Critics dispute this assertion, citing a 2007 study by Kansas State University which found that Roundup Ready soybean yields continue to lag behind those of conventional varieties.

Clive James of ISAAA points to the Asian experience with GM cotton, where he says small farmers are benefiting from biotech. More than 7 million farmers—representing some of the poorest in China—are seeing yields rise by 10 percent and pesticide use decline by half, he says. Farmer income is rising by approximately $220 a year, according to James.

But reviews of the Asian experience with GM cotton suggest that yield benefits are due more to good weather and other factors, not the use of biotech crops, and that GM cotton engineered for the shorter growing season in the U.S. sometimes fails to ward off targeted pests in India's longer growing season. It is true that insect resistant crops can reduce yield losses when infestation with targeted pests is severe. However, because cotton is afflicted with so many pests not killed by the built-in insecticide, biotech cotton farmers in India, China and elsewhere often apply as much chemical insecticide as growers of conventional cotton. But because they have paid up to four times as much for the biotech seed as they would for conventional seed, they often end up falling deeper into debt. Debt is an overriding problem among small farmers in developing countries, and any policies or technologies that deepen farmer debt have drastic consequences. Each year, hundreds of cotton farmers in India alone commit suicide from despair over insurmountable debts.

Even the U.S. Department of Agriculture (USDA) has found no economic benefit to farmers from growing GM crops in most situations.

SEED SERVITUDE

The agricultural biotechnology industry represents an historic merger of two distinct sectors—agrichemicals and seeds. In the 1990s, the world's largest pesticide makers—companies like Monsanto, DuPont, Bayer and Syngenta—began buying up the world's seed firms. These four biotech giants now control 41 percent of the world's commercial seed supply. Two factors drove this buying spree: the new technology of genetic engineering and the issuance of the first patents on seeds in the 1980s. Biotech firms saw that they could employ genetic engineering to develop herbicide-tolerant crops to exploit "synergies" between their seed and pesticide divisions. Seed patents enable owners to exert monopoly control over seeds, in part by enabling biotech firms to prevent farmers from saving seeds.

While patents on biotech seeds normally apply to inserted genes (or methods for introducing the gene), courts have interpreted these "gene patents" as granting biotech/seed firms comprehensive rights to the seeds that contain them. One consequence is that a farmer can be held liable for patent infringement even if the patented gene/plant appears in his fields through no fault of his own (e.g. cross-pollination or seed dispersal). Another consequence is that farmers can be sued for patent infringement—as well as for infringing sales contracts—if they save and replant seeds from their harvest, so-called "second-generation" seeds.

In the United States, industry leader Monsanto has pursued thousands of farmers for allegedly saving and replanting its patented

Roundup Ready soybean seeds. An analysis by the Center for Food Safety documented court-imposed payments of more than $21 million from farmers to Monsanto for alleged patent infringement. However, when one includes the much greater number of pretrial settlements, the total jumps to more than $85 million, collected from several thousand farmers.

Spurred on by the biotech multinationals, the U.S. and European governments are pressuring developing nations to adopt similar gene and seed patenting laws. This effort is being pursued through the World Trade Organization, which requires member nations to establish patent-style regimes for plants, as well as through bilateral trade agreements. Since an estimated 80 percent to 90 percent of seeds planted in poorer nations are produced on-farm (that is, they are saved from previous crops), the revenue to be gained from elimination of seed-saving in connection with the introduction of GM crops is considerable—conservatively estimated at tens of billions of dollars. If biotech/seed firms have their way, what farmer advocates call the "seed servitude" of U.S. farmers could soon become a global condition.

Biotech firms also have so-called Terminator and Traitor technologies waiting in the wings. Terminator is a genetic manipulation that renders harvested seed sterile, and represents a biological means to achieve the same end as patents: elimination of seed-saving. Traitor technology is similar, except that the second-generation seed sterility can be reversed upon application of a proprietary chemical. In this scenario, farmers would be allowed to save seed, but would have to purchase and apply a chemical to bring them back to life. While international outrage has thus far blocked deployment of Terminator, Monsanto recently purchased the seed company (Delta and Pine Land) that holds several major patents on the technology (together with the USDA). And while Monsanto has "pledged" not to deploy Terminator, the pledge is revocable at any time.

As the biotech multinationals tighten their stranglehold on the world's seed supply, farmers' choices are diminishing, and high-quality conventional seeds are rapidly disappearing from the marketplace. Biotech seeds presently cost two to four times as much as conventional varieties, or more. The price ratchets up with each new "trait" that is introduced. Seeds with one trait were once the norm, but are rapidly being replaced with two- and three-trait versions. As Monsanto put it in a presentation to investors, its overriding goal is "trait penetration" and investment in "penetration of higher-[profit-]margin traits." Monsanto and Dow recently announced plans to introduce GM corn with eight different traits (six insecticides and tolerance to two different herbicides). Farmers who want more affordable conventional seed, or even biotech seed with just one or two traits, may soon be out of luck. As University of Kentucky agronomist Chad Lee puts it: "The cost of corn seed keeps getting higher and there doesn't appear to be a stopping point in sight." While "trait penetration" is now chiefly a U.S. phenomenon, it is likely to be pursued throughout the world wherever GM crops become prevalent.

THE MANY USES OF BIOTECHNOLOGY

The tremendous hype surrounding biotech crops as a response to the food crisis does serve at least two purposes: as a "carrot" to persuade developing nations to adopt strict patent-style regimes for plants; and to divert attention from the underlying causes of the food crisis.

In 1991, the U.S. government and Monsanto funded development of a genetically modified virus-resistant sweet potato in collaboration with the Kenyan Agricultural Research Institute. Thirteen years later, the $6 million project was pronounced a dismal failure—the GM sweet potato did not resist the targeted virus, and yields were poor. However, it did help foster an atmosphere enabling introduction of other GM crops, and likely helped persuade Kenyan legislators to pass the Industrial Property Act in 2001, which according to patent expert Robert Lettington "may actually place very little restriction on the patenting of life forms at all." While the Kenyan project failed, a conventional breeding program in neighboring Uganda successfully bred a high-yielding, virus-resistant sweet potato in just a few years at a fraction of the cost. Many other biotech crop projects have also failed, including GM potatoes and tomatoes in Egypt, and GM corn and cotton in Indonesia.

Biotech mania has also diverted attention from the underlying social causes of the food crisis, which include diversion of food crops to make biofuels, and "trade liberalization" policies that have crippled developing country agriculture and made these nations dependent on subsidized surpluses from rich nations. "The structural causes" of the food crisis, says Anuradha Mittal, executive director of the Oakland Institute, "lie in policies of international financial institutions over the last 20 to 30 years, which have made developing countries so vulnerable in the first place." International Monetary Fund (IMF) and World Bank policies, she says, "eroded state and international investment in agriculture," as well as farmer support mechanisms such as state grain marketing agencies and subsidized agricultural services.

The IMF and World Bank also "promoted cash crops instead of domestic production of food for domestic consumption. All of those policies have basically removed the principle of self-sufficiency.

At the same time, you have had the lowering of tariffs which has resulted in the dumping of cheap, subsidized commodities from rich countries. With all of those policies, you find an erosion of the agricultural base of developing countries and their ability to feed themselves," says Mittal.

Eliminating agricultural self-sufficiency was an explicit objective of rich-country policies. As Reagan's agriculture secretary John Block expressed it with uncharacteristic candor in 1986: "The idea that developing countries should feed themselves is an anachronism from a bygone era. They could better ensure their food security by relying on U.S. agricultural products, which are available in most cases at lower cost."

The global food crisis underscores the bankruptcy of such policies. The flood of subsidized U.S. corn into Mexico facilitated by NAFTA has thrown at least 1.3 million Mexican farmers out of work. Haiti and the Philippines, once nearly self-sufficient in rice production, are now among the world's largest rice importers. Africa, a net food exporter in the 1960s, now imports 25 percent of its food. With the sharp rise in international grain prices, the reduced ability of poor nations to feed themselves presages increased hunger and poverty for many years to come. In fact, the food crisis recently prompted University of Minnesota food experts C. Ford Runge and Benjamin Senauer to double their projection of the number of the world's hungry by the year 2025, from 625 million to 1.2 billion. The UN-World Bank IAASTD report advocates "food sovereignty," defined as "the right of peoples and sovereign states to democratically determine their own agriculture and food policies."

TRUE SOLUTIONS

Another IAASTD recommendation is promotion of agroecological farming techniques suited to small farmers. Ever since the Green Revolution, the agricultural development establishment has focused primarily on high-tech crop breeding and expensive inputs (e.g. fertilizers, pesticides and "improved seeds"). These input-centered schemes offer potential market opportunities to multinational agribusinesses, but have generally favored wealthier growers over small farmers. In contrast, agroecology minimizes inputs, and relies instead on innovative cultivation and pest control practices to increase food production. A 2001 review of 200 developing country agricultural projects involving a switch to agroecological techniques, conducted by University of Essex researchers, found an average yield gain of 93 percent.

Control of insect pests through the introduction of natural predators has also achieved enormous success at low cost in Africa. One striking example is the introduction of insect predators to control a devastating cassava pest, which averted mass hunger in Africa in the 1980s and 1990s. A new dryland rice farming technique called the System of Rice Intensification dramatically increases yield, and is spreading rapidly in rice-growing nations, despite dismissal by the agricultural development establishment. Besides being low cost, agroecological techniques typically benefit smaller farmers.

GM REALITY CHECK

The tremendous hype surrounding biotechnology has obscured some basic facts. Most GM crops feed animals or fuel cars in rich nations; are engineered for use with expensive weed killers to save labor; and are grown by larger farmers in industrial monocultures for export.

"GM crops have nothing to do with feeding hungry people and nothing to do with sustainability," says Shand. "With the consolidation of the seed industry, seed companies' primary objective is to increase profits by restricting farmers' reliance on saved seeds."

For Class Discussion

1. How and where does Bill Freese summarize the protransgenic crops view and talk back to Prakash and Conko? How does his treatment of this opposing view contribute to the structure of his argument and to readers' impressions of his knowledge of the field and the reliability of his claims and evidence?

2. Freese claims that the biotech issue diverts attention from the underlying social causes of the food crisis. What evidence does he provide for this claim, and how does this explanation for third world poverty differ from that of supporters of transgenic crops?

3. Freese traces the history of biotech seeds and points out the stake that large corporations such as Monsanto and Syngenta hold in the development of biotechnology. How does he raise questions about values and the interpretation of facts? How does he develop the various economic and legal implications of transgenic seeds, for both its producers and its end users?

4. How does Freese argue against claims that biotechnology can create more healthful foods? What common arguments for biotech crops does Freese *not* address in this article?

5. What additional considerations has this article introduced into the debate on transgenic crops, and how has it contributed to your understanding of global hunger problems? ■

How We Can Feed the World
Mike Mack

Mike Mack is the chief executive officer of Syngenta, an agribusiness corporation that specializes in commercial seeds and crop protection products to "help growers worldwide raise the quantity and quality of their crops" and that is "committed to sustainable agriculture—farming with future generations in mind" ("Vision and Business Principles," syngenta.com). Mack has an MBA from Harvard University, and his previous positions within the company include Chief Operating Officer of Seeds and Head of Crop Protection, NAFTA Region. This article appeared in a special 2009 edition of *Newsweek* titled "How to Fix the World: A Guide for the Next President" under the subheading "The Economy."

> What political and economic issues does Mack allude to in this short policy argument on the importance of biotechnology?

The need to address food security has never been greater. In 2050 the world's population is expected to increase to 9 billion, up from 6.5 billion today. Recession and environmental stresses are deepening existing fears and insecurities associated with the future availability of quality, affordable food. Fortunately, one of the best assets we have to tackle these challenges is the U.S. farmer. With technology and global collaboration, farmers around the world can feed the growing population. As president of the United States, Barack Obama will be in a unique position to help in this endeavor by keeping global trade, agricultural policy, science and innovation high on America's agenda.

In the United States, farmers have successfully demonstrated the value of technology, not only through the use of seed- and crop-protection products like Syngenta's but also by adopting modern, advanced farming practices.

Unfortunately, however, many other nations have been less receptive to agricultural science and innovation. In the European Union, the use of biotechnology in crops has still not been accepted and further constraints are being placed on farmers' ability to use yield-enhancing crop-protection products. Europe needs a political and regulatory environment that is predictable and science-based, not politicized. Regulations currently being reviewed by the European Parliament would reduce wheat and other cereal production across Europe by 30 percent. Also, several biotech corn products that Europe's farmers could use to increase the quality and yield of their corn have received a positive risk assessment by the European Food Safety Authority, but they languish within the political process. In a world where food security affects every one of us, it is critical that farmers across the globe have access to the technology that will help them produce more food in a responsible and safe manner.

At the same time, many myths associated with modern farming practices must be debunked. Without the use of pesticides, for example, it is estimated that up to 40 percent of the world's crops would be lost to insects, weeds and disease. Both biotechnology and pesticides are highly regulated and rigorously tested by government agencies and manufacturers. What's more, agricultural science has demonstrated on many occasions the powerful, positive impact it can have on community welfare and poverty reduction.

The public needs to be better informed about these facts. A rising population puts increased pressure on the planet's limited natural resources. These strains are exacerbated by climate change and the increasing demands on our water supplies. Technology and sustainable land use offer solutions to tackle these limitations while helping farmers to produce higher yields. This applies to both food and crops for fuel. Today's first-generation biofuels are the building block for next-generation technology. This technology needs continued investment and support to achieve its potential.

In the past 50 years, we have vastly increased the production of high-quality affordable food thanks to innovation in farming practices and technology. Syngenta and other leading companies spend some $3 billion every year on agricultural research. And the more we discover, the more we realize the untapped potential of plants.

But as important as private-sector investment is, feeding the world will require greater governmental involvement. Governments must strengthen efforts in science education and increase research funding. They must also prioritize free trade, which has the potential to transform the agricultural sector. More open trade is the only way to get food to those who need it and are not able to produce enough themselves. President Obama should support the completion of the Doha Round of trade talks and recommit U.S. resources to hammering out bilateral agreements as well.

More open trade must also be accompanied by a coherent global framework for assessing food safety. The differences in safety standards that exist today among the biggest trading partners for major crops produced through biotechnology are only exacerbating food security challenges.

Nations that are more skeptical than the United States about new agricultural technology, such as the use of pesticides and biotechnology, should observe America's ongoing success in developing more food, feed and fuel without compromising food safety. Science-based regulations ensure that everyone wins—consumers, the environment, farmers and industry.

Given the size and power of the United States, the example set by the new administration will be critical in setting the tone for the future of food innovation. The challenge in agriculture today is to produce more with less. To do so, we need a progressive approach to policymaking that respects and advocates science and innovation and takes a global view. Farmers around the world are capable of producing enough food in a sustainable way. More trade, science-based regulation and the acceptance of innovation, coupled with renewed collaborative efforts by industry, are the only way to meet the growing challenges we all face. The world just needs committed, courageous leadership to pave the way.

For Class Discussion

1. How does this argument appeal to its primary audience, President Obama, and to the more general audience of the weekly news magazine?

2. How does Mack emphasize the U.S. role in global food security?

3. How do Mack's repeated appeals to science and innovation suggest his views on opponents of biotechnology?

4. "Sustainability" is a main concern of environmentalists and social activists. How do this article and Syngenta's vision statement define it? How might this differ from the concept of sustainability put forth by other authors in this chapter?

5. On what policy points do Mack and Freese disagree? How do their backgrounds, affiliations, and values inform their arguments on these points?

Competition
Ángel Boligán

Ángel Boligán works for the Mexico City newspaper *El Universal* and has received many international awards. His cartoons are syndicated and archived on www.cagle.com.

What argument does this cartoon make about the relationship between developing countries like Mexico and developed countries like the United States?

For Class Discussion

1. How do the images in this cartoon make an emotional appeal to readers? What knowledge does it assume?

2. Whom is this cartoon criticizing? Is this cartoon criticizing more than one group?

3. Political cartoons often appear in response to a specific occasion or event. What circumstances might have motivated Bolígan to produce this cartoon?

4. What deeper message does this cartoon convey about world hunger and poverty, developing countries, and developed countries?

5. Within this chapter, what new perspective on world hunger does this cartoon present? What arguments does it join, extend, or echo?

Gift of Food: How to Solve the Agricultural Crisis, the Health Crisis, and the Crisis of Poverty
Vandana Shiva

Vandana Shiva, who has a doctorate in physics, is an internationally known environmentalist, social activist, feminist, and vocal opponent of corporate globalization. She has authored several books about the corporate takeover of agriculture in India and other developing countries, including *Stolen Harvest: The Hijacking of the Global Food Supply* (2000), *Earth Democracy: Justice, Sustainability, and Peace* (2005), and most recently, *Soil Not Oil: Environmental Justice in an Age of Climate Crisis* (2008). She is director of the Research Foundation for Science, Technology, and Ecology and of Bija Vidyapeeth, the International College for Sustainable Living in Dehra Dun, India. In 1993, she won the Alternative Nobel Peace Prize (the Right Livelihood Award). She writes political/economic/environmental commentaries regularly, frequently for *Resurgence*, a magazine devoted to "connecting you to a world of ecology, art, and culture" (www.resurgence.org). This article was published in the August 2005 issue of *Resurgence*.

What deep values held by Vandana Shiva, concerning the spiritual and ethical view of food and nature, emerge in this argument?

The first thing to recognise about food is that it is the very basis of life. Food is alive: it is not just pieces of carbohydrate, protein, and nutrient, it is a being, a sacred being. Not only is food sacred, not only is it living, but it is the Creator itself, and that is why in the poorest of Indian huts you find the little earthen stove being worshipped; the first piece of bread is given to the cow, then you are required to find out who else is hungry in your area. In the words of the sacred texts of India, "The giver of food is the giver of life," and indeed of everything else. Therefore, one who desires wellbeing in this world and beyond should especially endeavour to give food.

Because food is the very basis of creation, food is creation, and it is the Creator. There are all kinds of duties that we should be performing with respect to food. If people have food it is because society has not forgotten those duties. If people are hungry, society has rejected the ethical duties related to food.

The very possibility of our being alive is based on the lives of all kinds of beings that have gone before us—our parents, the soil, the earthworm—and that is why the giving of food in Indian thought has been treated as everyday sacrifice that we have to perform. It is a ritual embodied in every meal, reflecting the recognition that giving is the condition of our very being. We do not give as an extra, we give because of our interdependence with all of life.

One of my favourite images in India is the kolam, a design which a woman makes in front of her house. In the days of Pongal, which is the rice harvest festival in South India, I have seen women get up before dawn to make the most beautiful art work outside their houses, and it is always made with rice. The real reason is to feed the ants, but it is also a beautiful art form that has gone on from mother to daughter, and at festival time everyone tries to make the best kolam as their offering. Thus, feeding the ants and works of art are integrated.

The indica rice variety's homeland is a tribal area called Chattisgarh in India. It must be about fifteen years ago that I first went there. The people there weave beautiful designs of paddy, which they then hang outside their houses. I thought that this must be related to a particular festival, and I asked, "What festival is it for?" They said, "No, no, this is for the season when the birds cannot get rice grain in the fields." They were putting rice out for other species, in very beautiful offerings of art work.

Because we owe the conditions of our life to all other beings and all other creatures, giving—to humans and to non-human species—has inspired annadana, the gift of food. All other ethical arrangements in society get looked after if everyone is engaging in annadana on a daily basis. According to an ancient Indian saying: "There is no gift greater than annadana, the giving of food." Or again, in the words of the sacred texts: "Do not send away anyone who comes to your door without offering him or her food and hospitality. This is the inviolable discipline of humankind; therefore have a great abundance of food and exert all your efforts towards ensuring such abundance, and announce to the world that this abundance of food is ready to be partaken by all."

Thus from the culture of giving you have the conditions of abundance, and the sharing by all.

If we really look at what is happening in the world, we seem to have more and more food surpluses, while 820 million people still go hungry every day. As an ecologist, I see these surpluses as pseudo-surpluses. They are pseudo-surpluses because the overflowing stocks and packed supermarket shelves are the result of production and distribution systems which take food away from the weak and marginalized, and from non-human species.

I went through the food department of Marks & Spencer the other day, and I went dizzy seeing all the food there, because I knew that, for example, a peasant's rice field would have been converted into a banana plantation to get luscious bananas to the world's markets. Each time I see a supermarket, I see how every community and ecosystem's capacity to meet its food needs is being undermined, so that a few people in the world can experience food "surpluses".

But these are pseudo-surpluses leading to 820 million malnourished people, while many others eat too much and get ill or obese.

Let us see how food is produced. To have sustainable food supplies we need our soils to function as living systems: we need all those millions of soil organisms that make fertility. And that fertility gives us healthy foods. In industrial cultures we forget that it is the earthworm that creates soil fertility; we believe that soil fertility can come from nitrates—the surplus of explosives factories; that pest-control does not come out of the balance of different crops hosting different species, but from poisons. When you have the right balance, living organisms never become pests: they all coexist, and none of them destroys your crop.

The recently released report of the Food and Agriculture Organization has chart after chart to show how in the last century we increased food productivity. But all they really calculated is labour displacement. They only looked at labor productivity—as how much food a human being produces by using technologies that are labour-displacing, species-displacing and resource-destroying. It does not mean that you have more food per acre; it does not mean that you have more food per unit used of water; it does not mean that you have more food for all the other species that need food. All of these diverse needs are being destroyed as we define productivity on the basis of food production per unit of labour.

We are now working on technologies, based on genetic engineering, which accelerate this violence towards other beings. On my recent trip to Punjab, it suddenly hit me that they no longer have pollinators. Those technologically obsessed people are manipulating crops to put genes from the Bt toxin (the soil bacterium Bacillus thuringiensis) into plants, so that the plant releases toxins at every moment and in every cell: in its leaves, its roots, its pollen. These toxins are being eaten by ladybirds and butterflies which then die.

We do not see the web of life that we are rupturing. We can only see the interconnections if we are sensitive to them. And when we are aware of them we immediately recognise what we owe to other beings: to the pollinators, to the farmers who have produced the food, and to the people who have nourished us when we could not nourish ourselves.

The giving of food is related to the idea that every one of us is born in debt to other beings: Our very condition of being born depends on this debt. So we come with a debt and for the rest of our lives we are paying back that debt—to the bees and the butterflies that pollinate our crops, to the earthworms and the fungi and the microbes and the bacteria in the soil that are constantly working away to create the fertility that our chemical fertilisers can never, never replenish.

We are born and live in debt to all Creation, and it becomes our duty to recognise this. The gift of food is merely a recognition of the need for constantly paying back that obligation, that responsibility. It is merely a matter of accepting and endeavouring to repay our debts to Creation, and to the communities of which we are a part. And that is why most cultures that have seen ecology as a sacred trust have always spoken of responsibility. Rights have flowed out of responsibility: once I ensure that everyone in my sphere of influence is fed, someone in that sphere is also ensuring that I am fed.

When I left university teaching in 1982, everyone said, "How will you manage without a salary?" I replied by saying that if ninety per cent of India manages without a salary, all I have to do is put my life in the kind of relationships of trust that they live through. If you give, then you will receive. You do not have to calculate the receiving: What you have to be conscious of is the giving.

> **The giving of food is related to the idea that every one is born in debt to other beings.**

In modern economic systems we also have debts, but they are financial debts. A child born in any Third World country already has millions of dollars of debt on her or his head owed to the World Bank, which has every power to tell you and your country that you should not be producing food for the earthworms and the birds, or even for the people of the land: You should be growing shrimps and flowers for export, because that earns money.

It does not earn very much money, either. I have made calculations that show that one dollar of trading by international business, in terms of profit, leads to $10 of ecological and economic destruction in local ecosystems. Now if for every dollar being traded we have a $10 shadow-cost in terms of how we are literally robbing food from those who need it most, we can understand why, as growth happens and as international trade becomes more "productive", there is, inevitably, more hunger: because the people who needed that food most are the ones who are being denied access to it by this new system of trading. This so-called free trade is taking away from them any way of looking after others' needs, or their own.

People ask me: "How can we protect biodiversity if we are to meet growing human needs?" My reply is that the only way to meet growing human needs is to protect biodiversity, because unless we are looking after the earthworms and the birds and the butterflies we are not going to be able to look after people either. This idea that somehow the human species can only meet its needs by wiping out all other species is a wrong assumption: it is based on not seeing how the web of life connects us all, and how much we live in interaction and in interdependence.

Monocultures produce more monocultures, but they do not produce more nutrition. If you take a field and plant it with twenty crops, it will have a lot of food output, but if any one of those individual yields—say of corn or wheat—is measured in comparison with that of a monoculture field, of course you will have less, because the field is not all corn. So just by shifting from a diversity-based system into a monoculture industrially supported with chemicals and machines, you automatically define it as more, even though you are getting less! Less species, less output, less nutrition, less farmers, less food, less nourishment. And yet we have been absolutely brainwashed into believing that when we are producing less we are producing more. It is an illusion of the deepest kind.

Trade today is no longer about the exchange of things which we need and which we cannot produce ourselves. Trade is an obligation to stop producing what we need, to stop looking after each other, and to buy from somewhere else.

In trade today there are four grain giants. The biggest of them, Cargill, controls seventy per cent of the food traded in the world; and they fix the prices. They sell the inputs, they tell the farmer what to grow, they buy cheaply from the farmer, then they sell it at high cost to consumers. In the process they poison every bit of the food chain. Instead of giving, they are thinking of how they can take out that last bit, from ecosystems, other species, the poor, the Third World.

In the early 1990s Cargill said, "Oh, these Indian peasants are stupid. They do not realise that our seeds are smart: We have found new technologies that prevent the bees from usurping the pollen." Now the concept of "the gift of food" tells us that pollen is the gift that we must maintain for pollinators, and therefore we must grow open-pollinated crops that bees and butterflies can pollinate. That is their food and it is their ecological space. And we have to make sure that we do not eat into their space.

Instead, Cargill says that the bees usurp the pollen—because Cargill has defined every piece of pollen as their property. And in a similar way, Monsanto said: "Through the use of Roundup we are preventing weeds from stealing the sunshine." The entire planet is energised by the life-giving force of the sun, and now Monsanto has basically said that it is Monsanto and the farmers in contract with Monsanto that, alone on the planet, have the right to sunshine—the rest of it is theft.

So what we are getting is a world which is absolutely the opposite to the "giving of food." Instead, it is the taking of food from the food chain and the web of life. Instead of gift we have profit and greed as the highest organizing principle. Unfortunately, the more the profit, the more hunger, illness, destruction of Nature, of soil, of water, of biodiversity, the more nonsustainable our food systems become. We then actually become surrounded by deepening debt: not the ecological debt to Nature, to the Earth and to other species, but the financial debt to the money-lenders and to the agents of chemicals and seeds. The ecological debt is in fact replaced by this financial debt: the giving of nourishment and food is replaced by the making of more and more profits.

What we need to do now is to find ways of detaching ourselves from these destructive arrangements. It is not just replacing free trade with fair trade: Unless we see how the whole is leading to the poisoning and polluting of our very beings, of our very consciousness, we will not be able to make the deeper shifts that allow us to create abundance again. In taking all from nature, without giving, we are not creating abundance; we are creating scarcity.

Growing world hunger is part of that scarcity. And the growing diseases of affluence are a part of that scarcity too. If we relocate ourselves again in the sacred trust of ecology, and recognise our debt to all human and nonhuman beings, then the protection of the rights of all species simply becomes part of our ethical norm and our ethical duty. And as a result of that, those who depend on others for feeding them and for bringing them food will get the right kind of food and the right kind of nourishment. So, if we begin with the nourishment of the web of life, we actually solve the agricultural crisis of small farms, the health crisis of consumers, and the economic crisis of Third World poverty.

For Class Discussion

1. How do Shiva's values structure the argument and influence its style? Where are her background, affiliations, and social activism most prominent in this argument?

2. What claims about industrial farming and the global food system are central to Shiva's argument? How does she explain poverty and world hunger?

3. How does Shiva appeal to the values, emotions, and imaginations of her target audience?

4. How would readers who don't share Shiva's particular kind of reverence for nature respond to this article? How would she need to rework her argument and approach to reach agribusinesses and biotech scientists?

5. Shiva concludes her piece with a proposal that relates to the subtitle of her article. How persuasive and rhetorically effective is this ending? ■

Power to the People
Eric Werker

Eric Werker is an assistant professor in the Business, Government, and International Economy Unit at Harvard Business School. His research explores the complex relationship between developed and developing economies. He has written numerous articles on foreign aid, foreign investment, and non-governmental organizations (NGOs) for both general and academic audiences, and previously worked with the U.S. government's Millennium Challenge Corporation, analyzing foreign aid projects in Africa, Latin America, and Eurasia. This policy proposal appeared in the November/December 2008 issue of *Foreign Policy*, a magazine that strives to publish "polemical, controversial, and powerful" arguments and whose mission is to "explain how the world works—in particular, how the process of globalization is reshaping nations, institutions, cultures, and, more fundamentally, our daily lives" ("About Us" www.foreignpolicy.com).

How does Werker's choice of words and examples help to identify the audience for this brief policy proposal?

Every nongovernmental organization has a mission statement. For example, CARE, one of the world's largest and best-funded NGOs, explains its mission as serving "individuals and families in the poorest communities in the world. Drawing strength from our global diversity, resources and experience, we promote innovative solutions and are advocates for global responsibility." Indeed, CARE has teams of experts with years of experience in more than 70 countries, and its efforts to tackle the "underlying causes of poverty" are impressive. Implicit in its mission statement, like those of most NGOs, is the notion that CARE is exceptionally knowledgeable about how to meet the needs of the world's poor. But does it know best?

Take one of the most confounding global problems today: the skyrocketing cost of food. Prices for staple crops such as rice and wheat have more than doubled since 2006, putting an enormous strain on the 1.2 billion people living on a dollar a day or less. In 2004, a typical poor farmer in Udaipur, India, was already spending more than half his daily dollar of income on food—and that was before grain prices went through the roof.

NGOs and relief agencies are on the front lines of this global crisis, distributing food and other forms of assistance to the hardest-hit victims. But food handouts may be the last thing that poor countries need right now. In many of the worst-stricken places, agriculture is the top employer. High food prices are offering a rare opportunity for farmers in these countries to make a tidy profit. Dumping imported food on the market will cut into many farmers' incomes and thus might do more harm than good. Low-wage work programs could help people avoid hunger, but they might also take farmers away from their fields just when farming is becoming lucrative.

Priorities, moreover, vary from person to person and from place to place. A West African farmer might choose to forgo next season's seeds and fertilizer to put food on the table today. A garbage collector in Jakarta might sacrifice trips to the doctor to keep from going hungry. Mexican parents might keep their kids home from school as the cost of education gets priced out of the family budget. Aid agencies can't always predict what the poor value most.

The first step in truly addressing the food crisis, therefore, is abandoning the idea that the donor knows best. Instead of more advice or another bag of rice, the poor should be given relief vouchers. The basic premise is simple: Give poor people a choice about what type of assistance they receive. Vouchers, backed by major donor countries, could be distributed to needy recipients in the areas hardest hit by the food crisis. The recipients could then redeem the vouchers in exchange for approved goods (such as food or fertilizer) or services (such as healthcare or job training). Relief vouchers would allow families to meet their most pressing needs without harming the very markets that can bring about permanent solutions. At the same time, they would give firms and NGOS an incentive to provide a wider array of services.

Relief vouchers could also save NGOs millions of dollars that victims never see. Figuring out what people need is hard enough during a natural disaster, when a helicopter flyover can reveal the physical damage. But the effects of the food crisis are much harder to diagnose. Each NGO must conduct household surveys, hire experts, meet with local government officials and foreign donors, and then write grant applications and raise funds before it can ever help its first victim. Meanwhile, monitoring these efforts eats up precious resources. With vouchers, agencies would simply follow the invisible hand of the market—in this case, the market for relief.

Relief vouchers would solve another problem: accountability. Most NGOs today answer only to the donors who fund their operations, not to their actual clients—the poor. Most major donors do their utmost to make sure their money is spent as promised. But even donors whose hearts are in the right place cannot anticipate the exact needs of so many

There's no free lunch.

different communities. With no mechanism for the poor to communicate their priorities, nonprofits and their donors are only accountable to themselves. A system of relief vouchers would change that.

Such a radical shift in accountability will have major ramifications. The development world is littered with projects that keep getting funded long after they are no longer useful. Under a voucher system, if an NGO delivered a product that no one needed, or failed to deliver what it promised, beneficiaries would stop coming to it for relief. This is why nonprofits working for vouchers wouldn't have to waste funds on expensive evaluations. After all, Pepsi does not have to prove whether its soda makes its customers better off. Products that people aren't willing to buy typically don't survive long. It is time to expose the nonprofit sector to the same market feedback.

If that scares some NGOs, it shouldn't. Too often, they must cater to the whims of donors when they would prefer to serve those in need. Without financial support, they would never be able to conduct their important work. But if a significant share of NGOs' financing came through voucher redemption, they would be able to focus their attention on the poor without worrying as much about pleasing large foundations and government agencies, which often have their own agendas.

Vouchers, of course, aren't a silver bullet. Corruption and fraud will be a concern. Moreover, some needs are best delivered at the community level, such as clean water, or at the national level, such as public-health campaigns. And in countries with well-developed national safety nets, such as South Africa, there may be no need to bypass functioning institutions by introducing vouchers. In some cases, relief vouchers would be impractical. Aid workers are fortunate if they can even reach those in need in a failed state like Somalia or a dictatorship like Burma.

Voucher schemes have already shown promise. Catholic Relief Services pioneered their use in 2000 by setting up "seed fairs" for farmers. In Ethiopia in 2004, the organization successfully introduced livestock vouchers for sheep, goats, and even veterinary services. The Red Cross distributed vouchers to vulnerable families in the West Bank in 2002 and 2003; the program was only discontinued for political reasons. Governments have long used other types of vouchers on larger scales: for schools, in many developing countries, and in the form of food stamps in the United States. Vouchers, in short, can work—and it's time to extend their logic to a much wider array of problems. It's time to give the poor the power of choice.

For Class Discussion

1. What is the core concept of this policy proposal? How does this proposal differ from the other arguments in this chapter regarding third world hunger?

2. What assumptions does Werker make about those providing aid? Those receiving it?

3. How effective is the application of business principles and examples in this piece?

4. How does Werker's direct manner and concise treatment of a big issue contribute to the persuasiveness of this argument?

5. What additional information would you need in order to assess Werker's proposal fully?   ∎

Where Does Your Food Come From?
FoodRoutes Network

FoodRoutes Network is a national nonprofit organization that works "to rebuild local, community-based food systems." The organization's Web site is designed to provide "timely information, resources, and market opportunities for the food and farming community, community-based nonprofits, the food-concerned public, policymakers, and the media" (www.foodroutes.org). This two-sided flier is part of the media kit it makes available to its users.

How do the images and text in this flier seek to appeal to readers' emotions, imaginations, beliefs, and values?

Where Does Your Food Come From?

Buy Locally Grown. It's Thousands of Miles Fresher.

Buy Fresh. Buy Local.

foodroutes.org

foodroutes.org

For Class Discussion

1. Look at how the photograph on the front of this flier is composed. How does the use of perspective and photographic technique emphasize certain elements? (To view this image in color, visit http://foodroutes.org/blcsheets.jsp.)

2. What are the strongest arguments for supporting local food systems conveyed by this flier? How does its text work rhetorically? Think about word choice and order, sentence length, and repetition.

3. What elements of the flier call for further action on the viewer's part? What resources are provided for further information?

FoodRoutes NETWORK

There Are Many Good Reasons To Buy Locally Grown Food

You'll get exceptional taste and freshness.
Local food is fresher and tastes better than food shipped long distances from other states or countries. Local farmers can offer produce varieties bred for taste and freshness rather than for shipping and long shelf life.

You'll strengthen your local economy.
Buying local food keeps your dollars circulating in your community. Getting to know the farmers who grow your food builds relationships based on understanding and trust, the foundation of strong communities.

You'll support endangered family farms.
There's never been a more critical time to support your farming neighbors. With each local food purchase, you ensure that more of your money spent on food goes to the farmer.

You'll safeguard your family's health.
Knowing where your food comes from and how it is grown or raised enables you to choose safe food from farmers who avoid or reduce their use of chemicals, pesticides, hormones, antibiotics, or genetically modified seed in their operations. Buy food from local farmers you trust.

You'll protect the environment.
Local food doesn't have to travel far. This reduces carbon dioxide emissions and packing materials. Buying local food also helps to make farming more profitable and selling farmland for development less attractive.

When you buy local food, you vote with your food dollar. This ensures that family farms in your community will continue to thrive and that healthy, flavorful, plentiful food will be available for future generations.

Buying local is this easy:

- Find a farmer, farmers' market, farm stand, or local food outlet near you, visit www.foodroutes.org.

- Shop at your local farmers' market or farm stand for the freshest, best tasting food available. It's easy to find local food. There are over 3,100 farmers' markets in the U.S. – one is probably near you!

- Encourage your local grocery stores and area restaurants to purchase more of their products from local farmers.

BUY FRESH BUY LOCAL

Where does your food come from? Learn more. www.foodroutes.org

Designed by **Sustain**

foodroutes.org

4. Which of the arguments and approaches to world hunger in this chapter does this flier support?

The Vegetable-Industrial Complex
Michael Pollan

Michael Pollan has written extensively on issues of food production and agricultural practices. His most recent books are *In Defense of Food: An Eater's Manifesto* (2008) and *The Omnivore's Dilemma: A Natural History of Four Meals* (2006), in which he addresses the increasing industrialization of our food, the degradation of the environment, and the confusion faced by Americans in trying to decide what constitutes healthy eating. Pollan served for many years as executive editor of *Harper's Magazine* and is now the Knight Professor of Science and Environmental Journalism at the University of California Berkeley. He is also a contributing writer for the *New York Times Magazine*, in which this policy argument appeared on October 15, 2006.

> How does this argument grow out of and respond to the current national concern about food contamination?

Soon after the news broke last month that nearly 200 Americans in 26 states had been sickened by eating packaged spinach contaminated with E. coli, I received a rather coldblooded e-mail message from a friend in the food business. "I have instructed my broker to purchase a million shares of RadSafe," he wrote, explaining that RadSafe is a leading manufacturer of food-irradiation technology. It turned out my friend was joking, but even so, his reasoning was impeccable. If bagged salad greens are vulnerable to bacterial contamination on such a scale, industry and government would very soon come looking for a technological fix; any day now, calls to irradiate the entire food supply will be on a great many official lips. That's exactly what happened a few years ago when we learned that E. coli from cattle feces was winding up in American hamburgers. Rather than clean up the kill floor and the feedlot diet, some meat processors simply started nuking the meat—sterilizing the manure, in other words, rather than removing it from our food. Why? Because it's easier to find a technological fix than to address the root cause of such a problem. This has always been the genius of industrial capitalism—to take its failings and turn them into exciting new business opportunities.

We can also expect to hear calls for more regulation and inspection of the produce industry. Already, watchdogs like the Center for Science in the Public Interest have proposed that the government impose the sort of regulatory regime it imposes on the meat industry—something along the lines of the Hazard Analysis and Critical Control Point system (Haccp, pronounced HASS-ip) developed in response to the E. coli contamination of beef. At the moment, vegetable growers and packers are virtually unregulated. "Farmers can do pretty much as they please," Carol Tucker Foreman, director of the Food Policy Institute at the Consumer Federation of America, said recently, "as long as they don't make anyone sick."

This sounds like an alarming lapse in governmental oversight until you realize there has never before been much reason to worry about food safety on farms. But these days, the way we farm and the way we process our food, both of which have been industrialized and centralized over the last few decades, are endangering our health. The Centers for Disease Control and Prevention estimate that our food supply now sickens 76 million Americans every year, putting more than 300,000 of them in the hospital, and killing 5,000. The lethal strain of E. coli known as 0157:H7, responsible for this latest outbreak of food poisoning, was unknown before 1982; it is believed to have evolved in the gut of feedlot cattle. These are animals that stand around in their manure all day long, eating a diet of grain that happens to turn a cow's rumen into an ideal habitat for E. coli 0157:H7. (The bug can't survive long in cattle living on grass.) Industrial animal agriculture produces more than a billion tons of manure every year, manure that, besides being full of nasty microbes like E. coli 0157:H7 (not to mention high concentrations of the pharmaceuticals animals must receive so they can tolerate the feedlot lifestyle), often ends up in places it shouldn't be, rather than in pastures, where it would not only be harmless but also actually do some good. To think of animal manure as pollution rather than fertility is a relatively new (and industrial) idea.

Wendell Berry once wrote that when we took animals off farms and put them onto feedlots, we had, in effect, taken an old solution—the one where crops feed animals and animals' waste feeds crops—and neatly divided it into two new problems: a fertility problem on the farm, and a pollution problem on the feedlot. Rather than return to that elegant solution, however, industrial agriculture came up with a technological fix for the first problem—chemical fertilizers on the farm. As yet, there is no good fix for the second problem, unless you count irradiation and Haccp plans and overcooking your burgers and, now, staying away from spinach. All of these solutions treat E. coli 0157:H7 as an unavoidable fact of life rather than what it is: a fact of industrial agriculture.

But if industrial farming gave us this bug, it is industrial eating that has spread it far and wide. We don't yet know exactly what happened in the case of the spinach washed and packed by Natural Selection Foods, whether it was contaminated in the field or in the processing plant or if perhaps the sealed bags made a trivial contamination worse. But we do know that a great deal of spinach from a great many fields gets mixed together in the water at that plant, giving microbes from a single field an opportunity to contaminate a vast amount of food. The plant in question washes 26 million servings of salad every week. In effect, we're washing the whole nation's salad in one big sink.

It's conceivable the same problem could occur in your own kitchen sink or on a single farm. Food poisoning has always been with us, but not until we started processing all our food in such a small number of "kitchens" did the potential for nationwide outbreaks exist.

Surely this points to one of the great advantages of a decentralized food system: When things go wrong, as they sooner or later will, fewer people are affected and, just as important, the problem can be more easily traced to its source and contained. A long and complicated food chain, in which food from all over the countryside is gathered together in one place to be processed and then distributed all over the country to be eaten, can be impressively efficient, but by its very nature it is a food chain devilishly hard to follow and to fix.

Fortunately, this is not the only food chain we have. The week of the E. coli outbreak, washed spinach was on sale at my local farmers' market, and at the Blue Heron Farms stand, where I usually buy my greens, the spinach appeared to be moving briskly. I tasted a leaf and wondered why I didn't think twice about it. I guess it's because I've just always trusted these guys; I buy from them every week. The spinach was probably cut and washed that morning or the night before—it hasn't been sitting around in a bag on a truck for a week. And if there ever is any sort of problem, I know exactly who is responsible. Whatever the risk, and I'm sure there is some, it seems manageable.

These days, when people make the case for buying local food, they often talk about things like keeping farmers in our communities and eating fresh food in season, at the peak of its flavor. We like what's going on at the farmers' market—how country meets city, how children learn that a carrot is not a glossy orange bullet that comes in a bag but is actually a root; how we get to taste unfamiliar flavors and even, in some sense, reconnect through these foods and their growers to the natural world. Stack all this up against the convenience and price of supermarket food, though, and it can sound a little . . . sentimental.

But there's nothing sentimental about local food—indeed, the reasons to support local food economies could not be any more hardheaded or pragmatic. Our highly centralized food economy is a dangerously precarious system, vulnerable to accidental—and deliberate—contamination. This is something the government understands better than most of us eaters. When Tommy Thompson retired from the Department of Health and Human Services in 2004, he said something chilling at his farewell news conference: "For the life of me, I cannot understand why the terrorists have not attacked our food supply, because it is so easy to do." The reason it is so easy to do was laid out in a 2003 G.A.O. report to Congress on bioterrorism. "The high concentration of our livestock industry and the centralized nature of our food-processing industry" make them "vulnerable to terrorist attack." Today 80 percent of America's beef is slaughtered by four companies, 75 percent of the precut salads are processed by two and 30 percent of the milk by just one company. Keeping local food economies healthy—and at the moment they are thriving—is a matter not of sentiment but of critical importance to the national security and the public health, as well as to reducing our dependence on foreign sources of energy.

Yet perhaps the gravest threat now to local food economies—to the farmer selling me my spinach, to the rancher who sells me my grass-fed beef—is, of all things, the government's own well-intentioned efforts to clean up the industrial food supply. Already, hundreds of regional meat-processing plants—the ones that local meat producers depend on—are closing because they can't afford to comply with the regulatory requirements the U.S.D.A. rightly imposes on giant slaughterhouses that process 400 head of cattle an hour. The industry insists that all regulations be "scale neutral," so if the U.S.D.A. demands that huge plants have, say, a bathroom, a shower and an office for the exclusive use of its inspectors, then a small processing plant that slaughters local farmers' livestock will have to install these facilities, too. This is one of the principal reasons that meat at the farmers' market is more expensive than meat at the supermarket: farmers are seldom allowed to process their own meat, and small processing plants have become very expensive to operate, when the U.S.D.A. is willing to let them operate at all. From the U.S.D.A.'s perspective, it is much more efficient to put their inspectors in a plant where they can inspect 400 cows an hour rather than in a local plant where they can inspect maybe one.

So what happens to the spinach grower at my farmers' market when the F.D.A. starts demanding a Haccp plan—daily testing of the irrigation water, say, or some newfangled veggie-irradiation technology? When we start requiring that all farms be federally inspected? Heavy burdens of regulation always fall heaviest on the smallest operations and invariably wind up benefiting the biggest players in an industry, the ones who can spread the costs over a larger output of goods. A result is that regulating food safety tends to accelerate the sort of industrialization that made food safety a problem in the first place. We end up putting our faith in RadSafe rather than in Blue Heron Farms—in technologies rather than relationships.

It's easy to imagine the F.D.A. announcing a new rule banning animals from farms that produce plant crops. In light of the threat from E. coli, such a rule would make a certain kind of sense. But it is an industrial, not an ecological, sense. For the practice of keeping animals on farms used to be, as Wendell Berry pointed out, a solution; only when cows moved onto feedlots did it become a problem. Local farmers and local food economies represent much the same sort of pre-problem solution—elegant, low-tech and redundant. But the logic of industry, apparently ineluctable, has other ideas, ideas that not only leave our centralized food system undisturbed but also imperil its most promising, and safer, alternatives.

For Class Discussion

1. In this argument, how does Michael Pollan persuade his general newspaper audience that a problem exists? What is wrong with a centralized food system?

2. Pollan claims that other arguments for eating local food can be somewhat sentimental. How does his justification for eating locally compare and contrast with the reasons presented by the FoodRoutes Network?

3. What evidence of external and internal threats does Pollan address with regard to the United States's food supply?

4. In his books, Pollan has made similar, extended arguments to the points addressed in this article. What points would you like to see developed more fully?

5. What contribution has he made to your understanding of the controversy over global versus local food systems?

Deepening Our Sense of What Is Local and Regional Food
Gary Paul Nabhan

Gary Paul Nabhan, Ph.D., is an Arab-American writer, lecturer, food and farming advocate, rural lifeways folklorist, and conservationist. He holds a professorship as a research social scientist based at the Southwest Center of the University of Arizona, and advises for many nonprofits, including the Renewing America's Food Traditions collaborative, an organization which he founded. He is the author of several books, including *Coming Home to Eat: The Pleasures and Politics of Eating Local Food* (2001), *Where Our Food Comes From: Retracing Nikolay Vavilov's Quest to End Famine* (2008) and, as editor, *Renewing America's Food Traditions: Saving and Savoring the Continent's Most Endangered Foods* (2008). This Web argument was published on October 25, 2007, at www.eatlocalchallenge.com, a group blog written by authors who are interested in the benefits of eating locally grown and produced food.

How does Nabhan establish a sense of shared values with his audience?

Now that *Time* magazine has done a cover feature article on the local foods movement and a book on the same topic by bestselling author Barbara Kingsolver and her family has climbed up the *New York Times* top-ten non-fiction list, we might want to ask what actually is it that we want to promote by using phrases like "Buy Fresh, Buy Local". I can assure you that there will be increasing criticism of the so-called local food movement, building on the Hudson Institute's feeble attempt to discredit it last fall in a variety of newspapers, with added absurdities being published in the *Economist* and by the American Farm Bureau. On the other hand, a reputable ethicist, Peter Singer, fears in his co-authored book *The Way We Eat* that 1) an emphasis on purchasing foods locally in U.S. communities will disadvantage needy producers in foreign countries—as if India's producers of Basmati rice actually gain much of the retail dollar spent on their rice in the U.S.—or 2) the un-ethically raised beef or chicken will suddenly take over farmers markets and CSAs—as if Conagra and Tyson execs will soon be hanging out in overalls selling antibiotic-laced breast meat on Saturdays at their local farmers markets. I can predict, however, that more substantive critiques will arise, and I, for one, welcome them. It is time that we deepen our sense of what we mean by local and regional, offer others better reasons as to why these concerns matter, and steadfastly resist any pressure to endorse simplistic formulas such as a 100-mile diet or an in-state diet.

Here are some ways we can deepen what we promote by the terms local and regional:

1. **Local means from a farm, ranch, or fishing boat that is locally-owned and operated, using the management skills and the labor of local community members.** A farm that is owned all or in part by an extra-local corporation, and which uses migrant workers who live outside the community does not benefit its community economically or culturally as much as it should.

2. **A regional food is one that has been tied to the traditions of a particular landscape or seascape and its cultures for decades if not for centuries.** If the same mix of mesclun greens is grown in greenhouses across the country and sold in every farmers market from Maine to New Mexico, it is more like a franchised product (from a seed company) than it is a local or regional food. Yes it may be produced five miles from your home and thereby reduce food miles, but its seeds are not saved and adapted to local or regional conditions, they are bought from afar every year.

3. **The miles a food travels ("food miles") must be placed in the size and volume of the mode of transport, its source of fuel, and its frequency of travel.** Using biodiesel in a larger truck may be more efficient, and leave less of a carbon footprint than using leaded gas in an old clunker. One in every five kilocalories in the American food production and delivery system now underwrites transportation, as well as packaging and cooling while in transit, so this will be an increasingly important issue to solve by using alternative fuels, carrying cost-efficient volumes, and ensuring that vehicles holding their full capacity in both directions, perhaps by carrying compost back to farms where the vegetables originated.

4. **On-farm energy and water use matter.** If a farm near Tucson Arizona is irrigated from a canal that transports Colorado River water hundreds of miles (and at high ecological cost to wild riverine species), or if it uses fossil groundwater set down during the Pleistocene pumped by fossil fuel set down in Iran during the Pennsylvanian era, what is to be gained by promoting its food?

5. **Other on-farm inputs matter just as much.** Where are the sources of hay for livestock, compost for garden crops or nitrogen for field crops? They should be locally if not regionally-sourced. Why call

lamb locally-produced in Idaho when its flock has wintered part of the year in California and its hay comes in from southern Colorado?

6. **Fair-trade with other cultures, localities and regions is fair game.** Circumvent the globalized economy for the items you truly need from other regions by establishing fair-trade exchanges. It is not that we don't care about farmers and ranchers elsewhere; we simply don't wish to see middlemen gaining more of each consumer dollar than the producers do. Producers inevitably plow money back into their communities and lands; intermediaries seldom do.

7. **Invest in the foods unique to your region that cannot or should not be grown anywhere else.** . . . Ancient food traditions based on climate, soil and culture, involve both native and immigrant foods that have adapted and been integrated into particular places. Because the U.S. currently lacks the geographic indicators such as denominations of origin that reinforce the links between place, culture and genetics of a particular food, these place-based foods are truly threatened by globalization. Invest in them and their original stewards.

For Class Discussion

1. In this definitional argument, Gary Paul Nabhan clarifies the criteria to be employed in talking about local and regional food. How have his definitions changed your understanding of local food?

2. Nabhan directly criticizes the claims of proponents of global trade. What reasons and alternatives does he suggest?

3. If this piece were written to a more skeptical audience, what assumptions would need to be explained? What language might need to be altered or what terms might need to be defined?

4. Compare the arguments made here to those made on the FoodRoutes Network poster. How does the target audience affect the writers' choices in presenting evidence?

5. What connections do you see between Nabhan's points about local food and those of Michael Pollan?

Health and Environment
United Nations Environment Programme

Part of a series of posters on the environment, poverty, energy, food, water, and health, this poster (p. 395), sponsored by the United Nations Environment Programme, appeared in an exhibition at the World Summit on Sustainable Development held August 26–September 3, 2002, in Johannesburg, South Africa.

www.unep.org, United Nations Environmental Programme

The United Nations Environment Programme's mission is "to provide leadership and encourage partnership in caring for the environment by inspiring, informing, and enabling nations and peoples to improve their quality of life without compromising that of future generations" ("About UNEP," www.unep.org). This poster refers to the recent studies showing that pesticides, chemical fertilizers, and other industrial wastes have contaminated soil, water, and the entire food chain. In the Arctic countries, the Inuits, the Aleuts, the Inupiats, the Siberian tribes, and the Saami—indigenous peoples who are dependent on whales and seafood—show high levels of toxins in their blood and breast milk.

What are your first impressions of and responses to this poster?

For Class Discussion

1. How does this poster reveal its dual purpose of educating and persuading? What role does emotion play in that purpose?

2. How do the use of light/dark, the images, the type, and the layout contribute to the rhetorical power of this poster? What effect were its designers trying to achieve?

3. What views sketched in the introduction of this chapter does this poster illustrate and support?

4. What does this poster contribute to the controversy over how to provide safe and adequate food for the world's 6.3 billion people? ■

Going Local on a Global Scale: Rethinking Food Trade in an Era of Climate Change, Dumping, and Rural Poverty

Kirsten Schwind

Kirsten Schwind is program director of Bay Localize, a San Francisco Bay Area group that works "to catalyze a shift from a globalized, fossil fuel-based economy that enriches a few and weakens most, to a localized green economy that strengthens all Bay Area communities" (www.baylocalize.org/about). Schwind holds a bachelor's degree in economics and public policy from Swarthmore College. Her graduate work focused on natural resources management, and she has worked with human rights in Guatemala. She has focused on food security, food sovereignty, trade, land access, labor conditions, and sustainable agriculture with several Bay Area nonprofits, including her former role as Food First's program director. Food First is an organization working to eliminate the injustices that cause hunger, with a particular emphasis on connecting the United States to global issues. This scholarly policy proposal was published in Food First's online *Backgrounder* in the spring–summer 2005 volume.

According to Kirsten Schwind, which stakeholders support local food and which stakeholders support a global food system and why?

Fresh, local food is a vision that unites community food security activists, environmentalists, slow food enthusiasts, and small-scale farmers globally. Supporting or rebuilding local food systems to bring fresh and culturally relevant food from local producers to local consumers catalyzes community and regional development in both the global North and the global South. Producing and marketing more food locally can help alleviate both global climate change and rural poverty. Building these local food systems requires rethinking the role of trade and the institutions that promote it.

TRADE FUELS CLIMATE CHANGE

Advocating for local food requires reexamining the deeply held economic theory of competitive advantage, which holds that each region should specialize in producing only what it can produce most cheaply, then trade with other regions for everything else. However, traditional economic calculations do not account for the true environmental cost of trade. For example, the potentially cataclysmic impacts of climate change mean that the environmental costs of transporting goods long distances are much higher than previously thought.

Most food travels hundreds, even thousands, of miles from farm to plate,[1] and the fossil fuel transportation infrastructure we rely on for all this trade emits greenhouse gasses that are contributing to climate change.[2] Climate change is raising sea temperatures and flooding coastal areas, and has the potential to increase crop failures, cause mass extinctions, and spur more destructive weather patterns such as hurricanes—all with profound implications for agriculture and human habitation.[3] Since the full consequences will not be felt for years after the greenhouse gasses have been emitted, it is exceedingly difficult to predict and price future ecological damage and add it to the energy costs of today's food system. Thus even prices that are adjusted to include current energy subsidies or minor "climate change taxes" are not reliable indicators of the ecological and social price of fossil fuel-driven global trade.

Buying local food can make a big difference to the environment. For example, in 1920 Iowa produced a wide variety of fruits and vegetables, but now most of its fruits and vegetables are shipped from elsewhere. If Iowans bought just 10 percent more of their food from within the state, they could collectively save 7.9 million pounds of carbon dioxide emission a year.[4] The Japanese environmental organization Daichi-o-Mamoru Kai (the Association to Preserve the Earth) found that if Japanese families consumed local food instead of imported food, the impact would be equivalent to reducing household energy use by 20 percent; the biggest impact would come from eating tofu products from soy grown in Japan instead of in the US.[5] And researchers in the

UK have calculated that purchasing local food has a greater positive impact on the environment than buying organic food that is not local.[6] While some food trade is inevitable, such as tropical products like coffee that are staples in colder climates, a surprising amount of trade is duplicative and ecologically wasteful. For example, Heinz ketchup eaten in California is made with California-grown tomatoes that have been shipped to Canada for processing and returned in bottles. In one year, the port of New York City exported $431,000 worth of California almonds to Italy, and imported $397,000 worth of Italian almonds to the United States.[7] This sort of unnecessary trade mortgages our children's planet for profits today.

GLOBALIZED, CONSOLIDATED FOOD TRADE UNDERMINES LOCAL ECONOMIES

Food trade can also undermine rural economies. For those who think that lack of food causes hunger, it's surprising to learn that the world currently has an overproduction of basic food crops, which results in low prices to farmers and low rural incomes.[8] Overproduction also results in dumping: the selling of imported food at less than it costs to produce it. Developing nations often point to the unfairness of this global food trading system. In response to low prices, many First World farmers receive subsidies, which can allow them to sell their harvests for less than the cost of production. Current trade rules permit this dumping, which can destroy nonsubsidized farmers' ability to compete. For example, rice, one of the world's most universal staple crops and a major US export, is sold on the world market at 20 to 34 percent less than what it costs the average US farmer to grow it—devastating competition for farmers who need to recoup their full production costs to survive.[9] In 2004, Indonesia banned rice imports to protect the livelihoods of its farmers, who produce enough rice to feed Indonesia's population.[10]

But if the farmers suffer, do the poor and hungry benefit from floods of cheap food? The surprising truth is that a vast majority of the world's poor make their living off agriculture, and 50 percent of the people who live with hunger globally *are* small-scale farmers.[11] The global overproduction of basic foods is a major factor driving low incomes and poverty in rural areas. Rural poverty drives urban poverty, as desperate economic refugees from failing farms drive down wages in urban areas.[12] Pro-poor development policies need to raise farm incomes for small-scale farmers. Reestablishing small farmers' access to local markets to sell their food is one such policy, and is the proposal put forth by Via Campesina, a network of nearly 100 major small-scale farmer organizations around the world.

The expansion of supermarket chains into areas that have long been supplied by local and regional farms through traditional markets is also working against small farmers and local food. From 1992 to 2002, supermarkets have increased their retail market share by 30 percent in East Asia (excluding China) and 45 percent in the South African region.[13] In addition, supermarkets are becoming highly concentrated in a few corporate chains—in South Africa, for example, the top 2 percent of food stores capture 55 percent of retail sales.[14]

As supermarket chains grow, they tend to centralize procurement for many stores in a few distribution centers, which buy in bulk from as few producers as possible, including importers of "cheap" commodities and large-scale farms, rather than from brokers that may purchase from smaller farms.[15] In addition to bringing food from farther away, supermarket procurement from a few large-scale suppliers drives a standardization of food that erodes diversity in taste, cultural heritage, and even nutrition.[16]

Supermarket concentration allows a few companies to demand ever-lower prices from farmers while driving locally owned food retail stores out of business. While chain supermarkets may offer lower prices to consumers, local businesses keep money circulating in the community and contribute more to overall community development. A Chicago study found that for every $100 in consumer spending with a local firm, $68 remains in the Chicago economy, versus $43 with a chain firm, and that for every square foot occupied by a local firm, local economic impact is $179, versus $105 for a chain firm.[17]Another study found that union-busting megastores such as Wal-Mart have been found to actually exacerbate poverty in US counties in which they are located, soaking up government subsidies to its stores and to its workers, who are forced to use public benefits to make ends meet.[18] Workers earning a living wage would not need to rely on artificially cheap food sold by Wal-Mart, and could support local farms and businesses instead.

TRADE IS BIG BUSINESS

Promoting systems to market food locally for healthier communities and ecosystems requires transforming policies and institutions currently dedicated to promoting ecologically and socially damaging trade. Policies that promote trade liberalization as a global panacea for poverty, hunger, and inequality drive unnecessary trade, but the biggest beneficiaries are large corporations seeking access to markets and greater profits. The International Monetary Fund (IMF) and the World Bank have long promoted rapid trade liberalization with no clear evidence that it helps the poorest populations. Taxpayer-supported export credit agencies spend over $100 billion a year funding loans to developing countries to import goods from corporations in the global North, increasing indebtedness.[19] Powerful countries set global rules in the World Trade Organization (WTO) and agreements such as CAFTA (the Central American Free Trade Agreement) that prevent communities, states, and sovereign nations from nurturing local production and regulating businesses according to the values of their citizens.[20] The US government, advised by a revolving door of big business executives, has demonstrated a willingness to go to war to protect corporate access to markets and trade.[21] These policies open market access for companies like the privately owned Cargill, one of the world's largest global food trading corporations, with profits surpassing $1.3 billion in 2003—almost triple those of 2000.[22]

GLOBAL MOVEMENTS FOR LOCAL FOOD

Local food activists in the US and around the world are rising to the challenge to make changes to allow local food systems to thrive. Citizens are passing innovative laws at the city, county, and state levels, including townships in rural Pennsylvania that are banning corporate ownership of farms.[23] Community builders aren't waiting for supermarkets to come to their neighborhood, but rather are growing or buying food through urban gardens, school gardens, farmer's markets, community supported agriculture, and food purchasing cooperatives. The Community Food Security Coalition is developing programs for schools and hospitals to source fresh, healthier food from local farmers.[24] Environmental groups such as the Sierra Club are hosting locally grown dinners to pressure businesses to sell local food.[25] And the Business Alliance for Local Living Economies (BALLE) network is linking farms with other local businesses to create community networks to support local products.[26] Progressive farm advocates such as the National Family Farm Coalition are promoting agricultural policies to address dumping and reinvigorate family farms, as well as opposing coercive trade agreements.

Global movements are also taking action to defend and rebuild local food systems, as a strategy for self-reliance, cultural survival, and pro-poor development. Via Campesina has developed a platform of food sovereignty, "prioritizing local agricultural production in order to feed the people," and is developing new trade rules based on this concept.[27] Small-scale farmers' organizations—Via Campesina members—from nearly fifty countries are uniting their power, lobbying their governments to remove agriculture from WTO negotiations. Before and during the 2003 WTO ministerial meeting in Cancún, grassroots pressure and protests from Via Campesina played a key role in convincing developing country representatives to end the talks rather than sign on to a damaging deal.[28]

The local food movement unites community activists, urban gardeners, small-scale farmers, environmentalists, teachers, chefs, nutritionists, local business owners, and eaters of fresh local food. The movement's potential to transform our food system is enormous. The successes of a cornucopia of community food programs have already demonstrated how local food can foster robust local development, improve food security and nutrition, build community, and support productive family farms. Going local can also be a part of the answer to reversing global environmental degradation and greatly reducing rural poverty. It's time to scale up and institutionalize these successes through organizing for policies that promote local food systems globally, and dismantling those that promote ecologically and socially damaging trade.

Notes

1. See Brian Halweil, *Eat Here: Reclaiming Homegrown Pleasures in a Global Supermarket* (New York: Norton, 2004) for an overview of studies on food miles. This very readable book is an excellent overview of the richness of the local food movement in the United States.
2. Hansen, et al., "Earth's Energy Imbalance: Confirmation and Implications." *Science* 2005 0: 11102522.
3. Canadian Department for International Development (DFID), et al., 2002, *Linking Poverty Reduction and Environmental Management: Policy Challenges and Opportunities.*
4. Rich Pirog, Timothy Van Pelt, Kamyar Enshayan, and Ellen Cook, 2001, *Food, Fuel, and Freeways: An Iowa Perspective on How Far Food Travels, Fuel Usage, and Greenhouse Gas Emissions*, Ames. IA: Leopold Center for Sustainable Agriculture, Iowa State University.
5. "Consumption of local food helps cut CO_2 emissions," March 2, 2005, *Kyodo News.*
6. J. N. Pretty, A. S. Ball, T. Lang, and J. I. L. Morison, 2005, "Farm Costs and Food Miles: An assessment of the full cost of the UK weekly food basket," *Food Policy* 30:1–19.
7. Katy Mamen, Steve Gorelick, Helena Norberg-Hodge, and Diana Deumling, 2004, *Ripe for Change: Rethinking California's Food Economy*, International Society for Ecology and Culture.
8. Food and Agriculture Organization (FAO), 2004, *The State of Agricultural Commodity Markets 2004.*
9. Institute for Agriculture and Trade Policy (IATP), 2005, *United States Dumping on World Agricultural Markets.*
10. "Imported Rice Ban Could Be Extended Until 2005," September 6, 2004, Jakarta Post; found on the website of the Embassy of Indonesia in Canada, http://www .indonesia-ottawa.org/information/details.php?type=news&id=83

11. Food and Agriculture Organization (FAO), 2004, *The State of Food Insecurity in the World 2004.*

12. Maxmilian Eisenburger and Raj Patel, 2003, *Agricultural Liberalization in China: Curbing the State and Creating Cheap Labor,* Food First Policy Brief #9, Oakland, CA: Food First.

13. T. Reardon, P. Timmer, C. Barrett, and J. Berdegué, 2003, "The Rise of Supermarkets in Africa, Asia and Latin America," *American Journal of Agricultural Economics* 85 (5):1140–1146.

14. Dave D. Weatherspoon and Thomas Reardon, 2003, "The Rise of Supermarkets in Africa: Implications for Agrifood Systems and the Rural Poor," *Development Policy Review* 21 (3):333–355.

15. Ibid. Supermarkets don't have to drive smaller farmers out of business or eradicate local food cultures; a few firms do purchase from local producers or producer cooperatives, and many more could. And government policy could promote this choice: an especially innovative government commission in the UK recommended that retailers convert part of their store to a local farmer's market, in exchange for property tax benefits on that portion of their floor space. See Brian Halweil's *Eat Here.*

16. Harriet V. Kuhnlein, 2004, "Karat, Pulque, and Gac: Three Shining Stars in the Traditional Food Galaxy," *Nutrition Review* 62 (11):439–442.

17. Civic Economics, 2004, *Andersonville Study of Retail Economics;* found at www.civiceconomics.com/Andersonville/html/reports.html

18. Stephan J. Goetz and Hema Swaminathan, 2004, "Wal-Mart and County-Wide Poverty," Pennsylvania State University Department of Agricultural Economics and Rural Sociology Staff Paper No. 371.

19. Aaron Goldzimer, 2003, "Worse Than the World Bank? Export Credit Agencies—The Secret Engine of Globalization," *Food First Backgrounder* 9(1).

20. CAFTA's chapter on investment, modeled on Chapter 11 of NAFTA, allows corporations to sue local or state governments for passing laws that may cause them to lose profits. This includes basic citizen protections such as environmental and labor laws.

21. Anuradha Mittal, 2003, "Open Fire and Open Markets: Strategy of an Empire," *Food First Backgrounder* 9 (3).

22. http://www.cargill.com/about/financial/financialhighlights.html# TopOfPage

23. Adam D. Sacks, 2005, "Rights Fight: Local Democracy vs. Factory Farms in Pennsylvania," *Food First Backgrounder* 11 (1).

24. For more information see the Community Food Security Coalition website, http://www.foodsecurity.org/ or Christine Ahn, 2004, "Breaking Ground: The Community Food Security Movement," *Food First Backgrounder* 10 (1).

25. See http://www.sierraclub.org/sustainable_consumption/true-cost/

26. See http://www.livingeconomies.org/
27. See http://www.viacampesina.org/art_english.php3?id_article=216& PHPSESSID= 3009460 b95082a11b59cb9ce44e880c2
28. Interview with Ibrahim Coulibaly, farmer organizer from CNOP in Mali, 4/4/05.

For Class Discussion

1. In this meaty researched policy proposal, what connections does Schwind posit among the issues? What rationale does she give for the need to reconstruct local food systems?

2. With what reasons and evidence does Schwind develop her claim that overproduction, not underproduction, is the cause of much world hunger?

3. Who is Schwind's primary audience in this piece? What values does this audience share with her? What assumptions does Schwind *not* explore in her argument?

4. What terms in this piece indicate something about the background knowledge of the target audience?

5. How could Schwind expand or change this argument to reach a neutral or indifferent audience? A hostile audience?

6. The title of this piece works out a new relationship with the words *global* and *local.* What is that relationship? How is it central to Schwind's proposal and part of its appeal?

Food that Travels Well
James E. McWilliams

James E. McWilliams is a fellow in the Agrarian Studies Program at Yale University and an associate professor of history at Texas State University. He has written on local economy, food preparation, pest control, and the environment in such books as *A Revolution in Eating: How the Quest for Food Shaped America* (2005), *American Pests: Our Futile Attempt to Conquer the Insect Empire from Colonial Times to the Death of DDT* (2008), and *Just Food: A Global Citizen's Guide to Virtuous Eating* (2009). In recent pieces for *Slate* (slate.com), McWilliams has argued questions such as the pollution potential of organic farming and the possible environmental benefits of genetically modified foods. This op-ed piece appeared in the *New York Times* on August 6, 2007.

> What values does McWilliams assume are shared by the audience for this piece?

AUSTIN, TEX. The term "food miles"—how far food has traveled before you buy it—has entered the enlightened lexicon. Environmental groups, especially in Europe, are pushing for labels that show how far food has traveled to get to the market, and books like Barbara Kingsolver's *Animal, Vegetable, Miracle: A Year of Food Life* contemplate the damage wrought by trucking, shipping and flying food from distant parts of the globe.

There are many good reasons for eating local—freshness, purity, taste, community cohesion and preserving open space—but none of these benefits compares to the much-touted claim that eating local reduces fossil fuel consumption. In this respect eating local joins recycling, biking to work and driving a hybrid as a realistic way that we can, as individuals, shrink our carbon footprint and be good stewards of the environment.

On its face, the connection between lowering food miles and decreasing greenhouse gas emissions is a no-brainer. In Iowa, the typical carrot has traveled 1,600 miles from California, a potato 1,200 miles from Idaho and a chuck roast 600 miles from Colorado. Seventy-five percent of the apples sold in New York City come from the West Coast or overseas, the writer Bill McKibben says, even though the state produces far more apples than city residents consume. These examples just scratch the surface of the problem. In light of this market redundancy, the only reasonable reaction, it seems, is to count food miles the way a dieter counts calories.

But is reducing food miles necessarily good for the environment? Researchers at Lincoln University in New Zealand, no doubt responding to Europe's push for "food miles labeling," recently published a study challenging the premise that more food miles automatically mean greater fossil fuel consumption. Other scientific studies have undertaken similar investigations. According to this peer-reviewed research, compelling evidence suggests that there is more—or less—to food miles than meets the eye.

It all depends on how you wield the carbon calculator. Instead of measuring a product's carbon footprint through food miles alone, the Lincoln University scientists expanded their equations to include other energy-consuming aspects of production—what economists call "factor inputs and externalities"—like water use, harvesting techniques, fertilizer outlays, renewable energy applications, means of transportation (and the kind of fuel used), amount of carbon dioxide absorbed during photosynthesis, disposal of packaging, storage procedures and dozens of other cultivation inputs.

Incorporating these measurements into their assessments, scientists reached surprising conclusions. Most notably, they found that lamb raised on New Zealand's clover-choked pastures and shipped 11,000 miles by boat to Britain produced 1,520 pounds of carbon dioxide emissions per ton while British lamb produced 6,280 pounds of carbon dioxide per ton, in part because poorer British pastures force farmers to use feed. In other words, it is four times more energy-efficient for Londoners to buy lamb imported from the other side of the world than to buy it from a producer in their backyard. Similar figures were found for dairy products and fruit.

These life-cycle measurements are causing environmentalists worldwide to rethink the logic of food miles. New Zealand's most prominent environmental research organization, Landcare Research-Manaaki Whenua, explains that localism "is not always the most environmentally sound solution if more emissions are generated at other stages of the product life cycle than during transport." The British government's 2006 Food Industry Sustainability Strategy similarly seeks to consider the environmental costs "across the life cycle of the produce," not just in transportation.

"Eat local" advocates—a passionate cohort of which I am one—are bound to interpret these findings as a threat. We shouldn't. Not only do life cycle analyses offer genuine opportunities for environmentally efficient food production, but they also address several problems inherent in the eat-local philosophy.

Consider the most conspicuous ones: it is impossible for most of the world to feed itself a diverse and healthy diet through exclusively local food production—food will always have to travel; asking people to move to more fertile regions is sensible but alienating and unrealistic; consumers living in developed nations will, for better or worse, always demand choices beyond what the season has to offer.

Given these problems, wouldn't it make more sense to stop obsessing over food miles and work to strengthen comparative geographical advantages? And what if we did this while streamlining transportation services according to fuel-efficient standards? Shouldn't we create development incentives for regional nodes of food production that can provide sustainable produce for the less sustainable parts of the nation and the world as a whole? Might it be more logical to conceptualize a hub-and-spoke system of food production and distribution, with the hubs in a food system's naturally fertile hot spots and the spokes, which travel through the arid zones, connecting them while using hybrid engines and alternative sources of energy?

> We must accept the fact, in short, that distance is not the enemy of awareness.

As concerned consumers and environmentalists, we must be prepared to seriously entertain these questions. We must also be prepared to accept that buying local is not necessarily beneficial for the environment. As much as this claim violates one of our most sacred assumptions, life cycle assessments offer far more valuable measurements to gauge the environmental impact of eating. While there will always be good reasons to encourage the growth of sustainable local food systems, we must also allow them to develop in tandem with what could be their equally sustainable global counterparts. We must accept the fact, in short, that distance is not the enemy of awareness.

For Class Discussion

1. How does James McWilliams establish himself as a member of his target audience? How might his claim then surprise his readers' expectations based on shared values?

2. What assumptions does McWilliams make about the feasibility of a largely or entirely local diet? How does McWilliams use cost-benefit analysis in this argument?

3. How do the following features influence the rhetorical effect of this argument: the use of terms such as "market redundancy," "factor inputs and externalities," "food miles labeling"; his choice of examples; and his use of questions? How do these features suit McWilliams' primary audience?

4. On what points might McWilliams and Gary Paul Nabhan agree? On what points might they disagree?

5. Op-ed pieces are too short for fully developed ideas. Which points in this piece would you need to investigate more in order to agree with McWilliams?

CHAPTER QUESTIONS FOR REFLECTION AND DISCUSSION

1. What are five major controversies about feeding the world now and in the future that are discussed in this chapter's readings?

2. What are the major differences among industrialized agriculture, biotech agriculture, organic farming, and small-farm or local agriculture?

3. The following pairs of writers disagree in major ways about how to provide food for developing nations. Choose one pair and discuss where these writers are most at odds. Are their major differences in their assumptions and values, their interpretations of the problems, their reasoning, or their interpretations of facts and uses of evidence? Why do you think one writer makes a stronger, more persuasive case for his/her view?

A. Bill Freese and C. S. Prakash/Gregory Conko or Mike Mack

B. Vandana Shiva and C. S. Prakash/Gregory Conko or Eric Werker

C. C. S. Prakash/Gregory Conko and Kirsten Schwind or Michael Pollan

4. People embrace the idea of nurturing a local food system for many different reasons. What is the case for local food in each of these views: from the perspective of the environment, food security, social justice, nutrition, and cultural heritage?

5. How do these writers try to open readers' eyes to the conditions under which food is produced and the economic forces that control this production: Scott Canon, Conko/Prakash, Bill Freese, Kirsten Schwind, Michael Pollan, and James E. McWilliams? Which piece had the biggest impact on you and why?

6. Using the introductions to the readings and perhaps doing some brief research on the Web, learn about the background, employment, and institutional affiliations of the following writers. How does this context appear to inform and shape the writers' views on problems with food systems and hunger?

   - C. S. Prakash and Gregory Conko
   - Mike Mack
   - Vandana Shiva
   - Eric Werker
   - Kirsten Schwind
   - Gary Paul Nabhan

7. Working individually or in groups, research one of the following hunger- and food-related issues and bring your findings and sources back to share with your class.

   A. Using Green Revolution advances such as chemical fertilizers, pesticides, herbicides, irrigation, antibiotics for animals, and large one-crop farms, agribusinesses (often called "high-yield farming") have transformed food production. Research the agribusinesses in your region and the crops they raise. What have these large farms contributed to the economy of your state and to the nation's food supply?

   B. Research the Web sites of the international agribusinesses Monsanto (www.monsanto.com) and Syngenta (www.syngenta.com). How do these companies portray themselves with respect to social responsibility and concern for the environment, farmers, sustainable farming, and developing countries? What is persuasive about their claims? What differences, if any, do you see in their public relations appeals?

   C. Seafood Watch is a program of California's Monterey Bay Aquarium designed to raise consumer awareness about the importance of buying seafood from sustainable sources (http://www.montereybayaquarium.org/cr/seafoodwatch.aspx). What criteria do they employ in evaluating wild-caught and farmed seafood? How do these criteria compare to those established by the Alaska Seafood Marketing Institute? If there is a fishing industry in your state, how do Seafood Watch's criteria compare to your state's laws or guidelines?

   D. Many people, including Michael Pollan, are concerned that a handful of food companies control much of the world's food production and sales. Research one of the following corporations and investigate how many brands and what range of food products each produces: Cargill, Nestlé, Pepsi, Coca-Cola, Philip Morris, Unilever, or ConAgra. Make a list of problems this consolidation could pose for consumers. A good source of information about food processing and food manufacturing companies is the Market Share Matrix (www.marketsharematrix.org).

   E. Via Campesina, the global alliance of small farmer organizations, presents a comprehensive policy statement about food sovereignty on its Web site, www.viacampesina.org. Research this statement and others you find on food sovereignty. What are the main principles of this policy? What is food sovereignty *against*? How does it relate to free trade and fair trade? How have outbreaks of mad cow disease, the use of animal antibiotics, and the presence of biotech crops increased global interest in food sovereignty?

WRITING ASSIGNMENTS

Brief Writing Assignments

1. Write a brief informal piece in which you describe and discuss the connections between your eating habits/favorite foods and your family's cultural heritage or the distinctive features of your home region's food.

2. Scott Canon claims that where we shop and the food we buy are political decisions with global consequences. Write a brief self-reflection in which you describe your awareness of food production before and after reading the articles in this chapter. What changes would you consider making in what you eat to help the environment, the laborers who work with food production, and your own health? What challenges face consumers in developed countries who want to focus on socially responsible eating?

3. Using ideas from the arguments you have encountered in this chapter, freewrite an informal defense or refutation of one of the following claims. Begin by summarizing the position you are opposing. To expand your thinking or as preparation for writing a formal argument on this food subissue, you might write for twenty or more minutes in support of the claim and then write for twenty or more minutes challenging it.

   A. Small farmers are more likely than corporations to be good stewards of the land and treat the environment well.

   B. The economics and politics of the global free trade system have been a main cause of hunger problems in developing countries.

   C. Individuals can make a substantial difference in the world hunger and poverty picture.

   D. Technology and scientific breakthroughs in agriculture offer the best hope to solve the world's need for more food to feed a growing population.

   E. Moving toward a local food system would be more beneficial for most people.

4. **Analyzing Arguments Rhetorically.** Many of the arguments in this chapter—for example, Vandana Shiva's "Gift of Food," C. S. Prakash and Gregory Conko's promotion of biotech food, and Gary Paul Nabhan's definitions of local and regional food—are clearly directed toward audiences receptive to their views. Choose one of these arguments, and thinking particularly about opposing views, analyze the argument rhetorically. Briefly discuss the strengths of the argument, its weaknesses, and possible ways the writer could reshape it for broader or less sympathetic audiences.

5. Think about the ways that food production and world hunger intersect with other topics in this text such as consumerism and free trade (Chapter 3), immigration (Chapter 5), environmental problems (Chapter 6), and cultural rights (Chapter 8). Then brainstorm a network of issue questions that highlight connected controversies: for example, How has the availability of cheap labor in the form of illegal immigrants encouraged agribusiness in the United States?

Writing Projects

1. **Analyzing Arguments Rhetorically.** Summarize a pair of readings in this chapter, such as those listed in item 3 of the "Chapter Questions for Reflection and Discussion," that particularly "talk" to each other. Then perform a rhetorical analysis of these pieces as effective arguments and contributions to the public conversation. Write for a general audience of news commentary magazine readers. You might discuss how each of these writers' arguments has influenced your view on global food production or hunger and why your audience might find one more persuasive than the other.

2. Many discussions of solving the world's hunger problems include mention of plant biotechnology. Write the most complete argument you can arguing in support of or a against the use of biotechnology in agriculture to combat hunger and poverty in the developing world. Your peers are the audience for this argument. You may want to do additional research to find your own evidence. Consider, for instance, the interesting claim made by Henry I. Miller and Gregory Conko in their book *The Frankenfood Myth: How Protest and Politics Threaten the Biotech Revolution* (2004): "We find it revealing that when biotech varieties have been made available to farmers in less developed nations, they have been adopted quickly and eagerly" (172). Does your research support or refute this claim?

3. As a child, when you dawdled over eating some vegetable, an adult relative might have said to you, "You should be happy to eat your vegetables; children in Africa are starving and would love that food." You may have wondered, How would you send that spinach on your plate to Africa? The readings in this chapter have tried to give you a sense of the complex problems causing hunger crises and the challenge of finding a solution. Write an argument that would interest and motivate fourth and fifth graders. Either (a) argue that what we eat does affect children in Africa or (b) propose what you believe is the best way to help alleviate hunger and malnutrition in Africa. You might want to include visuals in your argument. Synthesize and document the ideas that you have encountered in this chapter's readings.

4. Investigate the status of local food in your community by researching and perhaps interviewing local growers and people involved in Community Supported Agriculture (CSA) and subscription farming, farmers markets, urban agriculture, and food co-ops. What is the status of your region's local food system? Shape your research into one of these kinds of writing: (a) a brochure or flier for your community or your city that presents a practical plan for moving toward purchasing more food

from local growers; (b) an op-ed piece for your university or regional newspaper that argues the problems or advantages of reconstructing your local food system; (c) a policy argument directed toward your state legislators that explores the problems facing a regional food system and a proposal to bolster such a system.

5. Any plan to address hunger and food security issues effectively must also be sustainable: environmentally, economically, and socially. As the readings from this chapter illustrate, sustainability is not a fixed concept. Using the readings and your own research, write a researched argument in which you propose to an audience of your peers what you see as a realistic and practical definition of sustainable food. You may want to investigate Via Campesina (www.viacampesina.org), the Rural Development Institute (www.rdiland.org), the Sustainable Food Laboratory (www.sustainablefoodlab.org), or Sustainable Table (www.sustainabletable.org).

6. Scott Canon and Michael Pollan, among other authors in this chapter, briefly introduce a number of issues related to food production, relation-ships between first-world consumers and third-world producers, food safety, and food security. Investigate one of these issues to find out what problems exist, and write a researched argument to inform your peers about the issue and propose a solution they can use to make decisions about their food purchases and consumption. For example, you might in-vestigate Pollan's claim that feedlot conditions have contributed to out-breaks of E.coli or follow up on Canon's reference to why Starbucks makes its suppliers provide "shade-grown" coffee.

7. Research several of the following organizations, exploring how they are in-volved in the global controversies over food production. Then write an argu-ment directed at your peers in which you advise people from rich nations about the most effective way for individuals to contribute to solving world hunger problems.

Rural Development Institute (www.rdiland.org)

Consultative Group on International Agricultural Research (www.cgiar.org)

International Society for Ecology and Culture (www.isec.org.uk)

Food and Agriculture Organization (www.fao.org)

Food First Institute (www.foodfirst.org)

Feeding America (www.feedingamerica.org)

Urban Agriculture Network (www.cityfarmer.org)

Toronto Food Policy Council (www.foodshare.net/train11.htm)

Community Food Security Coalition (www.foodsecurity.org)

AgBioWorld Foundation (www.agbioworld.org)

Heifer International (www.heifer.org)

Merging and Clashing Cultures
Media, Technology, Music, and Film

QUESTION TO PONDER

The United Nations has declared these practices as cultural rights: digital literacy (the opportunity and ability to access information and communication technologies); linguistic diversity on the Internet; and all cultures' ability to promote their own cultural products digitally. Yet a huge "digital divide" exists between countries with digitally literate societies and those without. According to the International Telecommunication Union Digital Access Index of 2002, the following fifteen countries have the lowest access to digital resources in the world: Eritrea, Congo, Benin, Mozambique, Angola, Burundi, Guinea, Sierra Leone, Central African Republic, Ethiopia, Guinea-Bissau, Chad, Mali, Burkina Faso, and Niger.* Although the United Nations has established a fund to provide computers to developing countries, you are wondering if money and effort should first be invested in cell phones. Should your business club support fundraising for cell phone service or computers in Niger to encourage this country's economy and culture?

CONTEXT FOR A NETWORK OF ISSUES

Many big disputes about globalization center on culture. Of course, cultural exchange has been going on for millennia, and yet globalization has stepped up cultural contact through business, media, and travel. These contemporary

---

*"ITU Digital Access Index: World's First Global ICT Ranking Education and Affordability Key to Boosting New Technology Adoption." *International Telecommunications Union*, March 19, 2003. www.itu.int/newsarchive/press_releases/2003/30.html (accessed May 18, 2009).

cultural interactions have brought new possibilities and problems. Think of the effect of reality TV on the Arab world, of fast food on Asian countries, of Japanese anime (animation) on American cartoons, and of cell phones on South America. Because culture encompasses the material, intellectual, artistic, and spiritual practices of a society—including food and diet, art, music, literature, traditions and lifestyles, beliefs and values—it is bound up with national identity, preservation of heritage, cultural self-respect, and people's sense of home and belonging.

In discussions about globalization's impact on culture, Marshall McLuhan's concept of the **global village,** first articulated in 1964, figures prominently. McLuhan, a historian and prophetic cultural commentator, theorized about the cultural effects of mass communication, especially the impact of television on modern society. He explored how technology has extended—indeed, transformed—the ways that human beings relate to the world:

> After three thousand years of specialist explosion and of increasing specialism and alienation in the technological extensions of our bodies, our world has become compressional by dramatic reversal. As electrically contracted, the globe is no more than a village. Electric speed in bringing all social and political functions together in a sudden implosion has heightened human awareness of responsibility to an intense degree.*

The key words in this quotation—"extensions," "compressional," "contracted," "together," and "implosion"—suggest a double dynamic, a world that is expanding *and* shrinking. The metaphor of global society as a "global village" is problematic, however. The idea of the world's cultures drawn together in a global village raises questions about equal representation, reciprocal sharing, enriched diversity, and mutual understanding.

These complex ideas become more concrete when we look at examples of controversial cultural exchange:

- **The impact of American media and television networks.** In 2004, MTV calculated that around "eighty percent of its viewership is now outside the United States."† MTV executives claim that it adapts to each country by offering a mix of American programming, local versions of American programming, and programming that originates in the local culture. MTV also plans to bring some of the successful programming from MTV China and MTV Korea back to the United States to reach out to ethnic audiences. Yet some people in other countries are voicing concern about the pervasiveness of American television. For example, Ukrainian student Liliya Vovk points out that many viewers in her

---

*Marshall McLuhan, *Understanding Media: The Extension of Man* (Cambridge, MA: MIT Press, 1964), 5.
†David Bauder, "MTV Reaches Global Milestone," Associated Press (December 20, 2004).

country are becoming obsessed with American soap operas and that viewers have no control over what is shown; for example, horror films from the United States are shown any time of day, and children can easily see them.*

- **Global contact and the international popular music scene.** Some music critics say the American music industry is stimulating healthy competition, spurring musicians and performers to create more innovative expressions of their own national cultures. In a 2001 special edition of *Time* Magazine on global music, Executive Editor Christopher Porterfield claims that the Internet and television have created "a vast electronic bazaar through which South African kwaito music can make pulses pound in Sweden, or Brazilian post-mambo can set feet dancing in Tokyo".† However, other cultural critics point out that major labels and big money are not promoting world music. As Pino di Benedetto, the marketing director for EMI Africa, a main African recording company, has said, "There is a lot of music that comes out of Africa that would be marketable in the States and Europe. . . . Nobody gives us a chance. We just are not seen as hit makers."‡

One global organization that is addressing these tensions and attempting to shape global cultural exchange for the benefit of all countries is the **United Nations Educational, Scientific, and Cultural Organization** (UNESCO). In 2001, this group, consisting of about two hundred member nations, formed the Convention on Cultural Diversity and wrote the **Universal Declaration on Cultural Diversity,** grounded in the principles that "cultural diversity is as necessary for humankind as biodiversity" and that "cultural rights are an integral part of human rights."$ However, as any investigation of sites of cultural contact such as media, music, or food reveals, respecting cultural rights is challenging and the stakes in cultural globalization are high.

STAKES AND STAKEHOLDERS

Many stakeholders, including international institutions, nongovernmental organizations, transnational corporations, cultural critics, and citizen groups, are striving to influence the way that globalization affects their own

---

*"American Influence on Our Society," *Topics Online Magazine for Learners of English*, http://www.topics-mag.com/projects/ukraine/liliya.htm.

†"Planet Pop. Music Goes Global," *Time*, http://www.time.com/time/magazine/article/0,9171,1000785,00.html.

‡Sharon LaFraniere, "Africa, and Its Artists Belatedly Get Their MTV," *New York Times*, (February 24, 2005).

$UNESCO, Thirty-First Session, "Universal Declaration on Cultural Diversity" (Paris, November 2, 2001).

cultures and the cultures of other nations. Here are some of the big issue questions with which these groups are wrestling.

How Is Increasing Global Cultural Contact Affecting Cultural Diversity? Some activists and cultural critics assert that cultural contact is creating uniformity, standardization, **homogenization**—a global monoculture that is sterile, dull, and artificial. For example, some American travelers express their frustration when they find many foreign cities looking like home with Starbucks, Kentucky Fried Chicken, Wal-Mart, Pizza Hut, Taco Bell, Hard Rock Café, and the most current American films playing. More than monotony and homogenization, the issue for some linguists, anthropologists, activists, and spokespeople for indigenous cultures is the loss of cultural heritage and cultural identity. They are warning that whole cultures are on the brink of vanishing. Anthropologists, environmentalists, and activists are striving to preserve languages that are dying out as some formerly remote cultures are drawn into more contact with the outside world. Scholars and activists like Helena Norberg-Hodge, founder of the International Society for Ecology and Culture, argue that language is bound to culture and that culture is connected to the deep values and structures that hold societies together. Some advocates for indigenous cultures argue that many of the smaller threatened cultural groups—such as the people of Ladakh, an ancient culture nestled next to India, China, and Tibet—possess knowledge of peaceful lifestyles and social cooperation that the world needs. As Norberg-Hodge writes in her book *Ancient Futures* (1991), "There is more than one path into the future."*

In contrast, proponents of free trade, corporate leaders, some cultural analysts, and many citizens around the world applaud the opportunity and cross-fertilization engendered by globalization's stepped-up cultural contact and sharing. To people examining the international music scene like journalist Christopher Porterfield, the world has become a lively, richly stocked "bazaar," not a monoculture. These people contend that cultural globalization has brought new possibilities of pleasing everyone.

What Are the Power Dynamics of Cultural Globalization? Many critics contend that the United States and other rich countries are dominating developing countries through **cultural imperialism.** Just as rich nations imposed political power and economic control on third world countries in earlier centuries (and, indeed, became rich nations partly through this imperialism), many critics, policymakers, activists, and citizens assert

---

Ancient Futures: Learning from Ladakh (San Francisco: Sierra Club Books, 1991), 1.

that rich nations are imposing their own culture and undermining the cultural diversity and integrity of poor, developing nations. For example, how can poor countries lacking information and communication technologies and the financial resources to support their own domestic music, arts, and film possibly compete with the production and distribution systems of affluent Hollywood? Still other cultural critics and citizen groups in some countries say that it is arrogant and simpleminded to assume that American culture is "conquering" the cultures of countries around the world. Many critics reject sociologist George Ritzer's McDonaldization model and claim instead that **glocalization,** whereby local cultures take an active part in adopting and adapting foreign culture, is more accurate.* After all, many McDonald's restaurants are owned and managed by people from those countries, and MTV has incorporated much local programming.

Other critics argue that American and Western culture are mixed, diverse cultures themselves, having been changed by other cultures around the world for centuries. America and Europe have experienced an influx of people from developing countries and have become new composite cultures. Using words like *integration* and *cultural fusion*, these analysts claim that the mixing of cultures is inevitable, healthy, and enriching. Other arguers claim that many countries and groups of people are welcoming American and Western culture, which they see as modernization and progress. The people watching American movies and buying Kentucky Fried Chicken want to be included in the new global society and are embracing the modern Western "good life."

Can Cultural Exchange Be an Instrument for Promoting Global Understanding, Cooperation, and Peace? UNESCO supports the idea that protecting cultural rights and diversity has the potential to promote peaceful international relations. Its Universal Declaration on Cultural Diversity states that "[a]ffirming that respect for the diversity of cultures, tolerance, dialogue and cooperation, in a climate of mutual trust and understanding [is] among the best guarantees of international peace and security."†

---

*Sociologist George Ritzer posits the global spread of McDonald's as a business model and a cultural force in *The McDonaldization of Society* (2000). However, sociologist Ronald Robertson speaks of glocalization (a term combining *globalization* and *localization*). He adopted this term from Japanese business, which used it to describe customizing products made for the global market to fit local cultures. See Habibul Haque Khondker, "Glocalization as Globalization: Evolution of a Sociological Concept," *Bangladesh e-Journal of Sociology* 1, no. 2 (July 2004). Thomas Friedman's definition on glocalization is given in Chapter 1: "Exploring and Defining Globalization" on p. 6.

†UNESCO, Thirty-First Session, "Universal Declaration on Cultural Diversity" (Paris, November 2, 2001).

Thomas L. Friedman, a well-known American journalist, also posits connections between global cultural and economic exchanges and peaceful relations in his "Golden Arches Theory of Conflict Prevention." Friedman contends that the spreading of McDonald's is closely bound up with the economic development of a strong middle class and that "people in McDonald's countries [don't] like to fight wars anymore," preferring instead "to wait in line for burgers" and not risk their economic and cultural prosperity.* Friedman's critics, however, cite the number of McDonald's in other countries as an example of the United States' cultural imperialistic encroachment. Other analysts argue that because cultural imperialism—or at least, very imbalanced cultural exchanges—is usually the reality, increased cultural contact frequently does not foster peace; instead, it engenders resentment and antipathy, as seen in the Arab world's growing hostility toward American culture.

How Can Cultural Contact and the Marketing of Culture Be Regulated to Promote and Preserve Cultural Diversity? Friedman proposes that countries engage in active glocalizing by filtering powerful cultures. He urges cultures to become active agents learning how "to assimilate aspects of globalization into [their] country and culture in a way that adds to [their] growth and diversity, without overwhelming it."† However, Friedman admits that glocalization must be supplemented by other "filters" such as governmental intervention to ensure the preservation of cultural heritage, educational programs, and wise promotion of tourism. UNESCO's international and intercultural agreement, its Universal Declaration on Cultural Diversity, seeks to advance **cultural pluralism** and to prevent culture from being turned into a commodity controlled by transnational corporations. A legal agreement still in progress, the declaration calls on national governments, international governmental and nongovernmental organizations, civil society, and private businesses to work together to prevent consumerism from overrunning culture and to stop the free trade advocates, transnationals, and the WTO from controlling the marketing of culture. The UNESCO supporters of cultural diversity assert that national and local bodies must maintain the power to decide how cultural exchanges will be managed and must preserve the right to create and protect their own cultural industries.

This chapter—first in the "Student Voice," "International Voices," and "Global Hot Spot" sections and then in its readings—explores how the big issues of cultural identity, values, and quality of life are embedded in a variety of global cultural controversies.

The Lexus and the Olive Tree (New York: Anchor Books, 2000), 249.
†Ibid., 295.

STUDENT VOICE: Cross-Culturalization in Beijing
by Michael Caster

Many American students study abroad in order to learn about and appreciate other cultures. Student writer Michael Caster describes the experience of witnessing cross-culturalization in the ancient yet rapidly modernizing city of Beijing, China.

>   After my first year taking Chinese, I decided to spend a summer studying in Beijing. This experience not only provided me with an opportunity to improve my Chinese but also gave me a lived experience of the rapid, well-publicized changes in China. Although I had taken several courses on contemporary China and considered myself an expert, I was actually quite unprepared for the vision of Beijing that greeted me, one of diversity and metamorphosis.
>
>   A brick edifice, seemingly solid and immutable, may be transformed overnight as if by alchemy into a glass-windowed store selling postcards or pillows. A ceramics store selling artisan teapots one day may open its doors as a house of Tibetan treasures the next. Specialty T-shirt shops are replaced by shops with paper-cut Buddhas and Chinese gods, to be replaced again by shops selling expensive leather purses. Workmen chisel away at the brick to widen restaurants or carve new stores into the landscape. A small waffle stand, carved into the mortar of a cafe owned by a German and Mongolian couple, opened its doors for a week and then disappeared. A Chinese handcraft boutique at which I had planned to purchase a gift for my mother was replaced without warning by an art deco bar specializing in Belgium ales. On some days vendors set up on corners to sell sweet potatoes roasted on old oil drums filled with coal. These itinerant confectioners are more permanent than certain shops with doors and windows. Here stores, buildings, and dreams may pass away without dirge or burial to make way for the next eager entrepreneur.
>
>   I often studied late and stopped off for Chuan, a kind of Chinese kebab, roasted meats on a stick, on my way home. There was one place I especially liked to go because the people who worked there were always so friendly about helping me with my Chinese. While they roasted, we would banter about whatever topics I had learned the previous week. Occasionally they would ask me to help with some small English phrase. I asked questions about their hometowns. They had all come from the countryside, and their families were far from Beijing. We developed a rapport to the point where we would make jokes with our eyes about silly patrons and disoriented tourists. While neither of us spoke each other's language, we communicated with remarkable ease. They always knew what I wanted. Then, one

day on my way home after a long session of practicing calligraphy, I passed by and was dumbfounded at what I saw. Without a word, within the two days since I had last been there, my comfortable little haunt had been transformed into a shop selling novelty matchbooks with cover designs ranging from Mao to Obama.

This experience of urban metamorphosis repeated itself. I frequented a street called Nan Luo Gu Xiang. I would wind my way through with the well dressed and the destitute between cabs, bicycles, and handcarts. I remember the first time I walked into Nan Luo Gu Xiang, at the south end. Below an ornately carved and painted traditional Chinese gate, an inscription tells a brief history of the street. Originally built in 1267, it was designed in the quintessentially Chinese architectural style of residential blocks called hutongs, which jut off from a main cobbled roadway. From above, Nan Luo Gu Xiang, with its eight parallel hutongs, looks like a fishbone. It claims to be the only remaining traditional residential area in Beijing; others like it having been demolished for high rises and shopping centers. Here the vestiges of old Beijing, old men in dusty jackets who peddle flatbeds attached to their bicycles while hollering their idiosyncratic calls for collecting trash, cutting keys, and myriad other services blend with the modern as the affluent drive by in Audis and Mercedes.

Although Nan Luo Gu Xiang is a cultural preservation site, on this street I was inundated by the realities of cross-culturalization and change. Nan Luo Gu Xiang itself has become a commodity, with a store that sells T-shirts, caps, and posters with the acronym NLGX emblazoned in technicolor. I can't help wondering how far the changes will go, what part of the traditional culture is sacrosanct under the laws of preservation. Nan Luo Gu Xiang is a laboratory in which the art of living in a pluralistic global society is tested. The sociologist Zygmunt Bauman has poetically described us as living in the age of "liquid modernity" and perhaps there are few other places than Beijing where this liquidity is as palpable. After I left China, I wondered whether all this transformation was the artificial attempt to seem more cosmopolitan or the organic byproduct of a truly shifting collective identity.

INTERNATIONAL VOICES

Cultural contact is an ongoing, daily global occurrence, and citizens of countries everywhere are reflecting on the way that other cultures are changing their lives. In the following statement, posted on *TOPICS Online Magazine for Learners of English*,* a student from Korea comments on the influence of American fast food on Korean food and habits. As Yeunhwa Jang observes, changes in a culture's food are closely bound up with cultural identity and social relationships.

Yeunhwa Jang from Korea Comments on American Fast Food

American fast food has definitely affected Koreans. You can spot fast food restaurants from America everywhere and many of the younger generation don't like traditional Korean food anymore. Koreans are now using western spices such as ketchup, mayonnaise, and butter to cook regular meals. Salad with western style dressing is also popular now.

In addition, manners in restaurants are not the same as before. Waiters address us in a more westernized manner. We Koreans don't use individual dishes for eating something from main dishes. We have always eaten from one bowl, but now some people think that it is dirty or unsanitary.

Tipping is also new for us. In some luxurious restaurants, we are now supposed to give tips to the waiter. Basically, we have never valued service with money, but now every service is based on money. It's far from our traditional way of doing things.

Finally, new food is being invented. Korean food and American food are combined into fusion food, such as a modified pizza to which Korean spices have been added. These new foods are beginning to appeal to Korean people.

GLOBAL HOT SPOT: The Middle East

The introduction of reality TV to the Middle East has sparked enormous controversy over cultural rights, cultural identity, and cultural survival. This controversy has pitted young people against the older generation, liberals against conservatives, and business leaders against religious leaders, and has intensified animosity between the East and West. While some viewers throughout Syria, Egypt, Kuwait, Yemen, Lebanon, and Saudi Arabia— many of them young—are delighting in Arab versions of *American Idol, Fear Factor,* and *Survivor,* many outraged conservative Muslims are posting blistering responses on the Web. Denouncing *Star Academy,* an imitation of a French show, one critic wrote, "I am stunned by the corruption and blind imitation [of the West] on the program."[†]

One recent cultural argument focused on the reality TV show *Big Brother,* filmed in Bahrain's Amwaj Islands. This show featured young people living together in a house, violating Islamic cultural notions of privacy and gender roles, including the rule about veiling women's faces in public. A number of Islamic leaders have denounced this show and all media from

---

[*]http://www.topics-mag.com/globalization/food-korea.htm (accessed May 18, 2009).
[†]Zeina Karam, "Reality TV a Hit in Arab World, to the Horror of Conservatives," *Seattle Times,* March 4, 2004.

the West as a cultural imperialist plot by the United States to take over the Middle East by imposing Western values. In the following excerpt, journalist Samira Ragab challenges her audience to strengthen moderate Islamic values. This excerpt appeared in "Special Dispatch no. 707" for May 6, 2004, on the Web site of the Middle East Media Research Institute (MEMRI, www.memri.org), a nonpartisan organization that translates and analyzes Arabic, Farsi, and Hebrew media. This report gathered and quoted the public statements that led to the banning of *Big Brother*.

> From the Bahraini daily *Akhbar Al-Khaleej:* "The mistake is thinking that the 'Big Brother' program is only a television program that can be handled [merely] by objecting to its airing or filming in Bahrain. . . . [But] it is a media war directed at and planned for the youth, which is targeted in this war strategy. Thus, stimuli and temptations [are directed] at the youth, which perhaps will be unable to absorb them, reject them, or refrain from sinking to them. . . .
>
> "The solutions [to this] are in our hands, and begin with our homes. Educate your sons and daughters to free and logical speech, distant from the burden of traditionalist words within their minds. Let them suckle concepts of nationalism, loyalty, and belonging to this great land and homeland. Let them suckle concepts of Arab culture that emerged and grew under Islam and illuminated proper Islamic thought, not strict and extreme [Islamic thought]. Your children in your home are the weapons by which you will fight the impending Tatar and Crusader attacks."

News commentaries in the United States and Europe have discussed the mixed Arab responses to reality TV, including the support of business leaders, who see reality TV as a source of jobs, investment, and even positive cultural change. The following excerpt from the article "Can Reality TV 'Survive' in the Middle East?" by Samar Farah, correspondent of the *Christian Science Monitor*, appeared in that publication on March 26, 2004.

> Beirut and Adma, Lebanon, and Damascus, Syria— . . . It's Friday night, or "Prime" time for "Star Academy," one of the hottest incarnations of reality TV in the Arab world. There's no sex, no alcohol, and no swearing, but that hasn't diminished the enthusiasm of fans. . . . "There's no one in Lebanon who hasn't heard of ['Star Academy']," says Maythem Shamesdine, a Beirut college student. . . .
>
> For Arab producers, certain changes to the Western formats were a given. When water is involved on "Fear Factor," females don full-body wet suits. Cameras were removed from bathrooms, and bedrooms were segregated on "Star Academy." Arab "Big Brother" went further, providing separate common rooms and separate prayer rooms for men and women and forbidding

candidates to enter bedrooms of the opposite sex. For the rest, many producers rely on the participants' common sense.

"They've all grown up in Middle Eastern homes," says Roula Saad, producer and director of "Star Academy." "They know what is acceptable."

But both "Big Brother" and "Star Academy" still required single men and women to live together under the same roof—a notion new to most viewers and illegal in many Arab countries. Three girls leaving a trendy store in Damascus say that, initially, the idea of a coed house bugged them. . . .

According to some viewers, even the older generation is coming around. Yasmina Fayad, an assistant producer at Future Television, says her father is no longer protesting the living arrangements on "Star Academy." But she's quick to add, "If I were to tell my dad that I wanted to live with a guy—never!"

Can cultural exchange through reality TV improve international relations in the Middle East? In 2003, tens of thousands of Israeli teenagers voted twenty-one-year-old Firas Khoury the winner of the fifteen contestants who had been housed together and required to sing and dance to show their talent. Firas Khoury, the only Arab to participate in a reality TV show on Israeli satellite television, remarked that many of the Israeli contestants had never had an Arab friend. He hopes "to have an influence on Arab and Jewish youth . . ." and believes that "[s]ometimes you just need to close your eyes, and try to understand we are all human beings and we should love each other and there is nothing to fight for at the end."*

The readings in this chapter examine various cultural pressure points around the world by looking at cultural exchanges in the areas of media, technology, film, and music.

READINGS

When Here Sees There
George Packer

George Packer is an award-winning journalist who currently writes for the *New Yorker*. He has written many articles, works of nonfiction, and novels, including *Blood of the Liberals* (2001), *The Village of Waiting* (1988), the anthology *The Fight for Democracy* (2003), and *The Assassin's Gate: America in Iraq* (2005), all of which support liberal views regarding world issues. This op-ed piece appeared in the *New York Times* on April 21, 2002.

---

*David Chazan, "Arab Wins Israeli Reality TV Show," *BBC News*, November 28, 2003.

What does George Packer claim is wrong with "the global communication system" and its effects on the world?

An Arab intellectual named Abdel Monem Said recently surveyed the massive anti-Israel and anti-American protests by Egyptian students and said: "They are galvanized by the images that they see on television. They want to be like the rock-throwers." By now everyone knows that satellite TV has helped deepen divisions in the Middle East. But it's worth remembering that it wasn't supposed to be this way.

The globalization of the media was supposed to knit the world together. The more information we receive about one another, the thinking went, the more international understanding will prevail. An injustice in Thailand will be instantly known and ultimately remedied by people in London or San Francisco. The father of worldwide television, Ted Turner, once said, "My main concern is to be a benefit to the world, to build up a global communications system that helps humanity come together." These days we are living with the results—a young man in Somalia watches the attack on the south tower live, while Americans can hear more, and sooner, about Kandahar or Ramallah than the county next to theirs.

But this technological togetherness has not created the human bonds that were promised. In some ways, global satellite TV and Internet access have actually made the world a less understanding, less tolerant place. What the media provide is superficial familiarity—images without context, indignation without remedy. The problem isn't just the content of the media, but the fact that while images become international, people's lives remain parochial—in the Arab world and everywhere else, including here.

"I think what's best about my country is not exportable," says Frank Holliwell, the American anthropologist in *A Flag for Sunrise,* Robert Stone's 1981 novel about Central America. The line kept playing in my mind recently as I traveled through Africa and watched, on television screens from Butare, Rwanda, to Burao, Somalia, CNN's coverage of the war on terrorism, which was shown like a mini-series, complete with the ominous score.

Three months after the World Trade Center attacks, I found myself sitting in a hotel lobby by Lake Victoria watching Larry King preside over a special commemoration with a montage of grief-stricken American faces and flags while Melissa Etheridge sang "Heal Me." Back home, I would have had the requisite tears in my eyes. But I was in Africa, and I wanted us to stop talking about ourselves in front of strangers. Worse, the Ugandans watching with me seemed to expect to hear nothing else. Like a dinner guest who realizes he has been the subject of all the talk, I wanted to turn to one of them: "But enough about me—anything momentous happening to you?" In CNN's global village, everyone has to overhear one family's conversation.

What America exports to poor countries through the ubiquitous media—pictures of glittering abundance and national self-absorption—enrages those whom it doesn't depress. In Sierra Leone, a teenage rebel in a disarmament camp tried to explain to me why he had joined one of the modern world's most brutal insurgencies: "I see on television you have motorbikes, cars. I see some of your children on TV this high"—he held his hand up to his waist—"they have bikes for themselves, but we in Sierra Leone have nothing." Unable to possess what he saw in images beamed from halfway around the world, the teenager picked up an automatic rifle and turned his anger on his countrymen. On generator-powered VCR's in rebel jungle camps, the fantasies of such boy fighters were stoked with Rambo movies. To most of the world, America looks like a cross between a heavily armed action hero and a Lexus ad.

Meanwhile, in this country the aperture for news from elsewhere has widened considerably since Sept. 11. And how does the world look to Americans? Like a nonstop series of human outrages. Just as what's best about America can't be exported, our imports in the global-image trade hardly represent the best from other countries either. Of course, the world is a nonstop series of human outrages, and you can argue that it's a good thing for Americans, with all our power, to know. But what interests me is the psychological effect of knowing. One day, you read that 600 Nigerians have been killed in a munitions explosion at an army barracks. The next day, you read that the number has risen to a thousand. The next day, you read nothing. The story has disappeared—except something remains, a thousand dead Nigerians are lodged in some dim region of the mind, where they exact a toll. You've been exposed to one corner of human misery, but you've done nothing about it. Nor will you. You feel—perhaps without being conscious of it—an impotent guilt, and your helplessness makes you irritated and resentful, almost as if it's the fault of those thousand Nigerians for becoming your burden. We carry around the mental residue of millions of suffering human beings for whom we've done nothing.

It is possible, of course, for media attention to galvanize action. Because of a newspaper photo, ordinary citizens send checks or pick up rocks. On the whole, knowing is better than not knowing; in any case, there's no going back. But at this halfway point between mutual ignorance and true understanding, the "global village" actually resembles a real one—in my experience, not the utopian community promised by the boosters of globalization but a parochial place of manifold suspicions, rumors, resentments and half-truths. If the world seems to be growing more, rather than less, nasty these days, it might have something to do with the images all of us now carry around in our heads.

For Class Discussion

1. What assumptions about the benefits of technology might Packer's audience have? How does he challenge these assumptions?

2. According to Packer, how has the goal of "technological togetherness" failed? What reasons and evidence does Packer offer to support his claim?

3. Part of the rhetorical power of this piece derives from Packer's skillful use of language. List as many memorable phrases like "technological togetherness" and "the global-image trade" as you can and explain what ideas these phrases capture and why they are rhetorically effective.

4. Where and how does Packer acknowledge alternative views?

5. What has this article contributed to your thinking about the idea of a global village? ∎

Behind the Digital Divide
The *Economist*

The *Economist* is a London-based, weekly generalist magazine that analyzes international political and business concerns and advocates "free markets and free trade" (www.economist.com). Its target audience is British and international business leaders and political decision makers, and it is written by anonymous authors with the intention of creating a collective voice. This piece was first published on March 12, 2005.

> According to this article, why is it so difficult for economists and policymakers to determine how to integrate information and communication technologies (computers with Internet access) into the lives of citizens of developing countries?

Development: Much is made of the "digital divide" between rich and poor. What do people on the ground think about it?

In the village of Embalam in southern India, about 15 miles outside the town of Pondicherry, Arumugam and his wife, Thillan, sit on the red earth in front of their thatch hut. She is 50 years old; he is not sure, but thinks he is around 75. Arumugam is unemployed. He used to work as a drum-beater at funerals, but then he was injured, and now he has trouble walking. Thillan makes a little money as a part-time agricultural labourer—about 30 rupees ($0.70) a day, ten days a month. Other than that, they get by on meager (and sporadic) government disability payments.

In the new India of cybercafes and software tycoons, Arumugam and Thillan, and the millions of other villagers around the country like them, seem like anachronisms. But just a few steps outside their section of the village—a section known as the "colony", where the untouchables traditionally live—the sheen of India's technology boom is more evident in a green room equipped with five computers, state-of-the-art solar cells and a wireless connection to the Internet. This is the village's Knowledge Centre, one of 12 in the region set up by a local non-profit organisation, the M. S. Swaminathan Research Foundation (MSSRF). The centres, established with the aid of international donor agencies and local government support, offer villagers a range of information, including market prices for crops, job listings, details of government welfare schemes, and health advice.

A conservative estimate of the cost of the equipment in the Embalam centre is 200,000 rupees ($4,500), or around 55 years' earnings for Thillan. Annual running costs are extra. When asked about the centre, Thillan laughs. "I don't know anything about that," she says. "It has no connection to my life. We're just sitting here in our house trying to survive."

Scenes like these, played out around the developing world, have led to something of a backlash against rural deployments of new information and communications technologies, or ICTs, as they are known in the jargon of development experts. In the 1990s, at the height of the technology boom, rural ICTs were heralded as catalysts for "leapfrog development", "information societies" and a host of other digital-age panaceas for poverty. Now they have largely fallen out of favour: none other than Bill Gates, the chairman of Microsoft, derides them as distractions from the real problems of development. "Do people have a clear view of what it means to live on $1 a day?" he asked at a conference on the digital divide in 2000. "About 99% of the benefits of having a PC come when you've provided reasonable health and literacy to the person who's going to sit down and use it." That is why, even though Mr. Gates made his fortune from computers, the Bill & Melinda Gates Foundation, now the richest charity in the world, concentrates on improving health in poor countries.

The backlash against ICTs is understandable. Set alongside the medieval living conditions in much of the developing world, it seems foolhardy to throw money at fancy computers and Internet links. Far better, it would appear, to spend scarce resources on combating AIDS, say, or on better sanitation facilities. Indeed, this was the conclusion reached by the recently concluded Copenhagen Consensus project, which brought together a group of leading economists to prioritise how the world's development resources should be spent. The panel came up with 17 priorities: spending more on ICTs was not even on the list.

Still, it may be somewhat hasty to write off rural technology altogether. Charles Kenny, a senior economist at the World Bank who has studied the role of ICTs in development, says that traditional cost-benefit calculations are in the best of cases "an art, not a science". With ICTs, he adds, the picture is further muddied by the newness of the technologies; economists simply do not know how to quantify the benefits of the Internet.

THE VIEW FROM THE GROUND

Given the paucity of data, then, and even of sound methodologies for collecting the data, an alternative way to evaluate the role of ICTs in development is simply to ask rural residents what they think. Applied in rural

India, in the villages served by the MSSRF, this approach reveals a more nuanced picture than that suggested by the skeptics, though not an entirely contradictory one.

Villagers like Arumugam and Thillan—older, illiterate and lower caste—appear to have little enthusiasm for technology. Indeed, Thillan, who lives barely a five-minute walk from the village's Knowledge Centre, says she did not even know about its existence until two months ago (even though the centre has been open for several years). When Thillan and a group of eight neighbours are asked for their development priorities—a common man's version of the Copenhagen Consensus—they list sanitation, land, health, education, transport, jobs—the list goes on and on, but it does not include computers, or even telephones. They are not so much sceptical of ICTs as oblivious; ICTs are irrelevant to their lives. This attitude is echoed by many villagers at the bottom of the social and economic ladder. In the fishing community of Veerapatinam, the site of another MSSRF centre, Thuradi, aged 45, sits on the beach sorting through his catch. "I'm illiterate," he says, when asked about the centre. "I don't know how to use a computer, and I have to fish all day."

But surely technology can provide information for the likes of Thuradi, even if he does not sit down in front of the computers himself? Among other things, the centre in this village offers information on wave heights and weather patterns (information that Thuradi says is already available on television). Some years ago, the centre also used satellites to map the movements of large schools of fish in the ocean. But according to another fisherman, this only benefited the rich: poor fishermen, lacking motorboats and navigation equipment, could not travel far enough, or determine their location precisely enough, to use the maps.

Such stories bring to mind the uneven results of earlier technology-led development efforts. Development experts are familiar with the notion of "rusting tractors"—a semi-apocryphal reference to imported agricultural technologies that littered poor countries in the 1960s and 1970s. Mr Kenny says he similarly anticipates "a fair number of dusty rooms with old computers piled up in them around the countryside."

That may well be true, but it does not mean that the money being channeled to rural technology is going entirely unappreciated. Rural ICTs appear particularly useful to the literate, to the wealthier and to the younger—those, in other words, who sit at the top of the socio-economic hierarchy. In the 12 villages surrounding Pondicherry, students are among the most frequent users of the Knowledge Centres; they look up exam results, learn computer skills and look for jobs. Farmers who own land or cattle, and who are therefore relatively well-off, get veterinary information and data on crop prices.

Outside the Embalam colony, at a village teashop up the road from the temple, Kumar, the 35-year-old shop owner, speaks glowingly about the centre's role in disseminating crop prices and information on government welfare schemes, and says the Knowledge Centre has made his village "famous". He cites the dignitaries from development organisations and governments who have visited; he also points to the fact that people from 25 surrounding villages come to use the centre, transforming Embalam into something of a local information hub.

At the centre itself, Kasthuri, a female volunteer who helps run the place, says that the status of women in Embalam has improved as a result of using the computers. "Before, we were just sitting at home," she says. "Now we feel empowered and more in control." Some economists might dismiss such sentiments as woolly headed. But they are indicators of a sense of civic pride and social inclusiveness that less conventional economists might term human development or well-being.

A QUESTION OF PRIORITIES

Given the mixed opinions on the ground, then, the real issue is not whether investing in ICTs can help development (it can, in some cases, and for some people), but whether the overall benefits of doing so outweigh those of investing in, say, education or health. Leonard Waverman of the London Business School has compared the impact on GDP of increases in teledensity (the number of telephones per 100 people) and the primary-school completion rate. He found that an increase of 100 basis points in teledensity raised GDP by about twice as much as the same increase in primary-school completion. As Dr. Waverman acknowledges, however, his calculations do not take into account the respective investment costs—and it is the cost of ICTs that makes people such as Mr. Gates so sceptical of their applicability to the developing world.

Indeed, Ashok Jhunjhunwala, a professor at the Indian Institute of Technology in Chennai (formerly Madras), argues that cost is the "deciding factor" in determining whether the digital divide will ever be bridged. To that end, Dr. Jhunjhunwala and his colleagues are working on a number of low-cost devices, including a remote banking machine and a fixed wireless system that cuts the cost of access by more than half. But such innovation takes time and is itself expensive.

Perhaps a more immediate way of addressing the cost of technology is to rely on older, more proven means of delivering information. Radios, for example, are already being used by many development organisations; their cost (under $10) is a fraction of the investment (at least $800) required for a telephone line. In Embalam and Veerapatinam, few people actually ever sit at a computer; they receive much of their information from loudspeakers on top of the Knowledge Centre, or from a newsletter printed at the centre and delivered around the village. Such old-fashioned methods of communication can be connected to an Internet hub located further upstream; these hybrid networks may well represent the future of technology in the developing world.

But for now, it seems that the most cost-effective way of providing information over the proverbial "last mile" is often decidedly low-tech. On December 26th 2004, villagers in Veerapatinam had occasion to marvel at the reliability of a truly old-fashioned source of information. As the Asian tsunami swept towards the south Indian shoreline, over a thousand villagers were gathered safely inland around the temple well. About an hour and a half before the tsunami, the waters in the well had started bubbling and rising to the surface; by the time the wave hit, a whirlpool had formed and the villagers had left the beach to watch this strange phenomenon.

Nearby villages suffered heavy casualties, but in Veerapatinam only one person died out of a total population of 6,200. The villagers attribute their fortuitous escape to divine intervention, not technology. Ravi, a well-dressed man standing outside the Knowledge Centre, says the villagers received no warning over the speakers. "We owe everything to Her," he says, referring to the temple deity. "I'm telling you honestly," he says. "The information came from Her."

"I'm illiterate," says one fisherman. "I don't know how to use a computer, and I have to fish all day."

For Class Discussion

1. This article grows out of an effort to investigate how rural residents of India think and feel about computer centers (information and communications technologies, or ICTs) in their communities. What views emerge from informal surveys?

2. On the argument spectrum—from argument as inquiry and problem solving on one end to argument as hard-sell persuasion on the other end—where would you place this piece? In other words, what specifically is its purpose and how does it hope to affect its audience's views?

3. What views against providing computers for communities in developing countries does this article acknowledge?

4. What is the rhetorical effect on readers of the short narrative that concludes this article?   ∎

Cover Image from the *Economist*

The photo on page 429 appeared on the cover of the *Economist,* a weekly London-based political and economic news commentary magazine with a pro-free trade perspective, on March 12, 2005, the same issue that featured the article "Behind the Digital Divide."

What features of this cover photo are especially intended to appeal to this magazine's audience of business executives and political leaders?

Chris Sattlberger/Panos Pictures

Cover Image from the *Economist*

For Class Discussion

1. What makes this image arresting? What are some implications viewers might draw from this image?

2. What is rhetorically effective about having the cell phone be made out of mud? About the smiling boy?

3. From your interpretation of this cover image, what audience assumptions will the articles in this magazine challenge?

4. In what ways could this image be used in arguments about cultural rights and digital literacy? ▮

In Defense of Globalization: Why Cultural Exchange Is Still an Overwhelming Force for Good Globalization

Philippe Legrain

Formerly a special advisor in the World Trade Organization, Philippe Legrain is now a visiting fellow at the European Institute of the London School of Economics. He has been published in the *Times, Financial Times,* the *Wall Street Journal Europe,* the *Guardian,* the *Independent, Foreign Policy,* and many other leading political and economic news commentary journals. He is also the author of two books that support globalization while criticizing some of its flaws: *Open World: The Truth about Globalisation* (2002), and *Immigrants: Your Country Needs Them* (2007). This article appeared in the *International Economy,* a magazine about global policy, trade, and trends that is aimed at financial professionals and politicians, in summer 2003.

> Legrain is an economist who is directing his argument to readers who live in European Union countries. Where do you see evidence of the influence of his profession on his views, and evidence of his primary audience?

Fears that globalization is imposing a deadening cultural uniformity are as ubiquitous as Coca-Cola, McDonald's, and Mickey Mouse. Many people dread that local cultures and national identities are dissolving into a crass all-American consumerism. That cultural imperialism is said to impose American values as well as products, promote the commercial at the expense of the authentic, and substitute shallow gratification for deeper satisfaction.

Thomas Friedman, columnist for the *New York Times* and author of *The Lexus and the Olive Tree,* believes that globalization is "globalizing American culture and American cultural icons." Naomi Klein, a Canadian journalist and author of *No Logo,* argues that "Despite the embrace of polyethnic imagery, market-driven globalization doesn't want diversity; quite the opposite. Its enemies are national habits, local brands, and distinctive regional tastes."

But it is a myth that globalization involves the imposition of Americanized uniformity, rather than an explosion of cultural exchange. And although—as with any change—it can have downsides, this cross-fertilization is overwhelmingly a force for good.

The beauty of globalization is that it can free people from the tyranny of geography. Just because someone was born in France does not mean they can only aspire to speak French, eat French food, read French books, and so on. That we are increasingly free to choose our cultural experiences enriches our lives immeasurably. We could not always enjoy the best the world has to offer.

Globalization not only increases individual freedom, but also revitalizes cultures and cultural artifacts through foreign influences, technologies, and markets. Many of the best things come from cultures mixing: Paul Gauguin painting in Polynesia, the African rhythms in rock 'n' roll, the great British curry. Admire the many-colored faces of France's World Cup-winning soccer team, the ferment of ideas that came from Eastern Europe's Jewish diaspora, and the cosmopolitan cities of London and New York.

Fears about an Americanized uniformity are overblown. For a start, many "American" products are not as all-American as they seem; MTV in Asia promotes Thai pop stars and plays rock music sung in Mandarin. Nor are American products all-conquering. Coke accounts for less than two of the 64 fluid ounces that the typical person drinks a day. France imported a mere $620 million in food from the United States in 2000, while exporting to America three times that. Worldwide, pizzas are more popular than burgers and Chinese restaurants sprout up everywhere.

In fashion, the ne plus ultra is Italian or French. Nike shoes are given a run for their money by Germany's Adidas, Britain's Reebok, and Italy's Fila. American pop stars do not have the stage to themselves. According to the IFPI, the record-industry bible, local acts accounted for 68 percent of music sales in 2000, up from 58 percent in 1991. And although nearly three-quarters of television drama exported worldwide comes from the United States, most countries' favorite shows are homegrown.

Nor are Americans the only players in the global media industry. Of the seven market leaders, one is German, one French, and one Japanese. What they distribute comes from all quarters: Germany's Bertelsmann publishes books by American writers; America's News Corporation broadcasts Asian news; Japan's Sony sells Brazilian music.

In some ways, America is an outlier, not a global leader. Baseball and American football have not traveled well; most prefer soccer. Most of the world has adopted the (French) metric system; America persists with antiquated British Imperial measurements. Most developed countries have become intensely secular, but many Americans burn with fundamentalist fervor—like Muslims in the Middle East.

Admittedly, Hollywood dominates the global movie market and swamps local products in most countries. American fare accounts for more than half the market in Japan and nearly two-thirds in Europe.

Yet Hollywood is less American than it seems. Top actors and directors are often from outside America. Some studios are foreign-owned. To some extent, Hollywood is a global industry that just happens to be in America. Rather than exporting Americana, it serves up pap to appeal to a global audience.

Hollywood's dominance is in part due to economics: Movies cost a lot to make and so need a big audience to be profitable; Hollywood has used America's huge and relatively uniform domestic market as a platform to expand overseas. So there could be a case for stuffing subsidies into a rival European film industry, just as Airbus was created to challenge Boeing's near-monopoly. But France's subsidies have created a vicious circle whereby European film producers fail in global markets because they serve domestic demand and the wishes of politicians and cinematic bureaucrats.

Another American export is also conquering the globe: English. By 2050, it is reckoned, half the world will be more or less proficient in it. A common global language would certainly be a big plus—for businessmen, scientists, and tourists—but a single one seems far less desirable. Language is often at the heart of national culture, yet English may usurp other languages not because it is what people prefer to speak, but because, like Microsoft software, there are compelling advantages to using it if everyone else does.

But although many languages are becoming extinct, English is rarely to blame. People are learning English as well as—not instead of— their native tongue, and often many more languages besides. Where local languages are dying, it is typically national rivals that are stamping them out. So although, within the United States, English is displacing American Indian tongues, it is not doing away with Swahili or Norwegian.

Even though American consumer culture is widespread, its significance is often exaggerated. You can choose to drink Coke and eat at McDonald's without becoming American in any meaningful sense. One newspaper photo of Taliban fighters in Afghanistan showed them toting Kalashnikovs—as well as a sports bag with Nike's trademark swoosh. People's culture—in the sense of their shared ideas, beliefs, knowledge, inherited traditions, and art—may scarcely be eroded by mere commercial artifacts that, despite all the furious branding, embody at best flimsy values.

The really profound cultural changes have little to do with Coca-Cola. Western ideas about liberalism and science are taking root almost everywhere, while Europe and North America are becoming multicultural societies through immigration, mainly from developing countries. Technology is reshaping culture: Just think of the Internet. Individual choice is fragmenting the imposed uniformity of national cultures. New hybrid cultures are emerging, and regional ones re-emerging.

National identity is not disappearing, but the bonds of nationality are loosening.

Cross-border cultural exchange increases diversity within societies— but at the expense of making them more alike. People everywhere have more choice, but they often choose similar things. That worries cultural pessimists, even though the right to choose to be the same is an essential part of freedom.

Cross-cultural exchange can spread greater diversity as well as greater similarity: more gourmet restaurants as well as more McDonald's outlets. And just as a big city can support a wider spread of restaurants than a small town, so a global market for cultural products allows a wider range of artists to thrive. If all the new customers are ignorant, a wider market may drive down the quality of cultural products: Think of tourist souvenirs. But as long as some customers are well informed (or have "good taste"), a general "dumbing down" is unlikely. Hobbyists, fans, artistic pride, and professional critics also help maintain (and raise) standards.

> **A bigger worry is that greater individual freedom may undermine national identity.**

A bigger worry is that greater individual freedom may undermine national identity. The French fret that by individually choosing to watch Hollywood films they might unwittingly lose their collective Frenchness. Yet such fears are overdone. Natural cultures are much stronger than people seem to think. They can embrace some foreign influences and resist others. Foreign influences can rapidly become domesticated, changing national culture, but not destroying it. Clearly, though, there is a limit to how many foreign influences a culture can absorb before being swamped. Traditional cultures in the developing world that have until now evolved (or failed to evolve) in isolation may be particularly vulnerable.

In *The Silent Takeover*, Noreena Hertz describes the supposed spiritual Eden that was the isolated kingdom of Bhutan in the Himalayas as being defiled by such awful imports as basketball and Spice Girls T-shirts. But is that such a bad thing? It is odd, to put it mildly, that many on the left support multiculturalism in the West but advocate cultural purity in the developing world—an attitude they would tar as fascist if proposed for the United States. Hertz appears to want people outside the industrialized West preserved in unchanging but supposedly pure poverty. Yet the Westerners who want this supposed paradise preserved in aspic rarely feel like settling there. Nor do most people in developing countries want to lead an "authentic" unspoiled life of isolated poverty.

In truth, cultural pessimists are typically not attached to diversity per se but to designated manifestations of diversity, determined by their preferences. Cultural pessimists want to freeze things as they were. But if diversity at any point in time is desirable, why isn't diversity across time? Certainly, it is often a shame if ancient cultural traditions are lost. We should do our best to preserve them and keep them alive where possible. Foreigners can often help, by providing the new customers and technologies that have enabled reggae music, Haitian art, and Persian carpet making, for instance, to thrive and reach new markets. But people cannot be made to live in a museum. We in the West are forever casting off old customs when we feel they are no longer relevant. Nobody argues that Americans should ban nightclubs to force people back to line dancing. People in poor countries have a right to change, too.

Moreover, some losses of diversity are a good thing. Who laments that the world is now almost universally rid of slavery? More generally, Western ideas are reshaping the way people everywhere view themselves and the world. Like nationalism and socialism before it, liberalism is a European philosophy that has swept the world. Even people who resist liberal ideas, in the name of religion (Islamic and Christian fundamentalists), group identity (communitarians), authoritarianism (advocates of "Asian values") or tradition (cultural conservatives), now define themselves partly by their opposition to them.

Faith in science and technology is even more widespread. Even those who hate the West make use of its technologies. Osama bin Laden plots terrorism on a cellphone and crashes planes into skyscrapers. Antiglobalization protesters organize by e-mail and over the Internet. China no longer turns its nose up at Western technology: It tries to beat the West at its own game.

Yet globalization is not a one-way street. Although Europe's former colonial powers have left their stamp on much of the world, the recent flow of migration has been in the opposite direction. There are Algerian suburbs in Paris, but not French ones in Algiers. Whereas Muslims are a growing minority in Europe, Christians are a disappearing one in the Middle East.

Foreigners are changing America even as they adopt its ways. A million or so immigrants arrive each year, most of them Latino or Asian. Since 1990, the number of foreign-born American residents has risen by 6 million to just over 25 million, the biggest immigration wave since the turn of the 20th century. English may be all-conquering outside America, but in some parts of the United States, it is now second to Spanish.

The upshot is that national cultures are fragmenting into a kaleidoscope of different ones. New hybrid cultures are emerging. In "Amexica" people speak Spanglish. Regional cultures are reviving. The Scots and Welsh break with British monoculture. Estonia is reborn from the Soviet Union. Voices that were silent dare to speak again.

Individuals are forming new communities, linked by shared interests and passions, that cut across national borders. Friendships with foreigners met on holiday. Scientists sharing ideas over the Internet. Environmentalists campaigning together using e-mail. Greater individualism does not spell the end of community. The new communities are simply chosen rather than coerced, unlike the older ones that communitarians hark back to.

So is national identity dead? Hardly. People who speak the same language, were born and live near each other, face similar problems, have a common experience, and vote in the same elections still have plenty in common. For all our awareness of the world as a single place, we are not citizens of the world but citizens of a state. But if people now wear the bonds of nationality more loosely, is that such a bad thing? People may lament the passing of old ways. Indeed, many of the worries about globalization echo age-old fears about decline, a lost golden age, and so on. But by and large, people choose the new ways because they are more relevant to their current needs and offer new opportunities.

The truth is that we increasingly define ourselves rather than let others define us. Being British or American does not define who you are: It is part of who you are. You can like foreign things and still have strong bonds to your fellow citizens. As Mario Vargas Llosa, the Peruvian author, has written: "Seeking to impose a cultural identity on a people is equivalent to locking them in a prison and denying them the most precious of liberties—that of choosing what, how, and who they want to be."

For Class Discussion

1. Legrain's piece provides an overview of the controversies over globalization's effects on cultures around the world. What is the range of topics encompassed by this controversy over culture?

2. What is Legrain asserting about globalization and cultural exchange in this argument? What opposing views, including those made by liberal antiglobalization protesters, does he address?

3. What does Legrain mean when he defines his own outlook as "broadly liberal, socially and economically" (www.phillipelegrain.com)?

4. What defense does Legrain offer against the charges of the cultural domination of American consumerism? While acknowledging that cultural contact changes national identity, what does Legrain see as positive about cultural globalization?

5. This loosely structured argument throws example after example at readers. If you were creating a paragraph summary of this piece, what key points would you include? What examples would you include and why?

Great Mall of China
Henry Payne

Henry Payne is an editorial cartoonist for the *Detroit News*. His work has been published in the *New York Times*, the *National Review*, and *USA Today*, and he is a contributing cartoonist to *Reason*. This cartoon was originally published in the *Detroit News* and later reprinted in *Reason*.

> What knowledge of the Great Wall of China does the cartoonist assume that his audience has?

"THINGS HAVEN'T BEEN THE SAME SINCE WE OPENED OUR MARKETS..."

Henry Payne: © Detroit News/Dist. By United Feature Syndicate, Inc.

For Class Discussion

1. Which controversy over cultural exchange does this cartoon examine?
2. What claim does the cartoon support?
3. What questions about culture, free trade, and globalization does this cartoon raise? Whom does it appear to be satirizing?
4. What readings in this chapter would this cartoon agree with or support? ■

The Revolution Will Be Televised
Matt Pomroy

Matt Pomroy is a journalist for *Time Out* in the United Arab Emirates and deputy editor for the Middle East edition of *Men's Fitness*. This article appeared in *Time Out* in 2007, as well as in the online edition of *Arabian Business*, a weekly Middle Eastern business magazine published in both English and Arabic.

While this article was written for an audience of Middle Eastern business people, you as a reader may be more familiar with MTV's programming and identity. What cultural concerns does Pomroy address regarding the creation of MTV Arabia?

MTV is now older than most of the people who currently watch it. It was born on August 1, 1981, in New York and was launched with the sole purpose of showing music videos. As they flicked the switch, a disembodied voice said "Ladies and gentlemen, rock and roll," and with that, a cultural totem for a nation's youth sparked into life. The first song was "Video Killed The Radio Star" by the Buggles. Cheeky, irreverent, and appropriately prophetic, it was the perfect song to launch with. However, by song six they were playing Cliff Richard's "We Don't Talk Anymore"—no matter, as MTV would grow and morph into far more than just a video jukebox.

Today, MTV is seen in a total of 140 countries and has the power to reach two billion people. More significantly though, are the global franchises, with MTV Latvia, MTV Pakistan and MTV Japan among the 53 MTV channels that have launched outside of America, proving that globalisation needn't mean homogenisation. The spread of MTV has actually meant region-specific programming tying in with the channel's global ethos, rather than just transmitting a feed from the American parent station. Now the Middle East has joined the party and, although MTV Arabia is a relative latecomer, its launch could well be the most culturally significant since the original MTV was broadcast over 26 years ago.

"MTV Arabia is the region's first and only youth lifestyle brand, offering a platform for self-expression, while truly representing Arab youth." This is the statement from the channel's business plan and, as businesses go, it could be massive. The potential impact is staggering, as this free-to-air station has an estimated target audience of 190 million young people in 12 key regions: Saudi Arabia, Egypt, Syria, Lebanon, Bahrain, Jordan, Kuwait, Oman, Qatar, Yemen, Palestine and here in the UAE. The launch will be the biggest ever on 'day one' of any new MTV channel in its history due to the vast potential reach, and the fact that it's free to air. Culturally though, the significance may be even greater.

"We will be illustrating a more positive culture from the region, rather than the typical negative image," says Patrrick Samaha, MTV Arabia's General Manager. "The internet has exposed young people in the region to the rest of the world and now they want to be part of that—and this will be a platform for that expression. MTV will be affecting youth at a sensitive time of their lives."

Perhaps significantly, Abdullatif Al Sayegh, the CEO of Arab Media Group which will broadcast the channel, has stated that with regards to MTV, "AMG is committed to making a difference in the region by raising the standards of entertainment and championing pro-social initiatives."

It's interesting that MTV Arabia is launching at a time when the MTV network is at a critical juncture, not financially but in terms of content. The M in MTV stands for music, but the channel is moving away from that, to the annoyance of many (increasingly former) viewers. Even Justin Timberlake, while on stage at last month's MTV awards, made a stand and said "I want to challenge MTV to play more videos." The listings for MTV UK on November 7 illustrate the direction that the channel has taken in many regions. Of the 24 hours it broadcast that day, only three of them were actually showing music, and they were between the hours of 2–4am and then 6–7am in the morning. The rest of the day is devoted to reality TV and comedy aimed at the youth demographic, including eight episodes of That 70s Show.

MTV Arabia promise they will be committed to music with the ratio of music-to-programmes set roughly to 40/60, so music videos will be well represented and half of those screened will be from Arabic artists. But they insist that there is more to the station. "It's not about the music videos," Patrick says, "the word M means more than music these days and the objective is to become a youth station."

Giving the Arabic youth a credible outlet via MTV Arabia is going to be something of a balancing act. In America the channel is constantly condemned by parental watchdog groups as a corrupting influence, with a spokesperson from the Parents Television Council saying, "In an affront to families everywhere, MTV are trying to attract younger audiences with violence, sex and titillating language." At the same time the station is being criticised by others for censorship, with many music videos being banned or edited. For example, in Akon's video for 'Smack That', the phrase 'smack that' was censored in some parts.

But ironically for MTV Arabia, issues of censorship may work in their favour. "Of course there will be censorship," Patrick says smiling. "Our aim is quality and respect for culture. Some videos won't get on there simply because the quality is not good enough, others will be banned for cultural reasons. Although increasingly we are seeing good quality video clips from Arabic performers. But there will be a strict policy of respecting those with very high traditional values. MTV Arabia has to make the point that it's a global brand, but it's for Arabs and made by Arabs. Something made by people like them."

The adherence to local values has in many ways forced their hand: a total reliance on American imports would not be possible, so original programming was essential, as were the four months of field research. "The public decided what the station would be like—that was what we needed," Patrick explains. His team targeted people under the age of 24 and travelled around the region to schools and universities canvassing opinions. The aim was to see what it was they wanted, from what would eventually be their new channel. Patrick is also quick to point out that consultation with figures of authority also took place. "We also spoke to the governments, leaders and parents and said 'don't worry, it will be nice' so they know what's going on."

Many of the programmes will be made locally, with region-wide talent show *Hip HopNa* being the flagship series. The search for local hip-hop flair in the Middle East is perhaps the one show that will have the biggest impact, highlighting emerging Arabic artists.

Patrick explains, "you can't be MTV unless you start something new from day one, and Arabic hip-hop music is going to be huge.

"We've found some amazing talent. People said to us, 'how can you do hip hop without bad mouthing?' but we've done it."

Patrick believes that hip hop can be educational and, through music, young Middle Easterners will be telling their own stories. "They talk about their problems in a hip-hop way," he explains and the themes are pretty much the same ones that affect teenagers the world over. After all, far more teenagers have problems with family and school than they do with drive-by shootings and pretending to be a gangster. It's certainly far more honest. So what do the heads of MTV in America make of their Arabic cousin? Again Patrick cracks a grin. 'We are working closely with the MTV networks—it's a brand that we are new to, and it's a culture that they are new to, so we're both learning. But we may change as we go. Whoever says they don't want to change is actually saying they don't want to listen. We'll always listen—if at any point we say, "fine, this is it then we're on the wrong track."

If MTV is going to become the dominant voice of the youth once again, then this region could well be the place for it to happen. Young people represent 65 per cent of the population in the Middle East. AMG's Abdullatif Al Sayegh issued a rallying cry to this effect saying that, "MTV Arabia will celebrate a new era for our youth—it's time they were heard."

When MTV Arabia goes live, the world will have a prime opportunity to better understand and be entertained by not only the most misunderstood and maligned age demographic on the planet, but also the most misunderstood and maligned region. While MTV in other areas are content with screening sitcom re-runs, and sleazy reality shows with Paris Hilton, so MTV Arabia is giving a real voice to people who are essentially the future of the Middle East.

Despite increased censorship it's, in many ways, far more cutting edge than anything the American parent station is currently doing. Middle Eastern youth will have the centre stage and MTV is letting them show the world their ambitions, opinions and, of course, their music. Ladies and gentlemen, rock and roll.

For Class Discussion

1. What information has Pomroy included in this article to appeal to an audience of business people? Would you expect this audience to be more concerned with economic or cultural matters?

2. How does Pomroy address the opposing view that globalization leads to sameness everywhere? What evidence does he provide that this will not be the case with MTV Arabia?

3. The term glocalization is defined in Chapter 1, p. 6 by Thomas Friedman, and in the footnote on p. 415. Can you argue that MTV Arabia is an example of glocalization? Why or why not?

4. Who are Pomroy's sources in this argument? What other voices might he have consulted in order to make a more credible or convincing argument?

5. What background knowledge about MTV and its programming do you possess? In your view, what programs or music videos would seem culturally appropriate for MTV Arabia?

6. What indications does Pomroy provide that programs or videos produced for MTV Arabia might air elsewhere in the world? In other words, would this article provide any evidence that there will be a cross-cultural exchange? ∎

Mideast Rappers Take the Mic
Borzou Daragahi and Jeffrey Fleishman

Borzou Daragahi was born in Iran and grew up in the Chicago area and New York City. He is a Middle East correspondent for the *Los Angeles Times* and was a Pulitzer Prize finalist for his Iraq coverage in 2005 and 2007. Jeffrey Fleishman, also of the *Los Angeles Times*, has covered wars in Kosovo and Iraq and has traveled extensively through Europe and the Middle East. He is currently based in Cairo. This article appeared in the *Los Angeles Times* on April 7, 2009.

> While a traditional argument makes its main claim explicit, this piece contains a more implicit claim. What would you say is Daragahi's and Fleishman's purpose and how do they hope to change their audience's views?

Reporting from Cairo and Tehran—The police were polite but firm as they arrested Shahin Felakat, a lanky teen whose mussed-up strands of dirty brown hair reach in all directions, and charged him with singing lyrics that threatened Iran's Islamic order.

After a few days in jail, the 18-year-old rapper ran back to the studio to rejoin his homeboys.

"The authorities have a very negative view of rap," Felakat says. "They say rap has a corrupting influence. When you say the word 'rap,' they think it's about addiction, someone without parents who's only thinking of drugs and sex."

Another day, another hardship, another inspiration for the young men and occasional woman who turn out the lyrics and rhythms that are rapidly becoming the soundtrack for Middle East youths.

From the 021 to the 961 to the 962, the telephone codes for Tehran, Lebanon and Jordan, the vernacular of American rap music and street culture has infiltrated the lives of young people. These kids of the Middle East have adopted the beats and hyperbolic boasts of hip-hop, but they've also reshaped rap to fit their own purposes, tapping into its spirit of defiance to voice heartfelt outrage about their societies.

Iranians rhyme about stifled lives and street-level viciousness born of economic hardship. Lebanese rap subtly about sectarian blood feuds. Palestinians sling verses about misery in refugee camps and humiliation at Israeli checkpoints. Egyptians lament the fragmentation of the Arab world.

"The main theme is bringing about Arab unity, becoming one nation rather than being divided and conquered," says Sphinx, a rapper for the Cairo-based Arabian Knightz who grew up in Wilmington, Calif., and whose real name is Hesham Mohammed Abed.

The Arabian Knightz tone is spiritual, not religious; message-driven, not pious. It is the rap not of the gangsta and his trove of drugs and half-naked women, but of brash young men whose defiance coexists with tradition.

To connect with a Middle Eastern audience, Arabic and Persian hip-hop often weaves the beeps, bops and booms of Western rhythms into the distinctive rolls, punctuating clangs and soulful background singing of Asian pop. Producers sample clips from traditional horns and string instruments like ouds as well as electric guitar and synthesizers.

"To the extent that we can, we try to rap to Iranian rhythms," Felakat says.

Just as young men vent the pent-up rage, frustration and brutality of urban America through hip-hop music and graffiti, rappers in the Middle East mold ferocious rhymes and staccato rhythms into passionate odes to injustice, poverty and violence.

"We're struggling," says Lynn Fattouh, also known as Malikah, a 23-year-old Lebanese rap star who is one of the most famous female artists in the Arab hip-hop world.

"We're living a very hard life," she says. "We're witnessing war. We're witnessing hunger. We're living in countries where they don't even follow human rights. All the pain and all the stuff happening around us pushes us to express ourselves."

All eyes turn to Malikah as she hits the stage. Her taut frame, exuding toughness, sways hard back and forth, her fist curled tight around the microphone as she flows in Arabic:

I am talking to you woman to woman.
It's time to face up
It's time to plan.
Cry out for freedom . . .

Tanya Traboulsi

Lynn Fattouh, also known as Malikah, is one of the most famous female artists in the Arab hip-hop world.

Men have decided to manage your life and destiny.
Don't live in despair.
Go out and work and earn your dime.
Walk with me along this path.

"Onstage, I don't know what happens," she says. "I just flip. I can let go of all my stress and my anger. It's a part of me. It's the angry part of me. I can talk about politics, economy, social life, religion. I talk about me. What I see in the streets. It's the point of view of a Lebanese girl who lives in the Middle East."

Angst and anger drive much of the music. Rappers in the Middle East cite influences such as Eminem and the late Tupac Shakur, artists who tap wells of personal sorrow for inspiration.

"My songs have different subjects from love to drugs and street issues and social issues," says Felakat, part of an emerging crop of Iranian rappers. "Everything I write I try to incorporate aspects of my life. Otherwise it becomes empty."

Drugs and partying are an important part of the hip-hop scene.

Lebanese smoke hashish while Iranians use crystal methamphetamine, called *shisheh,* or glass, to stay pumped during overnight recording sessions.

The rappers are driven by the crumbling cityscapes that drove American hip-hop before it became all about glitter and cash.

"I rap about love, gangs, hitting, killing and stealing," says Mahdad, a boyish Tehran rapper of 19 who also goes by the name Maff.

"It's a joke of a city," he says of Tehran. "It's an absurd city where a bunch of limitations have been placed that don't allow anyone to live easily."

The young unshaven man speaks sparingly, sucking hard on cigarettes, batting away questions with one-word replies.

But Soroush Lashkari, Iran's best-known hip-hop artist, comes alive when he raps. His boyish jitters melt away. His lean frame sways with the rhythm. Electricity flows through the room.

This is Tehran.
That means a city where everything you see provokes.
Provokes your soul into the garbage bin.
You, too. You weren't a person. You were trash.
Everyone here is like a wolf. Do you want be like a lamb?
Let me open up your eyes and ears a bit.

Though restrictions on hip-hop rhetoric are harshest in the Islamic Republic, rappers in the rest of the Middle East have it tough as well. The Arabian Knightz must be careful when speaking about Egyptian President Hosni Mubarak. The group must submit its albums to state censors; if the censors' red pens are too heavy, the group's backup plan is to release its music in Dubai, or possibly Europe.

Though Egyptian rappers don't name names, they also don't hide their disgust. In the song "Not Your Prisoner," Sphinx sings:

Mr. Politician, I got a little question.
How come you're eating when your people isn't?

Rapper Fadi Abu Ghazallah, a Jordanian of Palestinian descent, remembers the time he recorded a politically charged song about the Arab-Israeli conflict. Security officials arrived shortly afterward at the Amman studio, erased the track and warned Ghazallah to stick to rhyming about parties and girls.

"I was, like, talking about peace in general, about how people should be living together in peace," recalls the chubby 24-year-old, who wears his hair in a ponytail and sports a goatee. "They told me, 'If you ever do that again, if you ever do a political track, if we ever catch you doing something like this, you are really busted.'"

Even in freewheeling Lebanon, artists censor themselves, refraining from lyrics that might be too provocative or explicit. Malikah, who boasts that "revolution is in my blood," decided not to record a song she wrote that lashed out at combatants in an outbreak of sectarian violence last year.

"Who is shooting who? Who are the innocents?" say the lyrics. "Some traitors ignited the situation. They should stop financing [the war], stop distributing arms, stop the slaughtering. . . . One group against another. Beirut is burning down slowly."

Middle East rappers also must adapt their music to traditional cultures and conservative families. At first, Malikah covered her face when she performed, lest her parents find out that she was a singer, an occupation often equated with prostitution in the Middle East.

"We are facing our own culture," said Sahand Quazi, an Iranian rapper who lived in Orange County before returning to Tehran, where he roams the streets in a dark tracksuit, his eyes shaded by the brim of a black baseball cap.

"I am facing my grandpa," he says. "I got to prove to my grandpa that hip-hop is good, that actually it is not bad. It is not corrupt."

Many of the best rappers have moved abroad, especially those from the Palestinian territories. Hip-hop artists in the Middle East occasionally craft lighter rhymes about partying with their homies, acquiring Dolce & Gabbana clothes or about who's the best rapper in town. But they return to themes of war, poverty and repression because often they've experienced little else.

"We don't do it like any other culture does it," Malikah says. "Not like they do it in the States or they do it France. When we rap, we use our language, our culture."

For Class Discussion

1. Written for a general newspaper audience, this piece assumes that the reader possesses some background knowledge of American hip-hop. How might you characterize the general view of hip-hop? What artists and subjects come to mind?

2. What is the main claim in this piece?

3. Who are Daragahi and Fleishman's sources in this article? How does their use of sources affect the credibility of their argument?

4. Compare the sources quoted in this piece to those quoted by Matt Pomroy. Based on their respective audiences, how effective would it be for Pomroy to have quoted Daragahi and Fleishman's sources and vice versa?

5. Using Thomas Friedman's definition of glocalization on page 6, make a case that the artists quoted or described by Daragahi and Fleishman do (or do not) exemplify successful globalization. Have they assimilated aspects of globalization into their own culture in a positive way? ∎

Why Is Bollywood Obsessed with Producing "Crossover Films"?
Rajal Pitroda

Bollywood, the subject of this article, is India's equivalent of America's Hollywood. This center of the Indian film industry produces over seven hundred films a year that are popular throughout Africa, Asia, and the Middle East. Typical Bollywood films are musicals that feature singing and elaborate choreography and cinematography. Bollywood films such as *Lagaan* (2001) are beginning to get attention from American audiences. While *Lagaan* is strictly an Indian film, *Bride and Prejudice* (2004)—called a "crossover film"—was intended to blend film cultures and to introduce America to Bollywood features. In this commentary, Rajal Pitroda, a Chicago-based writer and knowledgeable critic of the Indian entertainment industry, questions the value and cultural impact of such crossover films. This piece appeared in the *News India-Times,* published in New York, on March 11, 2005.

What audience does Pitroda particularly want to reach with this proposal argument, and what features appeal to that audience?

Gurinder Chadha's *Bride and Prejudice,* which opened last month in the U.S., is mainstream America's first exposure to India's singing and dancing tradition of cinema. Distributed in North America by Miramax Films, the publicity of *Bride and Prejudice* centered largely on its lead actress, Aishwarya Rai. Although a household name in India and other parts of the world familiar with Bollywood, Aishwarya was introduced to America through a series of television appearances, namely on *60 Minutes, Nightline* and *The Late Show with David Letterman.*

Almost immediately after each of the interviews was aired, Indians around America, and even at home in India, took to an analysis of her performance. Around dinner tables, on the Internet and in newspapers, we scrutinized her giggles, her grammar and the eternal question of what substance, if any, lay behind her looks. Headlines in India heralded 'Ash Does Fine,' while Internet interviews decreed her lack of sound judgment in choosing to wear a skirt over a sari. Almost all of us found some way to comment on Aishwarya's ability (or inability) to truly "crossover" into America. But why?

The reason, most likely, is that Aishwarya Rai is largely symbolic, a torchbearer of a larger revolution—one that takes Indian entertainment beyond the developing world, and into America.

However, instead of merely criticizing and evaluating her, we should be asking ourselves larger questions prompted by her presence—why, as a culture of global Indians, are we so obsessed with a marriage of Bollywood into the West? Why are so many of our filmmakers at home in India seeking to make the next big "crossover" film? And why—when we say that Bollywood is the largest film industry in the world, making movies for a global audience of nearly three billion—when one actress arrives in Hollywood, do we turn our entire focus on her? Are we just seeking appreciation and acceptance from the West? And what about our industry at home? What is actually happening to Bollywood in Mumbai?

Aishwarya's arrival in Hollywood, and its surrounding media blitz, needs to be viewed beyond the individual. She is cultural capital, a symbol of the Indian ethos, the Indian entertainment industry and a larger possibility. The challenge is to translate this into economic growth, and that is where the industry at home becomes critical.

India, and much of the world, is fixated on Hollywood because, despite making less than half the number of films as the Indian industry, it is the largest moneymaking film industry in the world. *Titanic*, released in 1997, earned $1.8 billion dollars at the global box office, more than the nearly 1,000 films combined released by the Indian industry in that year.

Hollywood, through its years, has built itself into this industry—it has created and shaped institutions that support talent, recognize achievement and respect the creative process.

Aishwarya offers India an entry point into Hollywood, and the global film industry. However, without the proper attention to our own processes, institutions and policies, the opportunity for global expansion may not materialize.

Recognized as an official "industry" by the government in 2001, the Indian film industry finally became eligible for bank finance and opened up to foreign investment, and thus, increased credibility. Despite these changes, it continues to operate much as it has in the past, with illegitimate sources of financing still rampant. The industry has not adequately studied its audiences with market surveys, and it is typical for films in India to not fully recoup their investment. These numbers, however, are difficult to monitor, as there is no single reputable source of box office receipt information. On any given week, all of the film trade journals may report different information on collections for a particular film, as producers, distributors and exhibitors do not fully disclose their particular cut of a deal.

In addition to financing and monitoring of funds, the Indian industry suffers from a severe lack in training institutions for creative talent. The once highly regarded Film and Television Institute of India is severely underfunded and understaffed, with equipment that has not been updated for over a decade. There are few other training schools for actors, writers, directors and more, contributing both to stale content and an ingrained lack of respect for creative pursuits, as they seemingly do not require a degree.

India has not cultivated institutions that support creative professionals either—there is no Directors Guild or Writers Guild to work with individuals on their rights and support them in their professions, within an Indian context.

All of these issues prevent India from creating and sustaining a stronger film industry at home, and one that is exportable beyond its borders.

Government institutions that support the entertainment industry are nearly defunct in their financing and international marketing abilities. Authorities are ineffective and uninterested in communicating with Western counterparts, and regulatory policies are altered on a whim, making it difficult for U.S. studios and distribution companies to keep up with policy changes that affect their interaction with India. Piracy is still rampant, high rates of entertainment tax plague distributors and exhibitors, and co-production treaties with countries such as Canada and Italy have been stalled for upward of three years.

Aishwarya Rai, whether giggling or not, draws interest and attention to our industry, and is paving the way for a greater international audience. The globalization of the Indian entertainment industry may begin with one actress, but it cannot be sustained by her alone. India requires a movement that develops its own talent while drawing production to its borders, much like the software industry did in the 1990s, supported by institutions like the IITs, and organizations like Nasscom and TiE. In order to create a truly international industry, one that not only moves West but also builds East, we must first cultivate Bollywood at home, and continue to entertain billions of people as only we do best.

For Class Discussion

1. What cultural interaction and what Bollywood conditions is Pitroda protesting in this piece?

2. What proposal does she put forth?

3. How does she persuade readers of her knowledge and of the importance of her proposal?

4. How rhetorically effective is Pitroda's conclusion in wrapping up her argument and persuading her audience?

5. What theories or principles of cultural globalization discussed in the introduction to this chapter does Pitroda's argument support?   ∎

Shocked by Slumdog's Poverty Porn
Alice Miles

Alice Miles is a columnist for *The Times* of London, writing mainly on politics and national issues such as education and health. The film that she critiques, *Slumdog Millionaire*, released in late 2008, was wildly popular and won several Oscars. This opinion piece was published on January 14, 2009, in *The Times*, a traditionally right-of-center publication that has long been considered the newspaper of record in the United Kingdom.

As indicated by its title, this opinion piece has a bold, outspoken tone. What effect might Alice Miles' tone and choice of language have on her audience?

There are many reasons why you might want to see *Slumdog Millionaire*—it is directed by the brilliant Danny Boyle, it is set in the sensual feast that is Mumbai and it has won awards for music, directing and acting. And then there is the fact that critics and its own publicity have branded it a feel-good movie. Call me shallow, but that ultimately swung it for me.

A few hours later I was wincing in my seat. The film opens with a scene of horrible violence: a man hanging from the ceiling of a police station, being tortured to unconsciousness, a trickle of blood running from his mouth. It moves swiftly into scenes of utter misery and depravity, in which small starving children are beaten, mutilated and perverted.

Mothers die horribly in front of their sons, small girls are turned into prostitutes, small boys into beggars. I hope it won't spoil the feel-good surprise if I tell you that one particularly sadistic scene shows a young boy having his eyes burnt out with acid to maximise the profits of street begging. Charities working with street children in India seem unaware of any instances of this, although Save the Children emphasises that similar violence against children by beggar mafia is well documented.

The film is brilliant, horrifying, compelling and awful, the relentless violence leavened only by an occasional clip of someone working his way through the questions on the Indian version of *Who Wants to Be a Millionaire*? You might want to look away, but you can't and, despite the banal storyline, I can see why it is pulling in the awards.

Yet the film is vile. Unlike other Boyle films such as *Trainspotting* or *Shallow Grave*, which also revel in a fantastical comic violence, *Slumdog Millionaire* is about children. And it is set not in the West but in the slums of the Third World. As the film revels in the violence, degradation and horror, it invites you, the Westerner, to enjoy it, too. Will they find it such fun in Mumbai?

Like the bestselling novel by the Americanised Afghan Khaled Hosseini, *A Thousand Splendid Suns, Slumdog Millionaire* is not a million miles away from a form of pornographic voyeurism. *A Thousand Splendid Suns* is obsessed with rape and violence against women, the reader asked to pore over every last horrible detail. *Slumdog Millionaire* is poverty porn.

Here is the British Board of Film Classification (BBFC) summary of the film. It judged it suitable for viewers aged 15 or over (I would add another ten to that): "Strong violence is seen in a scene where a group of Muslims are attacked and killed in the street—together with general chaos and beatings, there are some stronger and more explicit moments, such as the deliberate setting of a man on fire. . . . We also later see strong violence that includes a knife held to a woman's throat as she's forcibly snatched off the street, an impressionistic blinding of a young beggar boy, and torture by electricity in a police station. The BBFC has placed this work in the COMEDY genre."

Comedy? So maybe that's it: I just didn't get the joke.

I wonder if India will, or whether, as with Aravind Adiga's Man Booker prize-winning novel, *The White Tiger*, people will feel more ambivalent than in the West. An editorial in dnaindia.com, a Mumbai-based online newspaper, read: "The miserable existence of the average slum dweller, which we in India know so well, is novel to the Western viewer. . . . The awarding of the Booker Prize to *The White Tiger* shows that the seamier side of the Indian dream continues to have a resonance in Western sensibilities. *The White Tiger's* victory left many Indians underwhelmed; who is to say that when Indian audiences finally see *Slumdog* they will not be equally put off?"

The film is brilliant, horrifying, compelling and awful.

As a review on the same website by Vrinda Nabar, an Indian professor at a US university, put it: "*Slumdog's* eventual victory comes at a price. When the selective manipulation of Third World squalor can make for a feel-good movie in a dismal year, the global village has a long way to go."

Quite. The *Mumbai Mirror* dubbed it "Slum Chic", and notes that the term "slumdog" is not widely recognised in India: "It appears to be a British invention to describe a poor Dharavi kid in a derogatory way."

I am being highly selective: mostly, India seems in thrall to the brilliance of *Slumdog* and how it has put Mumbai and Bollywood on the map.

That said, most Indians have not seen the film, because it will not open there until next week, a delay that has raised an eyebrow or two: did Mumbai not deserve to see *Slumdog* first? Instead, pirated copies are doing the rounds while America watches a film that Hollywood refused to fund, because "who wants to see misery and street kids?"

Boyle describes the film as "very subversive". He has forestalled potential criticism about plundering another country's horror as entertainment by employing many Indian actors, including Bollywood stars and an Indian composer. Much of the dialogue is in Hindi.

And it may be that the brilliance of the film rescues Boyle from criticism: he is a film-maker, not a social commentator, and nobody doubts its cinematic brilliance. As the *New York Times* put it: "It's hard to hold on to any reservations in the face of Mr. Boyle's resolutely upbeat pitch and seductive visual style."

That very seductiveness is the problem. But if Boyle may be absolved from criticism, I am not sure the same can be said of the audience. "Slumderful!" declared the *New York Post*. When we are suckered into enjoying scenes of absolute horror among children in slums on the other side of the world, even dubbing them comedy, we ought to question where our moral compass is pointing. Boyle's most subversive achievement may lie not in revealing the dark underbelly of India—but in revealing ours.

For Class Discussion

1. What evidence from the film does Miles cite to support her claim? Would fewer examples have been sufficient to make her point? In other words, what is the cumulative effect of the many instances of violence that she lists?

2. Miles's direct style in this argument is often associated with a form of argument called *polemic*, in which the author expresses a sense of outrage at a given situation. How effective is her choice of tone and language in conveying her position?

3. Although she calls the film "vile," Miles maintains that the director Danny Boyle may be absolved from criticism. Do you agree with her assessment of who is to blame?

4. How rhetorically effective is Miles's admission that she is "highly selective" in her presentation of Indian points of view?

5. One criticism of globalization is its tendency to exoticize foreign cultures, allowing those in the Western world to act as cultural voyeurs. How does Miles's argument support this point of view?

Slumdog Millionaire
Robert Koehler

Robert Koehler is a film critic for *Variety*, *Cinema Scope*, *Cineaste* and the *LA Weekly*. He is a member of FIPRESCI (the International Federation of Film Critics) and has served as a juror at several film festivals including Cannes, Vancouver, Mexico City, Buenos Aires, Guadalajara, Palm Springs, Los Angeles, and San Francisco Latino festivals. This review of the film *Slumdog Millionaire* appeared in the Spring 2009 issue of *Cineaste*, a quarterly magazine which offers a social, political, and esthetic perspective on the cinema.

What charges does Koehler level against audiences and critics of the film?

Danny Boyle's *Slumdog Millionaire* is the film of the moment for the "new middlebrow"—that audience able to perceive momentous changes in the world and culture when they're reported in, say, the *New York Times*, but one, at the same time, that wouldn't have the slightest clue that the most thrilling new rushes of creative filmmaking since the nouvelle vague originate in the apartments and editing rooms of Manila, Kuala Lumpur, Barcelona, and Buenos Aires. This new middlebrow has a fresh object of adoration in Boyle's entertainment, since it quite conveniently summarizes and expresses so many wishes, hopes, and romantic yearnings of the West toward what is perceived as the troubled East—with today's West resembling nothing so much as the West of the Sixties and its taste for turning Indian style into various forms of Hippie Chic. (*Slumdog* is paisley cinema, pure and simple.) Boyle's feverish, woozy, drunken, and thoroughly contrived picaresque also conveniently packages misperceptions about India (and the East) that continue to support the dominant Western view of the Subcontinent, making the film a potent object to examine not only what is cockeyed about an outsider's view (particularly, an Englishman's view) of India, but even more, what is misperceived by a middlebrow critical establishment and audience about what comprises world cinema.

Suitably then, the creative godfather of *Slumdog*, more than Bollywood musical fantasies, is Charles Dickens. Certain Bollywood tropes are obediently followed, such as the innocent hero rising above terrible circumstances, the determined pursuit of a love against all odds and that stock Bollywood type, the snarling (often mustachioed) nemesis. But, including the much discussed group-dance finale, these are tropes included almost by necessity and play onscreen in a notably rote fashion. They are alien to Boyle, which is why the Dickens model is more culturally and even cinematically germane when addressing the issues inside *Slumdog*. Dickens's picaresque novels about young underdog heroes struggling and managing to eventually thrive in social settings weighed heavily against them were grist for, first, Vikas Swarup's novel, *Q & A*, and then, Simon Beaufoy's loosely adapted screenplay, which greatly compresses the novel's episodes and sections, renames characters and—for as outlandish as the final film is—actually tones down the adventure's more incredible events and coincidences.

If Dickens's milieu was the early years of the Industrial Revolution, the film's setting is the new era of globalism, in which India is undergoing its own revolution. Jamal (Dev Patel) is Pip, Nicholas Nickleby, and Oliver Twist rolled into one, a lad who by sheer gumption has managed to land a spot as a contestant on the hugely popular *Who Wants to Be a Millionaire?* even though he's a humble (but oh so smart) *chai wallah* (or tea servant) at a cell-phone sales center. When he's first seen on screen, though, Jamal is in trouble: A fat cop is abusing him in a police station, though that's nothing next to the electrocution he receives from the chief inspector (veteran Indian actor Irrfan Khan), who's convinced that Jamal has cheated on the show. How, his caste-based logic goes, could a "slumdog" like Jamal have won ten million rupees (and only one question away from winning 100 million) without cheating? Even the most scurrilous and bigoted of Mumbai cops likely wouldn't go all Abu Ghraib on a poor teen boy for cheating on TV, and it's just the start of the film's endless supply of stunning exaggeration-for-effect gambits that are more like a two-by-four upside the head than anything that might be termed in polite company as "dramatic touches." Boyle appears to have absorbed this exaggeration into his directorial bloodstream, since, in at least the film's first half and lingering long into the second, he indulges in a rush of shots filmed with an obsessively canted camera, the technique lovingly nurtured by Orson Welles to convey states of eruption and dislocation, but grievously abused by Boyle through repetitive excess until it reeks of desperation.

So, we get it: Jamal has everything stacked against him as he must convince these thugs with badges how he knew the questions thrown to him by the show's supercilious and remarkably condescending host, Prem (Anil Kapoor), and that he will—it is written—prevail. From here, the rest of the movie comprises Jamal's case, which begins with the wildly implausible notion that Jamal remembers more or less everything in his life inside the framework of a Dickens novel, and ends with his endless and, um, dogged pursuit of his only true love, the beautiful (can she be anything else?) Latika (Frieda Pinto). Of course, wild implausibility has been Boyle's general stock-in-trade for some time, beginning with his *Clockwork Orange* pastiche, *Trainspotting* (which followed his *Hammer* pastiche, *Shallow Grave*, and preceded his Roland Emmerich pastiche, *The Beach*, a film so awful that it would have killed many lesser mortals' directing careers on the spot, and nearly killed Boyle's). *28 Days Later* was intrinsically implausible—about zombies apparently ready to race Usain Bolt in the Olympics—but so burly, aggressive, and spectacularly rude that it didn't allow a moment's pause for reflection. Is Boyle's last movie, *Sunshine*, about a space crew on a mission straight for the sun, any more ridiculous than *Slumdog Millionaire*, which suggests that a little Muslim boy raised in Mumbai's worst hellholes can become rich and famous? (Well, maybe a little more.)

Because *Slumdog* isn't conceived as a genre piece with its own built-in conventions (horror, sci-fi) but is rather a self-consciously contrived picaresque situated in the real world of Indian class structure, Muslim/Hindu religious conflicts, underworld crime rings, and pop media, the sheer impulse to push the story into a frothy romance functions as a betrayal of its fundamental material. In the end, when Jamal has won (because, as the viewer is reminded more times than is worth counting, his victory is destined to happen), he becomes India's new superstar, its latest populist hero, a seeming sensation, a bolt out of the blue. So where is he? Squatting ever so quietly, alone, unmolested, unnoticed by anyone in Mumbai's central train station, where he spots Latika, also alone, and where they then run to each other and break into a Bollywoodstyle number. The effect of this scene turned the first audience at Telluride, based on eyewitness accounts, all goofy in the head. ("I wanted to run outside and scream and holler at the mountains," one starry-eyed survivor told me.)

It's hard to argue against such sentiment or reaction; for sure, early viewers of Julie Andrews running down that Austrian meadow in *The Sound of Music* were similarly nutty. Some are just mad for *Slumdog Millionaire*—including far, far too many critics—and they won't hear a discouraging word. As the cultlike object of many in the new middle-brow, no argument is heard, and some express outright shock when their beloved new movie is broken apart, knocked, or outright dismissed as what it is—a really, really minor movie, with really, really big problems. Just as the score by composer A.R. Rahman, a crafty and fairly cynical Bollywood hand, is bogus "Indian" music from top to bottom, with an excess of quasi-hiphop stylings, electronic beat patterns and vocalese gumming up the works and sounding like the kind of backgrounds one might hear in a TV travel advert, so the closing number is bogus Bollywood following on the heels of bogus social drama.

The problem, for the fresh-scrubbed middlebrow and for the rest of us, is that if the real thing isn't known—that is, genuinely Indian cinema—how to judge the Fox Searchlight facsimile?

Really, though, *Slumdog* is fun, so let your quibbles just drift away, sit back, relax and let it spill all over you like a nice mango lassi. That's certainly the refrain of too many of the post-Telluride reviews, which recognized Boyle's brazen manipulations and absurd storytelling jumps of even marginal logic for what they were

> *Slumdog* is fun; so let your quibbles just drift away, sit back, relax.

but still joined in the cheering (a word that I counted in at least ten reviews). And they're right; it is fun—fun as a cultural fabrication to question. Consider this overlooked yet central aspect of the film's many conceits: *Slumdog* uses TV as a national arena, and precisely as the medium wherein Jamal not only escapes his class, but (when the show is reviewed on tape during the police station interrogation) uses it as a tool to justify his existence. The film at once reinforces the myths of reality game show TV as actual rather than manufactured suspense and as a machine for getting rich quick, while—in total contradiction—suggests that TV can also be a partner with the police in torture. As at so many other points, Boyle and Beaufoy try to have it both ways: Jamal proves his mettle by deploying his life experiences in order to be the ideal game show star, while the show itself (via Prem, who says that he "owns" the show and reveals that he's also from the slums) collaborates with police to persecute and torture Jamal, even though Prem also knows—an important point—that Jamal isn't cheating. The basis for arranging for Jamal's arrest is a collapsing house of cards on close inspection, since the arrest is not only a surprise to the show's producer, but couldn't have possibly been managed by Prem, who has after all been on the show during airtime. Perhaps Prem is jealous of his fellow slum-dog? An interesting, even profound, character point—one that's right there, hanging like ripe narrative fruit, and which would have been even more interesting had Beaufoy and Boyle bothered to pluck it. The Dickensian sensibility, with its ironies and coincidences, is imposed here but never truly developed and only selectively applied—Dickens's picaresque tales, laden with social criticism and narrative athleticism, never fail to point a harsh finger at unjust authority (something Boyle is clearly uncomfortable doing) through a romance of the hero's ulti-mately improbable triumph over odds (something Boyle bases his whole movie on, culminating with the ersatz Bollywood finale). As a re-sult, the exchanges of colonialism in *Slumdog Millionaire* are too deli-cious not to notice. In a single film, we have: the celebration of the ex-port of a British gameshow to the Indian viewing public; a narrative structured on the show itself and the (British) Dickens picaresque; a dis-astrously tone-deaf and colorblind depiction of the world experienced by Muslim lower classes as decorated in gloriously erotic and lush col-ors as perhaps only a European-based director (Boyle) and cinematogra-pher (the usually brilliant and ingenious Anthony Dod Mantle) could manage; a British-themed call center as the opening of opportunity and upward mobility for Jamal.

In its expressly liberal intentions to depict an India in which a sin-gle Muslim boy can win a nation's heart, *Slumdog Millionaire* massages the Western viewer's gaze on a country and culture they barely know, save for a vague sense of cultural exports like the occasional Bollywood movie or song. Perhaps especially now, after the fearsome attacks by Islamist extremists on Mumbai's most cherished institutions and on Western tourists, Boyle's film is just the soft pillow for concerned Western viewers to plump their heads; surely, there's hope, when even a Muslim lad who is abused, scorned, and rejected can recover his dignity, win the girl and thrive in a world free of terror. It's precisely the India of which Westerners, starting with its former British masters, heartily dream, an India where everything is possible.

The Indian reality, of course, is far more complex, and it has taken filmmakers of sublime artistry and a subtle grasp of the huge Indian spectrum like Mani Ratnam, Shonali Bose, Buddhadeb Dasgupta, Girish Kasaravalli, and Murali Nair to express that complexity on screen. Opportunities for lower classes to free themselves from the old con-straints are indeed greater now in India than ever before, largely through the jobs created by the nation's exploding hightech and man-ufacturing sectors, which have literally created a middle class where one barely existed before. That new middle class is full of Jamals, using the new social streams fostered by computers and the Web to find types of work that simply never existed before in the Indian economy. The now infamous call centers—an aspect Boyle's film hardly glances at—are mere slivers of this new economy. But it is new, and therefore has only just begun to make its presence felt in a nation of such vast stretches and distances of geography, culture, religious traditions, and economic status.

It's here that Boyle's vision of India goes truly south, since it reinforces his target audience's general ignorance of reference points in Indian cinema. An affectionate nod in an early sequence to the Bollywood spectacles starring Amitabh Bachchan is typical: His enduring superstar status aside, the particular Amitabh movies visually cited in Slumdog Millionaire are actually too old for Jamal—a lower-class boy born in the late Eighties—to have seen (except, perhaps, on videotape). The brief Amitabh film reel in *Slumdog* is more properly seen as reflective of Boyle's own personal memory bank of the Bollywood movies seen in his youth, and therefore useful for Boyle's purposes, since Amitabh remains the one Bollywood superstar widely known in the West. (He's also something of an insider's joke here, since he was the original host of the Indian Millionaire show titled, *Kaun Banega Crorepati*? (*Who Will Become a Crorepati?*).

> A truer manifestation of globalization is the explosion of world cinema itself.

Slumdog Millionaire may be minor, but in one way it's important: It serves as the ideal vehicle for the new middlebrow's perception of what makes up world cinema. For starters, as a non-Indian movie with Indian actors (pros based in the U.K. and India, plus newcomers and nonpros), dialogue, settings and music, it provides a comfortable substitute for a genuine Indian film (say, by the above-mentioned, neglected and under-seen Ratnam, Dasgupta, or Nair). The new middlebrow can thus say they've covered their current Indian cinema; after all, they've seen—and enjoyed—*Slumdog Millionaire*.

Boyle's film has been celebrated as an expression of globalization, and it's certainly true that the story itself couldn't exist in a world before globalization took effect in once-protectionist India, and that Jamal's progress is globalization incarnate. But a truer manifestation of globalization is the explosion of world cinema itself, and how the past decade and a half has seen the spread of national cinemas to an unmatched degree in the art form's history. This has been possible only through the combined forces of globalization and the absorption of previous experimentation in film grammar and theory; the ways in which local filmmakers in their local conditions have responded to the challenges of making cinema on their own terms has made the current period probably the most exciting ever from a global perspective.

India is an interesting example in this regard, since its many languages and regions have produced a wide range of filmmaking styles and voices, most of which continue to struggle (like Ratnam, who himself dances between more genres and forms than Steven Soderbergh) to be seen abroad. We're living in the midst of a paradoxical climate, however: Just as world cinema and its locally-based voices (and not glib fly-by-night tourists like Boyle) are more aggressively active than ever, and more exciting in their expressions, the outlets in the U.S. for this work are shrinking. Distributors, burned by too many subtitled films that bomb at the box office, have narrowed their shopping lists at festivals and markets. Alternative outlets, from festivals to pay-per-view, can contain only so many titles. Video is the last refuge, meaning that cinema made by artists ends up being seen (if at all) on TV.

Boyle is obviously keenly aware of this condition in his own film about characters raised speaking Hindu: He manages to compress the Hindu dialogue into about fifteen minutes' total running time (a fraction of the full running time of 116 minutes), and then offer up subtitles for the Hindu in distractingly snazzy lines of text that dance all over the screen like a hyperkinetic TV ad—apparently the perfect solution for otherwise worldly minded folks who hate reading subtitles. In the future, *Slumdog Millionaire* might be seen as a talisman of a potentially degraded film culture, in which audiences were sufficiently dumbed-down to accept the fake rather than the real thing and, in a new middlebrow haze, weren't able to perceive the difference.

Slumdog Millionaire Produced by Christian Colson; directed by Danny Boyle; codirected (India) by Loveleen Tandan; screenplay by Simon Beaufoy, based on the novel *Q&A* by Vikas Swarup; cinematography by Anthony Dod Mantle; production design by Mark Digby; costumes by Suttirat Anne Larlarb; edited by Chris Dickens; music by A.R. Rahman; starring Dev Patel, Frieda Pinto, Madhur Mittal, Anil Kapoor, Irrfan Khan CQ, Tanay Hemant Chheda CQ, Tanvi Ganesh Lonkar, Ashutosh Lobo Gajiwala. 116 mins. A Fox Searchlight release.

For Class Discussion

1. For what audience is this argument written? What clues are there in the cultural references, vocabulary, and subjects that would help you identify the audience?

2. Like Miles, Koehler is critical of how audiences in Western cultures have responded to *Slumdog Millionaire*. How does his argument differ? Why does he find the film and its reception problematic?

3. Koehler points out that the idea of television as a way for Jamal to escape his class is an "overlooked" aspect of the film, and also mentions his job at

a British call center. What view of globalization do these aspects of the film seem to suggest?

4. Where Miles would excuse director Danny Boyle for his cultural missteps, Koehler takes him to task. How do you account for the difference in their positions, given the two articles' respective audiences?   ■

The Slumdog Look
Hemant Morparia

Hemant Morparia, M.D., is a radiologist whose popular cartoons appear daily on the front page of the *Bombay Times*. This cartoon was published on March 3, 2009.

What two issues of global interest does this cartoon combine in a humorous way?

EITHER RECESSION HAS HIT THE FASHION WORLD HARD TOO, OR IT'S THE 'SLUMDOG' LOOK...

Hemant Morparia/artizans.com

For Class Discussion

1. Fashion designers often borrow inspiration from other cultures. How does this cartoon present a humorous take on that practice?

2. Though this cartoon is a satire and does not necessarily represent a real trend, how might critics of globalization view this co-optation of Indian culture? How might Indians feel about those aspects of their culture that are represented by this trend?

3. Can you think of any similar instances where American fashion, music, food, or film have borrowed from another culture? How important is it to understand the context for the cultural artifacts that have been adapted?

4. How does this cartoon speak to the global cultural concerns raised by Alice Miles and Robert Koehler in their critiques of the film *Slumdog Millionaire?*   ■

A "Slumdog" in Heat: Interview with Danny Boyle

Fareed Zakaria

Fareed Zakaria is the editor of *Newsweek International* and writes a regular column for *Newsweek*, which also appears in *Newsweek International* and in the *Washington Post*. Zakaria was the managing editor of *Foreign Affairs*, the widely-circulated journal of international politics and economics. He is the author of several books, including *The Future of Freedom* (2003) which has been translated into twenty languages, and most recently, *The Post American World* (2008). This interview was published in the February 9, 2009, issue of *Newsweek*, a weekly news magazine for a general audience covering global affairs, business, science, technology, society, arts, and entertainment.

> How does Zakaria frame his questions to acknowledge the criticism that the film has faced?

Produced with a budget of only $15 million, *Slumdog Millionaire* is this year's Hollywood rags-to-riches story—in more ways than one. The film follows the fortunes of Jamal (Dev Patel), a young man from the Mumbai slums who becomes a contestant on *Who Wants to Be a Millionaire,* only to be accused of cheating. The movie—part thriller, part romantic comedy, part musical—has earned nearly $100 million worldwide and is the front runner for the best-picture Oscar. But back in India, the movie has become a cultural lightning rod, a target for protesters and charges of "slum voyeurism." A lawsuit alleges it defames Mumbai's urban poor, and many take offense at the appearance of "dog" in the title. *Newsweek's* Fareed Zakaria spoke with the director, Danny Boyle, about the film's creation and the resultant uproar. Excerpts:

Zakaria: *Slumdog Millionaire* feels like a big movie in its commercial aspirations, but did you expect it to get the kind of critical acclaim it's received?

Boyle: No. With every film you make you have what I call "the bathroom moment," where you look at yourself and you think, OK, this is the one. But you never could expect what's happened with this film. Having said that, I remember moments while making the film— Mumbai is such an exhilarating, extraordinary place to be that you do think, If I could capture some of this city, some of what a lot of people don't realize is here, it will be fascinating.

Do you think part of the appeal of the movie stems from people's fascination with India?

That's one of the reasons I wanted to make the film. I didn't want to make the film because of *Who Wants to Be a Millionaire*. I have to say, though, I've rethought that aspect. Although that is an element, for the public it's the universality of the story. People want to root for Jamal. It doesn't matter where he comes from.

It struck me as a very Dickensian story.

When I asked Simon Beaufoy, the writer of the script, what it was like writing it, he said, "You can't escape the shadow of Dickens, dealing with these extremes within an extraordinary city."

In India itself, there's been a cloud over the film, with some activists claiming that the title is demeaning. What did you mean by "slumdog"?

This is one of the saddest things for me. People are absolutely entitled to say whatever they think about the film. Protest is a healthy part of life in India, provided it doesn't become violent. Basically it's a hybrid of the word "underdog"—and everything that means in terms of rooting for the underdog and validating his triumph—and the fact that he obviously comes from the slums. That's what we intended.

Some people seem to feel that you are shining a spotlight on Indian poverty.

It's an entertainment, not a documentary. But we wanted to depict as much of the city as possible, and you cannot ignore that part of life in Mumbai—nor would I want to. It's one of the most extraordinary things that hits you about the city, the way that the slums sit beside everything else. They're not ghettoized. For me, the slums were extraordinary. Part of you expects abject poverty, but what you find, of course, is an extraordinary energy. You sense a kind of resilience against all odds. As a filmmaker, I wanted to try and capture that energy, as well as show the circumstances in which people are forced to live. I hesitate to use the word inspiring, but on a human level it is inspiring. If we could all live our lives as resourcefully as people with so little do! Whereas we live in such luxury, yet complain about things and moan about things.

Do you worry that the movie will face further backlash in India? Have you taken any legal precautions?

No, not legal. Our priority at the moment is the young actors, especially the two that come from very poor backgrounds. I also worry about any kind of violence. In terms of furor, criticism, debate, you realize that part of your responsibility as a filmmaker is to stand up and be counted if you're proud of the film. I'm proud to do that.

How long did you spend in Mumbai?

I spent about a year there. As soon as you touch India, specifically Mumbai, you feel electric, in good ways and bad ways. A pulse just charges through you. That hasn't changed since we started the film. I feel more alive than I've ever felt in my career.

It sounds like India had a huge impact on you. Can you just walk away from it?

Well, you can get on a plane, but you can't walk away from it. It's always going to be with you.

Do you think you will make another movie set in India?

I would love to make a thriller in the city. We made basically a picaresque film with elements of a thriller, romance, comedy. But all the time you're there, you're thinking, this would be the most extraordinary place for a thriller. I don't think I'll do it next, but I would love to do it. I've begun talking to a couple of people about that idea.

Do you have your Oscar speech prepared in case you win?

Because the film features Benjamin Franklin—he's in the bit where the kid gets the $100 note—I can use his great quote, that "nothing is certain in life except death and taxes." To which I would add, "and law cases and protests." You have to make sure that you thank the right people, but that comes from your heart. So, no.

Is there anything else you'd like to add?

Just an acknowledgment to Mumbai and everybody who lives in that extraordinary city. It's a gift for a filmmaker, going there. And I will always be eternally obliged to it—and that's to everyone, to those who love us and those who hate us. Somebody sent me a quote from Plato: "Be kind, for everyone you meet is fighting a hard battle." That kind of approach helps you deal with everything, really, and that's how we tried to behave in Mumbai. Hopefully in the long run people will appreciate that.

For Class Discussion

1. How can this interview be read as a rebuttal argument by director Danny Boyle against the charges leveled by writers such as Alice Miles and Robert Koehler?

2. What tone does Boyle use in his responses to Zakaria's questions? How rhetorically effective is this tone in responding to the "uproar" the film has created?

3. What charges does Boyle address in this brief interview? What questions would you have liked to see him address more directly?

4. In your opinion, is Boyle effective in convincing *Newsweek's* readership of his position? What about the protesters in India?

5. Zakaria mentions that the film has been accused of "slum voyeurism." Based on the readings in this chapter about this film, does it seem that it is more helpful or harmful in promoting respectful attitudes toward other cultures and cross-cultural understanding?

Marvel Comics and Manifest Destiny

David Adesnik

David Adesnik, a research analyst in Washington DC, received his doctorate in international relations from Oxford University. Doublethink Online sponsors his blog as a "bright young mind of the Right." This cultural analysis was posted January 28, 2005, on the Web site of the *Daily Standard* (www.weeklystandard.com), a British daily online publication affiliated with the *Weekly Standard*, a news commentary magazine.

> This piece is more exploratory than argumentative. What claims does it make about comic superheroes? What questions does it raise about popular culture and cross-cultural exchanges?

Devarajan's aspirations are noble, yet it's interesting to wonder if American audiences will recognize this Spider-Man after his translation into the local idiom. Or, conversely, if Devarajan, born in New York to parents from India, will preserve too much of Spider-Man's American heritage and wind up with a character that won't resonate with Indian audiences.

In short, Devarajan's attempt to transform Peter Parker into Pavitr Prabhakar forces him to confront the age-old challenge of separating the universal aspects of human nature from the particular characteristics of a specific culture. The success (or failure) of Devarajan's effort matters, because it may tell us something important about the validity of Americans' faith in the universality of our most cherished ideals.

The first issue of *Spider-Man: India* demonstrates that Devarajan was dead serious when he spoke of preserving the Spider-mantra that "with great power comes great responsibility." In 1962, Spider-Man learned this enduring lesson when a security guard asked him to stop an armed robber in the midst of making his getaway. At that time, Peter Parker was an embittered teenager with no sense of obligation to the greater good. He refused to apprehend the robber.

Later that same night, Peter returns home to find out that his beloved Uncle Ben has been murdered. Enraged, Peter hunts down the murderer, only to discover that it is the tough he let go. This tragic coincidence provokes his epiphany.

In *Spider-Man: India*, young Pavitr Prabhakar learns his lesson in an almost identical manner. While swinging across Mumbai, Pavitr hears the cries of a young woman surrounded by a gang of thugs. He does nothing and swings away. Moments later, Pavitr's beloved Uncle Bhim hears the cries of the same young woman and decides to confront her assailants. They warn Uncle Bhim that they will hurt him if he does not walk away. Bhim stays. He is murdered. Later that night, Pavitr learns of his uncle's death, hunts down the murderers, and experiences an epiphany of his own.

Although its innovations seem trivial, *India*'s reworking of the Spider-myth brilliantly enhances the painful irony of the American original. Whereas Ben's murder is a matter of pure coincidence, Bhim dies because he had the courage to confront precisely the same evil that his nephew wouldn't. In both instances, the punishment for selfishness is the death of a loved one. Yet in *India*, that loved one is also a martyr whose death becomes the embodiment of the ethos to which Spider-Man must aspire.

The counterpoint to *India*'s subtle reworking of the death of Uncle Ben is its ambitious recasting of Spider-Man's powers as the worldly incarnation of a purposeful, mystical force rather than the accidental outgrowth of a scientific experiment. In a recent interview, Devarajan observed that the diametrically opposed forces of science and magic represent the fundamental contrast between Eastern and Western culture.

At a time when IBM is outsourcing thousands of high-tech jobs to Bangalore, it may seem strange to hear an Indian-American insist that magic is the essence of Eastern culture. Nonetheless, Devarajan's decision to build his story on a mythological foundation provides a much better testing ground for the hypothesis that the superhero ethic is part of a "universal psyche" rather than an American one.

As a literary device, the replacement of science with magic functions smoothly. In both accounts of Spider-Man's origins, there is a seamless integration of plot and metaphor. Although Peter Parker is now a married man in his thirties, he was a bespectacled teenage bookworm when Spider-Man debuted in the 1960s. A friendless outcast, Parker devoted all of his time to academic pursuits, such as the public science exhibit at which he was bitten by a radioactive spider. Although nominally an accident, the spider bite is a metaphorical expression of the American faith that knowledge is power and that science is the engine of progress. Initially taunted because of his devotion to science, Parker ultimately becomes all the more powerful because of it.

In *Spider-Man: India*, Pavitr Prabhakar is an outcast not because of his academic talent, but because of the traditional clothing that he wears to an expensive private school in cosmopolitan Mumbai. As a scholarship student from a small village in the countryside, it is all Pavitr can afford. One day, while being chased by the bullies who taunt him for wearing harem pants reminiscent of the glory days of MC Hammer, Pavitr stumbles upon an ancient mystic who warns him of an impending battle between ancient forces of good and evil. The old man endows Pavitr with the power of the spider and tells him "This is your destiny, young Pavitr Prabhakar. Rise to the challenge . . . fulfill your karma." In the same manner that Parker embodies the ideals of modern America, Prabhakar embodies those of traditional India.

At first, the suggestion that Pavitr has a destiny that he must fulfill may strike some readers as un-American. In the land of opportunity, we reject out of hand the notion that individuals must resign themselves to their fate. Instead, we believe that there are no limits to what can be achieved by a combination of hard work and ingenuity.

Yet is the concept of destiny really so foreign? Was it not under the banner of Manifest Destiny that the young United States claimed for it-self the Great Plains and the northern reaches of Mexico? Was it not Ronald Reagan who constantly reminded the citizens of the United States that they had a "rendezvous with destiny"? To what else did George W. Bush refer to in his second inaugural address when he stated that "History has an ebb and flow of justice, but history also has a visible direction, set by liberty and the author of liberty"?

The most important difference Spider-fans will notice between the Indian and American notions of destiny is the Indian belief that tyranny and evil are primal forces no less powerful than freedom and good. Yet there is also a considerable measure of doubt embedded in the American vision of progress. Although one scientific accident gave Spider-Man his powers, other scientific accidents were responsible for the creation of his arch-nemeses, Dr. Octopus and the Green Goblin. In the final analysis, that which makes Pavitr Prabhakar authentically Indian does not make him in any way un-American.

Today the Republic of India is the most populous democracy on the face of the Earth. Someday, it may rival the United States in terms of wealth and power. Conventional thinking suggests that the emergence of a second superpower would threaten the security of the United States of America. Yet if India's first superhero recognizes that with great power there also comes great responsibility, perhaps we should look forward to the emergence of an Indian superpower.

For Class Discussion

1. What are the main changes that Devarajan has made in translating Spider-Man into an Indian comic book superhero?

2. What does this cultural analysis suggest are the important connections between nations' popular heroes and their values and identities?

3. What is the rhetorical effect of the title of this article? How does Adesnik use the concept of "Manifest Destiny"?

4. Do you think the *Spider-Man: India* comic exemplifies a positive or a negative cultural exchange? Why?

Image from *Spider-Man: India*
Jeevan J. Kang

This image is part of the Gotham Comics press release of the *Spider-Man: India* series, drawn by famous Indian artist Jeevan J. Kang. The comic ran for four issues in India in 2004, and in 2005 was released to a U.S. audience. The series was later collected into a trade paperback. In this comic, Pavitr Prabhakar, a poor Indian boy from the country and the counterpart of Peter Parker, discovers his karma and embraces the fight against evil. See the cover images at http://www.marvel.com/digitalcomics/titles/SPIDER-MAN~colon~_INDIA.2004.

As an American reader, what is your spontaneous response to the drawing of this character?

Spider-Man:™ and © 2005 Marvel Characters, Inc. Used with permission. Illustration by Gotham Studios Asia.

SPIDER-MAN © 2004 Marvel Characters Inc.

For Class Discussion

1. In its press release, Gotham Comics calls *Spider-Man: India* a "transcreation," by which it means an Indian retelling of the American superhero's story. What signs of adaptation and cultural contextualizing do you see in this image?

2. What other characters from popular U.S. culture have crossed cultures in this way?

3. Based on what you have read in David Adesnik's article, do you think these kinds of cultural transpositions are effective, creative, and interesting? Why? Why do you think American audiences would or would not enjoy this new comic?

4. How could you make a case that "transcreation" is an example of "glocalizing" rather than an example of cultural imperialism?

CHAPTER QUESTIONS FOR REFLECTION AND DISCUSSION

1. Several of the readings in this chapter focus on problems with the way that media are shaping people's perceptions of other cultures. What problems do George Packer and the writers of the pieces on *Slumdog Millionaire* identify? How do these writers interpret, support, or attack the idea of the global village?

2. The main perspectives on global cultural exchange discussed in this chapter can be summarized by these labels: cultural loss, cultural superiority, cultural imperialism, cultural homogenization, cultural assimilation, cultural fusion, preservation of cultural rights, cultural diversity, cross-culturalization, and cultural pluralism. In your own words, how would you describe each of these views of intercultural exchange? From the readings and your own experience or research, find examples to illustrate these views. For instance, what is an example of cultural fusion?

3. Some critics argue that cultural homogenization and Western domination are endangering other cultures around the world. Drawing on the articles by Rajal Pitroda, Philippe Legrain, Matt Pomroy, and Daragahi and Fleishman, how would you refute this claim?

4. Several of the arguments in these readings turn on the quality and quantity of their examples. From a logical, philosophical, and ethical perspective, why is this "arguing by example" problematic? Illustrate your response with particular readings.

5. Which reading or readings in this chapter make the most effective and persuasive use of appeals to readers' values, imaginations, and emotions? Which examples, narratives, and quotations appeal most powerfully to the

writers' target audiences? Which authors are the most knowledgeable, credible, reliable, and reasonable?

6. Choose one of the following pairs of readings and map out their points of agreement and disagreement. Consider their target audiences, their assumptions and values, their main claims and reasons, and the points that each overlooks or ignores:

   - George Packer and the *Economist* or Matt Pomroy
   - Philippe Legrain and Rajal Pitroda
   - Matt Pomroy or Borzou Daragahi/Jeffrey Fleishman
   - Rajal Pitroda and David Adesnik
   - Alice Miles and Robert Koehler
   - Alice Miles or Robert Koehler and Fareed Zakaria

7. This chapter's Global Hot Spot addresses issues surrounding the introduction of reality TV to the Middle East. How do the readings on MTV Arabia and Middle Eastern hip-hop introduce additional concerns, or possibly lessen some of those concerns?

8. The film industry, the comic book industry, and the music industry are thriving in the United States, yet other countries are developing strong industries or have the potential to develop strong industries. Research Bollywood or the film industry in Europe or Africa; anime or the comic book industry in Japan, the Philippines, Egypt, or India; or the music industry in a specific country. If you look at Bollywood, you might also consider the crossover film by British writer/director Gurinder Chadha *Bride and Prejudice* (2004) and this director's other popular film *Bend It Like Beckham* (2002), or Mira Nair's *Monsoon Wedding* (2001). If you look at comic book industries, you might explore the local comic book industries in the Philippines (Mango Comics, Summit Publishing, and Culture Crash), anime in Japan, AK Comics from Cairo, or *Spider-Man: India* and other Indian comics. If you look at music, you might explore the Middle Eastern hip-hop scene, the different genres of Afro Pop in Africa, or *corrido* or *rock nacional* in Mexico.

WRITING ASSIGNMENTS

Brief Writing Assignments

1. Thinking about your own identity, personal style, and cultural choices, briefly explain what part of foreign or international culture is most important to you. You could focus on food, music, clothing, sports, film, animation, language, television programming, religion, art, philosophy, or literature.

2. Using the readings in this chapter as a source of inspiration and the global quiz in Chapter 1 on pages 3–5 as a model, create a quiz about cultural

phenomena (food, clothing, sports, film, music, art, trendy brands, advertising, architecture, and comics) for an audience of your peers. Create ten to fifteen multiple choice items. You will need to choose different regions in the world and research specific cultural areas for those regions (for example, the main professional competitive sports in Australia; the main protest singers in South America). Include answers separately and keep track of your sources so that your classmates can take your quiz or pursue these topics further.

3. Write freely and informally for twenty minutes in response to this question: From this chapter, which article on the impact of globalization on culture surprised, intrigued, disturbed, or persuaded you the most and why?

4. Choose one of the following claims and write for twenty minutes in support of it or against it. Use evidence from the readings and from your own experience to develop your claim persuasively. To force yourself to think from a different point of view, you may want to try writing in agreement with the statement and then writing against it:

   A. Americans can't get away from home because home—the American way of life—is everywhere.

   B. Countries and regions should have complete control of what culture they export and import.

   C. The marketing, buying, and selling of culture is inevitable and mostly benefits everyone.

   D. Media have increased global understanding and cooperation.

   E. Cultural exchanges can fuel peaceful relations among countries.

5. Choose an internationally marketed product, such as a soft drink, brand of car, food, or television franchise, and research how that product is marketed differently in different countries. You might consult the producer's Web pages for different countries to view their branding or print advertising, or check YouTube (www.youtube.com) to locate international commercials. What aspects of the advertising remain consistent across cultures, and what attempts are made to "glocalize" the product? Write up your findings as a report to your peers, or consider creating a poster or a PowerPoint presentation.

6. Using George Packer's piece as inspiration, think of an international news item that you saw or heard in the media, and follow up on the story. How is the event covered in newspapers from other countries? From the country of origin? Write a brief for your peers that updates them on the story to date.

Writing Projects

1. Following the example of Michael Caster's reflective narrative, pondering the signs of cross-culturalization in Beijing on pages 417–418, describe and reflect on a site of cultural change that shows the effects of globalization.

Your site could be one you experienced while traveling, or could be some city, community, or region with which you are familiar. Just as Michael's narrative is informed by the cultural theory of Zygmunt Bauman, your narrative should show the influence of the ideas about global exchange you have encountered in this chapter or through other reading. As an alternative to this topic, you could write a narrative reflecting on why a community or region has *not* felt the effects of globalization. Write your reflective narrative for your university community, imagining that you are going to be part of a discussion forum on experiencing globalization.

2. Writing for an uninformed audience, build a strong case that one of the cultural forms below—or one you know from your own experience—has had a profound, transformative influence on American life:

   A. Anime (from Japan)

   B. Music from Africa, Latin America, or the Caribbean

   C. Food from Asia

   D. Film from India or Europe

   E. Television programs from Britain

   F. Dance from Africa

   G. Soccer from Europe or South America

   You might write an argument as a feature story for your university or local newspaper.

3. Investigate the contemporary music scene of some country such as Brazil, Mexico, South Africa, or Japan—perhaps focusing on a particular style of music (such as hip-hop, punk rock, folk). You might think of Jamaican reggae artists Bob Marley and his son Ziggy; Nigeria's Femi Kuti; Brazil's samba and hip-hopper Max de Castro and Marisa Monte of samba and art-pop fame; diva Brenda Fassie from South Africa; Shakira from Colombia; Thalia from Mexico; and Charlotte Church from Wales. Argue that that country's music has had an important effect on world music. Or you could argue that this music/music style/recording artist should receive world attention. You will need to provide criteria to evaluate the importance of this music or artist. Tailor your argument to your chosen audience.

4. Tourism can be a force for good, inspiring cultures to spend money to preserve their own cultural heritages and enabling people from other countries to experience these cultures. But tourism can also speed up the destruction of cultural heritages by fueling rampant development and foreign investment and control. In some cases, tourism can be constrictive to the people who actually live there, preventing them from advancing in an effort to retain what tourists find exotic about the culture. Choose a country with an especially old culture (such as Ladakh, Bhutan, Indonesia, Peru, Ecuador, or Egypt) and research how tourism has had an impact on

the culture. Depending on the information that your research yields, argue that tourism needs to be curtailed, better controlled, or encouraged. Write your argument for a tourist magazine that caters to well-educated, wealthy Americans.

5. Research the image that a country or the tourist business uses to market that country. You could begin by thinking of the architectural and geographical icons that come readily to mind (for example, the Eiffel Tower and Notre Dame in Paris; London Bridge and Big Ben in London; Uluru [Ayers Rock] and the Outback in Australia; Machu Picchu with its Inca ruins in Peru). Write an op-ed piece for your university or city newspaper in which you argue that the cultural marketing of a country or region of a country does (or does not) promote cross-cultural understanding. How simplistic and reductive is the country's popular image? What positive or negative effects does this cultural marketing have on global perceptions of this country?

6. **Analyzing Arguments Rhetorically.** Choose two of the readings in this chapter about films and India (the arguments by Alice Miles, Robert Koehler, and Rajal Pitroda), and write a comparative rhetorical analysis considering their target audiences, their respective genres, their assumptions and values, their main claims and reasons, and the points that each emphasizes and overlooks. Write for a general magazine audience interested in learning about globalization and film. Which argument do you find the most insightful and provocative in building cultural understanding?

7. Research the status of information and communication technology in a developing country in Africa, South America, or Asia, and write a brief policy proposal arguing what a local business, university club, or nongovernmental organization could do to provide more cell phones and/or computers and Internet access to this country.

8. Write a researched exploratory essay, following the example of Patrick Scholze's exploratory essay on blood diamonds in Chapter 3, pp. 119–122. To launch your research, formulate a question about cultural diversity, the global free trade system, and some specific cultural form or practice in a specific region of the world (for example, the effect of the marketing of reality TV or MTV in the Middle East, the selling of American fast food in Asia, or some development in the music industry). In formulating your question, you might think in terms of the definitions of glocalization offered in Chapter 1 on p. 6 and in this chapter on p. 415–416. Consult at least four sources representing different kinds of publications and different viewpoints. Summarize and respond to each source as you narrate the way each has changed your understanding of your research question. By the end of your essay, either discuss the answer to your question that you have constructed or explain why your question would require further investigation and thinking. You might find these organizations useful as background information.

The International Network on Cultural Diversity (INCD)
Communication Rights in the Information Society (CRIS)
UNESCO and the Universal Declaration on Cultural Diversity
American Library Association (which is interested in public access to
    cultural diversity)

You could direct this argument to UNESCO or to an audience of your peers.

Defending
Human Rights
Trafficking and Child Labor

QUESTION TO PONDER

Estimates are that "more than 27 million people are enslaved" around the world and that more than fifteen thousand people are forcibly brought to the United States yearly.* These people are trafficked—moved across national borders against their will, intimidated by the loss of their visas and passports and by threats to their families, and coerced through violence to work for minimal or no pay. Often they are mistaken for illegal immigrants. The U.S. Department of Health and Human Services has created a set of outreach and training materials to aid local social service organizations, law enforcement, and health care professionals in identifying and offering support to trafficking victims. You are wondering, What can U.S. citizens do to stop human trafficking?

CONTEXT FOR A NETWORK OF ISSUES

Many people think all slavery ended several centuries ago. Britain's Abolition Act of 1833 launched the abolition of slavery throughout its empire; the United States banned the importation of slaves in 1808 and abolished slavery with the Thirteenth Amendment in 1865; and Brazil ended slavery in 1888. Yet a new form of slavery—human trafficking—is illicitly thriving around the globe despite progress with human rights.

Since World War II, the United Nations and advocacy groups have brought human rights to the attention of the world. The **Universal Declaration of Human Rights,** adopted by the General Assembly of the United Nations on December 10, 1948, declares that "recognition of the inherent dignity and of the equal and inalienable rights of all members of

*Free the Slaves & Human Rights Center, University of California–Berkeley, "Hidden Slaves: Forced Labor in the United States," September 2004, http://www.freetheslaves.net/.

the human family is the foundation of freedom, justice, and peace in the world" (www.un.org/en/documents/udhr). Humanitarian advocacy groups such as Amnesty International, founded in 1961 to defend prisoners of conscience, have turned a spotlight on human rights violations. Today, human rights encompasses basic rights: the political freedoms of speech, assembly, and suffrage, and the right to religion, work, welfare, and health. However, the trafficking of women and children and forced labor represent serious violations of these rights.

The illegal business of **trafficking** of human beings, involving the buying and selling of people who are forced to work for the profit of others, is a problem affecting most countries, including European Union nations, Canada, and the United States. Girls and boys as well as men and women are "trafficked": that is, transported within countries or across national borders, traded for money, and kept subjugated by violence and brutality. The United Nations defines trafficking as

> the recruitment, transportation, transfer, harbouring or receipt of persons, by means of the threat or use of force or other forms of coercion, of abduction, of fraud, of deception, of the abuse of power or of a position of vulnerability or of the giving or receiving of payments or benefits to achieve the consent of a person having control over another person, for the purpose of exploitation. Exploitation shall include, at a minimum, the exploitation or the prostitution of others or other forms of sexual exploitation, forced labour or services, slavery or practices similar to slavery, servitude or the removal of organs.[*]

Although the exact number of persons trafficked is difficult to pin down because this trade is criminal, Human Rights Watch, a leading human rights organization, estimates that between 700,000 and four million persons are trafficked annually (www.hrw.org). The **International Labor Organization** reports that about "8.4 million children are caught in 'unconditional' worst forms of child labour, including slavery, trafficking, debt bondage, and other forms of coerced labour, forced recruitment for armed conflict, prostitution, pornography, and other illicit activities."[†] These large numbers of adults and children become caught in trafficking through abduction; through their vulnerability in orphanages, refugee camps, street life, poverty, and unemployment; or through the abuse of their earnest desires for a better life.

Shocking statistics only begin to convey the depth of human suffering that trafficking inflicts. For example, one of the main trafficking patterns involves the removal of women and girls from the former Soviet Union republics for sale and exploitation in Europe, the Middle East, and Japan.

---

[*]Protocol to Prevent, Suppress, and Punish Trafficking in Persons, Especially Women and Children, Supplementing the United Nations Convention Against Transnational Organized Crime (2000).

[†]"Child Labor Remains 'Massive Problem,'" *World of Work*, no. 43 (June 2002): 4–5.

Lured and deceived by false job offers, women are sold for $2,500, raped and beaten into submission, and forced to service ten to thirty men a night, making between $75,000 and $250,000 a year for their "owners."* Terrorized into submission, these women are exposed to psychological abuse, rape, torture, and sexually transmitted diseases, including HIV/AIDS. When they are not working, they are often kept locked up, sometimes in filthy conditions. Similar exploitation is present in the burgeoning sex tourism industry in Southeast Asia, where girls as young as twelve are trafficked from Burma to Thailand, from Nepal to India, and from Vietnam to Cambodia.

Children, officially anyone under age eighteen, are also being sold and held in hopeless, dehumanizing labor. Activists distinguish between child labor, which is customary in some developing countries to supplement family income, and bondage. While the former can involve dangerous conditions, long hours, and low pay, the latter involves the abduction of children from their homes and entrapment in harmful, degrading work in other parts of their countries or outside their countries. Anti-Slavery International notes that only a small percentage of child labor is involved in manufacturing items for export. However, hundreds of thousands of children in Sri Lanka, Cambodia, India, Pakistan, Nepal, and African nations are trapped in bleak, arduous, isolated work as domestic laborers, and are often exploited sexually as well.

While this human suffering should arouse our compassion, these violations of human rights should also concern us because human trafficking feeds crime domestically and contributes to the political and social destabilization of many regions of the world. The global trafficking of women and girls in the sex trade has fueled the AIDS pandemic, which in turn advances social disintegration, political instability, and potential terrorism. Currently, sex trafficking, the spread of AIDS, and subsequent social unraveling are threatening India, Nepal, and China. Human trafficking also fuels organized crime and the growth of corruption; the huge potential profits attract organized crime, and wealthy traffickers can easily bribe local government officials and police. After trade in drugs and weapons, the traffic of women and children is the most lucrative criminal business. Often the drug trade and the sex trade nurture each other by using the same routes and contacts. In addition, forced child labor jeopardizes the future of societies and perpetuates countries' cycles of poverty as worn-down children are denied education and opportunities to acquire skills that could help them improve their economic status.

The United Nations, the United States and many other countries, and numerous nongovernmental organizations (NGOs) are trying to address these human rights problems. The United Nations has formally proscribed trafficking and forced labor in Article 4 of its Universal Declaration of Rights: "No one shall be held in slavery or servitude; slavery and the slave

---

*Victor Malarek, *The Natashas: Inside the New Global Sex Trade* (New York: Arcade Publishing, 2003): 4–5.

trade shall be prohibited in all their forms" (www.un.org/en/documents/ udhr). Similarly, Article 32 of the UN Convention on the Rights of the Child adopted by the United Nations General Assembly on Nov. 20, 1989, declares, "State Parties recognize the right of the child to be protected from economic exploitation and from performing any work that is likely to be hazardous or to interfere with the child's education or to be harmful to the child's health or physical, mental, spiritual, moral, or social development." In 2000, the U.S. Congress passed the Trafficking Victims Protection Act that established the Tier System for measuring countries' efforts to combat human trafficking. Tier 1 includes the most cooperative countries and Tier 3 includes the least diligent in fighting trafficking.* This approach is intended to work by using shame and economic pressure to compel countries to confront their human trafficking problems. The United States has banned sex tourism involving children in the PROTECT Act of 2003 and has called on other nations to criminalize such behavior. Numerous organizations are working with governments on preventative strategies, detection and prosecution of traffickers, and rehabilitation of victims. For example, the Angel Coalition of the Moscow Trafficking Assistance Center has begun educational programs in orphanages and schools warning of trafficking, and has established a free telephone helpline for Russian-speaking women and girls trafficked to Europe. As this chapter shows, the immensity and complexity of the human trafficking problems necessitate local and regional efforts as well as international cooperation.

STAKES AND STAKEHOLDERS

Many stakeholders such as national governments, international advocacy groups, and civil society organizations around the world are struggling to grasp the causes and extent of human trafficking and are investigating solutions to this global problem. In addressing this problem, they are focusing on a number of subcontroversies.

How Has Globalization Affected the Trafficking of Women and Children?
Free trade proponents believe that many of the current violations of human rights, especially in developing countries, are part of the temporary conditions of economic development. They argue that global trade and growing prosperity will bring new freedoms and improve the societal and economic conditions that make people vulnerable to human trafficking. These advocates object to using economic sanctions to penalize countries for their human rights violations and trafficking problems. Some free trade supporters

---

*For more information on tier rankings of different countries, see U.S. Department of State, Office to Monitor and Combat Trafficking in Persons, *Trafficking in Persons Report 2009*, June 16, 2009.

and governments and businesses in developing countries themselves argue that making money from their women and children, although harsh and unpleasant, is a practical way of dealing with economic needs, of paying their countries' debts, and of entering the global market.

In opposition, social activists and critics of economic globalization hold multinational corporations and free trade accountable for forcing rapid economic change, for undermining the social order and traditional societies in these countries, and for creating ready global markets for trafficked people. Kevin Bales, author of *Disposable People: New Slavery in the Global Economy* (1999) and activist in Anti-Slavery International, asserts that the emphasis on profits and speedy modernization has nurtured these countries' tolerance of human trafficking and that the lure of big money has fostered corruption in developing countries. Many critics also fault multinationals for indifference to human rights violations in developing countries.

Some analysts and critics stress the role of global communication and connections in facilitating the smuggling of slaves across national borders and the falsifying of passports, airline tickets, visas, and work contracts. Investigative journalist Victor Malarek, in his book *The Natashas: Inside the New Global Sex Trade* (2003), argues that the Internet is fueling the sex trade. Malarek calls the Internet "the biggest whorehouse on the planet,"[*] and claims that "in no time porn kings, pimps and traffickers were online promoting their products and services. Indeed, many observers believe that the Net is singularly responsible for the incredible explosion in the trafficking of women and girls worldwide."[†]

Who Should be Protecting Human Rights? Despite various treaties and agreements, the global community is in conflict about who should enforce them. NGOs, activists, and some policymakers are calling for more UN and U.S. involvement in establishing laws to catch and punish traffickers and those who benefit from trafficked persons. Some advocacy groups and NGOs want the U.S. Department of State to emphasize human rights in applying its Tier System more rigorously. These activists and analysts criticize multinational corporations, trade agreements, institutions such as the World Trade Organization, and governments for valuing property over human lives, and they challenge them to make human trafficking unprofitable and, therefore, unattractive. These activists contend that protecting human rights is a good business practice that creates political and economic stability beneficial for investment.

How Big is the Human Trafficking Problem and What Are the Motives of Activists? Some critics and public health officials argue that NGOs are exaggerating the problem in order to gain more governmental aid. The human

---

[*]Malarek, p. 80.
[†]Ibid., p. 81.

trafficking issue has brought together conservative Protestants, Catholics, Jews, Buddhists, and feminists in the cause of international human rights; yet some politicians and critics suggest that these social activists are using the sex trade issue to fuel their campaign against prostitution. Some researchers, politicians, and analysts also contest the idea that certain groups of child laborers and sex workers are being trafficked, disagreeing over who are victims and who are willing workers using prostitution and servitude knowingly as solutions to their economic problems.

How Can We End Trafficking and Help Current and Potential Victims? Controversies swirl around whether we need more legislation or better enforcement of the legislation we have. Many stakeholders are asking, How can countries be held to their commitment to treaties such as the Convention on the Rights of the Child and their own laws? Some NGOs, politicians, and activists point out that the people who have the highest stakes in human trafficking, the victims themselves, are first silenced by coercion and then by the legal processes that criminalize them or penalize them as illegal migrants. These activists are campaigning for new laws and procedures for victims to have access to greater protection and aid. Trafficking Programme Officer of Anti-Slavery International Elaine Pearson recommends "increased employment and migration opportunities; protection and support for those trafficked, including temporary or permanent residence in countries of destination; and opportunities for legal redress and compensation."*

NGOs, researchers, and policymakers disagree about what strategies and solutions to pursue. Some target root causes, prevention, and the connection between trafficking and poverty, noting that the dominant global patterns of trafficking are from east to west and south to north, from poorer countries to richer ones. Kevin Bales asserts that the trafficking victims and the poor need to own their own lives; he recommends that we "give them access to credit, let them choose their work, get rid of corruption, offer rehabilitation programs, and provide education."† Some activists focus on the global market, for example, challenging sex work as an industry, promoting the curbing of sex tourism, or asking consumers to buy or not buy items produced by child workers. Other analysts, activists, and policymakers call for public support of local in-the-field groups that are in tune with specific regional conditions. Still others demand a rethinking of human trafficking in terms of migration patterns or global health problems.

The three sections that follow—"Student Voice," "International Voices," and "Global Hot Spot"—take you deeper into local and global, personal and social connections to the trafficking of women and children.

---

*"Trapped in Traffic," *New Internationalist,* no. 337 (August 2001): 26.
†*Disposable People* (Berkeley: University of California Press, 1999): 257.

STUDENT VOICE: A Human Connection by Victoria Herradura

Although Americans may feel removed from the problems of sex trafficking and forced labor, student writer Victoria Herradura shows how she became aware of these human rights abuses and decided to offer help.

As a first generation Filipino in the United States, I have been sheltered from the many hardships that my parents faced while growing up in the rural areas of the Philippines. My parents wanted to raise me as Americanized as possible, which meant not living the frugal lifestyle that they were raised in. Of course, this did not mean abandoning my relatives still trapped in the motherland unable to obtain visas. Every season, my mother would rummage through my belongings to find forgotten toys, clothes, and even unused school supplies to send overseas to my cousins in the Philippines. I would always put up a battle with her. There was no way I would let my mother simply give away my belongings to my cousins whom I had never met. I figured that if both of my parents were able to make it from the islands to America, there should be no reason why my aunts and uncles could not relocate here if that was what they truly desired.

As the years passed, I grew out of my bratty childhood attitude and personally sorted through my clothes and other belongings to send overseas. My mother thought that I was being more altruistic, but secretly I just wanted to make more room in my closet for better clothes, better shoes, and better accessories. During my junior year in high school, just before the seasonal closet clean-out, I purchased a pair of pastel pink Converse high-tops for a spirit day at school. Unfortunately, I was only able to wear those shoes once because a few days later, my mother packed them up and shipped them off. Several months after that, I found the need for those pastel pink shoes again. I searched through my closet, under my bed, in the backyard, and in the basement until my mother told me that my less-fortunate cousin in the Philippines was wearing them at that moment. The thought that she would dare give away something I bought with my own money to someone I did not even know temporarily made me livid.

It was not until the middle of senior year, when I watched the Lifetime movie, *Human Trafficking,* and saw the dire conditions and economic crisis of families in foreign countries, that I realized how horribly skewed my thoughts about my relatives had been. The movie traces three different stories, three different journeys out of human trafficking: that of a little girl, a teenager, and an older woman. The purpose of the film is to show that human trafficking is a global human rights issue, targeting women of all ages. In countries where there seems to be little hope of economic stability, any door that leads to opportunities and security is accessed without question, which allows the rich to take advantage of the poor and ignorant.

It seems odd that a four-hour movie highlighting the struggles of a form of prostitution could make me grasp the difficulties of life in the Philippines, but the story of the little girl did just that. The film portrays an American preteen girl, on vacation in the Philippines with her parents, who befriends a poor Filipino boy lurking in the street market for girls to sell into prostitution. While her parents are searching for her, she meets a younger Filipina who was sold by her parents for a year to do physical labor for a rich European businessman. Sadly, parents from rural areas of the Philippines often sell their children to men who claim that their children will be well taken care of and returned in good condition without any idea of the actual work they have to endure. I now know that jobs in America with a minimum wage are not offered everywhere and that the opportunities of making a successful life are not the same for everyone. My cousins are not being sold to foreign human traffickers, but it is just as challenging for them to earn money and get by on their own. They appreciated every used item my mother sent more than I did when those very same items were new.

Since watching that movie, I have willingly donated my belongings, not only to my relatives, but also to local charities. I have even convinced my parents to sponsor children in the Philippines because what is considered pocket change to Americans is just enough to meet a child's daily basic needs and prevents one more child from entering the world of human trafficking. Although I am disgusted at my initial views of life outside of the comforts of the U.S. borders, I realize that we often need exposure to the outside world to feel the need to help globally.

INTERNATIONAL VOICES

Among the many ongoing global conversations about forced child labor are the research contributions of scholars who are trying to determine how widespread and how detrimental forced child labor is. The passage that follows is a case study from a research project funded by the United Nations Children's Fund (UNICEF) in September 2000. Omolar Dakore Oyaide, from the department of gender studies at the University of Zambia, investigated child workers in Zambia, Africa. This passage comes from her published study "Child Domestic Labour in Lusaka: A Gender Perspective."

Testimony of a Child Domestic Worker in Zambia

This case study describes a thirteen-year-old orphaned girl worker, who didn't have money to go to school. At the time of this interview, she had been paid two months' wages for four months of work. She described her daily duties in these terms:

"I wake up at 0500 hours [5 a.m.]. I sweep the house and prepare breakfast for all the members of the house. I wash the dishes. I bathe the children and get them ready for school. I take them to school. I sweep the surrounding of the house. Then I wash the blankets of the young ones because they wet their bed and [wash] the clothes of everybody. I prepare lunch after this and serve lunch to everybody. I wash dishes and clean the dishes and then I iron clothes for the children and their parents. Then I start preparing dinner and after everyone has eaten, I wash up and tidy the kitchen. I prepare packed lunch for school for the children for the following day. I lock the door after everybody has gone to bed before I can sleep. I go to bed at 23 hours [11 p.m.] and sleep on the floor of the living room. My employer likes to shout at and insult [me] and is very rude. My employer's younger brother takes advantage of me sexually. If I refuse, he threatens me that he will tell them that I went out of the yard instead of working.

While child domestic workers are silenced by their youth; by social, economic, and often racial discrimination; and by their isolation, the girls and women entangled in sex trafficking experience these repressions as well as the power of the criminal forces that ensnared them and that continue to subjugate them. Consequently, only a few of these victims have shared their horrendous personal experiences. The following testimony is from the U.S. House of Representatives, Committee on International Relations Hearing on the Implementation of the Trafficking Victims Protection Act, November 8, 2001 (http://commdocs.house.gov/committees/intlrel/hfa76351.000/hfa76351_0f.htm). This testimony reveals that the United States is also involved in sex trafficking.

Testimony of a Trafficked Woman in the Sex Trade

My name is Maria. I am in disguise today because I am in fear that my captors will recognize me and place my life and that of my family in danger.

My story begins in May of 1997 in Vera Cruz, Mexico, when I was approached by an acquaintance about some jobs in the United States. She told me that there were jobs available in restaurants and that I will earn enough money to support my daughter and my parents in Mexico. I accepted the offer and a coyote brought me to Texas.

I was transported to Florida and there one of the bosses told me I would be working in a brothel as a prostitute. I told him he was mistaken, and that I was going to be working in a restaurant, not a brothel. He said I owed him a smuggling debt and the sooner I paid it off, the sooner I could leave. I was 18 years old and had never been far from home. I had no money or way to get back.

I was constantly guarded and abused. If anyone refused to be with a customer, we were beaten. If we adamantly refused the bosses would show us a lesson by raping us brutally. We worked 6 days a week, 12 hours a day.

. . . I never knew where I was. We were transported every 15 days to different cities. I knew if I tried to escape I would not get far because everything was unfamiliar. The bosses said that if we escaped they would get the money from our families. . . .

GLOBAL HOT SPOT: The Balkans and Eastern Europe

The sex trafficking of women is a global problem; recently, however, prime trafficking sites with the greatest number of women involved have been the states that were formerly part of the Soviet Union: Ukraine, Belarus, Moldova, Armenia, Georgia, Azerbaijan, Kyrgyzstan, and Kazakhstan. Girls and women trafficked from these impoverished countries end up most frequently in Europe and the Balkans and sometimes in the Middle East, Japan, the United States, and Canada. The following report was written by Mara Radovanovic, head of Lara, a women's organization devoted to helping women who have been trafficked from the former Soviet Union republics to Bosnia and Herzegovina. This report appeared on the Web site of Kvinna till Kvinna, a women's support foundation (http://www.kvinnatillkvinna.se/article/2001) in October 2002.

. . . .We contacted our local police station and the police at the border to inform them about the importance of paying attention to girls or boys that could be victims of trafficking. It worked out well. The police started to contact us so that we could take care of those affected and give them a secure place to stay while trying to help them. Our goal is to help them return to their countries, but they also need access to food, clothes, medical and psychological assistance. It is also very important that they have interpreters present so the victims can give a testimony of their experiences. So far we have helped 60 persons, and we have listened to their stories, one worse than the other.

Many people mix up trafficking with prostitution. Consequently, they claim those affected should not be treated as victims, since they have made a choice. Even the police and the authorities sometimes regard those affected by trafficking as prostitutes who have come to Bosnia and Herzegovina to make money. But we know how trafficking works, how the dealers do it.

They reach out to poor girls from the east, for example Ukraine, Moldavia or Romania and they promise them a good job in Bosnia and Herzegovina. Already when they cross the border, they are sold for the first time to professional traffickers, and after that they are sold again at every border, each time at a higher price. . . . They are then transported to trafficking centers, for example in Belgrade and Serbia, where trafficked women from many countries are gathered. There the women are deprived of their identity. Their passports are taken from them, and they are given false names, birth dates and sometimes even a new country of origin. We helped two twin sisters who looked exactly the same, but one of them had a Ukrainian passport while the other had a Romanian one. . . .

We have done research to get all the details and now we struggle to spread information and raise awareness of the situation with as many people as possible. In Bijeljina we have succeeded to build opinion against the slave trade and both politicians and the public support us. As a result, all the bars involved in such activities have had to close down. But a lot of work remains to be done and we continue the struggle, both locally and internationally. We co-operate with several women's organizations in the Balkans and the rest of Europe, since the traffickers work in a similar way everywhere.

Mara Radovanovic's account gives insight into the governmental, legal, and social channels that need to be enlisted to combat human trafficking. However, testimonies of sex trafficked girls and women, like those posted on the Protection Project Organization Web site (www.protectionproject. org), reveal the huge obstacles to solving this problem. The arguments in this chapter, which present policy statements, scholarly research, and calls to action, will introduce you to the political, economic, social, and ethical dimensions of human trafficking and child labor, and will help you formulate your own views.

READINGS

Human Trafficking
David A. Feingold

David A. Feingold is an anthropologist, author, filmmaker, and director of the Ophidian Research Institute, a nongovernmental organization focused on human trafficking. He has worked for UNESCO Bangkok as international coordinator for HIV/AIDS and Trafficking Projects. His documentary film *Trading Women*

(2003) exposes the complexities of trafficking in Southeast Asia. In his film and writing, Feingold calls for more research and more accurate statistics. He says that trafficking involves two main elements, "migration and coercion," and that "trafficking is like a disease" that is constantly mutating and needs responses that are continuously being adjusted and refined in order to get at the underlying factors and to find an effective solution.* He favors work with local NGOs to improve the status and job opportunities of potential victims. This article appeared in the September–October 2005 edition of *Foreign Policy,* a politically nonbiased magazine about international politics and economics that is "dedicated to reaching a broad, nonspecialized audience who recognizes that what happens 'there' matters 'here,' and vice versa" (www.foreignpolicy.com).

> How does Feingold show his double purpose of clarifying and complicating his audience's understanding of human trafficking?

Judging by news headlines, human trafficking is a recent phenomenon. In fact, the coerced movement of people across borders is as old as the laws of supply and demand. What is new is the volume of the traffic—and the realization that we have done little to stem the tide. We must look beyond our raw emotions if we are ever to stop those who trade in human lives.

"MOST VICTIMS ARE TRAFFICKED INTO THE SEX INDUSTRY"

No. Trafficking of women and children (and, more rarely, young men) for prostitution is a vile and heinous violation of human rights, but labor trafficking is probably more widespread. Evidence can be found in field studies of trafficking victims across the world and in the simple fact that the worldwide market for labor is far greater than that for sex. Statistics on the "end use" of trafficked people are often unreliable because they tend to overrepresent the sex trade. For example, men are excluded from the trafficking statistics gathered in Thailand because, according to its national law, men cannot qualify as trafficking victims. However, a detailed 2005 study by the International Labour Organization (ILO) found that, of the estimated 9.5 million victims of forced labor in Asia, less than 10 percent are trafficked for commercial sexual exploitation. Worldwide, less than half of all trafficking victims are part of the sex trade, according to the same report.

Labor trafficking, however, is hardly benign. A study of Burmese domestic workers in Thailand by Mahidol University's Institute for Population and Social Research found beatings, sexual assault, forced labor without pay, sleep deprivation, and rape to be common. Another study, by

---

*Vicki Silverman, "*Trading Women* Shatters Myths about Human Trafficking," America.gov, September 11, 2003, http://www.america.gov/st/washfile-english/2003/September/20030911115501namrevlisv0.2781031.html (accessed June 15, 2009).

the German Agency for Technical Cooperation (GTZ), looked at East African girls trafficked to the Middle East and found that most were bound for oppressive domestic work, and often raped and beaten along the way. Boys from Cambodia and Burma are also frequently trafficked onto deep-sea commercial fishing boats, some of which stay at sea for up to two years. Preliminary research suggests 10 percent of these young crews never return, and boys that become ill are frequently thrown overboard.

The focus on the sex industry may galvanize action through moral outrage, but it can also cloud reason. A recent example is the unsubstantiated press reports that tsunami orphans in Indonesia's Aceh province were being abducted by organized gangs of traffickers. How such gangs could operate in an area bereft of roads and airstrips remains unclear, but that did not stop some U.S. organizations from appealing for funds to send "trained investigators" to track down the criminals. Although the devastation wrought by the tsunami certainly rendered people vulnerable—mostly through economic disruption—investigations by the United Nations have yet to identify a single confirmed case of sex trafficking.

"TIGHTENING BORDERS WILL STOP TRAFFICKING"

Wrong. The trafficking issue is often used—some would say hijacked—to support policies limiting immigration. In fact, the recent global tightening of asylum admissions has increased trafficking by forcing many desperate people to turn to smugglers. In southeast Europe, a GTZ study found that more stringent border controls have led to an increase in trafficking, as people turned to third parties to smuggle them out of the country.

Similarly, other legal efforts to protect women from trafficking have had the perverse effect of making them more vulnerable. For example, Burmese law precludes women under the age of 26 from visiting border areas unless accompanied by a husband or parent. Although Burmese officials say the law demonstrates the government's concern with the issue, many women believe it only increases the cost of travel (particularly from bribe-seeking police) and decreases their safety by making them dependent on "facilitators" to move them across the border. These women incur greater debt for their passage, thus making them even more vulnerable to exploitation along the way.

"TRAFFICKING IS A BIG BUSINESS CONTROLLED BY ORGANIZED CRIME"

False. Trafficking is big business, but in many regions of the world, such as Southeast Asia, trafficking involves mostly "disorganized crime": individuals or small groups linked on an ad hoc basis. There is no standard profile of traffickers. They range from truck drivers and village "aunties" to labor brokers and police officers. Traffickers are as varied as the circumstances of their victims. Although some trafficking victims are literally kidnapped, most leave their homes voluntarily and become trafficked on their journey.

Trafficking "kingpins," along the lines of the late cocaine boss Pablo Escobar, are rare. Japanese mafia, or yakuza, do control many of the venues in Japan where trafficked girls end up, but they are more likely to purchase people than transport them. Doing research in Thailand in 1997, I located the Luk Moo ("Piglet") network, which was responsible for about 50 percent of the women and girls smuggled into Thailand from Burma, China, and Laos to work in brothels. There were also other networks, such as the Kabuankam Loy Fah ("Floating in the Sky") network that specialized in girls for restaurants and karaoke bars. However, these networks have since faded in importance, owing to changes in the structure of the sex industry.

The worldwide trade in persons has been estimated by the United Nations Office on Drugs and Crime at $7 billion annually, and by the United Nations Children's Fund at $10 billion—but, of course, no one really knows. The ILO estimates the total illicit profits produced by trafficked forced laborers in one year to be just short of $32 billion. Although that is hardly an insignificant amount, it is a small business compared to the more than $320 billion international trade in illicit drugs.

"LEGALIZING PROSTITUTION WILL INCREASE TRAFFICKING"

It depends on how it's done. The intersection of the highly emotive issues of sex work and human trafficking generates a lot more heat than light. Some antitrafficking activists equate "prostitution" with trafficking and vice versa, despite evidence to the contrary. The U.S. government leaves no doubt as to where it stands: According to the State Department Web site, "Where prostitution is legalized or tolerated, there is a greater demand for human trafficking victims and nearly always an increase in the number of women and children trafficked into commercial sex slavery." By this logic, the state of Nevada should be awash in foreign sex slaves, leading one to wonder what steps the Justice Department is taking to free them. Oddly, the Netherlands, Australia, and Germany—all of whom have legalized prostitution—received top marks from the Bush administration in the most recent Trafficking in Persons Report.

Moreover, some efforts to prohibit prostitution have increased sex workers' risk to the dangers of trafficking, though largely because lawmakers neglected to consult the people the laws were designed to protect. Sweden, for example, is much praised by antiprostitution activists for a 1998 law that aimed to protect sex workers by criminalizing their customers. But several independent studies, including one conducted by the Swedish police, showed that it exposed prostitutes to more dangerous clients and less safe-sex practices.

Others argue that giving sex workers a measure of legitimacy short of legalization would actually discourage trafficking. In Thailand, many opposed to the commercial sex industry support extending labor and social security laws to sex workers. Such a move could hamper trafficking by opening establishments to inspection, allowing labor organization, and exposing underage prostitution.

"PROSECUTION WILL STOP TRAFFICKERS"

Not likely. In the United States, an odd but effective coalition of liberal Democrats, conservative Republicans, committed feminists, and evangelical Christians pushed a law through Congress in 2000 that aimed to prosecute traffickers and protect victims at home, while pressuring other countries to take action abroad. The Victims of Trafficking and Violence Protection Act recognized trafficking as a federal crime for the first time and provided a definition of victims in need of protection and services.

Despite the political energies expended on human trafficking, there is little evidence that prosecutions have any significant impact on aggregate levels of trafficking. For example, U.S. government figures indicate the presence of some 200,000 trafficked victims in the United States. But even with a well-trained law enforcement and prosecutorial system, less than 500 people have been awarded T visas, the special visas given to victims in return for cooperation with federal prosecutors. In fact, between 2001 and 2003, only 110 traffickers were prosecuted by the Justice Department. Of these, 77 were convicted or pled guilty.

Given the nature of the trafficking business, so few convictions will have little effect. Convicting a local recruiter or transporter has no significant impact on the overall scale of trafficking. If the incentives are right, he or she is instantly replaced, and the flow of people is hardly interrupted.

"SANCTIONS WILL STOP TRAFFICKING"

Wrong. The same U.S. law that made trafficking a federal crime also gave the United States the right to punish other states that do not crack down on human trafficking. The State Department is required to send a report to Congress each year ranking countries according to their success in combating trafficking and threatening sanctions for those with the worst records.

But international humanitarian agencies see the threat of U.S. sanctions against foreign governments as largely counterproductive. Practically speaking, sanctions will likely be applied only against countries already subject to sanctions, such as Burma or North Korea. Threatening moderately unresponsive countries—such as China, Nigeria, or Saudi Arabia—would likely backfire, causing these countries to become less open to dialogue and limiting the flow of information necessary for effective cooperation.

Although some countries certainly lack candor and create false fronts of activity, others actively seek Uncle Sam's seal of approval (and the resources that often follow) with genuine efforts to combat trafficking. Bangladesh, for example, received higher marks from the State Department this year by taking significant steps against trafficking, despite the country's poverty and limited resources. Incentives, instead of sanctions, might encourage others to do the same.

"TRAFFICKING VICTIMS SHOULD BE SENT HOME"

Not always. Sending victims home may simply place them back in the same conditions that endangered them in the first place, particularly in situations of armed conflict or political unrest. If criminal gangs were involved in the trafficking, they will likely threaten the safety of victims and their families.

To complicate matters, people may have no "home" to which they can return. Lack of legal status is a major risk factor in trafficking, impeding and often precluding victims' return and reintegration. That problem is particularly true for minorities, indigenous peoples, and informal migrants who often have no way to prove their nationality. In Thailand, for example, studies by the United Nations Educational, Scientific and Cultural Organization have demonstrated that a lack of proof of citizenship is the single greatest risk factor for a hill tribe girl or woman to be trafficked or otherwise exploited. Without citizenship, she cannot get a school diploma, register her marriage, own land, or work outside her home district without special permission. Lack of legal status prevents a woman from finding alternate means of income, rendering her vulnerable to trafficking for sex work or the most abusive forms of labor.

In developing countries, one's lack of legal status usually begins at birth. Without a birth certificate, a child typically has no legal identity: That is why international laws such as the Convention on the Rights of the Child stress that children have the right to be registered at birth. Many activists have never considered that a fix as simple as promoting birth registration in developing countries is one of the most cost-effective means to combat human trafficking.

"TRAFFICKING IS DRIVEN BY POVERTY"

Too simple. Trafficking is often migration gone terribly wrong. In addition to the push of poverty or political and social instability, trafficking is influenced by the expanded world views of the victims—the draw of bright lights and big cities. The lure of urban centers helps to account for why, in parts of Africa, girls from medium-sized towns are more vulnerable to trafficking than those in rural villages.

To fill the demand for ever cheaper labor, many victims are trafficked within the same economic class or even within a single country. In Brazil, for example, girls may be trafficked for sex work from rural to urban areas, whereas males may be sold to work in the gold mines of the Amazon jungle. In the Ivory Coast, children are frequently sold into slavery to work on cocoa plantations. In China, girls are trafficked as brides in impoverished rural areas, which are devoid of marriage-age females as a result of China's one-child policy and families' preference for baby boys.

Does this mean that "destination" countries or cities are the beneficiaries of trafficking? Not necessarily. What one area or industry may gain in cheap, docile labor, others—especially those situated near national borders—often pay for in terms of security, health costs, and, sometimes, political unrest. Trafficking may answer a demand, but the cost is too steep for this ever shrinking world to bear.

For Class Discussion

1. What common views of human trafficking is Feingold criticizing? What is his main claim about human trafficking?

2. What evidence strikes you as the most effective and persuasive?

3. How well does Feingold convince you of his knowledge and authority and of the reliability of his evidence?

4. This piece has been structured to fit *Foreign Policy*'s "Forum," a regular feature that presents a loose, informal debate. If Feingold were to rewrite this piece as another kind of argument genre (for example, an op-ed piece, policy brief, or open letter to a public official), what claims, reasons, and evidence would you suggest he include? Think of the audience he would be trying to reach and the length and depth of the article.

5. How has Feingold influenced your view of human trafficking? What questions do you have after reading this article?

Put Your Money Where Their Mouths Are

Nicholas D. Kristof

Nicholas D. Kristof holds degrees from Harvard College and Oxford University and is the winner of two Pulitzer Prizes in international reporting (along with his wife, Sheryl WuDunn). With her, he has written *China Wakes* (1995) and *Thunder from the East* (2001) about China's economic and political transformation, and *Half the Sky: From Oppression to Opportunity for Women Worldwide* (2009). He has worked as the *New York Times* bureau chief in Hong Kong, Beijing, and Tokyo, and has written numerous provocative editorials on sweatshop labor and prostitution in the developing world (see his blog "On the Ground" on the *New York Times* Web site). This op-ed piece appeared in the April 3, 2004, issue of the *New York Times*.

> What general audience and what specific audience does Kristof address in this op-ed piece? What relationship does he establish with his dual audiences?

With Democrats on the warpath over trade, there's pressure for tougher international labor standards that would try to put Abakr Adoud out of work.*

Abakr lives with his family in the desert near this oasis in eastern Chad. He has never been to school and roams the desert all day with his brothers, searching for sticks that can be made into doors for mud huts. He is 10 years old.

It's appalling that Abakr, like tens of millions of other children abroad, is working instead of attending school. But prohibiting child labor wouldn't do him any good, for there's no school in the area for him to attend. If child labor hawks manage to keep Abakr from working, without giving him a school to attend, he and his family will simply be poorer than ever.

And that's the problem when Americans get on their high horses about child labor, without understanding the cruel third world economics that cause it. The push by Democrats like John Kerry for international labor standards is well intentioned, but it is also oblivious to third world realities.

Look, I feel like Scrooge when I speak out against bans on sweatshops or on child labor. In the West, it's hard to find anyone outside a university economics department who agrees with me. But the basic Western attitude particularly among Democrats and warm-and-fuzzy humanitarians

---

*The labor issue in Kristof's op-ed piece relates to Ed Finn's argument in Chapter 2 (see pp. 29–31) and to the sweatshop discussion in Chapter 3: "Trading Goods: Consumerism, Free Trade, and Sweatshops."

sometimes ends up making things worse. Consider the results of two major American efforts to ban imports produced by child labor.

In 1993, when Congress proposed the U.S. Child Labor Deterrence Act, which would have blocked imports made by children (if it had passed), garment factories in Bangladesh fired 50,000 children. Many ended up in worse jobs, like prostitution.

Then there was the hue and cry beginning in 1996 against soccer balls stitched by children in their homes (mostly after school) in Sialkot, Pakistan. As a result, the balls are now stitched by adults, often in factories under international monitoring.

But many women are worse off. Conservative Pakistanis believe that women shouldn't work outside the home, so stitching soccer balls is now off limits for many of them. Moreover, bad publicity about Pakistan led China to grab market share with machine-stitched balls; over the next two years, Pakistan's share of the U.S. soccer ball market dropped to 45 percent from 65 percent.

So poor Pakistani families who depended on earnings from women or children who stitched soccer balls are now further impoverished.

I'm not arguing that child labor is a good thing. It isn't. But as Jagdish Bhagwati, the eminent trade economist, notes in his new book, *In Defense of Globalization,* thundering against child labor doesn't address the poverty that causes it.

In the village of Toukoultoukouli in Chad, I visited the 17 girls and 31 boys in the two-room school. Many children, especially girls, never attend school, which ends after the fourth grade.

So a 12-year-old boy working in Toukoultoukouli has gotten all the education he can. Instead of keeping him from working, Westerners should channel their indignation into getting all children into school for at least those four years and there is one way that could perhaps be achieved.

It's bribery. The U.N. World Food Program runs a model foreign aid effort called the school feeding program. It offers free meals to children in poor schools (and an extra bribe of grain for girl students to take home to their families). Almost everywhere, providing food raises school attendance, particularly for girls. "If there were meals here, parents would send their kids," said Muhammad Adam, a teacher in Toukoultoukouli.

School feeding costs just 19 cents per day per child.

So here's my challenge to university students: Instead of spending your energy boycotting Nike or pressing for barriers against child labor, why not sponsor school meals in places like Toukoultoukouli?

I spoke with officials at the World Food Program, and they'd be thrilled to have private groups or individuals help sponsor school feedings. (See www.nytimes.com/kristofresponds for details.) Children in

Africa will be much better off with a hot meal and an education than with your self-righteous indignation.

For Class Discussion

1. What is Nicholas Kristof's main claim in this proposal argument?

2. In this piece, Kristof is criticizing humanitarians, liberals, and activists for their approach to child labor. What does he say is wrong with their approach? How does he defend his criticism of them and support his own view?

3. What do Kristof's informal, conversational tone and style contribute to his argument?

4. How has this piece influenced your thinking about the connections among child labor, poverty, and the citizens of rich nations?   ∎

A World Fit for Us
Children's Forum (Special Session on Children—UNICEF)

The three-day Children's Forum sponsored by UNICEF took place during May 2002 in New York City. Its purpose was to involve children in influencing their governments and NGOs in implementing programs to benefit children. Two children per government and NGO were invited to participate. This speech, "A World Fit for Us," was written by the Children's Forum and delivered to the United Nations General Assembly Special Session on Children on May 8, 2002, by two child delegates: thirteen-year-old Gabriela Azurduy Arrieta from Bolivia and seventeen-year-old Audrey Cheynut from Monaco. This speech is printed on the Special Sessions link of UNICEF (www.unicef.org/specialsession/documentation/childrens-statement.htm).

> How does this speech, with its special occasion, speakers, and audience, seek to establish children as primary stakeholders in human rights issues?

We are the world's children.
We are the victims of exploitation and abuse.
We are street children.
We are the children of war.
We are the victims and orphans of HIV/AIDS.
We are denied good-quality education and health care.
We are victims of political, economic, cultural, religious and environmental discrimination.
We are children whose voices are not being heard: it is time we are taken into account.

We want a world fit for children, because a world fit for us is a world fit for everyone.

In this world, we see respect for the rights of the child:

- governments and adults having a real and effective commitment to the principle of children's rights and applying the Convention on the Rights of the Child to all children,
- safe, secure and healthy environments for children in families, communities, and nations.

We see an end to exploitation, abuse and violence:

- laws that protect children from exploitation and abuse being implemented and respected by all,
- centres, and programmes that help to rebuild the lives of victimized children.

We see an end to war:

- world leaders resolving conflict through peaceful dialogue instead of by using force,
- child refugees and child victims of war protected in every way and having the same opportunities as all other children,
- disarmament, elimination of the arms trade and an end to the use of child soldiers.

We see the provision of health care:

- affordable and accessible life-saving drugs and treatment for all children,
- strong and accountable partnerships established among all to promote better health for children.

We see the eradication of HIV/AIDS:

- educational systems that include HIV prevention programmes,
- free testing and counselling centres,
- information about HIV/AIDS freely available to the public,
- orphans of AIDS and children living with HIV/AIDS cared for and enjoying the same opportunities as all other children.

We see the protection of the environment:

- conservation and rescue of natural resources,
- awareness of the need to live in environments that are healthy and favourable to our development,
- accessible surroundings for children with special needs.

We see an end to the vicious cycle of poverty:

- anti-poverty committees that bring about transparency in expenditure and give attention to the needs of all children,
- cancellation of the debt that impedes progress for children.

We see the provision of education:

- equal opportunities and access to quality education that is free and compulsory,

- school environments in which children feel happy about learning,
- education for life that goes beyond the academic and includes lessons in understanding, human rights, peace, acceptance and active citizenship.

We see the active participation of children:

- raised awareness and respect among people of all ages about every child's right to full and meaningful participation, in the spirit of the Convention on the Rights of the Child,
- children actively involved in decision-making at all levels and in planning, implementing, monitoring and evaluating all matters affecting the rights of the child.

We pledge an equal partnership in this fight for children's rights. And while we promise to support the actions you take on behalf of children, we also ask for your commitment and support in the actions we are taking, because the children of the world are misunderstood.

We are not the sources of problems; we are the resources that are needed to solve them.
We are not expenses; we are investments.
We are not just young people; we are people and citizens of this world.

Until others accept their responsibility to us, we will fight for our rights.
We have the will, the knowledge, the sensitivity and the dedication.
We promise that as adults we will defend children's rights with the same passion that we have now as children.
We promise to treat each other with dignity and respect.
We promise to be open and sensitive to our differences.

We are the children of the world, and despite our different backgrounds, we share a common reality.
We are united by our struggle to make the world a better place for all.
You call us the future, but we are also the present.

For Class Discussion

1. What image of children does this speech seek to convey?

2. Repetition, antithesis (contrasting statements), and the use of examples are the main rhetorical devices employed most prominently in this speech. Why are these effective in a speech? What effects do you think these devices had on the immediate listeners?

3. What words would you use to describe the tone of this speech?

4. How has this piece influenced your view of the violation of children's rights discussed in this chapter?

Chadian Eight-Year-Old Soldier Smoking

Luc Novovitch

Advocacy organizations believe that around 300,000 children from more than thirty countries are fighting in wars around the world. Many of these children—both boys and girls—have been abducted or coerced into military service, tortured, sexually

abused, forced to participate in violence, and compelled to witness terrible atrocities. These children are fighting in armies in Nepal, Sri Lanka, Indonesia, Colombia, Guatemala, Burma, Peru, Sudan, Uganda, Sierra Leone, and Liberia, among other countries. Many countries have signed the UN protocol of 2002 to stop the military recruitment of children; however, Asian and African signatories who have violated the protocol have not been brought before the International Criminal Court. This photo, one of many taken by news agencies reporting the problem of child soldiers, shows an eight-year-old soldier in Chad.

The more readers know about the horrors experienced by child soldiers, the more disturbing photos of these children are. What details of this photo stand out for you?

For Class Discussion

1. What features of this photo suggest that this boy has suffered?

2. With this photo in mind, list some of the psychological problems that child soldiers may have while they are serving in these armies and when they are liberated.

3. Investigate the problem of child soldiers by consulting the Web sites for such advocacy organizations as Human Rights Watch (www.hrw.org/), the Anti-Slavery Society (www.anti-slaverysociety.addr.com), and Save the Children (www.savethechildren.org/). What key facts from these sources would you use in a report for your peers on this human rights issue? What makes a photo rhetorically effective to protest child soldiers?

4. How has this photo influenced your thinking about forced child labor? ∎

Trafficking and Health
Joanna Busza, Sarah Castle, and Aisse Diarra

Joanna Busza and Sarah Castle are lecturers at the Center for Population Studies at the London School of Hygiene and Tropical Medicine. Busza has researched reproductive and sexual health issues in Southeast Asia, and from 1997 to 2001, she focused on HIV prevention with migrant sex workers. Sarah Castle spent fifteen years in Mali, Africa, working with out-migration. Aisse Diarra, an independent consultant, has extensive experience with women's health and women's rights issues in Mali. This policy proposal appeared in the scholarly publication the *British Medical Journal* on June 5, 2004.

This article follows a surprising-reversal format in that it sets up a common view of the trafficking of women and children and then argues that this view is erroneous and misinformed. What is the common view that Joanna Busza, Sarah Castle, and Aisse Diarra challenge? What is the new, surprising view that they seek to establish?

Trafficking in women and children is now recognised as a global public health issue as well as a violation of human rights. The *UN Protocol to Prevent, Suppress, and Punish Trafficking in Persons, Especially Women and Children* states that trafficking involves force, threat, or fraud and intent to exploit individuals.[1] Intermediaries often smuggle victims across international borders into illegal or unsafe occupations, including agriculture, construction, domestic labour, and sex work. A recent study identified trafficking to be associated with health risks such as psychological trauma, injuries from violence, sexually transmitted infections, HIV and AIDS, other adverse reproductive health outcomes, and substance misuse.[2] These risks are shaped by lack of access to services in a foreign country, language barriers, isolation, and exploitative working conditions. However, as this article shows, efforts to reduce trafficking may be making conditions worse for voluntary migrants.

RESPONSE TO TRAFFICKING

Multinational, governmental, and non-governmental groups working to counter trafficking sometimes misinterpret the cultural context in which migration occurs.[3] They often seek to eradicate labour migration rather than target specific instances of exploitation and abuse.[4,5] Regulatory measures, such as introducing new requirements for documentation and strengthening of border controls, criminalise and marginalise all migrants, whether trafficked or not. This exacerbates their health risks and vulnerability by reducing access to appropriate services and social care. Such approaches do not adequately distinguish between forced and voluntary migrants, as it is extremely difficult to identify the motivations of migrants and their intermediaries before travel.[6]

We illustrate these concerns with evidence from research conducted among child migrants in Mali who had been returned from the Ivory Coast and Vietnamese sex workers in Cambodia. The evidence draws from studies conducted between 2000 and 2002.[7,8] In both settings, the international media has reported emotively on the existence of "child slaves," "sex slaves," and "trafficking" and oriented donors and non-governmental organisations to this agenda.[9–11]

CHILD MIGRANTS IN MALI

Although no substantiated figures exist, an estimated 15,000 Malian children have been "trafficked" to the cocoa plantations in the Ivory Coast.[12] This study responded to a demand from several international non-governmental organisations that wanted to improve their understanding of the situation.[7] We compiled a sampling frame with the assistance of nongovernmental organisations working with children and their governmental partners. It included young people from communities deemed to be at high risk of trafficking, as well as intercepted or repatriated children thought to have been trafficked. However, a survey of nearly 1000 young people from this list found that only four could be classified as having been deceived, exploited, or not paid at all for their labour. Rather, young people voluntarily sought employment abroad, which represented an opportunity to experience urban lifestyles, learn new languages, and accumulate possessions. For both boys and girls, the experience provided a rite of passage with cultural as well as financial importance.

For many of these migrants, movement across international borders depended on assistance from intermediaries, often family members. In Mali there is a longstanding tradition of using intermediaries to facilitate a range of social and economic activities, such as looking for employment, negotiating purchases, handling disputes, and even seeking a spouse. Our research found that intermediaries could protect the migrants during their journey and help them search for work. In destination areas, they advocated for young people in cases of non-payment of salary or abrupt termination of employment. Migrants also relied on intermediaries to negotiate with corrupt authorities that demanded bribes at international borders. Classifying such assistance as "trafficking" simplifies a much deeper cultural reality.

Local anti-trafficking policies and interventions, however, have not acknowledged these complex dynamics and have instead posed obstacles to safe, assisted migration. For example, interviews with Malian legal experts showed that new legislative measures do not enable them to distinguish between a trafficker with intent to exploit and an intermediary who, for a fee, facilitates a young migrant's journey and search for housing and employment. Local anti-trafficking surveillance committees have been established; these have come to view all migration as negative and local leaders seem to seek to arrest children if they attempt to leave. At the national level, a new child's passport is required for all children under the age of 18 who wish to travel. In reality, young people find the document difficult to obtain, and failure to possess it provides an easy excuse for law enforcement officers to extort additional bribes at borders.

These measures discourage community members from assisting in traditional labour migration and have the potential to force migrants to rely increasingly on corrupt officials to waive travel documents or provide forgeries. Clandestine migrants are generally more difficult to reach at destination points, as they may be reluctant to seek health care or other help if they fear being forcibly repatriated or detained. Child migrants who left home of their own free will report being returned home against their wishes by non-governmental organisations, only to leave for the border again a few days later.

The study found that rehabilitation centres for trafficked children run by two non-governmental organisations in the Malian town of Sikasso were usually empty. Such interventions are neither appropriate nor cost effective and do not tackle the exploitative conditions encountered by children in the Ivory Coast. Children would be better served through services offered in the Ivory Coast or support through protective networks of intermediaries and community members.

VIETNAMESE SEX WORKERS IN CAMBODIA

As with Malians in the Ivory Coast, it is difficult to obtain accurate data on the number of Vietnamese migrants in Cambodia. Some estimates suggest that up to 10,000 Vietnamese women are sex workers in Cambodia.[13] The research presented here was conducted in collaboration with a local non-governmental organisation as part of a wider investigation of sex workers' perceptions, motivations, and experiences.[8] The study formed one component of a service delivery programme to about 300 brothel based Vietnamese sex workers in Svay Pak district, Phnom Penh. Before the research, medical services, outreach, and counselling had been provided to sex workers for over five years, and a trusting relationship had been established between non-governmental organisation staff and both sex workers and brothel managers. Young, female, Vietnamese speaking project staff familiar to the sex workers conducted indepth interviews with 28 women and focus group discussions with 72 participants to explore patterns of entry into sex work.

Most women knew before they left Vietnam that they would be engaged in sex work under a system of "debt bondage" to a brothel. The work would repay loans made to them or their families. Some women showed clear ambition in their choices to travel to Cambodia for sex work, citing economic incentives, desire for an independent lifestyle, and dissatisfaction with rural life and agricultural labour. As in Mali, intermediaries from home communities were instrumental in facilitating safe migration. Many women were accompanied by a parent, aunt, or neighbour who provided transport, paid bribes to border patrols, and negotiated the contract with brothel managers.

Of the 100 participants in this qualitative study, six women reported having been "tricked" into sex work or betrayed by an intermediary. Many sex workers, however, expressed dissatisfaction with their work conditions or stated that they had not fully appreciated the risks they would face, such as clients who refused to use condoms, coercion from brothel owners, and violence from both clients and local police.

A policy focus on combating "trafficking" again seemed to threaten rather than safeguard migrants' health and rights. Local and international non-governmental organisations conducted raids on brothels during which sex workers were taken to "rehabilitation centres," often against their will. Police sometimes assisted in these raids, although they also conducted arrests independently.

Our research found that "rescued" women usually returned to their brothel as quickly as possible, having secured their release through bribes or by summoning relatives from Vietnam to collect them. Furthermore, police presence in the raids scared off custom[ers], thus reducing earnings, increasing competition for clients, and further limiting sex workers' power in negotiating improved work conditions. Bribes and other costs were added to sex workers' debts, increasing their tenure in the brothel and adding pressure to take on additional customers or agree to condom-free sex to maximise income. Raids and rescues could also damage the relationship between service providers and brothel managers, who restricted sex workers' mobility, including access to health care, to avoid arrest. These findings mirror recent reports from other sex worker communities throughout the region.[14–16]

THE WAY FORWARD

Our research in Mali and Cambodia shows disturbing parallels in ways that anti-trafficking measures can contribute to adverse health outcomes. Without wanting to minimise the issue of trafficking, these studies show that a more flexible and realistic approach to labour migration among young people is required. The needs of vulnerable young migrants, whether trafficked or not, can be met only through comprehensive understanding of their motivations and of the cultural and economic contexts in which their movements occur. Criminalising migrants or the industries they work in simply forces them "underground," making them more difficult to reach with appropriate services and increasing the likelihood of exploitation.

We do not dispute that in both settings migrants have suffered hardship and abuse, but current "anti-trafficking" approaches do not help their problems. The agendas need to be redrawn so that they reflect the needs of the populations they aim to serve, rather than emotive reactions to sensationalised media coverage. This requires deeper investigation at both local and regional levels, including participatory research to inform interventions from the experiences of the migrants and their communities. From the research that we have conducted in Mali and Cambodia, we recommend the following:

- Policy makers need to recognise that migration has sociocultural as well as economic motivations and seeking to stop it will simply cause migrants to leave in a clandestine and potentially more dangerous manner. Facilitating safe, assisted migration may be more effective than relying on corrupt officials to enforce restrictive border controls.
- Instead of seeking to repatriate migrants, often against their will, interventions should consider ways to provide appropriate services at destination points, taking into consideration specific occupational hazards, language barriers, and ability to access health and social care facilities.
- Programmes aimed at improving migrants' health and welfare should not assume that all intermediaries are "traffickers" intending to exploit migrants. Efforts to reach migrants in destination areas could use intermediaries.
- Organisations that have established good rapport with migrant communities should document cases of abuse and advocate for improved labour conditions. In the case of sex work, however, this can be politically difficult. For example, the United States Agency for International Development recently announced its intention to stop funding organisations that do not explicitly support the eradication of all sex work.

Ultimately, trafficking and other forms of exploitation will cease only with sustainable development in sending areas combined with a reduction in demand for cheap, undocumented labour in receiving countries. Non-governmental organisations and government partners therefore need to focus on the root causes of rural poverty and exploitation of labour as well as mitigating the health risks of current migrants. At the moment, trafficking is big business not just for traffickers but also for the international development community, which can access funds relatively easily to tackle the issue without investing in a more comprehensive understanding of the wider dynamics shaping labour migration.

References

1. United Nations. *Protocol to prevent, suppress and punish trafficking in persons, especially women and children, supplementing the United National Convention Against Transnational Organized Crime.* New York: United Nations, 2000.
2. Zimmerman C, Yun K, Shvab I, Watts C, Trappolin L, Treppete M, et al. *The health risks and consequences of trafficking in women and*

adolescents. Findings from a European study. London: London School of Hygiene and Tropical Medicine, 2003.

3. Butcher K. Confusion between prostitution and sex trafficking. *Lancet* 2003;361: 1983. [CrossRef][ISI][Medline]
4. Marshall P. *Globalization, migration and trafficking: some thoughts from the South-East Asian region.* Bangkok: UN Inter-Agency Project on Trafficking in Women and Children in the Mekong Sub-region, 2001. (Occasional paper No 1.)
5. Taran PA, Moreno-Fontes G. *Getting at the roots.* UN Inter-Agency Project Newsletter 2002;7: 1–5.
6. Coomaraswamy R. *Integration of the human rights of women and the gender perspective: violence against women: report of the special rapporteur on violence against women, its causes and consequences.* New York: UN Economic and Social Council, 2000.
7. Castle S, Diarra A. *The international migration of young Malians: tradition, necessity or rite of passage?* London: London School of Hygiene and Tropical Medicine, 2003.
8. Busza J, Schunter BT. From competition to community: participatory learning and action among young, debt-bonded Vietnamese sex workers in Cambodia. *Reprod Health Matters* 2001;9: 72–81. [CrossRef[ISI][Medline]
9. Bobak L. For sale: the innocence of Cambodia. *Ottawa Sun* 1996 Oct 24.
10. Chocolate slaves carry many scars. *Daily Telegraph* 2001 Apr 24.
11. Child slavery: Africa's growing problem. *CNN* 2001 Apr 17.
12. United States Agency for International Development. *Trafficking in persons: USAID's response.* Washington, DC: USAID Office of Women in Development, 2001: 10–6.
13. Unicef. Unicef supports national seminar on human trafficking. www.unicef.org/vietnam/new080.htm (accessed 11 Nov 2003).
14. Jones M. Thailand's brothel busters. *Mother Jones* 2003 Nov/Dec.
15. Phal S. *Survey on police human rights violations in Toul Kork.* Phnom Penh: Cambodia Women's Development Association, 2002.
16. Sutees R. Brothel raids in Indonesia—ideal solution or further violation? *Research for Sex Work* 2003;6: 5–7.

For Class Discussion

1. This proposal argument addresses the complexities of child labor in Mali and Africa, and of Vietnamese sex workers (many of them young girls) in Cambodia. What clashes among stakeholders on the trafficking controversy and what complexities do Busza, Castle, and Diarra want readers to understand?

2. What claims do these writers make about stakeholders' conflicting agendas for dealing with global child labor and the sex trade?

3. In this researched policy proposal, how do the writers establish their credibility and authority? What makes their use of evidence effective and persuasive?

4. How has this article influenced your view of the trafficking of children and women? In what ways do you think free trade advocates would agree with the writers of this article?

For Sale
International Organization for Migration

The International Organization for Migration is a fifty-year-old global organization that seeks to "assist in meeting the growing operational challenges of migration management; advance understanding of migration issues; encourage social and

© International Organization for Migration (IOM), taken from the Southern African Counter-Trafficking Assistance Programme. www.iom.org.za/CounterTrafficking.html

economic development through migration; and uphold the human dignity and well-being of migrants" (from its mission statement, www.iom.org). IOM works with governments and civil society on every continent. Its countertrafficking projects focus on information campaigns, counseling services, research, safe conduct and assistance for victims, and working with governments on their legal systems to stop trafficking.

What are your first impressions of this poster?

For Class Discussion

1. How would you describe the girl on this poster?

2. What is the emotional effect of the combination of the photo of the girl, the words "FOR SALE," and the placement of the words?

3. What primary and secondary audiences do you think this poster is attempting to reach?

4. Examine the information provided on the Web site of this organization (www.iom.int/). How does this organization on its Web site and in this poster establish the connections between migration and human trafficking? What are some of those connections?

5. What readings in this chapter does this poster support? ∎

Confusion Between Prostitution and Sex Trafficking
Kate Butcher

Kate Butcher is a public health consultant with John Snow Research International and Training, a leading provider of consultation on public health based in the United Kingdom. She has worked extensively with HIV/AIDS programs in Africa and Asia, and she has written much about combating AIDS, including her 2001 article "Danger and Opportunity: Responding to HIV with Vision," published in the journal *Gender and Development*. Her policy proposal here was originally published in the *Lancet* on June 7, 2003. The *Lancet*, a well-known and highly reputable British medical journal dating from 1823, is "an independent and authoritative voice in global medicine." It has always sought to "combine publication of the best medical science with a zeal to counter the forces that undermine the values of medicine, be they political, social, or commercial" (from "About *The Lancet*" at www.thelancet.com/about).

How does the thesis of Butcher's argument suit the reformist purpose of this medical journal?

In May, 2003, the US government passed the Leadership Against HIV/AIDS, Tuberculosis and Malaria Act of 2003, which outlines the areas and support that the US administration is prepared to endorse in the fight against these diseases. The act includes the limitation that "No funds made available to carry out this Act . . . may be used to provide assistance to any group or organization that does not have a policy explicitly opposing prostitution and sex trafficking."[1]

This statement might go unnoticed, but it deserves attention. The juxtaposition of the terms prostitution and sex trafficking demonstrates a belief that both share similar characteristics, and thus reflects moral ideology rather than objective reality.

The distinction between trafficking and prostitution is important because it pivots on individual agency. Trafficking, though variously defined,[2] covers coercion, forced labour, and slavery. Prostitution describes the sale of sex, by no means necessarily without consent or with coercion. At a time when trafficking is increasing, as are international efforts to tackle it, it is critical to clarify the differences between the issues.[3]

The merging of these issues is not new, nor confined to the USA. In Asia, where human trafficking (both for prostitution and for bonded labour) has a longer history than in Europe, responses by governments and feminist groups alike have often been to call for eradication of prostitution, and therefore trafficking.

But this approach overlooks an important fact; millions of women have made the decision to sell sex, usually but not always, on economic grounds. Selling sex is a pragmatic response to a limited range of options. If you can earn the equivalent of UK £100 in a night, why knit sweaters or sweep floors to earn the same money in a month?

When women's groups call for rehabilitation and rescue of trafficked and prostituted women they argue from their own moral perspective and not that of the women they are seeking to save. The situation is complex, in that a spectrum can exist between trafficking and prostitution, with trafficked girls at one end and women who have decided to work as prostitutes at the other. Some women who have been trafficked may eventually begin to define themselves as sex workers. The longer a woman is involved in the sex industry the more likely this is to be the case; 6 years after being trafficked to India a Nepalese woman told me: "Why would I want to return to Nepal? I have friends here, I make good money. In Nepal what would I do? Look after goats and have no money! I'm good at my job and I know it. I don't want to return to Nepal."

Of course there will be other women and men who may wish to leave the sex industry. The responsibility of public health, development, and human rights workers is to ensure that individuals enjoy the same level of human rights whatever their involvement in the sex industry.

The prominence of debate about sex work and trafficking has grown largely as a result of the HIV epidemic.[4] Sex workers, initially identified as a public health threat, embodied in phrases such as "pools of infection" and "vectors of disease", were recruited to promote safer sex. Sex workers around the world have been practising safer sex and educated many of their clients to do the same.[5] Their importance in responding to the HIV epidemic is evident, but evidence of improved rights for these men and women is harder to find.

Key rights listed in the UNAIDS handbook for legislators on HIV, law, and human rights include:

- Non-discrimination and equality before the law
- Freedom from inhuman or degrading treatment or punishment
- Autonomy, liberty, and security of the person

All over the world these basic entitlements are violated in the context of sex work. It is rare to read of a successful lawsuit made by a sex worker against a rapist, violation from a policeman, or unlawful arrest.

By merging trafficking and prostitution, the agency of sex workers is overlooked. Rather than promoting opposition to prostitution we would do better to promote human rights. The right to resist being drawn into prostitution by trafficking certainly, but so too the right to work with the law's protection from harm, be it rape, violence, robbery, or other violations.

We can expect sex workers to continue contributing to the fight against HIV and thus to public health: it is after all in everyone's interest including their own. We should also expect public health and development professionals to support their so doing without fear for their lives or their safety—in sum, by advocating for the human rights of sex workers.

Notes

1. HR 1298 US leadership against HIV/AIDS, tuberculosis and malaria act of 2003. http://www.thebody.com/govt/global_aids.html (accessed May, 2003).
2. Luckoo F, Tzvetkova M. Combating trafficking in persons: a directory of organisations. London: Change, 2002.
3. Human Rights Caucus. UN trafficking protocol: lost opportunity to protect the rights of trafficked persons. December, 2000. http://www.unodc.un.or.th/factsheet/fact2001_trafficking.htm (accessed May, 2003).
4. Kotiswaran P. Preparing for civil disobedience: Indian sex workers and the law. *21 Boston College Third World Law J,* no 2, Spring, 2001.
5. Network of Sex Work Projects. Making sex work safe. http://www.nswp.org/safety/msws/ (accessed May, 2003).

For Class Discussion

1. According to Butcher, what is the complex relationship between sex trafficking, prostitution, human rights, and the AIDS epidemic? In this policy proposal, developed in part through a definitional argument, what does Butcher claim is the distinction between prostitution and sex trafficking?
2. Whom is Butcher criticizing and rebutting in this article?

3. What reasoning and evidence does Butcher offer to support her views?

4. What assumptions must readers have to agree with this argument?

5. Butcher has worked extensively in global public health. How does knowledge of her background influence your response to this argument? ■

Slavery in 2004
John R. Miller

Former ambassador John R. Miller has been a Republican congressman from the state of Washington and was the director of the State Department's Office to Monitor and Combat Trafficking in Persons from 2002 to 2006. He is known for his bold, uncompromising stance against human trafficking. This op-ed piece appeared in the *Washington Post* on January 1, 2004.

What economic solution does Miller propose to deal with trafficking and human rights problems?

Do U.S. sanctions move other countries toward progress on human rights? Of one thing I am sure: On the emerging human rights issue of the 21st century—modern-day slavery—the threat of cutting U.S. aid has brought forth efforts that will free thousands from bondage.

That slavery exists as we enter 2004 may shock many. Nonetheless, slavery in many forms, particularly sex and forced labor, reaches into almost every country. Sex slavery affects thousands of women and children and has caused trafficking in human beings to become the third-largest source of money for organized crime, after the drug and arms trades. That grim reality motivated President Bush this fall to become the first world leader to raise the slavery issue at the U.N. General Assembly. He called for new international efforts to fight the slave trade and pledged to almost double U.S. resources devoted to this cause.

The U.S. government estimates that 800,000 to 900,000 men, women and children are trafficked across international borders every year, including 18,000 to 20,000 into the United States. Some estimate total worldwide slavery to be in the millions.

In September I visited a number of countries to meet with the human beings behind such numbers. If you talk with Sasha, a former sex slave in Amsterdam, or with Lord, a former factory slave in Bangkok, you quickly understand the toll this takes on individual bodies and spirits. The story that one victim, Maria, told Congress a few years ago is typical. Lured with the hope of a restaurant job from Vera Cruz, Mexico, and trafficked through Texas, Maria was finally delivered to a brothel in Florida. There she resisted but—frightened, threatened, beaten and raped in a strange land—she succumbed and "worked" to pay off the debts that traffickers claimed she owed them.*

Cases such as hers and the urgings of faith-based and feminist organizations led Congress to pass legislation that not only strengthened U.S. prosecution of traffickers and assistance to victims but also mandated the State Department to report on slavery and the slave trade around the world.

And here we see how the threat of economic penalties has started to play a crucial role. For the first two years the law was in effect, there were zero consequences. But this year, Congress provided that countries rated by the State Department as having made no significant efforts be faced with the potential loss of U.S. military aid, educational and cultural assistance, and support from the World Bank and International Monetary Fund.

In the three months before the slavery report came out this past June, my office saw more progress in some countries than in the previous two years. Laws against trafficking in persons were passed in places from the Philippines to Haiti to Burkina Faso. Victims were rescued and massive arrests of traffickers were made in Cambodia and Serbia.

The U.S. law provided that for those countries poorly rated in this year's report, there would be a three-month period to make antislavery efforts. In 10 countries, including military allies of the United States, there was a flurry of activity.

Turkey set up and implemented new screening procedures that recognized 200 victims. Georgia appointed special officers with responsibility for trafficking and started broadcasting hotline numbers for victims on national television. The Dominican Republic launched a national educational billboard campaign and set up a national anti-trafficking police unit with special prosecutors. In these and other countries there were numerous arrests and prosecutions.

Of course not all these actions resulted from the threat of aid cuts. Many government officials, finally recognizing the enormity of the human crises, wanted to act. Some undoubtedly were embarrassed by the State Department's report. Strenuous efforts by diplomats in many U.S. embassies were crucial.

We continue, however, to face the problem that many countries' economies have links to slavery. Corrupt and complicit police pose a challenge in many nations. And there is the difficulty of trying to fight diseases such as HIV-AIDS at the same time we are fighting the sex trafficking that causes so much of that disease.

To meet these challenges we need support and action at home and antislavery allies abroad. But we also need the willingness to impose economic penalties that give antislavery laws and diplomacy meaning.

---

*Maria's story is quoted in the "International Voices" section of this chapter on page 479.

For Class Discussion

1. Political conservatives (Republicans) and especially free trade proponents and libertarians oppose economic intervention as a means to pressure foreign governments to attend to their problems with human rights and trafficking. What is John Miller's stance?

2. How does Miller build a case for his main claim?

3. What features of this article show Miller's attempting to bring American citizens into the controversies over human trafficking and to move them to agree with his views?

4. Who do you think opposes John Miller's views and on what basis?

5. Miller has frequently objected to the use of the term "sex worker," claiming that it mischaracterizes the women and children who endure abuse and slavery (http://www.humantrafficking.org/updates/524). How do you think language influences people's understanding of and attitudes toward human trafficking?

Ending Abuses and Improving Working Conditions for Tomato Workers
Eric Schlosser

Eric Schlosser is an award-winning investigative journalist whose work appears in the *Atlantic Monthly, Rolling Stone,* the *Nation,* and the *New Yorker.* He is perhaps most famous for his advocacy book *Fast Food Nation: The Dark Side of the All-American Meal* (2001), a best-seller translated into twenty languages that has contributed to changing the way Americans think about what they eat. This excerpted testimony was given before the U.S. Senate Committee on Health, Education, Labor, and Pensions on April 15, 2008, as part of a larger hearing on ending abuses and improving working conditions for migrant farm workers.

How does Eric Schlosser's use of the word *slavery* and of the concept influence the reaction of an audience to his argument?

I'd like to thank the Committee for inviting me to testify here today. I have been involved for more than a decade in the effort to improve the wages and working conditions of America's farmworkers. . . . What is happening right now in the tomato fields of Florida is so bad that it almost defies description, let alone belief.

This January Senator Bernie Sanders and I happened to be visiting Immokalee, Florida, the heart of the state's tomato-growing region, when the U.S. Justice Department released its indictments in the latest farmworker slavery case. The defendants in the case have been accused of threatening, slapping and kicking workers, beating workers, locking them inside trucks, chaining them to a pole, deliberately keeping them in debt and forcing them to work for free. The indictments read like something you might encounter in the year 1868, not 2008. The defendants have been charged, among other things, with violating the Thirteenth Amendment of the United States Constitution. That is the amendment outlawing slavery and involuntary servitude.

I find it incredible that in the year 2008—the two hundredth anniversary of the abolition of the slave trade—there is still slavery in the United States. I find it even more incredible that the tomato growers of Florida and some of their largest customers continue to deny that such abuses exist. . . .

I think most Americans would agree that the practice of slavery in the United States is unacceptable. But that sense of outrage does not seem to extend to the tomato growers of Florida and some of their fast food customers. During the same week that three tomato pickers climbed through the ventilation hatch of the box truck where they were being held against their will and escaped to freedom, setting in motion the Justice Department's latest slavery case—during that very same week, representatives of the Florida Tomato Growers Exchange and the Burger King Corporation staged a press junket in nearby fields, introducing reporters to happy farmworkers with "no complaints" and strongly denying that involuntary servitude or slavery was a problem. Perhaps the growers and some of their fast food customers are sincerely unaware that tomato pickers are being exploited. But such earnest pleas of ignorance bring to mind the scene in the film *Casablanca* when a French policeman, Captain Renault, is "shocked, shocked" to find out that gambling is occurring—at the casino where he regularly gambles.

The plight of tomato pickers in Florida needs to be understood in a broader historical context. Farmworkers are now, and have long been, among the poorest workers in the United States. The historian Cletus E. Daniel has described early twentieth century efforts to recruit farmworkers for California's fruit and vegetable harvest as "the search for a peasantry." In 1951 the President's Commission on Migratory Labor condemned the abysmal working conditions that farmworkers endured. "We depend on misfortune to build up our force of migratory workers," the commission concluded, "and when the supply is low because there is not enough misfortune at home, we rely on misfortune abroad to replenish the supply." During the 1970s, campaigns led by Cesar Chavez and the United Farm Workers union raised wages and greatly improved working conditions. But most of those gains were lost during the 1980s and 1990s. According to the U.S. Department of Labor, the typical farmworker earns roughly $10,000 to $12,000 a year. That figure may be somewhat inflated, due to the inclusion of supervisory workers in the most recent wage survey. In 2001 the Department of Labor estimated that the typical farmworker earned about $7,500 a year. It is hard to see how some of the most desperate workers in the United States gained a pay increase of 50 percent or more during the past seven years. Whatever the actual figure, there is little dispute that farmworkers rank near the very bottom of the American pay scale.

Farmworkers not only do hard manual labor for low wages, but they also suffer enormous stress and uncertainty about the prospects of employment. Almost all harvest work is considered "at will." There is no contract, no seniority, no obligation from the employer beyond the day-to-day. A farmer hires and fires workers as necessary, without need for explanation. It makes no difference whether the worker has been an employee for ten days or ten years. The terms of employment are laid down on a daily basis. A migrant usually does not know how long he or she will work on a given day—or even if work will be available. On a good day, the wages that can be earned may be high. But a good day may be followed by weeks without any work. This system gives an extraordinary amount of power to farmers and their labor contractors.

I spent a year investigating the poverty of farmworkers in California, the state with by far the largest number of migrants. I found that migrants were living in garages, abandoned cars, labor camps unfit to be horse barns. Right now there are thousands of farmworkers living outdoors in the hillsides of northern San Diego County. At one of the hillside encampments I visited, migrants slept beneath plastic garbage bags at night and did their laundry each week in a neighboring stream. The farmworkers I met seemed to embody a great many of the virtues that we cherish in the United States. These migrants were hardworking, deeply religious, devoted to their families— and yet were being exploited. It seemed wrong to me, pure and simple. In this country, hard work should get you out of poverty, not keep you in it.

> **Migrants were living in garages, abandoned cars, labor camps unfit to be horse barns.**

Bad as things are for the migrant workers in California, the migrants in Florida seem to have it even worse. Organizations like the United Farm Workers union and California Rural Legal Assistance provide some outlet for migrant grievances and some hope for a better future in that state. The primarily Latino workforce in Florida agriculture is much more isolated, with little institutional support. And the abuse of farmworkers in Florida has a uniquely dark history. Various systems of peonage, forced labor, and slavery thrived there long after the end of the Civil War. . . . Today the living conditions among migrant workers in Immokalee, Florida, though deplorable, are not as bad as in some rural California communities. But the power that farmers wield in Florida seems much more complete. The early morning scene in Immokalee's town square—where crowds of migrants gather at dawn hoping to find work, and labor contractors pick

workers like cattle at an auction—feels like a scene in a nineteenth century novel. "Harvest of Shame," the documentary about migrants made
by Edward R. Murrow in 1960, opens with a similar scene, showing
migrants being selected and packed into trucks. Much of "Harvest of
Shame" was filmed in Florida. In the documentary, a Florida farmer describes his workforce in terms that remain unfortunately relevant today:
"We used to own our slaves—now we just rent them."

Tomato pickers in Immokalee now earn about 40 to 50 cents for
each thirty-two pound bucket that they harvest. . . . Tomato pickers are
hired mainly by labor contractors, who try to shield farmers from legal
responsibility. The labor contractors often charge migrants for food,
housing, and transportation, deducting the costs straight from the
migrant's paycheck. Labor contractors often pay the smuggling fees of
new migrants, then force them to work off the debt. This system is an
invitation to abuse. Many of the recent slavery cases in Florida involve
illegal immigrants being held in servitude by their labor contractors. But
this is not primarily an immigration problem. It is a human rights problem. U.S. citizens have been enslaved lately in Florida, as well.

The seven major slavery cases prosecuted in Florida over the past
decade have all been handled by the Department of Justice. In keeping
with the brutal history of farm labor in Florida, state officials have done
little to prevent or punish cases of involuntary servitude. Not a single
Florida farmer has thus far been prosecuted in the seven federal slavery
cases, which have involved hundreds of migrants.

The Department of Justice has done a fine job pursuing slavery cases
in Florida. But it can devote even more resources to the fight against trafficking and involuntary slavery. And a much stronger effort can be made
to hold farmers legally responsible for the enslavement of their workers.
Farmers in Florida must be held accountable for what they suffer and permit to happen on their land. At the moment, a loophole in the Trafficking
Victims Protection Act makes it difficult to prosecute farmers in slavery
cases. That loophole should be closed, and those who "know or have reason to know" about involuntary servitude should face criminal charges.
The Department of Labor should devote greater resources to enforcing the
labor laws not only in Florida agriculture, but also in agriculture throughout the United States. And a significant increase in the federal minimum
wage—which, adjusted for inflation, has declined by about 40 percent
since the late 1960s—would greatly improve the lives of the nation's poorest workers. The immediate solution to these problems, however, does not
lie with the federal government or with state officials in Florida. The
largest purchasers of Florida tomatoes must take responsibility for the labor conditions in which those tomatoes are produced. Fruit and vegetable
farmers today are under enormous pressure to cut operating costs. They
face increased competition from overseas suppliers and price reductions
imposed by their largest customers. . . .

Today the major fast food chains stand atop America's food chain. Their purchasing decisions can transform entire sectors of the nation's agricultural economy. The fast food chains issue strict product specifications to suppliers and insist that they be met. When McDonald's introduced the Chicken McNugget in the mid-1980s, it fundamentally changed how poultry are raised, bred, processed and sold in the United States. When McDonald's decided in 2000 not to purchase any genetically modified potatoes, it effectively eliminated the market for those potatoes. In recent years, the animal welfare demands of the leading chains have prompted huge changes in the industrial practices of the American meatpacking industry.

The Coalition of Immokalee Workers recognized years ago that the fast food industry has enormous influence over what happens in the tomato fields of Florda. The coalition is a non-profit group that works on behalf of migrants in Florida. It has led the campaign to increase the wages of tomato pickers by one penny per pound, thereby significantly raising their wages. And it has helped the Department of Justice investigate most of the slavery cases prosecuted since the mid-1990s. In recognition of this work, the coalition has received awards from the Robert F. Kennedy Memorial Foundation and Anti-Slavery International, the world's oldest human rights group. The Coalition of Immokalee Workers has been one of the few brave and effective defenders of migrants in the state of Florida. I have been a strong critic of the fast food industry for years. But I applaud Yum Brands Inc., the parent company of Taco Bell and Pizza Hut, for its commitment to ending the exploitation of tomato pickers in Florida. Its agreement with the Coalition of Immokalee Workers provides a model for how wages can be meaningfully increased and working conditions can be carefully monitored. The additional penny per pound that Yum has agreed to pay, given directly to the workers, imposes no hardship upon Florida tomato farmers and does not increase the consumer price of any Yum Brands product. The McDonalds Corporation deserves credit for agreeing to a similar arrangement.

> **The fast food industry has enormous influence over what happens in the tomato fields.**

The admirable behavior of these two industry giants makes the behavior of Burger King and its ally, the Florida Tomato Growers Exchange, seem completely unjustifiable. It is hard to see how the payment of an extra penny per pound for labor costs would violate U.S. antitrust laws, as the tomato growers claim. . . . Burger King, for its part, has argued that Florida tomato pickers are actually well-paid—and at the same time has made a well-publicized donation to a charitable group devoted to the children of those workers. It is hard to see why the children of migrants who are being paid a decent wage would need any charity whatsoever.

The tomato pickers in Florida are not asking for charity. They are seeking a fair wage for their hard work and an end to slavery.

Instead of making charitable donations, Burger King should be showing the same sort of concern for human rights that it recently demonstrated on behalf of animal rights. "Our corporate conscience drives our commitment to animal welfare," a Burger King executive said on March 27th. "For almost a decade we have used our purchasing power to encourage positive steps in animal agriculture. We are proud to set an example for the restaurant industry." If Burger King can partner with People for the Ethical Treatment of Animals to improve the lives of chickens, it can certainly work with the Coalition of Immokalee Workers, a far less controversial group, to improve the lives of migrant workers in Florida.

The head of the Florida Tomato Growers exchange has called the proposed one-penny surcharge for migrants "un-American." I think most Americans would strongly disagree. Slavery, indentured servitude, desperate workers living in fear—that's what most people would consider unacceptable and un-American. The exploitation of farmworkers should not be tolerated in Florida. It should not be tolerated anywhere in the United States. There are many social problems that are extremely difficult to solve. This is not one of them. A few years ago I calculated how much it would cost the typical American household if the wages of every migrant farmworker was doubled. The answer was about $50 a year—and even that amount is probably too high. By paying a few pennies extra, an enormous amount of misery can be ended. The large fast food chains and supermarket chains must insure that those pennies are paid, and that the money goes directly to farmworkers. A little bit of compassion will go an awfully long way.

For Class Discussion

1. What view of migrant labor is Eric Schlosser advocating in this testimony?

2. How does Schlosser use narrative, personal testimony, and industrial precedent to build his argument? What pieces of evidence has he embedded in this narrative?

3. If Schlosser's immediate audience is a Senate committee, who is his ultimate audience? Which elements of his argument and its presentation show an awareness of what might persuade that audience? How does he affect his credibility by stating that the immediate solution to abusive labor practices does not lie with federal or state officials?

4. What opposing views does Schlosser acknowledge and how does he respond to them?

5. Schlosser insists that "this is not primarily an immigration problem. It is a human rights problem." What terms or concepts from this chapter does he use to illustrate the distinction? How effectively does he make these connections for the reader?

Look Beneath the Surface
National Human Trafficking Resource Center

This poster is one of a series that appears on the U.S. Department of Health and Human Services' National Human Trafficking Resource Center Web site under Campaign Toolkits. The NHTRC's goal is to "connect community members with additional tools to raise awareness and combat human trafficking in their local areas, as well as guide service providers and law enforcement personnel in their work with potential trafficking victims" (http://www.acf.hhs.gov/trafficking/index.html, "What We Do"). The Department of Health and Human Services has created this poster for social service organizations as part of its campaign against trafficking.

Even if you had little knowledge of the human trafficking issue and the main problems it poses, what ideas could you glean from this poster?

Administration for Children & Families

For Class Discussion

1. One problem in fighting human trafficking is identifying the victims. A number of campaigns are directed at equipping workers such as law enforcement officers and social services and medical personnel to identify victims. What features of this poster indicate its main target audience?

2. What assumptions is this poster addressing and arguing against?

3. After studying the image, the text, the use of type, and the layout of this poster, reconstruct the thinking of its creators. What creative choices did they make and why?

4. One of the projects of the NHTRC is a community-based campaign called "Rescue and Restore," currently established in twenty-four cities, regions, and states. If you were part of a design team assigned to create a comparable poster for your city or state for law enforcement or health care professionals, what image, text, and layout would you choose for your poster and why? ∎

CHAPTER QUESTIONS FOR REFLECTION AND DISCUSSION

1. According to this chapter's readings, what obstacles and problems do trafficked victims face when they try to break free from the people and situations that are controlling them?

2. Where do David Feingold, Nicholas Kristof, the National Human Trafficking Resource Center, and Joanna Busza and her coauthors differ in their claims about child labor and in their assumptions. Do they disagree in their underlying values or in their interpretation of facts?

3. Where do David Feingold, Kate Butcher, the International Organization for Migration, Joanna Busza and her coauthors, and John R. Miller differ in their claims about sex trafficking and in their assumptions, reasons, interpretation of facts, and use of evidence? What are the major disagreements?

4. What do this chapter's readings suggest are the main economic and legal issues related to forced labor and the trafficking of women and children for sexual exploitation?

5. Which readings do each of the visual arguments in this chapter support?

6. The human rights violations discussed in this chapter suggest many questions for further investigation. Choose one of the following questions and do some research to help you formulate an informed answer.

A. Many policymakers discourage the boycotting of companies and products as a way to combat human rights violations; however, consumer power was successful in the Rugmark Campaign in improving the treatment of child workers in the rug and carpet industry in India. How did this campaign achieve its success?

B. A number of NGOs have decided to involve children in their search for ways to stop the exploitation of children. Choose one of the following organizations and examine its Web site. What are some of the ways that this organization is including children and working to help them?

Global Movement for Children (www.unicef.org/gmfc/)

The Childwatch International Research Network (www.childwatch
.uio.no/)

Save the Children (www.savethechildren.net/)

South Asian Coalition on Child Servitude (Bachpan Bachao Andolan) (http://www.bba.org.in/)

C. While the United Nations is a leader in working for human rights, in some cases peacekeeping troops have taken advantage of women and children refugees in war-torn regions. Research the "sex for food" problems and the cases of brutality in Congo, Sudan, or another African country. How do these situations complicate the global community's responsibility to protect the human rights of women and children?

D. Research Nicholas Kristof's numerous columns about the sex trade written for the *New York Times* since 2003. Summarize Kristof's main views. Prepare to share with your class both his main points and some of his most moving emotional appeals.

E. Children are being abducted and forced to be camel jockeys, soldiers, and domestic and agricultural workers. Research one of these abusive practices and the efforts to stop it. What strategies offer the most hope?

7. What connections do you see among free trade, immigration, and the trafficking of women and children? You might consult Chapters 3 and 5.

WRITING ASSIGNMENTS

Brief Writing Assignments

1. Write for twenty minutes informally about what surprised, shocked, or disturbed you the most about the trafficking of women and children and which reading had the most impact on you.

2. After considering the readings in this chapter, use one of the following prompts to begin sorting out your own thinking on the views of human rights you encountered in this chapter:

   A. The arguments in this chapter have particularly clarified my understanding of _____ (some aspect of the human trafficking issue).

   B. The arguments in this chapter have changed my views on the (urgency, magnitude, or nearness) of the trafficking and forced labor problem in these ways _____.

   C. After reading these articles (fill in titles), I have major questions about _____.

3. In your own words, write a brief explanation in response to one of the following questions:

   A. What is the relationship between the international flesh trade and free trade?

   B. How is globalization affecting human trafficking?

   C. What can consumers in rich nations do to end human rights violations such as forced labor?

4. **Analyzing Arguments Rhetorically.** Locate a poster, brochure, public service announcement, or other visual argument regarding human rights and/or trafficking, and compare it to one of the visual arguments in this chapter. What is persuasive about the piece you have located? How do your piece and the piece from the chapter compare in terms of their angle of vision, presentation of information, intended audiences, and emotional appeals made?

5. Summarize one of the arguments in this chapter with which you disagree. Then briefly explain where you might find common ground with this writer in your values or views. Finally, present two or three points where you diverge from this argument and briefly discuss why.

Writing Projects

1. **Analyzing Arguments Rhetorically.** Write a rhetorical analysis essay in which you analyze two arguments from this chapter and then explain how these pieces have changed or shaped your view of the trafficking of women and children and human rights issues. Choose one of the following pairs of authors and map out their points of agreement and disagreement. Consider their target audiences, their assumptions and values, their interpretation of the problem, their proposed solutions, and the points that each overlooks or ignores. In a final synthesis section of your essay, show how both authors have contributed to your informed view. Write your essay for a group of people who have turned to you for guidance in understanding the human rights issues involved in trafficking.

   • David Feingold and John R. Miller or Nicholas Kristof

   • Kate Butcher and John R. Miller or Joanna Busza/Sarah Castle/Aisse Diarra

   • Joanna Busza/Sarah Castle/Aisse Diarra and David Feingold or John R. Miller

   • Eric Schlosser and John R. Miller

2. Suppose a friend said to you, "Okay, I am sickened by the horrible treatment of women and children in Russia, Cambodia, and Bosnia, and I hate the idea of people being bought and sold, but I don't see how the sex trade in Bosnia or children's debt bondage in Southeast Asia affects me or how I could influence these issues."

   Respond to your friend in one of these ways:

   A. Write a narrative like Victoria Herradura's in the introduction to this chapter on pp. 477–478 that shares your personal experience and reasons for caring about these human rights issues.

   B. Write an open letter to your friend, using the ideas and information from the readings in this chapter. Make your letter an argument directed to your friend but also to a larger audience (your university community or city) whose views you want to enlarge or change.

3. Investigate the status of antitrafficking legislation and programs in your state and determine if trafficking is a state crime and if your state has an antitrafficking task force. What social services resources are

available to help trafficking victims? For instance, you might consult the California Attorney General's SafeState page on human trafficking (http://safestate.org), and the preparation of other states. Consider your state's geographical location, borders, ports, and waterways; main sources of revenue such as agriculture; and major cities. Based on your fieldwork and research, write a letter to your state legislator proposing a bill to create antitrafficking resources for your state or to implement ideas that have been successful in other states and communities.

4. Identify a major controversy within the human trafficking issue such as (a) which methods of combating human trafficking within Eastern Europe or Southeast Asia are the most promising; (b) how effective economic sanctions are in motivating countries to fight human trafficking; or (c) whether legalizing prostitution helps or hinders NGOs' and governments' fight against sex trafficking. Based on your reading and thinking about this issue, formulate a claim that articulates your position, and construct an argument developing this claim. Write your argument for an uninformed, neutral audience of your peers.

5. Sometimes when issues are as complex as human trafficking, we become overwhelmed and discouraged. However, at that point, we need to think about activists such as Don Cesare Lo Deserto and his home for rescued victims of the sex trade in Italy; Mara Radovanovic of the Lara organization in Bosnia; politician Linda Smith and Shared Hope, her organization to help women and children; former Ambassador John Miller and the antitrafficking legislation he has sponsored; and Brazilian mother Pureza Lopes Loyola and her courageous search for her trafficked son. Investigate and research one of these activists or one you discover on your own. Then write an editorial or journalistic profile for your university or community newspaper explaining what you found impressive and inspirational about this person's contribution to the fight against trafficking violations of human rights.

6. Unless people pressure their governments to call for stricter laws and more enforcement of laws to punish traffickers, human trafficking will continue to grow. A number of Web sites of advocacy groups and NGOs are committed to educating the public about the horrors of the trafficking of women and children and enlisting support. Among some of the most active ones are these:

Human Rights Watch (www.hrw.org)
Anti-Slavery International (www.antislavery.org)
Save the Children (www.savethechildren.org)
The Protection Project (www.protectionproject.org)
Global Movement for Children (www.unicef.org/gmfc/)
United Nations Children's Fund (UNICEF) (www.unicef.org)

Using three or four of the following criteria or some of the ideas in Chapter 2: "Analyzing and Writing Arguments," write an evaluation argument about the effectiveness of the public appeal of the Web site of one of these organizations:

A. Functional and attractive layout and design of the site

B. Clear explanation of the problem and information to support the organization's position

C. Strong appeal to readers' emotions, sympathies, and values

D. Good credibility or currency of the information presented

E. Clear requests and directives indicating what the organization wants readers to do

Argue that this organization's site does (or does not) measure up to your criteria. In your evaluation argument, written for voters in your age group, show why you would (or would not) recommend this site to someone who is seeking to understand human trafficking.

7. Write a letter to your U.S. representative or senator arguing that the United States (a) should take a tougher stand on the trafficking of women and children; (b) should focus more on helping countries tackle the root causes of human trafficking; (c) should allocate more money to provide education in developing countries; or (d) should adopt some other proposal of your choice to combat this new slavery. Make your letter clear, focused, and specific, and show that you are knowledgeable about this issue by accurately citing any sources that you use. As an alternative, you might write a policy proposal intended to motivate voters in your state to support your perspective on combating human trafficking.

Glossary of Globalization and Argument Terms

agribusiness   An industry engaged in the production, processing, manufacture, or distribution of farm goods.

alternative energy   Energy derived from sources such as biofuels, solar and hydro power, or wind, tidal, and geothermal energy that is proposed as an alternative to the continued consumption of nonrenewable resources such as oil, natural gas, and coal.

amnesty   The granting of a pardon for offenses against a government, often related to issues of political dissent.

angle of vision   The lens of values through which an argument's writer is interpreting the issue.

appeal to ethos   The ethical character of a writer that comes across in the argument in the writer's credibility, knowledge, and treatment of other viewpoints.

appeal to logos   The logical structure, consistency, and development of an argument.

appeal to pathos   How a writer engages the emotions and imaginations of the audience and taps into the audience's values in an argument.

argument   A persuasive text that makes a claim and develops it with reasons and supporting evidence.

assumptions   The principles behind the reasons given for an argumentative claim.

asylum seeker   A type of refugee seeking relief from political or religious persecution.

attributive tags   Language used by a writer to indicate that the ideas being expressed belong to another author.

audience   The people whom a writer has in mind when making an argument, or the people whom the writer hopes to persuade of his/her position on an issue.

blue collar   Pertaining to working-class employees who perform manual labor such as factory work.

brain drain   A phenomenon in which college-educated persons and professionals leave developing countries in order to take advantage of better conditions and substantially higher pay for their skills in developed countries.

capital   Wealth and durable produced goods that are used in the production of other goods—farm equipment, property, or money, for example.

Central America–Dominican Republic–United States Free Trade Agreement (CAFTA–DR)   A free trade agreement, similar to the North American Free Trade Agreement, between the United States and most Central American countries, legalized in 2005.

claim   A statement that asserts an arguable answer to an issue question and functions as the core of an argument.

Clean Air Act   A set of laws originally passed in 1963 that has since been expanded and revised. These laws aim to improve air quality and focus specifically on the ozone layer, acid rain, and emissions standards for factories and vehicles.

climate change   Changes in global temperatures and weather patterns that can result in changing patterns of rainfall and drought, greater intensity and frequency of storms, and melting of polar ice caps and glaciers. Formerly referred to as global warming, the phenomenon is currently discussed in relation to issues of atmospheric pollution caused by greenhouse gases.

colonialism   Political, economic, social, and cultural domination and exploitation of a territory by a foreign power. This system was popular among the European powers in the nineteenth century, a notable example being Great Britain's presence in India.

commons   A concept that considers the earth's resources as belonging equally to all nations and peoples of the world. Examples include air, fresh water, the oceans, and animal and plant biodiversity.

communication technology   Technologies used to transmit data or exchange information.

communism   A political system in which the government owns the means of production and equitably distributes the common goods among the people.

communitarianism   A political philosophy, created in response to the rugged individualism of liberalism, that advocates the preservation and enhancement of the community.

comparative advantage   David Ricardo's theory of economics stating that all countries benefit when each nation specializes in producing and exporting goods it can produce at relatively lower cost, and imports goods it produces at higher cost.

cost-benefit analysis   A method of determining whether the benefits of a proposed policy outweigh the losses.

creative destruction   In economics, an outcome of offshore outsourcing where the destruction of a company's existing infrastructure provides the opportunity for reorganization, redevelopment, and innovation, potentially creating new, different jobs.

cultural diversity   Differences in race, ethnicity, language, nationality, or religion among various groups within a community or nation.

cultural homogenization   The act of making a formerly diverse cultural population uniform.

cultural imperialism   Promoting the domination of the culture or language of one nation over another, disregarding cultural diversity.

cultural pluralism   The existence of multiple culturally diverse groups within a larger shared culture.

dependency theory   A theory of international relations that states that rich countries stay rich and keep poor countries poor by exploiting the resources and wealth of poor countries.

deregulation   The reduction or elimination of government control of private economic activities, usually to the benefit of corporations.

derivative   A contract based on a stock, bond, or commodity that specifies the selling of future cash flows, often described as a way to buy and sell risk. The contract transfers the risk of a credit asset, without transfer of the underlying asset itself. Examples include stock options, futures, and credit default swaps.

developed countries/industrialized countries/first world countries   The wealthiest nations of the world, which enjoy high levels of education, health standards, and technological advancement.

developing countries/emerging economies/third world countries   The poorer countries of the world, which are attempting to industrialize or reach the economic level of the developed countries.

diaspora   People settled far from the homelands of their ancestry.

direct trade   A form of trade in which private and respectful price-setting agreements are made directly between the grower or producer and the company selling that product so that both parties benefit.

economic development   Usually measured by an increase in a population's standard of living, economic development involves increases in technology, resources, and human capital.

economic globalization   The movement from separate, national economies toward an international or global economy in which goods, money, and workers are able to flow across national borders freely.

economic growth   An increase in the total output of a nation over time, usually measured in terms of gross domestic product (GDP).

embargo   A legal refusal to sell goods to a disfavored country.

emissions   The release of greenhouse gases into the atmosphere.

Environmental Protection Agency   An agency of the U.S. government created in 1970 to oversee coordinated governmental protection of the environment and natural resources.

ethnicity   Cultural characteristics that distinguish one group of people from another.

ethos   See *appeal to ethos.*

European Union (EU)   A federation of European states, originally created after World War II to prevent another war through economic integration by means of the establishment of a common currency and free movement of goods across borders. Currently, the European Union maintains common economic, foreign, and security policies. The agreement between fifteen countries (Austria, Belgium, Denmark, Finland, France, Germany, Greece, Ireland, Italy, Luxembourg, the Netherlands, Portugal, Spain, Sweden, and the United Kingdom) has expanded to twenty-seven countries, including

Bulgaria, Cyprus, the Czech Republic, Estonia, Hungary, Latvia, Lithuania, Malta, Poland, Romania, Slovakia, and Slovenia.

evidence   Examples, facts, numerical data, testimonies and quotations, or further reasoning that support an author's claim in an argument.

Export Processing Zone (EPZ)   A region within a country aimed at attracting foreign investment from multinational corporations by relaxing tax and labor restrictions. Examples include apparel and textile factories in Saipan and the Philippines, and Motorola and Intel factories in Costa Rica. EPZs are often associated with sweatshops.

fair trade   A trade movement characterized by concern for human rights and social responsibility that demands workers and farmers be treated and paid fairly and that works to remove middlemen.

fatwah   A statement issued by an Islamic religious figure.

Federal Reserve   An institution of the U.S. government responsible for monetary policy, meaning the regulation of banks, adjustments of the money supply, and the control of inflation.

financial literacy   An understanding of the multiple and cumulative ways that global financial institutions and personal financial choices affect individuals and others around the world, including an ability to understand financial regulations and agreements.

first world   Originally used to indicate democratic nations during the Cold War, the term now describes the highly developed, rich nations of the Western world.

food security   The ability of countries independently to provide adequate and reliable food at reasonable cost for their own people in socially acceptable ways to sustain healthy living.

food sovereignty   The right of people to define their own food and agriculture, free from pressures of the international market.

fossil fuels   Fuels formed over millions of years from dead plants and animals; examples include oil, natural gas, and coal.

free trade   An economic philosophy of reducing barriers to unrestricted trade, such as tariffs, taxes, subsidies, and quotas, in an effort to move raw materials, goods, and services freely across international borders. This ideology is largely embraced and promoted by the World Trade Organization, the International Monetary Fund, and the World Bank as the best way to benefit both developed countries and developing countries.

Free Trade Area of the Americas (FTAA)   A proposed trade agreement that would expand the benefits of the North American Free Trade Agreement to the entire Western Hemisphere.

fundamentalism   The belief in strict adherence to certain traditional doctrines and practices of a religion and the tendency to interpret scriptures literally.

General Agreement on Tariffs and Trade (GATT)   Created in 1947, GATT is a negotiating framework for international trade aimed at eliminating tariffs and quotas in order to achieve free trade. GATT was absorbed by the WTO.

genocide   Deliberate and systematic annihilation of a racial, political, or cultural group.

genre   The type, kind, or category of argument, such as an editorial, scholarly argument, or advocacy advertisement.

global capitalism   The expansion of the system of capitalism (individual and corporate ownership of the means of production) as the primary economic system around the globe.

global financial system   The international interdependence of banks and other financial institutions, corporations, and governments.

globalization   A contested term, globalization is generally used in one of two ways: (1) to describe the way that transportation, communication, and technology have facilitated the movement of materials, goods, and ideas across continents and national borders; and (2) in reference to the dominant model and system of economic globalization.

global village   The drawing together of the world's diverse cultures through the advent of mass communication and technology, first articulated in 1964 by Marshall McLuhan.

glocalization   A term used by Japanese business to describe ways to tailor global products to local markets. Thomas L. Friedman popularized the term, describing it as the ability of a culture to assimilate aspects of other cultures in a way that enriches the home culture rather than overwhelms or replaces it.

grassroots   A political movement organized by a network of citizens at the local level.

Green Revolution   A dramatic increase of agricultural production, in both developed and developing countries, between the 1940s and 1970s as a result of the widespread use of pesticides, chemical fertilizers, hybrid seeds, and animal antibiotics.

gross domestic product (GDP)   The total monetary value of goods and services produced by and within a country during a specific period.

gross national product (GNP)   The total monetary value of goods and services produced by a nation at home and abroad during a specific period.

guest worker program   A plan proposed by former President George W. Bush that would enable both potential immigrants to the United States and those already working in the country illegally to apply for renewable three-year worker visas.

H-1B visa   A work visa allowing skilled international professionals and/or international students in specialty areas to work in the United States for up to six years. The visa is favored by high-tech, healthcare, and scientific companies, and allows the holder to bring a spouse and family and to apply for a Green Card (legal permanent residency).

hegemony   The dominance of one power over another and a simultaneous acceptance of the commanding power's right to rule.

ideology   A unifying system of beliefs, values, philosophies, and attitudes that guides a society, particularly in the form of its government.

imperialism   The practice of one country's extending its control over the territory, political system, or economic life of another country.

information technology (IT)   All forms of technology that deal with computers, telecommunications, or the storage, transmission, or retrieval of information.

infrastructure   The system of public works in a country that makes business activities possible—for example, roads, buildings, telephone service, electricity, and public transportation.

International Labor Organization (ILO)   A UN agency created in 1919 to maintain and promote fair and socially just international labor standards.

International Monetary Fund (IMF)   An international organization, one of the three main global economic institutions created in 1944, designed to lend finances to nations with debt problems and provide solutions that will enable international free trade, monetary cooperation, and economic growth. Some people protest IMF policies because membership is undemocratic; the countries that contribute the most money have the most voting power.

issue question   A controversial question that can have many contestable answers and can lead to many different claims.

kairos   The timeliness of an argument, as related to the motivating occasion.

Kyoto Protocol   An international agreement negotiated in 1997 in Kyoto, Japan, and effective in 2005, to reduce the rate of fossil fuel emissions to acceptable levels through legally binding commitments. The United States decided not to sign this agreement or adhere to its standards.

land reform   Redistribution of land ownership to small farmers and peasants in order to destroy the concentration of landholdings among a few powerful landowners or corporations.

leverage   The ability of a small amount of capital to control bigger investments; securitization is a form of leverage.

liberalism   A political philosophy from the nineteenth century that embraces individual rights, civil liberties, and private property.

libertarianism   An economic philosophy that promotes free trade and emphasizes the importance of personal freedom in economic and political affairs and the limitation of government intervention in the lives and choices of individuals.

local food   Food produced in the same region in which it is sold or consumed, often linked to traditional regional or cultural diets.

logos   See *appeal to logos*.

macroeconomics   Factors that reveal the big picture of a state's economy, including GDP growth, inflation, interest rates, and productivity.

market   A place where buyers and sellers interact and supply and demand control the fluctuation of prices of goods.

Marxism   Marx's theory of socialism that includes class struggle and a dictatorship of the proletariat working toward the eventual realization of a classless society.

Millennium Development Goals   Eight goals set by the United Nations to tackle and conquer some of the world's worst problems, including the scarcity of safe water, extreme poverty and hunger, child mortality, HIV/AIDS, and to achieve universal primary education, gender equality, environmental sustainability, and global partnership for development. The proposed time for reaching these goals is 2015.

monoculture   The growing of plants or animals of a single species, absent of biodiversity.

most favored nation (MFN)   A trade principle utilized by the WTO that states that all of a nation's trading partners must receive the lowest tariff rates the country offers.

motivating occasion   The event, occasion, problem, or condition that prompts an arguer to speak out.

multinational/transnational corporations   Corporations that have divisions in more than two countries.

nationalism   Complete loyalty to and belief in the greatness of one's nation.

nation building   Constructing or structuring a nation using the power of the state, often in the realms of political development, economic growth, and social harmony.

neoliberalism   A political-economic philosophy that encourages deregulation, favors corporations, and suggests that the best way to achieve justice, progress, and growth is through free market economics.

nongovernmental organization (NGO)   A nonprofit agency unconnected to government or corporate or private actors and interests that is devoted to issues of social justice and resource management. Examples include Catholic Relief Services, the International Red Cross, the World Wildlife Fund, and Human Rights Watch.

nonrenewable resources   Natural resources that are finite and exhaustible because of their scarcity or the length of time it takes for them to be replenished; examples include minerals and oil.

North American Free Trade Agreement (NAFTA)   A trade agreement ratified in 1993 and put into effect in 1994 between the United States, Canada, and Mexico, created to encourage free trade and investment among the three countries.

organic food   Food grown or raised without the use of man-made fertilizers, pesticides, additives, antibiotics, or growth hormones.

outsourcing/offshore outsourcing   Subcontracting some or all of a business's functions to a foreign company. This term is most often used to describe the movement of jobs to developing countries.

pathos   See *appeal to pathos*.

potable water   Water that is safe for human consumption.

privatization   Turning over or selling state-owned industries to the private sector.

productivity   The efficiency with which things are produced, usually with a focus on the amount of labor and time involved.

protectionism   Any policy used to protect domestic industries against competition from imports; tariffs are the most common form of protectionism.

pull factors   The conditions enticing people to move from developing countries to developed countries, such as the promise of higher-paying jobs and the suggestions made in the media about the superiority of the developed nation's lifestyle and customs.

purpose   The writer's goal in making an argument.

push factors   The conditions compelling people to move from developing countries to developed countries, such as the displacement of subsistence farmers from their traditional lands and livelihoods.

quota   A form of protectionism that limits the total quantity of imports of a good during a set period of time.

rational choice theory   The theory of human nature and interaction that states that people calculate the costs and benefits of any action and rationally decide which course of action would be the best to take.

real politik   A German term describing foreign policy that is based on practical concerns as opposed to theoretical or ethical concerns.

reasons   In argument, the statements that support the claim being made, explicitly and implicitly, and with the claim create the core of an argument.

recession   A period of reduced economic activity characterized by rising levels of unemployment, a decline in GDP, and slowed production.

renewable resources   Natural resources such as forests or fisheries that renew themselves through natural processes.

rhetoric/rhetorical   The persuasive use of language to accomplish certain ends in specific situations.

sectarianism   Adherence to a particular form or sect of a religion to the exclusion of other sects.

secularism   A governmental system that embodies the separation of church and state.

securitization   A structured finance process in which cash flow-producing financial assets (such as credit card debt, car loans, mortgages, and other assets) are pooled and repackaged into securities which are then sold to investors.

Smith, Adam   The founding father of economics and capitalism, most famous for *The Wealth of Nations* (1776), in which he argued that people should be free from government interference to follow their own self-interests in the market, which would regulate economic activity like an "invisible hand." However, Smith believed that government intervention in the economy was at times necessary to provide public works such as roads and schools that would not be profitable for individuals to produce on their own.

social safety nets   Programs and benefits provided by a government that exist independently of a person's employment status. Examples include socialized health care in the European Union and Canada.

socialism   A political and economic system in which a democratic community owns the means of production and distributes the benefits equitably among the community members.

sovereignty   A principle of government that holds that a state exercises absolute power over its territory and population.

stakeholders   People who have investments in the answers to issue questions.

STAR criteria   The criteria for evaluating evidence in an argument. STAR stands for sufficiency, typicality, accuracy, and relevance.

Structural Adjustment Programs (SAP)   The package of free market reforms designed to create economic growth and to generate income to pay off a nation's debt. These policies were promoted by the IMF and World Bank. Third world nations agree to SAPs in exchange for debt relief.

structured finance   A broad term used to describe a sector of finance that was created to help transfer risk using complex legal and corporate entities.

style   The level of formality and complexity, tone, and use of language employed by a writer in an argument.

subcontracting   To use a third party to complete all or part of the work required for a job.

subsidy   Financial help from the government to the private sector of the economy.

sustainable development   Development that meets the needs of the present while conserving resources so that future generations will be able to meet their own needs.

sweatshop   A factory in which employees work for long hours under unhealthy or dangerous conditions for low pay.

tariff   A tax on each unit of an imported good.

theocracy   A political system in which political organization is based upon religious organization.

third world   Used during the Cold War to describe nations aligned with neither communism nor democracy, this term is now used to describe developing countries.

totalitarianism   A political system characterized by dictatorial, one-party rule. Totalitarian regimes generally do not tolerate political opposition and attempt to control all aspects of citizen life.

trade barriers   Policies utilized by governments to restrict importing and exporting with other countries; tariffs are the most common form of trade barriers.

Trade-Related Intellectual Property Rights (TRIPs)   Laws governing patents, copyrights, and other goods related to information which are hotly disputed in the international trading system; one example is patents in the pharmaceutical industry.

trafficking   An illegal activity involving the international transport of drugs, weapons, or people, the latter by threat, force, or fraud.

transgenic crops/biotech crops   Crops that have been experimentally altered by genetic material from another organism.

Troubled Assets Relief Program (TARP)   A $1.5 trillion program funded by the United States Congress in 2008 and 2009 so that the U.S. Treasury Department could allocate the funds to banks and financial institutions weakened in the global financial crisis. In return, the Treasury Department takes a position of ownership in the bank or financial institution in the form of preferred stock.

United Nations   An international organization created in 1945 by fifty-one countries to preserve peace and security through international cooperation and collective action. Current membership is 191 countries.

United Nations Educational, Scientific, and Cultural Organization (UNESCO)   An international organization with about two hundred member nations that includes among its goals the assertion of cultural rights as human rights and the preservation of cultural diversity.

Universal Declaration on Cultural Diversity   An international and intercultural agreement written by UNESCO in 2001 that seeks to make legal the principles that cultural diversity is a necessity for humankind and contributes to international peace and security, and that cultural rights are integral to human rights.

Universal Declaration of Human Rights   A document adopted by the General Assembly of the United Nations on December 10, 1948, that recognizes the equal rights of all humans globally.

Uruguay Round   The final set of trade negotiations under GATT that began in 1986 and closed in 1993. This round created the WTO as a permanent arena to address issues of international free trade.

wastewater   Used water that carries wastes like soap, chemicals, or fertilizers from homes, businesses, or industries.

white collar   Pertaining to employees who do nonmanual desk work, often for higher compensation than blue-collar workers receive.

World Bank   An international financial institution, one of the three main global economic institutions created in 1944, whose purpose is to lend funds and provide assistance for economic development in poorer countries, often prescribing policies that promote free trade.

World Health Organization (WHO)   An agency of the United Nations, founded in 1948 to promote the attainment of the highest level of human health through research, technical cooperation among countries, international conferences, and various other programs.

World Trade Organization (WTO)   An international organization created in 1994 and active as of 1995, responsible for the legislation and regulation of trade rules and the adjudication of trade disputes, aimed at maintaining free trade in the international trading system.

xenophobia   Fear or hatred of foreigners.

Films on Global Issues

Chapter 1 Exploring and Defining Globalization

Being Hmong Means Being Free. Documentary. Produced by Larry Long. 56 min. 2000.

The Corporation. Documentary. Directed by Mark Achbar and Jennifer Abbott. 145 min. 2003.

Granito de Arena. Documentary. Directed by Jill Friedberg. 60 min. 2004.

The New Rulers of the World. Documentary. Directed by Alan Lowery. 53 min. 2001.

Chapter 3 Trading Goods: Consumerism, Free Trade, and Sweatshops

Another World Is Possible. Documentary. Directed by Mark Dworkin and Melissa Young. 24 min. 2002.

The Battle in Seattle. Action, Drama. Directed by Stuart Townsend. 99 min. 2007.

Behind the Labels: Garment Workers on U.S. Saipan. Documentary. Directed by Tia Lessin. 45 min. 2001.

Black Gold. Documentary. Directed by Marc Francis and Nick Francis. 78 min. 2006.

Cappuccino Trail: The Global Economy in a Cup, a.k.a. *Tales from the Global Economy: The Cappuccino Trail.* Documentary. Directed by Jeremy Newson. 50 min. 2002.

Life and Debt. Documentary. Directed by Stephanie Black. 86 min. 2001.

Made in L.A. POV Documentary. Directed by Almudena Carracedo and Robert Bahar. 70 min. 2007.

A Struggle (Zheng Zha). Documentary. Directed by Haolun Shu. 50 min. 2001.

Talking to the Wall: The Story of an American Bargain. Documentary. Directed by Steve Alves. 57 min. 2004.

This Is What Democracy Looks Like. Documentary. Directed by Jill Friedberg and Rick Rowley. 72 min. 2000.

Wal-Mart: The High Cost of Low Prices. Documentary. Directed by Robert Greenwald. 95 min. 2005.

Chapter 4 Trading Financial Risk and Jobs: The Global Economic Crisis

American Jobs. Documentary. Directed by Gregg Spotts. 60 min. 2004.

Commanding Heights: The Battle for the World Economy. Documentary miniseries. Directed by William Cran and Greg Barker. 360 min. 2002.

The Crisis of Credit Visualized. Educational. Jonathan Jarvis.
http://crisisofcredit.com. 12 min. 2009.

Enron: The Smartest Guys in the Room. Documentary. Directed by Alex Gibney.
110 min. 2005.

Globalization: Winners and Losers. Documentary. Directed by Keely Purdue.
42 min. 2000.

Legacy of Shame. Documentary. Directed by Maurice Murad. 52 min. 2002.

1-800-INDIA. Documentary. Produced by Anna Carter; directed by Safina
Uberoi. 60 min. 2005.

Outsourced. Comedy. Directed by John Jeffcoat. 98 min. 2007.

The Seattle Syndrome. Documentary. Directed by Steve Bradshaw. 25 min. 2000.

Benoit Mandelbrot Thinks We're All Screwed. Interview with Naseem Taleb and
Benoit Mandelbrot. YouTube. 6 min. 2008.

30 Days, Season II: "Outsourcing." Documentary. Directed by Morgan Spurlock.
288 min. 2008.

Chapter 5 Crossing Borders: Immigration

Abandoned: The Betrayal of America's Immigrants. Documentary. Directed by
David Belle and Nicholas Wrathall. 55 min. 2000.

The Beautiful Country. Drama. Directed by Hans Petter Moland. 125 min. 2005.

Crossing Arizona. Documentary. Directed by Joseph Mathew and Don DeVivo.
96 min. 2006.

A Day Without a Mexican. Comedy. Directed by Sergio Arau. 95 min. 2004.

Death on a Friendly Border. Documentary. Directed by Rachel Antell.
26 min. 2001.

Farmingville. Documentary. Directed by Carlos Sandoval and Catherine
Tambini. 72 min. 2003.

Head-On. Drama. Directed by Faith Akin. 118 min. 2004.

In My Own Skin: The Complexity of Living as an Arab in America. Documentary.
Directed by Nikki Byrd and Jennifer Jajeh. 16 min. 2001.

Lone Star. Drama. Directed by John Sayles. 134 min. 1996.

The Namesake. Drama. Directed by Mira Nair. 122 min. 2007.

The New Americans. Documentary miniseries. Directed by Susana Aikin et al.
408 min. 2004.

New World Border. Documentary. Directed by Jose Palafox and Casey Peek.
28 min. 2001.

Suspino: A Cry for Roma. Documentary. Directed by Gillian Darling Kovanic.
72 min. 2003.

30 Days, Season II: "Immigration." Documentary. Directed by Morgan Spurlock.
288 min. 2008.

Under the Same Moon. Drama. Directed by Patricia Riggen. 109 min. 2008.

The Visitor. Drama. Directed by Thomas McCarthy. 104 min. 2008.

Chapter 6 Protecting the Environment: Water Issues and Emerging Energy Technologies

Blind Spot. Documentary. Directed by Adolfo Doring. 88 min. 2008.

Blue Gold: World Water Wars. Documentary. Directed by Sam Bozzo. 90 min. 2008.

Blue Vinyl. Documentary. Directed by Judith Helfand and Daniel B. Gold. 98 min. 2002.

DAM/AGE: A Film with Arundhati Roy. Documentary. Directed by Aradhana Seth. 50 min. 2002.

The 11ᵗʰ Hour. Documentary. Directed by Nadia Conners and Leila Conners Petersen. 95 min. 2007.

The End of Suburbia: Oil Depletion and the Collapse of the American Dream. Documentary. Directed by Gregory Greene. 78 min. 2004.

Extreme Oil. Documentary. Directed by Dominic Allan, Paul Burgess, William Cran, and Rebecca John. 180 min. 2004.

Flow. Documentary. Directed by Irena Salina. 83 min. 2008.

Garbage Warrior. Documentary. Directed by Oliver Hodge. 87 min. 2007.

The Next Industrial Revolution: William McDonough, Michael Braungard and the Birth of the Sustainable Economy. Documentary. Directed by Chris Bedford and Shelley Morhaim. 55 min. 2001.

Running Dry. Documentary. Directed by Jim Thebaut. 90 min. 2005.

Sustainable Futures. Documentary. Produced by Unesco-Opeongo Line Co-Production. 39 min. 1999.

Thirst. Documentary. Produced and Directed by Alan Snitow and Deborah Kaufman. 62 min. 2004.

Waste=Food. Documentary. Directed by Rob van Hattum. 51 min. 2007.

Chapter 7 Feeding the World: Biotechnology, Culture, and Local Food

Darwin's Nightmare. Documentary. Directed by Hubert Sauper. 107 min. 2004.

Deconstructing Supper: Is Your Food Safe? Documentary. Directed by Marianne Kaplan. 48 min. 2002.

Fragile Harvest. Documentary. Directed by Robert Lang. 49 min. 1987.

The Future of Food. Documentary. Directed by Deborah Koons. 88 min. 2004.

The GMO Trilogy: Unnatural Selection. Documentary. Produced by Jeffrey M. Smith. 60 min. 2006.

Seeds of Plenty, Seeds of Sorrow. Documentary. Directed by Manjira Datta. 52 min. 1994.

Silent Killer: The Unfinished Campaign Against Hunger. Documentary. Produced by Hana Jindrova and John de Graaf. 57 min. 2005.

Strong Roots: The Landless Workers Movement in Brazil. Documentary. Directed by Aline Sasahara and Marie Luisa Mendoça. 41 min. 2001.

Chapter 8 Merging and Clashing Cultures: Media, Technology, Music, and Film

Akira: The Special Edition, a.k.a. *Akira*. Action animation. Directed by Katsuhiro Otomo. 124 min. 1988.

Bride and Prejudice: The Bollywood Musical. Musical comedy. Directed by Gurinder Chadha. 111 min. 2004.

Howl's Moving Castle. Fantasy animation. Directed by Hayao Miyazaki. 119 min. 2004.

Lagaan: Once Upon a Time in India. Musical. Directed by Ashutosh Gowariker. 225 min. 2001.

Mondovino. Documentary. Directed by Jonathan Nossiter. 135 min. 2004.

Sierra Leone's Refugee All Stars. Documentary. Directed by Banker White and Zach Niles. 80 min. 2007.

Slumdog Millionaire. Drama. Directed by Danny Boyle. 120 min. 2008.

Spirited Away. Adventure animation. Directed by Hayao Miyazaki. 125 min. 2001.

Taking Pictures. Documentary. Directed by Les McLaren and Annie Stiven. 56 min. 1996.

Chapter 9 Defending Human Rights: Trafficking and Child Labor

Blood Diamond. Action, Drama. Directed by Edward Zwick. 143 min. 2006.

Born into Brothels: Calcutta's Red Light Kids. Documentary. Directed by Zana Briski and Ross Kauffman. 85 min. 2004.

The Garden. Documentary. Directed by Ruthie Shatz and Adi Barash. 85 min. 2004.

Immokalee: A Story of Slavery and Freedom. Documentary. Directed by Jeff Imig. 21 min. 2004.

In My Country. Drama. Directed by John Boorman. 103 min. 2005.

The Invisible Children (Rough Cut). Documentary. Directed by Jason Russell, Bobby Bailey, and Laren Poole. 55 min. 2003.

Journey from the Fall. Drama. Directed by Ham Tram. 135 min. 2007.

Rain in a Dry Land. POV Documentary. Directed by Anne Makepeace. 82 min. 2007.

Stolen Childhoods. Documentary. Directed by Len Morris and Robin Romano. 85 min. 2005.

Trade. Drama. Directed by Marco Kreuzpaintner. 119 min. 2007.

Trading Women. Documentary. Directed by David A. Feingold. 77 min. 2003.

Answers to Chapter 1 "Global Pursuit," pp. 3–5

1. h

2. c

3. Baht—Thailand; Krona—Sweden; Euro—Slovenia; Ruble—Russia; Yuan—China

4. a, d

5. c

6. **Organization for Economic Co-Operation and Development**, an international organization committed to democracy and the market economy. There are currently thirty full members and the organization is headquartered in Paris. **Organization of the Petroleum Exporting Countries**, a cartel of thirteen oil-producing nations: Algeria, Angola, Ecuador, Iran, Iraq, Indonesia, Kuwait, Libya, Nigeria, Qatar, Saudi Arabia, the United Arab Emirates, and Venezuela. Since 1965, the organization has been headquartered in Vienna.

7. United States

8. b

9. Finance. They are all names associated with major stock exchanges or stock market indexes. NASDAQ— New York; Hang Seng—Hong Kong; FTSE 100—London; Deutsche Börse—Frankfurt

10. California, Arizona, New Mexico, Texas

11. None. Several nations have made claims to territories within Antarctica but the region as a whole is administered and regulated according to the 1959 Antarctic Treaty.

12. True. Both France and Italy are members of the European Union. Providing you did not have a criminal record or any relevant outstanding legal issues, the terms of the European Union agreement in theory place no restrictions on this type of mobility.

13. b

14. b

15. The Tour de France bicycle race, the world's premier cycling event. The yellow jersey is awarded on each day of the grueling 2,000+ mile race to the rider with the fastest time for that day.

16. b

17. c

18. c

19. a

20. d

Credits